AFRICA SOUTH OF THE SAHARA

TEXTS IN REGIONAL GEOGRAPHY
A Guilford Series

Edited by

James L. Newman
Syracuse University

Africa South of the Sahara: A Geographical Interpretation
ROBERT STOCK

AFRICA
SOUTH OF THE SAHARA

✳

A Geographical Interpretation

ROBERT STOCK

THE GUILFORD PRESS
New York   London

©1995 The Guilford Press
A Division of Guilford Publications, Inc.
72 Spring Street, New York, NY 10012

Marketed and distributed outside North America by Longman Group
Limited.

Printed in the United States of America

This book is printed on acid-free paper.

Last digit is print number: 9 8 7 6 5 4 3 2

Library of Congress Cataloging-in-Publication Data

Stock, Robert
    Africa south of the Sahara : a geographical interpretation /
Robert Stock.
       p.   cm. – (Texts in regional geography series)
    Includes bibliographical references and index.
    ISBN 0-89862-406-1
    1. Africa, Sub-Saharan–Geography.   2. Africa, Sub-Saharan–
History–1960– I. Title. II. Series.
DT351.S917 1994
967'.0329–dc20   94-34329
                                                           CIP

In memory of three friends:

"Alhaji" (Alhaji Isa Pantai)
"B/G" (Babangida Ahmed Tage)
"Phaku" (Dr. Sandram Phiri)

Preface

Africa in the 1990s is a very different region from the Africa I first encountered a quarter century ago. It is a more complex, more cosmopolitan continent, yet one where the optimism of the past has given way, for the most part, to a deep pessimism about prospects for the future. Nevertheless, this fascinating continent continues to be blessed with the enduring strength of its land and its peoples.

There has also been a fundamental transformation in the way we as geographers study regions such as Africa south of the Sahara. The old regional geography, with its emphasis on "where" and "what"–political divisions, precipitation, populations, products, and places–has been superseded by new perspectives emphasizing the political, social, economic, and environmental dynamics of how regions function.

This book attempts to take a fresh look at the geography of Africa south of the Sahara, focusing on the contemporary issues that challenge Africans in the 1990s, but always in the context of their historical genesis. Hopefully, it will contribute in a small way to the creation of a more informed public, less willing to accept long-established myths and conventional truisms about Africa and its people. Hopefully, it will be for many but an initial step in a longer process of learning about Africa, and finding ways of supporting, even if from afar, the African quest for self-determination and development.

The preparation of this book began more years ago than I care to admit. I would like to acknowledge with thanks the patience of The Guilford Press in waiting (and waiting . . .) for the first and revised drafts of the manuscript to materialize. Jeff Bellinger helped with basic research in the early stages of the project. Ross Hough of Queen's University prepared the maps and diagrams. Many of the photographs came from CIDA's photo library; special thanks to Pierre Vachon for his assistance in using the CIDA collection. Jim Newman's careful reading of the manuscript provided many useful suggestions on how it might be improved. Thanks are due to many others for their encouragement and suggestions, among them Jonathan Crush (particularly with respect to Chapter 26), Barry Riddell, Hamish Main, Charles Anyinam, and Geoff Williams. Students in my Geography 255 class in Belleville provided invaluable feedback as initial users of the book; special thanks to Helena Crews for her editorial notes. I owe a deep debt of gratitude to my wife, Evelyn Peters, who not only put up with years of "book" conversation but also gave unwavering encouragement for the endeavor as well as many useful suggestions. I would not have reached this stage without her support. Finally, to Matthew and Rachel, hugs and kisses from your too-often-busy Dad.

Contents

SOCIAL GEOGRAPHY

RESOURCES

AFRICAN ECONOMIES

POLITICAL GEOGRAPHY: REGIONAL CASE STUDIES

CONCLUSION

INTRODUCTION

Africa in the 1990s

Roots of Crisis

During the 1950s, Africa was a continent awakening to the prospects of independence. Ghana's independence in 1957 received extensive publicity; not only was it the first black African state to regain its independence, but it also had in Kwame Nkrumah a charismatic leader who gave voice to the aspirations of people throughout the continent.

Africa in the 1960s could be characterized as a continent in transition. During the decade, 31 countries in Africa south of the Sahara became independent, 17 of them in 1960 alone. It was a time of great optimism because independence implied that Africans would again control their own destinies. Governments could pursue policies that would be in the national interest, rather than for the benefit of colonial overlords. Development theorists, among them Walter Rostow and W. Arthur Lewis, believed that modernization was imminent, provided that appropriate policies were put in place to encourage savings and investment. Volunteers from the American Peace Corps and from other countries arrived by the thousands, optimistic that their energy, enthusiasm, and training could speed the development process.

By the early 1970s, much of the initial optimism had faded; Africa was a continent in limbo. Development had proved much more complex and difficult to achieve than modernization theorists or political leaders had envisaged. Although the first decade of independence had brought some notable progress—large increases in school enrollment, for example—the benefits were very unevenly distributed. Regional, ethnic, and political tensions were unleashed, resulting in violent clashes and coups. As the decade proceeded, the economies of more and more countries faltered in the face of world petroleum price increases, coupled with stagnating demand and low prices for other primary products. The 1970s also witnessed the Sahelian drought and with it the widespread recognition of an African environmental crisis. While some analysts saw the growth of economies in a few countries, particularly Kenya and Côte d'Ivoire, as signs of hope, many others viewed the future with growing pessimism.

During the 1980s, it became clear that Africa was a continent in decline. The news from Africa was almost always bleak—starving children in Ethiopia and Somalia; civil wars in Sudan, Angola, and other countries; and the slaughter by poachers of elephants and other wildlife. Countries such as Zambia and Tanzania had to abandon their African socialist models of development because of reduced export revenues and growing debts. The growing burden of debt affected all countries, even those such as Côte d'Ivoire that had seemed most prosperous. Few new development projects could be undertaken. Existing infrastructure–roads, for example–deteriorated because there was not enough money for maintenance. Farm production stagnated, and the cost of food and other necessities increased greatly.

By the 1990s, the prevailing view was that Africa was a continent in crisis. The rapid spread of AIDS has begun to pose an ominous threat to economies, societies, and health care systems. In addition, the economic situation has continued to deteriorate. Even in countries like Ghana, where interventions by the International Monetary Fund (IMF) and the World Bank have succeeded in creating a semblance of stability, the situation is better characterized as stable poverty rather than stable prosperity. In Liberia, Somalia, and Rwanda, bloody civil wars have brought about the collapse of the state, and with it increasing anarchy and suffering. What is most depressing is the lack of new, innovative ideas on how real progress toward development might be achieved. It is increasingly clear that if there is to be a solution to the African crisis, it will have to come from within.

Seeds of Hope

While the overall situation in Africa south of the Sahara has deteriorated, in the early 1990s there have been several positive political developments, the most dramatic of which are occurring in South Africa, where the dismantling of apartheid has proceeded faster than had previously seemed possible. The release in 1990 of Nelson Mandela, after 27 years of imprisonment, set the stage for negotiations on a constitution to give all South Africans, irrespective of race, rights of participation in the political process and rights of residence and property ownership anywhere in the country. In a referendum in March 1992, white South Africans voted strongly to endorse the ongoing reform process, allowing President de Klerk to move forward toward an agreement. Prolonged negotiations produced an agreement for constitutional reform among groups representing most South Africans, leading to the country's first fully democratic, nonracial elections in April 1994, and a successful transition to black majority rule. While it is too early to predict the future geography of South Africa, the division of space, power, and possibly wealth will be very different from what had prevailed in the past.

These developments in South Africa are already bringing about important changes elsewhere in the region. After many years of pressure to leave Namibia, South Africa withdrew in 1990 and handed over power to an elected government led by the South West African People's Organization (SWAPO), the movement that had led the anticolonial struggle for three decades. South Africa ended almost two decades of efforts to destabilize Angola and Mozambique. South Africa's withdrawal of support for insurgent groups has made possible political accommodation and reconstruction in these countries for the first time since they achieved independence in 1975. In the longer term, the end of apartheid has created opportunities for increased trade and regional cooperation between South Africa and neighboring countries.

Elsewhere the 1990s have seen a rapidly growing movement toward political pluralism. In response to increasing public pressure, the majority of military dictatorships and one-party states have moved toward multiparty political systems. Democratic changes in government have taken place peacefully in several countries, including Zambia and Benin. While it remains to be seen how thorough and successful the democratization movement will be, any development that makes autocratic leaders more accountable to the people is cause for hope.

The end of the Cold War promises to benefit Africa as a whole, even though the reduced flow of aid seems to have been one of its immediate consequences. Several wars and insurrections were fueled in the past largely by superpower rivalries. Millions of Africans have died in Ethiopia, Sudan, Angola, and Mozambique, to name only the most important examples, in wars sustained by arms shipments from the superpowers whose primary interest in the conflicts was to counter each other.

Future development in Africa south of the Sahara will depend increasingly on the mobilization of local resources and know-how. The results of efforts based on imported ideas have usually been very disappointing; neither socialist/Marxist nor conventional capitalist principles have worked very well. Furthermore, international development aid is diminishing. However, if this means that more attention is paid to indigenous resources, significant benefits may be gained. In fields such as peasant agriculture and ethnomedicine, researchers are beginning to better appreciate the logic and inherent value of African ways of doing things. The possibility of supporting and ultimately building upon what ordinary Africans already know and do represents an exciting alternative to development strategies that rely exclusively on the state and that denigrate what people themselves can contribute to the development process.

Organizing Themes in the Geography of Africa South of the Sahara

This book is intended to be an introduction to contemporary Africa south of the Sahara. It examines the sociocultural, political, and economic processes that help to explain the patterns of human utilization of the continent and its resources and the dynamics of change in Africa's geography.

The focus is Africa south of the Sahara. The five countries of North Africa – Egypt, Libya, Tunisia, Algeria, and Morocco – have stronger cultural and historical ties to the Mediterranean and southwestern Asia and, thus, have been excluded. The Indian Ocean island nations of Mauritius and Seychelles, although members of the Organization of African Unity, have been excluded. Not only are these

states demographically and culturally distinct, but also their socioeconomic paths have increasingly diverged from those of continental African states. Other island nations – the Comoros, Madagascar, Cape Verde, Equatorial Guinea, and São Tomé e Príncipe – have been included because of their closer proximity, both spatially and socioeconomically, to continental Africa. South Africa has been included, despite its unique political and social history and greater modern development. There are strong regional economic ties between South Africa and several of its neighbors, and the cultures and many aspects of the economies and histories of the the majority of South Africans are characteristically African. With the transition to majority rule, South Africa will no doubt take its place as one of the most influential members of the family of African nations.

The book is divided into nine units of three chapters each. Individual chapters explore different aspects of broad topic areas such as demography, natural resources, and urban economies and societies, each of which represents a distinct area of scholarship with its own questions and debates. While individual chapters explore particular topics, there are a number of broad themes that draw the chapters together. These represent some of the more important points of debate in African studies and, as such, are themes around which further reading or term assignments could be structured. Several of these themes will be introduced below.

Unity in Diversity

The question of whether Africa south of the Sahara is better characterized by its unity or by its diversity has had a long history of debate within African studies. This book acknowledges the importance of both perspectives, but gives precedence to the theme of unity, that is, "unity in diversity."

Unity and diversity are both evident in Africa's physical geography. The ancient Precambrian rocks of Africa have been warped, faulted, weathered, and eroded over hundreds of millions of years, giving rise to a landscape characterized by vast plateaus and plains with comparatively few complicating physical features. Yet closer inspection reveals considerable topographic diversity, ranging from snowcapped volcanoes to deep rift valleys. The continent may be divided into vast regions sharing a similar climate and ecology: desert, semidesert, savanna, and tropical forest. Nevertheless, when these ecological regions are compared, the differences between them are immense. The physical geography of Africa south of the Sahara is explored in Chapter 2.

Unity and diversity are evident in the cultural geography of Africa south of the Sahara. There are thousands of distinct ethnic groups, each possessing a particular set of cultural attributes; several individual countries are home to between 100 and 300 ethnic groups. Despite the evident complexity of the cultural map of Africa south of the Sahara, we can equally point to significant dimensions of cultural unity. This common cultural heritage of black Africa, which Jacques Maquet has called "Africanity," is discussed in Chapter 3.

Unity and diversity are evident in the economic geography. African countries face significant problems of underdevelopment, including inadequate infrastructure, a weak industrial sector, and heavy reliance on raw-material exports. All have dual economies, comprised of a large indigenous sector of small-scale producers and a small, foreign-dominated modern sector. Not all African economies are identical, however. Some depend on mineral exports, whereas others rely on agriculture. In addition, Africa's economic geography reflects attempts at different times and in different countries to implement a wide range of economic models: socialist, capitalist, and mixed.

The thematic structure of this book serves to emphasize the striking similarities in cultural heritage, historical evolution, and contemporary political and economic development, rather than the inevitable differences found among the 46 political units that constitute Africa south of the Sahara. The vignettes included in each chapter serve as a reminder of the complexity and diversity of the unique geographies of particular localities.

Underdevelopment and Development

Africa south of the Sahara is the poorest of the world's megaregions. Of the 40 countries with per capita annual incomes of $500 or less, 28 are located in Africa south of the Sahara. In two-thirds of these countries, economic growth failed to keep pace with the rate of population increase between 1975 and 1990. Social indicators, ranging from access to basic education to life expectancy provide further evidence of African underdevelopment.

Except for Liberia, all parts of Africa south of the Sahara have experienced European colonial rule. Structures established during the colonial era have contributed significantly to African underdevelopment. The colonial legacy includes national boundaries that pay little regard to physical and cultural realities and externally oriented economies based on the export of raw materials. The cultural legacy of colonialism is evident in religion (Christianity), education, language, and values. These imprints have proved to be very resilient indeed.

While the colonial era has shaped contemporary Africa in many ways, the historical legacy of precolonial Africa is also important, especially in a symbolic sense. For inspiration and a sense of identity, African intellectuals look back to the accomplishments of their ancestors: the art of Ife and Benin; the architecture of Zimbabwe and Lalibela; the intellectual, political, and economic accomplishments of ancient Ghana and Mali.

The history of comparatively recent times often has had a more tangible significance. In countries such as Guinea-Bissau and Zimbabwe, prolonged struggles for independence have created a strong sense of national identity. Several countries, including Ethiopia, Uganda, Sudan, and Angola, have had lengthy periods of civil war and unrest that have undermined whatever prospects for development might have existed. Then there are the legacies of particular rulers that some countries have inherited: for example, Nyerere (Tanzania), who could be characterized as a visionary, or Amin (Uganda), as a brutal despot.

Debates concerning Africa's prospects for development, and the best strategy for achieving it, have raged continuously since the advent of independence. Prospects at first seemed very good; modernization theorists promised that an age of prosperity could be achieved through savings, investment, and specialization. When the results of such policies proved to be disappointing, there came into focus dependency theories emphasizing that the Third World had been underdeveloped, not developed, as a result of the European presence.

During the late 1970s and early 1980s, the underdevelopment versus development debate continued, albeit with an altered focus. Development theories shifted from an emphasis on the top-down, macroscale approaches of modernization theory to bottom-up approaches emphasizing small-scale development projects benefiting local communities. Meanwhile, underdevelopment theories became more Marxist in their analysis, emphasizing the self-interest of ruling classes in independent African states as a factor in perpetuated underdevelopment.

Since the early 1980s, the locus of development debates has shifted again. The IMF and World Bank have imposed structural adjustment policies emphasizing currency devaluation, reduced government involvement in the economy, and other measures designed to stimulate economic growth. The IMF and World Bank argued that inefficiency and inappropriate policies account for the disappointing pace of development. Underdevelopment theorists, conversely, have attributed the deepening crisis to the massive burden of debt and the heavy-handed intervention of the IMF and World Bank.

Development is a universal goal. Individual families struggle to make ends meet and to find some means of bettering the lot of their children. Groups of men and/or women come together and pool their resources in cooperative societies, hoping for mutual gain. Every community and region hopes for investment to spur local development; many agitate long and hard to gain official favor. At a national level, macroscale economic and social policies are designed and implemented with the objective of achieving progress. Likewise, the international discourse about aid and the global economy always focuses on development as an ultimate goal.

Among the themes explored in this book is the context and significance of development decision making at different levels of resolution, ranging from the individual farmer's choice of what crops to produce to the decisions that governments make about development objectives and strategies. This is not to imply that there is necessarily a wide range of choice; individuals and governments may be equally constrained in their choices because of factors beyond their control. Moreover, members of a single family or community are bound to have diverse priorities for development and different opportunities and constraints that affect what they can accomplish. In short, development, whether in theory or in practice, is a very complex and patchy process.

Probably the most important constraint on development is Africa's vulnerability within the global political economy. World markets for African raw-material exports have been characterized by large price fluctuations and a general downward trend, making sound longer-term planning precarious at best. Large increases in external debt, and in the cost of servicing that debt, have accompanied the declining terms of trade. To retain access to international credit, African governments have had to accept the intervention of the IMF and World Bank, which some have characterized as a new form of colonialism. Moreover, although it has more need for development assistance than any other continent, aid to Africa has been stagnating. International tensions have declined, and other regions, particularly Eastern Europe, have emerged as competitors for limited aid money. Beyond the immediate hardships caused by reduced flows of aid is the larger question of whether aid donors have effectively abandoned Africa south of the Sahara to its underdeveloped fate.

Aspects of the continuing debates about development and underdevelopment recur throughout this book and are of great importance in the interpretation of the condition of African societies and economies. Varying perspectives are presented on key development/underdevelopment debates. It is important that you think carefully about the issues involved, do further research on the subject, and make up your own mind. Nevertheless, it should be noted that my own views generally conform to an underdevelopment perspective that identifies various external influences, starting with the establishment of the slave trade and continuing to the present day, as a primary reason for the underdevelopment of Africa south of the Sahara.

The Cultural Roots of African Societies

African cultures emphasize the importance of cooperation and continuity—the chain of life from past to present to future. Social units such as the extended family, community, and ethnic group assume great importance; individual rights and individual accomplishments do not have much importance in African tradition. The importance of maintaining the strength of social units through reproduction is one of the factors accounting for fertility rates that are still the highest in the world.

The organization of production also shows strong cultural influences. The techniques of production are often specific to a culture and depend on knowledge passed from one generation to another. So too are rituals and traditions widely undertaken in conjunction with planting, harvesting, and other productive activities. Modern science, which long ignored or dismissed indigenous knowledge, has begun to appreciate the sophistication and relevance of such knowledge for contemporary development.

While the role of cultural inheritance may be less obvious in the daily lives of urban Africans, especially those who have substantial Western education, it does continue to influence values and behaviors. The continuing strength of extended families in the city and the maintenance of strong economic and so-

cial ties between urban-based and rural-based family members are examples of how cultural heritage persists.

Cultural geographers have begun to recognize that when culture is treated unitarily, there is danger that the importance of cultural differences *within* society, particularly between men and women and between different social classes, may not receive adequate recognition. This argument has particular relevance for the study of African societies, where there tends to be clear differentiation between the cultural and economic lives of men and women, as well as important differences between the lives of those who are rich and poor, and urban and rural.

The relevance of gender is particularly evident in the division of labor. Women are not only responsible for child rearing and housework, but also, in most societies, for food production and obtaining water and fuelwood for household use. Development planners have only belatedly recognized the crucial role that women play in African economies, and the importance of women's organizations, whether economic or cultural. Past development efforts often have failed because of the assumption that in order to succeed programs needed only to target men as the heads of households. The belated recognition of the importance of gender differences has given rise not only to development initiatives focusing specifically on the needs of African women but also to a growing literature in which many aspects of the lives of African women are explored.

The Environment as the Material Basis for Development

The economies and societies of Africa south of the Sahara are based fundamentally on the environment as a sustenance base. As such, environmental health, economic health, and societal health are inevitably interwoven.

A significant majority of Africans are primary producers—farmers, herders, fishers, and hunters—who depend directly on environmental resources for their sustenance. For farmers, access to reasonably fertile soil and favorable weather conditions are necessary to obtain a reasonable crop. Not only profits but often the survival of the family and community are jeopardized when crops fail. African primary producers are very concious of the importance of the environmental resources upon which they depend, as is evident in traditional strategies of resource protection.

The prosperity of other Africans is also linked to the environment as a sustenance base. Most export earnings are derived from primary products, principally agricultural goods and minerals. Many urban-based Africans are employed in the large-scale processing of primary products, ranging from oil seeds to wood and minerals. Moreover, the cost of living is greatly affected by the availability of food, which in turn reflects environmental and other factors bearing on productivity in the countryside.

With the increasing global awareness of environmental issues, and particularly with the publication in 1987 of *Our Common Future*, the report of the World Commission on Environment and Development, the question of development sustainability has assumed great importance. Sustainability implies that strategies to meet the needs of current generations must also ensure that the ability of future generations to do likewise is not compromised.

The sustainability of development takes on particular significance in the African context. The continuing depletion of the natural-resource base, especially soil, forests, water supplies, and wildlife, is of growing concern. Recurring episodes of drought and crop failure point to the seriousness of these environmental crises. Most scientists studying the so-called greenhouse effect believe that droughts will become increasingly frequent and severe, especially on the dry margins of areas used for farming and herding. The consequences for those directly affected by environmental decay may well include poverty, famine, ill health, and forced migration.

What happens to the environment, as society's sustenance base, cannot be separated from larger-scale development decisions, ranging from official directives to cultivate soil-depleting crops like cotton to the construction of large dams that may force farmers and herders onto less productive and more vulnerable lands. In decisions of this sort, the prospects of immediate returns have often taken precedence over questions of sustainability and dangers of long-term environmental effects.

It is hardly new that ignorance of the needs and structures of African societies and economies has given rise to inappropriate development decisions. People of European heritage often have referred to Africa as "the dark continent," implying not only that its people were dark skinned but also that African societies were mysterious and primitive. This book attempts to provide a broad and balanced introduction to the geography of Africa south of the Sahara, thus contributing to a greater knowledge of the continent, its peoples, its problems, and its prospects.

Further Reading

Africanists make use of a large number of national and international bibliographic sources that include the following:

African Historical Dictionary (a series of source books for individual countries)
Cambridge Encyclopedia of Africa
A Current Bibliography on African Affairs
International African Bibliography

There are several journals of African studies that contain a wide variety of articles on topics of historical and contemporary interest. Some of the more important of these journals are the following:

Africa
African Affairs
African Studies Review
Canadian Journal of African Studies
Journal of African History
Journal of Modern African Studies
Journal of Southern African Studies
Review of African Political Economy
Rural Africana
Third World Quarterly

Current events and recent trends can be followed using these popular periodicals:

Africa
Africa Report

African Business
New Internationalist
South
Weekly Review
West Africa

For a list of organizations with a primary interest in some aspect of African development, see *Review of African Political Economy*, no. 54 (1992), pp. 126–132.

OVERVIEW

The three chapters in this section serve as a brief introduction to Africa south of the Sahara and set the stage for the sections which follow.

Chapter 1 introduces the map of Africa. As in any new field of study, many of the names will be unfamiliar at first. Time spent now becoming better acquainted with the countries of Africa, their locations relative to other countries, and some of their basic characteristics will pay dividends later. "Knowing the map" is essential for grasping the geographical context of situations and events, past or present.

Chapter 2 is a brief description of the African enviornment and the processes shaping it. Although this book is about the human geography of Africa south of the Sahara, the fundamental importance of the environment for human activity cannot be denied. This is particularly the case in Africa, where the great majority of people are primary producers relying directly on the environment for their sustenance, and where so many concerns have been raised in recent years about the nature and significance for humans of environmental degradation.

In Chapter 3, the focus turns to the people of Africa. In this chapter, I discuss some of the characteristics that are typical of African cultures, and I argue that culture—a shared set of fundamental values, beliefs, and ways of doing things—is a glue that binds Africa south of the Sahara. Many attempts at development have failed because the cultural context has been disregarded. In Chapter 3, I discuss the various cleavages that divide Africans as a whole, as well as Africans who are members of a particular cultural group. These cleavages include ethnicity, religion, social class, and gender. Thus, I emphasize the importance not only of the unity but also the diversity of African peoples.

1

The Map of Africa

The English satirist Jonathan Swift, writing in the early 18th century, commented on the prevalent ignorance about Africa and the African people:

> So geographers in Afric maps
> With savage pictures fill the gaps
> And o'r uninhabitable downs
> Placed elephants for lack of towns

A century later, Africa remained, in the public mind, "darkest Africa," a mysterious and virtually unknown continent. As the end of the twentieth century approaches, Africa is still the least-known continent. The names of certain African countries are often in the news, but people generally know too little about these countries to give what they read and hear meaning. Where is Mali? Is Malawi a different place? Is it Ghana or Guyana that is in Africa? What was the former name of Burkina Faso? Is Equatorial Guinea a part of Guinea? Simple questions such as these are difficult even for college-educated Westerners.

Africa covers a vast territory. At its widest from west to east and at its longest from south to north the distance is almost the same: approximately 7,500 km. To put this into context, the distance from Los Angeles to New York is 4,470 km. Or, if you prefer, with a surface area of 24.6 million sq km, Africa

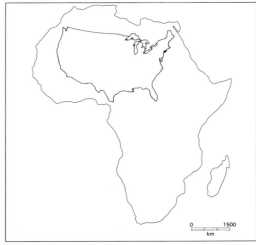

Figure 1.1. Africa and the continental United States: relative sizes.

south of the Sahara is about three times the size of the continental United States (see Figure 1.1).

Just as Africa has occupied a relatively small part of the conciousness of most Westerners, it has also been portrayed on world maps in a way that makes it appear smaller than it actually is. The widespread use in the past of the Mercator and other scale-distorting map projections has contributed to misperceptions about the relative sizes of land masses. Because distortion with a Mercator projection increases markedly with distance from the equator, places at higher latitudes, such as Greenland and Canada, appear much larger than places of comparable size nearer the equator. For example, while Greenland appears to be roughly the same size as Africa on a Mercator projection, it is actually only 7.3% as large, or slightly smaller than Sudan or Zaire. Maps that result in the continent appearing smaller than it is help to perpetuate ignorance about the importance and complexity of Africa.

The Political Map

The contemporary political map of Africa south of the Sahara bears little resemblence to that of a hundred years ago when the scramble to carve up the continent among the European imperialist powers was in full swing. The details of how the colonial division of Africa was accomplished are discussed in Chapter 5. What is important at this point is to recognize that African boundaries are recent and often unrelated to either local cultural/

Figure 1.2.. The countries of Africa.

Table 1.1. Countries of Africa South of the Sahara

	Capital	Area (1,000 km²)	Population (millions)	Per capita income	Human development index
Angola	Luanda	1246	9.5	$610	.150
Benin	Porto Novo	113	4.9	380	.114
Botswana	Gaberone	600	1.2	1600	.524
Burkina Faso	Ouagadougou	274	9.3	340	.081
Burundi	Bujumbura	28	5.7	220	.177
Cameroon	Yaoundé	475	11.9	1000	.328
Cape Verde	Praia	4	.4	780	.428
Central African Republic	Bangui	623	3.1	390	.166
Chad	N'Djamena	1284	5.8	190	.087
Comoros	Moroni	2	.5	460	.274
Congo	Brazzaville	342	2.4	940	.374
Côte d'Ivoire	Yamoussoukro	322	12.4	790	.311
Djibouti	Djibouti	22	.4	NA	.083
Equatorial Guinea	Malabo	28	.4	330	.186
Eritrea	Asmara	94	3.2	NA	NA
Ethiopia	Addis Ababa	1130	49.6	120	.166
Gabon	Libreville	267	1.2	2690	.510
Gambia	Banjul	11	.9	240	.064
Ghana	Accra	239	15.3	390	.311
Guinea	Conakry	246	5.9	430	.066
Guinea-Bissau	Bissau	36	1.0	180	.088
Kenya	Nairobi	583	25.0	360	.399
Lesotho	Maseru	30	1.8	470	.432
Liberia	Monrovia	111	2.6	NA	.220
Madagascar	Antananarivo	587	12.0	230	.371
Malawi	Lilongwe	118	8.8	180	.179
Mali	Bamako	1240	8.7	270	.072
Mauritania	Nouakchott	1031	1.9	500	.140
Mozambique	Maputo	802	16.1	80	.155
Namibia	Windhoek	824	1.5	1030	.440
Niger	Niamey	1267	7.9	290	.079
Nigeria	Abuja	924	99.0	250	.242
Rwanda	Kigali	26	7.1	320	.213
São Tomé e Príncipe	São Tomé	1	.1	340	.399
Senegal	Dakar	196	7.6	650	.189
Sierra Leone	Freetown	72	4.2	220	.048
Somalia	Mogadishu	638	8.0	170	.118
South Africa	Pretoria	1221	38.9	2470	.766
Sudan	Khartoum	2506	25.8	NA	.164
Swaziland	Mbabane	1	.8	900	.462
Tanzania	Dodoma	945	25.2	130	.266
Togo	Lomé	57	3.8	390	.225
Uganda	Kampala	236	16.9	250	.204
Zaire	Kinshasa	2345	38.6	260	.299
Zambia	Lusaka	753	8.3	390	.351
Zimbabwe	Harare	391	10.1	650	.413

political realities or natural features. Sometimes this artificiality leads to international disputes, as indicated by the examples of Vignette 1.2

Another unfortunate colonial legacy is the extreme fragmentation of the political map.

In all, there are 46 independent states, some of which are too small to be considered economically viable. The small size and national populations of the majority of African states (Table 1.1) is a continuing constraint on development. Certain states have shapes that are

Vignette 1.1. Lesotho and Zambia: Landlocked and Vulnerable

The fifteen landlocked states include the majority of Africa's poorest and least developed countries. While there is no single explanation for this poverty, landlocked states share a common disadvantage of dependence on neighboring countries for access to the sea. Economic development and even political stability may depend on keeping these transportation routes open. Lesotho and Zambia are telling examples of the importance of dependable access to the sea and of the obstacles that landlocked countries may face in attempting to secure such access.

Lesotho is clearly the most vulnerable of Africa's landlocked states. As an enclave completely surrounded by South Africa, Lesotho was forced to remain virtually silent about apartheid and about periodic infringements by South Africa on Lesotho's sovereignty. In 1986, South Africa, claiming that "terrorists" belonging to the African National Congress were being permitted to stay in Lesotho, imposed a total blockade, which was only lifted after Lesotho's compliant government was overthrown in a coup and replaced by one even more subservient.

Zambia would appear to be less vulnerable since it borders on eight other countries, five of which have ocean ports. However, when an international embargo on trade with Rhodesia was imposed following that country's unilateral declaration of independence in 1965, the route by which Zambia had exported its copper and imported oil and other goods was cut off. The alternate route via Zaire and Angola could not be used because of the state of insurgency in Angola. Mozambique could not be used because of insurgency and the lack of an established route.

To overcome the blockade, Zambia arranged to have a pipeline and a rail line constructed to the port of Dar es Salaam in Tanzania. Western countries were unwilling to finance the Tazara railway, so Zambia turned to China. The railway was an engineering success, but because of the great distances involved, port congestion, and low volumes of freight, it has proved to be of limited usefulness. While Zambia has been less vulnerable since Zimbabwe achieved independence and South Africa abolished apartheid, its long-term prospects remain constrained by its landlocked status.

unusual and unhelpful. Gambia is the most extreme example. It extends 325 km along the Gambia River and is no more than 30 km wide. In addition, except for a short coastline, Gambia is completely surrounded by Senegal.

Fifteen African states are landlocked (Figure 1.3). Most of these states share a common legacy of colonial disinterest and neglect, because of the perception that they had few possibilities for development. Countries such as Mali, Niger, and Chad served as labor-reserve areas from which workers could be recruited for the planations and mines of more prosperous colonies. The (relative) exceptions to this pattern of colonial neglect were Uganda, once described by Winston Churchill as the "pearl

of Africa," and Southern and Northern Rhodesia (now Zimbabwe and Zambia), which were prosperous centers of mining and commercial agriculture. Ethiopia joined the ranks of Africa's landlocked states in 1993 after its coastal province of Eritrea, annexed in 1954, succeeded in gaining its independence after three decades of armed struggle.

Africa's landlocked states continue to be very poor and underdeveloped. Only four of them (Zimbabwe, Botswana, Lesotho, and Swaziland) have annual per capita incomes greater than $400. They also tend to have small populations; only Ethiopia and Uganda have more than 10 million people. However, their greatest source of vulnerability results

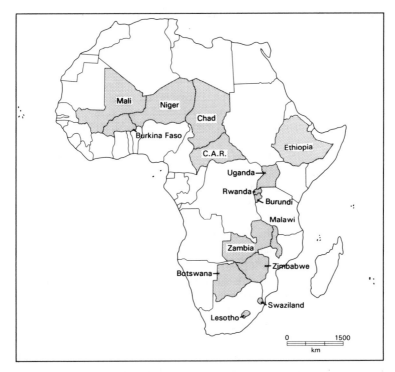

Figure 1.3. Africa's landlocked states. Ethiopia became Africa's 15th landlocked state in 1993 when Eritrea became independent.

from a perpetual dependence on neighboring states for an outlet to the sea. This problem is exacerbated by the frequent absence of reasonable transportation linkages. Five of the landlocked states have no railroads, and even where linkages exist, political tension between neighbors or within neighboring states may preclude the use of these railroads (Vignette 1.1).

One of the ongoing tasks for those involved in African studies is to "relearn" the map periodically as changes are made in place names or administrative structures (see Table 1.2). In several cases, name changes at independence or after independence represent an attempt to replace colonial names with ones more historically and culturally relevant. Several countries have also relocated their capital cities. In each case, the change is justified as a means of bringing government closer to the people by abandoning colonial seats of government for smaller, more centrally located places.

Levels of Development

Maps are a powerful tool for displaying and analyzing spatial distributions, such as variations in wealth and the quality of life. The maps in Figures 1.5 and 1.6 illustrate contrasting approaches to the definition of development in the continent of Africa.

While Africa south of the Sahara is, taken as a whole, very poor, extreme variations of wealth and development exist across the continent. There are significant differences between the most and least developed countries in income, economic diversity, and quality of life. There are also large differences within each country—between urban and rural areas, between different regions, and between the rich and the poor.

There is no universally accepted measure of development, in part because development is multidimensional and in part because there are disagreements about what development entails. The most widely used measure is per

Vignette 1.2. Disputed Borders

On several international borders, disputes about territory have occurred as part of the legacy of the arbitrary political division of Africa under colonialism. These disputes have been most serious in places where colonial borders have divided a particular ethnic group between two countries or where it has been felt that historical–political affiliations have not been recognized.

The postage stamps shown below (Figure 1.4) illustrate how certain governments have sought to correct what they have perceived as long-term injustices.

The first stamp is from Somalia and shows the neighboring Ogaden region of Ethiopia as part of Somalia. This region has a predominantly Somali population and has long been claimed as part of "Greater Somalia." In 1977, Somalia invaded Ethiopia in an unsuccessful attempt to take over the Ogaden. Although the Somalis have been less aggressive in pursuing their territorial claims in recent years, they have not abandoned their belief that the Ogaden is rightfully theirs.

The second stamp is from Mauritania and celebrates the annexation of the southern part of Spanish (now Western) Sahara. In 1974, Spain decided to abandon its colony in large part because of the growing threat of a Moroccan invasion. Ignoring a judgment from the International Court of Justice that rejected the claims of Morocco and Mauritania, Spain signed a treaty in November 1975 with those two countries, under which Spanish Sahara was to be divided between Morocco and Mauritania. The Saharan people were not consulted about this arrangement, and the Saharan liberation organization called POLISARIO has pursued a fierce guerrilla war for independence. Although the total population of Western Sahara was only about 100,000, POLISARIO managed to force the Mauritanians to withdraw and renounce their territorial claims in 1978. The struggle against Moroccan occupation continues.

a
b

Figure 1.4. "Lay claim to thy neighbor." (a) Somalia, 1964. The map shows parts of neighboring countries as Somali territory. (b) Mauritania, 1976. The stamp celebrates Mauritania's ill-fated attempt to annex part of Western Sahara.

capita gross national product (GNP). In only six African countries south of the Sahara is per capita GNP above $1,000, while in seven countries it is less than $200 (see Table 1.1 and Figure 1.5). The $2,690 GNP per capita of Gabon is 34 times that of Mozambique, which at $80 has the continent's lowest reported per capita GNP. However, while variations in per capita income are certainly important, aggregate national income data do not show

how wealth is distributed in a society, or whether available wealth has been used to improve productivity or the quality of life.

Another measure, which is being used with increasing frequency, is the Human Development Index (HDI) (see Table 1.1 and Figure 1.6). In the *Human Development Report, 1990*, published under the auspices of the United Nations Development Program, the HDI is described as an index of the range and quali-

Table 1.2. Some Important Postindependence Changes to the Map of Africa

Countries renamed at time of independence

New name	Former name
Botswana	Bechuanaland
Djibouti	French Somaliland
Ghana	Gold Coast
Lesotho	Basutoland
Malawi	Nyasaland
Zambia	Northern Rhodesia
Zimbabwe	Rhodesia

Countries renamed since independence

New name	Former name
Benin	Dahomey
Burkina Faso	Upper Volta
Malagasy Republic	Madagascar
Congo-Kinshasa	Zaire
Tanzania	Tanganyika and Zanzibar

Name changes to capital cities

New name	Former name	Country
Banjul	Bathurst	Gambia
Harare	Salisbury	Zimbabwe
Kinshasa	Léopoldville	Zaire
N'Djamena	Fort Lamy	Chad
Maputo	Lorenço Marques	Mozambique

New capital city established

New capital	Old capital	Country
Abuja	Lagos	Nigeria
Dodoma	Dar es Salaam	Tanzania
Lilongwe	Zomba	Malawi
Yamoussoukro	Abidjan	Côte d'Ivoire

ty of options available to people to shape their own destinies. The index is calculated by using measures of life expectancy, education, and per capita income, which are combined according to a methodology described in the report

The HDI is a serious attempt to move beyond the limitations of per capita GNP. However, if another mix of variables, or a different weighting of variables was used, somewhat different results would emerge. Moreover, national HDI scores may be quite misleading for countries such as South Africa where there are very large differences in human welfare between social groups within the country. Thus, care should be exercised in drawing conclusions based on the proportional size of HDI scores for different countries or on the ranking of countries when their HDI scores are fairly similar. Nevertheless, this index is useful in focusing attention on broad differences in levels of national development and in identifying countries whose people are the most disadvantaged.

Regional and Political Groupings

In a continent as large and diverse as Africa, it is inevitable that various groupings of countries will be identified. One approach to the definition of such groups is membership in regional economic and political organizations or membership in global organizations based on shared culture and history. The most important political organization linking African states is the Organization of African Unity. All African states, with the exception of Western Sahara, are members. Among the regional political–economic organizations, two stand out: ECOWAS (Economic Community of West African States), which links 16 countries in West Africa, and SADC (Southern African Development Community), composed of 10 states in southern Africa that came together with the objective of reducing their dependence on South Africa (see Figure 1.7a). There are a number of smaller, less important regional-development organizations, one of which is the Mano River Union linking Sierra Leone, Liberia, and Guinea.

Several African nations are members of the Commonwealth of Nations or of La Francophonie (see Figure 1.7b). The former organization brings together states from all continents which were formerly British colonies. The latter brings together the former French and Belgian colonies of Africa with other French-speaking nations. These groupings provide opportunities for formal policy coordination, as in the case of the Commonwealth's former boycott of trade with South Africa.

In addition to groups defined by membership in an organization, regional groupings are often defined on the basis of geographical proximity and perceived similarity. Figure 1.8 shows some of the commonly used informal

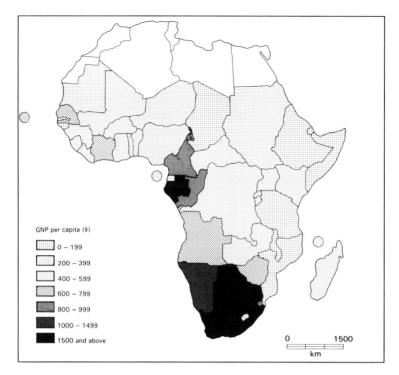

GNP per capita ($)

0 – 199

200 – 399

400 – 599

600 – 799

800 – 999

1000 – 1499

1500 and above

0   1500
km

Figure 1.5. GNP per capita, 1989. Countries with the highest GNPs per capita include most of the continent's major mineral producers. Data source: World Bank. *World Development Report, 1991.* New York: Oxford University Press, 1991.

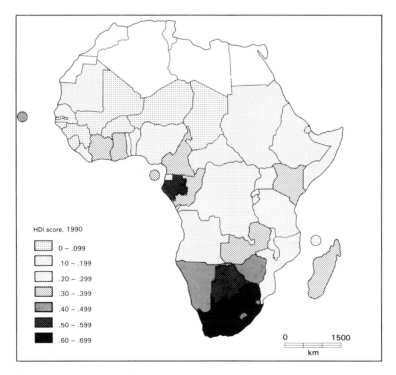

HDI score, 1990

0 – .099

.10 – .199

.20 – .299

.30 – .399

.40 – .499

.50 – .599

.60 – .699

0   1500
km

Figure 1.6. Human Development Index score, 1990. Comparing Figures 1.5 and 1.6, there appears to be a broad correlation between GNP per capita and HDI score. Data source: United Nations Development Program (UNDP). *Human Development Report, 1991.* New York: Oxford University Press, 1991.

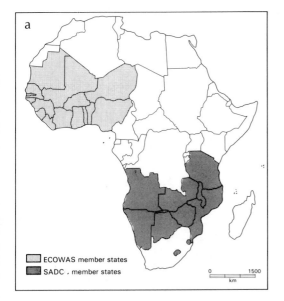

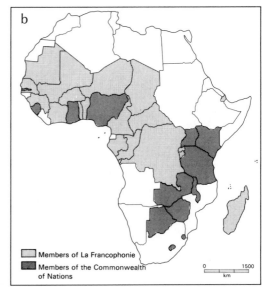

Figure 1.7. Examples of major political and economic groupings: (a) Economic Community of West African States and Southern African Development Community States. (b) La Francophonie and Commonwealth of Nations.

regional groupings of countries in Africa south of the Sahara. Note that there is no single defining characteristic and less than complete agreement on which countries should be included in each group.

The term *West Africa* commonly refers to countries to the west of the Cameroon–Nigeria border, an important physical and cultural dividing line in the continent. The Sahelian countries form a significant subregion within

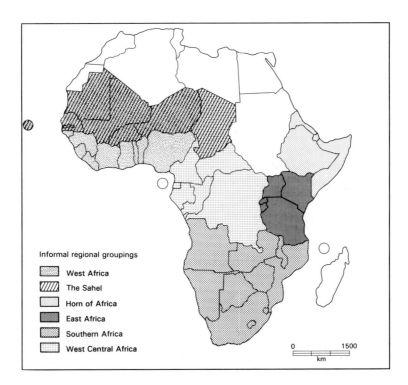

Figure 1.8. Informal regional groupings of countries

Figure 1.9. Major rivers, lakes, and coastal waters.

West Africa characterized by desert–margin environments and, especially in recent years, recurring drought. *East Africa* consists of Kenya, Uganda, and Tanzania, the former members of the East African Common Market, but Rwanda and Burundi are usually included because of their strong economic ties with the others. With political changes in South Africa, *Southern Africa* is becoming much more meaningful as a grouping than the formerly common Frontline States, a grouping that had consisted of countries defined by their opposition to apartheid and nearness to South Africa. Other informal groupings include the four countries of the Horn of Africa (Ethiopia, Eritrea, Somalia, and Djibouti; Sudan is sometimes included in this group) and the states of west central Africa anchored by Cameroon to the north and Zaire to the south.

The Physical Map

At first glance, the physical map of Africa looks rather uninteresting. The coastline of the continent is often straight and uncomplicated; there are only a few identifiable seas, gulfs, and other adjoining bodies of water. Topographically, the vast, gently undulating plateaus create an impression of uniformity, especially when there are no great mountain ranges such as the Himalayas or Rockies to catch one's eye.

Table 1.3. Largest Rivers in Africa South of the Sahara

River	Length (km)	Length Rank[a]	Drainage basin (km²)	Drainage basin Rank	Discharge rate (m²/sec)	Discharge rate Rank
Nile	6,670	1	3,349	3	2,830	NA
Congo (Zaire)	4,630	10	3,822	2	39,000	2
Niger	4,100	14	2,092	9	5,700	37
Zambezi	2,650	33	1,331	15	7,070	29
Ubangi	2,460	40	773	33	7,500	28
Orange	2,250	50	855	26	215	NA

[a]Rank among world rivers.
Source: *World Facts and Figures,* 3rd ed., 1989.

A closer inspection, however, reveals considerable variety in Africa's topography. For example, there are spectacular escarpments up to 2,000 m fringing the southern African coast; the escarpment known as the Drakensberg Mountains in South Africa is particularly spectacular. Then there is the world's largest rift-valley system, extending from southern Mozambique through eastern Africa to the Red Sea and beyond. And to this list can be added the magnificent volcanic peaks, notably Mounts Kenya, Kilimanjaro, Elgon, and Cameroon, which rise to between 4,000 m and almost 6,000 m above sea level.

A half-dozen major river systems together drain some four-fifths of Africa south of the Sahara (Table 1.3 and Figure 1.9). Four rivers stand out: the Nile, the Congo, the Niger, and the Zambezi. Others of regional note are the Orange, the Limpopo, the Kasai, the Ubangi, the Benue, the Volta, and the Senegal.

Because the coastline is regular and has very few substantial indentations, Africa south of the Sahara has few good natural harbors. The scarcity of harbors, along with the presence of escarpments and major rapids near the mouths of many of the largest rivers, impeded early European attempts to explore and exploit the continent. The nature of the coastline, specifically the scarcity of good harbors, remains a significant impediment to development in many countries.

Becoming familiar with the locations of prominent physical features as well as other elements of the African map is not a particularly important end in itself. However, familiarity does provide a basis for interpreting specific issues and situations, each of which occurs in a particular context that is spatial, environmental, social, political, and economic. Thus, the maps in this chapter serve to establish the spatial context for our study of the geography of Africa south of the Sahara.

Further Reading

Thematic and national atlases are available that address in considerable detail various aspects of the geography of Africa south of the Sahara. The list that follows identifies a broad selection of these valuale sources.

For a handy and easily used survey of Africa in maps, see the following source:

Griffiths, I. L. L. *An Atlas of African Affairs.* 2nd ed. London: Routledge, 1994.

There are several excellent African historical atlases:

Griffiths, I. L. L. *Africa on Maps Dating from the Twelfth to the Eighteenth Century.* Leipzig, Germany: Editions Leipzig, 1968.
Ajayi, J. F. A., and M. Crowder. *Historical Atlas of Africa.* London: Longman, 1985.
Fage, J. D. *An Atlas of African History.* New York: Africana, 1980.
Kwamenha-Poh, M., J. Tosh, R. Waller, and M. Tidy. *African History in Maps.* London: Longman, 1982.

For a fascinating case study of fact and fiction in early maps of Africa, see the following source:

Bassett, T. J., and P. W. Porter. "From the best authorities: The mountains of Kong in the cartography of West Africa." *Journal of African History,* vol. 32 (1991), pp. 367–414.

There are two valuable series of atlases each volume of which pertains to a particular country:

Barbour, K. M., J. S. Oguntoyinbo, J. O. C. Onyemelukwe, and J. C. Nwafor. *Nigeria in Maps.* London: Hodder and Stoughton, 1982. (Other volumes in the series deal with Sierra Leone [1966], Malawi [1972], Tanzania [1971], Zambia [1971], Liberia [1972].)

Barbour, K. M., J. S. Oguntoyinbo, J. O. C. Onyemelukwe, and J. C. Nwafor. *Les Atlas Jeune Afrique: République Centraficaine.* Paris: Editions Jeune Afrique, 1984. (The Jeune Afrique atlas series also includes volumes on Africa [1973], Congo [1977], Niger [1980], and Senegal [1980].)

The following are a few examples of thematic atlases on Africa:

Diesfeld, H. J., and H. J. Hecklau. *Kenya: A Geomedical Monograph.* Heidelberg, Germany: Springer, 1978.

Food and Agriculture Organization of the United Nations (FAO). *Atlas of African Agriculture.* Rome: FAO, 1986.

Murray, J. *Cultural Atlas of Africa.* New York: Facts on File, 1982.

Thompson, B. W. *The Climate of Africa.* Oxford: Oxford University Press, 1965.

For ideas on African underdevelopment in global perspective, see the following source:

Kidron, M., and R. Segal. *New State of the World Atlas.* Rev. ed. London: Heineman, 1987.

2

✸

The Physical Environment

In Africa, as elsewhere, human organization is affected in countless ways by characteristics of the physical environment. At the same time, "nature" continues to be modified, sometimes profoundly, by human actions. This chapter provides a brief description of the African physical environment and touches upon some of the most important environmental processes. It begins with a survey of Africa's geology and physiography, then moves to the dynamics of climate, and concludes with brief descriptions of the interlinkage of climate, vegetation, and soils in each of Africa's physical megaregions (biomes). This survey sets the stage for a closer examination in other chapters of various human–environmental linkages.

Geology and Physiography

The African continent has an exceptional degree of physiographic uniformity, which is particularly evident in the relative uniformity and vastness of its plains and high plateaus, the long escarpments abruptly separating one physiographic unit from another, and the infrequently indented coastline. The appearance of regularity partly reflects the widespread occurrence of Precambrian bedrock; most exposed materials consist of Precambrian

outcrops, the weathered remnants of Precambrian formations, or sedimentary deposits originally derived from Precambrian rocks. The fact that particular tectonic and weathering processes have operated at a grand scale, both spatially and temporally, has also contributed to the broad uniformity of the physical landscape that we see today.

Geographers often distinguish between "Low Africa" and "High Africa," separated by a line running from northern Angola to northwestern Ethiopia (Figure 2.1). "Low Africa," located northwest of this line, is characterized by low plains and sedimentary basins usually under 500 m above sea level. It also contains several isolated upland regions with altitudes of 1,000 to 4,000 m, the most important of which are (1) the Tibesti, Aïr, and Hoggar Massifs in the Sahara and (2) the Guinea and Adamawa Highlands further south. "High Africa," the southeastern portion of the continent, is dominated by plateaus and plains 1,000 to 2,000 m above sea level. The plateaus are bounded by often spectacular escarpments, including the Great Escarpment paralleling the coast of southern Africa from Angola to southern Mozambique, a distance of 5,000 km. There are also several prominent high plateaus and mountain systems, most notably the Drakensburg Mountains (Lesotho and South Africa), the Mitumba Mountains (Zaire,

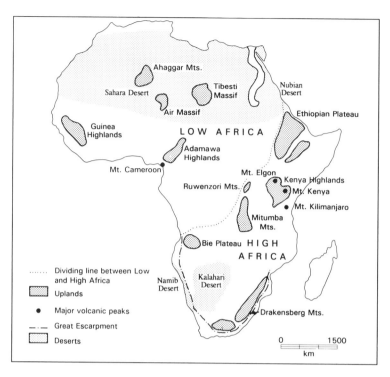

Figure 2.1a. Physiography: major physiographic features.

Rwanda, and Burundi), the Kenya Highlands, and the Ethiopian Plateau.

Tectonic Influences

The physiography of Africa reflects tectonic movements that have occurred over hundreds of millions of years. In fact, the very existence of the continent is the result of tectonic forces that caused the breakup of the ancient megacontinent Gondwanaland some 250 million years ago. The coastline closely follows the line of breakup of Africa from other land masses that formerly constituted Gondwanaland (South America, Antarctica, Australia, Madagascar, Saudi Arabia, and India).

The evidence that Gondwanaland once existed is varied and convincing. The shapes of its consituent parts, when placed side by side like pieces in a jigsaw puzzle, fit quite closely. The adjoining parts of the reassembled megacontinent have similar rock types, identical fossil glacial deposits, and otherwise unique fossil life-forms. The configuration of

ocean-bottom geological formations also points to progressive separation of land masses that at one time formed a single continent.

The Great Rift Valley systems of eastern Africa (Vignette 2.1) are the result of continuing continental fragmentation owing to tectonic forces. In short, the processes that gave rise to Africa are continuing to reshape it. While these processes are hardly discernible in relation to the scope of human history, when viewed in geological time they are quite recent and fast developing.

The volcanism commonly associated with this massive fracturing of the earth's crust has created a number of impressive volcanic peaks. Mount Kenya, Mount Kilimanjaro (Figure 2.2), and Mount Elgon, among others, provide spectacular evidence of past and continuing volcanism along Africa's rift valleys. Soils of volcanic origin are usually extremely fertile and often support high population densities where rainfall is adequate.

The breakup of Gondwanaland precipitated a series of continental uplifts. Africa was

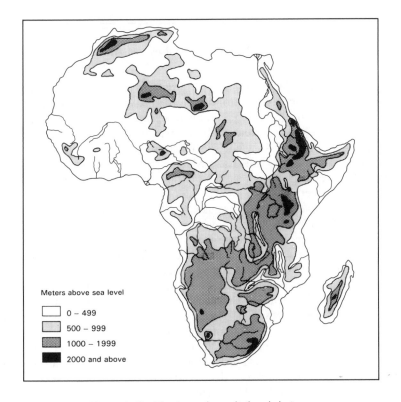

Figure 2.1b. Physiography: relief and drainage.

Figure 2.2. Mount Kilimanjaro, Tanzania. This magnificent volcanic peak, 5,895 m above sea level, is the highest mountain in Africa. Photo: CIDA.

Vignette 2.1. The Rift Valleys of Africa

The rift valleys of eastern Africa (Figure 2.3) are among the world's most impressive physiographic features. They extend from the Jordan River valley, through the Red Sea and East Africa, to central Mozambique. This represents a distance of over 7,000 km. Africa has two major rift-valley systems. The Eastern Rift extends from central Ethiopia to central Kenya (see Figure 2.4), while the Western Rift runs from north of Lake Victoria through Lake Tanganyika and Lake Malawi to the Mozambique coast.

These rift valleys developed as a result of faulting caused by tension within the earth's crust. A central block between two parallel fault lines is displaced downward, creating a linear valley. The sides of the valley are usually steep and sometimes precipitous. Africa's rift valleys are 40 to 60 km wide and vary from a few meters to 2,000 m deep. The vertical displacement of geological strata is sometimes even greater–up to 6,000 m in eastern Africa. The difference between apparent depth and the actual displacement of strata is attributable to the erosion of the valley sides and the accumulation of eroded sediments and sometimes volcanic lavas in the valley bottom. In the vicinity of Lake Naivasha in Kenya, some 1,800 m of volcanic lavas have been deposited on top of the original valley floor. Volcanic activity associated with the rift valleys has also created several spectacular volcanic peaks, the largest of which is Mount Kilimanjaro.

Eastern Africa's large lakes, with the notable exception of Lake Victoria, are located within the rifts. Lake Tanganyika, Lake Malawi, and Lake Turkana are the largest of these rift-valley lakes. These are very deep; the floor of Lake Malawi is up to 700 m below sea level. Several, including Lake Turkana, are salt lakes that have no drainage outlet. Soda ash is mined from the saline deposits of Kenya's Lake Madgadi.

The rift valleys of Africa are of interest not only because they provide spectacular landscape features that help us to understand the evolution of the continents, but also because they have provided the earliest fossil evidence of early human and protohuman life on the planet. Among the most important of these rift-valley locations have been the Olduvai Gorge in Tanzania and Lake Turkana in Kenya. At these locations, archeologists have uncovered not only skeletal remains but also tools, weapons, and other evidence of the evolution of early human life. This evidence points to Africa as being the very cradle of human development.

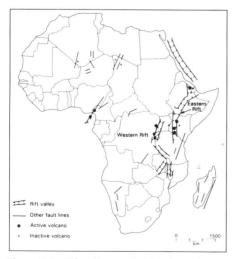

Figure 2.3. Rift valleys and volcanic peaks.

Figure 2.4. Escarpment along the edge of the Great Rift Valley near Naivasha, Kenya. Photo: author.

elevated from 1,300 to 1,700 m in the south and the east (High Africa), but much less in the north and east (Low Africa). The uplift caused major rivers (e.g., the Congo and the Niger), which had formerly been confined to inland drainage basins, to erode downward and to eventually establish paths to the sea. According to the geomorphologist Lester King, there have been five major cycles of uplift and erosion since the demise of Gondwanaland, each lasting for millions of years and bringing about a renewed cycle of erosion. As cycles of erosion proceeded, valleys were widened and valley-side escarpments receded. King has attributed the characteristic stepped landscape of Africa, with its broad plains bounded by escarpments, to these cycles of repeated uplift and erosion.

More recent uplifting has facilitated the cutting of deep gorges occupied by major rivers. Rivers confined to such deep valleys or flowing over escarpments into them (as the Zambezi does at Victoria Falls) provide sites of great potential for the generation of hydroelectric power, although very little of this potential has been exploited. Among the hydroelectric projects that have proceeded are the Kariba and Cabora Bassa dams on the Zambezi and the Inga project on the Zaire. On the other hand, the high cost of transversing the escarpments and gorges has been a major impediment to the development of transportation systems.

Superimposed on this general pattern of uplift is a complex pattern of tectonic downwarping that has created a series of wide basins. Five of these basins are occupied by a great river system (the Niger, the Congo, the Zambezi, the Nile, and the Orange), which together drain three-quarters of Africa south of the Sahara. Two other basins, the Chad and Kalahari, have internal drainage systems without any outlet to the sea. The central parts of the large drainage basins contain relatively young sedimentary rocks derived mainly from the erosion of the uplifted zones separating the basins.

Climatic Influences

Climate has shaped African topographic landscapes in several, and sometimes unexpected, ways. Even small glaciers are to be found, adjacent to the equator, at the summits of Mount Kenya, Mount Kilimanjaro, and the Ruwenzori Mountains.

Desert aridity is responsible for diverse landforms, including (1) crescent-shaped and longitudinal sand dunes, (2) flat-bottomed water courses known as wadis, (3) alluvial fans, and (4) salt pans. Salt pans are formed in basins when evaporation of rainwater leaves deposits of mineral salts behind. Residents of the Sahara have exploited these salt pans for centuries as a source of many valued types of mineral salts.

In more humid regions (over 1,000 mm of rainfall), processes of deep chemical weathering have created a number of characteristic landforms, including inselbergs and laterite-capped hills. These processes are most successful when there is a combination of open-jointed Precambrian rocks, high temperatures, relatively abundant rainfall, and the presence of decaying vegetative matter that can increase the acidity of infiltrating rainwater. Chemical weathering causes the rock to lose certain constituent minerals and to begin disintegrating.

The soils derived from the chemical weathering of rock in the humid tropics are called laterites. These brick-red soils have heavy concentrations of insoluble iron and aluminum oxides but have lost most of their other nutrients because of the leaching action of rainwater as it seeps through the soil. When exposed by the clearance of vegetation, these dense, iron-rich soils often develop a hardpan surface, known as ferricrete, which renders farming almost impossible.

Inselbergs—massive, solitary domes of Precambrian rock rising above the surrounding plains—are common features of the moister savannas and to a lesser extent of the forests (see Figure 2.5). It is believed that they originated as subsurface masses of rock resistant to chemical weathering. They remain solid and unaltered, while weathering disintegrates the surrounding areas of more open-jointed rocks. The inselberg is exposed later when erosion strips away the surrounding weathered rock. The exposed inselberg continues to resist weathering and gradually assumes a dome shape through the successive peel-

Figure 2.5. Inselberg near Abuja, Nigeria. The smooth, rounded form is typical of inselbergs.

1. Chemical weathering weakens open-jointed rock; certain formations resist weathering.

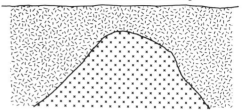

2. Erosion removes most of weathered rock; resistant masses emerge as inselbergs.

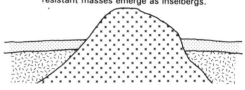

▨ Rocks susceptible to chemical weathering

▨ Resistant rocks

▨ Laterites

Figure 2.6. Schematic drawing of the formation of inselbergs. The processes of chemical weathering and erosion that give shape to inselbergs occur gradually over millions of years.

ing away of surface layers of rock (see Figure 2.6).

This brief overview cannot do justice to the diversity of African landscapes and the range of processes that have given shape to them. Nevertheless, it points to the importance of major tectonic forces, such as faulting of the earth's crust and continental drift operating over many millions of years on a vast scale, and also the regional variations in climate and geology which give rise to a range of distinctive, continuously evolving landform assemblages.

Dynamics of Climate

Virtually all of Africa south of the Sahara lies within 35 degrees of the equator, so tropical climates occur in all but its southern extremity. The climatic patterns found north and south of the equator are essentially mirror images of each other.

African climates are best understood in relation to seasonal patterns of air circulation which derive from global circulation systems. Altitude, topography, and ocean currents also affect climate and may be extremely important determinants locally and regionally.

Most of Africa south of the Sahara gets its rainfall from air originating over the Atlantic Ocean and moving inland toward an equatorial zone of low pressure, the Intertropical Convergence Zone (ITCZ). The main exception is eastern Africa, from Somalia to South Africa, which is affected by air masses from the Indian Ocean. The other exception is the South African Cape, which has a Mediterranean climate and receives rainfall in winter when midlatitude westerlies achieve their northernmost position.

To understand the seasonal changes and regional variations in African climates, it is useful to start by considering the patterns of air circulation. The basic sequence is as follows:

- Winds converge in the equatorial zone of low pressure (the ITCZ), where air rises, spreads out and moves poleward in the upper atmosphere.
- This air descends, hot and dry, in the zones of high pressure centered on the Tropics of Cancer and Capricorn. The air then moves away from the tropics, including toward the ITCZ.
- The zones of high and low pressure – in fact, the entire circulation system – shift seasonal-

ly in harmony with the apparent movement of the sun's position, north of the equator during Northern Hemisphere summers and south of the equator in Southern Hemisphere summers.

- Two contrasting air masses, tropical continental and tropical maritime, converge at the ITCZ. Tropical continental is the hot, very dry air mass that has descended at the tropics and is returning to the ITCZ. Tropical maritime originates over the ocean and is moisture laden as it moves onshore. When it is forced to rise, whether owing to convection, frontal uplift, or relief (orographic effect), rainfall may well occur.

Figure 2.7a shows the pattern of air pressure, prevailing winds, and rainfall during January when the sun appears overhead in the Southern Hemisphere. Rainfall north of the

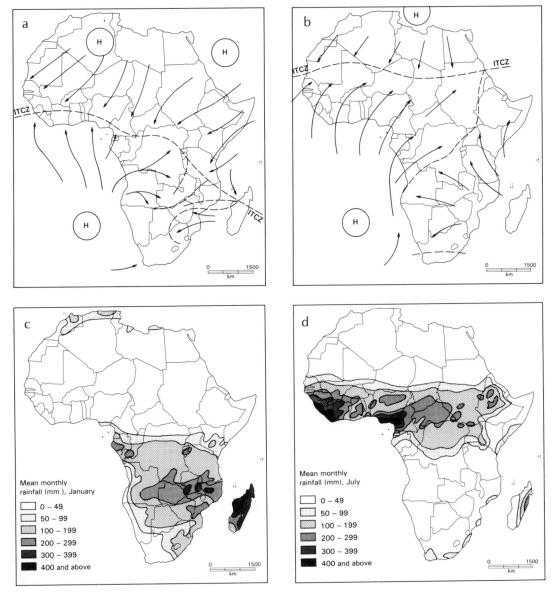

Figure 2.7. Seasonal variations in atmospheric pressure, winds, and precipitation. (a) Pressure and winds, January. (b) Pressure and winds, July. (c) Mean monthly precipitation (mm), January. (d) Mean monthly precipitation (mm), July.

equator is minimal. South of the equator, on-shore southwesterly winds from the Atlantic bring heavy rainfall to the Congo Basin and lesser amounts to its north and south. In East Africa, south of the ITCZ, large tropical cyclones move onshore from the Indian Ocean. Eastern Madagascar and parts of the coastal mainland between southern Tanzania and South Africa are particularly affected and are liable to receive high winds and torrential rainfall in coastal areas. North of the ITCZ in East Africa the predominant northeasterly winds bring dry continental air originating over central Asia, so that there is little rainfall.

In July, that is, during summer in the Northern Hemisphere, the ITCZ shifts far to the north and lies over the southern Sahara (Figure 2.7b). Southwesterly winds bring tropical maritime air and, consequently, rainfall to West Africa. These winds from the Atlantic penetrate as far east as the Ethiopian Highlands. Almost the entire breadth of the continent receives rainfall at this time.

The occurrence of rainfall is closely related to the cross-sectional structure of the ITCZ (Figure 2.8). The moist tropical maritime air forms a wedge under the dry continental northeasterlies at the ITCZ. Where the wedge is very thin, the weather is hot and humid, but rainfall is unlikely to occur. Some 400 to 600 km back from the surface position of the

convergence, the wedge is sufficiently thick (perhaps 5,000 m) to permit the development of cumulonimbus clouds and thunderstorms. Further back still, the wedge of moist air continues to become thicker, but there is a more stable atmospheric configuration and little rainfall, despite high humidity and heavy cloud cover.

Rainy seasons are longer close to the coast than farther inland because the coastal regions are under the influence of tropical maritime air for longer periods. However, because maximum precipitation occurs in the part of the wedge of medium thickness, places near the coast tend to have a double maximum pattern of rainfall; that is, there are two periods of higher rainfall each year. The first maximum occurs in spring as the ITCZ moves poleward, and the second occurs in early fall as the ITCZ retreats toward the equator. Farther from the equator, where the wedge of moist maritime air does not remain thick and stable long enough to impede rainfall, there is a single midsummer period of heavy precipitation.

Most rainfall in Africa is convectional, that is, the result of local surficial heating and updrafts that facilitate the development of cumulus and cumulonimbus clouds. Convectional rainfall tends to occur in small systems and, therefore, gives very spotty spatial coverage. Marked variations in the growth of crops may

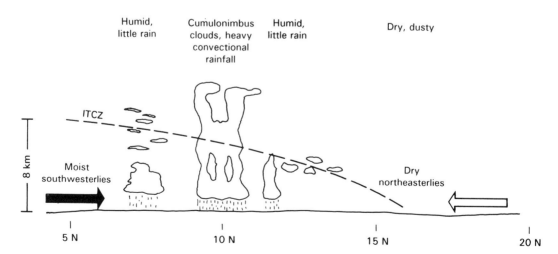

Figure 2.8. Schematic cross section of the Intertropical Convergence Zone (ITCZ) showing associated weather conditions. After A. T. Grove. *Africa*. 3rd ed. Oxford: Oxford University Press, 1978, p. 14.

Vignette 2.2. Climate Change

Africa has experienced substantial changes in climate over the past 15,000 to 20,000 years. During the last ice age, it appears that the climate of Africa was significantly cooler and drier than it is now. Desert sand dunes formed up to several hundred kilometers beyond the limits of the present-day Sahara and Kalahari Deserts. The major vegetation zones all shifted closer to the equator. Glaciers descended over 1,000 m down the slopes of the high mountains of East Africa.

As the ice caps of Europe and North America began to retreat some 15,000 years ago, Africa's climate became warmer and wetter and the desert margins retreated. What is now the Sahara became a fertile, savanna-type environment with substantial rivers and lakes. Fossils and well-preserved rock paintings provide evidence of the profusion of wildlife and the presence of human hunters and herders in the present-day Sahara. The Lake Chad Basin and Kalahari Basin both contained very large lakes.

About 5,000 years ago, the climate of the Sahara and other comparatively arid environments became much drier and less variable. All but the largest rivers disappeared and Lake Chad began to shrink. As desertification intensified, most humans retreated from the Sahara with their herds. While the climate of Africa has since remained relatively stable, fluctuations are known to have taken place, particularly during the period known as the "Little Ice Age" in Europe (from the 16th to the 18th centuries) and during the late 19th century. During these times the climate of Africa tended to be more moist than usual.

Since the early 1970s, a series of serious droughts have affected various parts of the continent. They have brought about significant environmental effects, as well as effects on human societies and economies. The effects on ecosystems include lower river discharges and lower lake levels, as well as stress on flora and fauna. Desertification has occurred on a large scale in marginal semiarid environments.

What has been particularly significant in these recent episodes of drought and associated damage to ecosystems is the degree to which population growth, the utilization of marginal arid lands, and inappropriate development strategies have made these effects, both ecological and human, more severe. The number of people living in ecologically vulnerable areas has increased greatly during the 20th century. Some were attracted during the preceding wet phase by abundant land and the construction by government agencies of wells and other modern infrastructures. Others came because they had been displaced from more productive regions by development projects like irrigation schemes. The end result was increased pressure on marginal lands and the virtual certainty that people and their livestock would do serious damage to vegetation and soil when the rains failed and normal vegetative growth could not occur.

Most climatologists now believe that these recent trends in Africa's climate are part of a global pattern of climate change and that the rate of change can be expected to accelerate in the very near future. These changes are linked to the increased concentration of carbon dioxide, methane, CFCs (chlorofluorocarbons), and other "greenhouse" gases in the atmosphere; it is predicted that the concentration of these gasses by the year 2050 will be twice what it was before the industrial revolution. The major sources of these gases include pollution by automobiles and industry and the cutting and burning of forests. Unlike earlier periods of climatic change, the present phase of global warming is very much the creation of human beings.

Africa south of the Sahara is not a major source of "greenhouse" gases; none of its coun-

cont.

Vignette 2.2. (cont.)

tries ranks among the world's 20 largest sources of air pollutants. However, the majority of climatologists are predicting that it will be one of the areas most seriously affected by the "greenhouse effect." It is expected that humid climates will become even wetter and that semiarid and arid areas will become significantly hotter and drier. More frequent and more serious droughts are expected to occur in desert-margin and savanna environments, causing not only desiccation but also more frequent crop failures, severe food shortages, and the displacement of vast numbers of people. It has been predicted that global sea levels will rise by up to 1.5 m by the mid–21st century because of global warming. Rising sea levels would threaten to inundate low-lying coastal areas, including much of the Comoros and coastal cities like Lagos and Abidjan.

The consequences of climate change for Africa are expected to be extremely serious. The number of Africans potentially threatened is very large indeed. Perhaps one-quarter of the population of Africa south of the Sahara lives in comparatively arid areas where the threat of drought and desertification is already high and where climatic change would mean diminished agricultural potential and increased probability of mass starvation. Many millions more who live in coastal areas face the prospect of being displaced from their homes by rising sea levels.

Because of Africa's poverty, the kinds of public programs that may help people in wealthier countries to cope with rapid changes to their environment are unlikely to be available to Africans. African nations and individual families can be expected to be essentially on their own as they attempt in the future to cope with rapid and profound environmental changes.

---

result, particularly in areas of seasonal rainfall. For example, one village may have healthy, knee-high grain while adjacent villages may be awaiting their first substantial rainfall of the year.

In some regions, highlands force moisture-laden air to rise and produce rain, known as orographic rainfall. It is more common in East than in West Africa owing to the more extensive areas of high plateaus and mountains. However, although rainfall increases owing to orographic lifting on the windward side of major relief features, it decreases on the leeward side as the air descends.

The climatic processes that have been discussed above give rise to great variations in regional climates, ranging from the uniformly hot and perpetually rainy climates of the equatorial zone, to the very arid climates of the Sahara and Kalahari deserts. These regional variations in climate, and associated variations in vegetation and soils, are discussed in the following section.

African Biomes

A *biome* may be defined as a large region whose climate, vegetation, fauna, and soils are characterized by broad uniformity. A biome is usually named after the predominant vegetation in the region. Emphasis should be placed on the *broad uniformity* of a biome because within each biome there is considerable variation and complexity, reflecting the diversity of interrelated processes that shape the environment. Moreover, while there is an obvious relation between the elements that constitute a biome, this does not mean that the boundaries between different vegetation types and those separating related climate regions and soil regions will correspond exactly with each other.

The associations of vegetation, climate, and soil that characterize Africa's major biomes are summarized in Table 2.1 and are discussed below. Their resulting spatial patterns are shown in Figures 2.9, 2.11, and 2.12, respectively.

Vegetation zones in Africa (Figure 2.9) show a pattern of roughly concentric rings centered on the Congo Basin. While rainfall is especially important for vegetation, other factors such as altitude, soil characteristics, and drainage are locally significant. Human use of the environment—selective clearing and planting of species, grazing, and the use of fire—continues to modify vegetation patterns. Therefore, it is important to remember the limitations of "natural" vegetation as a meaningful concept. Large areas of vegetation that initially seem undisturbed have actually been altered greatly by human use.

Figure 2.11 shows the major climatic regions, together with climate graphs for places that have been selected as "typical" examples of each climate type. These help to illustrate a useful general rule, namely, that equatorial climates have extremely regular patterns of temperature and rainfall and that the degree of variability increases in successive zones away from the equatorial zone.

Prevailing climatic conditions in each biome produce specific processes, such as physical and chemical weathering, which are fundamental to soil formation. The interrelations of climate, vegetation, and soils are complex. For example, climatic conditions govern both the production of biomass, which is the source of organic matter for the soil, and the rate at which nutrients from decayed vegetation and other sources are leached from the soil. Human use of soil resources is also of great importance, for example, through cropping practices such as monoculture that may contribute to soil erosion or accelerate the depletion of soil fertility.

Tropical Rain Forest

The tropical rain forest occurs in close association with equatorial climates. Equatorial climates are characterized by heavy rainfall and a dry season that is either very short or absent. These climatic conditions permit the development of the most biologically diverse of the world's biomes but also contribute to the development of soils, called Oxisols, that contain few nutrients and little organic matter. The tropical forest is the biome with the greatest diversity of animal life, a reflection of the countless ecological niches that exist in it.

Monrovia, Calabar, and Tamatave are examples of places with an equatorial climate (Figure 2.11). Equatorial climates are characterized by very heavy rainfall (e.g., 5,131 mm at Monrovia, 3,070 mm at Calabar, and 3,256 mm at Tamatave) that occurs virtually year round (10 to 12 months with 50 mm or more). Temperatures are high, averaging about 25°C. Both annual and diurnal temperature ranges are very low. Compared to other parts of Africa with an equatorial climate, West African locations tend to have slightly higher total precipitation, a better-defined short dry season, and seasonal reversals of prevailing winds. These areas are classified as tropical monsoon in certain climate classification systems.

Vegetation is very luxuriant and consists of many different species in close proximity. Vegetation typically occurs in three layers, namely, a shrub layer of relatively low species, a canopy of densely packed trees of medium size, and an emergent layer of isolated tall trees extending far above the canopy. Where the forest has remained undisturbed, the ground level may be quite open but dark. Where the canopy has been disturbed, permitting much more light to penetrate to ground level, a dense and tangled mass of vegetation develops.

Human activities, especially farming and lumbering, pose a severe and growing threat

Table 2.1. Africa's Major Biomes

Vegetation type	Related climate type	Related soil types
Tropical rain forest	Equatorial	Oxisols
Guinea savanna	Humid tropical	Oxisols, Alfisols, Ultisols
Sudan savanna	Tropical wet and dry	Alfisols (Ustalfs)
Semidesert (Sahel)	Tropical steppe (semiarid)	Alfisols, Aridisols
Desert	Desert	Aridisols
Mediterranean	Mediterranean	Alfisols (Xeralfs)

a   b

c   d

Figure 2.9. Views from four vegetation regions. (a) Tropical rain forest, southern Cameroon. (b) Sudan savanna, south central Kenya. (c) Semidesert, southern Kenya. (d) Desert, Eritrea. Photos: (a) CIDA: R. Lemoyne; (b), (c) author; (d) M. Peters.

to tropical rain forests. The forest ecosystem is very delicate, and indiscriminant clearing can jeopardize the ecosystem's survival. More than 1 million sq km of Africa's tropical forests have been lost, and the rate of loss is growing.

The soils of the tropical rain forest are subject to heavy leaching, a consequence of the region's high temperatures and heavy rainfall. Most minerals nutrients have been leached from the topsoil, leaving iron-rich laterite behind. While the forest provides an abundant supply of biomass, these soils contain very little organic matter. The warm, moist environment is ideal for soil bacteria that cause the rapid decomposition of organic matter. Because these Oxisols are so infertile, subsistence farmers in tropical-forest environments practice shifting cultivation, moving their farms every two or three years as the soil's limited store of plant nutrients is exhausted.

Moist (Guinea) Savanna

The distribution of Guinea savanna vegetation approximates that of humid tropical climates. These areas have less rainfall than the equatorial zone, generally about 1,000 to 2,000 mm per year. The rainfall tends to peak twice during the year (the double maximum pattern described previously), with the peaks separated by relatively short but distinct dry seasons. Kinshasa, Yaoundé, and Kampala are examples of places with a humid tropical climate.

The characteristic vegetation is a mixture of trees and tall grasses. Where rainfall is relatively high and human influence low, there may be quite a dense canopy of evergreen trees. The effect of agriculture on the savanna ecosystem is especially evident in the "derived savannas" of the forest margins, where overly intensive utilization has caused a degradation from forest to savanna. Fires, often deliberately set by farmers, herders, and hunters, affect the evolution of savanna vegetation by selectively eliminating species that are not fire resistant.

The soils of the Guinea savanna are diverse, a reflection of the transition here from forest to relatively dry savanna. Oxisols and Ultisols, both highly leached and relatively infertile, occur where precipitation is above average for this zone. In drier parts, Alfisols are found. The name *Alfisol* reflects the high aluminum (*Al*) and iron (*fi*) content of these soils, which tend to be heavily leached but have somewhat greater organic matter and fertility than the Oxisols and Ultisols associated with moister environments.

Dry (Sudan) Savanna

Dry-savanna vegetation tends to occur in areas with tropical wet and dry climates. These climates have a lengthy dry season, typically 5 to 8 months in duration. Places such as Kano and Addis Ababa that are located in the Northern Hemisphere receive rainfall between May and September, whereas Lusaka in the Southern Hemisphere has rain from November to March. As distance from the humid tropical zone increases, the duration, amount, and reliability of rainfall decrease. Precipitation is usually between 500 and 1,000 mm per year; the higher total at Addis Ababa reflects the orographic effect of the Ethiopian Plateau.

The annual and diurnal (daily) temperature ranges are greater in the tropical wet and dry zone than in zones closer to the equator. There are cooler temperatures at Addis Ababa and Lusaka than at Kano because of their greater elevation above sea level.

Many of the characteristics of the dry-savanna vegetation reflect the longer dry seasons and lesser amounts of rainfall, as compared to the Guinea savanna. Trees are usually

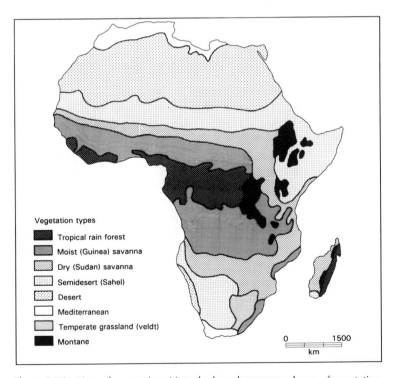

Vegetation types

- Tropical rain forest
- Moist (Guinea) savanna
- Dry (Sudan) savanna
- Semidesert (Sahel)
- Desert
- Mediterranean
- Temperate grassland (veldt)
- Montane

0   1500
km

Figure 2.10. Natural vegetation. Note the broad correspondence of vegetation, climate, and soils zones shown on the map and summarized in Table 2.1.

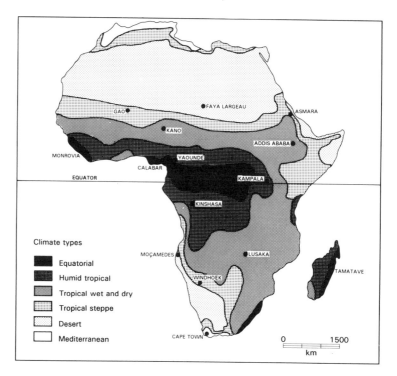

Figure 2.11a. Climate types. Climate graphs for representative places in each of the broad climatic regions are shown in Figure 2.11b. After *The Atlas of Africa*. Paris: Atlas Jeune Afrique, 1977, p. 75.

more scattered and the grass is not as tall. The species found here are adapted to the more difficult climatic conditions; acacia trees, for example, have very small leaves that are shed seasonally and a tough outer bark and thorns that discourage browsing by animals.

Savanna environments have less diversity of wildlife than tropical-forest ecosystems. However, East Africa's dry-savanna environments are famous for their herds of grazing species and associated predators.

Ustalfs, a type of Alfisol, are the main soil type. These soils are often relatively fertile. Ustalfs usually contain fine dust brought by winds from the desert during every dry season. They are less heavily leached than soils in areas with moister climates and may have a fairly high organic content.

Semidesert (Sahel)

Between the tropical wet and dry and the desert climates there is a transitional semi-arid zone. Places such as Asmara, Gao, and Windhoek that have semidesert (tropical steppe) climates receive approximately 250 to 500 mm annually during a rainy season of one to three months. The sparse, unreliable rainfall makes agriculture a very risky activity because crop failure occurs frequently.

On the desert margins, where rainfall is low and the rainy season is very short, the drought-resistant properties of plants are crucial for their survival. Trees tend to have thick bark and small, waxy leaves that do not lose much moisture through transpiration. Some species conserve moisture by shedding their leaves during the dry season.

Semidesert vegetation is very vulnerable to damage from fire, overgrazing, and agriculture and is therefore easily prone to desertification. Healthy stands of vegetation are crucial for stabilizing the soil and reducing soil erosion by wind and water.

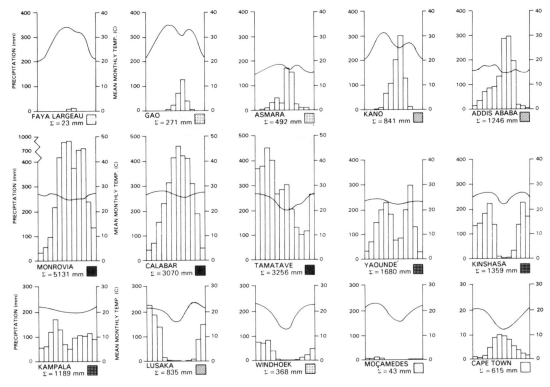

Figure 2.11b. Climate graphs for selected stations. The lines indicate temperature; bars are rainfall per month. For the locations of sampled stations, see Figure 2.11a.

Desert

Desert climates have little and unreliable rainfall (e.g., 23 mm at Faya Largeau and 43 mm at Moçamedes). There are extreme diurnal ranges of temperature and significant annual variations. For example, the differences between mean monthly minimum and maximum temperatures at Faya Largeau range from 15 to 18°C, three times higher than at Calabar in the equatorial zone. The mean monthly maximum temperature exceeds 40°C (104°F) during five months of the year. Moçamedes is somewhat cooler because of its coastal location and the effects of the cold Benguela Current offshore.

Desert vegetation occurs in both the Sahara and Kalahari, although rather different species are typical of the two deserts. Desert plant life must be highly adapted to the sparse and infrequent rainfall and poorly developed, often saline, soils. Vegetation is likely to be denser and more varied along water courses than in the open desert.

The Aridisols of desert environments are poorly developed and have a very low organic content, reflecting the dry climate and lack of vegetation. Under certain conditions, layers of salts or calcium carbonate may accumulate on or below the surface.

Mediterranean

Mediterranean climates occur at the southern tip of South Africa, as well as north of the Sahara. Rainfall is received in the winter (April to September in Cape Town) when the mid-latitude westerlies penetrate farthest toward the equator. Precipitation is quite low; Cape Town, for example, receives 615 mm annually.

The South African Cape has a drought-resistant scrub vegetation that resembles the maquis scrub found in other areas of Mediter-

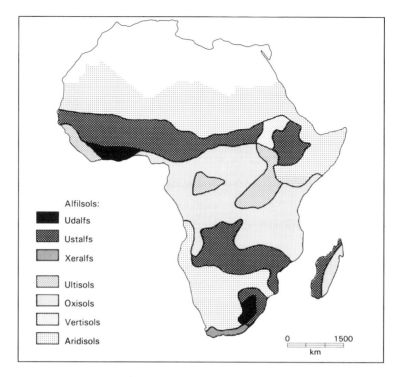

Figure 2.12. Major soil groups.

ranean climate, such as southern California and the Mediterranean Basin. However, the Cape region has many indigenous plant species that are unique to South Africa.

Xeralfs are the soils usually associated with Mediterranean environments. These brownish-colored soils often have quite high natural fertility.

In this chapter, I have given a very brief introduction to Africa's physical environment and have pointed to the existence of many discernible linkages among geology, landforms, soils, climate, and vegetation. What remains to be explored in greater detail in several later chapters, as one of the broad organizing themes of the book, is the relation between physical environment and the human geography of the African continent.

Further Reading

Various aspects of the geomorphology of Africa are discussed in the following sources:

Bridges, E. M. "Africa." In E. M. Bridges, ed.,

World Geomorphology, pp. 30–65, Cambridge: Cambridge University Press, 1990.

Buckle, C. *Landforms in Africa*. London: Longman, 1978.

Hastenrath, S. *The Glaciers of Equatorial East Africa*. Dordrecht, Holland: D. Reidel, 1984.

King, L. C. *The Morphology of the Earth*. Edinburgh: Oliver and Boyd, 1962.

Pritchard, J. M. *Landform and landscape in Africa*. London: Edward Arnold, 1979.

Thomas, M. F. "Geomorphology and land classification in tropical Africa." In M. F. Thomas and G. H. Whittington, eds., *Environment and Land Use in Africa*, pp. 103–145. London: Methuen, 1969.

The following sources contain important studies of Africa's climate:

Griffiths, J. F., ed. *Climates of Africa*. Amsterdam, Netherlands: Elsevier, 1972.

Nieuwholt, S. *Tropical Climatology*. Chichester, England: Wiley, 1977.

Thompson, B. W. *The Climate of Africa*. New York: Oxford University Press, 1965.

On climate change in Africa, past and present, see the following sources:

Grove, A. T., and A. Warren. "Quaternary landforms and climate change on the south side of the Sahara." *Geographical Journal,* vol. 134 (1968), pp. 193–208.

Nicholson, S. E. "Climatic variations in the Sahel and other African regions during the past five centuries." *Journal of Arid Environments,* vol. 1 (1978), pp. 3–24.

Sulaiman, M., ed. *The Greenhouse Effect and Its Impact on Africa.* London: Institute for African Alternatives, 1990.

Aspects of African ecosystems are discussed in the following sources:

Battistini, R., and G. Richard-Vindard. *Biogeography and Ecology in Madagascar.* Amsterdam: W. Junk, 1972.

Goodall, D. W., ed. *Ecosystems of the World.* Amsterdam: Elsevier, 1982–1993. (This is an excellent series of reference volumes describing ecosystems in different parts of the world.)

Hopkins, B. *Forest and Savanna.* London: Heinemann, 1965.

Lewis, L. A., and L. Berry. *African Environments and Resources.* Boston: Unwin Hyman, 1988.

Werger, M. J., ed. *Biogeography and Ecology of Southern Africa,* 2 vols. The Hague, Netherlands: W. Junk, 1978.

Whitlow, J. R. "The study of vegetation in Africa: A historical review of problems and progress." *Singapore Journal of Tropical Geography,* vol. 5 (1984), pp. 88–101.

African soils are discussed in the following sources:

Pullan, R. A. "The soil resources of West Africa." In M. F. Thomas and G. W. Whittington, eds., *Environment and Land Use in Africa,* pp. 147–192. London: Methuen, 1969.

United Nations Educational, Scientific, and Cultural Organization (UNESCO). *Soil Map of the World.* Vol. 6, *Africa.* Paris: UNESCO, 1977.

3

✷

Culture and Society

This chapter explores two contrasting perspectives on the people of Africa south of the Sahara. On the one hand, Africans share a remarkable cultural unity, which the French anthropologist Jacques Maquet has called "Africanity." On the other hand, Africa is riven with ethnic, linguistic, religious, and class cleavages.

Cultural Unity

Shared characteristics, shared experience, and a shared worldview give the people of Africa south of the Sahara a common identity, which prevails despite the vast size of the continent and the great diversity of languages, ethnic identities, and religions. Identities are defined not only by a group's self-image but also by the group's image in the eyes of others. Non-Africans possess a limited number of often stereotypical images of Africa and Africans, garnered from such diverse sources as the media, film, missionaries, and politicians' speeches. Many Africans are well aware of these international images, and their sense of identity is shaped, in part, in response to them.

The fact that the African identity cannot be defined with absolute precision does not make it any less real. Here is how Maquet (1972) expresses this point:

Life-styles and work-styles are the heart of the matter; human behavior and things made in a social group. Its not the sunshine or the black skin that gives the impression of African unity. It is sunny and hot in all the tropical areas of the world, but that doesn't give one the feeling of being in Africa. There are black sections in many American cities. But Harlem, even on a sunny day when it is more humid than Kinshasa in the rainy season, still is not Africa. This unity, strongly yet vaguely experienced by the traveler returning to Africa, is a cultural unity. Culture is . . . the totality of knowledge and behavior, ideas and objects, that constitutes the common heritage of a society. (p. 4)

To view Africa south of the Sahara as a single cultural entity is not to deny the significance of the continent's diversity. African peoples may be subdivided into several broad groups, defined according to their primary economic activity (e.g., hunter–gatherers, farmers, pastoralists), language family (e.g., Khoisan, Bantu), or another criterion. In turn, these broad categories incorporate hundreds of ethnic groups, each with its own cultural identity. African society, therefore, may be seen as a nested hierarchy—hundreds of ethnic groups belonging to several large groups all of which share a common African identity.

Several constituent elements of the African identity may be described, the first being possession of a black skin. Being black does not necessarily make one African, but blackness is a shared characteristic of Africans from south of the Sahara. While Maquet argues against reliance on racial criteria, he tacitly acknowledges its importance in his subtitle *The Cultural Unity of Black Africa*.

Africans conceptualize the relation between humankind and nature in a way very different from that conceptualized by people in Western societies. Christian theology tends to see nature as separate from God and to see humankind as outside and above nature. African traditional religions emphasize that spiritual forces are manifest everywhere in the environment. Gods and spirits are associated both with the major elements of the physical environment (e.g., rivers, thunder) and with such landmarks as rock outcrops and tree groves. Gods and spirits are thought to be concerned about the daily affairs of humans. They make it possible for humans to reap the gifts of nature but can deny these blessings and cause misfortune if angered. Drought and crop failure, for example, may be attributed to the wrath of gods denied proper respect.

The deities are honored in sacrifices and ceremonies, often undertaken at specific times of the year and conducted by priests devoted to their worship. The power of gods and spirits is also reflected in the daily behavior of individuals—for example, the avoidance of places like sacred groves that are believed to harbor spirits.

Past and future generations of Africans are linked in a continuing "chain of life," which is maintained by remembering appropriately the spirits of generations past and by nurturing the next generation of Africans. Human fertility provides assurance of the group's survival; large families are preferred, and childlessness is viewed as a tragedy. One of the keys to maintaining the "chain of life" is the education of young people in the traditions of the group. This education often includes formal instruction conducted in conjunction with initiation into adulthood. Africans living in modern cities sustain the "chain of life" through visits and gifts to relatives in the home village and sometimes by sending their children to be raised in the village by relatives.

The African identity is closely tied to the land. African communities have traditionally depended on hunting, herding, and farming for sustenance; most Africans still do. The African dependence on the land reinforces a sense of closeness to nature. The very survival of individuals, families, and communities is dependent on natural phenomena: abundant rainfall and the absence of natural catastrophes. Prosperity cannot be taken for granted but must be cultivated with appropriately deferential behavior toward the gods. African societies protect access to the land by treating it as communal, rather than individual, property. Individuals have essentially custodial rights—from the gods and for future generations—to land and resources from the land.

Respect for wise and judicious authority is an African attribute. The African chief, chosen by elders for his strength and integrity, is a spiritual as well as political figure, whose leadership determines the prosperity, health, and safety of the group. At the village level, the authority of community elders, acting as guardians of the common welfare, is respected. In return, "big men" with political and economic power are expected to use it generously for the benefit of their followers. Their support takes the form of gifts during festivals, financial support for marriages and other ceremonies, and help in times of crisis.

Patron–client relationships exist within families, as well as at the community level. African families are extended rather than nuclear, including not only parents and their children but also grandparents, cousins, nieces, nephews, and other relatives, some of whom are adopted.

The arts, particularly sculpture, music, dance, and storytelling, are crucial to the expression of the African identity. Artistic expression serves a variety of purposes, ranging from the veneration of ancestors and glorification of rulers to the education of the young. Africa has two overlapping artistic traditions: One is court art done by professionals at the behest of chiefs, and the other is popular culture in which all ordinary Africans participate to a greater or lesser extent.

The African identity today incorporates a

deep sense of pride about the outstanding accomplishments of Africans, both past and present. The powerful leaders of the past, who advanced their subjects' fortunes or fought valiantly to save them, are remembered. Also revered are Africa's contemporary heroes, ranging from political leaders championing African causes to international sports champions.

A shared history of colonialism contributes to the sense of unity. That different forms of colonial rule may have varied in brutality is not significant. Rather, all forms of colonialism were forcefully imposed and maintained. All forms of colonialism left Africans feeling humiliated and oppressed. The protracted struggle for freedom from colonial rule took many forms—including countless acts of passive resistance, political activism, and armed struggle—and involved all Africans. For Africans in all parts of the continent, the prolonged and now successful fight for freedom by black South Africans provided a potent symbol of the meaning of colonialism.

Societal Diversity

Despite the unifying themes there are few places in the world where the extent of societal diversity is as great as in Africa south of the Sahara. These sociocultural cleavages have marked effects on political life and patterns of development.

During the 1960s, the term *pluralism* was widely used to refer to the complex patterns of ethnicity, language, and religion in African nations. The forging of a national identity from often seemingly incompatible groups was considered to be a major challenge for the newly independent states. Unfortunately, studies of pluralism were mostly descriptive and provided little guidance about policies for facilitating nation building. More recently, studies of social structure have focused less on horizontal cleavages such as ethnicity and religion and more on the class structure of African societies. The self-interest of ruling classes has been linked to policies that perpetuate underdevelopment, and the conflicting interests of different classes have been linked to internal discord.

Ethnicity

Ethnicity may be defined as affiliation or loyalty to a group sharing a common sense of origin, real or artificially constructed. Most ethnic

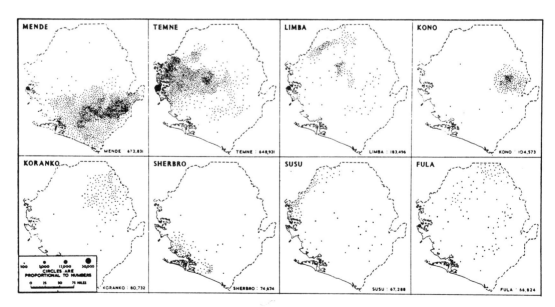

Figure 3.1. Sierra Leone: Distribution of major ethnic groups. Note that while groups tend to occupy a relatively easily identified core region, ethnic territories are seldom discrete and exclusive to a single group. Source: J. Clark. *Sierra Leone in Maps.* New York: Africana, 1972. ©1969 by J. I. Clarke, S. J. A. Nelson, and K. Swindell. Reprinted by permission.

Figure 3.2. Calabash carvers, Jigawa State, Nigeria. Much African art involves the decoration of everyday objects with designs that are often intricate and imbued with cultural meaning. Photo: author.

groups share the same language, culture, and political and economic institutions. *Ethnicity* has replaced the perjorative terms *tribe* and *tribalism*, with their connotations of primitive feuding between hostile rivals. Ethnicity is a deceptive construct since ethnic divisions are often surprisingly imprecise. Certain African groups share a common ethnic identity that overrides evident cultural differences, while other groups with no significant cultural differences claim separate ethnic identities.

Some tribes were essentially colonial creations. Ethnic identities were heightened by strengthening the power of chiefs as nominal rulers and by establishing new ethnically defined administrative units. Certain loosely affiliated groups were for the first time given chiefs and other traditional institutions.

The colonial tribalization of Africa south of the Sahara was instrumental in legitimating colonial rule, not only the colonial conquest that allegedly brought peace to a feuding continent but also the policies of separate development for different groups. Ethnic indentities were defined in relation to characteristics, such as supposed cultural sophistication, ascribed to various groups by colonial rulers. Certain groups were considered to be dependable workers, while others were deemed lazy and recalcitrant. Such labeling not only helped to shape and justify policies that created gross regional inequities in development but also sanctioned the forceful recruitment of migrant labor from certain regions and ethnic groups.

Irrespective of how feelings of ethnic identity originated, they did not wither after independence. African nations, however, vary greatly in ethnic diversity. A few nations, notably Somalia, Lesotho, Swaziland, and Botswana, are ethnically homogenous and contain no substantial ethnic minorities. At the other extreme are ethnically diverse nations such as Tanzania, Cameroon, and Nigeria, which contain hundreds of ethnic groups.

In Tanzania and Cameroon no ethnic group is large enough to be politically dominant. However, Nigeria has three very large and powerful ethnic groups that dominate the almost 300 smaller groups in the country. Within Nigeria, the Hausa, Yoruba, and Igbo, whose current populations are approximately 20 to 25 million each, are more appropriately considered ethnic *nations*. Minority groups such as the Nupe, Ijaw, Tiv, and Kanuri, with 1 to 4 million members, are comparatively small in the context of Nigeria but are hardly insignificant. The national populations of 16 African countries are less than the 2.5 million

a

b

Figure 3.3. Islam in Africa. (a) Mosque, Niamey, Niger. The mosque is the focal point for religious, and often political life in Islamic communities. (b) Islamic scholar at prayer, Niger. Photos: R. Lemoyne.

population of the Tiv in Nigeria, yet the Tiv are only the eighth-largest Nigerian ethnic group.

Political conflicts with ethnic dimensions have always received considerable attention in the Western media. The 1966 riots and the subsequent civil war in Nigeria, the recurrent Hutu–Tutsi conflicts in Rwanda and Burundi, and political disputes in Uganda under Idi Amin are typical examples of crises in which the Western media have chosen to emphasize interethnic conflicts. Unfortunately, contrary evidence has not received the attention it deserves. Not only have ethnic rivalries not been a major problem in numerous countries in Africa, but the intensity of ethnic rivalries has receded in many African countries. By giving excessive coverage to ethnic disputes, the media has helped to reinforce the colonial image of Black African nations as hopelessly divided and unviable.

Language

Africa south of the Sahara has great linguistic diversity; there are well over 1,000 distinct African languages. Linguists continue to disagree about the best way of classifying African languages. Even where languages are seen to be related, the processes underlying the relation usually remain a mystery.

Students of African languages have identified over 100 groups of languages–that is, two or more closely related languages or a single language unrelated to any other–belonging to four major language superfamilies, of which Niger–Congo is the largest. It includes both the many languages of West Africa and the approximately 400 Bantu languages that constitute a subfamily within Niger–Congo. Numerous languages of the Afro-Asiatic group are found in the area adjoining the Sahara, both in West Africa and in the Horn of Afri-

Vignette 3.1. "Ethnicity" and Political Violence in Rwanda

The curse of ethnic enmity and ethnic violence has been a recurring theme in coverage by the Western media of events in Africa. The Nigerian civil war, hostilities in Uganda and Rwanda, and violence in the black townships of South Africa, to name only a few cases, have been analyzed simply as "tribal" conflicts. Other dimensions of these conflicts have received very little attention. The result has been to solidify in the minds of the Western public the idea that "tribalism" is an *African* problem, even in the midst of bloody fratricidal violence in the former Republic of Yugoslavia and the former Soviet Union.

The background to the violence in Rwanda during 1994 that has resulted in the deaths of an estimated 500,000 people illustrates the importance of looking beyond stereotypes of tribal conflict. The violence that occurred in Rwanda was mostly the result of ethnic differences, but not exclusively so. Moreover, the ethnic dimension of the crisis reflects a complex history of relations between different segments of Rwandan society, extending over many centuries. Of particular importance in this history is the alteration and manipulation of ethnic relations that occurred under colonialism.

The people of Rwanda, the Banyarwanda, embrace three subgroups: the Hutu (approximately 85% of the population), the Tutsi (about 15% of the population), and the Twa (about 1%). The groups commonly intermarry, speak the same language, and share a common culture. The Tutsi were the ruling class in the Kingdom of Rwanda before the arrival of colonial powers, maintaining a "feudal" domination of the Hutu and Twa. Status and wealth, vested in their ownership of cattle, were associated with being Tutsi. Tutsi who lost their cattle and became poor would generally come to be identified as Hutu, and Hutu who became wealthy could become Tutsi. The system was more one of class than of ethnicity.

The imposition of German, and later (after World War I) Belgian, colonialism deepened the rift between the groups. People were classified formally as Hutu or Tutsi on the basis of cow ownership; anyone with fewer than 10 cows was deemed to be Hutu. In communities that had Hutu chiefs, the chiefs were replaced by Tutsi. Chiefs were made to administer a brutal regime of forced labor and taxation that made life unbearable for the Hutus and for the poorer Tutsis. Educational opportunities were reserved almost exclusively for Tutsi.

As independence approached, the Belgians reversed their policy of using the Tutsi as administrators, and supported the emergence of an all-Hutu political party. Communal violence broke out in 1959, resulting in the deaths of many chiefs and citizens. The Beligians seized the opportunity to replace many Tutsi chiefs with Hutu. In January, 1961, with Belgian support and in defiance of the United Nations, the Tutsi monarchy was abolished and Rwanda declared a republic.

The years follwing independence saw recurring violence, direted primarily by the governing Hutu majority against the Tutsi. Many thousands were killed. By 1964 an estimated 150,000 Banyarwandan refugees had fled to neighboring countries. The government continued to play on ethnic fears; for example, people were required to carry identity cards that named the group to which they belonged. Nevertheless, Hutus and Tutsis continued to live and work side by side, usually without undue tension.

Banyarwanda refugees who had fled to countries such as Uganda became essentially stateless. Rwanda refused to allow repatriation, claiming that the country was overpopulated and that many wishing to enter Rwanda were Banyarwanda who for generations

cont.

Vignette 3.2. (*cont.*)

had been citizens of other countries. Banyarwanda in Uganda continued to be viewed as outsiders and, because of their ability to succeed economically, were subjected to hostility and, on occasion, widespeard violence. The sense of alienation among Banyarwanda refugees lay behind the formation of the Rwanda Patriotic Front (RPF) and its attempt to invade Rwanda in 1989.

After over 3 years of intermittent fighting, the RPF and the Rwandan government signed the Arusha Accord in 1993. It was to end fighting between the RPF and the government, and provided a formula for power-sharing between the opposing sides. However, the government moved slowly to implement the accord. The death of the president in a plane crash, in April 1994, unleashed a wave of genocidal violence across Rwanda, perpetated primarily by government paramilitary groups. Although the majority of the victims were Tutsi, many Hutus distrusted by the governing faction–whether for ideological reasons or by virtue of their region of origin–were also killed. There were, without doubt, also many acts of retaliation by the RPF and its supporters. As violence escalated, the RPF began to move on the capital, Kigali. The government stepped up its campaign of fear by warning that "the lords" were trying to return. In this climate of terror and fear, it is hardly surprising that, following the defeat of government forces by the RPF, nearly 2 million Rwandans fled to Zaire and other neighboring countries, fearing for their lives.

The RPF has vowed to end the fratricidal violence and, in appointing Hutus to the top two positions in the new government, has made an important start. Nevertheless, it will take much more than good intentions to bring about the repatriation of the vast refugee population and to restore a climate of trust and cooperation in the country.

Primary source: U.S. Committee for Refugees. *Exile from Rwanda: Background to an Invasion.* Washington, D.C.: 1991.

---

ca. Hausa and Amharic are its most important members. The Nilo–Saharan languages of north central Africa and the Khoisan languages of southwestern Africa constitute the other two distinct language superfamilies. Both are spoken by far fewer people than either the Niger–Congo or Afro-Asiatic.

The distribution and importance of individual African languages has gradually but continuously evolved. Many of the more obscure languages, spoken by a few dozen to a few thousand people, are dying out and are being replaced by expanding lingua franca, pidgins, and official European languages.

In many regions, people from different cultural backgrounds must use a common lingua franca to converse (Figure 3.4). Swahili, which developed along the East African coast from a fusion of Arabic with local Bantu languages, is now spoken throughout East Africa. It is also increasingly prevalent in adjacent parts of central Africa. Hausa, spoken by at least 50 million people, is the most important lingua franca in West Africa, particularly in Nigeria and Niger. Arabic is widely spoken in Islamic societies, especially in Sudan. A few other languages, including Malinke in Senegal and neighboring countries and Bemba in south central Africa, are used as regional lingua francas. Creole and pidgin languages, which are derived from English and other European tongues combined with local African languages, serve as lingua francas in certain coastal areas of West Africa that have had a long history of African–European contact.

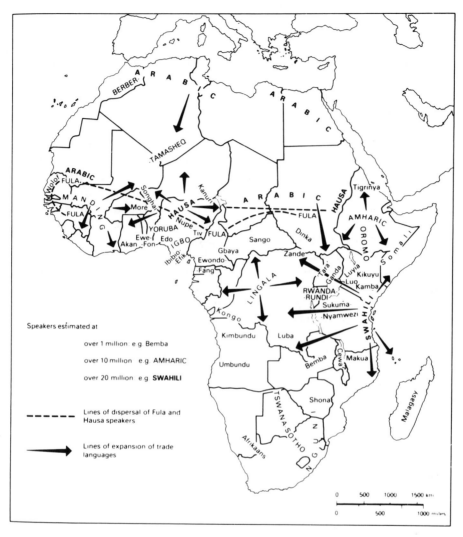

Figure 3.4. Lingua francas and other important African languages. Arabic, Hausa, and Swahili are the most important and fastest growing of Africa's lingua francas. Source: D. Dalby. "African languages." *Africa South of the Sahara, 1991.* London: Europa, 1990, p. 96. ©1990 by Europa Publications Limited. Reprinted by permission.

African lingua francas possess various advantages that permit them to expand at the expense of small, local languages. They are widely used in the printed and spoken media and have their own literatures. The use of lingua francas as languages of instruction in the school systems of countries where they are spoken has facilitated their spread. The growth of lingua francas has contributed significantly to the lessening of ethnic rivalries and the emergence of stronger national identities. In Kenya, Tanzania, and Uganda, Swahili is strong enough to be recognized as an official national language.

The colonial languages—English, French, Portuguese, and Spanish—have continued to spread because of increasing access to education. The continued use of English and French is virtually assured because of their importance as international languages of science and technology. European languages will retain their position as official national languages because most countries have no indigenous language suitable for this purpose.

Religion

Traditional religion encompasses all the belief systems and religious practices that are specific to a culture. Various kinship and occupational groups typically depend on specific deities for protection and prosperity and take primary responsibility for performing the rituals needed to ensure continuing good fortune. The deities have a variety of characteristics and are commonly associated with particular elements in the natural environment.

The persistence of traditional religions varies greatly, reflecting both the duration and strength of Christian and Islamic missionary activity and the resilience of individual cultures. Certain groups, such as the Mossi of Burkina Faso, have strongly resisted conversion. The boundaries between religions are blurred by the retention of elements of traditional belief systems by African Christians and Muslims. Many Africans have essentially a dual religious affiliation, to either Islam or Christianity as well as to a traditional religion. As Vignette 3.2 shows, even where Islam or Christianity becomes very firmly established,

beliefs and practices based on indigenous religion may continue to be important, although they may be expressed in new ways.

Christianity is widely distributed in Africa south of the Sahara. The Christian population is proportionally highest in southern Africa and west central Africa (Figure 3.5). African Christianity dates from A.D. 400 when two Christian kingdoms emerged: Nubia, in what is now Sudan, and Axum, in the region that is now Ethiopia. The Ethiopian Orthodox Church, the state church of the Ethiopian Empire, remained essentially isolated from the rest of Christendom until the 20th century.

Except for sporadic missionary efforts during the era of slavery, European interest in converting Africans to Christianity only commenced in the 19th century. The continent was then subdivided into religious spheres of influence dominated by different Protestant and Catholic missions, each promoting its own version of Christianity. Missionaries were actively involved in providing health care and education, which were used as inducements to conversion. The missions were often the

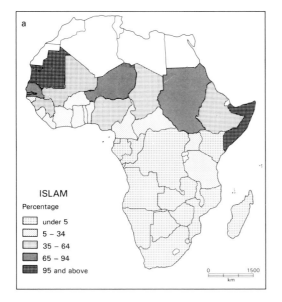
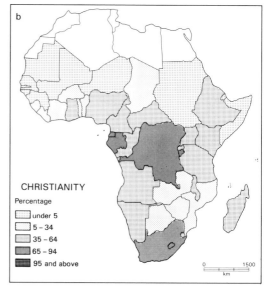

Figure 3.5. The distribution of (a) Islam and (b) Christianity. Islam predominates in the states adjacent to the southern edge of the Sahara, Christianity further south. Nigeria and Ethiopia are the only states with large proportions of both.

Vignette 3.2. Continuity and Change in the Hausa Cult of *Bori*

The word "tradition" usually evokes an image of reverence for the ideas and rituals of the past and perhaps of resistance to change. This case study illustrates that "traditional" religious–cosmological belief systems in reality may be extremely fluid, reflecting and responding to changes that are taking place in the broader social milieu. It also provides an example of a cultural institution that has come to be interpreted and used very differently by men and women.

Bori is a spirit possession cult widely practiced in segments of Hausa society in northern Nigeria and Niger. Bori is based on a belief in an invisible spirit world that parallels the visible world of humans. There are spirits of every social origin and status and of every disposition. They are deeply involved in the daily lives of humans. Some spirits seek to establish a friendly relationship with humans and may bring them prosperity. Others are antisocial and cause various types of misfortune. Bori adepts act as intermediaries between the spirit and human worlds and are especially involved in the treatment of diseases believed to be caused by spirit attack.

The origins of bori are to be found in the pre-Islamic religion of the Hausa people, now observed only in a few isolated rural areas where people have resisted conversion to Islam. This religion involves several types of rituals to mediate the relationship between the spirit world and humanity. For example, heads of households make sacrifices to the spirits prior to the agricultural season to ensure that a good crop is obtained. The details of these sacrifices are carefully specified—for example, the exact coloring of the animal to be killed as well as the location, timing, and method of sacrifice.

Where Islam is firmly established, most of the rituals associated with traditional Hausa religion have long since been discontinued. However, bori continues to be practiced widely, even in the most thoroughly-Islamic urban areas. The majority of bori members in the city are women. Most men condemn bori as un-Islamic and claim that its adepts are usually prostitutes or, in the case of male participants, homosexuals. For women, whose social role has been regulated by the implementation of Islamic traditions such as seclusion (purdah), bori provides a medium of social interaction that is relatively free of male authority. The ceremonies of spirit possession become metaphors for the concerns of women, ranging from the frequent death of children, whose diseases are attributed to spirits, to rivalry among cowives in polygamous households. Women are often able to use the requirements of bori to negotiate concessions from their husbands who fear the consequences of antagonizing the spirits.

During the colonial era, the British attempted to ban bori, fearing that it could become a medium for political resistance. However, it survived and experienced a strong resurgence in the 1950s. Bori has become an important force in political life in Hausaland, not only because it facilitates women's political participation but also because it promises politicians a way of enlisting supernatural support for their campaigns.

Far from being merely a repository of "tradition," bori is a mirror of social change. While formerly important concerns, such as smallpox, have receded owing to modern vaccination, new social problems, such as the urban breakdown of traditional values and authority, have come to the fore in Hausaland. These new forms of social malaise are attributed by many Hausa to changes in the spirit world, such as the arrival of previously unknown spirits. The ability of the bori cult to reflect and respond to the changing times, more than anything else, accounts for its survival and continuing relevance.

only source of such services in areas neglected by the colonial state.

As a response to the uncompromising attitude of most missionaries toward traditional customs and religions, numerous independent African churches emerged. These independent churches combine Christian teachings and ceremonies with elements of African culture and traditional religion. Examples of independent churches are the Zionists of South Africa, the Cherubim and Seraphim of Nigeria, and the Kabunga of Zaire. Although these churches generally remained aloof from anticolonial struggles, their original rejection of European religious dominance had real political undercurrents.

The geography of Islam reflects longstanding patterns of interaction between Africa and the Islamic societies of Arabia and North Africa. Initially, Islam was mainly the religion of the ruling classes; it began to take hold south of the Sahara when the ruling class of the ancient kingdom of Ghana converted in the 12th century. Islam grew remarkably during the 19th century as a result of militant Islamic reform movements centered in present-day Sudan, Nigeria, and Mali. In each case, charismatic leaders launched jihads (holy wars) and established orthodox Islamic states.

The militant tradition of Islam provided the impetus for determined resistance to colonial expansion and, later, passive resistance to colonial rule. Islamic fundamentalism has posed a continuing challenge to the governments of certain states, particularly Sudan and Nigeria, since independence. Many Muslims are worried about the implications of increasing Western influences. While most Muslims seek a comfortable accommodation of the two, a determined minority continues to advocate the establishment of orthodox Islamic states purged of corrupting Western influences.

Muslims have continued to expand their influence rapidly, both numerically and spatially, as a result of their own proselytizing activities. Muslims often describe Islam as a religion for black people, and, by contrast, characterize Christianity as a white religion. New converts are attracted by the apparent unity and discipline of Islamic communities.

They may also be attracted by the relative ease of becoming a Muslim; the process commences with a simple profession of faith and typically proceeds gradually over many years and even generations. Islam has tended to be more patient than Christianity regarding the reluctance of converts to abandon traditional cultural and religious practices. On the other hand, in certain countries, the association of Islam with particular ethnic groups or a specific region has contributed to resistance to conversion elsewhere. In southern Sudan, for example, there has been determined local resistance to attempts by northerners to promote Islam and establish an Islamic state.

Social Class

Social classes reflect the unequal distribution of political and economic power in a society. Ruling classes are in a position to exploit the weak and consolidate their own privileged position, using tools ranging from alliances, both internal and international, to ideology. Class divisions cut across ethnic, linguistic, and religious categories.

The study of social formations has remained mostly the preserve of Marxist scholars. Liberal and conservative writers have tended to focus on horizontal cleavages such as ethnicity and religion or to use variables such as income or occupation as indicators of status. There is no attempt in the following discussion to precisely define the various social classes or to adhere to Marxist categories. Rather, the objective is to describe in general terms the changing character of vertical cleavages in African societies and to emphasize that the dynamics of class interaction are at least as important as those of ethnicity and religion.

Class composition and the dynamics of class relations evolve in response to changing economic, political, and sociocultural circumstances. In Africa south of the Sahara, marked changes occurred in the class structure of societies, first, after the imposition of colonial rule, and then again, following independence.

In precolonial times, many African societies were structured hierarchically, with chiefs and royal families at the top. The ruling classes consolidated their power using their control over access to land, customary obligations and taxes payable to them, and their ability to wage war. Other precolonial societies were more egalitarian, with no tradition of chieftaincy.

Patterns of stratification were radically different in the colonial state. Europeans occupied the top positions in the social hierarchy. There emerged a new class of indigenous elites, with some Western education and access to certain official positions. These small "assimilated" classes had legal status that conferred limited political rights in the Portuguese, Belgian, and French colonies. The power of traditional chiefs was most often eroded under colonialism; although the chiefs retained their positions, they had very little meaningful power. However, chiefs who in some areas had previously wielded limited power rose to prominence during the colonial era.

Although most Africans continued to rely on agriculture for their sustenance, farmers became more differentiated during the colonial era. Some achieved relative prosperity through commercial cropping and trade, but many disadvantaged farmers were forced to leave home to seek seasonal employment to earn money for their taxes.

The class structure shifted once again after independence. Europeans either left or assumed less visible roles. The dominant class was a "state bourgeoisie," consisting of politicians, civil servants, teachers and other professionals, and senior military officers. Not only were areas of power formerly reserved for colonial officials opened to Africans, but the entire state apparatus was precipitously expanded and diversified. Entry and promotion depended on educational qualifications and connections to those in power. However, opportunities have become progressively more limited for those lacking political connections. Meanwhile, the formal power of traditional rulers has continued to recede.

In most countries, the attitudes and behavior of the dominant classes have generated much cynicism from the masses. The Wa Benzi, as they are called in East Africa, are blamed for mismanagement and the deepening economic crises. While relatively few of them own Mercedes Benz cars, take shopping trips in Europe, live in palatial estates, and wear luxurious clothing, these supposed symbols of success are popularly viewed as indicators of corruption and betrayal.

In addition to the ruling classes, several groups with varying levels of wealth and power are to be found in the city:

- Often relatively prosperous petty capitalist traders, transporters, and artisans
- Lower-status employees of larger businesses and governments
- Poor people who make ends meet in informal sector jobs they have often created for themselves
- Marginal people who are essentially unemployed and mostly dependent on others for their sustenance

The rapid growth of cities, coupled with the increasing dominance of permanent rather than migratory residents in the cities, has influenced the social structure of African nations. Distinctly urban social classes have emerged and made their mark. While the urban masses are effectively excluded from decision making in most countries, governments have tacitly recognized their potential for protest by implementing certain policies benefiting the urban poor. For example, many countries subsidized urban consumers by importing staple foods for sale below market prices. Many of these policies were reversed during the 1980s as a result of the implementation of structural adjustment packages. Policy measures such as reducing or ending subsidized food imports, reducing public-sector employment, and imposing fees for health care and education have greatly increased the cost of living, not only for the poor, but also for the urban middle class.

With few exceptions, most rural people have fared poorly since independence. Although more services are now provided in rural areas, the rural–urban gap in service provision continues to grow. Government policies such as importing cheap food and imposing heavy indirect taxes on exported produce have depressed rural incomes and stimulated massive urbanward migration. Benefits from rural development projects have gone mostly to large farmers and entrepreneurs and have accelerated the growth of a landless class that survives by selling its labor. Despite their numerical dominance, the rural masses have even less political clout than their urban counterparts and have usually been ignored by those in power.

The flow of people and money between rural and urban areas contributes to class formation in both settings. For example, rural–urban migration has been the primary source of growth for urban classes, especially the urban poor. Migrants to the city commonly maintain ties to their ancestral homes through gifts, investments in property, and involvement in hometown improvement associations. The "big men" in rural society are often urban based, although they will not necessarily be "big men" in the city.

While the classes identified above are found throughout Africa, their size and status vary from country to country. Many factors, ranging from indigenous cultures, to the social, economic, and political policies of colonial powers, to the models of development adopted by individual countries after independence, contribute to the diversity of African social formations.

Gender

Men and women in African societies occupy separate, albeit overlapping, spheres. For women, the primary foci of activity are home and children. Nevertheless, the scope of the domestic sphere is large, encompassing in most African societies food production (farming) and obtaining household necessities such as firewood and water. For men, public life and the marketplace are the primary foci of activity. This is not to deny the importance of the role played by many African women in commerce or of many African men in food production.

Not only are the roles of men and women different, but so too is the power and influence they wield in both traditional and modern African society. The separate and unequal position of women was perpetuated and often deepened during the colonial period through policies that, for example, gave priority to male education or stressed cash crop production by men with no regard for the primary role women played in agriculture. The struggle of African women, for greater security and greater opportunity for themselves and their children, continues.

Exploring the Diversity of African Society

Africa's writers have provided a rich and diverse body of literature in which many of the themes introduced in this chapter are explored through the eyes of ordinary Africans who in the course of simply living their lives are forced to grapple with the challenges and dilemmas of societal change. Works by African writers can be an invaluable resource for geographers wishing to develop a better understanding of the dynamics of tradition and change in African societies.

There has been much writing of note by authors communicating in French and Portuguese, but the largest and most accessible body of African fiction is that written in English. More and more novels are also being written in African languages such as Swahili, Kikuyu, Yoruba, and Igbo in some parts of the continent.

Nigeria has produced many writers of note, including Wole Soyinka (who won the 1986 Nobel Prize for Literature), Chinua Achebe, Cyprian Ekwensi, Festus Iyayi, and Buchi Emecheta. Novels written by Ghana's Ayi Kwei Armah and Kofi Awoonor have also been widely acclaimed. East Africa has a thriving literary tradition, in which the Kenyan novelist Ngugi wa Thiong'o has achieved prominence. In South Africa, the violence of apartheid has been the focus for provocative works not only by members of the oppressed communities but also by white liberal writers such as Alan Paton and Nadine Gordimer. A number of classic works originally produced in French have been translated into English, including novels by Ousmane Sembene (Senegal) as well as Ferdinand Oyono and Mongo Beti (Cameroon).

Unity and diversity, continuity and change. These paired constructs may appear to be contradictory, but collectively they epitomize the essence of modern African society. Africa has a rich diversity of cultures that is further compounded by religious, class, and gender differences within each society. Nevertheless, there is a common cultural inheritance and unity among African peoples that transcends these societal cleavages.

Further Reading

The following sources are recommended as introductions to the cultural identity of Africa:

Clark, L. *Through African Eyes: Cultures in Change.* New York: Praeger, 1969.

Maquet, J. *Africanity: The Cultural Unity of Black Africa.* New York: Oxford University Press, 1972.

Mazrui, A. *The Africans: A Triple Heritage.* Boston: Little, Brown, 1986. (This volume was written to accompany an excellent PBS documentary series with the same title.)

Paden, J., and E. J. Soja. *The African Experience.* 2 vols. Evanston, IL: Northwestern University Press, 1970.

There are many sources on ethnic issues in specific countries. For general surveys on ethnicity and language, see the following sources:

Du Toit, B. M., ed. *Ethnicity in Modern Africa.* Boulder, CO: Westview Press, 1978.

Greenberg, J. *The Languages of Africa.* Bloomington: Indiana University Press, 1966.

Kuper, L., and M. G. Smith, eds. *Pluralism in Afri-*
ca. Berkeley: University of California Press, 1969.

Murdock, G. P. *Africa: Its Peoples and Their Culture History.* New York: McGraw-Hill, 1959.

Shaw, T. "Ethnicity as the resilient paradigm for Africa: From the 1960s to the 1980s." *Development and Change,* vol. 17 (1986), pp. 587–605.

An extensive literature on African religion includes the following sources:

Clarke, P. B. *West Africa and Islam.* London. Edward Arnold, 1982.

Parrinder, G. *African Traditional Religion.* London: Sheldon, 1974.

Sanneh, L. O. *West African Christianity: The Religious Import.* Maryknoll, NY: Orbis, 1983.

Trimmingham, J. S. *A History of Islam in West Africa.* Oxford: Oxford University Press, 1962.

Issues related to social class in Africa are discussed in the following sources:

Allen, C., and G. Williams, eds. *Sub-Saharan Africa: The Sociology of "Developing Societies."* New York: Monthly Review, 1982.

Cohen, D. L., and J. Daniel, eds. *Political Economy of Africa: Selected Readings.* Harlow, England: Longman, 1981.

Gutkind, P., and P. Waterman. *African Social Studies: A Radical Reader.* New York: Monthly Review, 1977.

Lubeck, P., ed. *The African Bourgeoisie.* Boulder, CO: Lynne Rienner, 1987.

Sklar, R. "Patterns of social conflict: state, class, and ethnicity." *Daedalus,* vol. 111 (Spring 1982), pp. 71–98.

For an introduction to themes explored in African novels, read the following source:

Riddell, J. B. "Let there be light: The voices of West African novels." *Journal of Modern African Studies,* vol. 28 (1990), pp. 473–486.

AFRICA IN
HISTORICAL PERSPECTIVE

All geography is in some sense historical geography. The importance of maintaining a clear sense of historical perspective is especially important in studying the geography of Africa where, for example, the legacy of colonial rule is so frequently evident in the present-day economic, political, and social circumstances of the continent.

Chapter 4 provides a brief survey of Africa prior to the colonial era. It surveys the origins, organization, and accomplishments of several early empires, refuting the formerly widespread notion that Africa had no history of its own. The chapter also looks at the extent, organization, and effects of the centuries-long slave trade that saw many millions of Africans transported to the New World and elsewhere.

Chapter 5 examines the historical geography of colonialism, starting with the late–19th-century scramble of European powers to carve up the continent. The specific legacies of European rule varied from colony to colony, depending on the choice of economic development and government models. Some colonies, such as Northern Rhodesia and Southern Rhodesia, were transformed by the alienation of land for white settlement and the development of resource-extraction industires. Other colonies, such as Chad, were considered to have little value and were neglected, except as a source of labor. Although the colonial era was, in historical terms, very brief, its continuing legacy has been pervasive.

Chapter 6 explores several themes related to Africa's struggle for independence, and the subsequent struggles for repsonsive government, development, and survival. The optimism of the early 1960s has given way to a more sober realization of the complexities of development in a changing world system. Not only is Africa's influence in global affairs extremely limited, but so too is its ability to control even basic aspects of its own destiny. Three decades after colonialism's demise, neocolonialism thrives.

4

✳

The African Past:
Historical Geography of Africa
South of the Sahara

Available archeological evidence, together with recent genetic and linguistic research, points to Africa as the very cradle of humanity. *Homo sapiens* is thought to have first appeared in Africa some 150,000 to 200,000 years ago. About 100,000 years ago, modern humans appear to have swept out of Africa, quickly displacing archaic hominids in other parts of the world.

The evolutionary succession leading to modern humankind has been traced back some 4 million years. Considerable fossil evidence about these early hominids, the australopithecines, has been uncovered in South Africa, the East African rift valleys, and the Afar Depression in Ethiopia. The australopithecines shared certain physical characteristics—brain size, the shape of teeth and jaws, and skeletal characteristics affecting posture and locomotion—that clearly differentiated them from both the higher apes and the human species (*Homo*) that appeared later.

In tracing the evolution of humans, anatomical change becomes increasingly less important over time relative to intellectual and cultural development—social organization and the use of tools, for example—that made possible the human utilization of increasingly diverse environments. Around 2.4 million years ago, a more advanced hominid, *Homo habilis* (known as the "tool maker") appeared. *Homo habilis* had a larger brain than the australopithecines, used simple stone tools, and lived in encampments. *Homo erectus,* which superseded *Homo habilis* some 1.8 million years ago, had a more erect posture and larger brain, and devised a variety of more sophisticated tools. Like *Homo habilis* and the australopithecines, *Homo erectus* apparently lived in savanna environments, particularly near larger bodies of water.

Africa has yielded only scattered evidence related to the appearance of early *Homo sapiens* 150,000 to 200,000 years ago. Over the past 50,000 years, the pace of cultural development of *Homo sapiens* has steadily accelerated. Early advances included the development of more varied and sophisticated stone tools and the first human colonization of tropical rainforest environments.

The Agricultural and Iron Revolutions

In the totality of human history, the agricultural revolution is a recent event, having first occurred in Mesopotamia approximately 10,000 B.C. The agricultural revolution in Africa south of the Sahara is even more recent, although the actual date remains a subject of debate. Rock paintings show that pastoralism, initially based on sheep and goat herding and later on cattle rearing, was well established in the central Sahara during the moist climatic phase between 8000 and 4000 B.C. Grinding stones have been found in their settlements, suggesting that they harvested grain. As the climate became progressively drier, communities in the savanna regions south of the Sahara that had depended on fishing turned increasingly to crop cultivation and pastoralism to secure their food supply. Farming and pastoralism became widespread in this savanna belt between 3000 and 1000 B.C. By 1000 B.C. farming was also well established throughout the forest zone. Unlike the savanna zone where grain crops were predominant, farmers in the forest zone specialized in the cultivation of root crops and bananas.

Agricultural innovation occurred in four culture hearths in Africa south of the Sahara: the Ethiopian Plateau, the West African savanna, the West African forest, and along the forest–savanna boundary in west central Africa. Within each of these regions, a variety of crops were domesticated and methods of cultivation suited to the local environment were developed. From these foci, crops and agriculture diffused to other parts of Africa south of the Sahara. Cultigens were also exchanged with other agricultural hearths, especially Egypt and the Middle East. The spread of agriculture frequently accompanied the Bantu migrations into central and southern Africa; these migrations are discussed later in the chapter.

The list of plants apparently domesticated in Africa is impressive. The following are among the more important of them:

- Cereals: teff, finger millet, bulrush millet, sorghum, African rice
- Roots and tubers: yams
- Pulses: Bambara groundnuts, cowpeas
- Oil crops: oil palm, castor oil, shea butter
- Starch and sugar plants: ensete
- Vegetables: okra, garden eggs
- Fruits: watermelons, tamarind
- Stimulants: coffee, cola
- Fiber plants: cotton

The next great human revolution, that of making iron, began in Africa around 500 B.C. in Nubia in present-day Sudan. Other early foci of iron making developed at Nok in central Nigeria and in the vicinity of Lake Victoria (Figure 4.1). Unlike other parts of the world, Africa south of the Sahara did not experience a bronze age between the stone and iron ages, except in Nubia. The introduction of iron making permitted the construction of improved weaponry and tools and enabled iron-making peoples to expand territorially at the expense of those using only stone tools and weapons.

Bantu Migrations

Some 5,000 years ago, one of the most important migrations in human history began in central Nigeria, for reasons which remain a mystery. The Bantu migrations occurred in stages over five millenia, eventually reaching the southern extremity of the continent. Archeologists and historians have used diverse evidence—linguistic, cultural, technological, and cultural—to determine with increasing precision the timing of migrations and relationships among the various Bantu peoples.

Two major thrusts of Bantu migration from West Africa have been identified. The eastern stream proceeded toward the Lake District of East Africa, then southward through East Africa, and beyond into the southeastern part of the continent, initially following the savanna corridors. The second (western) migratory stream involved the spread of Bantu peoples and cultures south through Cameroon into the rain forests of west central Africa. By the third century A.D. the expansion of western Bantu peoples into all parts of the rain forest was complete.

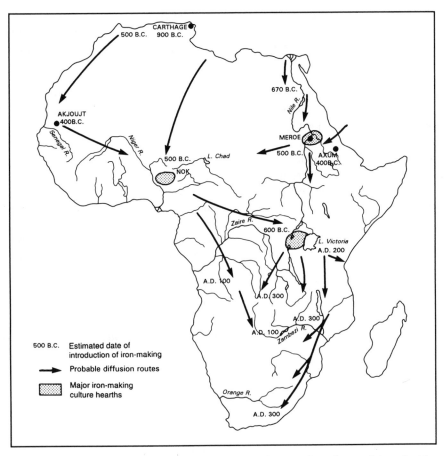

Figure 4.1. The diffusion of the technology of iron making. Nok, Nubia, and the Lake Victoria region are the three earliest centers of iron making in Africa south of the Sahara. After K. Shillington. *History of Africa*. London: Macmillan, 1989, p. 38.

The Bantu migrations seem to have occurred gradually and unevenly. Periodically, a group of people led by an ambitious subchief would secede and move on. Their migrations brought them into contact with indigenous stone-age societies who would either be forced into retreat or absorbed into the dominant Bantu culture. Through intermarriage and cultural fusion, distinct new cultures emerged wherever Bantu subgroups settled. Today, the similarity of languages and other cultural traits, and closely related blood types provides evidence of the common origins of people in eastern, central, and southern Africa.

The Bantu were agriculturalists who used iron tools and weapons. Their migrations were cultural and technological as well as demographic. They brought agricultural, herding, and iron-making technologies, introduced new forms of social organization, and established important empires, such as Zimbabwe and Kongo.

The migration of the Bantu peoples is but one of several known major movements of people that have given rise to the present-day population of Africa south of the Sahara. Madagascar was settled by people of Indonesian origin who arrived more than 1,500 years ago. Peoples of Caucasian origin originating in the Sahara and North Africa, as well as in the Arabian Peninsula, occupied several areas south of the Sahara. Along the Red Sea and the East African coast, cities established by Arab settlers became important points of trade and cultural development. Arab settlement also expanded inland, down the Nile Valley and beyond to Darfur in present-day western Sudan. In West Africa, the pastoral Fulani extended their grazing territory between the 11th and 16th centuries, occupying much of the savanna from their base in Senegambia eastward to Lake Chad. Indeed, the Fulani still continue to expand their territorial range. These recurrent processes of migration, diffusion, and assimilation have been extremely important in the evolution of the ethnic and cultural maps of the continent.

African Empires

The story of the empires in Africa south of the Sahara extends almost 3,000 years, beginning with the establishment of the empire of Kush. Other empires later developed in Ethiopia and West Africa. At the time of the colonial conquest, each of the major regions of the continent had several examples of advanced kingdoms or empires. Only a few details pertaining to the most important empires are related in this chapter, but these should serve to disprove the common notion that African development began with the colonial conquest.

Eastern Africa

The Nile River has a long history as a corridor for the movement of peoples, ideas, and trade goods between Egypt and Africa south of the Sahara. About 1000 B.C., the state of Kush in the Nile Valley of present-day Sudan was able to assert its independence from Egypt. Kush conquered Egypt in the eighth century B.C. and ruled it for several decades. The Kushitic civilization flourished following the rise to ascendancy of Meroe as the capital city, starting in the sixth century B.C. The

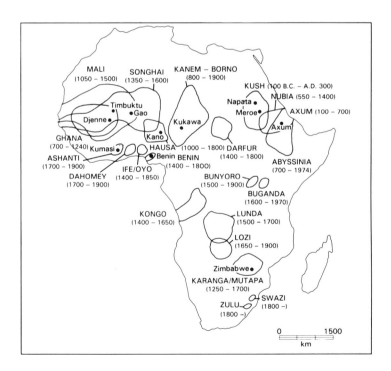

Figure 4.2. Major African states and empires. The map shows the names, locations, and approximate dates of existence for the most important precolonial states.

sophistication of Kush was reflected in its impressive stone architecture, irrigation systems, a large iron industry, its own script, and a well-developed sense of nationhood. The first great empire of Africa south of the Sahara experienced its greatest development during the final three centuries B.C. Its collapse around A.D. 300 seems to have been precipitated by the decline of its agricultural base owing to soil exhaustion and of its iron industry owing to the overexploitation of forests for charcoal.

Three Christian kingdoms, collectively known as Nubia, were established in the Sudanese Nile Valley in the 6th century A.D. These kingdoms flourished until the 8th century, when the spread of Islam effectively isolated Nubia from the rest of Christendom. The Christian kingdoms of Nubia finally expired in the 15th century.

Long before the emergence of Christian Nubia, the empire of Axum had embraced Christianity. Axum, located in the northern Ethiopian highlands, emerged in the first century A.D. through its control of the ivory trade from Africa to Arabia. Axum was predecessor to the Ethiopian or Abyssinian Empire, which for centuries was based at Gondar. In spite of constant pressure from neighboring Islamic states and many centuries of isolation from other Christians, the Ethiopian Empire survived until 1974, when Emperor Haile Selassie was deposed in a military coup. The spectacular 12th century A.D. churches of Lalibela, which were carved out of solid rock, provide enduring evidence of the vitality of Ethiopian civilization.

West Africa

Between the 9th and 19th centuries, a series of Islamic empires rose to prominence in the savanna of West Africa; the most important of them were Ghana, Mali, Songhai, Kanem-Borno, the Hausa States, and Sokoto. All had agricultural economies, but their control of one or more of the major trade routes across the Sahara provided the main source of wealth. Slaves, gold, cloth, and ostrich feathers were sent to North Africa in significant quantities; and weaponry, coins, and cloth were import-

ed in return. The savanna states also controlled the movement of salt from Saharan mines toward markets in the southern savanna and forest zones.

Ghana, a kingdom located in present-day Senegal and Mali, rose to prominence during the 9th century. During the 11th century, the rulers and many of the people of Ghana converted to Islam. Accounts of Arab travelers such as Al Bekri, who visited Ghana in 1067, provide insights into the size and splendor of the kingdom. Al Bekri noted, for example, that Ghana could field an army of 200,000 warriors. However, the kingdom of Ghana experienced a steady decline during the 12th century, following the opening of new, rich goldfields at Bure, beyond Ghana's borders, and the resultant shifting of trade routes.

By the mid–13th century, the empire of Mali had emerged in the upper Niger and Senegal Valleys, forged through the skilled leadership of the legendary Sundiata. Mali became extremely rich as a result of its control of the Bure goldfields and valuable salt deposits. Mansa Musa, then emperor of Mali, traveling as a pilgrim through Cairo to Mecca in A.D. 1324, was accompanied by 500 porters each bearing a staff of gold weighing about 65 oz (Vignette 4.1). The Malian state was organized and administered on Islamic principles. Universities were established at Timbuktu and Jenne, well before any existed in northern Europe. Large quantities of books were imported, and scholars from Greece, Egypt, and Arabia were employed.

The decline of Mali during the 15th century coincided with the emergence of Songhai, centered at Gao on the bend of the Niger River. Several independent Hausa states had also developed in present-day northern Nigeria and the sultanate of Kanem-Borno had established control over the area around Lake Chad.

By the 13th century, advanced states had been established in the forest zone. The Yoruba states of southwest Nigeria, and the related kingdom of Benin were the most prominent of them. Their wealth was also based on trade, principally the sale of kola nuts, ivory, and gold to the savanna states. Only after the arrival

Vignette 4.1. The Empire of Mali

The 14th-century Arab geographer, Al Omari, provides us with a graphic description of Mali and the visit of Emperor Mansa Musa to Cairo in A.D. 1324 while traveling on a pilgrimage to Mecca. Exerpts from Al Omari's writings follow.

> The king of this country [Mali] . . . is the most important of the Muslim Negro kings; his land is the largest, his army the most numerous; he is the king who is the most powerful, the richest, the most fortunate, the most feared by his enemies, and the most able to do good to those around him.
>
> [He] presides in his palace on a great balcony called bembe where he has a great seat of ebony that is like a throne fit for a large and tall person: on either side it is flanked by elephant tusks turned toward each other. His arms stand near him, being all of gold, sabre, lance, quiver, bow and arrows. He wears wide trousers . . . of a kind which he alone may wear. Behind him there stand about a score of Turkish or other pages which are bought for him in Cairo; one of them, at his left, holds a silk umbrella surmounted by a dome and a bird of gold. His officers are seated in a circle about him, in two rows, one to the right and one to the left; beyond them sit the chief commanders of his cavalry. . . . Their army numbers one hundred thousand men of whom there are about ten thousand mounted cavalry.
>
> During my first journey to Cairo and sojourn there I heard talk of the arrival of the Sultan Mansa . . . when he came into the Sultan's [of Egypt] presence, we asked him to kiss the ground. But he refused and continued to refuse, saying: "However can this be?" Then a wise man of his suite whispered several words to him that I could not understand. "Very well," he thereupon declared, "I will prostrate myself before Allah who created me and brought me into the world." Having done so, he moved toward the Sultan. The

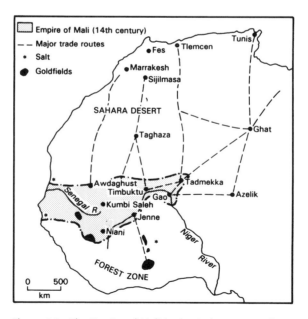

Figure 4.3. The Empire of Mali in the 14th century. After K. Shillington. *History of Africa.* London: Macmillan, 1989, p. 95.

Vignette 4.1. (cont.)

---

latter rose for a moment to welcome him and asked him to sit beside him: then they had a long conversation.

[He] spread upon Cairo the flood of his generosity; there was no person, officer of the court or holder of any office of the [Cairo] sultanate who did not receive a sum in gold from him. The people of Cairo earned incalculable sums from him, whether by buying and selling or by gifts. So much gold was current in Cairo that it ruined the value of money.

Excerpt from Al Omari. "Mali in the Fourteenth Century." In B. Davidson, *The African Past*, pp. 83–87. Harmondsworth, England: Penguin, 1966.

---

of Europeans along the coast did slaves become an important component of the forest kingdoms' trade. Although agriculture was the basis of their economies, the forest states were decidedly urban in character. The larger towns were divided into distinct wards and surrounded by a wall. European visitors to Benin during the 16th and 17th centuries remarked about the considerable size and orderliness of the city and the grandeur of the palace and found it comparable to the major European cities of the time.

Central and Southern Africa

Little is known of the kingdoms of central and southern Africa, most of which were very remote from early European contact. Karanga is best known because of the remarkable ruins of stone towers and walls at its capital city, Great Zimbabwe (Figure 4.4). The kingdom flourished from the 13th to the 15th century. Its people were skilled metalworkers who mined and crafted gold and copper and smelted iron on a large scale. Archeological evidence shows that Zimbabwe was the center of a flourishing trade in gold six to nine centuries ago. Trade goods from as far as India and China have been found at the ruins of Great Zimbabwe.

Between the 14th and 18th centuries, three major kingdoms—Luba, Lunda, and Kongo—emerged, flourished, and then declined in parts of what is now southern Zaire and north-

ern Angola. The prosperity of Kongo depended on a productive agricultural base, metalworking, and a flourishing interregional trade in foodstuffs, metals, and salt. The arrival of the Portuguese, whose main interest was to use the region as a source of slaves, led to the destabilization and finally the collapse of Kongo in the late 16th century.

The Slave Trades

For 12 centuries, starting in the seventh century, slaves were a principal export from Africa south of the Sahara (Figure 4.5). Scholars have long debated the actual numbers sent, but recent estimates suggest a total approaching 25 million! This brutal trade in human beings not only reduced the populations of many parts of Africa but also affected local and regional economies, social and political stability, and the environment.

The Trans-Saharan Trade

Trade between North Africa and black Africa increased greatly from the seventh century A.D., following the introduction of the "ship of the desert," the camel. The trans-Saharan route became the conduit for a diverse and mutually beneficial interaction between the savanna states of Africa and the Islamic world. Armaments, books, textiles, and beads moved southward, while gold, ivory, and slaves went

Figure 4.4. Section of the wall, Great Zimbabwe. These massive stone walls have remained intact for hundreds of years, even though no mortar was used to construct them. Photo: CIDA: B. Paton.

northward along a small number of routes. Islamic religious and cultural influences also crossed to the south side of the Sahara. Thus, slaves constituted but one element, albeit a very important one, in trans-Saharan commerce.

As many as 9.4 million slaves were exported via the Saharan routes between A.D. 650 and 1900. The journey across the desert on foot was so arduous that it was common for the majority of those sent to perish on the way. Perhaps two-thirds were young women destined to become concubines or house servants in North Africa and Turkey. Male slaves were often employed as soldiers or courtiers; some wielded considerable power and influence in these positions.

East African Slave Trade

An estimated 5 million slaves were exported from eastern Africa as part of the large and diverse maritime trade linking Africa to Arabia, Oman, Persia, India, and even China. Trade along the East African coast dates from the early centuries A.D., but its magnitude increased during the 8th century. Initially gold and ivory were the main items of trade, with slaves being of relatively little importance. However, the sale of slaves later increased in importance, especially during the 18th and 19th centuries when the slave trade grew dramatically. Slaves from eastern Africa, like those sent across the Sahara, were primarily women and children destined to become concubines and household servants.

As the Indian Ocean trading system grew in importance, increasing numbers of Arab merchants settled in towns along the East African coast. A distinctive Islamic culture incorporating African and Arab elements evolved in these coastal centers. Some 40 of them developed into dynamic city–states; among the most important were Kilwa, Malindi, Mombasa, Zanzibar, Mogadishu, and Dar es Salaam. Their prosperity was reflected in the construction of impressive coral-stone mosques, palaces, and homes. The language kiSwahili is one of the most important legacies of the synthesis of African and Arab civilizations in the cities of the East African coast. Although virtually all visible evidence of the Indian Ocean trading system was confined to the coast, its cultural and economic effect was manifest as far inland as the East African lakes and Zimbabwe.

The Portuguese arrived in 1498 and proceeded to attack and pillage some of the main towns. While the Indian Ocean trade continued under Portuguese control, the Swahili civilizations of the East African coast waned.

Trans-Atlantic Slave Trade

Desite the enormity of the trans-Saharan and East African slave trades, they cannot rival the European-controlled slave trade, either in the number of people transported or in the resultant distortion of ecomomic, social, and political structures. Commodities other than slaves ceased to be a factor in African–European trading relationships; virtually the entire commercial economy of the western coast of Africa between the 16th and 19th centuries was organized to facilitate the capture, transportation, and sale of slaves.

Direct European involvement in the acquisition of African slaves began in the 15th century as Portuguese navigators explored the West African coast. The real growth of the trade, however, followed the European conquest of the Americas. African slaves were identified as an ideal source of labor for the plantations and mines of the New World, especially after the decimation of the American indigenous population. By the late 16th century, the English, Danes, Dutch, Swedes, and French had joined the initial slave traders, the Portuguese and Spaniards. The trade continued to grow; approximately 80% of slaves transported across the Atlantic were sent between 1700 and about 1870, when the trade ended.

The slave trade was one element of the "triangular trade" linking Europe, Africa, and the Americas. European ships carried guns, alco-

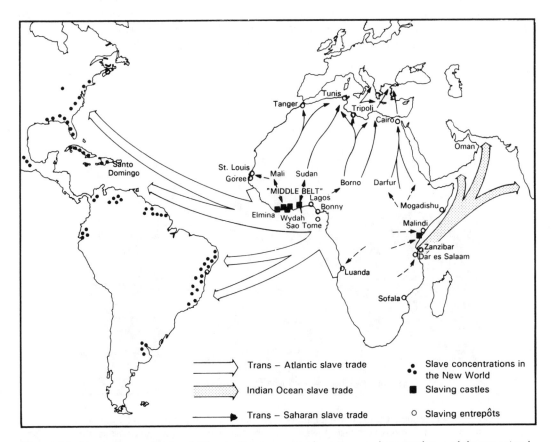

Figure 4.5. Three slave trades. In addition to these export trade systems, indigenous forms of slavery existed in many African societies.

hol, and cheap manufactured goods from Europe to West Africa. These goods would then be exchanged for slaves, and the slaves transported to the New World. The money obtained from selling the slaves financed the purchase of gold, silver, tobacco, sugar, and rum, which would be transported to Europe. This trading system provided great profits for shipowners and merchants, and also spurred the development of slaving ports such as Liverpool.

Europeans maintained only a tenuous presence in Africa. Castles were established along parts of the coast, especially in present-day Ghana, as centers for slave trading. Angola was the only other area in which substantial permanent bases were maintained. Elsewhere, Europeans relied completely on African intermediaries to assemble slaves at the coast, to be exchanged for manufactured goods during irregular visits by trading ships.

The slave trade was a major force in the underdevelopment of West Africa. The most widely accepted estimate of the number of slaves sent across the Atlantic is slightly less than 10 million. Many more died in transit, in slave raids and wars, and from the famine, disease, and economic disruption associated with the trade. Manning, who has written extensively about the demography of the slave trade, estimates that the population of tropical Africa in 1850 was only about one-half of what it would have been in the absence of slavery and the slave trade.

The demographic effect of the slave trade varied greatly over time and space. It appears that West African kingdoms seldom waged war explicitly to capture slaves prior to the climax of the slave trade in the 18th and early 19th centuries, but rather sold excess captives obtained in wars fought for other reasons. Thereafter, heightened demand for slaves brought about an increase in the frequency and scale of slave raiding. On some parts of the Atlantic coast of Africa, particularly in Senegal and Angola, the majority of slaves were captured relatively far inland. Elsewhere, such as along the Bight of Benin (coastal Nigeria

Figure 4.6. Elmina Castle, Ghana. Elmina is the oldest and largest of some 20 fortifications built by various European powers along the Ghanaian coast as the bases for the slave trade. The construction if this mammoth Portuguese castle began in 1482. Photo: author.

and Benin), most slaves were captured locally during protracted wars among neighboring kingdoms.

For many smaller and weaker ethnic groups in areas such as the Middle Belt of West Africa, located between the savanna and coastal slaving states, the slave trade brought about significant population decline. However, the populations of some coastal slave-trading states, such as Dahomey, seem to have increased in conjunction with the slave trade. Most of their female and child captives were retained rather than sold, and as a result high rates of fertility prevailed in these societies.

The slave trade disrupted agriculture, manufacturing, and trade, especially in the areas where slave raiding was most severe. Weaker communities were often forced to abandon their homes and seek refuge in remote or mountainous regions. Millions of young people were removed early in their most productive years; the development of countless communities was retarded by the loss of their energies and skills. The trade goods received in return by the slaving aristocracies were mostly armaments and luxury goods, neither of which provided any impetus for development. In states participating in the slave trade, the growing wealth and power of the aristocrats enabled them to dominate the peasants and to threaten and enslave their weaker neighbors.

In the Americas, slave labor was crucial for the functioning of the enormously profitable mines and plantations where sugar, tobacco, indigo, and cotton were produced. Even after the abolition of slavery, the plantation remained the main production unit in many countries; former slaves frequently remained as sharecroppers or indentured laborers. Slaves, however, provided much more than mere labor. Many of them possessed skills such as ironmaking and weaving that were greatly needed in the plantation and mining economies. They also had special knowledge about the cultivation of tropical crops and not only grew their own food but also commonly produced a surplus on small plots allocated to them.

Europe's rulers and merchants benefited materially from the slave-based economic activity. Slavery also fostered the development of racist stereotypes and myths in Europe. Africans were portrayed as shiftless savages; to enslave them was actually rationalized to be a means of rescuing them from their hopeless lives of misery! To justify the enslavement of Africans, Europeans first had to dehumanize them.

An intense debate began in Britain in the late 18th century, which culminated in the abolition of slavery. The momentum for abolition developed from several perspectives, including liberal opposition to the treatment of slaves, concern about growing rebelliousness among slaves in certain colonies, and the belief that so-called legitimate commerce could be more profitable and successful in supplying the burgeoning demand for tropical raw materials to supply British industry. Gradually, the abolition of slavery was adopted or enforced elsewhere, and by 1870 the Atlantic slave trade came to an end.

African Slave Trade

In Africa, as in many parts of the world, the institution of slavery has had a very long history. However, the export slave trade was associated with a massive increase in internal slavery and altered both the nature of slavery in African societies and the organization of economic activity.

The number of slaves retained within Africa, primarily women and children along the Atlantic coast and mostly men in the savanna region and in East Africa, increased as the export slave trade grew. Slave raiding made available many different kinds of captives, not just those most in demand for the export trade. The collapse of the trans-Atlantic slave trade in the 19th century did not end the wars and raids that had fed the trade. By the end of the 19th century, many African states were more than half slave, with systems of production primarily based on the use of slave labor. Slaves had become so important in the economiy of northern Nigeria, for example, that the British chose not to abolish slavery outright immediately after the colonial conquest for

Vignette 4.2. African History and Culture in Western Museums

The portrayal of African history and culture in non-African museums is a contentious issue that has at times pitted African intellectuals and political leaders, and often African Americans as well, against European and North American archeologists, museum curators, and academics interested in African culture. These disputes form part of a larger struggle by aboriginal and colonized peoples to reclaim ownership of their heritage.

The majority of the finest works of African art is to be found in museums and private collections outside of Africa. Many of these works were seized as war booty during the colonization of Africa. Others have been stolen—and continue to be stolen—from religious shrines, palaces, and museums in Africa, eventually finding their way into Western art markets. The attempts by African governments to have these artifacts returned have generally been rebuffed, largely because of the fear that a repatriation of antiquities long held by Western museums would set a precedent leading to the eventual decimation of their collections. Africans argue that many of the objects of art held by Western museums are very significant cultural and religious symbols and as such belong at home rather than in a museum display.

African concerns about Western museums extend beyond the ownership of antiquities and sacred objects to the way in which Africans are portrayed. Consider, for example, the controversy that erupted just prior to the 1992 Barcelona Olympic Games over the display in the museum at Banyoles, Spain, of the stuffed remains of an African, believed to have been stolen from a grave about 1830 by two French naturalists. "The Negro," as the exhibit is known, has been on display since 1916. A local African cultural center referred to the exhibit as a disgrace, a horror, and a serious mistake. The International Olympic Committee, at the request of several African nations, asked that the exhibit be withdrawn, but the town council refused and rejected claims that the exhibit was racist.

A rather more complex controversy erupted at the Royal Ontario Museum in Toronto in 1990 over an exhibit entitled "Into the Heart of Africa." Through the display of photographs Canadian missionaries had taken and artifacts they had collected, the exhibit was intended to explore the cultural arrogance of these missionaries who worked in Africa in the 19th and early 20th centuries. However, opponents denounced the display because it contained negative and stereotyped images of Africans; they argued that the display could misinform rather than educate impressionable young viewers. The display was withdrawn, but not before there had been heated debate about the messages conveyed by museum displays and the rights of particular communities to be involved in deciding how their own histories and cultures should be interpreted.

---

fear of bringing about economic and social chaos.

Not only did slavery within Africa grow, but the nature of the institution changed. With wealth and power increasingly determined by the control of slave labor, slaves became increasingly commoditized. Customary rights of slaves within African societies, such as strict limits on the sale of the children of slaves, were progressively eroded.

The Contemporary Significance of African History

It used to be said, in some quarters, that Africa south of the Sahara had no history of its own. This view, convenient for those intent on the subjugation and exploitation of Africa, has never borne any close scrutiny. However, in recent decades the careful work of archeologists, historians, and other social scientists has

---

Vignette 4.3. African Cultural Imprints in the New World

Africans sent to the Americas brought not only their ability to work but also a cultural heritage. African cultural influences have survived despite the adverse conditions under which enslaved Africans arrived. The enslaved Africans had originated in many different regions that shared neither a common language nor a specific common culture. Moreover, they had virtually no power to control their own destinies in the New World.

New African American cultures evolved from the interaction of African cultures and the incorporation of European cultural influences in particular settings. African elements survived more readily in the Caribbean and Brazil than in the United States, where blacks formed a much smaller proportion of the total population.

African influences on contemporary African American culture include the following:

- Language: Creole languages combining elements of African and European tongues developed as vehicles of communication within slave communities and between masters and slaves. These creole languages still show clear evidence of their African roots. For example, studies of Gullah, the dialect spoken in the Sea Islands of South Carolina and Georgia, have found that the dialect incorporates words from some 30 West African languages.
- Religion: African religious constructs, particularly the belief that supernatural forces control the destiny of humankind, persist in many parts of the African diaspora. The Caribbean and Brazil have a great variety of flourishing religious cults in which the worship of African deities is combined with the veneration of Christian saints. These cults include Macumba, Xango, and Umbanda in Brazil, and Santeria (primarily in Cuba and Puerto Rico) and Voodoo (Haiti) in the Caribbean. African American religions are now growing in the United States, owing to the recent wave of immigration from Cuba, Puerto Rico, Brazil, and Haiti.
- Folklore: African influences are evident in the folklore of African Americans—for example, techniques for craft production and herbal medicine. Folk tales such as 'Brer Rabbit are derived from a rich African tradition of storytelling used to educate the young and to subtly ridicule the rich and powerful.
- Arts: The profound influence of African American cultures on the arts and especially music is widely recognized. Spirituals, gospel, blues, jazz, rock and roll, soul, and reggae share common African roots. The themes of the music reflect the life experiences of 20th-century African Americans, but the structure and rhythm of the music are African. For example, the "call and response" (leader and chorus) structure of African work songs and traditional drumming is very commonly found in African American spirituals and jazz. Modern abstract sculpture and painting have been influenced in important ways by African traditional art. Pablo Picasso, the father of cubism, acknowledged that African traditional sculpture had been his primary source of inspiration.

shed increased light on the richness of Africa's history and the importance of African contributions to the collective history of humankind.

While the global significance of African history is well recognized, the portrayal of African history and culture, especially in Western museums, has been hotly disputed (Vignette 4.2). Africans question the morality of the continued possession and sometimes the insensitive display in Western museums of African treasures of great historical and cultural significance, more often than not stolen or seized as spoils of war.

Africans have turned to their rich historical traditions as a source of inspiration and identity. The contemporary map of Africa displays several names that are identical to those of ancient African kingdoms. Ghana, Mali, Benin, and Zimbabwe have all been resurrected as country names during the past 30 years. The trend was started by Kwame Nkrumah, who insisted that the colonial name Gold Coast be replaced with Ghana. The fact that ancient Ghana and modern Ghana occupied totally different territories was of no significance. Changing the name to Ghana replaced a name that symbolized British colonial oppression with one symbolizing both new beginnings and ancient roots, thus affirming that the underdevelopment of Africa was neither an original nor a natural state.

For peoples of African descent in the Americas and elsewhere in the African diaspora, African history represents an important reference point. It is particularly significant that despite the passage of time and past tendencies to ignore or even to attack the African cultural heritage, so many elements of this cultural heritage are still evident throughout the New World (Vignette 4.3). African history is also a part of American history.

Further Reading

The following sources provide general surveys of African history:

Ajayi, J. F. A., and M. Crowder, eds. *Historical Atlas of Africa*. New York: Cambridge University Press, 1985.

Curtin, P., S. Feierman, L. Thompson, and J. Vansina. *African History*. Boston: Little, Brown, 1978.

Fage, J. D., and R. Oliver. *Cambridge History of Africa*. 7 vols. New York: Cambridge University Press, 1975–1977.

Freund, W. *The Making of Contemporary Africa*. Bloomington: Indiana University Press, 1984.

Shillington, K. *History of Africa*. London: Macmillan, 1989.

Various themes in African prehistory are examined in the following sources:

Clark, J. D. *The Prehistory of Africa*. New York: Praeger, 1970.

Leakey, R., and R. Lewin. *Origins: What New Discoveries Reveal about the Emergence of our Species and its Possible Future*. New York: Dutton, 1977.

Phillipson, D. W. *African Archaeology*. New York: Cambridge University Press, 1985.

Wilson, A. *Origins Reconsidered*. New York: Little, Brown, 1992.

The book by Davidson is particularly recommended as a readable, profusely illustrated introduction to the empires of Africa:

Davidson, B. *African Kingdoms*. New York: Time-Life Books, 1966.

Vansina, J. *Kingdoms of the Savanna*. Madison: University of Wisconsin Press, 1966.

Vansina, J. *Paths in the Rainforest*. Madison: University of Wisconsin Press, 1990.

The slave trade, particularly the Atlantic trade, has been the subject of much research that has attempted to find the size and geographical organization of the trade, as well as its effects:

Curtin, P. *The Atlantic Slave Trade: A Census*. Madison: University of Wisconsin Press, 1969.

Inikori, J. E., ed. *Forced Migration: The Impact of the Export Slave Trade on African Society*. New York: Africana, 1982.

Lovejoy, P. *Transformations in Slavery: A History of Slavery in Africa*. Cambridge: Cambridge University Press, 1983.

Manning, P. *Slavery and African Life: Occidental, Oriental and African Slave Trades*. Cambridge: Cambridge University Press, 1990.

The sociocultural history of peoples of African descent in the New World has been explored by many authors:

Fikes, R. "Blacks in Europe, Asia, Canada and Latin America: A bibliographic essay." *A Current Bibliography on African Affairs*, vol. 17 (1984–1985), pp. 113–127.

Murray, D. W. "The slave trade and slavery in Latin America and the Caribbean." *Latin American Research Review*, vol. 21 (1986), pp. 202–215.

Nunez, B. *Dictionary of Afro-Latin American Civilization*. Westport, CT: Greenwood, 1980.

5

✸

The Colonial Legacy

European rule in most parts of the African continent had been in existence for only 60 to 80 years in 1960 as the colonial era moved rapidly toward its end. However, though the colonial era was short, it brought profound and lasting changes to the social, political, and economic geographies of Africa south of the Sahara. The crises now afflicting Africa are seldom comprehensible without reference to specific aspects of the colonial legacy. This is not to imply that the impress of colonialism was identical in all settings. On the contrary, it is important to recognize the variability over time and space of colonial policies and effects. Moreover, colonial rule should not be seen as an omnipotent force; Africans often resisted colonial edicts and found their own ways of adapting to the new reality.

Prelude to Colonization

The 19th century brought about profound changes in the relationship between Africans and Europeans. At the beginning of the century, the slave trade was still in full swing; by the end, the trade had been abolished. At the beginning of the century, Africa away from the coast was virtually unknown to Europeans; by the end, Europeans had set eyes upon virtually every part of the continent. At the begin-

ning of the century, political maps of Africa were almost blank; at the end, the maps carried a patchwork of pink, green, yellow, mauve, and orange to identify different colonially controlled areas of the continent.

In 1807, Great Britain abolished the African slave trade and moved to impose this policy on other slave-trading countries. For a number of African coastal states, the transition from an economy based for centuries on the slave trade to one based on legitimate commerce in primary products such as palm oil and groundnuts was very traumatic. In several states, the coercive powers of traditional rulers were challenged by newly emerging commercial and religious leaders. The resulting unrest made it possible for European trading companies, adventurers, and consular representatives to exert increasingly comprehensive influence. These trends intensified in West Africa starting in the 1860s, when declining terms of trade in African commodities forced many independent African and European traders to become middlemen working for the large trading companies.

European fascination with Africa began to increase in the late 18th century, particularly after James Bruce returned in 1783 from his quest to find the source of the Blue Nile. Several European explorers followed Bruce, including Park who twice attempted to follow the Niger River to the sea, Burton and Speke who followed the White Nile to its source in Lake Victoria, and Livingstone who explored large parts of central Africa. Much of the funding of this European exploration of Africa came from a number of scientific and geographical societies funded by wealthy individuals and companies. Returning explorers presented their findings to the sponsoring societies and wrote articles for their journals. These journeys of discovery generated great interest in a public intent on knowing much more about the world, and among merchants and industrialists eager to discern what trade opportunities might exist in the unknown interior of Africa.

During the 19th century, there was a growing interest in the establishment of Christian missions in Africa. The new missions, like the explorers and commercial agents, helped to pave the way for the establishment of formal colonial rule by heightening public interest in Africa and the fate of Africans. Missionaries, most notably David Livingstone, returned to Europe after visiting the African interior and talked passionately about the importance of the "civilizing mission," which involved combating the slave trade, starting schools, and encouraging the development of commerce in conjunction with the primary objective of spreading the gospel. The missionary project was fundamental to the European conviction that colonialism was a charitable undertaking by a morally and technologically superior race.

The Scramble for Africa

Prior to 1880, perhaps 90% of Africa south of the Sahara was still ruled by Africans (see Figure 5.1). Two decades later, the only uncolonized states were Ethiopia and Liberia.

Small European enclaves along the coast had existed for centuries, starting with the establishment of slaving castles in the late 15th century. Several of these enclaves were consolidated and extended during the 19th century. The French were well established in Senegal and Dahomey, the British in Gambia, Sierra Leone, and South Africa; and the

Portuguese were in Angola and Mozambique. However, by about 1880 tensions among the major European powers increasingly began to be focused on Africa. The French were angered by Britain's annexation of Egypt to safeguard its interests in the Suez Canal. In South Africa, the British extended their control inland from the Cape of Good Hope, following the discovery of rich diamond deposits at Kimberley. The French sought to expand into the upper Niger region by means of a rail link to Dakar, started in 1879. In the Congo, King Leopold of Belgium sent emissaries to annex territory and establish the Congo Free State as a personal estate. The Germans moved on several fronts, proclaiming Togo, Cameroon, Tanganyika (Tanzania), and South West Africa (Namibia) as protectorates.

Africa's would-be colonizers held a conference in Berlin in 1884 to 1885 in an atmosphere of intense distrust to establish ground rules for the carving up of the continent. Spheres of influence were traded like prizes in some great game of Monopoly. It was decreed that new annexations would not be recognized unless the territory had been effectively occupied. The scramble for Africa was beginning in earnest; whether "effective control" was established by means of military conquest or through bogus, one-sided "treaties" did not change the end result for Africans.

The French moved inland from several of their existing coastal bases toward Lake Chad—east along the savanna corridor from Senegal, north from Côte d'Ivoire and Dahomey, northeast from Gabon, and south from Algeria. In the process, they hoped to confine and outflank the British and gain control of as much territory as possible. The French also annexed Madagascar and a few smaller islands off the East African coast.

The British consolidated and extended their positions on the West African coast. While they claimed far less territory than the French, they managed to secure the most productive and populous areas. In southern Africa, Cecil Rhodes was the driving force behind British imperialist expansion, sending a military unit north to occupy territory and obtain mining concessions in Bechuanaland (Botswana) and

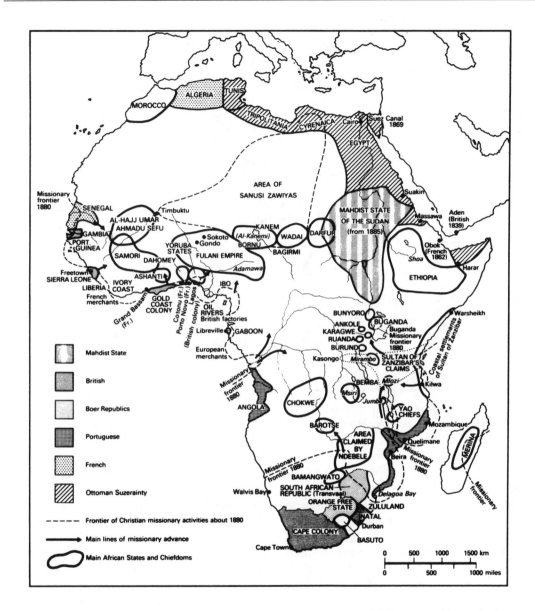

Figure 5.1. Africa on the eve of the colonial conquest. European control did not extend beyond a few footholds along the coast. Source: *Africa South of the Sahara, 1991*. London: Europa, 1990, p. 12. ©1990 by Europa Publications Limited. Reprinted by permission.

Rhodesia (Zimbabwe and Zambia). Rhodes was responsible for the powerful "Cape to Cairo" metaphor, which envisaged the establishment of continuous British rule and a rail line between Africa's southern and northern extremities. British control of southern Africa was consolidated as a result of the Boer War of 1899 to 1902, in which the formerly separate Boer republics of Transvaal and Orange Free State were defeated and later incorporated into the Union of South Africa. Britain's long-standing interest in East Africa intensified during the mid-1880s, in response to the newly-established German presence in Tanganyika. In East and central Africa, British control was initially exercised by commercial interests, the Imperial British East Africa Company and the British South Africa Company, respectively.

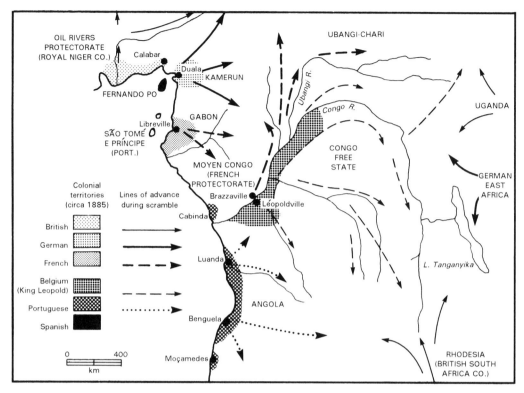

Figure 5.2. The scramble for the Congo Basin and Angola. Similar scrambles for territory occurred in all parts of the continent in the decade following the Berlin Conference. After K. Shillington. *History of Africa.* London: Macmillan, 1989, p. 312.

The other major colonial powers, the Germans and Portuguese, extended control inland from the bases they had established prior to the Berlin Congress. The Italians established themselves in Eritrea and Somaliland, but failed to conquer Ethiopia as a result of their resounding defeat at Adowa in 1896 by Ethiopian forces led by Emperor Menelik II. The Spanish also maintained a minor presence on the Guinea coast in present-day Equatorial Guinea. The Congo Free State was also enlarged, with tactics that were exceptionally brutal even for those times. Only in 1914 did King Leopold relinquish control of "his" Congo Free State to the Belgian government.

The colonial scramble for Africa was not the unproblematic claiming of territory that it has sometimes been made out to be. Africans mounted what was often a determined resistance to the advancing colonial regiments. In a few places, such as northern Niger and western Uganda, armed resistance continued

into the 1920s. Moreover, rival colonial powers often clashed over the demarcation of boundaries. The political decisions eventually made in the capitals of Europe over the location of boundaries were frequently arbitrary and ill conceived. The boundaries that the colonial powers created often divided ethnic groups and traditional political units between neighboring countries. To give but one example, the grand sultanate of Kanem-Bornu, founded in the 11th century, was divided among the British (Nigeria), Germans (Cameroon), and French (Niger and Chad).

By the early 1900s, the map of colonial spheres of influence was largely fixed. The most important subsequent change occurred when Germany was forced to relinquish control of its colonies after World War I. Britain, France, Belgium, and South Africa were granted the trusteeship of particular German colonies by the League of Nations. With the exception of a few administrative changes, such as the creation of the Federation of Rhodesia and Nyasaland in 1953, the political map of Africa did not change significantly for the rest of the colonial era.

The Colonial State

The colonial state was run by a small cadre of administrative and military officers and was operated as an extension of the European metropolitan state. The broad outlines of colonial policy were developed in Europe and generally reflected the political climate of Europe rather than the needs of Africa. The primary role of colonial officials was to interpret and implement policy directives from the metropole in relation to the particular situations found in specific regional settings. The goals of the colonial state focused on maintaining law and order and promoting particular kinds of development deemed to be in the interest of the metropole. The goals did not include fostering the development of modern, self-reliant nation–states, a notion inconceivable in light of the racist assumptions that underpinned colonialism (see Vignette 5.1).

The actual structure of colonial states varied greatly. In colonies with a substantial white-settler presence, most notably Kenya and Rhodesia, the settlers had considerable power, which they used to consolidate and legitimate their special privileges. Restrictions were placed not only on the economic and social choices available to Africans but also on those of Asian and Arab populations. For example, certain kinds of crops were reserved exclusively for settler–producers. Colonial governors

b

a

Figure 5.3. "Our colonialism, their colonialism." (a) "John Bull" reluctantly accepts responsiblity for the orphan Uganda abandoned on his doorstep. (b) The German eagle swoops in on defenceless villagers. Source: *Punch,* (a) April 21, 1894, and (b) April 26, 1890.

Vignette 5.1. "Africa Decivilized": Accounting for the Ruins of Zimbabwe

Colonial rule was justified, in large part, on the myth that the "Dark Continent" had no history worthy of the name. If Africans were believed to be incapable of indigenous development colonialism could be considered a charitable undertaking, rather than an exercise in conquest and exploitation.

Where there was tangible evidence of past achievements, it tended to be discounted or ignored, even falsified. The misinterpretation—indeed, the deliberate distortion—of the history of the ruins of Great Zimbabwe provides an interesting example of the "decivilization" of Africa under colonial rule.

Cecil Rhodes and other early European visitors to Zimbabwe were fascinated by the ancient gold workings and awesome stone structures they found. Local African legends spoke of the ruins as having been constructed by African ancestors countless generations earlier. But Rhodes ignored this explanation and, instead, alluded to legends about long-distance voyages by the ancient Egyptians and Phoenicians. He paid archeologists to study the ruins and to conclude that the seat of power of Solomon and the Queen of Sheba had been found.

Radiocarbon dating and other archeological evidence revealed that Great Zimbabwe had flourished after 1000 A.D., far too late for the Queen of Sheba myth to have any basis. For decades after it had been demonstrated conclusively that Africans had constructed this edifice, Rhodesian history books, museum literature, and other government publications continued to claim otherwise. Archeology was deliberately censored; to acknowledge African history and African achievement was too painful for those who wished to maintain white domination.

The history of Great Zimbabwe became an important symbol to both sides in the struggle for black majority rule, after white Rhodesia had declared unilaterally its independence in 1964. For Africans, Zimbabwe was a potent symbol of African achievement, as well as the chosen name of the future country for which they were prepared to sacrifice their lives. For the white Rhodesian state, Zimbabwe symbolized the unthinkable—namely, that Africans could (and would) prevail.

The following exerpt from "Zimbabwe: 'Bantu theory' v. truth: Link with Arabia," which appeared in a 1972 issue of *Property and Finance* magazine, demonstrates the continuing denial of truth and acknowledges why it was considered so important to do so.

In these days of deliberate subversion of civilized authority, the international New Liberalism attempts to mould all aspects of life including the sciences, to its glorification of the Negro. Archaeology, the study of antiquities, is a natural victim, for it can be used as a means of creating an artificial cultural respectibility for Black nationalism and, accordingly, a justification of Black rule. Against all objective evidence, Zimbabwe is again being promoted as a Bantu achievement.

Based on J. Frederickse. *None but Ourselves: Masses vs. Media in the Making of Zimbabwe.* London: Heinemann, 1982.

in the settler-dominated colonies sometimes acted as a brake on settler self-interest. The overexploitation of African labor, for example, could be counterproductive for the colony and even for European employers if it meant that Africans did not have sufficient time, money, and land to produce enough food for themselves and their families.

At the other extreme were regions where the British implemented a system of indirect rule, which involved keeping and modifying traditional political structures to suit European needs. Indirect rule was a pragmatic approach implemented in settings where few European officials were available and where there were well-established indigenous political systems. Local authorities could be given responsibility for unpopular measures such as tax collection and the recruitment of labor for the colonial state's projects. Indirect rule was commonly used as a reason for paying little attention to the development of economic and social infrastructures, on the pretext that local authorities were responsible for financing and implementing projects—for example, primary education. However, the apparent powers retained by indigenous rulers were an illusion. These rulers were handpicked by their colonial overseers, were told what to say and do, and were replaced if they were incompetent or too independent minded. Indirectly ruled areas such as northern Nigeria emerged from the colonial era experiencing very little development. This neglect, combined with the use of different administrative models in other parts of these same countries, has contributed in no small way to an on-going history of interregional misunderstanding and occasional violence.

Where there was no history of chieftancy, as among the Swahili in Tanganyika or the Igbo in Nigeria, the colonial powers often created chiefs and used them to perform unpopular tasks. These new chiefs were regarded with suspicion, especially in the French and Belgian colonies where their role as colonial puppets was particularly obvious. Moreover, these "chiefs" were often outsiders or low-status individuals chosen only because they could be counted on for total obedience.

To maintain law and order, the colonial administrations relied heavily on African recruits commanded by European officers, and to run the lower levels of the bureaucracy, the colonial administrations relied on educated Africans. These supporting cadres were often recruited from subordinate classes, such as former slave families, or from other regions. As such, these cadres owed their status to the colonial state and could be counted upon to implement its repressive policies, often enthusiastically. The French, Belgians, and Portuguese attempted to consolidate African support for the colonial state by granting special "assimilated" status to Africans who were Western educated. These educated Africans

Figure 5.4. "The black man's burden," German East Africa (Tanzania), circa 1910. Photo: O. Haeckel.

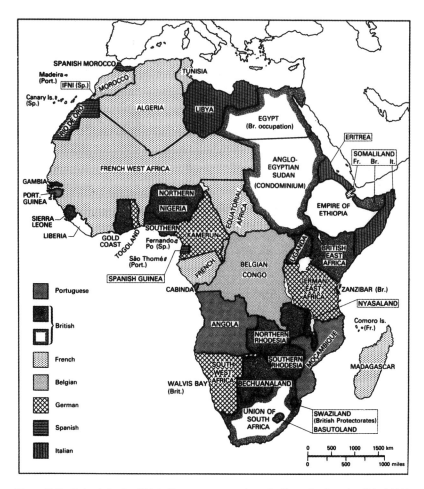

Figure 5.5. Colonial rule, 1914. Germany was stripped of its colonies after World War I, but otherwise the colonial map remained essentially the same. Source: *Africa South of the Sahara, 1991*. London: Europa, 1990, p. 14. ©1990 by Europa Publications Limited. Reprinted by permission.

received certain political and social privileges denied to the African masses but remained clearly subordinate to Europeans in the colonial social hierarchy.

Colonial Economic Policy

Colonial economic policy is often described in relation to the construction of infrastructures and the introduction of new crops and new modes of production. Without doubt, developments of this sort represent the most tangible legacy of colonial economic policy.

Railroads and roads were constructed, often across difficult terrain. Mines were developed and plantations established in many parts of the continent. Africa became a major source of groundnuts, cocoa, rubber, coffee, palm oil and other agricultural products, tropical woods, and minerals, particularly copper, diamonds, and gold. New cities were established to serve as administrative and commercial centers. Western education and health care were introduced.

The economic contribution of colonialism was long considered to be the incorporation of Africans into the modern world economy as productive workers and farmers. The growth of production in colonial economies was interpreted as evidence of progress in the broad "civilizing mission" used to justify the colonial project. Conversely, the people in areas that did not become important sources of production were portrayed as being backward and, hence, not meriting much attention.

The spatial pattern of colonial development that evolved was highly uneven and reflected expectations of profit rather than altruism. It is useful to generalize about this uneven development in relation to the three basic models of development that were employed in colonial Africa. The three approaches—namely direct European investment, African smallholder production, and labor supply—created distinctive socioeconomic structures and landscapes in the areas affected by each.

Direct European investment occurred in a relatively few areas of the continent. These enclaves of European capital included such mining regions as the Copper Belts of Northern Rhodesia and Belgian Congo, such commercial plantations as the sisal farms of Tanganyika, and such areas of European settlement as Kenya's "White Highlands."

The success of European ventures in these areas depended on three critical elements: control of the most desirable land, a secured supply of cheap African labor, and access to markets. The three elements are integrally linked. As white farmers gained legal title to large tracts of desirable land, Africans who had occupied these lands for countless generations were left without attractive options. In many cases, they were forced to move to newly created reserve lands that were often located in areas with less fertile soils and that were, as a rule, overcrowded. In Kenya, the imposition of soil conservation programs on African reserve lands deprived farmers of even more of their scarce land and time, causing the women who had been most adversely affected to mount a campaign of resistance (Vignette 5.2). To make ends meet, most families in the reserve lands had to rely on selling their labor to European farmers. Even when Africans were able to remain behind on part of their ancestral lands, it was usually as sharecroppers or as laborers on European farms. The imposition of taxes on all Africans, as well as legislated restrictions on Africans' access to commercial markets for livestock and cash crops, further ensured a ready supply of labor.

Figure 5.6. "The shephard and the sheep." This early 20th century postcard illustrates the often patronizing worldview of early Christian missionaries in Africa. Photo: Mission des Péres Blancs.

Figure 5.7. Preparing a new plantation, Nyasaland (Malawi), 1920s. The production of cash crops, in this case probably tobacco, involved the use of forced labor in many areas. Photo: Nyasaland Pharmacies.

Even then, the colonial state often had to resort to forced-labor recruitment to guarantee enough workers for commercial European ventures.

Perhaps the greatest contribution of the colonial state to the development of these enclaves of European capitalism was the construction of railroads and ports to permit the mineral and agricultural products to reach overseas markets. The development of this infrastructure to benefit European capital was often extremely costly, not only in money but also in suffering and loss of life (Vignette 5.3).

In countries such as Nigeria, Ghana, and Senegal, which were unattractive to European settlers, quite densely populated, and characterized by well-developed indigenous farming systems, a different colonial development strategy emerged. African farmers were encouraged, if necessary by coercion, to grow crops for export to Europe. For African farmers, the incentive to grow cash crops was both negative (the need to get cash to pay taxes) and positive (the opportunity to accumulate wealth and purchase manufactured goods). Non-African entrepreneurs, both larger trad-

ing companies and Asian and Arab family businesses, profited from the expansion of African smallholder production. They purchased and exported the cash crops, imported and sold consumer goods, and often financed export crop production with advances of seed or cash loans, typically charging extremely high rates of interest.

Capitalists and the colonial state reaped great profits from the most productive of the areas of smallholder production, even when the course of development did not conform to that which had been planned. The British, for example, hoped to obtain vast amounts of cotton for its textile industry from the Kano region in northern Nigeria. Hausa farmers did not respond as the British hoped, largely because of the difficulty of incorporating large-scale cotton production into the farmers' existing agricultural systems. However, when local traders began to promote groundnuts as a cash crop and sent representatives into the countryside to advance credit for farmers to grow the crop, the response was overwhelming. Groundnut production in Kano Province increased tenfold between 1912 and 1913. The government was so unprepared for the

---

Vignette 5.2. Resistance under Colonialism: A Kenyan Example

Africans responded to colonial rule with many forms of active and passive resistance. The revolt of Kenyan women against imposed soil conservation schemes provides an example of such resistance. This protest arose as a result of the combined effects of environmental deterioration, changing class and gender roles, and contradictions in colonial policy.

Starting in the 1930s, the alleged degradation of land farmed by Africans became an issue of major concern. It was claimed that poor farming practices were causing increased soil erosion and that enforced conservation programs were needed to protect the environment. Behind the overt concerns about conservation lay the real issue, namely, the struggle by white settlers to consolidate and legitimate their control of the White Highlands.

Following the imposition of colonial rule, African lands were indeed farmed much more intensively and without many traditional conservation practices. However, these changes reflected the pressures of accommodating a growing population on a much reduced land base. Traditional strategies such as crop rotation, intercropping, and extended fallowing had to be sacrificed in order to address immediate needs for sustenance. The growing substitution of Irish potatoes for sweet potatoes and of maize for millet increased the susceptibility of land to erosion. Moreover, as the interests and responsibilities of men and women changed in the now monetarized economy, women's traditional rights to land increasingly became the focus of competition.

The response of the colonial state was to institute soil conservation programs such as planting lines of Napier grass on erosion-prone slopes and making compost pits. What started as a voluntary program became increasingly compulsory, and chiefs were made responsible for meeting established targets. After World War II, the program's focus shifted to the construction of bench terraces along the contours of slopes. The new approach was strongly opposed by women because it required so much of their land and their time. For every 1-m drop between contour terraces, up to 2 m of land was lost. The colonial state insisted that several days of unpaid forced labor be devoted each month to the onerous work of building terraces.

Women mounted widespread acts of resistance, both visible and invisible, against compulsory soil conservation work. In April, 1948, resistance escalated into a full-scale "Women's Revolt" in Murang'a District. The women arrived, 2,500 strong, at the district headquarters to announce their refusal to do more soil conservation work, stating that they had "quite enough to do at home." Attempts to persuade them to return to work were rebuffed. A few weeks later, after their protests continued to escalate, the women involved were arrested and fined.

While this protest was remarkable for its size and intensity, it was not an isolated incident. Throughout Africa, ordinary people mounted protracted and often subtle resistance to colonial rule, and in doing so certainly hastened the end of colonialism.

Based on F. Mackenzie. "Political economy of the environment, gender and resistance under colonialism in Murang'a District, Kenya." *Canadian Journal of African Studies*, vol. 25 (1991), pp. 226–256.

Figure 5.8. Steam-powered boats, Kinshasa, Belgian Congo (Zaire), circa 1930. The one boat is loaded with sacks of produce, quite likely brought up-country for export. Photo: E. Nogueira.

deluge of groundnuts that it was unable to transport the entire crop to the port of Lagos before the next harvest.

The effect of introducing cash crops into smallholder farming systems was not always positive, or even benign. These crops required heavy investments of labor and often had to be grown on the best land. Certain crops, notably cotton, make heavy demands on soil nutrients and facilitate increased soil erosion. Although the expansion of cash crops often brought higher incomes, it also increased malnutrition because of the reallocation of land and labor from food to cash-crop production.

Many parts of Africa were perceived by colonial authorities to have little potential for modern development. They were far from ports and railroads and typically had rather infertile soils or semiarid climates. The people in these regions were often portrayed as "backward." Still, these areas were expected to contribute their share to the upkeep of the colonial state. Their contribution was in the form of migrant labor for areas of mining and export-oriented agriculture often located many hundreds of kilometers away. Taxation and

forced labor recruitment were used to ensure that labor was made available, even when wages were extremely low and working conditions brutal (Vignette 5.3). Labor reserve areas such as Mali, Niger, Chad, and Basutoland (Lesotho) received very little indeed by way of infrastructural development. Moreover, local economies often suffered because of the loss of labor from food production.

Evaluating the Colonial Legacy

Africa's colonizers saw themselves as benign interlopers, carrying the torch of civilization to a primitive, "dark" continent. They emphasized the imposition of peace among warring rivals; the introduction of Western medicine and education; the construction of cities, ports and rail systems; the transformation of African economies through the development of mining and of commercial agriculture; and the creation of legal and administrative systems. The development process was seen as difficult, often frustrating, but ultimately very rewarding because of the many benefits

Vignette 5.3. The Human Cost of Colonial Development

It is in the labor reserves of Africa south of the Sahara that the great costs and minimal benefits of colonial development policies are best illustrated. The story of the Sara people of southern Chad is a compelling example.

The French referred to the Sara as "la belle race" ("the beautiful people") because of their fine physiques and peaceful dispositions. These qualities, together with their political disorganization, made them primary targets for forced labor recruitment as porters, railroad workers, and soldiers.

Between 1921 and 1934, the French colonial administration undertook the construction of a railway, 450 km long, from Ponte-Noire to Brazzaville in French Equatorial Africa. The railway passed through extremely rough and heavily forested territory. Construction involved cutting down countless trees, moving an estimated 10 million cubic meters of rock and soil, carving 12 tunnels up to 1.6 km in length through the rock, and constructing 162 large bridges and 92 viaducts. The arduous work of chopping down trees, digging tunnels and moving soil all had to be done by hand using very simple tools; heavy equipment was not available.

More than 120,000 African laborers were involved in building the Congo–Brazzaville railway, about one-fifth of whom were Sara. Their working conditions were appalling, especially in the first years of the project. They worked for 12 hours per day in sweltering heat (between November and May) and torrential rains (May to October). Construction accidents were common. There were frequent epidemics of malaria, sleeping sickness, and other diseases. The food provided was monotonous and inadequate for the type of work the laborers were doing. The death toll among workers is indicative of their suffering; it is estimated that half of the 120,000 perished. But according to the colony's governor, "Either we accept the sacrifice of six to eight thousand men or we renounce the railroad."

The Sara mounted a determined resistance to forced labor on the railroad. As Sara resistance increased, the French resorted to more and more drastic recruitment methods. Recruitment quotas were established for each village, and chiefs who failed to fill them faced the prospect of being sent to jail. The most unwilling of the "recruits" were actually tied together by rope for the long journey on foot from Chad to Bangui and onward to the construction site.

The Sara gained nothing from this suffering. African workers received a mere one franc per month in the early years of the project. From 1930 on, wages increased to about 100 francs per month, still a pittance. The Sara community suffered a grievous demographic and economic cost through the loss of more than 10,000 healthy young men who were sent to work on the railroad and never came home. All of this was done for a railway that ended 1,200 km from the Sara homeland.

Based on M. Azevedo. "The human price of development: The Brazzaville railroad and the Sara of Chad." *African Studies Review*, vol. 24 (1981), pp. 1–19.

that the "civilizing mission" brought to Africans.

Writers within the modernization perspective, which prevailed in development studies during the 1960s, continued to see the colonial legacy, as well as the path of development in the postcolonial era, in much the same way. This is illustrated in the following exert that portrays colonial officials and entrepreneurs as "eager beavers," diligently creating opportunity and transforming African society:

Figure 5.9. Indigo dying, Kano, Nigeria. Kano's textile industry, like most precolonial industries, was pushed toward extinction by the importation of European manufactured cloth. Photo: author.

Roads and railways link the administrative nodes and provide, in turn, channels through which modernizing innovations seep. . . . Modernization in all its innovative aspects is distributed from the major sources through the tarred arteries and laterite capilliaries of the land and society. Some innovations have economic implications–coffee revolutionizes Kilimanjaro, sisal spreads around Tanga and Morogoro, cotton seeps through Sukumaland–and commodity flows swirl through the road network, feeding back information to the administrators who upgrade, realign, and tar the dirt tracks of the previous year. (P. Gould. "Tanzania 1920–63: The spatial impress of the modernization process." *World Politics*, vol. 22 (1970), pp. 149–170.)

The view that the essence of the colonial legacy was the dynamic transformation of the "blank map" of Africa was challenged vigorously by writers from the dependency school. They pointed to the undermining under colonialism of indigenous economies and societies and argued that whatever changes had taken place were implemented primarily for the benefit of Europeans, not Africans. Colonialism developed Europe and underdeveloped Africa. Walter Rodney's book *How*

Europe Underdeveloped Africa (Washington, D.C.: Howard University Press, 1974) was particularly influential in the radical reinterpretation of the colonial era. Rodney argues that

colonial Africa fell within that part of the international capitalist economy from which surplus was drawn to feed the metropolitan sector. As seen earlier, exploitation of land and labour is essential for human social advance, but only on the assumption that the product is made available within the area where the exploitation takes place. Colonialism was not merely a system of exploitation, but one whose essential purpose was to repatriate the profits to the so-called "mother country." From an African view-point, that amounted to consistent expatriation of surplus produced by African labour out of African resources. It meant the development of Europe as a part of the same dialectical process in which Africa was underdeveloped. (p. 162)

While more recent evaluations of the colonial legacy tend to be subtler than Rodney's, the interpretation is usually much the same. Europe may have transformed Africa, but the process was far from unproblematic. Colonialism built, but it also destroyed, inflicting pro-

Vignette 5.4. Postage Stamps: A Window on the Geography of Colonial Africa

Postage stamps reflect the changing political geography of the colonial era, and reveal much about the colonial attitude toward Africa and Africans.

The place names on early stamps include many country names that have disappeared or remain only as the names of regions within present-day states. Examples pictured in Figure 5.10 include the Portuguese Congo (a), Oil Rivers Protectorate (b) located in southeastern Nigeria, Zululand (c) and British-occupied Orange Free State (d), both now part of South Africa, and German South-West Africa (e), now Namibia. Early stamps also reflect the pivotal role played by commercial interests in the colonial project. Rhodesian stamps continued to bear the name of the British South African Company until 1917 (f), while chartered companies such as the Mozambique Company (g) remained in control of parts of Mozambique as late as 1941.

While colonial postage stamps showed a variety of images of Africa and Africans, a few themes were predominant. Africans were often portrayed in "romantic primitive" mode [see (h) and (i)]; images of bare-breasted women and proud warriors were especially common on French colonial stamps. African wildlife was another very popular theme [see (j) and (k)]. Where historical events were commemorated, they were of European achievements, such as Caille's exploration of West Africa (l) or the founding of the City of Mozambique (m).

The end of the colonial era was celebrated with commemorative stamps in every newly independent country, including Ghana (n) and Nigeria (o). The transition to independence was not always smooth. Stamps record the failed attempt by Katanga Province to secede from Congo-Kinshasa in 1960 (p), and of the white minority government in Rhodesia to retain power through a unilateral declaration of independence from Great Britain in 1965 (q).

Figure 5.10. The colonial era in stamps.

found damage to indigenous societies and the environment. Whatever benefits Africa realized from, for example, the introduction of modern medicine, were trivial compared to the benefits reaped by Europe from the exploitation of African labor and resources. Moreover, far from being an altruistic undertaking, the colonial project was underpinned by a racist ideology and enforced by using Europe's superior military technology to maintain dominance over the African people.

It is perhaps ironic that it took European colonialism to inform Africans that they were African. Europe created not only the map of Africa as we know it, but also a sense of common identity among Africans who experienced the domination and humiliation of colonialism. This sense of identity was manifest in a continentwide movement for independence and calls in some quarters for an African political union. Ironically, these calls for union were frustrated by other African leaders who insisted that the colonial political map of independent Africa should closely conform to that established under colonialism.

Further Reading

General discussions of the history of colonialism and its effect on African societies include the following sources:

Crowder, M. *West Africa under Colonial Rule*. Evanston, IL: Northwestern University Press, 1968.

Fanon, F. *A Dying Colonialism*. New York: Grove Press, 1967.

Gann, L. H., and P. Duignan, eds. *Colonialism in Africa, 1870–1960*, 5 vols. London: Cambridge University Press, 1969–1975.

Mazrui, A. *The Africans: A Triple Heritage*. Boston: Little, Brown, 1986. (See, in particular, Chapter 5.)

Rodney, W. *How Europe Underdeveloped Africa*. Washington, DC: Howard University Press, 1974.

Wallerstein, I. "The three stages of African involvement in the world-economy." In P. C. Gutkind and I. Wallerstein, eds., *The Political Economy of Contemporary Africa*, pp. 30–57. Beverley Hills, CA: Sage, 1976.

The implementation of colonial rule varied considerably among the various colonial powers and often reflected the circumstances encountered in different countries. Studies of particular forms of colonial rule include the following sources:

Berman, B. *Control and Crisis in Colonial Kenya: The Dialectic of Domination*. London: James Currey, 1990.

Clarence-Smith, G. *The Third Portuguese Empire*. Manchester, England: Manchester University Press, 1985.

Crowder, M. *Senegal: A Study in French Assimilation Policy*. London: Oxford University Press, 1967.

Suret-Canale, J. *French Colonialism in Tropical Africa, 1900–1945*. New York: Universe, 1971.

Colonialism had a variety of effects on African societies. See, for example, the following sources:

Chimhundu, H. "Early missionaries and the ethnolinguistic factor during the invention of tribalism in Zimbabwe." *Journal of African History*, vol. 33 (1992), pp. 87–110.

Clark, L. *Through African Eyes: Cultures in Change*. New York: Praeger, 1970.

There is a large literature on the transformation of economies under colonialism in particular settings. See, for example, the following sources:

Arrighi, G. "Labour supplies in historical perspective: A study of the proletarianization of the peasantry in Rhodesia." *Journal of Development Studies*, vol. 6 (1970), pp. 197–234.

Brett, E. A. *Colonialism and Underdevelopment in East Africa*. New York: Nok, 1973.

Shenton, R. W. *The Development of Capitalism in Northern Nigeria*. Toronto, Ontario: University of Toronto Press, 1986.

Watts, M. *Silent Violence: Food, Famine and Peasantry in Northern Nigeria*. Berkeley: University of California Press, 1983.

6

✳

Independent Africa:
The Struggle Continues

The year 1960 was an important watershed in the history of Africa south of the Sahara: The number of independent countries increased from 5 to 22. Nevertheless, it is important to put 1960 into perspective. The events of that year would have been impossible but for decades of determined resistance to colonial rule. Moreover, 1960 was only a beginning. It took many more years before countries like Angola, Zimbabwe, and Namibia were able to achieve independence; in South Africa, the struggle for majority rule was not completed until 1994. Finally, gaining independence has proved to be only one step along an immensely difficult path toward stability and development.

The Struggle for Independence

The struggle for independence proceeded on two fronts. On the one hand, there was an intellectual battle against colonial rule, led initially by a number of Africans studying in Europe and the United States who became involved in the Pan-African movements of W. E. B. Du Bois and Marcus Garvey. Pan-Africanism and its credo, "Africa for the Africans," were advanced through a series of six international meetings held between 1900 and 1946 (see Vignette 6.1). The second front in the struggle against colonialism consisted of an uncoordinated but sustained pattern of armed and passive resistance mounted by ordinary Africans. Later, and especially after World War II, these two forms of resistance merged together. Intellectual leaders such as Nkrumah in the Gold Coast (Ghana) and Azikiwe in Nigeria returned to Africa and established political parties, trade unions, and independent newspapers that worked for closer cooperation among those involved in the fight for justice and self-determination.

The actual path of the independence struggle varied greatly, depending among other things on the nature of the local colonial state and the extent to which independent thinking and dissent were tolerated. In a few countries, the quest for independence involved protracted armed struggle against the colonizers. In approximately one-quarter of the colonies, large, organized campaigns of political agitation, protest, and civil disobedience preceded independence. Elsewhere, political organization was less advanced, and independence tended to come as a result not of intensive local pressure, but of changing colonial policies in response to events elsewhere.

The following sketches of the path to independence in five colonies give some indication of the diversity of experiences.

Gold Coast

In the Gold Coast, the struggle for independence began in earnest in 1947 following the return of Kwame Nkrumah from America, where he had studied and was active in the Pan-African Movement. After joining the United Gold Coast Convention (UGCC), he organized a campaign of passive resistance, with self-government as the ultimate goal. In 1948, the violent suppression by the police of a peaceful demonstration of ex-servicemen, followed by the jailing of Nkrumah and other leading Ghanaians, served only to radicalize the movement for self-government. After his release from prison, Nkrumah left the UGCC to form a new political organization, the Convention People's Party (CPP), and to pursue a more militant strategy to achieve "self-government now." Nkrumah was again imprisoned, but the CPP still won a resounding 90% of the vote in municipal elections in 1951. Recognizing the implications of this mandate, the British granted internal self-government, followed in 1957 by full independence.

Côte d'Ivoire

The path to independence was rather less dramatic in Côte d'Ivoire. Felix Houphuët-Boigney, a wealthy farmer, became the leading Ivoirian politician and served in several French cabinets during the 1950s. He supported a gradual transition to self-government, and strongly opposed the aspirations of several

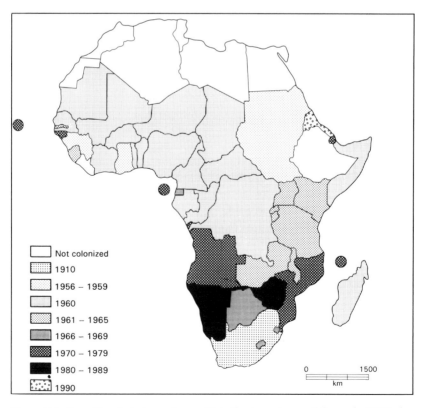

Not colonized
1910
1956 – 1959
1960
1961 – 1965
1966 – 1969
1970 – 1979
1980 – 1989
1990

0   1500
km

Figure 6.1. Transition to independence. Note the importance of the early 1960s for the attainment of political independence.

Vignette 6.1. The Origins of the Organization of African Unity

In 1958, the Pan-African Movement came home to Africa with the launching of the First Conference of Independent African States, held in Accra in April, 1958. Except for South Africa, all independent states (Ghana, Liberia, Ethiopia, and Sudan, as well as four North African states) were present. The movement was at this time guided by nine fundamental principles:

1. Africa for the Africans and total rejection of colonialism
2. Political unification (United States of Africa) as a goal
3. A renaissance of African morale and culture
4. African nationalism supplanting the tribalism of the past
5. Economic development according to socialist principles
6. Democracy as the most desirable method of government
7. Rejection of violence, except to resist military repression
8. Solidarity of black peoples everywhere
9. Positive neutrality, except in regard to African interests

For Ghana's Kwame Nkrumah, the achievement of national independence was only a necessary first step toward the ultimate objective of African unity. In an attempt to put theory into practice, Ghana, Guinea, and later Mali, agreed to unite in 1959. However, the Ghana–Guinea–Mali union agreement was never implemented, and other African states increasingly expressed concern about the need to protect their sovereignty.

With many more states achieving independence in 1960, the question of unity became increasingly complex. Two major groups emerged in 1961: the Casablanca powers and the Monrovia powers. The Casablanca Group brought together seven of the more radical states, led by Ghana. Four months later, 20 states met in Monrovia and put forward an alternate vision of Africa's future. This group contained a dozen former French colonies (called the Brazzaville Group) and eight other states, the most prominent being Nigeria and Ethiopia. They argued strongly against formal political union, focusing instead on the need for a mutual recognition of equality and sovereignty, noninterference in each others' internal affairs, and cooperation in economic, cultural and scientific fields. Subsequently, the Monrovia Group continued to grow stronger, while the Casablanca Group became less united.

The leaders of Nigeria, Guinea, and Ethiopia were instrumental in bringing the two sides together at the first successful summit of African leaders at Addis Ababa in May 1963. Nkrumah renewed his call for a revolutionary union of all African states, modeled on the USA or USSR, but was rebuffed. Instead, delegates were inspired by the appeal of Algeria's Ben Bella to set aside bickering and unite in support for Africans still struggling to achieve independence. The outcome of the meeting was the signing of the charter for an Organization of African Unity (OAU).

In its 30-year history, the OAU has had its share of both successes and failures. It has played an active role in the struggles against Portuguese colonialism and apartheid and has been instrumental in mediating several disputes between neighboring states. However, it has not provided any real leadership on such issues as Africa's slide into debt bondage or reconciliation in recent civil wars, notably in Somalia and Sudan.

other leaders from French Africa for a rapid transition to independence and a federation of French West African states. Fearing that its wealth would be used to subsidize the poorer Sahelian regions of French West Africa, Côte d'Ivoire opted for independence in 1960 to forestall any move toward a regional federation. Houphuët-Boigney remained president for over 30 years, until his death at age 88 in 1993. Throughout his years in power, he remained perhaps Africa's staunchest advocate of conservative positions on economic, political, and social matters.

Kenya

Kenya had a large number of white settlers who farmed much of the best land and used their control of the colonial state to advance their own interests. British military expeditions succeeded in quelling armed resistance between 1896 and 1905, but Kenyan Africans continued to engage in passive resistance and staged many organized protests against land, labor, and taxation policies of the colonial state. Political organizations, principally the Young Kikuyu Association and after 1944 the Kenya African Union, spearheaded the protests. From 1952 to 1958, the Mau Mau secret society launched guerrilla attacks on white settlers and black allies of the British. The British responded with a series of repressive measures to end the rebellion and jailed thousands of Africans. While the Mau Mau revolt did not result in immediate independence, it convinced the British that change was inevitable. In 1963, Kenya became independent under the leadership of Jomo Kenyatta, who had been imprisoned for his alleged involvement in the Mau Mau.

Namibia

Namibia achieved independence only in 1990 after a quarter century of armed struggle by SWAPO. The German colony of South-West Africa was made a South African trust territory after World War I. South Africa virtually annexed the colony in 1949, and proceeded to implement many elements of apartheid.

Figure 6.2. Independence monument, Lomé, Togo. This impressive monument portrays independence as breaking the chains of bondage. Photo: author.

Starting in the late 1940s, several major strikes were launched by African workers to protest social and labor conditions. SWAPO began its war of independence in 1966, the same year that the United Nations declared South African rule illegal. Guerrilla activities were concentrated in the northern part of the country near the border with Angola, where SWAPO had established several bases. South Africa waged a protracted and bloody counterinsurgency campaign in both Namibia and Angola, but could not defeat SWAPO. Meanwhile, there was growing international pressure on South Africa to get out of Namibia. South Africa finally agreed in 1989 to hold elections leading to independence. Their strategy of last resort was to work to elect a compliant regime that would not seriously challenge South African interests. However, SWAPO won a convincing victory, and shortly thereafter Namibia gained its hard-won independence.

Eritrea

Africa has had numerous secessionist movements, among the most important being the attempted secessions of Katanga from the Congo (Zaire) in 1960 and 1961, Biafra from Nigeria in the late 1960s, and Somaliland from Somalia in the early 1990s. However, Eritrea represents the only country to have succeeded in winning independence in this way. Formerly a colony of Italy, Eritrea was awarded to Ethiopia by the United Nations in 1952. The armed struggle for independence began in 1961 and lasted for three decades. The Eritrean People's Liberation Front continued to control all but the largest towns, despite massive, protracted campaigns by the Soviet-backed Ethiopian military to crush the rebellion. The collapse of the Ethiopian government in 1991 resulted in large part from the debilitating effects of its unsuccessful Eritrean campaigns. The new regime adopted a more conciliatory stance and agreed to a referendum on independence. The referendum of April 1993 produced a 99% vote in favor of independence, setting the stage for Eritrean independence a month later.

The Struggle for Responsive Government

Throughout the world, relatively few governments can be said to be truly representative and responsive to the needs and aspirations of its citizens, and this dearth of responsive governments has been especially evident in Africa south of the Sahara. It is reflected in the small number of democratically elected regimes, the many military dictatorships, and the brutal terrorism that certain regimes have inflicted on their own citizens.

Much of the weakness in African political institutions can be traced to the colonial period, particularly the transition to independence. Nowhere had Africans had a truly effective voice either in government or in administration. Moreover, there were concerted efforts by colonial powers to handpick new leaders who would not seriously challenge the interests of the metropole. Independence often came quickly, with little advance preparation and with unworkable European-inspired constitutions.

In the former Belgian Congo, later Zaire, political chaos commenced almost immediately after the Belgians precipitately declared it independent. The United Nations intervened to end the attempted secession in Katanga Province, but several additional years of violence ensued. In many Western circles, the Congo instantly became the symbol of Africa's unreadiness for independence–the evidence that chaos and corruption would be the hallmark of independent African states.

The political history of Zaire since 1965, when the military dictatorship of Mobuto Sese-Seko was established, is encapsulated in the following quotation from I. Griffiths, *An Atlas of African Affairs* (London: Methuen, 1984): "The Mobuto regime drifts in a sea of corrupt incompetence unable to defend itself, propped up by the United States and France who are intent on safeguarding their own political and economic interests" (p. 75). This reference to foreign intervention points to a telling characteristic of many authoritarian regimes, namely, that their hold on power is as much or more dependent on external backing as on local support. In the case of Zaire, foreign troops have intervened three times since the mid-1970s to quell anti-Mobutu uprisings.

Following independence, African regimes faced a rising tide of expectations with few resources and little time to respond. In these circumstances, many opted for single-party states, believing that interparty maneuvering was a luxury they could not afford at such a crucial time in their history. Institutions such as the military, trade unions, and civil service typically were brought under closer government control, and decision making became increasingly concentrated in a few hands. In several countries, the course of development was closely controlled by a charismatic leader–Nkrumah and Kenyatta, for example–whose legitimacy was based on leadership of the anticolonial struggle.

Not surprisingly, the absence of a political

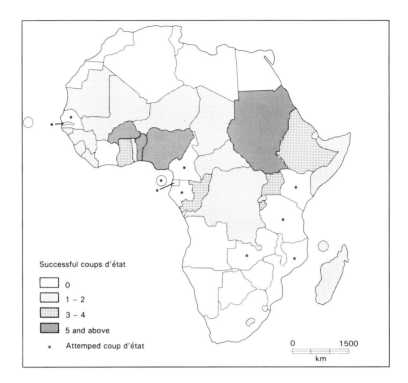

Figure 6.3. Successful coups d'état. Coups have been much less common in East and southern Africa than elsewhere in the continent. Data source: C. Cook and D. Killingray. *African Political Facts since 1945,* 2nd ed. London: Macmillan, 1991.

opposition provided a ready excuse for sections of the military to intervene and overthrow allegedly ineffective, corrupt, or unresponsive civilian regimes. Between 1960 and 1992, there were over 70 successful coups d'état in 31 countries and many more attempts which did not succeed (see Figure 6.3). The record of Africa's military governments has been as mixed as that of its civilian regimes. Some military regimes have provided relatively stable governments and have managed to balance regional, ethnic, and religious interests more effectively than the civilian regimes that they replaced. For example, the Nigerian military regimes headed by Gowon, Mohammed, Obasanjo, and Babangida provided a standard of government that compared favorably to that of intervening civilian regimes. Other military governments–exemplified by Idi Amin's regime in Uganda–have been thoroughly inept and have relied on terror to retain power.

Despite the preeminent role of the military in bringing about change in African governments, not all transfers of power have been by force. Ghana and Nigeria, among other countries, have had military regimes that relinquished power to elected civilian governments; in these countries, however, the history has been one of renewed military intervention. Some countries, including Senegal and Tanzania, have had orderly transitions of power from one regime to another and no military coups.

The 1990s have brought significant change to the political landscape of Africa south of the Sahara. Responding to internal crises and to international events such as the replacement of communist regimes in Eastern Europe, Africans began to agitate for responsible, democratically elected governments. In the majority of countries, those in power have agreed, often reluctantly, to permit opposition

Vignette 6.2. The Rocky Road of Ghanaian Politics, 1957 to 1993

In no country in Africa south of the Sahara was there more optimism, international as well as local, about postindependence prospects than in Ghana. However, the postindependence history of Ghana has been characterized by recurrent economic and political crises and descent into deepening poverty.

Kwame Nkrumah led Ghana to independence in 1957 and remained in power until 1966. He moved ambitiously to broaden Ghana's economic base beyond cocoa, of which Ghana was the world's first-ranked producer. The massive Volta River project was launched to provide power for industrial development, the new port city of Tema was built, and state farms were set up to modernize agriculture. However, the economic situation worsened, caused by cocoa prices that fell by over 75% and by too many overly ambitious and poorly implemented development initiatives. Meanwhile, political power became increasingly centralized, first through the creation of a one-party state and then through Nkrumah's promotion of a pervasive "cult of personality."

With political opposition effectively gone, the military remained the only force capable of challenging Nkrumah. There was widespread public support when he was removed from office by the National Liberation Council (NLC) in 1966. During three years of NLC rule, the economy continued to deteriorate, owing to the weakness of cocoa prices, the collapse of many of Nkrumah's projects, and a growing debt burden. Ghanaians rejoiced when the soldiers agreed to return power to civilians in 1969.

The civilian regime of Dr. Kofi Busia was unable to sustain its initial popularity; the root causes of economic crisis were beyond its control. Attempts to encourage a market-driven economic recovery failed, forcing Busia to devalue the currency and introduce austerity measures. For the first time, there was a shortfall in food production.

Ghanaians were neither very sad about Busia's removal from power nor very optimistic about future prospects when Lt. Col. I. K. Acheampong seized power in a coup in January 1972. The new regime's austerity program, including currency devaluation and drastic limitations on imports, meant increased hardship for ordinary citizens. Attempts were made to encourage food production and greater self-reliance through "Operation Feed Yourself." However, the economic situation continued to worsen despite a temporary revival of cocoa prices largely because so much of the crop was being smuggled into neighboring countries to be sold for hard currency. Politically, Acheampong became increasingly isolated, especially after his proposal for the military to share power with civilians was widely opposed.

Acheampong was replaced in an officer's coup led by Lt. Gen. Affuko in 1978. The new regime promised to facilitate a return to civilian rule, but public discontent continued to grow because of the deepening economic crisis. The currency was massively devalued in a severe "austerity budget." Market prices for food and other necessities rose sharply. The government's response to a series of strikes by hard-pressed civil servants and workers was to declare a state of emergency.

When junior officers under the leadership of Lt. Jerry Rawlings seized power in 1979, there was widespread euphoria. Rawlings not only removed the hated Acheampong–Affuko regime, but also offered an action-oriented, populist alternative. The former leaders and others accused of corruption were tried in public tribunals and in some cases executed as part of a "housecleaning" campaign. The return to civilian rule was accelerated; multiparty elections were held; and only three months after Rawlings took power, Hilla Limann's civilian regime was sworn in.

cont.

Vignette 6.2. (cont.)

Limann's Third Republic government lasted just over a year. Its weakness was the result not only of the continuing economic crisis but also of Rawlings's watchful presence in the background. In December, 1981, Rawlings staged a coup, widely referred to as the "second coming." This time, however, he did not promise to relinquish power.

Rawlings's Provisional National Defence Council (PNDC) held power for more than a decade. As a new regime, the PNDC emphasized grassroots democracy, particularly in the form of neighborhood defense committees to mobilize popular participation in the revolution. Economic ties with the USSR and other socialist states in Africa and elsewhere were strengthened. These strategies suggested a return to an Nkrumah-like approach to government. However, the continuing socialist rhetoric of the regime has been eclipsed by economic policies that emphasize austerity and free-market principles. Because of these policies, Rawlings has become the rather unlikely hero of those favoring structural adjustment as the solution to Africa's economic woes.

The cornerstone of Ghana's economic policy since 1983 has been the Economic Recovery Program, developed under the direction of the World Bank and IMF. The devaluation of the currency continued; by the late 1980s the Ghanaian *cedi* (a unit of currency) retained less than one-thousandth of its initial value under Nkrumah. Prices were increased and subsidies on imported food removed in order to encourage increased production of export and food crops. Large cuts were made in the civil service and in social expenditure. User fees were introduced in the education and health sectors to compensate for some of the lost government revenue allocations.

Compared to the years before, the economic performance since 1983 has been a major success. The economy has grown by up to 8.6% annually, although the average annual growth between 1980 and 1989 was a more modest 2.8%. Export revenues have grown considerably and inflation has declined. However, most of the increased revenues have gone to service the debt, which had grown to $2.3 billion in 1989. The cost of debt servicing took half of Ghana's exports in 1989, compared to only one-eighth in 1980. The fact that the average Ghanaian in the mid-1980s consumed only 76% of the Food and Agriculture Organization of the United Nations (FAO) basic calorie standard is one indication of how hard life has continued to be.

During 1992, a new constitution was approved as the basis for the restoration of democracy. After declaring himself a candidate for the presidency just days before the election, Rawlings won a massive victory. While the opposition claimed that the election had been rigged, it seems clear that the Ghanaian public had chosen a continuation of the status quo in preference to a less predictable future under a new leader.

---

groups to organize and undertake political activities. Incumbents have been voted out of office in several countries, including Zambia, Cape Verde, and Benin. Even in Malawi, with perhaps the most repressive regime in Africa, mass public protests have succeeded in challenging the govenment.

The struggle for democracy has been less successful in other countries. In Zaire, for ex-

ample, President Mobutu has managed to rebuff internal and international pressures for democratization. In Angola, the results of elections sponsored by the United Nations were rejected by the leadership of Unita, which then proceeded to resume and expand its campaign of guerrilla warfare. As a result, Angola is even more devastated than it had been before. In Ghana, the military leader, General Rawlings, held on to power after entering the 1992 election at the last minute. In Nigeria, the military intervened to annul what had appeared to be a fair and decisive vote in the 1993 election for a civilian president.

The struggle for democracy may ultimately yield little in the way of concrete results. The record of failure over three decades of rule by countless African governments provides little encouragement that future democratically elected regimes will achieve significant progress. All governments, civilian or military, one-party or multiparty, face the daunting task of addressing the urgent needs and expectations of a growing population with limited and generally declining resources.

The Struggle for Development

The time of independence was characterized by an optimism that reflected economic trends and ideas about progress not only in Africa but also in other parts of the world. During the 1950s, production and consumption had increased greatly in Europe and North America, spurred by postwar reconstruction and a prevailing mood of optimism. Demand for African raw materials rose; so, too, did the prices of these commodities. A wave of new investment led to the opening of mines and plantations and in the more prosperous colonies led to the first industries' producing goods for local markets. The Alliance for Progress was launched in Latin America, with the promise of an economic revolution like the one achieved by the Marshall Plan in Europe. It was confidently predicted that Africa would now be able to follow this same path toward development.

Needless to say, results were very discouraging. Commodity prices leveled off or fell, and demand for a number of products failed to keep pace with rising production. Moreover, the attempts of many governments to stimulate growth and to diversify their economies—for example, by establishing industries—were ill conceived and ineptly implemented. More and more coffee from more and more countries simply brought about lower prices and created large unsold surpluses. Development initiatives were often severely-handicapped by the lack of basic infrastructures, such as a good road network, a reliable and cheap supply of electrical energy, and an educational sector capable of training skilled people of all kinds.

African countries have experimented since independence with several models of political, economic, and social development. These approaches may be grouped into three broad categories: (1) capitalism, (2) populist socialism, and (3) Afro-Marxism. The three strategies will be outlined briefly at this point and then described in greater detail in Chapter 22.

Prior to independence, the modern economies of all African countries were organized on capitalist principles. Major investments in commercial agriculture, resource extraction, manufacturing, communications, and trade had been undertaken during the colonial period by large European trading companies. Independent entrepreneurs from Europe, the Middle East, and the Indian subcontinent were very active in the agricultural and trading sectors, often with great success, as the growth and diversification of Asian-owned enterprises in East Africa shows. In many colonies, African capitalists expanded the range and size of their enterprises; indigenous entrepreneurs achieved particular success in Nigeria, Ghana, and Senegal.

Countries such as Côte d'Ivoire, Kenya, and Malawi have followed an explicitly capitalist development strategy since independence. They have emphasized economic growth rather than equity as a primary development objective. Compared to other African countries, they have developed quite open economies. Private investment, both domestic and foreign, has generally been welcomed. Still, there have been limits to openness. Capitalist governments have often become partners with capitalist investors in joint ventures; and in Kenya and several other countries, legislation has been passed to closely regulate the economic role of resident entrepreneurs of non-African origin.

Several countries searched for an alternative to capitalism, which was criticized as being exploitative and incompatable with the African traditions of cooperative production and communal ownership of land. African socialism was proposed as a strategy that would bring about more equitable development. The state assumed a dominant role in the economies of Ghana, Tanzania, and other African socialist countries. The role of capitalist companies was severely restricted, and parastatal companies were formed to undertake high-priority economic projects. Priority was given to rural development, with the objective of reducing social and economic disparities between city and countryside.

Mozambique, Angola, and Ethiopia, among others, adopted Afro-Marxism as a state ideology. In several of these countries, this commitment to Marxism was forged in the context of armed struggle for independence. Economic strategies concentrated on gaining control of the "commanding heights" of the economy through state direction. State farms and state-owned factories were organized along the lines of enterprises in the Soviet Union and other communist states. For the most part shunned by the West, Afro-Marxist states became very dependent on trade and aid linkages with communist states.

Afro-Marxism as an official ideology has been virtually doomed, at least for now, by a number of factors, including its failure to bring about real economic progress, growing pressure from international financial institutions for economic liberalization, and the demise of communism in Europe and the Soviet Union. These same pressures have forced the populist socialist states to reorganize their social and economic policies to conform much more closely to free-market principles.

The development policies of African states began to converge during the 1980s and have become increasingly alike during the 1990s. This trend has been facilitated by the intervention of global financial institutions, particularly the IMF, and the growing assertiveness of major aid donors. In the present global order, there appears to be no viable alternative. However, the achievements of African states adhering to imposed structural adjustment reforms have been very modest indeed. Thus,

there will continue to be interest in alternate development models for Africa, models that pay much more attention than those currently fashionable to the alleviation of the suffering of the people and also to the achievement of balanced and sustainable growth.

The Struggle Ahead

African countries can point to some notable accomplishments in the years since independence. For example, all countries have greatly expanded their health and education systems and provide much improved accessibility and a far greater range of services than was available in 1960. Nevertheless, Africa has increasingly become a continent in crisis. The African state has been severely weakened by its declining ability to address the basic needs, much less the aspirations, of its citizens. With the stagnation or decline of both export and aid revenues and the growing cost of debt servicing, few governments have the means to properly maintain existing services and infrastructures, much less to commence significant new development projects.

While the intervention of the World Bank and IMF has provided some immediate support for African states in trouble, their assistance has come with a very high price. The structural-adjustment measures that they have imposed, including currency devaluation, severe cutbacks in social spending, the introduction of user fees for health and education, and the removal of food subsidies, have been immensely unpopular with the public and in some cases have led to strikes and protests by frustrated citizens. In several countries, most notably Tanzania, governments have been forced to adopt policies that are fundamentally opposed to their own long-established strategies and philosophies of development. The relation between African governments and the international financial institutions has been seen, justifiably, as a new form of neocolonialism, more concerned with debt repayment than with African development.

For Angola and Mozambique, the struggle

Figure 6.4. Photographer's signboard, Hadejia, Nigeria. The name "Struggling Man Joe" epitomizes the daily struggle of hundreds of millions of ordinary Africans to survive and to progress. Photo: author.

for survival has been in the first instance the fight against destabilization by South Africa. Military intervention by South Africa, especially in Angola, and guerrilla warfare supported by South Africa caused a great many deaths, forced millions to flee their homes, destroyed economic and social infrastructures, and paralyzed activities throughout the countryside. Fortunately, South Africa's destabilization efforts began to decline around 1990, with Namibia's attainment of independence and with the belated acceptance in South Africa of the inevitability of fundamental political change at home.

Many African communities have been severely threatened by environmental and political crises in which states have been unable and sometimes unwilling to help. Sometimes, the very survival of communities and ways of life have been at stake. For example, pastoral communities have often been threatened by droughts that have decimated livestock herds and forced migration into new, contested territories (see, e.g., Vignette 10.2). Pastoralists have also suffered greatly as a result of civil wars in Uganda, Somalia, and Sudan. But pastoralists have not been the only victims, as shown by the existence of almost 10 million African refugees who have fled to the relative safety of countries other than their own.

Clearly, the struggle for survival is most acutely evident in the refugee camps that house victims of devastating famines and political turmoil. In recent years, the most compelling images of this struggle for survival have come from Somalia, Liberia, Sudan, Ethiopia, Mozambique, and Rwanda. However, the struggle for survival in all countries is also very tangible for the majority of urban workers coping with rising prices and significantly declining real wages and for peasants coping with environmental degradation, among other problems. In African societies that are modernizing, the gradual erosion of knowledge, institutions, and resources that formed the basis of traditional strategies for coping with adversity, leaves African communities increasingly vulnerable and dependent for assistance on governments and international donors whose help is at best uncertain.

Figure 6.5. Tank graveyard near Massawa, Ethiopia (now Eritrea). African countries too often served as pawns in superpower struggles for global supremacy. For Ethiopia, these struggles have meant untold misery and the tragic diversion of scarce resources from crucial development needs. Photo: M. Peters.

The attainment of independence was a major accomplishment for Africa, particularly in countries where armed struggle was needed to bring about decolonization. In the subsequent struggles for stability and development, there have been some successes and many disappointments. Recent trends, particularly the involvement of the IMF and World Bank, have significantly eroded African sovereignty.

During the early 1970s, the motto of the independence movements in the colonies then ruled by Portugal was "a luta continua"–"the struggle continues." This motto epitomizes the situation that still prevails in Africa south of the Sahara.

Further Reading

On the struggle for independence, see the following sources:

Kenyatta, J. *Facing Mount Kenya*. London: Secker and Warburg, 1953.

Legum, C. *Pan-Africanism: A Short Political Guide*. New York: Praeger, 1965.

Nkrumah, K. *I Speak of Freedom*. New York: Praeger, 1961.

Wallerstein, I. *Africa: The Politics of Independence*. New York: Vintage, 1961.

The following sources provide useful assessments of the African situation at various points in time:

"Africa: A generation after independence." Special theme issue of *Daedalus*, vol. 111, no. 2 (1982).

Chabal, P. *Power in Africa: An Essay in Political Interpretation*. Basingstoke, England: Macmillan, 1992.

Crowder, M. "Whose dream was it anyway? Twenty-five years of African independence." *African Affairs*, vol. 86 (1987), pp. 7–24.

Davidson, B. *The Black Man's Burden: Africa and the Curse of the Nation State*. New York: Times Books, 1992.

Duignan, P., and R. H. Jackson, eds. *Politics and Government in African States, 1960–1985*. London: Croom Helm, 1986.

Legum, C., I. W. Zartman, S. Langdon, and L. Mytelka. *Africa in the 1980s: A Continent in Crisis*. New York: McGraw-Hill, 1979.

Martin, P. M., and P. O'Meara, eds. *Africa,* 2nd ed. Bloomington: Indiana University Press, 1986. (In particular, see Chapters 1, 17 and 18.)

Mazrui, A. *The African Condition: A Political Diagnosis.* London: Cambridge University Press, 1980.

Onimode, B. *A Political Economy of the Africa Crisis.* London: Zed, 1988.

Paden, J., and E. W. Soja, eds. *The African Experience.* Evanston, IL: Northwestern University Press, 1970.

Ray, D. I., P. Shinnie, and D. Williams, eds. *Into the 1980s: Proceedings of the Eleventh Annual Conference of CAAS.* 2 vols. Vancouver: Tantalus, 1981.

The accomplishments of the OAU are assessed in the following sources:

Amate, C. O. C. *Inside the OAU: Pan-Africanism in Practice.* London: MacMillan, 1986.

Cervenka, Z. *The Unfinished Quest for Unity: Africa and the OAU.* New York: Africana, 1978.

For a political and economic history of Ghana since independence, see the following source:

Rimmer, D. *Staying Poor: Ghana's Political Economy, 1950–1990.* Oxford: Permagon, 1990.

The effect of IMF and World Bank intervention is discussed in the following source:

Onimode, B. *The IMF, the World Bank and the African Debt. Vol. 1: The Economic Impact; Vol. 2: The Social and Political Impact.* London: Zed, 1989.

The African alternative to structural adjustment is described in the following source:

United Nations Economic Commission for Africa (UNECA). *African Alternative Framework to Structural Adjustment Programme for Socio-Economic Recovery and Transformation.* Addis Ababa: UN-ECA, 1989.

DYNAMICS
OF POPULATION

Geographers have long recognized the importance of examining carefully the dynamics of population, eccompassing population distribution, population growth, and population mobility. Where people live and where populations are growing, whether through natural increase or migration, often reflects the relative health—ecological, economic, social, and political—of different places. At the same time, rapid population change may both reflect and contribute to the destabilization of what had apparently been relatively stable situations.

Many of the characteristics of Africa's present population distribution and patterns of change reflect processes that have operated for decades, centuries, or even millenia. For example, population distribution reflects in certain ways not only postindependence migrations, like those from the countryside to the city, but also the colonial reshaping of Africa's political and economic map; population distribution even reflects major historical migrations such as those of the Bantu peoples.

Chapter 7 looks at the uneven distribution of population in African south of the Sahara. Some of the explanations that have been used to account for population distributions, including both environmental and historical factors, are noted. The uneven distribution of population may have a variety of effects, ranging from environmental degradation in vulnerable, heavily exploited environments to the limited prospects for diversified development that exist for many countries with small national populations.

In Chapter 8, the focus turns to the rapid growth of African populations, explanations for rapid growth, and its implications for the continent's future. With a growth rate of 3% per year, population is expanding faster in Africa than anywhere else in the world. Connections are often drawn between population growth and various problems, whether damage to ecosystems or food shortages. However, while few would deny that rapid population growth has serious implications, the assertion that population growth is the primary cause of these problems remains open to debate.

Chapter 9 focuses on population mobility in Africa. Several distinct explanations have been advanced to account for Africa's high rates of mobility and the resultant differential effects on various regions, depending on whether they are source areas or destinations for migrants. While the flow of labor migrants to islands of economic development, first established in colonial times, continues to be very important, the flight of refugees to safety from areas of political or ecological distress has become an increasingly prominent form of migration.

7

✳

Population Distribution

The population of Africa south of the Sahara is very unevenly distributed – a situation that reflects a variety of ecological and histori-cal–cultural factors and that has notable im-plications for development. Mean national population densities (Figure 7.1) range from less than 2 persons per sq km in Mauritania to 290 per sq km in Rwanda. The least dense-ly populated countries, those with under 10 persons per sq km, account for just over one-eighth of the total population but occupy 46% of the total area (Table 7.1). The 11 coun-tries that have these very low densities are very diverse, as the following partial listing will show: Mali, Sudan, Gabon, Congo, Angola, and Namibia. They occur throughout the con-tinent and in all of the major biomes – tropical forest, savanna, semidesert, and desert. Con-versely, countries with the highest population densities (over 80 per sq km) account for about 25% of the total population but only 5% of the area. This group of 6 countries is domi-nated by Nigeria, which accounts for over three-quarters of the high-density group's to-tal population and area.

Areas of high or low population density sel-dom, if ever, correspond to national units. It is not uncommon for regions of exceptional density to cut across national boundaries. Moreover, substantial regional variations in population density are found *within* virtually all nations. Vignette 7.1 looks at the uneven distribution of population in one country, Zambia, and touches upon some of the fac-tors that help to account for these spatial var-iations in population density.

Localized pockets of high population den-sity are to be found in most countries, espe-cially in the vicinity of major cities. Of greater interest are several larger clusters of high den-sity, the most important of which are the fol-lowing:

1. Several areas in Nigeria, particularly the Igbo homeland in southeastern Nigeria, the Yoruba heartland in southwestern Niger-ia, and the close-settled zones surround-ing the Hausa cities of Kano, Zaria, and Sokoto in northern Nigeria
2. A zone extending from Burundi and Rwan-da along the western and northern shore-lines of Lake Victoria through southern Uganda and western Kenya
3. Other more localized pockets in East and Central Africa found in southern Malawi, northeastern Tanzania, the hinterland of Nairobi in Kenya, and central Ethiopia
4. The bantustans created by the South Afri-can government as "homelands" for its black population
5. The island nations of the Comoros, Cape Verde, and São Tomé e Príncipe

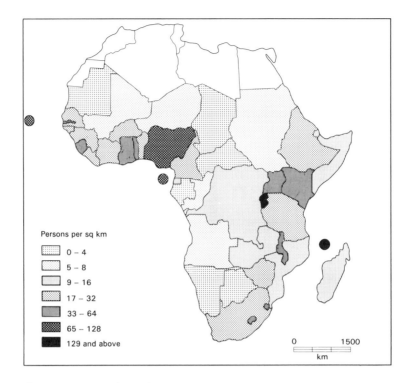

Figure 7.1. National population densities. The large number of countries with low to very low densities is especially striking. Data source: UN. *Demographic Yearbook 1991.* New York, 1991.

The following areas are characterized by particularly low densities and only localized concentrations of settlement:

1. The Sahara Desert, together with the Sahelian zone along its southern fringe

2. The desert and semidesert regions of Botswana, Namibia, Angola, and western South Africa

3. Large parts of west central Africa between Chad and Angola, including most of the tropical forest zone in Congo, Gabon, and

Table 7.1. National Population Densities in Relation to Area, 1990

Density/km²	Percentage of population	Cumulative percentage	Percentage of area	Cumulative percentage
0–4	2.9	2.9	19.0	19.0
5–9	10.6	13.5	27.2	46.2
10–19	15.7	29.2	21.3	67.5
20–39	23.1	52.3	18.2	85.7
40–79	23.3	75.6	9.5	95.2
80–159	21.8	97.4	4.6	99.8
160 and over	2.6	100.0	0.2	100.0

Compiled from *World Resources, 1990–91.* New York: Basic Books, 1991; amended to take into account preliminary figures from the 1991 Census of Nigeria.

Zaire, and varied savanna environments in Central African Republic, southern Sudan, and Angola

It is often hard to ascertain the specific causes and effects of exceptional densities in particular regions. The following section identifies some of the factors that help to account for variations in population density.

The Ecology of Population Distribution

Geographers have long grappled with the notions of carrying capacity and population pressure. Clearly, there are great differences in the ability of environments to produce the resources that human populations need to survive. However, it has not been possible to develop widely accepted measures of carrying capacity and population pressure. One of the most common approaches is to determine the amount of arable land per person working in agriculture. However, while this measure helps to identify areas where population density may

be a problem, it is not sufficiently reliable as a basis for a careful analysis of the balance between people and land.

Population distribution is influenced by many factors, some pertain to the physical environment and its capacity to support populations, and some reflect social and political characteristics. Often, present-day distributions reflect events or situations that occurred decades or even centuries in the past. The *redistribution* of population may well occur as circumstances change, but redistribution tends to be a very prolonged process.

Precipitation, specifically the amount, seasonal distribution, and reliability of rainfall in particular regions, is the most important of the climatic factors related to the distribution of population. Where rainfall is low and the rainy season short and uncertain, as in drier savanna and semidesert regions, low densities are the rule. The reverse is not necessarily true; the majority of tropical forest and moist savanna environments, where adequate precipitation is not a limiting factor, also have low population densities.

Humid tropical environments with low pop-

Figure 7.2. Densely settled rural landscape, Rwanda. Despite the mountainous terrain, this is one of the most heavily populated regions of Africa, with average densities approaching 300 per sq km. Photo: CIDA.

Vignette 7.1. Case Study: Population Distribution in Zambia

Patterns of population distribution within each country reflect the influence of unique combinations of physical and historical–cultural influences. Zambia's 7.6 million people are spread over 753,000 sq km, for an average density of less than 10 per sq km. The population, however, is very unevenly distributed.

The largest area of relatively high density follows the main railway line from Livingstone (Victoria Falls) northeast to Lusaka and beyond to the Copper Belt near the Zairean border (Figure 7.3). Close to half of all Zambians live within about 40 km of this railway; Zambians refer to this linear region as the "line of rail." Compared to Nigeria, Rwanda, or central Ethiopia, the densities of 15 to 50 per sq km typical of the line of rail are relatively low. However, within Zambia there is a marked contrast between the line of rail and most of the rest of the area, including the virtually uninhabited valleys of the Kafue and Luangwa rivers, which flank it on either side.

Virtually all of Zambia's modern economy is found along the line of rail—the larger

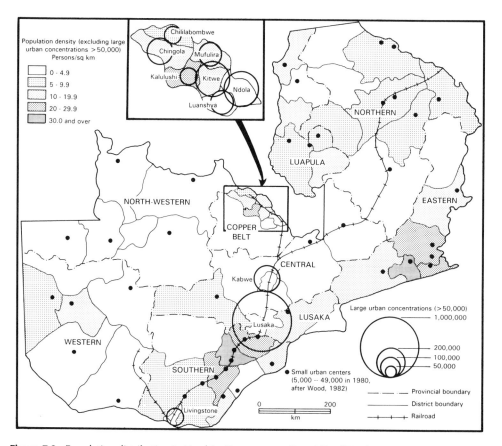

Figure 7.3. Population distribution in Zambia. Data sources: Republic of Zambia. *1990 Census of Population, Housing and Agriculture: Preliminary Report.* Lusaka: Central Statistical Office, 1991. A. P. Wood. "Population trends in Zambia: A review of the 1980 census." In A. Findlay, ed., *Recent National Population Change*, pp. 102–125. Durham, England: Institute of British Geographers Study Group, 1982.

cont.

Vignette 7.1. (cont.)

---

cities, the northern copper mining areas, and the commercial farming region near Lusaka. This concentration of modern economic activity, which dates from the early colonial era, has been a powerful magnet for young people, especially young men, from Zambia's periphery.

The line of rail supports higher densities, in part, because it has relatively fertile and well-drained soils. In the low-density river valleys, soils tend to be either very shallow and infertile or poorly drained. Moreover, the valleys are infested with tsetse, while the area along the line of rail is free of tsetse. Poor soils and a legacy of tsetse-transmitted sleeping sickness are of widespread significance as explanations of the very low densities (under 5 per sq km) found in most of peripheral Zambia.

High densities are found in the southeastern region close to Malawi and Mozambique, where comparatively fertile soils are intensively cultivated. The high densities also reflect the legacy of Portuguese colonialism and the flight of Mozambicans from a regimen of forced labor; population densities are much lower immediately across the border in Mozambique, despite a physical environment and ethnic profile closely resembling southeastern Zambia. Small areas of quite dense settlement also occur in the northwest, near Lake Mweru on the Zaire border.

The regional imbalances in population and the very large area of extremely sparse population are major constraints on Zambia's development. The overwhelming concentration of modern economic activity has fostered a persistent migration of Zambians from the resource-poor and opportunity-poor periphery to the heartland and has helped to perpetuate regional disparities in development. Because of the prolonged decline of Zambia's economy, funds to improve transportation and services in the low-density periphery are very scarce indeed.

---

ulation densities often have infertile laterite soils that are unsuitable for intensive cultivation. Many of these areas support only shifting cultivation systems in which farmed plots are abandoned every two or three years and left fallow for prolonged periods of time. The primary exceptions are the scattered pockets of very fertile volcanic soils that can be farmed intensively on a permanent basis. These often support very dense populations, as in Rwanda and Burundi. Lowlands with relatively young alluvial soils may also support densities that are above average for their region. Such is the case in the valleys of the Gambia, the Senegal, and the upper Niger rivers of West Africa.

The relation between soil productivity and population is not one-way; human activities may enhance or reduce the "natural" potential of the environment. Overcultivation and overgrazing, especially on marginal and hilly land, may increase rates of wind and water erosion. In tropical forest ecosystems suitable for shifting cultivation, too frequent clearance and cropping results in the degradation of both vegetation and soil resources. On the other hand, careful husbandry that makes appropriate use of manure, ground cover, intercropping, fallowing, and other fertility-enhancing techniques increases yields and ensures the long-term usefulness of the land. In the Kano region in Nigeria, for example, very intensive application of manures and the use of methods such as intercropping explain the ability of this fairly dry area to support rural populations as high as 400 persons per sq km.

Patterns of risk from debilitating and often deadly diseases such as sleeping sickness and river blindness are often reflected in the distribution of population. Vignette 7.2 illustrates

Vignette 7.2. River Blindness and Population Distribution in Ghana

John Hunter's studies of river blindness in northern Ghana have provided valuable insights into the effect of ecological hazards on the health of local societies. Since this research was first undertaken in the late 1960s, new hope has emerged that the disease and its effects can be substantially controlled.

River blindness—onchocerciasis—is caused by a parasitic worm transmitted from person to person by the bite of the fly called *Simulium damnosum*. Adult worms breed within the human subject; in a heavily infected person their numbers may be in the billions. Eventually, the parasites may invade the eye socket and, if sufficiently numerous, cause blindness. Because the flies breed in fast-flowing water and usually have a restricted flight range, the probability of being bitten increases as one approaches a riverine breeding site.

Hunter's research in the 1960s showed that between 1 and 27% of Nangodi's population was heavily infected and that the highest rates were in chiefdoms closest to the Red Volta River. The study showed how high rates of infectivity threatened the viability of communities. Heavily infected individuals cannot participate fully in the work of the household, so that food production and family incomes decline and the workload, including the care of the blind, has to be done by fewer people. The people of Nangodi responded by abandoning severely affected villages for locations that were farther from the river.

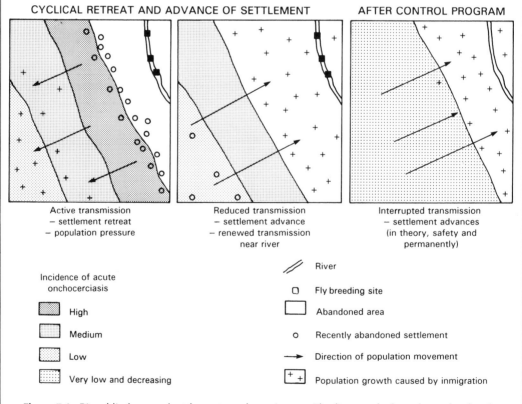

CYCLICAL RETREAT AND ADVANCE OF SETTLEMENT   AFTER CONTROL PROGRAM

Active transmission
– settlement retreat
– population pressure

Reduced transmission
– settlement advance
– renewed transmission
near river

Interrupted transmission
– settlement advances
(in theory, safety and
permanently)

Incidence of acute
onchocerciasis

High

Medium

Low

Very low and decreasing

River

Fly breeding site

Abandoned area

Recently abandoned settlement

Direction of population movement

Population growth caused by inmigration

Figure 7.4. River blindness and settlement: a schematic map. The first panels show the cycle of settlement advances and retreat described by Hunter. The last panel suggests that disease control programs may eliminate the rationale for this cycle, that is, permit permanent settlement of the valleys.

Vignette 7.2. (cont.)

In some of these areas of refuge, population densities increased to over 500 per sq km. Intensified land use contributed to soil exhaustion, erosion, and hunger. Emigration, particularly of young males, became necessary for household survival.

Hunter identified a long-term cycle of settlement advance and retreat in Nangodi (Figure 7.4). As the disease becomes more prevalent, the most seriously threatened villages cannot sustain themselves and are abandoned. The displaced people add to the pressure on already overutilized resources elsewhere in the district. Eventually, population pressure, the attraction of fertile river bottomlands, and the apparent reduction of the disease threat lead to a decision to resettle formerly abandoned lands. With more people living near the fly's riverine breeding sites, a renewed cycle of infectivity and socioeconomic crisis becomes likely.

Since the mid-1970s, an international campaign has sought to control river blindness by using chemical sprays to destroy the fly vector at its larval stage. Transmission has been effectively interrupted in 90% of the project area in Ghana and six other countries. People have begun to return to the fertile valleys to establish farms and set up settlements near the treated rivers.

The long-term success of the program, after spraying ends in 1995, remains in doubt. Will the flies eventually become resistant to the chemical sprays, or the vector to the drugs used to treat infected individuals? Will this bring about a renewed cycle of infectivity and the reabandonment of the valleys?

Primary source: J. M. Hunter. "Population pressure in a part of the West African savanna: A study of Nangodi, northeast Ghana." *Annals of the Association of American Geographers*, vol. 57 (1967), pp. 101–114.

---

at a relatively local scale how otherwise attractive environments may be depopulated because of the effect of disease. Sleeping sickness has been identified as a primary cause of low population densities in parts of the savanna and tropical forest with heavy infestations of tsetse. Such is the case in large parts of Zambia, for example (see Vignette 7.1). Nevertheless, pockets of high density are found in many tsetse-infested areas. Indeed, maintaining high densities and clearing the bush were strategies used by precolonial African societies for tsetse control.

The contemporary distribution of population reflects not only the nature of the environment but also historical processes of development and underdevelopment. For example, the slave trade had effects on population distribution that are still evident today. Regions, such as parts of West Africa's Middle Belt, from which many slaves were taken lost population, while certain highland areas, such as Nigeria's Jos Plateau, served as defensive refuges from the slave trade and became more densely populated as a result.

The reshaping of the political–economic map of Africa under colonial rule caused major changes in population distribution. Many new cities were established and developed as administrative and trade centers. The economic landscape was transformed through the development of mines and areas of cash crop production to which migrant labor came. For most Africans, interregional mobility became much easier because of greater political stability and improved transportation.

Ecological changes occurring because of colonial policies also affected local population distributions. Diseases as well as people migrated along the transportation corridors, and newly created forest reserves provided environments where disease vectors could proliferate. In certain areas, long-established communities were abandoned as a result of new disease hazards. However, the opposite trend occurred in some areas, namely, previously avoided areas became accessible to new settlers owing to locally successful vector and disease control programs.

Among the developments since independence that continue to change the distribution of population, two of the most important have been disparities in development and political/military conflicts. Development disparities—the concentration of modern economic development and services in the largest cities and a few favored regions—has caused increased rural–urban, interregional, and international migration. While resettlement has sometimes been undertaken deliberately, as in the construction of large dams and reservoirs, more often migration has been the inevitable but unplanned consequence of unbalanced development strategies. Instability and conflicts, whether political or ethnic in nature, have resulted in a massive dislocation of people; millions have fled from their homes

as refugees to adjacent countries or to safer places within their own countries.

In South Africa, the enforcement under apartheid of policies of racial segregation and compulsory relocation created pockets of very high density in the homelands (Figure 7.5). Under apartheid, a mere 13% of the land base was allocated to the three-quarters of the population that was black. An estimated 3.5 million people were forcibly removed from their homes between 1960 and 1983, most into the already overcrowded homelands. The population of the 10 homelands increased from 7 million in 1970 to 11.3 million in 1980 and 16.9 million in 1991. The most dramatic increase was in QwaQwa, which grew from 23,000 in 1970 to 453,000 in 1991, primarily because of removals.

The results from forcibly removing millions of people to these reserves without providing them with adequate means of survival have been predictable. Overall, some 20 to 40% of the rural population has no access to land or livestock; landlessness is considerably greater in some areas. Most plots are too small and too infertile to provide sufficient subsistence. Up to 40% of infants and small children are

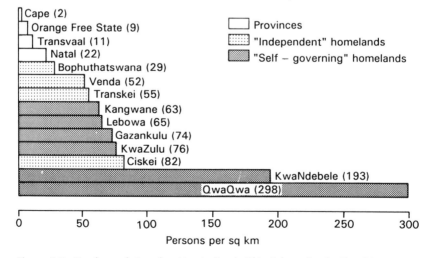

RURAL POPULATION DENSITIES, 1980

Cape (2)
Orange Free State (9)
Transvaal (11)
Natal (22)
Bophuthatswana (29)
Venda (52)
Transkei (55)
Kangwane (63)
Lebowa (65)
Gazankulu (74)
KwaZulu (76)
Ciskei (82)
KwaNdebele (193)
QwaQwa (298)

☐ Provinces
▨ "Independent" homelands
▩ "Self − governing" homelands

0   50   100   150   200   250   300
Persons per sq km

Figure 7.5. Rural population densities in South Africa's homelands. Densities are especially high in comparison to those in the rest of South Africa. After F. Wilson and M. Ramphale. *Uprooting Poverty: The South African Challenge.* Cape Town, South Africa: David Phillip, 1989, p. 36.

undernourished. The intensive utilization of marginal land has accelerated soil erosion. Labor migration to centers of economic development in South Africa has been the only viable means of support in the homelands, but this option has not been available to the majority.

In its *Official Yearbook* (1989–90, p. 86), the government of South Africa made no reference to the effect of forced removals on the population of the homelands. Instead, the government attributed the high densities of the homelands to their being "located in the well-watered eastern regions of the subcontinent . . . together with the traditional system of land ownership and utilisation." Despite the more recent elimination of restrictions on where people may legally reside, the legacy of four decades of removals will not soon disappear, if only because of the extreme poverty in which most of the nonwhite population now lives.

In Zimbabwe, as in South Africa, official policies of land apportionment became a primary determinant of population distribution. By 1930, over 50% of all land had been set aside for Europeans, despite the fact that Europeans never accounted for more than 5% of the population. Africans living in areas designated for European use were faced with the choice of moving to the reserves or remaining as laborers or rent-paying tenants on European farms. Population pressure and environmental degradation increased steadily on the reserves. The most fertile regions in the central part of the country were designated for European settlement, while the African reserves included large areas that were marginal and unable to support many people.

The injustice of this situation culminated in civil war during the 1970s, ending in 1980 with the establishment of an independent black government. Disparities in population density increased during the war; certain commercial farming areas lost population because of guerrilla activity, while the reserves became places of refuge for displaced Africans.

Population pressure and land apportionment were issues that, for ecological, economic, and political reasons, could not be ignored by the new government. Vacant and underutilized European farms were purchased for the resettlement of landless African families. The former large farms were subdivided into village units in which each settler family was allocated a plot of land in the village, 5 ha (hectares) of arable land, and communal grazing rights. Large unorganized movements of African squatters into formerly European lands occurred in some areas. However, the government has attempted to slow the pace of migration by improving producer prices, extension services, and transportation in the former reserve areas and by decentralizing urban functions from Harare and Bulwayo to smaller cities.

Despite Zimbabwe's repeal of discriminatory land legislation, the inequitable distribution of population in relation to land resources will not soon disappear. Developing effective programs of resettlement and balanced regional growth to address problems of land degradation and poverty on the former reserves will continue to be a major challenge. Nevertheless, the success of Kenya two decades earlier in resettling many landless farmers on formerly European lands, while managing to expand agricultural production for domestic and export markets, gives reason for optimism.

Urban and Rural Settlement

The population of Africa south of the Sahara is still predominantly rural; less than one-third of the population resides in urban centers. East Africa, with 20% of its population in cities as of 1990, is considerably less urbanized than West Africa (with 32%), central Africa (with 38%), or southern Africa (with 42%). Individual countries fall along a continuum that ranges from Burundi, Rwanda, and Burkina Faso (under 10% urban) to South Africa (60%) and Djibouti (81%).

Average annual growth rates for African urban populations have been about 5%, well above rates in Asia and Latin America. The urban population of West Africa rose from 10.6 million in 1960 to 56.3 million in 1990

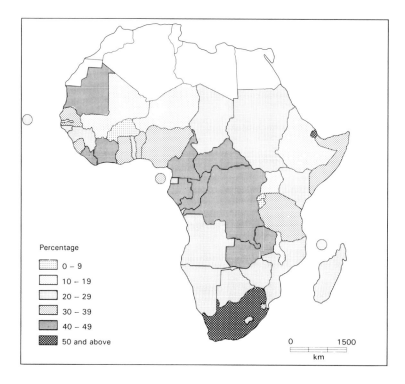

Figure 7.6. Urbanization as a percentage of the total population, 1990. Africa is the least urbanized of the continents, but rates of urbanization vary greatly from country to country. Data source: UNDP. *Human Development Report, 1991.* New York: Oxford University Press, 1991.

and is projected to be 97.0 million in 2000. Urbanization has increased at an even greater rate in East Africa, from 5.7 million in 1960 to 32.7 million in 1990 – and is projected to be 73.6 million in 2000. An increase from 6.3 to 47.3 million is predicted for central Africa from 1960 to 2000.

Very few countries have well-developed urban systems with a substantial number of cities of varying sizes and functions. The countries with the most extensive urban systems are South Africa and Nigeria. Uganda is typical of the majority of countries, in that it has a primate city system. The population of Kampala, Uganda's largest city, is almost ten times that of the second-ranked city, Jinja. In a primate system, the largest city has a much larger population than other cities, as well as a disproportionate share of modern economic and political functions. Primacy is partly attributable to the recency of urbanization in

most of Africa and the fact that most countries have small and mostly rural populations. It has been argued that such concentrations of population, wealth, and power in a single city perpetuate and deepen regional disparities and promote accelerated rural–urban migration.

Rural settlement patterns are a reflection of the various ways in which particular cultural groups approach the social organization of space (Figure 7.7). Some rural dwellers live in nucleated settlements varying in size from a few families to several thousand inhabitants. Elsewhere, rural settlement is dispersed, with each individual family living on its own plot of land. The dispersed farm compounds may each have an extended family group consisting of several nuclear families belonging to a single lineage.

Patterns of rural settlement are important for the provision of education and health care

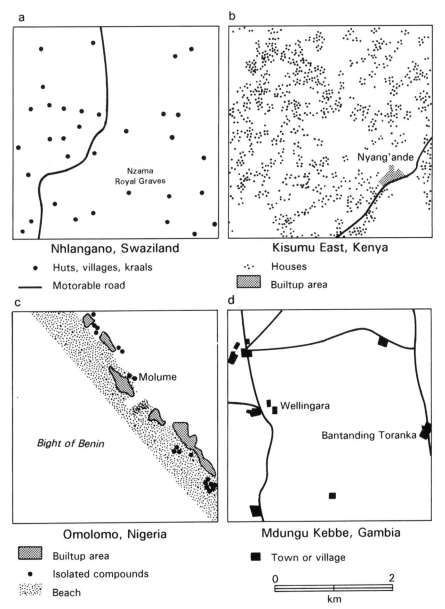

Figure 7.7. Examples of rural settlement types. (a) Dispersed compounds, Swaziland. (b) Very dense dispersed settlement, western Kenya. (c) Linear pattern of nucleated fishing villages, Nigeria. (d) Nucleated agricultural settlements, Gambia.

and the integration of rural people into national life. It is much more difficult to provide services to dispersed compounds than to village-based populations. It is also harder to mobilize dispersed populations to participate in state-sponsored development initiatives. The apparent advantages of nucleated settlements have led several governments to group dis-

persed rural populations in villages. Tanzania's ambitious program of developing *ujamaa* villages is the best known of these programs. Developing villages, however, has tended to be infinitely more complicated in practice than in theory. Rural dwellers have often resisted because they have preferred their ancestral lands or have distrusted the government. Official plans for resettlement have often been too ambitious, given the scarcity of needed resources and widespread reluctance in the countryside. For example, Tanzania has effectively abandoned its *ujamaa* program because of its high cost, widespread peasant resistance to resettlement, and the disapproval of international lending agencies.

The problems of service delivery and integration are most acute among pastoral nomads. Many countries have programs to encourage pastoralists to settle permanently and to send their children to school. Most pastoral peoples have jealously guarded their independence and resisted resettlement initiatives. On the other hand, growing crises of civil unrest, drought, disease, and environmental degradation, as well as the loss of access to traditional grazing lands, threaten the viability of pastoral ways of life in several coun-

tries, forcing many pastoralists to adopt a sedentary lifestyle.

National Populations

It is ironic, given the widespread concern about rapid population growth and high population densities, that the small size of national populations is a developmental constraint in many African countries. Only 14 out of 46 countries in Africa south of the Sahara have national populations greater than 10 million while 7 have less than 1 million citizens. Nigeria alone has almost four-fifths as many people as the total of 115 million living in the 31 countries that have less than 10 million each.

Figure 7.8 assigns to each country an area proportional to its national population. The

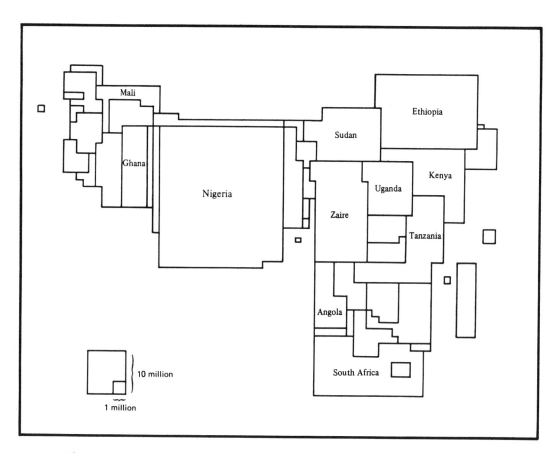

Figure 7.8. Population cartogram. Areas on the map are proportional to national populations.

Table 7.2. National Populations, 1991

Population (in thousands)	No. of countries	Examples of countries
0–999	7	Gambia, Swaziland, Comoros
1,000–4,999	13	Liberia, Togo, Congo
5,000–9,999	12	Guinea, Somalia, Zambia
10,000–19,999	7	Ghana, Uganda, Zimbabwe
20,000–49,999	6	Sudan, Zaire, Ethiopia
50,000–99,999	1	Nigeria

overall shape of the cartogram, as compared to the normal base map of Africa south of the Sahara, is distorted significantly by the position of the large and high-density population of Nigeria adjacent to the sparsely populated states of west central Africa. The cartogram is an effective illustration of the dominance of Nigeria's population. Elsewhere, the block of relatively populous countries in East Africa together with Zaire contrast markedly with the plethora of small-population states in southern, west central and West Africa.

Countries that are both small in population and poverty-stricken may be unable to undertake many types of large-scale development. Their domestic markets cannot support most large-scale or specialized industries. They often remain dependent on foreign aid to balance their budgets and on other countries for such professional services as education and specialist health care. In general, Africa's small-population states do not possess the special advantages of resource wealth, location, local capital, and skilled labor that have permitted some small countries elsewhere in the Third World–Singapore, Hong Kong, and the Bahamas, for example–to achieve notable economic success.

Governments and development agencies are increasingly aware of the importance of population size and population distribution for national, regional, and local development. They are concerned about the rapid growth of cities and concurrent decline of many rural economies, as well as the apparent relation between population pressure and environmental degradation in many parts of rural Africa. They express interest in the development of sparsely populated regions, some of which have considerable potential. Unfortunately, the political will to address these issues seriously has only rarely been present, and the resources to bring about effective and comprehensive change have been even less available.

Problems of population distribution, however, represent only one component of the larger population picture. Comprehensive population policies must also address problems of rapid growth–on average 3% annually–in African populations, as well as the dramatic migrations that are redistributing the African population. The following chapter examines patterns of population growth, the significance of rapid growth, and prospects for slowing the rate of natural increase. Chapter 9 focuses on the importance of migration, both voluntary and involuntary, as an element of population change.

Further Reading

Data on population distribution in Africa are very uneven in its coverage, quality, and accessibility. Academic studies of population distribution are similarly uneven. For some countries, you may be able to obtain census data from national census reports or annual statistical handbooks. Published population distribution maps are available for some countries.

Various aspects of population distribution are considered in the following sources:

Barbour, K. M., J. S. Oguntoyinbo, J. O. C. Onyemelukwe, and J. C. Nwafor. *Nigeria in Maps.* New York: Africana, 1982. (In this "in Maps" series of national atlases, look for other volumes on Liberia, Malawi, Sierra Leone, Tanzania and Zambia.)

Davies, H. "Population growth, distribution and density change, and urbanization in Zimbabwe: A preliminary assessment following the 1982 census." *African Urban Notes,* vol. 2 (1987), pp. 13–23.

Dumanowski, B. "The influence of geographical environments on the density and distribution of population in Africa." *Africana Bulletin,* vol. 9 (1968), pp. 9–33.

UNECA. *Population Distribution and Urbanization in ECA Member States.* New York: United Nations Economic Commission for Africa, 1983.

Kloos, H., and A. Adugna, "The Ethiopian population: growth and distribution." *Geographical Journal,* vol. 155 (1989), pp. 35–51.

Mortimore, M. "Population distribution, settlement and soils in Kano Province, Northern Nigeria, 1931–1962." In J. C. Caldwell and C. Okonjo, eds., *The Population of Tropical Africa,* pp. 298–306. London: Oxford University Press, 1968.

Moss, R. P.. and R. J. Rathbone. *The Population Factor in African Studies.* London: University of London Press, 1975.

Ominde, S. H. *Population and Development in Kenya.* London: Heinemann, 1984.

Zinyama, L., and R. Whitlow. "Changing patterns of population distribution in Zimbabwe." *Geojournal,* vol. 13 (1986), pp. 365–384.

The question of land apportionment and population density in South Africa is considered in the following sources:

Simpkins, C. *Four Essays on the Past, Present and Future Distribution of the Black Population of South Africa.* Cape Town: South Africa Labour and Development Research Unit, 1983.

Wilson, F., and M. Ramphele. *Uprooting Poverty: the South African Challenge.* Cape Town: David Philip, 1989. (Chapter 2 is especially useful.)

Issues related to population pressure are discussed in the following sources:

Higgins, G. M. *Potential Population Supporting Capacities of Lands in the Developing World.* Rome: Food and Agricultural Organization of the United Nations, 1982. (This book contains a technical report and maps portfolio.)

Hunter, J. M. "Population pressure in a part of the West African savanna: A study of Nangodi, northeastern Ghana." *Annals of the Association of American Geographers,* vol. 57 (1967), pp. 101–114.

Prothero, R. M. *People and Land in Africa South of the Sahara.* London: Oxford University Press, 1972.

8

✴

Population Growth

Population growth is occurring much faster in Africa than ony other continent. The average annual growth in the 1985 to 1990 period was 3.0% in Africa, compared to 2.1% in South America, 1.6% in Asia, and 0.3% in Europe. São Tomé e Príncipe is the only country in Africa south of the Sahara currently growing at less than 2.0% annually.

Such rates of growth have serious implications for development planning. Among the most obvious are the employment needs of young people reaching adulthood and the continuing growth in demand for services such as health care and education. In the many areas where rural economies are under pressure, population growth increases the incentive of young people to move to the city. Without steady economic growth the increasing demand for essential services and jobs cannot be met.

Patterns of Population Growth

Populations may grow in two ways: (1) by natural increase, that is, births minus deaths, or (2) positive net migration, that is, inmigration (arriving at a place) minus outmigration (leaving a place). National population changes in many African countries have been almost entirely attributable to natural increase, with net migration across international frontiers being relatively unimportant. Some African countries, however, have experienced considerable gains or losses because of refugee movements or international migration of labor to areas of economic opportunity. The estimated 1 million Mozambican refugees in Malawi in 1992 equal one-fifteenth of Mozambique's population and one-eighth of Malawi's. The 1.2 million labor migrants from Burkina Faso in Côte d'Ivoire represent almost one-sixth of the source country's total population and perhaps one-eighth of the Ivoirian population.

At current rates of natural increase, 3.1% annually, the population of Africa south of the Sahara can be expected to double every 23 years. The high rate of natural increase reflects very high rates of fertility and occurs despite crude death rates that are significantly above the average for Third World countries.

Crude birth rates have been more stable than crude death rates, declining by more than 10% in only 8 countries over the 20 year period from 1970 to 1991. During this period, birth rates increased in 10 countries; these increases were 10% or more in Congo, Gabon, Central African Republic, Guinea-Bissau, and Ethiopia. With few exceptions, death rates declined by 15 to 35% between 1970 and 1991.

African birth and death rates differ consider-

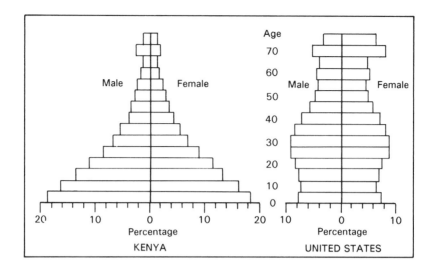

Figure 8.1. Population pyramids for Kenya and the United States. Kenya—a young, rapidly growing population, and the United States—an older, slow-growth population.

ably from those found in most other parts of the Third World, including large and relatively poor countries like India, China, and Mexico. Between 1970 and 1991, crude birth rates fell 27% to 30 per 1,000 in India, 31% to 22 per 1,000 in China, and 35% to 28 per 1,000 in Mexico. Crude death rates fell 45% to 10 per 1,000 in India, 34% to 7 per 1,000 in China, and 50% to 5 per 1,000 in Mexico during the same period.

High rates of population growth are clearly reflected in the age structure of the population (see Figure 8.1). The African population is very young; between 40 and 50% of the population consists of children aged 0 to 15 years, while less than 5% of the population is over 65 years of age. By way of comparison, children make up 22% and adults over 65 years 12% of the U.S. population.

Similar differences in age structure and rates

Table 8.1. Natural Increase in Selected African Countries

Country	CBR[a]	% change in CBR 1970–1991	CDR[b]	% change in CDR 1970–1991	Pop. growth 1980–1991 (% per year)
Burundi	46	0	17	−26	2.9
Burkina Faso	47	−2	18	−28	3.0
Congo	49	+14	16	0	3.4
Ethiopia	50	+16	21	+5	2.7
Guinea	49	−6	21	−22	2.6
Kenya	45	−15	11	−39	3.8
Lesotho	35	−15	11	−45	2.8
Nigeria	44	−14	14	−33	3.0
South Africa	31	−20	9	−36	3.5
Zambia	47	−4	15	−21	3.6

[a]CBR: crude birth rate (births per 1,000 people per year).
[b]CDR: crude death rate (deaths per 1,000 people per year).
Source: World Bank, *World Development Report, 1993.*

of growth characterize the populations of the four apartheid-defined racial groups in South Africa. While the age structure of the white population of South Africa resembles older, slower growing populations in Europe and North America, that of the black populations in South Africa is typical for Africa south of the Sahara. The age structures of the Asian and colored populations fall between those of blacks and whites in South Africa.

Because of the very high rates of natural increase today, it is inevitable that the population of Africa will continue to grow substantially. Even if birth rates were to fall precipitously, the youthfulness of the population ensures that population numbers will continue to grow for decades to come. The one factor that could conceivably halt the rapid growth of the African population in the near future is the AIDS epidemic; some demographers are predicting a situation in which Afri-

can birth rates will remain high and death rates will increase (Vignette 8.1).

Explaining Africa's High Fertility

Fertility patterns in particular settings reflect a variety of influences, of which attitudes toward children, infant mortality patterns, marriage customs, and family planning are among the most important.

Based on present age-specific fertility rates, women in Africa south of the Sahara give birth an average of 6.7 times each (Figure 8.2). The very high fertility rates are in accord with the widespread preference in Africa for large families. According to the World Fertility Survey, the average desired family size among women in Africa south of the Sahara is 6.5 children. Young women (15 to 19 years) are as likely to prefer large families as older wom-

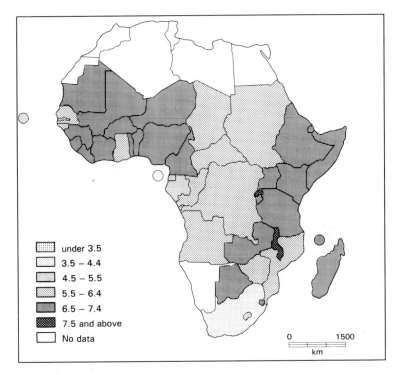

under 3.5
3.5 – 4.4
4.5 – 5.5
5.5 – 6.4
6.5 – 7.4
7.5 and above
No data

0   1500
km

Figure 8.2. Total Fertility Rate, 1990. Total fertility rate: the average number of children per woman, based on current age-specific fertility rates. Data source: UNDP. *Human Development Index, 1991.* New York: Oxford University Press, 1991.

Vignette 8.1. AIDS: What Effect on Africa's Population Growth?

With the AIDS epidemic in Africa still in its infancy, its implications for Africa's demographic future remain a matter of debate. Nevertheless, attempting to predict these effects is extremely important for devising appropriate responses to the disease. What follows is a brief summary of the findings of recent research on this subject, conducted under the auspices of the Center for International Research, U.S. Bureau of the Census.

The rates of HIV infection vary greatly between countries, between urban and rural areas, between different regions within countries, and between low-risk and high-risk populations. Prostitutes and persons with other sexually transmitted diseases are examples of high-risk groups. In some parts of the continent surveys have found little or no sign of HIV. At the other extreme is Uganda, where surveys suggest that over three-quarters of the high-risk group, a quarter of low-risk urbanites, and one-eighth of low-risk rural dwellers were HIV-positive by 1990. As a general rule, infectivity is higher in urban than rural areas and is especially great among high-risk groups.

Africa is affected by two distinct strains of the HIV virus that causes AIDS: HIV-1 and HIV-2. HIV-1 has been identified in all countries in Africa south of the Sahara but is especially concentrated in the "AIDS Belt" that stretches across central Africa (Figure 8.3). There are two major centers of infectivity: One is in Uganda, Rwanda, eastern Zaire, and northwest Tanzania; another is in the lower Congo River basin focused on Kinshasa. HIV-2 is found primarily in West Africa, especially in Mali, Côte d'Ivoire, Guinea-Bissau, and adjoining countries. HIV-2 has not been detected in the areas where HIV-1 is most prevalent.

The two strains of HIV affect different age groups (Figure 8.4). The prevalence of HIV-2 increases with age; persons under 30 years of age account for only about 10% of cases. Conversely, HIV-1 is most prevalent among adults aged 15 to 49, with young

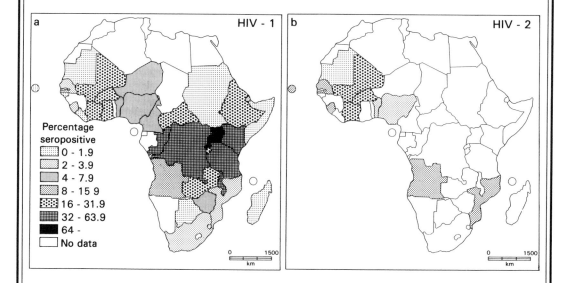

Figure 8.3. Distribution of (a) HIV-1 and (b) HIV-2 in urban high-risk populations. HIV-1 is more prevalent and represents a greater demographic threat. Data source: B. Torrey and P. Way. "Seroprevalence of HIV in Africa, Winter, 1990." *CIR Staff Paper 55.* U.S. Bureau of Census, 1990, p. 25.   *cont.*

Vignette 8.1. *(cont.)*

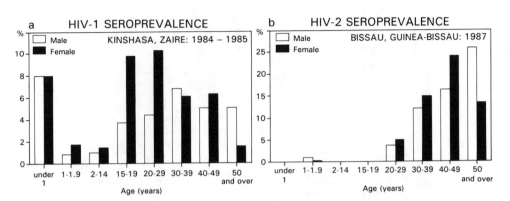

Figure 8.4. Age–sex distribution of (a) HIV-1 and (b) HIV-2. Note the high incidence of HIV-1 among young women. Data source: B. Torrey and P. Way. "Seroprevalence of HIV in Africa, Winter, 1990." *CIR Staff Paper 55.* U.S. Bureau of Census, 1990, p. 24.

women aged 15 to 29 having the very highest rates of infectivity. There is also a significant cluster of newborns with HIV, who have contracted the virus prior to birth.

These differences in age–sex distribution have considerable demographic importance. HIV-1 can significantly retard or even reverse population growth because of its concentration in young adults of childbearing age and in the infant children of HIV-positive women. HIV-2 affects older age cohorts and thus does not have the same deep effect on birth rates and infant survival.

Mathematical modeling has been used to predict the effect of AIDS, given population and HIV-occurrence profiles typical of the "average" in Africa south of the Sahara about 1990. The model showed HIV infectivity increasing sevenfold between 1990 and 2015 – from 4 to 16% in urban areas and from 0.5 to 5,0% in rural districts. At this level of infectivity, a total of 70 million would be HIV-positive in Africa south of the Sahara by 2015. The predicted annual number of AIDS deaths would be 4.6 million, out of a total of 13.8 million deaths. Urban crude death rates are projected to be twice as high as would be expected without AIDS. However, because of high birth rates, continued population growth is predicted. It is projected that the total population would be about 5% lower than it would have been without AIDS.

In countries such as Uganda and Rwanda where HIV rates are much above average, AIDS will surely have a much more devastating effect than that predicted by the general model. In these areas, the high rates of infectivity among young women may become especially important in reducing fertility and child survival rates. As a result, some countries may eventually experience a significant decline in population because of AIDS.

Considering Africa south of the Sahara as a whole, the model predicts a large and growing number of AIDS deaths, but not the catastrophic population collapse expected by some observers. Only time will tell whether this model will have succeeded in anticipating the medium-term effect of AIDS on Africa's population.

Based on P. Way and K. Stanecki. "The demographic impact of an AIDS epidemic on an African country." *CIR Staff Paper 58.* U.S. Bureau of Census, 1991. B. Torrey and P. Way. "Seroprevalence of HIV in Africa, Winter, 1990." *CIR Staff Paper 55.* U.S. Bureau of Census, 1990.

Figure 8.5. Children, Ogun State, Nigeria. With a median age that is below 20 in most countries, Africa has the world's most youthful population. Photo: author.

en (45 to 49 years), which suggests that attitudes about family size are not changing.

Both sociocultural and economic factors account for the desire for large families. The social reasons include the prestige associated with large families and deeply ingrained belief systems that emphasize fertility as the key to the survival and prosperity of any society. The economic benefits of high fertility are the help that children can give with work on the farm and in the household and the security that children provide for parents in their old age. In societies where children are both wanted and economically important, childlessness is considered to be a major tragedy.

High rates of fertility exist not only because of the strong desire for large families, but also because of the high rates of infant and childhood mortality. It is not uncommon, especially in poorer rural communities, to encounter women who have watched half of their offspring die. As long as the survival of children to adulthood remains uncertain, Africans will continue to have many children.

Enhanced health care programs can have contradictory effects on fertility. Child-health programs hold the promise of reduced infant mortality and, ultimately, lower fertility rates.

Rates of vaccination coverage have increased markedly since the early 1980s, thanks to the Expanded Immunization Program sponsored by the United Nations International Children's Emergency Fund (UNICEF) and the World Health Organization (WHO). Other strategies to lower infant and child mortality include promoting breast-feeding and the use of oral rehydration solution to treat diarrhea. In the short run, however, improved health care may actually increase birth rates by improving the care of pregnant women and reducing chronic venereal infections that cause infertility.

The desire for large families helps to account for a very high rate of marriage among young adult women. Traditional African societies have strongly favored early marriage of women; puberty is considered to be the ideal age for marriage in many societies. Consequently, most women spend the great majority of their fertile years (approximately 15 to 45 years of age) married. This maximizes the potential fertility of individual women and collectively of the entire society.

Thus far most Africans have resisted attempts to introduce modern birth-control technology. Zimbabwe, Benin, and Kenya are the only countries where more than 15% of women of reproductive age use any form of modern birth control. In most countries less than 5% of women use modern contraceptives (Figure 8.6a). These low rates contrast strikingly with those from many other parts of the Third World–71% in China, 50% in Brazil, and 35% in India, for example.

Although many African governments officially support family-planning programs, none can be said to be aggressive supporters of such programs. Several countries offer no support for family planning and even prohibit the sale of contraceptives (Figure 8.6b). Some countries are pronatalist, that is, have as official policy the promotion of higher birth rates. Support for family-planning initiatives tends to be low in west-central Africa, a region with certain countries (e.g., Gabon, Central African Republic) that have rather low fertility levels and small national populations. Most Islamic countries (e.g., Somalia, Mauritania) do not support family planning programs.

Family-planning programs have often been introduced as part of larger foreign-aid packages. Acceptance, therefore, may be a pragmatic decision having nothing to do with support for making birth control more readily available. Governments that are ambivalent about family planning are unlikely to commit the resources needed for a successful program. Moreover, the programs become susceptible to rumors that they are neocolonial and un-African or that the use of contraceptives has caused health problems among women. Such rumors increase popular resistance to birth control and are very hard to counteract.

The common assumption that modern birth control is being introduced into a vacuum ignores important mechanisms whereby individuals and societies have limited fertility. Extended sexual abstinence following birth, together with the fertility-limiting effect of prolonged breast-feeding, provide extremely effective traditional means of spacing births. African women commonly breast-feed their babies for 18 to 30 months and abstain from intercourse on the grounds that becoming pregnant too soon would jeopardize the health of the breast-feeding baby. However, as modern education and the promotion of infant formula change attitudes about the care of infants, especially among urban dwellers, traditional birth-limiting strategies are practiced less carefully, causing some increase in fertility.

While high fertility is the norm in African

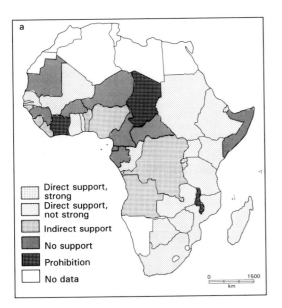

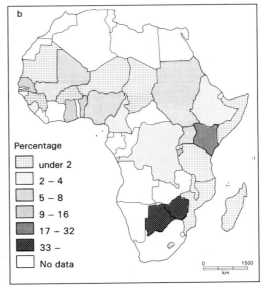

Figure 8.6. Population policies and family planning, mid-1980s. (a) Government policy with respect to family planning. (b) Use of modern contraception by married women of reproductive age (percentage). Data source: World Bank. *World Development Reports, 1986–1990.* New York: Oxford University Press, 1991.

a

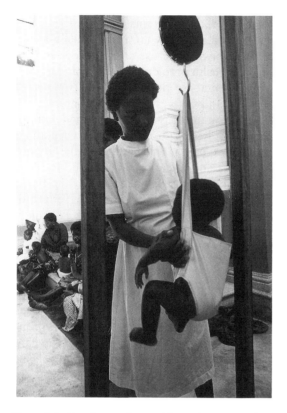

b

Figure 8.7. Two keys to less rapid population growth. (a) Infant being weighed, Mozambique. Improved maternal and child health care help to reduce infant mortality and ultimately pave the way for smaller families. (b) Family planning clinic, Zimbabwe. Zimbabwe's family planning program, among Africa's most successful, is closely linked to the health care system. Photos: CIDA: (a) B. Paton, (b) D. Barbour.

societies, smaller families are becoming increasingly common among urbanites with above-average incomes and education levels. Urbanites have comparatively easy access to information and technology for all aspects of child rearing and birth control, and they consider smaller families to be the key to obtaining better educational chances for their children and better opportunities for material progress themselves. Birth control also makes it easier for upwardly mobile women to combine child rearing and a career.

The recent experience of Zimbabwe is noteworthy because of the country's exceptional success in reducing fertility. Zimbabwe's crude birth rate fell from 53 in 1970 to 36 in 1991. This achievement has been attributed to the country's strong commitment to fami-

ly planning in conjunction with broad-based economic development, improved health care, and enhanced opportunities for women. By promoting birth control as a means of birth *spacing* rather than birth *limitation*, much of the cultural resistance to the technology has been overcome. The Zimbabwean example points to the possibility of an African fertility transition comparable to that experienced elsewhere in the Third World when effective population planning occurs as part of a sound strategy of socioeconomic development.

Explaining Africa's High Mortality

Although crude rates of mortality in Africa south of the Sahara have declined markedly since the 1960s, the reduction has been less spectacular than in other parts of the world. Mortality rates for children under the age of 5 remain particularly high (Figure 8.8). The mortality rate for children under 5 is one of the most sensitive measures of underdevelopment and poverty; the survival of children is influenced by multiple factors, including health care, nutrition, sanitation, and parents' education. The poorest countries continue to have the highest rates of infant and child mortality. Sample surveys in certain very poor rural areas have found that one-third or more of children die before the age of 5. However, under-5 mortality rates such as 91 per 1,000 live births in South Africa, 139 in Côte d'Ivoire, and 167 in Gabon show that nations that are better off also continue to have unacceptably high infant and child mortality. The

key is not wealth but the uses to which that wealth is put.

Between 1970 and 1991, national rates of infant mortality declined by an average of about 30%. Childhood vaccination programs have made possible much of this reduction, especially since the implementation during the 1980s of the UNICEF–WHO Expanded Immunization Program to protect children against the main deadly diseases, including measles, whooping cough, tetanus, and polio.

Because of the high levels of mortality, especially infant mortality, life expectancies are significantly lower than in other parts of the world. Life expectancy at birth is below 50 years in 21 countries and below 60 years in 40 countries. Botswana, South Africa, Zimbabwe, and Cape Verde are the only countries where life expectacy is above 60 years.

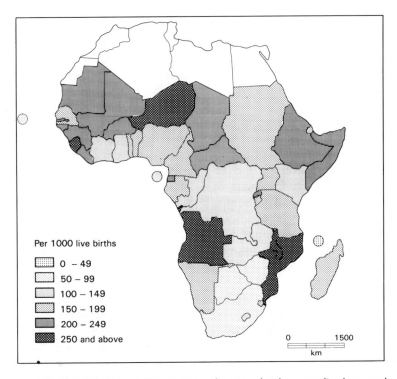

Figure 8.8. Under-5 mortality rate. Mortality rates for the most disadvantaged groups within each country are often well above the already high national values. Data source: UNDP. *Human Development Report, 1991.* New York: Oxford University Press, 1991.

By way of comparison, Haiti is the only country in the Western Hemisphere where life expectancy is less than 60 years.

Conventional explanations of Africa's high mortality have focused on extensive poverty and an unhealthy environment. During the colonial era, the pervasiveness of environmental health risks was emphasized. Disease, malnutrition, and poverty were seen as parts of a vicious circle preventing development. This pessimistic assessment of the African condition helped to legitimate colonial rule, first by singling out disease vectors and parasites as the main cause of underdevelopment, and second by casting Europeans in the role of saviors who would eventually liberate Africa from its disease burden.

Now as then, even the most "environmental" of diseases reflect the political and economic milieu in which they occur. Malaria is the most deadly of such diseases, killing an estimated 500,000 African children each year and contributing to the deaths of many more who succumb to opportunistic infections that often follow malaria. Malaria is less often fatal to adults, but recurrent bouts of fever, which occur as new batches of malarial parasites are released into the blood stream, cause weakness, susceptibility to other infections, and decreased productivity.

Malaria is transmitted from person to person by the female anopheles mosquito. Thus, the mosquito population, the sizes of infected and susceptible human populations, and the opportunities for mosquito–human contact all affect the probability of the spread of the disease. Sources of stagnant water where mosquito larvae may develop—small ponds and rain barrels, for example—are ubiquitous in poor communities that are crowded, poorly drained, and deprived of modern amenities. Such communities are likely to have not only the highest rates of infectivity but also inadequate or nonexistent health care facilities where cases of malaria may be treated. Moreover, malaria and the infections that accompany it are likely to be most debilitating and fatal among those who are undernourished. The recent resurgence of malaria throughout Africa is part-

ly attributable to the decline in nutritional status among the poor in both urban and rural areas.

During the 1960s the WHO launched a global campaign to eradicate malaria. Breeding sites were drained or sprayed with a thin film of oil to suffocate the mosquito larvae, and homes were sprayed with residual-action insecticides. Antimalarial drugs were used to treat malarial patients and were given as a prophylactic to susceptible populations. This chemical onslaught against malaria failed, primarily because the mosquitoes developed resistance to pesticides and the malarial parasites became resistant to the widely used antimalarial drugs. Moreover, budgetary cutbacks resulted in malaria control programs that were intermittent at best. The strains of malaria now prevalent are much deadlier and harder to control than those of the past.

Schistosomiasis, which afflicts perhaps 200 million Africans, is another disease that is only superficially environmental. Transmission from one person to another takes place indirectly. The eggs of schistosoma (a blood fluke) pass via urine into a freshwater source. After hatching, the larvae mature within the bodies of certain species of snails, before reentering the water. The transmission cycle is completed when the schistosoma penetrate the skin of someone entering the water. This "environmental" disease continues to thrive because of the development priorities of governments and aid agencies. The establishment of irrigation projects without programs to control snails has caused the disease to proliferate among farmers who work in snail-infested irrigation water. The construction of dams and reservoirs has also increased transmission; infection rates commonly exceed 75% in lakeside communities. At the same time, the failure to provide adequate sources of safe water means that the majority of rural Africans must still rely on infected natural sources for their domestic water supplies.

Cholera is another disease of underdevelopment that is less environmental than it initially seems. Cholera is spread through food or water that has been contaminated with feces from an infected person. It is almost always confined to the poor, whether residents of crowded and unsanitary slums or villagers forced to use local wells or streams because safer water is not available. The demise of cholera does not await a miracle cure, only a sustained commitment to public health and social justice.

Other infectious and parasitic diseases similarly reflect the broader political economic environment. Measles, for example, is still one of the leading causes of childhood death. While the periodic recurrence of measles epidemics is inevitable, the same cannot be said for the deaths each year of hundreds of thousands of children from measles and its complications. The vaccine that prevents these deaths in industrialized countries costs pennies per child. Yet, until very recently, childhood vaccination programs in Africa were poorly and sporadically organized. Again, it has been the rural poor who have suffered most from this neglect.

While the long-established "environmental" diseases continue as major causes of death, excess mortality is increasingly related to the sale of potentially lethal products in the African marketplace and to the deepening crises of underdevelopment. These newer causes of disease and death are included in Table 8.2 (see numbers 8 to 10), which identifies several types of health problems linked to underdevelopment.

Third World markets have become increasingly important for transnational companies as demand for products such as tobacco and infant fomula shrink in the industrialized countries because of slow-growing populations, changing lifestyles, and health education. Tobacco sales in Africa have increased fivefold in 20 years in response to heavy advertising; the inevitable proliferation of lung cancer and other smoking-related diseases has begun to occur. The use of infant formula has continued to grow in response to aggressive marketing campaigns, despite the poor economic situation that makes formula prohibitively expensive for most Africans. The advertisements for infant formula promise healthier babies, but

the reality is exactly the opposite for poor mothers unable to prepare sufficient, safe, sterile formula for their babies. Several studies point to the inappropriate use of formula results as the most important cause of infant deaths in Africa.

The health costs of continuing insurrections and wars are staggering—communities abandoned for the relative safety of refugee camps, crops unsown or unharvested because of fighting, health centers destroyed, medicines diverted to treat military casualties, and so on. To give one small example, Angola leads the world in amputations per capita, the legacy of over 30 years of anticolonial struggle and externally funded insurrection.

While the link between health and development is very widely acknowledged, liberal and radical scholars differ in how these linkages are interpreted. Liberals have tended to see such problems as the unintended side-effects of naive development initiatives and have seen more health-sensitive planning as the solution. Radicals have argued that ill health is intregally and inevitably linked to profit-driven capitalist underdevelopment. They point to the frequent repetition of past mistakes, long after their thorough exposure in the development literature, as evidence that the health effects of the capitalist quest for profit are neither accidental nor unanticipated.

The following discussion of debates about rapid population growth elaborates upon the importance of analytic perspective, showing how it affects the choice of questions asked and the kinds of solutions that are likely to be proposed.

Evaluating the Causes and Consequences of Rapid Population Growth

The plight of nations with rapidly growing populations has been the subject of strenuous debate. While all agree that rapid population growth is significant, there is no agreement about the nature of the problem or appropriate solutions. The four major perspectives are

Table 8.2. Diseases of Underdevelopment

Development processes related to increased health risks	Examples of the resultant health problems
1. Changes in society–environment relationships (e.g., resettlement in a different ecological milieu)	Epidemics of infectious and parasitic diseases (e.g., sleeping sickness, malaria, river blindness)
2. Increased population movements owing to improved transportation and quest for opportunity	Previously uninfected people exposed to tuberculosis, malaria, and other infections
3. Changes in water flow and use (e.g., with dams and irrigation schemes)	Increased risk of waterborne diseases, (e.g., schistosomiasis and guinea worm)
4. Changes in vegetation cover affecting habitat of disease vectors	Increased risk of vectored diseases (e.g., sleeping sickness, river blindness, and yellow fever)
5. Microenvironmental changes (e.g., in house construction and neighborhood density)	Cerebrospinal meningitis, tuberculosis, cholera, and other infectious diseases
6. Changes in value systems and erosion of traditional values	Stress, mental illness, suicide, malnutrition, AIDS
7. More environmental pollution and introduction of industrial and agricultural chemicals	Cancers, respiratory diseases, fetal abnormalities, poisoning of food chains (e.g., fish)
8. Marketing of potentially harmful consumer goods (e.g., tobacco, infant formulas, alcohol, drugs)	Malnutrition, infant diarrhea, cancers, respiratory diseases, addiction, allergic reactions
9. Increased armed conflict within and between nations, directly and indirectly affecting health	Hunger and malnutrition from economic disruption, psychosocial, and physical trauma
10. Debt crises forcing states to cut social services, raise taxes, reduce public sector employment	Hunger and malnutrition, psychosocial stress, shortages of essential drugs

Based on C. C. Hughes and J. M. Hunter. "Disease and development in tropical Africa." *Social Science and Medicine*, vol. 3 (1970), pp. 443–493. R. Stock. "Disease and development or the underdevelopment of health." *Social Science and Medicine*, vol. 23 (1986), pp. 689–700.

as follows: (1) neo-Malthusian, (2) diffusionist, (3) dependency, and (4) Marxist.

Thomas Malthus, a 19th-century economist, developed a theory of population growth and resource scarcity that is still very influential, especially in conservative circles. Malthus predicted inevitable misery as the geometric growth of population outstripped food supplies. He stated that without preventative checks to reduce fertility, population growth would be halted by rising mortality. For modern neo-Malthusian writers such as Paul Ehrlich and Garret Hardin, a classic example of the catastrophe predicted by Malthus is now emerging in Africa. The solutions proposed by neo-Malthusians are often drastic; Hardin, for example, has advocated "lifeboat ethics," a survival-of-the-fittest doctrine that argues for the abandonment of most poverty-stricken

states and the use of drastic salvage measures in other Third World countries that have strategic importance.

The diffusionist view is that population growth is a serious problem that threatens global stability but that technological innovations in birth control, medicine, and agriculture provide the ingredients for a solution. The primary challenges, then, are to make the requisite technology easily accessible and to convince people to adopt it. This has been the view espoused by most governments and international development agencies.

Dependency theorists emphasize that population size and growth are less important than the maldistribution of resources at a global scale. The per capita consumption of resources by Africans is only a fraction of that of North Americans and Europeans. Therefore, dependency theorists insist that the focus should be on an equitable redistribution of the earth's resources rather than population control. Socially just development would naturally bring about the demographic transition to low birth and death rates and eliminate the need for coercion.

Marxists also reject the view that population growth is the cause of socioeconomic crises in Africa. Rather, they focus on capitalist exploitation that concentrates ownership of land and wealth in fewer and fewer hands and exploits a proletariat that must sell its labor to survive. In fact, the growth of population may be functional for capitalism since it has enabled rural economies to survive despite outmigration to the cities. Marxist analysts reject reformist solutions and call for fundamental political and social change to reorganize society and, thereby, mobilize the resources needed to sustain present and future populations.

The relation between development theory and practice continues to shift, reflecting changing geopolitical dynamics as well as new development ideas and priorities. In the post–Cold War era of the 1990s, the commitment of many aid donors to assisting Africa's poorest countries seems to be waning. A neo-Malthusian approach, whereby aid to many of Africa's poorest nationsis being reduced or eliminated, is replacing the previous diffusionist approach with its emphasis on aid as a stimulus for development. Meanwhile, many radical critics of conventional aid programs, ironically, are decrying these cutbacks in the kinds of development initiatives they have long condemned.

With populations doubling every 20 to 25 years, the nations of Africa south of the Sahara face an enormous challenge. The growing population stretches resources to the limit even in comparatively wealthy countries such as Côte d'Ivoire and Zimbabwe. In poor, ecologically vulnerable and already densely populated countries such as Burundi and Burkina Faso, the future is much more precarious. There is no reason to expect that the crises of basic sustenance that have received so much global attention since 1970 are about to end.

Given the economic, political, and social status quo of the early 1990s, there is ample reason for pessimism about Africa's ability to avert catastrophe. Rapid population growth, however, is not the preeminent problem; the present crises would in all probability have occurred even if the population had remained stable. To focus on population control as *the key* to solving Africa's problems is inappropriate and futile, for African women will continue to bear many children as long as so many of them die unnecessarily from diseases of underdevelopment.

Further Reading

The following is a useful sourcebook on African demography:

Gregory, J., D. Cordell, and R. Gervais. *African Historical Demography: A Multidisciplinary Bibliography*. Los Angeles: Crossroads, 1984.

For current data on population growth, see the following annually published sources:

Population Reference Bureau. *World Population Data Sheet*.
United Nations. *Demographic Yearbook*.
World Bank. *World Development Report*.

The nature and significance of population growth are examined in the following sources:

Goliber, T. J. "Africa's expanding population: Old problems, new policies." *Population Bulletin*, vol. 44, no. 3 (1989).
Kelley, A. C., and C. E. Noble, *Kenya at the Demographic Turning Point?* Washington: World Bank, 1990.
Sai, F. T. "The population factor in Africa's development dilemma." *Science*, vol. 226 (1984), pp. 801–805.
United Nations. *Population Growth and Policies in Africa south of the Sahara*. New York, 1986.

For additional sources focusing on African fertility, see the following sources:

Adegbola, A. "New estimates of fertility and child mortality in Africa south of the Sahara." *Population Studies*, vol. 31 (1977), pp. 467–486.

Caldwell, J. C. "The economic rationality of high fertility: An investigation illustrated with Nigerian survey data." *Population Studies*, vol. 31 (1977), pp. 5–28.

Cochrane, S., and S. Farid. *Fertility in Sub-Saharan Africa: Analysis and Explanation*. Washington: World Bank, 1990.

Doenges, C. E., and J. L. Newman. "Impaired fertility in tropical Africa." *Geographical Review*, vol. 79 (1989), pp. 101–111.

Gregory, J. W., and V. Piche. "African population: reproduction for whom?" *Daedalus*, vol. 111 (1982), pp. 179–209.

The following studies look at patterns of disease and death and their explanation:

Hughes, J., and J. M. Hunter. "Disease and development in tropical Africa." *Social Science and Medicine*, vol. 3 (1970), pp. 443–493.

Prothero, R. M. "Disease and human mobility: a neglected factor in epidemiology." *International Journal of Epidemiology*, vol. 6 (1977), pp. 259–267.

Packard, R. "Industrial production, health and disease in sub-Saharan Africa." *Social Science and Medicine*, vol. 28 (1989), pp. 475–496.

Spencer, B. G., and I. Winkowska. "A multivariate analysis of mortality in rural Africa." *African Studies Review*, vol. 34 (1991), pp. 81–96.

Stock, R. "Disease and development or the underdevelopment of health." *Social Science and Medicine*, vol. 23 (1986), pp. 689–700.

Turshen, M. *The Political Ecology of Disease in Tanzania*. New Brunswick, NJ: Rutgers University Press, 1984.

9

Population Mobility

Africans are highly mobile, and their oral histories indicate that this has been so since time immemorial. The effects of migration extend far beyond gains or losses in population numbers: Migrants bring with them their fertility, their wealth, their skills, their culture, and a host of personal characteristics, modifying in the process both the communities of destination and of origin.

Explanations of African Population Mobility

The reasons why people migrate are extremely varied—sometimes the quest for new opportunities, sometimes the flight to safety from turmoil or ecological disaster, and sometimes the observance of social or religious custom. Three types of explanations are often advanced to account for high mobility rates in Africa south of the Sahara:

1. Some writers have examined population mobility as an important dimension of African culture, viewing modern migrations as a continuation of the continent's long tradition of population mobility.
2. Some have focused on the importance of perceived economic opportunities as a stimulus for migration.

3. Others have argued that migration in Africa occurs primarily as a response to forces that essentially compel people to move.

Africans' long history of mobility is reflected not only in countless local legends of the migration of ancestors but also in major migrations that occurred over several centuries and that have been verified. The Bantu colonization of the southern half of the continent, which took place as a many-staged process over five millenia, is the most important of many known historical migrations. Studies of the interrelation among languages, patterns of diffusion of particular cultural practices and technologies, and genetic analysis not only prove that past migrations occurred but also help to unravel the complex relation between patterns of mobility and the sociocultural evolution of the continent. Several more recent large-scale migrations, such as the exodus of the Ndebele from South Africa to Zimbabwe in the mid–19th century, are part of the modern historical record.

More localized forms of circulation associated with seasonal rhythms in traditional economies are also rooted in antiquity. For example, many pastoralists move between seasonal pastures in order to have access to adequate water and fodder for their animals and to minimize risks from ecological dangers.

Another example is provided by the seasonal movement of many agriculturalists from their home farms to riverine sites where irrigation is possible. Other types of mobility associated with trade and craft production also existed long before European rule was imposed.

For many Africans, religious and social obligations have been an important stimulus for migration. Since the 14th century reign of Emperor Mansa Musa of Mali, West African Muslims have been traveling to Mecca and other holy places of Islam. Many West Africans have settled permanently along the entire savanna corridor through Sudan once followed by most pilgrims (see Vignette 9.1). The pilgrimage is an example of a long-established migration stream that grew significantly in the more stable political environment of the colonial era.

The scale and diversity of past migrations have been cited as evidence that Africans have always been mobile and that they have a propensity to migrate. Colonial officials sometimes used this evidence to justify the recruitment of migrant labor. The interpretation of migration as traditional has occasionally been extended to the analysis of contemporary labor migrations, which have been characterized at times as a modern rite of passage for young African males—essentially a part of their initiation into manhood.

Many studies have focused on the economic context within which population mobility has taken place, particularly during the colonial and postcolonial eras. The various economic explanations of migration focus on the disparities of development between stagnant migrant source areas and the "islands of economic development" to which migrants are attracted. These economic models conceptualize mobility as a voluntary response by individuals who are motivated to take advantage of opportunities, particularly the availability of jobs. It is generally assumed that migrants have sufficient knowledge of opportunities at potential destinations to be able to make rational choices.

One of the leading economic theorists of migration is Michael Todaro, who claimed that artificially high urban wages maintained by government policy attract migrants to the city from the rural periphery. While this migration may be perfectly rational for the individual, it can be counterproductive for the society and economy because too many migrants respond to the high urban wages. Therefore, Todaro advocated that wage differentials be eliminated to reduce rural to urban migration.

The Todaro model formalizes earlier descriptive models of migration behavior, notably the push–pull and "bright lights" models. The first of these draws an analogy between the forces underlying migration and the physical forces of push and pull: Push factors are those that encourage the potential migrant to leave an unsatisfactory home environment, while pull factors are attractive aspects of a place of opportunity. The attraction of the "bright lights" of the city is another simple analogy used to explain migration behavior. The "bright lights" are seen as being especially influential for young people who have attended school and developed aspirations for a modern lifestyle.

Individual response to perceived opportunities certainly is reflected in migrant behavior. Political economists, however, question whether the primary determinant of mobility is the perception of opportunity elsewhere or the structural factors impinging on the lives of potential migrants. They point to the historical effects of deliberate colonial policies that sought to cause laborers to migrate, such as the imposition of a head tax. In parts of the continent located far from the coast and from transportation routes, the production of cash crops was not a viable option, forcing people to earn tax money by selling their labor in more commercially developed regions. The function in the colonial economy of these labor reserves was to provide a source of cheap, captive labor. Other colonial policies also effectively forced Africans to sell their labor to survive. The expropriation of lands for European agriculture and forest reserves undermined the viability of indigenous economies; African producers were forced in many cases to relocate in smaller, less fertile areas. Epidemics of rinderpest and trypanosomiasis occurred near forest reserves, often decimating

Vignette 9.1. The Overland Pilgrimage to Mecca

Each year, hundreds of thousands of West Africans travel by air to Saudi Arabia as pilgrims to Islam's holy places. A few thousand still follow the overland route from Nigeria through Chad and Sudan to the Red Sea, a route used by pilgrims for three centuries (Figure 9.1). The overland pilgrimage reached its maximum extent between the 1920s and 1950s; the consolidation of colonial rule made the journey safer, the introduction of trucks made it faster and easier, and the opportunities for work along the way made it financially attainable.

The significance of the pilgrimage extends beyond its religious meanings. The pilgrimage route has served as a cultural conduit along which innovations such as new crops, farming techniques, and styles of architecture have spread, both eastward and westward. The journey is seldom completed in less than three years and may be spread over two to three decades. Pilgrims traditionally have taken jobs along the way to finance the journey. They work as farm laborers, porters, petty traders, barbers, and in other mostly menial jobs. Their economic role has been especially significant in the Gezira irrigation scheme.

West Africans, or "Fellata" as they are called in Sudan, have established many villages along the pilgrimage route and also have their own neighborhoods (*zongos*) in the larger towns. Pilgrims en route stay in these communities and obtain information about the journey and employment opportunities. Hausa is the lingua franca of the Fellata, reflecting the predominance of northern Nigerians among the pilgrims. There are more than 1 million Fellata in Sudan, representing some 5% of the national population. Although many have been there for several generations, the Fellata are regarded as temporary residents by the Sudanese government. As outsiders who often speak Arabic poorly and who willingly accept unattractive jobs, they have low social status. Both the Nigerian and Sudanese governments occasionally have found it expedient politically to demand the repatriation of the Fellata. However, only token repatriations have occurred.

The diverse effects of the overland pilgrimage illustrate an important facet of African population mobility, namely that the characteristics and meanings of particular migrations are seldom as simple as they first appear.

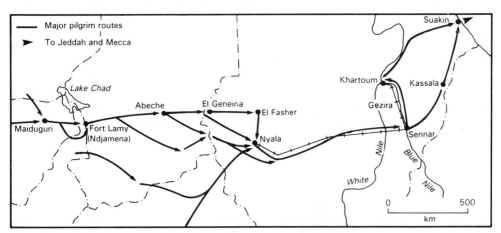

Figure 9.1. The overland pilgrimage from West Africa to Mecca. After J. S. Birks, "Overland pilgrimmage in the savanna lands of Africa." In L. A. Kosinski and R. M. Prothero, eds., *People of the Move.* London: Methuen, 1975, p. 303.

Vignette 9.2. The Struggle for Swazi Labor

The discovery of the Witwatersrand gold fields in 1886 had profound consequences for then-existing economies and societies in southern Africa. Out of the insatiable demand of the gold mining industry for cheap, unskilled male labor and the resistance of Africans to being uprooted from the land emerged South Africa's notorious migrant labor system. By 1915, some 200,000 black migrant workers were employed in 60 mines.

The recruitment of African labor into South Africa's commercial economy has often been characterized as having taken place smoothly and inevitably. In reality, African workers resisted being forced to work in the mines and found various ways of responding creatively to the challenges they faced.

The incorporation of Swazi workers into this system took place unevenly between 1890 and 1920. Three general phases, pre-1900, 1900 to 1910, and 1910 to 1920, can be discerned in this process of incorporation. Each phase was characterized by a different set of circumstances and responses by the Swazi.

During the first phase, the Swazi remained virtually immune to the demands of the mining industry. Colonization and the first imposition of colonial taxes did not take place until 1895 to 1897. The kingdom of Swaziland was a highly structured sociopolitical system, in which all males were members of national age regiments and duty bound to perform certain tasks on behalf of the king. Moreover, the country's agricultural productivity was so great that the Swazi had no economic reason to migrate.

The first surge of Swazi migrants occurred in 1898 and 1999 in response to a series of ecological crises—four years of drought, locust invasions, and a rinderpest epidemic

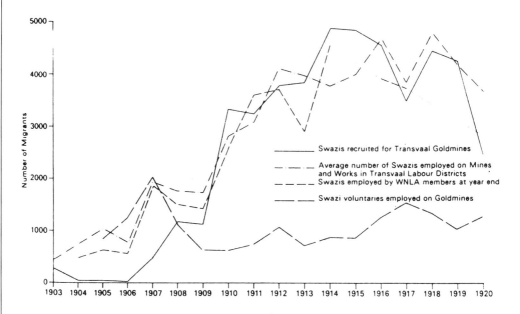

Figure 9.2. Swazi employment in South African gold mines, 1903 to 1920. WNLA (Witwatersrand Native Labour Association) was established by a group of mines to recruit workers. Source: J. S. Crush. "Swazi migrant workers and the Witwatersrand gold mines, 1886–1902," *Journal of Historical Geography*, vol. 12 (1986), pp. 27–40. ©1986 by Academic Press. Reprinted by permission.					*cont.*

Vignette 9.2. (cont.)

---

that killed 80 to 90% of the cattle. Most of the migrants avoided the labor recruiters who had flooded the country, preferring instead to make their own way to the mines. The work environment they encountered was brutal and unsafe—and for many, fatal.

The next surge of migrant labor did not occur until 1907 and 1908 (Figure 9.2). Because of their distaste for the squalid and dangerous conditions in the mines, many Swazi had taken advantage of other work opportunities on plantations, in coal mines, and in the cities. The 1907–1908 wave of migration to the mines took place because many of these other jobs had been lost owing to economic depression. Moreover, the colonial state was aggressively pursuing tax offenders, and labor migration was now being encouraged by Swazi chiefs who needed to raise money to contest colonial land policies. Most workers went independently and, thus, sought to avoid the most dangerous mines and tasks.

After 1909, Swazi employment patterns changed. Not only did the numbers going to the mines more than double, but the majority for the first time signed on with labor recruiters. Local traders who operated as recruiters provided cash advances and other incentives to secure workers for particular mines.

By 1920, the growth of labor migration had undermined traditional political institutions. Working in the mines had become an integral part of Swazi economic and social life.

Based on J. S. Crush. *The Struggle for Swazi Labour, 1890–1920.* Kingston, Ontario: McGill-Queen's University Press, 1987.

---

herds of cattle and forcing pastoralists to resort to labor migration.

Because wages in the modern sector were low, African migrant workers continued to rely on subsistence production in their home localities to make ends meet. In effect, they had to maintain one foot in the rural periphery and the other in the cash-economy core and had to migrate back and forth between them. The term labor migrancy has sometimes been used to describe this situation in which survival became dependent on combining wage labor and peasant subsistence production.

Political independence has altered but not diminished the influence of structural processes on migration. For example, modern development schemes involving irrigation and large-scale commercial agriculture displace small producers from their farms, contributing to increased population pressure in areas of land shortage. The deterioration of marginal environments used too intensively has contributed to widespread crop failures and

hunger, while wars and civil unrest have forced millions to flee their homes.

The danger with purely structural explanations, however, is that the behavior of ordinary Africans may be seen as entirely determined by, and purely in the interest of, capitalism. People in socialist economies have also migrated for essentially the same reasons. Moreover, despite the importance of structural determinants, Africans have always made some choices about how and where they earned their incomes, and their choices have not always been those with the greatest apparent benefits for capitalism (see Vignette 9.2).

Colonial and Postcolonial Labor Migration

Colonialism created a pattern of uneven development characterized by isolated nodes of modern economic activity, but with a univer-

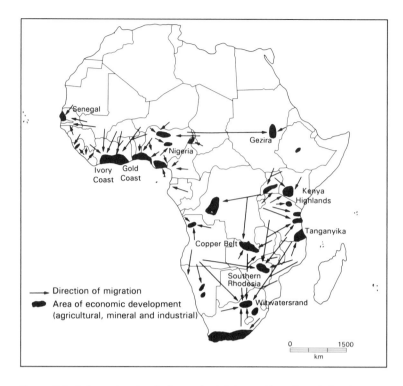

Figure 9.3. Labor migration in late colonial times. Note the relation between the various labor reserve areas and the destinations, that is, islands of economic development. After R. M. Prothero. *Migrants and Malaria.* London: Longman, 1965, p. 42.

sal requirement to participate in the cash economy. Consequently, it was inevitable that major migration streams would emerge between economic cores and their regional peripheries. Figure 9.3 shows the generalized pattern of labor migration as it evolved in Africa south of the Sahara during colonial times. On a continental scale, the spatial differentiation of migration streams is apparent. Labor migrants were attracted to areas with developed cash economies, each of which had its own neglected periphery from which labor was drawn. When migrants sought jobs, the following were the major foci of the migrants' job search:

- South Africa, especially the Witswatersrand mining region and major agricultural areas
- Central Africa, particularly areas of European agriculture in Zimbabwe and the Copper Belts of Zaire and Zambia

- East Africa, notably the former White Highlands of Kenya
- West Africa, especially the major cash-cropping areas of Ghana, Côte d'Ivoire, Senegal, and Nigeria

It is neither possible nor necessary to provide a detailed description of all the major movements of labor in Africa south of the Sahara. The general similarity of the patterns, processes, and meanings of migration in different parts of the continent is such that the discussion of these themes can be confined to a single region—in this instance, migration to and from Ghana and Côte d'Ivoire.

In colonial times, hundreds of thousands of seasonal migrants were attracted to export-cropping zones in southern Ghana and southern Cote d'Ivoire. Most came from the more arid savanna states of the former French West Africa (Burkina Faso, Mali, Niger) and from the northern fringes of Ghana and Togo. In the early decades of colonial rule, direct and indirect forms of coercion were employed to mobilize labor. Migration involved many hundreds of kilometers of travel that often had to be undertaken on foot owing to the poor development of transportation. Prior to 1960, Ghana received more migrants than any other West African country; most migrants came to work on cocoa farms.

In addition to the seasonal migrations of wage labor, permanent migrations of resettlement and agricultural colonization occurred. The expansive migrations of the Akwapim and Krobo peoples in Ghana to establish new cocoa plantations is the best known of these colonial resettlement migrations. At a local scale, many villages were relocated away from ancient defensive sites to downslope locations better suited to farming.

Since independence, the steady decline of the Ghanaian economy has reduced the country's attractiveness for migrants. Recurrent political tensions with Togo, which had been the largest source of migrants to Ghana, and the implementation of the Aliens Compliance Order of 1969, by which all foreign workers without a valid residence permit were expelled, also affected the size of Ghana's migrant population. The combined result was a net loss of about 400,000 foreign nationals between 1965 and 1975.

In contrast, migration to Côte d'Ivoire, especially from Mali and Burkina Faso, continued to increase after 1960. Some 1.4 million people, about one-fifth of the Ivoirian population, was of foreign nationality by the late 1960s. The proportion of immigrants was especially high in Abidjan (one-third of the population) and in other southern districts where export agriculture and forestry are concentrated. The data in Table 9.1 demonstrate the overwhelming importance of Côte d'Ivoire as a destination and of Burkina Faso as the primary source of migrants in this regional migration system. The trends established in the 1960s and 1970s, with the migrant population growing faster than the indigenous population, especially in urban areas, have subsequently continued.

As Ghana's economic crisis deepened after 1970, increasing numbers of Ghanaians left for other countries. Nigeria was very attractive because of the rapid growth of its economy, fueled by petroleum exports. The Ghanaian population in Nigeria differs from the classic African labor migrant population because it contains large numbers of professionals, including teachers, nurses, pharmacists, engineers, and university lecturers. The increasing visibility of immigrants prompted a backlash against them; the Nigerian government ordered all aliens without valid papers to leave in 1983 and again in 1985. An estimated total of 1.5 million non-Nigerians, including 700,000 Ghanaians, were expelled in 1983. These expulsions, however, only temporarily reversed the flow of Ghanaians to Nigeria.

Perhaps the single most important postin-

Table 9.1. Foreign Nationals by Country of Nationality and Country of Enumeration, circa 1975 (in thousands)

Country of Nationality	Country of Enumeration						Total
	Ghana	Côte d'Ivoire	Burkina Faso	Togo	Liberia	Mali	
Ghana	–	43	17	30	7	NA	97
Côte d'Ivoire	18	–	44	NA	2	8	72
Burkina Faso	159	726	–	8	NA	48	941
Togo	244	12	3	–	NA	NA	259
Liberia	5	3	1	NA	–	1	10
Mali	13	349	22	NA	1	–	385
TOTAL	449	1133	87	38	10	57	

After: K. C. Zachariah and J. Conde, *Migration in West Africa: Demographic Aspects.* New York: Oxford University Press, 1981, p. 35.

Figure 9.4. Seasonal labor migrants from Niger, returning home to the farm after working in Côte d'Ivoire. These migrants are likely to return to Côte d'Ivoire in 3 to 4 months, after the farming season. Photo: author.

dependence trend has been the increasing urban orientation of migration streams. While migrants still go to rural areas and work in agriculture, the relative importance of rural-bound migrations has decreased significantly. For example, over half of Côte d'Ivoire's immigrants live in cities, compared to only one-third of the indigenous Ivoirian population. The growth of rural to urban migration reflects the ever-increasing urban–rural disparities in wealth. While rural areas remain neglected and economically stagnant, cities hold out the promise of success for migrants.

The growing rural–urban gap has important implications for women. Women left behind in the countryside have to cope with increased responsibilities because of the absence of so many men. They reap few benefits from migration, since men tend to spend most of what they earn as migrants for their own purposes.

Present-day labor migrants are staying for a longer time. Unlike the colonial era, circulatory movements now very commonly last for more than one dry season. A large proportion of migrants intend to stay in their new place of residence permanently, or at least for several years. They bring their families with them or marry in their new communities. Thus, cities are growing rapidly and an ever-growing proportion of their residents are becoming true urbanites.

Refugees

Africa has the largest concentration of refugees in the world. In 1990 and 1991, the United Nations High Commission for Refugees (UNHCR) had registered 4.8 million refugees in Africa south of the Sahara. The distribution of these registered refugees is shown in Figure 9.5. However, the actual number forced to flee is much larger; a substantial proportion of international refugees is not registered with UNHCR, and many do not report to authorities in their countries of refuge. They may be able to blend unnoticed into the broader population of economically motivated migrants and are sometimes from the same cultural background as the local population. Moreover, available refugee data exclude the many displaced people who migrate to safer places inside their home countries.

The African refugee problem is both pervasive and complex. About three-quarters of the countries of Africa south of the Sahara have been affected significantly as either the origin or destination of at least 10,000 refugees since 1980. Ten countries have both generated and accommodated large numbers of refugees. In some cases, such as Somalia and Rwanda, the number of refugees has been equivalent to 10% or more of the national population.

The following general characteristics describe the recent distribution of refugees and the development of the refugee problem in Africa south of the Sahara since about 1960:

1. There are large clusters of refugees in the Horn of Africa, central Africa, and south-central Africa. There were comparatively few in West Africa until the late 1980s, but Liberia, Sierra Leone, and Mauritania have since become major source of refugees.

2. Both the number of refugees and the number of countries involved have continued to grow since the early 1960s.

3. The flow of refugees has been very uneven, both spatially and temporally.

4. A considerable majority of refugees—perhaps three-quarters—consists of women and children.

5. There are several examples of borders that have been crossed by refugees moving in opposite directions at different points in time. For example, although Sudan has served as a refuge for Ethiopians, at other times Sudanese refugees have fled to Ethiopia.

Refugees are forced to move as a result of various political and ecological disasters. The political causes have included warfare between

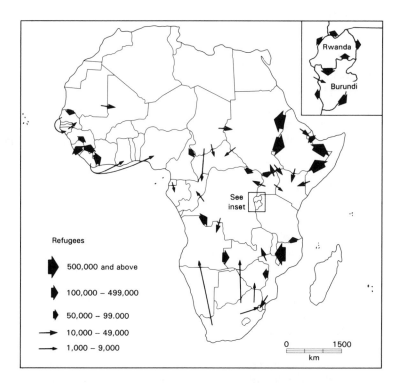

Figure 9.5. Major refugee movements as of 1990 to 1991. These data on official refugee movements often represent only a fraction of the number of people displaced from their homes. Data source: UNHCR. *UNHCR Activities Financed by Voluntary Funds: Report for 1991–92. Part I: Africa.* Geneva: UNHCR, 1992.

Figure 9.6. UNHCR camp for Ethiopian refugees in Sudan. Photo: CIDA: R. Lemoyne.

neighboring countries, anticolonial wars, armed insurrection by guerrilla forces, interethnic conflict, religious persecution, and political repression. The ecological causes include natural disasters like volcanic eruptions and crop failures caused by drought. The distinction between political and ecological causes is blurred because people living in areas of armed conflict often are unable to produce food.

Major influxes of refugees pose a dilemma for the countries to which they have fled. Most refugees arrive with neither material possessions nor any means to support themselves. Thus, it is not enough to simply grant permission for refugees to stay: Their basic needs of food, drinking water, shelter, and health care cannot be ignored. While the UNHCR and other voluntary and governmental agencies provide considerable assistance, much of the burden ultimately falls upon the country of refuge.

For decades, Sudan has been a major destination for refugees fleeing from conflicts in neighboring countries—Zaire, Uganda, Chad, and Ethiopia. The number of officially enumerated refugees increased from 10,000 in the early 1960s to 100,000 in the mid-1970s, 400,000 in the early 1980s, and 1,200,000 in 1986. This number had declined to 750,000 by 1990.

The refugee burden is especially onerous in a country like Sudan, already struggling with inadequate health, education, and transportation systems, recurrent economic crises; widespread drought and hunger; and unresolved religious and political tensions. Sudan discourages the spontaneous resettlement of refugees, directing them instead to government-organized farming settlements where they can grow crops and move toward greater self-reliance. These villages are meant to provide refuge only until repatriation can be done safely, not to facilitate permanent resettlement.

Sudan's acceptance of so many refugees, irrespective of the large costs involved, is in marked contrast to the formidable barriers refugees encounter in many far wealthier countries. Unfortunately, other concurrent policies of the Sudanese government have helped to make southern Sudan one of Africa's largest sources of refugees. Southern Sudanese have fought for three decades to achieve the regional autonomy they consider essential to preserve their own cultures and religions within the Islamic state of Sudan. The prolonged, bitter campaign to quell this insurrection has cost many lives and has forced hundreds of thousands of southern Sudanese to flee their homes.

Beyond the statistical story of millions of Africans forced to move are the individual human stories of personal, family, and community loss. The continuing, massive flow of refugees is not only a symptom of the diverse crises affecting Africa but also a key cause of underdevelopment in both source and destination countries. While effective short-term programs are needed to help poorer countries to cope with refugee influxes and to ensure that the basic needs of refugees are met, the longer-term priority must be to address the political, economic, and ecological disasters that continue to displace so many millions of Africans from their homes.

The Effect of Migration

Migration has diverse demographic and economic effects both in areas of origin and destination. Such effects vary in relation to the type (e.g., labor or refugee), volume, and duration of migration and the characteristics of the migrating population.

Migration alters not only the size of the population but also its composition. Age–sex pyramids for two Liberian regions, one a rural area of heavy outmigration and the other an urban receiving area, demonstrate the predominance of young adult males in African labor migration streams (Figure 9.7). The paucity of young adults, especially young men, in River Cess contrasts markedly with the excess population of young males in Monrovia. The large child population in River Cess occurs because many Liberian parents, even long-term residents of urban centers, prefer to have their children raised in a rural environment.

The proportion of longer-term and permanent migrants to areas of modern-sector employment is increasing. As the duration of stay increases, family migration has increased in prevalence. Nevertheless, urban residents generally maintain important social and economic ties with their ancestral homes. They may make periodic social visits, send school fees to relatives, and invest in a business or construct a house for their eventual retirement.

Migration is commonly said to benefit the economies of sending and receiving areas. In reality, the benefits are very unevenly dis-

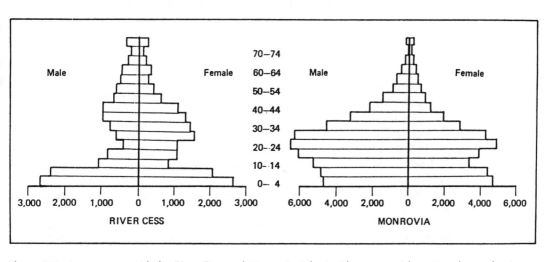

Figure 9.7. Age–sex pyramids for River Cess and Monrovia, Liberia. These pyramids portray the predominance of young males that is typical of rural–urban migration streams in Africa. Data source: Republic of Liberia. *Demographic Annual of the Population Growth Survey, 1970.* Monrovia, Liberia: Department of Planning and Economic Affairs, 1971.

tributed, and the costs often exceed benefits. Recipient economies benefit from the availability of a ready supply of cheap, compliant, and expendable labor. These benefits accrue primarily to employers; the arrival of a "reserve army" of would-be workers adversely affects the job security, wages, and working conditions of the established labor force.

Regions of outmigration may benefit by a somewhat reduced population pressure and the infusion of remittances – money sent home to purchase necessities for family members, to buy consumer goods, or to start a business. However, there are significant costs. Farming production often declines because of the loss of labor. Crops requiring high labor inputs may be replaced by less labor-intensive but inferior alternatives. For example, the substitution of cassava for yams and grain crops saves labor but adversely affects nutrition. Crafts industries and local trade decline because of the loss through migration of producers and consumers. The burden of holding together rural economies and societies is increasingly delegated to the women who remain behind. Despite the constant infusion of remittances from migrants, most source areas have remained as poor as ever. Whatever remittances are received are poor compensation for the loss of the talents and energies of the young people who leave. What remains is a stagnant relict economy.

Further Reading

For discussions of theoretical issues related to African migration, see the following sources:

Gould, W. T. S., and R. M. Prothero. "Space and time in African population mobility". In L. A. Kosinski and R. M. Prothero, eds. *People on the Move*. pp. 39–49. London: Methuen, 1975.

Gregory, J. W., and V. Piche. "African migration and peripheral capitalism." *African Perspective*, no. 1 (1978), pp. 37–50.

Todaro, M. P. "A model of labour migration and urban unemployment in less developed coun-

tries." *American Economic Review*, vol. 99 (1969), pp. 138–148.

For studies on labor migration in various regions of Africa, see the following sources:

Amin, S. *Modern Migrations in Western Africa*. London: Oxford University Press, 1974.

Arthur, J. A., "International labour migration patterns in West Africa." *African Studies Review*, vol. 34 (1991), pp. 65–89.

Clark, J. I., and L. A. Kosinski, eds. *Redistribution of Population in Africa*. London: Heinemann, 1982.

Crush, J. S. *The Struggle for Swazi Labour, 1890–1920*. Kingston, Ontario: McGill-Queen's University Press, 1987.

Crush, J. S., A. Jeeves, and D. Yudelman. *South Africa's Labour Empire: A History of Black Migrancy to the Gold Mines*. Boulder, CO: Westview, 1991.

Murray, C. *Families Divided: The Impact of Migrant Labour in Lesotho*. Cambridge: Cambridge University Press, 1981.

Pottier, J. *Migrants No More: Settlement and Survival in Mambwe Villages, Zambia*. Bloomington: Indiana University Press, 1988.

Van Onselen, C. *Chibaro: African Mine Labour in Southern Rhodesia 1900–1933*. London: Pluto, 1976.

Zachariah, K. C., and J. Conde. *Migration in West Africa: Demographic Aspects*. Oxford: Oxford University Press, 1981.

Zegeye, A., and S. Ishemo, eds. *Forced Labour and Migration: Patterns of Movement within Africa*. London: Hans Zell, 1989.

To learn more about refugees in Africa, see the following sources:

Black, R. "Refugees and displaced persons: Geographical perspectives and research directions." *Progress in Human Geography*, vol. 15 (1991), pp. 281–298.

Harrell-Bond, B. E. *Imposing Aid: Emergency Assistance to Refugees*. Oxford: Oxford University Press, 1986.

Refugees (a journal published by UNHCR).

Rogge, J. *Too Many, Too Long: Sudan's Twenty-Year Refugee Dilemma*. Totowa, NJ: Rowman and Allanheld, 1985.

Rogge, J. *Refugees: A Third World Dilemma*. Totowa, NJ: Rowman and Littlefield, 1987.

RURAL ECONOMIES

*The majority of Africans live in rural areas and work as primary producers, rely-
ing on their skills as farmers, herders, fishers, and hunters to secure the necessities of life from the natural environment. The chapters in this section concentrate
on primary production as the focus of rural economies. This topic provides many
opportunities for examining such core themes as the importance of the environment for human sustenance, the cultural foundations upon which systems of
production rest, and the significance for rural societies of colonial and postcolonial
development initiatives.*

*Chapter 10 describes the major indigenous systems of food production, em-
phasizing the logic of these systems—the diverse strategies whereby sustenance
is obtained from often difficult environments. These systems of production are
an integral part of the African cultural endowment; each society has its own set
of strategies and divisions of labour for the production of food. However, despite
the resilience of indigenous systems of production, their health if not survival has
been threatened in many areas by inappropriate policies, population growth, and
environmental degradation.*

*Chapter 11 examines the legacy of a century of attempts to modernize African
agriculture, with often disappointing and sometimes disasterous consequences.
The colonial policy of introducing cash crops was designed primarily to incorporate Africans into the commercial economy and to create a source of tropical
products valued by Europeans, rather than to improve the lot of rural Africans.
A variety of agrarian development strategies has been tried in recent decades,
but the models for development have usually been foreign, costly, and unsustainable. Newer approaches that build upon existing systems of production and
focus on small farmers provide some reason for optimism.*

*In Chapter 12, the subject is the food crisis in Africa, a crisis that has grown
so much in magnitude that images of starvation have come to epitomize Africa
for many in North America. The occurrence of critical food shortages have been
very uneven in space, in time, and within the societies of affected regions. The*

chapter examines the distinction between chronic hunger, which occurs year after year in certain settings, and acute food shortages of famines. The diverse explanations of hunger—environmental, demographic, technical, and political—are also considered. It is apparent that just as hunger is an urban as well as a rural phenomenon, its alleviation depends on changes not only in the countryside but also in urban Africa.

10

✳

Indigenous Food Production Systems

Most Africans continue to derive their liveli-hood as primary producers, specifically from farming, raising livestock, fishing, hunting, and gathering. Indigenous systems of food produc-tion are predominant virtually everywhere on the continent. Even in European-controlled regions of South Africa and Zimbabwe, and the small foci of plantation agriculture in sever-al countries, African farm employees utilize indigenous methods of production to obtain food for household consumption.

This chapter focuses on the logic of in-digenous production systems. Research on African agriculture has repeatedly shown the sophistication of these systems as means of extracting a living from often difficult and fragile environments. African primary producers simultaneously pursue several goals: maximizing yields, minimizing the risks as-sociated with drought and other catastrophes, diversifying production for household self-sufficiency, and protecting the resource base. Growing recognition of the importance of en-vironmental protection, the sustainability of systems of production, and dietary diversity, among other issues, is fostering an increased appreciation of African indigenous systems of production.

The term *indigenous* is used in the chapter

in preference to the widely used *traditional*. The word *traditional* may seem to imply that these production systems have been rigid and unchanging. On the contrary, they have con-tinued to evolve in response to diverse in-fluences, including changing ecological circumstances, population growth, market op-portunities, and the introduction of new tech-nologies. One of the most important changes was the adoption of cash-crop cultivation dur-ing the colonial era. Africa's farmers found ways of incorporating these crops into their existing systems of production. More recent-ly, technologies like animal-drawn ploughs, chemical fertilizers, and improved-variety seeds have been adopted and effectively in-corporated into the existing system by many small-scale producers. On the other hand, plantation agriculture, large-scale irrigation, European mechanized agriculture, and cattle ranches are not merely introduced *technologies* but entire introduced *systems* of production.

Food Production

Indigenous food production methods may be grouped into three broad categories: (1) food-crop cultivation; (2) raising livestock, including pastoralism; and (3) fishing, hunting, and gathering.

While it is possible, in theory, for primary producers to rely exclusively on one of these three sources of food, most rural Africans utilize all three. However, the relative importance of each varies greatly from culture to culture and among households in particular communities (Figure 10.1). Most agriculturalists supplement their farm-produced diets with livestock such as chickens and goats, and collect edibles from the wild. Many pastoralists cultivate crops, as well as hunt and gather. Systems of mixed farming, in which raising livestock and cultivating crops are integrated and of relatively equal importance, are widely practiced in certain cultures, as with the Serer of Senegal and the Amhara of Ethiopia.

African primary producers also rely on the marketplace as a supplemental source of food for household use. The marketplace provides access to a variety of locally produced food stuffs, as well as foods produced outside the community, including commercial products like flour and pasta.

African primary producers, to a varying extent, also market what they have produced. In addition to conventional "cash" crops like cocoa and cotton, foods of many kinds are sold: grains and other foodcrops, livestock and livestock products, fish, game, and other foods from the wild. Many farmers have shifted resources into the production of foodstuffs for sale, taking advantage of increasing demand and rising prices in urban areas. These trends point to the blurring of boundaries between categories such as food crops and cash crops, or subsistence and commercial agriculture, around which discussions of African agriculture are often structured.

Fishing, Hunting, and Gathering

Hunting and gathering societies in Africa, as elsewhere, are on the verge of extinction. The

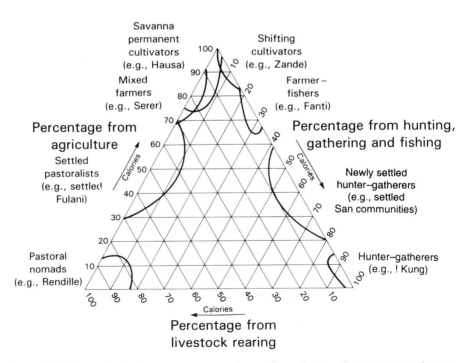

Figure 10.1. Types of subsistence economies. The graph emphasizes the varying significance of agriculture; livestock rearing; and hunting, fishing, and gathering as sources of sustenance.

!Kung San of the Kalahari and The Mbuti (Pygmies) of the Zairean rain forest are societies where hunting and gathering have continued to be practiced widely. Studies of !Kung gathering strategies have shown that they are able to obtain an extremely diverse and nutritious diet with relatively low labor inputs. Game, hunted by adult males, contributes about one-third of calories in the !Kung diet, while vegetable foods, most collected by women and children, account for the remainder. While the !Kung consume numerous plant foods either seasonally or throughout the year, their staple is the highly nutritious mongongo nut. This diet permits the !Kung to live longer and healthier lives than most African farmers.

The marine resources of many parts of the African coast, as well as lakeshore and riverine environments, are an important source of food. For the Fante of the Ghanaian coast and numerous other societies, fishing and agriculture constitute the dual bases of economic activity. Fishing is a year-round activity involving the majority of the economically active population, but most families also farm. The work is usually divided according to gender, with men doing the fishing and women most of the farming, as well as the selling and preparing of fish.

For most Africans, fishing, hunting, and gathering are secondary to the practice of agriculture or pastoralism. The kinds of edible flora and fauna that are harvested seem almost infinite. Such foodstuffs are often gathered seasonally and provide variety and nutritional balance, as well as dietary energy during times of seasonal hunger or crop failure. In many African societies, bush meat—meat from wild animals—and locally harvested fish are important sources of protein. The utilization of wild fauna and flora is discussed further in Chapters 20 and 21.

Farming Systems

Indigenous farming systems in Africa share a number of common characteristics. Farms are small, typically one to five hectares. While the small size of farms sometimes reflects a scarcity of land in heavily populated areas, it more often reflects the limited labor resources available in rural households. Unless hired labor or labor-saving technology is available, the size of farms will be limited to the area that a household can manage during periods of heaviest labor demand—planting, weeding, and harvesting. Trade-offs may be made, depending on the availability of land, between careful, labor-intensive cultivation of small farms and less intensive cultivation relying on lengthy fallows to restore soil fertility in sparsely populated areas.

In most parts of Africa south of the Sahara, women have primary responsibility for food production. In societies where women do the farming, the involvement of men in food production tends to be limited to a few specific tasks, such as land preparation prior to planting. Children play an active role in food production. Their participation not only enables the household to increase its total production of food but also provides invaluable opportunities for socialization and instruction in farming techniques (Vignette 10.1).

Various methods of enhancing yields and protecting the environment, including intercropping, crop rotation, and bush fallowing, are widely used. Intercropping is the practice of planting two or more crops together in a field to maximize yield, reduce soil erosion, and take advantage of complementary nutrient requirements. For example, legumes (e.g., beans and peanuts) that convert atmospheric nitrogen into a form that other plants can use are intercropped with nitrogen-dependent grain crops. In crop rotation different combinations of crops are grown in each year of a cropping sequence. Bush fallowing is a method of restoring soil fertility by temporarily abandoning farmland so that it can be recolonized by natural vegetation.

African cultivators have developed several farming strategies, each of which involves its own set of adaptations to local social, economic, and environmental conditions. The following paragraphs examine the organizational structure and logic of the most important of these cropping systems: shifting cultivation,

Vignette 10.1. Learning to Farm: The Socialization of Children in Rural Sudan

What children learn about the environment and how to use it as a basis for sustenance is crucial for the survival of rural economies and societies from generation to generation.

In the village of Howa in eastern Sudan, as in most traditional African communities, learning occurs in conjunction with work and play. Children are active participants in the activities of the household. They help their parents with agricultural tasks such as clearing the farm, planting, weeding, and harvesting. They play an important role in the care of livestock. They are often made responsible for collecting firewood and obtaining water for domestic use. They are sent to gather wild foods such as fruits and green vegetables that consitute an important part of rural diets.

Work of this sort provides unlimited opportunities for learning about the environment. Children learn by observing their parents and older siblings as they work with them in the fields. They learn by asking questions, and they learn from mistakes; if, for example, they mistakenly weed out a useful plant, their parents will explain what should have been done.

Children in rural Sudan also learn through play. One example is when boys trap small birds to be roasted and eaten and sometimes to be sold for a few pennies. The line between work and play isn't always well defined; trapping birds for fun may help to supplement the family diet and may contribute to the control of crop-destroying pests.

Changes in the economy and the ecology brought about by development initiatives may change the nature and significance of traditional learning. In Howa, the development of a large irrigation scheme has brought about an increase in the work of children. For example, collecting firewood takes longer because it is less readily available close to the village. The labor requirements of irrigated cotton production are greater than those for crops grown previously. Households need more income to survive in the increasingly commercial local economy, and children have to contribute their share.

The irrigation scheme has increased economic disparities within the community and has resulted in the widespread alienation of land. As a result, most Howa children are unlikely to be able to have their own farms in the future. Many will work as farm laborers, and others will seek employment in the city.

There is a growing discontinuity between what the children of Howa have learned and the opportunities they will have as adults. Modern, formal education often appears to be a more relevant preparation for this new reality. However, the growing workload of children in the local economy has become a significant barrier to school enrollment; enrollments are not increasing as might have been expected given the socioeconomic changes that have taken place.

Based on C. Katz, "Sow what you know: The struggle for social reproduction in rural Sudan," *Annals of the Association of American Geographers*, vol. 81 (1991), pp. 488–514.

rotational bush fallow, and permanent cultivation. Nevertheless, it is important to emphasize that the actual implementation of each of these systems varies greatly in particular settings. It is also common for individual farmers to use different strategies in different fields, for example, cultivating fields close to home far more intensively than those located farther away.

Shifting Cultivation

In shifting cultivation, soil fertility and farm productivity are maintained by changing the

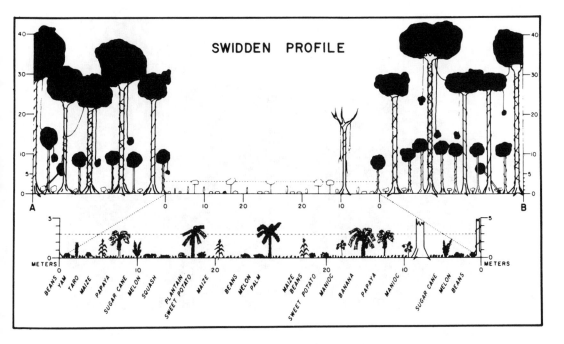

Figure 10.2. Cross-section of a shifting cultivation farm. The diagram illustrates the diversity of intercropped species, mimicking the structure of the forest. Source: M. Hammond. *From Riches to Rags: A Critique of the Transformation of Shifting Cultivation Societies in Contact with Expanding Political Economies of Nation States.* M. A. Thesis, Michigan State University, 1977.

location of cultivation. It involves clearing and burning natural vegetation to produce ash, then farming the cleared area for a few cropping seasons, and finally abandoning the plot for another to permit soil renewal. Because high land-to-population ratios are needed, it is a system for sparsely populated regions. It is practiced in a variety of environments, including the tropical forest, moist (Guinea) savanna, and grassy (Sudan) savanna; but it is especially suited to the infertile laterite soils found in the tropical forest. The dense vegetation is nourished by decaying plant matter covering the forest floor. Once the leaf-fall cycle that replenishes the litter layer is interrupted, soil fertility begins to decline.

The cultivation of a plot begins with the cutting and burning of vegetation, which releases phosphorous and other minerals from the vegetation into the soil and temporarily lowers soil acidity. Higher yields of ash are generally related to improved crop yields. Shifting cultivators plant several crops together in a way that mimics the diversity and layered

structure of the natural ecosystem (Figure 10.2). Legumes are intercropped to increase nutrient supply, reduce soil erosion and baking, and inhibit weed growth.

After a couple of years, when yields have declined, the clearing and cropping sequence is repeated elsewhere. Plots are small and surrounded by forest, so they are soon recolonized by natural vegetation. The stability of the system depends on the maintenance of fallows long enough to permit soil rejuvenation. Fallows vary in relation to local conditions, but average about 10 to 20 years in forest regions. The duration of cultivation may be longer in savanna regions where nutrients are leached more slowly than in very humid forest ecosystems. Crop rotation is used to prolong the cultivation cycle. Crops such as sorghum, sweet potatoes, and yams that require nutrient-rich soils may be planted initially and then replaced in the second or third year with less demanding crops such as cassava. Other crops such as beans, squash, and maize are intercropped with the major staples.

Figure 10.3. Shifting cultivation, southeastern Côte d'Ivoire. The random mixing of several different crops is characteristic of shifting cultivation systems. Photo: author.

To the uninformed observer, shifting cultivation appears to be a primitive, inefficient, and disorganized system that needlessly destroys natural vegetation and is not amenable to modernization. However, soil scientists and agronomists have come to see shifting cultivation as a sophisticated and effective approach to farming in marginal environments that produces a variety of crops, uses virtually no purchased inputs and, when used appropriately, does not cause lasting ecological damage.

Rotational Bush Fallow

With increasing population density and shorter fallows, inadequate for soil rejuvenation, shifting-cultivation systems may have to give way to more intensive forms of cultivation such as rotational bush fallow. Rotational bush fallow involves the development of a regular system of fallows in which farmland never reverts to natural forest or savanna vegetation. Strategies such as crop rotation and intercropping, greater use of animal manure, and intensive cultivation of floodplains and household gardens are used to compensate for the shorter fallows.

Intercropping and crop rotation are crucial to the success of rotational bush fallow. Unlike shifting cultivation, relatively few crops — typically two to four complementary crops — are cultivated together. Farmers employ a detailed knowledge of local environmental conditions to select the best combinations and sequences of crops. For example, the varieties grown in well-drained and wet soils may be different. Some parts of the farm may support the most favored crops for 3 to 5 years before it is necessary to resort to cassava, while poorer soils nearby may be planted with cassava after only 1 year.

In many rotational fallow systems, the soil is heaped into ridges or mounds to permit the concentration of fertile topsoil and ash around the roots of plants. Ridges and mounds also improve drainage and aeration, reduce soil erosion, and help to control weeds. Manure is commonly used to enhance fertility in areas where there are substantial livestock populations. Manure may be collected and spread on the farm, or pastoralists may be asked to graze their herds on the farm in the dry season and thereby convert crop refuse into manure. "Green-manure" crops—crops grown to be ploughed into the soil to increase organic content—are grown in some rotational fallow systems.

Production from comparatively small but intensively farmed household gardens and floodplains becomes increasingly important as growing population densities exert pressure on finite land resources. Heavy applications of manure and household refuse, together with careful cultivation techniques, ensure continual high yields. Economically valuable trees such as oil palm and mango are deliberately cultivated to increase farm productivity.

Permanent Cultivation

Permanent cultivation as an indigenous system of production occurs in relatively few parts of Africa south of the Sahara. In general, areas of permanent cultivation are notable for the intensity and sophistication of agricultural development, as indicated by their very high densities of agriculture-dependent population. Far from being confined to any particular ecological milieu, intensive, permanent cultivation is found in areas as diverse as the tropical-forest fringe in southern Nigeria and the rich volcanic soils of the high plateau of southern Uganda, Rwanda, and Burundi. The organization of production varies considerably, reflecting the diversity of local social, demographic, economic, and ecological conditions. To illustrate this diversity of permanent systems of cultivation, the organization of production among the Hausa and Igbo in Nigeria will be compared.

Permanent cropping is characteristic of the close-settled zones of large Nigerian Hausa cities such as Kano, Zaria, and Sokoto. The Kano close-settled zone contains about 6 million people with rural population densities of 250 to 500 per square kilometer. All arable land is cultivated every year and is enriched with heavy applications of animal manure, household refuse, and night soil. Waste products to fertilize the soil are hauled to the countryside from the large cities and taken by farmers living in rural settlements to their nearby fields. The use of commercial fertilizer has increased in recent years.

Hausa farmers maximize yields from their small farms by intercropping beans and peanuts—legume crops—with millet and sorghum. Crop varieties are carefully matched to specific ecological conditions in each field. Chickens, goats, and sheep scavenge or are fed crop refuse and provide a source of dietary

a

b

Figure 10.4. Gender and agriculture. (a) Men cultivators, Côte d'Ivoire. (b) Women preparing yam mounds, Ghana. Although women produce most of Africa's food, men are likely to be involved, even when women have primary responsibility for food crop production. The preparation of yam mounds is a good example of a male-dominated task; not only is the work heavy, but the yam crop is a valuable source of cash—hence, its attraction for men. Photos: CIDA: (a) R. Lemoyne, (b) B. Paton.

Figure 10.5. Ploughing with oxen, Tigre Province, Ethiopia. Two small stone barriers are visible behind the ploughman; these structures have been built to trap rainwater and impede soil erosion. Photo: M. Peters.

protein. Many types of foodstuffs and other useful products are obtained from flora growing in villages, on farms, and along farm boundaries. Farmers who have access to a floodplain and a source of water for irrigation will farm the floodplain very intensively, especially during the dry season, often to produce high-value vegetables for sale.

Permanent cultivation in the Igbo heartland of southeastern Nigeria applies many of the same principles and practices but otherwise bears little resemblance to Hausa agriculture. The agricultural landscape of Igboland is dominated by the ubiquitous presence of the oil palm, once an important source of export earnings. The long rainy season enables crop production almost year-round, unlike Hausaland where most production is confined to the 4- to 5-month rainy season. The primary staples are root crops (yams, cocoyams, and cassava), rather than grains. The presence of tsetse severely limits possibilities for raising cattle, sheep, and other livestock; the Igbo consume considerably less animal protein than the Hausa.

Igboland has extremely high population densities, despite the prevalence of relatively infertile and erosion-prone soils. Permanently farmed areas around settlements have the appearance of carefully tended gardens. Productivity is sustained at a high level through intercropping and the heavy application of manure, ashes, and crop refuse. In outlying fields, fertility is protected with short fallows during which soil-rebuilding legumes are grown.

Livestock Production

While raising animals as a source of food and income is the work of many pastoral societies, livestock production is not monopolized by pastoralists. Most African farmers own poultry, and many own goats, sheep, donkeys, and cattle. Nevertheless, the focus of this section is pastoralist and mixed farming systems, where food production and the care of livestock are integrally linked. In the farming systems previously discussed, livestock are very commonly raised but are seldom a necessary element of the production system.

Pastoralism

Vast areas of savanna, semidesert, and desert are utilized primarily, if not exclusively, by pastoralists to produce livestock and such livestock products as milk. Pastoralism is notable for its ability to utilize marginal environments that are too dry, too rocky, or too steeply inclined for successful farming. Cattle are the most important and most valued livestock for virtually all African pastoralists, except in desert and near-desert environments where camels are kept. Most pastoralists also keep significant herds of sheep and goats.

The size and quality of family herds of cattle have traditionally been considered to be the preeminent measure of status and wealth. Gifts of cattle and sacrifices of cattle are reserved for ceremonial occasions like weddings and religious holidays. Cattle, especially females of breeding age, are sold with reluctance. Sheep and goats usually have less sociocultural significance and, thus, are managed in a more utilitarian manner.

Cattle are the primary sustenance base for most pastoralist societies. Milk and yogurt are the preferred and most important foods for many pastoralists. Some East African groups consume blood taken from their cattle. Meat tends to be eaten quite rarely, except on ceremonial occasions. However, livestock are a form of "consumable capital" that can be sold or eaten in times of emergency. Cattle may also perform other utilitarian functions, such .as pulling ploughs and carts or carrying loads.

Spatial mobility is fundamental to the pastoralist way of life, for it permits an orderly utilization of available water and pasture throughout the year. The resources needed by pastoralists to sustain their herds are very unevenly distributed in time and space. Water and pasture are plentiful during the rainy season but become increasingly scarce as the dry season progresses. Thus, pastoralists gravitate during the dry season to moister environments and move as often as necessary to secure adequate forage. Seasonally varying risks such as livestock diseases also affect migration patterns. Many of the dry-season grazing grounds must be abandoned at the commencement of the rains when tsetse become more numerous and widespread, thus increasing the risk of trypanosomiasis.

Pastoralism takes a variety of forms. "True nomads," who move their herds in an apparently random fashion and maintain no permanent base camps, are very few in number. A more common pattern involves the maintenance of permanent settlements that are occupied throughout the year by women, children, and some men. Agriculture is often practiced around these settlements. Herders, together with the livestock, spend part of the year at the settlement and the rest on seasonally utilized pastures. The basic patterns of movement between seasonal pastures are generally well established. Particular lineages or families gravitate toward places where they have an intimate knowledge of the environment and where their access to wells and grazing lands has become customary as a result of many years of use and cooperative interaction with local inhabitants.

The seasonal migrations of pastoralists take place within several distinct ecological frameworks (Figure 10.6). Many pastoralists move between upland pastures occupied during the rainy season and floodplains occupied during the dry season when pasture and water become increasingly scarce. In upland areas such as the Fouta Djallon and Abyssinian Highlands, seasonal mobility is between higher-altitude pasture and lowland pasture. In certain regions, mobility is governed by the seasonal oscillation of the boundary between tsetse-infested and safe zones; when fly density and range increase during the rainy season, pastoralists retreat to protect the health of their herds. Another pattern, common in densely farmed areas, is organized in relation to the farming calendar. Dry-season camps are established near farming communities to take advantage of the possibilities for trade and to utilize crop refuse as fodder. However, livestock are moved to sparsely occupied areas during the rainy season so that the animals do not damage crops.

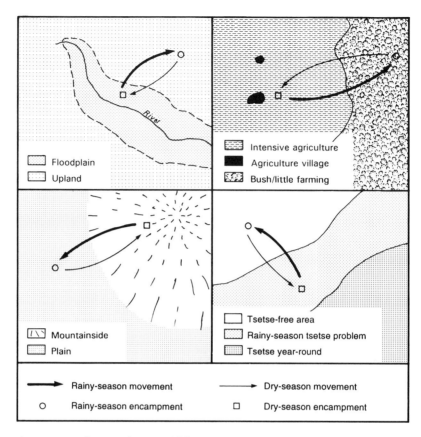

Figure 10.6. Schematic drawing of different types of spatial mobility among pastoralists. Mobility enables herders to use seasonally varying resources effectively, increasing returns and limiting ecological damage.

In the marginal environments generally utilized by herders, environmental crises such as droughts may occur quite often. The survival of pastoral families and their herds depends on a correct and timely "reading" of environmental signals. During particularly bad years when normally utilized resources fail to materialize, longer, emergency migrations may be necessary to find suitable pasture and water. Decisions to deviate from established patterns of mobility are not made lightly; such migrations are risky because of the added stress of a longer journey for the livestock and the herders' imprecise knowledge of unfamiliar territory and its resources. Moreover, movement into new territory brings increased risk of conflict with farmers over land and the right to use it (see Vignette 10.2).

Herd dispersal is another risk-minimizing strategy used by many pastoralists. Instead of maintaining one very large herd, two or more smaller herds may be created. Herd dispersal gives some protection against possible losses caused by drought, disease, and theft, and it reduces the rate at which the grazing resources in a given location are exhausted.

Production techniques used by pastoralists have often been said to be uneconomic. Their cattle produce very little milk—usually 2 to 5 l per day, a small fraction of the average production of cattle in modern dairy enterprises in the industrialized world. African pastoralists have also been accused of keeping excessively large herds, resulting in overgrazing, and are said to be very reluctant to market their livestock. However, careful ana-

---

Vignette 10.2. The Political Ecology of Peasant–Pastoralist Conflict in Northern Côte d'Ivoire

---

Cultural ecologists studying indigenous production systems have tended to emphasize how such systems may practice an orderly allocation of resources and how they represent ideal strategies for the exploitation of particular environments.

Reality is often rather more complicated. The allocation of scarce resources may be the focus of intense conflict between different ethnic groups or social classes. Thus, environmental stress needs to be interpreted in relation to the broader context of political developments that affect decision making by households at a local level. Such studies, which combine the concerns of ecology and political economy, are often called the "political ecology" of environmental degradation.

A case in point is the recent occurrence of conflicts between indigenous Senufo farmers and recently arrived Fulani herders in northern Côte d'Ivoire. The arrival of substantial numbers of Fulani from Mali and Burkina Faso began in the early 1970s, at the time of the Sahelian drought. The Fulani had previously avoided the area because of tsetse, which posed a substantial risk to the health of their animals. The Ivoirian government has encouraged the settlement of Fulani as a means of strengthening the domestic livestock industry and reducing the country's dependence on imported meat.

The position of the Fulani in northern Côte d'Ivoire remains very tenuous. Because of the enhanced risk from tsetse, the Fulani migrate with their herds very frequently. Moreover, as outsiders they do not have traditional land use rights. The Senufo have strongly resisted the incursion of the Fulani into their territory, focusing on the financial losses they have suffered because of crop damage caused by Fulani-owned cattle. A survey of Senufo farmers showed that damage was very widespread and quite extensive, amounting on average to perhaps one-fifth of household income. Cotton and rice were the crops most frequently affected. In the great majority of cases, the farmers could not secure compensation; most of the damage occurs at night, so there is no proof of which animals were responsible.

Conflicts over land and compensation for crop damage have resulted in a growing anti-Fulani sentiment in northern Côte d'Ivoire, which culminated in violent clashes during 1980, 1981, and 1986. In 1986, some 80 Fulani were killed in Korhogo District, and hundreds of camps were abandoned as pastoralists fled north of the frontier with their cattle.

Policies of the government livestock development agency, SODEPRA, have helped to raise the ire of the Senufo. In particular, giving rights to the Fulani was seen as undermining the Senufo earth priests' authority over land use rights and improvements. The clashes have seriously jeopardized the government's attempts to find a way of accommodating the Fulani in Côte d'Ivoire.

Based on T. Bassett, "The political ecology of peasant-herder conflicts in the northern Ivory Coast," *Annals of Association of American Geographers*, vol. 78 (1988), pp. 453–472.

---

lyses of pastoral economies have refuted these criticisms. Although the cattle produce little milk, they do so using scanty and unreliable resources; American cattle would neither produce much milk nor survive for long in most environments occupied by Africa's pastoralists. Moreover, studies of herd size have demonstrated that herds are seldom larger than the minimum needed to provide sustenance for a family and reasonable assurance against the possible impact of drought and disease.

a

b

Figure 10.7. Pastoralists. (a) Pastoralist with a herd of sheep, Mali. (b) Pastoralist family breaking camp, Mali. Because they move frequently with their herds, nomadic pastoralists tend to have relatively few material possessions. Photo: CIDA: P. St. Jacques.

For some pastoralists, growing crops has become a necessary adjustment because of the inadequate size of herds. The loss of livestock during the droughts of recent years has forced many pastoralists into much greater reliance on agriculture. In Somalia, for example, many pastoral nomads turned to farming and fishing after almost all of their animals perished. Pastoralist agriculture has developed in many other settings as a strategy for economic diversification and profit. However, there is often a class-based or gender-based division of labor

Figure 10.8. Pastoralist's cattle grazing on crop refuse, Kaduna State, Nigeria. The photo illustrates one aspect of the symbiotic relationship between farmers and pastoralists; as the cattle graze, they deposit manure on the farmer's fields. Photo: author.

between livestock raising and cropping; agriculture is usually left for women or subordinate classes.

Pastoralists have come under increasing pressure because of the encroachment of agriculture and other forms of development into their traditional territories, ecological damage in part caused by increasing animal and human populations, and the devastation of drought and disease. They have been pressured by governments to "be more economic" in their behavior and sometimes to abandon their migratory traditions. Despite such major pressures, pastoral societies are still resilient. The key to their survival has remained their sophisticated knowledge of animal husbandry and production systems that carefully and effectively utilize marginal environmental resources.

Mixed Farming

While most farmers in Africa south of the Sahara own some livestock, true mixed farming, in which there is a functional integration of livestock raising and crop husbandry, is uncommon. For example, farmers who own cattle or sheep, but do not have sufficient resources to grow dry-season fodder for the animals, often entrust the care of their livestock to local pastoralists. The Serer of south central Senegal and the Amhara and Gurage of Ethiopia are examples of groups that do practice mixed farming.

The Serer own cattle and cultivate crops and, thus, provide an African example of true mixed farming. Because of land scarcity, Serer agriculture involves heavy applications of animal manure to enhance yields. Cropped land and pasture are rotated in a systematic fashion. Cattle are also used extensively as draft animals to pull plows and carts.

Mixed farming is practiced in much of Ethiopia, the country with the largest number of livestock in Africa. The Amhara are mixed farmers who fully integrate cropping and animal husbandry. The Gurage of southwest Ethiopia practice a distinctive and extremely intensive form of mixed farming in which ensete is the main crop. Ensete is a bananalike plant, the stem of which is used to make a starchy food. Manure from confined or communally pastured livestock is essential to the maintenance of this unique form of agriculture.

Indigenous systems of food production, as practiced by the Amhara and Gurage, are still the very heart of Africa's rural economies. Nevertheless, such systems are under pressure in many places, as a consequence of forces as diverse as environmental degradation, population pressure, the loss of a land base to competing uses, and counterproductive government policies. The continuing health of these systems cannot be taken for granted.

The long-standing conviction that indigenous systems of production are primitive, unchanging, and of little relevance to Africa's future—widespread among African government officials, aid workers, and agricultural scientists—is beginning to change. Newer research has provided a much better understanding of the logic and effectiveness of systems such as shifting cultivation and pastoralism, which, far from being primitive and rigid, continue to change in response to a variety of influences.

The ideal rural development strategy is one that not only is compatable with existing systems of production but that also builds upon the strengths and potentialities of those systems. Unfortunately, as the next chapter will show, this lesson has been learned very slowly.

Further Reading

Classic studies of hunting and gathering societies include the following sources:

Marshall, L. *The !Kung of Nyae Nyae.* Cambridge: Harvard University Press, 1976.
Turnbull, C. *The Forest People.* New York: Simon and Schuster, 1968.

There are many studies that examine the logic of African indigenous farming systems. The Morgan article provides a good introduction to this topic. The other sources are more detailed studies of particular farming systems, or regional patterns:

Morgan, W. B. "Peasant agriculture in tropical Africa." In W. F. Thomas and G. W. Whittington, eds., *Environment and Land Use in Africa*, pp. 241–272. London: Methuen, 1969.

Jones, W., and R. Egli. *Farming Systems in Africa: The Great Lakes Highlands of Zaire, Rwanda and Burundi*. Washington, DC: World Bank, 1984.

Knight, C. G. *Ecology and Change: Rural Modernization in an African Community*. New York: Academic, 1974. (See, in particular, Chapters 4 and 5.)

Lagemann, J. *Traditional African Farming Systems in Eastern Nigeria*. Munich: Weltforum, 1977.

McLoughlin, P. F. M. *African Food Production Systems: Cases and Theory*. Baltimore, MD: Johns Hopkins University Press, 1970.

Netting, R. M. *Hill Farmers of Nigeria: Cultural Ecology of the Kofyar of the Jos Plateau*. Seattle: University of Washington Press, 1968.

Norman, D. W., E. M. Higgins, and H. M. Hays. *Farming Systems in the Nigerian Savanna: Research and Strategies for Development*. Boulder, CO: Westview, 1982.

Richards, P. *Indigenous Agricultural Revolution: Ecology and Food Production in West Africa*. Boulder, CO: Westview, 1985.

The following sources examine pastoral societies and economies in contemporary Africa, and consider their future prospects:

Adamu, M., and A. H. M. Kirk-Greene, eds. *Pastoralists of the West African Savanna*. Manchester, England: Manchester University Press, 1986.

Bassett, T. J. "Fulani herd movements." *Geographical Review*, vol. 76 (1986), pp. 233–248.

Carr, C. J. *Pastoralism in Crisis: The Danasetch and their Ethiopian Lands*. Chicago: University of Chicago, Department of Geography, 1977.

Galaty, J. C., and P. C. Salzman. *The Future of Pastoral Peoples: Proceedings of a Conference in Nairobi, Kenya*. Ottawa, Ontario: International Development Research Centre, 1982.

Herskovits, M. J. "The cattle complex in East Africa." *American Anthropologist*, vol. 28 (1926), pp. 230–272, 361–388, 494–528, 633–644.

Monod, T., ed. *Pastoralism in Tropical Africa*. London: International African Institute, 1975. (In particular, see Monod's introductory essay, pp. 99–183.)

Stenning, D. J. *Savanna Nomads*. London: Oxford University Press, 1959.

11

✶

Agrarian Development
and Change

Africa has more unexploited arable land than any other continent. Officials and development planners have often expressed optimism about Africa's potential and have made innumerable proposals over the years for the transformation of African agriculture and pastoralism. Attempts at major structural change, such as the establishment of plantations or state farms, have usually achieved poor results. The alternate approach to rural development, presently favored by many development agencies, focuses on the productive capacity of small farmers.

Colonial Effects on Indigenous Production Systems

Colonial rule brought significant changes to African agriculture and pastoralism. While many of the effects of colonial rule were evident almost immediately, others developed gradually over several decades. The colonial legacy remains one of the most important determinants of the shape of African agriculture today. Prior to the emergence of dependency theory, the effect of colonialism on rural economies and societies was usually viewed in a positive light. Emphasis was given to the apparent benefits to Africa of the introduction of new crops, new market opportunities, and new technologies. While coercion was sometimes used to bring about desired changes, such measures were seen to be fully justified. This notion of colonial altruism was dismissed by scholars from the dependency school. Rather, the motivation behind colonial policies was seen as blatant self-interest. These policies undermined the viability of indigenous systems by squeezing resources from small producers and upsetting ecological balances that, it was argued, Africans had maintained for centuries.

Large areas of land were expropriated and reserved for European farms and plantations, most notably in Kenya, Southern Rhodesia, and South Africa. Africans expelled from their lands were relocated in confined reserves where less fertile soils and necessarily shorter fallow periods caused declining productivity. The tax burden in settler-dominated colonies was placed squarely on the shoulders of Africans. Dual pricing systems were established that granted significantly higher prices for European crops and livestock.

Forest and game reserves were created, with often serious implications for farmers and pastoralists who had traditionally used these territories. Pastoralists lost vital seasonal pastures and had their normal migration routes severed. The increasingly dense vegetation and growing wildlife populations in these reserves created ideal conditions for the proliferation of tsetse, which in turn made the surrounding countryside increasingly dangerous for humans and livestock.

Throughout Africa south of the Sahara, rural labor was appropriated to serve the interests of the colonial state. Every colonial power relied at times on forced labor to recruit troops, porters, construction workers, and plantation laborers. For the peasantry, time lost from agriculture meant smaller harvests and often hunger. Farmers cultivated increasing amounts of cassava in place of preferred and more nutritious crops. Other forms of labor appropriation, such as the "voluntary" seasonal migration of peasants to earn money for taxes, had similar implications for peasant agriculture, despite their more benign appearance.

Cash crops were promoted as a means of involving Africans in the commercial economy and ensuring a supply of tropical products for European industry. Some of these crops, including cotton, groundnuts, and oil palm, had been widely cultivated in precolonial Africa, while others were introduced for the first time. Africans frequently resisted the introduction of cash crops because it diverted scarce resources away from food crop production. Some cash crops were more compatable than others with existing farming systems. For example, groundnuts could be intercropped with millet and actually increased grain yields by fixing nitrogen in the soil, whereas cotton was viewed as a "soil robber" and poorly suited to intercropping.

When fairly attractive prices were offered for cash crops that were compatable with traditional farming systems, African farmers could become enthusiastic adopters. Vast areas of unfarmed forest in the Gold Coast (Ghana) were planted with cocoa by migrant farmers. However, the prices offered to African farmers were seldom attractive, and cash cropping often clashed with food cropping. In these circumstances, peasant resistance to cash cropping made sense. Producer prices were kept

far below world market values by granting trading monopolies to a few companies or to a produce marketing agency. This appropriation of profits through taxation and monopoly pricing was justified as a means of obtaining capital for development. However, little of what was actually spent on development was of much benefit to rural areas.

Colonial agricultural agents attempted to introduce various changes in indigenous agricultural practice; these innovations reflected European views of how farming should be done. For example, mixed farming integrating cropping and raising livestock was often promoted but with little success because few African farmers had sufficient land and wealth to successfully engage in mixed farming. Monoculture was also promoted, despite some evidence that traditional farming practices such as shifting cultivation and intercropping were actually superior.

African farmers' disinclination to change seemed to confirm their backwardness. The myth of the unprogressive peasant helped to sustain the view that Africa's land and labor could be most effectively exploited by developing European-style farms, plantations, and ranches. The role of Africans would be to supply labor and to produce their own sustenance.

Postcolonial Policies and the Neglect of Agriculture

Agricultural research and aid initiatives in the 1960s emphasized the expansion and diversification of cash cropping. For many countries, increased cash-crop sales were the obvious vehicle to finance development in the form of industrial growth and modern agriculture. Farmers paid a "hidden tax" in the form of the low prices that they received from government agencies for cash crops. These prices typically were set well below prevailing world market prices (Table 11.1). Moreover, increased production often brought reduced prices in world markets because demand for products such as coffee and cocoa is relatively inelastic (i.e., consumption is un-

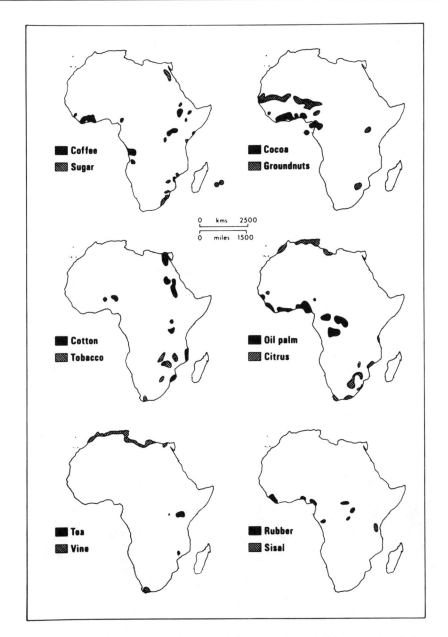

Figure 11.1. Major zones of cash-crop production. Source: I. Griffiths. *An Atlas of African Affairs.* London: Methuen, 1984, p. 121. ©1984 by Methuen and Co. Reprinted by permission.

likely to change much in response to changes in price). For other commodities, competition from other sources (e.g., American mechanized peanut farms) or from substitute products (e.g., synthetic products that can be used to replace sisal) have depressed both demand and price.

Prior to the opening of the International Institute for Tropical Agriculture in Ibadan in 1968, food crops were virtually ignored in agricultural research and development. Very little was known about the logic of indigenous production systems or the potential utility of improved food-crop varieties and related in-

Table 11.1. The "Hidden Taxation" of Cash Crops in Selected Countries: 1976–1980 Producer Price as a Percentage of Fair Market Price[a]

	Cocoa	Coffee	Cotton	Groundnuts	Tobacco
Cameroon	45	36	79		
Malawi			75	59	28
Mali			44	43	
Sudan			60	67	
Togo	25	23	79		
Zambia				71	88

Note. Blank entries indicate that the country does not produce a significant amount of the product.
[a]World price minus transport and marketing costs.
Based on World Bank, *Accelerated Development in Sub-Saharan Africa,* 1981 (Box D, p. 56).

novations. When the need to actively encourage greater food production was finally recognized, many African nations were already suffering from recurrent food shortages.

The most common response to food deficits was to increase food imports, especially wheat and rice that had become an important component of diets in urban areas. Imported foods were often sold at less than the market prices of locally produced foods. While food subsidies reduced the likelihood of unrest among urban populations, it also undercut indigenous food producers. Depressed prices for both food crops and cash crops created a massive disincentive for peasants to increase production and invest in their farms.

The overall structure of development in postindependence Africa has hastened the decline of agriculture. While some schools and health clinics have been constructed in rural districts, social services in urban areas remain vastly superior. The probability of migration is also increased by educational systems that have very seldom promoted agriculture or

Figure 11.2. Tea plantation, Tanzania. Although Africa produces only a small percentage of the world's tea, it is locally important in several East and central African countries. Photo: CIDA: D. Barbour.

provided skills designed to foster rural development. Rather, the "hidden curriculum" of schools has tended to extol the values of modern, urban life. It is little wonder that more and more African youth aspire to an urban future and have no enthusiasm for agriculture or rural life. Certain countries, such as Tanzania, have given priority to improving rural living standards, but most have paid lip service to rural development and made little real progress.

Attempts to Restructure African Agriculture

African governments, eager to boost food production and export earnings, have experimented with various development schemes to restructure agriculture. In doing so, they have sought to emulate the experiences of technically more advanced economies, whether capitalist or socialist, and to accommodate offers of aid from diverse sources.

Most African countries have gone through phases of importing modern agricultural machinery and establishing or promoting the development of large-scale farm enterprises. There have been a few qualified successes, but these approaches have generally had minimal effect on national production. In contrast, these approaches have typically had an adverse effect on indigenous production systems, often by alienating land normally used by peasants and pastoralists and by diverting developmental resources away from small-scale producers.

The following discussion outlines some characteristics and problems of four types of initiatives: (1) state farms, (2) planned resettlement, (3) irrigation schemes, and (4) large-scale capitalist agriculture.

State Farms

The first experiments with state farms occurred in the early 1960s in Ghana and Guinea. The collective farms of Eastern Europe provided the model for agrarian transfor-mation. The experiments failed badly, largely because of poor management. Heavy investments in farm machinery were wasted because of parts shortages, poor maintenance, and adverse environmental conditions. Peasants were reluctant to commit themselves fully to collective work on state farms, preferring instead to farm their own land.

Mozambique, Angola, and Ethiopia attempted to establish state farms as a part of a broader socialist transformation. In the former Portuguese colonies, farms formerly owned by white settlers were consolidated to form state enterprises. Mozambique invested heavily in tractors and combine harvesters but was unable to mobilize either adequate management or peasant enthusiasm. The results were so poor that most of the farms were abandoned by the mid-1980s.

While state farms have most often been associated with Marxist regimes, they have also been tried by moderate socialist and capitalist regimes. For example, Tanzania has established large-scale mechanized wheat farms with Canadian assistance (discussed in Vignette 22.2). Zambia's experiment with state farms was particularly unusual; each of several huge model farms was set up and managed as a foreign aid project by a different country (USA, USSR, China, and Canada, among others). Zambia has derived few benefits from this experiment, in which the quest for foreign aid took precedence over the development of a coherent national strategy of agricultural development built around an assessment of the country's own needs and resources.

Planned Resettlement

Planned resettlement has been initiated in a number of African countries, using a variety of models. One of the most common reasons for resettlement programs has been to accommodate people displaced by dams and other major projects. Resettlement has been used in several countries as a strategy for political and economic transformation. The settlement of Africans on farms reclaimed from European settlers in Kenya, the organization of

Vignette 11.1. Kenya's Smallholder Resettlement Schemes

The Kenyan experience with resettlement schemes provides useful insights into the development potential of African farmers.

By the late 1950s, the British were exhausted after several years of bloody Mau Mau rebellion and had accepted Kenyan independence as inevitable. Among the problems they faced was the future of the "White Highlands" where land had been reserved exclusively for Europeans. Many whites now wished to leave. Hundreds of thousands of Kenyans who had worked on these farms, or lived as squatters in the white reserves, or struggled to live on densely populated African reserves, hungered for these lands.

A series of resettlement projects were developed in which the government purchased European farms, subdivided them into smaller units, and sold them to Kenyans. The preparation for resettlement involved careful evaluation of soil fertility and studies to determine optimum sizes for viable farms. Colonial officials also were determined to disperse the blocks of resettlement and to segregate different ethnic groups from each other.

The initial schemes focused not on the landless but on middle-class farmers who could afford to invest in relatively large farms. Two settler categories were established: yeomen who were allocated about 20 ha each, and peasants who were to get about 6 ha. Settlers could obtain some financial assistance and were provided with elaborate extension services to facilitate the development of successful capitalist farms.

As news of the settlement program spread, many landless families began to descend on the designated areas, and fears of renewed Mau Mau violence grew. The resettlement program was now expanded to accommodate some of these people and curtail their sense of frustration. The new project, known as the Million-Acre Scheme, was designed to accommodate 35,000 families and many thousands of squatters who were allowed to remain in situ. Colonial officials had little confidence in these poor and apparently inexperienced farmers. They received very small plots on often inferior land and were allocated minimal assistance.

The performance of Kenya's resettlement schemes confounded the expert predictions. Total agricultural output increased 4% per year during the 1960s and early 1970s. Despite having inferior resources, smallholders were soon obtaining higher yields and higher profits than the middle-class yeomen and peasants were. A study in 1974 found that output per hectare was 19 times greater on farms smaller than ½ ha than on farms larger than 8 ha. Small-scale farmers specialized in both food crops, especially hybrid corn, and cash crops, especially tea, coffee, and pyrethrum. It had been assumed that growing these crops would be beyond the abilities of small-scale farmers.

Smallholders' success partly reflects their total reliance on farming for their living, whereas middle-class farmers often divided their energies between farming and other businesses. We cannot assume that small farmers will always be more productive, but Kenya's experience reminds us to never underestimate the potential of ordinary African producers. It also gives us reason to be skeptical about the World Bank's Integrated Agricultural Development Projects (IADPs) that focus heavily on assistance for wealthier "progressive" farmers.

ujamaa villages in Tanzania, and the removal of Ethiopians from the drought-striken plateau to the sparsely populated periphery provide varied examples of politically informed reset

tlement. While several approaches to resettlement have been attempted, few have achieved the anticipated benefits.

One of the largest and most successful resettlement programs was undertaken in Kenya during the early 1960s (Vignette 11.1). After the Mau Mau revolts and with independence imminent, many European farmers in the White Highlands wished to leave. Their farms were purchased and subdivided into moderate-sized holdings for African farmers. The extensive promotion of commercial farming innovations, including hybrid maize, various cash crops, and dairy cattle, was one of the keys to the success of the Kenyan program. A similar approach was used in Zimbabwe to reorganize the rural landscape following the departure of many European farmers at the time of Zimbabwean independence.

Tanzania's establishment of *ujamaa* villages represents a different approach to rural transformation. Tanzania's scattered rural population was encouraged to form new villages where social services could be provided more easily and agricultural development could be encouraged. *Ujamaa* villagers were to devote a significant proportion of their time to communal efforts, including work in collective village farms. The villagers also had their own family plots. The early promise of Tanzania's village scheme waned, especially when increasing levels of coercion were applied in what had begun as a voluntary program. Moreover, with its total economy in decline, Tanzania was less and less able to provide material support for rural development.

The socialist government of Ethiopia began to organize the resettlement of families from the densely settled heartland of the country to the sparsely populated western and southwestern peripheries. The resettlement program was greatly expanded at the time of the 1984 to 1985 drought; over half a million people were moved in just over one year. The government perceived the program as a cure-all for the famine and its deeper environmental roots and as a means of lessening its dependence on foreign assistance by opening up fertile, underutilized territory. The program was implemented hastily without careful planning and without sufficient government resources to ensure that the transition would be orderly and successful.

At the height of the resettlement effort, the program was denounced by a French organization as genocidal. The government was charged with forcing people to leave their homes, and it was claimed that tens of thousands had perished because of inadequate planning. These claims seem to have been overstated. While many resettled persons were coerced into moving–unemployed urban youths, for example–most did so voluntarily, albeit because of their desperate circumstances during the famine. Although many settlers experienced considerable initial hardship, there is no conclusive evidence that there was heavy mortality. Some settlers later returned to their former homes, but most have remained behind and have made the transition from famine victims to successful peasants in a new environment. After 1986, the Ethiopian government greatly reduced the program, primarily because of the lack of resources to support successful resettlement. The lack of enthusiasm for resettlement among many aid donors meant that it would have to be funded by diverting scarce funds from other desperately needed programs.

Irrigation Projects

Large-scale irrigation schemes have long been seen as a means of increasing the prosperity of semiarid regions. During the colonial era, the Inland Delta scheme in Mali and the Gezira irrigation scheme in eastern Sudan were lauded as great achievements. The Inland Delta project was inaugurated in 1919, with the objective of irrigating nearly 1 million ha by using water from the Niger River to grow cotton and rice. As of 1960, only 36,000 ha were under cultivation. Its failure was the result of the poor quality of much of the soil, the prohibitive costs of developing the project, salinization, and difficulty in attracting settlers to the scheme. The Gezira scheme, located near the junction of the Blue and White Niles, has been more successful than the Inland Delta scheme, largely because of more fertile soil and a dependable supply of water. Nevertheless, the future of this 1 million-ha scheme depends on overcoming increasingly serious problems of waterweed growth, siltation, salinization, and pesticide pollution.

The Sahelian drought of 1970 to 1974 further increased interest in irrigation as a strategy for agricultural development. Irrigation seemed to promise increased production—two annual crops instead of one—and greater security from drought. Various economic arguments were advanced to justify investment in irrigation. Domestic food production, including wheat and rice cultivation to reduce imports, was stressed in some schemes. Elsewhere, the possibilities for export earnings from selling vegetables, flowers, and sugar have been emphasized.

Major irrigation schemes, such as the Senegal Valley and Kano River projects, have not been worth the price, whether measured according to monetary, social, or ecological criteria. (see Vignette 11.2). Nigeria's three largest schemes had a total development cost of approximately $1.8 billion, equivalent to $25,000 per hectare of land developed. Maintenance and operating costs are very high. This heavy investment cannot be justified as drought security; there is seldom enough water for irrigation during droughts. The real cost of irrigation development includes the loss of land normally used by pastoralists for dry season grazing and by farmers for cropping.

Large-Scale Capitalist Agriculture

Most African countries contain substantial capitalist agricultural ventures, owned by domestic or foreign companies. While large-scale capitalist agriculture is comparatively minor in most of Africa south of the Sahara, it is well developed in certain countries, such as Côte d'Ivoire and Botswana. It is also growing rapidly in other countries. Nigeria now allocates large estates to transnational corporation so that they may produce more of their own raw materials (e.g., cotton for textile mills and grain for breweries) and grow food for sale in domestic markets. The costs and benefits of this approach cannot yet be assessed. Nevertheless, it conforms to the long-standing conventional vision of those in power, namely, that future prosperity depends on modernizing agriculture rather than developing fully the potential of indigenous farming systems. According to this vision, rural Africans will increasingly work as wage laborers rather than as independent producers. In most cases, it also implies that non-Africans will exert control over scarce agricultural resources for their own profit.

a

b

Figure 11.3. Modern agriculture. (a) Modern dairy farm, near Lusaka, Zambia. (b) Large, mechanized wheat farm, Rift Valley, Kenya. Modern wheat farms have been established in several countries including Tanzania, Kenya, and Sudan, in an effort to reduce dependence on imported wheat. Photos: author.

Vignette 11.2. Irrigation Schemes and the Hidden Costs of Development

Large-scale irrigation has been promoted widely as a means of increasing agricultural output and alleviating the effects of drought. In Nigeria, large irrigation projects have been built in the Sokoto Valley, the Kano River basin, and near Lake Chad; numerous smaller dams and reservoirs also have been constructed. In several studies, these dams were found to have significantly decreased river discharge and the amount of river bottomlands flooded. As a result, the economies of downstream communities have been devastated.

These projects were designed without due consideration to downstream effects on the ecology and economies of river valleys. River flooding, which occurs during and immediately following the 3- to 6-month rainy season, has traditionally formed the basis for an important floodplain economy based on fishing and farming. Flood-tolerant varieties of rice and sorghum are grown, and as the flood recedes, wheat, vegetables, and other crops are planted to take advantage of residual moisture left in the soil. Floodplain farming involves small areas but is very lucrative and has been essential to the well-being of many communities in densely populated parts of northern Nigeria.

W. M. Adams studied the Bakalori Project on the Sokoto River and found it had caused a 51 to 90% decline in the area flooded. The area planted with flood-dependent crops such as vegetables and rice declined dramatically, and the quantity and value of fish caught was greatly reduced. Adams estimated that the value of crops lost because of dam construction amounted to about 3.1 million naira per year, far above the 2 million naira in rice production that the economic analysis for the project had too optimistically predicted for the new irrigation scheme. Moreover, the negative effects of the dam were borne throughout the Sokoto Valley downstream from the project. Even if the planned benefits of the project had materialized, they would have been confined to the very small area of the irrigation project.

Hamish Main studied the effects of two small dams built in Kano State. Official estimates show that some 4,500 were resettled after their villages and farms were flooded; many more had to relocate without government help. The villagers lost two-thirds of their farm plots, including 85% of their valuable floodplain plots. Ownership of the remaining floodplain land has become highly concentrated in the hands of the villages' wealthiest people and in the hands of outsiders. For many of the rest, who have been unable to generate as much income from their new land and new settlement circumstances, migration has become the only viable alternative. The majority have gone to Kano; most started off doing seasonal labor migration before taking the major step of moving permanently to the city with their families.

Sources: W. M. Adams. "The downstream impacts of dam construction: A case study from Nigeria." *Transactions of the Institute of British Geographers*, vol. 10 (1985), pp. 292–302; and H. A. C. Main, "Dam projects and urbanization in Kano State, Nigeria," *Singapore Journal of Tropical Geography*, vol. 11 (1990), pp. 87–98.

Focus on the Small Farmer: The World Bank

In a 1973 speech, the president of the World Bank, Robert McNamara, signaled an important policy shift, arguing that the key to solving Third World poverty lay in raising the "low productivity of millions of small farms." World Bank lending for agrarian development has since emphasized projects that it claims assist the rural poor. Although most other development agencies have since jumped onto the "small farmer bandwagon," the World Bank has remained its greatest proponent.

The World Bank has developed a basic model, the Integrated Agricultural Development Project (IADP), which has been applied in many parts of Africa and elsewhere in the Third World. While specific details vary to reflect local ecological and socioeconomic realities, the overall strategy remains much the same.

The IADPs stress the importance of promoting a "package" of innovations and investments designed to attack possible barriers to progress simultaneously. For example, many of the benefits of improved yields will be lost if storage, transportation, and marketing systems remain deficient. The most important parts of the IADP package consist of improved varieties of seeds and agricultural chemicals – fertilizers, herbicides, and pesticides – and a supply network to make these inputs accessible to farmers. Various relatively inexpensive technological innovations, such as improved ploughs and small pumps for irrigation, are also promoted. Improved agricultural extension, particularly at the village level, is emphasized as a key to convincing farmers to adopt the recommended practices. So-called progressive farmers are targeted for extension services on the assumption that they will convince others to participate.

IADP programs typically include an improved services component. Investments in village water supply, schools, and clinics enhance potential productivity, while better roads bring more efficient marketing. By introducing new methods of crop storage, the volume and quality of marketed and locally consumed produce may be improved, and farmers' profits enhanced. The World Bank also encourages reforms to government policy to facilitate agricultural development. Free-market commodity pricing, rather than government-fixed pricing, is considered vital to stimulate rural productivity and marketing efficiency. Improved rural credit is needed so that farmers can obtain production inputs.

The IADP approach to rural development has received mixed reviews. Few would dis-

agree that the integration of several dimensions of rural development is a vast improvement over previous approaches that focused narrowly on selected innovations, such as hybrid seeds, without considering other factors affecting their utility. The IADPs have also been praised for attempting to integrate innovations into traditional production systems and for creating a symbiosis between traditional and modern agriculture not found in the earlier, large-scale agrarian development schemes. Supporters of the IADPs also point to significantly increased production in several of its projects. The gains have not always been in the targeted areas. For example, the Funtua, Gusau, and Gombe IADPs in Nigeria did not attain their primary objective of increasing cotton production, although farmers did achieve a significant increase in their production of food crops.

Critics of the IADPs have focused primarily on the high cost of the IADPs, the increased dependence on foreign inputs and capital, and the unequally distributed benefits of these projects. World Bank loans to finance IADPs have significantly increased the indebtedness of a number of African countries. Unfortunately, the decline in trade has meant that the projected increases in export crop revenues that were to pay for the loans have not materialized. Meanwhile, the cost of technological inputs has continued to rise. Because most African countries must import virtually all of the hybrid seeds, agricultural chemicals, and other material inputs essential to the IADP approach, external dependence is increased. This strategy runs counter to the present objectives of African nations, stated in the 1989 *African Alternative Framework to Structural Adjustment Programme*, to seek greater stability through self-reliance.

The IADPs are often criticized for increasing socioeconomic inequality in rural areas. Because each project is normally confined to a particular region, other parts of the country are left behind. Moreover, the focus on "progressive farmers" tend to increase inequality within communities. As with the Green Revolution in Asia, the basic tehnology is too expensive for poor farmers. Local elites benefit from "progressive-farmer" incentives to obtain IADP technology and then use the profits to expand their holdings at the expense of poorer farmers.

The environmental effects of IADP technology have also caused concern. The proliferation of agricultural chemicals, a few of which have been banned in industrialized countries, threatens human health and endangers fauna and flora. Increasing reliance on a few varieties of hybrid seeds reduces the biotic diversity that has always been a primary safeguard for farmers against the threat of drought, pests, and diseases.

The World Bank projects are no panacea, either for Africa's peasantry or for countries that are attempting to achieve food security and increased agricultural exports. The cost of the package is too high for the IADP model to be implemented at a national scale, given current debt burdens and gross national products. Indeed, increasing indebtedness and falling world commodity prices threaten the viability of existing projects. African governments may learn a number of valuable lessons from the IADP experiments, but in the present economic climate they must explore alternatives that are less costly, spatially and socially more equitable, and less dependent on global market forces. Even if financial constraints can be eased, the key question remains, "What kind of development and for the benefit of whom?" Rural progress does not necessarily depend on elite "progressive farmers" as the World Bank contends; African peasants have repeatedly responded positively to genuine opportunities that are compatable with the status quo.

The Way Ahead

The way forward, beyond the IADP approach, involves several facets. It must start with a genuine commitment by governments to broadly based rural development. This commitment needs to be expressed in concrete ways, such as the reallocation of resources from urban elites to the rural masses and the

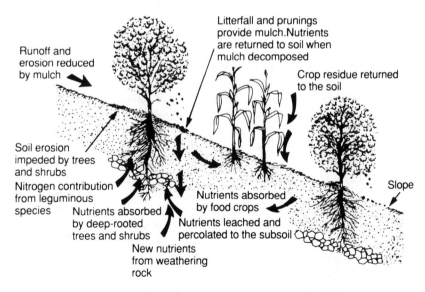

Figure 11.4.. Alley cropping. The diagram shows some of the ecological dynamics that make alley cropping a sustainable farming system, even in marginal tropical forest environment. Source: B. T. Kang and L. Reynolds, eds. *Alley Cropping in the Humid and Sub-Humid Tropics.* Ottawa: International Development Research Centre (IDRC), p. 18. ©1989 by IDRC. Reprinted by permission.

Figure 11.5. Crop research at the International Institute of Tropical Agriculture, Ibadan, Nigeria. Research to develop improved cropping practices and new varieties of tropical crops like cassava, shown here, is of cruciall importance for the future of African agriculture. Photo: CIDA: B. Paton.

development of marketing and pricing policies that give primary producers a just return.

Greatly increased research on indigenous agriculture is an essential component of progressive agrarian development. Research would explore indigenous agricultural practices in detail, focusing on elements that facilitate self-reliance. Careful studies of local crop varieties would identify those most suitable for particular ecological settings and those that yield well irrespective of fertilizer application.

Appropriate low-cost innovations can greatly improve the prospects for traditional agriculture. For example, the development of alley cropping at the International Institute of Tropical Agriculture has provided an ecologically sound, low-cost alternative to shifting cultivation. Alley cropping involves planting rows of food and cash crops between rows of leguminous shrubs that add nitrogen to the soil and reduce soil erosion (Figure 11.4). The use of alley cropping in marginal tropical forest ecosystems eliminates the need for lengthy fallow periods and the continual shifting of farm

locations. It provides an excellent working model of a practical, sustainable agricultural system.

Progressive agricultural development must also foster more self-reliant involvement of rural people in local development. For example, small erosion-control devices, tree planting, and the construction of roads and clinics can be accomplished with local materials and labor at a low cost. The nature of official support for local improvements is crucial if local initiative is to be mobilized; peasant skepticism about communal projects remains as a legacy of the colonial exploitation of forced labor and the heavy-handed alienation of rural resources by some postindependence governments.

Further Reading

An extensive bibliography listing sources on agricultural change can be found in the following source:

Rummel, L. "African agricultural development: A bibliography of recent works." In S. K. Commins, M. F. Lofchie, and R. Payne, eds., *Africa's Agrarian Crisis: The Roots of Famine*, pp. 210–229. Boulder, CO: Lynne Rienner, 1986.

Aspects of colonial agricultural development are discussed in the following sources:

Hopkins, A. G. *An Economic History of West Africa*. London: Longman, 1973.

Tosh, J. "The cash crop revolution in Tropical Africa: A Reappraisal." *African Affairs*, vol. 79 (1980), pp. 79–94.

There is a vast literature on agricultural change and policies in Africa. The following sources are particularly useful:

Barker J., ed. *The Politics of Agriculture in Tropical Africa*. Beverly Hills, CA: Sage, 1984.

Bates, R., and M. Lofchie, ed. *Agricultural Development in Africa: Issues of Public Policy*. New York: Praeger, 1980.

Chambers, R. *Rural Development: Putting the Last First*. New York: Longman, 1983.

De Wilde, J. C., et al., eds. *Experiences with Agricultural Development in Tropical Africa*. 2 vols. Baltimore, MD: Johns Hopkins University Press, 1967.

Ghai, D., and S. Radwan, eds. *Agrarian Policies and Rural Poverty in Africa*. Geneva, Switzerland: International Labour Organization, 1983.

Hart, K. *The Political Economy of West African Agriculture*. New York: Cambridge University Press, 1982.

Pingali, P., Y. Bigot, and H. P. Binswanger. *Agricultural Mechanization and the Evolution of Farming Systems in Sub-Saharan Africa*. Baltimore, MD: Johns Hopkins University Press, 1987.

Richards, P. "Farming systems and agricultural change in West Africa." *Progress in Human Geography*, vol.7 (1983), pp. 1–39.

Contrasting perspectives on the impact of the World Bank on African agriculture are given in the following sources.

Lele, U., ed. *Aid to Africa Agriculture: Lessons from Two Decades of Donor's Experience*. Baltimore, MD: Johns Hopkins University Press, 1992.

Gibbons, P., K. J. Havnevik, and K. Hermele. *A Blighted Harvest: The World Bank and African Agriculture in the 1980s*. London: James Currey, 1993.

The following case studies involve diverse agricultural initiatives, including irrigation, resettlement and state farms:

Barnett, A. *The Gezira Scheme: An Illusion of Development*. London: Frank Cass, 1977.

Hanlon, J. *Mozambique: The Revolution under Fire*. London: Zed, 1984.

Hyden, G. *Beyond Ujamaa in Tanzania: Underdevelopment and an Uncaptured Peasantry*. Berkeley: University of California Press, 1980.

Leo, C. "The failure of the 'progressive farmer' in Kenya's million acre scheme." *Journal of Modern African Studies*, vol. 16 (1978), pp. 619–638.

Pankhurst, A. *Resettlement and Famine in Ethiopia: The Villagers' Experience*. Manchester: Manchester University Press, 1992.

12

✳

The Food Crisis

The intense coverage by the international news media of major famines in the Sahel, Ethiopia, Sudan, and Mozambique, among others, has indelibly marked Africa as the continent of hunger. Stories have emphasized the importance of ecological factors (drought and desertification) and political factors (instability and conflict) as explanations for these catastrophes. Such factors are very relevant, but provide only partial insights into Africa's food crisis. As Carl Eicher (1982) says, "The crisis stems from a seamless web of political, technical and structural constraints which are a product of colonial surplus extraction strategies, misguided development plans and priorities of African states since independence, and faulty advice from expatriate planning advisers. These complex, deep-rooted constraints can only be understood in historical perspective" (p. 157).

Dimensions of the African Food Crisis

This chapter examines the nature and significance of the main types of food crises confronting Africa: chronic undernutrition and abnormal food shortages (famine). Chronic undernutrition occurs when there are significant food deficits year after year. Famines accompany unusually large food deficits that occur because of crop failures or other catastrophes. Famines may afflict areas of chronic shortage or regions that normally have adequate food supplies.

According to the World Bank, the crisis in African agriculture is reflected in the following trends:

1. The growth rate of agricultural production has declined, and is almost everywhere less than the rate of population growth.
2. African agricultural exports have stagnated.
3. Commercial imports of food grains have increased three times as fast as population, and food aid has increased greatly.
4. Increased food imports, in the form of wheat and rice, have changed food preferences and increased food dependency since demand for these foods can seldom be met by local producers.

Hunger is usually attributed to food-production problems, but it is also the result of problems of food inaccessibility. It is the poor who go hungry and starve because they lack the resources necessary to purchase adequate sustenance or to grow their own food. Thus, food crises need to be placed in socioeconomic context, in which disparities in access to food are related to social structure and political–economic processes.

this chapter, however, is on undernutrition, that is, a shortfall in dietary energy supplies.

Nutritional Status

The Fifth World Food Survey of the FAO provides some basic data on the nutritional status of the world's population. It confirms the existence of a large and growing gap between rich and poor countries in access to food energy. The average dietary energy supply (DES) in Africa south of the Sahara is 2,070 kcal per capita (person) per day, which is 22% below the world average (2,660 kcal) and almost 40% less than the average for developed nations (3,390 kcal).

The DES represents only one of the components of a nutritious diet. The human body also requires many different minerals, vitamins, and proteins in varying quantities. In discussing nutrition, the FAO distinguishes between undernutrition, defined as insufficient DES, and malnutrition, which arises from deficiencies in specific nutrients. Several diseases of malnutrition, such as anemia, rickets, and pellagra, are common in Africa. The focus of

Food Production, Imports, and Aid

Most Africans are farmers or pastoralists, and Africa's food comes primarily from domestic sources. The available evidence indicates that food production has failed to keep pace with the increased demand for food caused by rapid population growth. In 25 years from the early 1960s to the mid-1980s, the per capita production of food in Africa south of the Sahara fell by about 25% (Figure 12.1). The precipitous decline in African production is in remarkable contrast to the per capita increases that have been recorded in Asia and Latin America.

The poor quality of agricultural statistics leaves some doubt whether food production has fallen as much as Figure 12.1 suggests. Certainly, there has been a decline in foods entering the formal marketplace. It is possible, however, that more food is being consumed in rural households or sold on the black market, in which case the apparent decline in

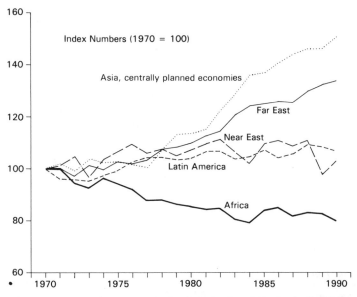

Figure 12.1. Trends in per capita food production: Africa and other Third World regions compared. Africa's performance has lagged far behind that of other Third World regions. After *World Resources, 1990–91.* New York: Basic Books, 1990.

Table 12.1. Food Imports and Food Aid: Cereal Grains

	Food production index 1986–1988 (1979–1981 = 100)	Cereal imports (exports)[a] 1986–1990 (1,000 tons/year)	Food aid as percentage of food imports	Tons/1,000 people/year (net imports)
Angola	87	301	26	31
Benin	110	102	9	22
Botswana	69	158(+2)	28	132
Burkina Faso	116	165(+3)	35	19
Burundi	100	17	26	3
Cameroon	97	251(+8)	3	22
Cape Verde	105	67	80	186
Central African Republic	87	45	32	11
Chad	103	81	46	14
Comoros	109	35	21	76
Congo	92	113	1	51
Côte d'Ivoire	104	549	1	47
Djibouti	NA	56	0	136
Equatorial Guinea	NA	12	25	29
Ethiopia	89	807	86	16
Gabon	97	53	0	48
Gambia	95	71	21	84
Ghana	108	249	32	17
Guinea	93	225	24	40
Guinea Bissau	139	60	20	63
Kenya	89	263(+107)	45	7
Lesotho	80	193(+4)	21	112
Liberia	92	133	32	53
Madagascar	97	143(+18)	65	13
Malawi	85	158(+5)	53	19
Mali	97	126	49	15
Mauritania	89	222	34	117
Mozambique	83	466	82	30
Namibia	NA	67	0	39
Niger	83	125	46	14
Nigeria	103	805	0	17
Rwanda	82	25	51	4
São Tomé e Príncipe	67	13	57	108
Senegal	106	597	15	83
Sierra Leone	101	147	32	37
Somalia	100	240	100	39
South Africa	NA	NA(+2604)	0	(+74)[b]
Sudan	89	749(+247)	88	18
Swaziland	93	45	14	183
Tanzania	89	345(+55)	52	3
Togo	88	86(+20)	12	19
Uganda	121	27	63	2
Zaire	98	382	25	11
Zambia	96	85	100	11
Zimbabwe	81	89(+324)	17	(+34)

[a]Numbers in parentheses are exports.
[b]Net exports.
Sources: FAO. *Trade Yearbook*, 1990.
     FAO. *Food Aid in Figures*, 1990.
     UNDP. *Human Development Report*, 1991.

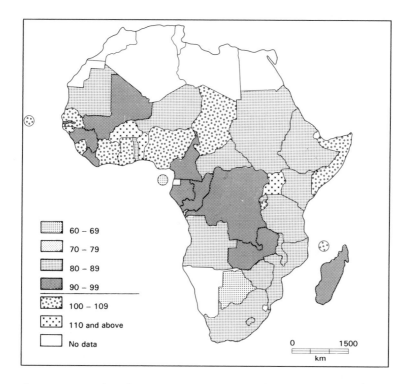

Figure 12.2. Food production per capita: 1986 to 1988 as a percentage of 1979 to 1981. Only a handful of countries managed to increase food production per capita during the 1980s. Data source: UNDP. *Human Development Report 1991.* New York: Oxford University Press, 1991.

The map legend shows:
- 60 – 69
- 70 – 79
- 80 – 89
- 90 – 99
- 100 – 109
- 110 and above
- No data

0   1500
km

production would not be as severe. The reliability of production data is very important, since contemporary agrarian policies have been heavily influenced by these data and the image of crisis that they project.

Food aid and food imports have, in part, compensated for shortfalls in production. Table 12.1 shows the degree to which African countries depend on food from other countries, using data on the volume of cereal grain imports and cereal food aid and on grain receipts per capita. Zimbabwe and South Africa are, in normal years, net exporters of cereal grains. However, even these countries have to rely on imports during times of severe drought, as in 1991 and 1992. At the other extreme are Nigeria, Ethiopia, Sudan, and Senegal, which import at least 500,000 t (metric tons) of grain per year from other countries. This degree of dependence on aid and imports is relatively modest in comparison to

several other parts of the Third World. Egypt, for example, acquires twice as much food from overseas sources as Nigeria, Ethiopia, Sudan, Mozambique, and Senegal combined. However, the data on per capita receipts of food show that several mostly smaller nations of Africa south of the Sahara are heavily dependent on food aid and imports. Nine countries obtain between 100 and 200 t of imported cereals per 1,000 people per year.

Food aid is channelled to countries identified by the United Nations as having a low income and a food deficit. Comparatively wealthy countries such as Nigeria and Côte d'Ivoire purchase significant amounts of grain but receive little or no food aid. Food aid has also been used to provide emergency relief to feed refugees, drought victims, and others affected by abnormal food shortages. Food imports and aid may be a valuable resource for countries plagued with famines or refugee in-

---

Vignette 12.1. The Wheat Trap

The rapid growth of food imports may encourage—and, in turn, be spurred by—new patterns of consumer demand. Gunilla Andrae and Bjorn Beckman's *Wheat Trap* is a study of the implications of Nigeria's growing reliance on imported wheat during the 1970s and early 1980s. Similar processes of "taste transfer" to imported foods are found virtually everywhere in Africa south of the Sahara.

Nigeria's annual imports of wheat and flour increased 18-fold from 1960 to 1964 to 1980 to 1982. Wheat is not part of the traditional diet in most parts of Nigeria. However, by the 1980s, bread had become one of the most important foods of the masses in both urban and rural areas. Three factors that help to explain the growth of bread consumption are (1) its convenience, (2) its compatability with local diets, and (3) its low cost compared to other staples.

The Nigerian government permitted wheat imports to increase because they helped to ensure that urban populations would have access to cheap food. However, the high cost of imported wheat provided the justification for massive investment in irrigation schemes to grow wheat. Once this commitment to domestic production had been made, continuing wheat imports could be treated as an interim measure, pending the availability of local supplies. However, this was an illusion because of the high cost and technical difficulty of growing wheat under irrigation in a tropical setting. A provisional estimate put the true cost of growing one hectare of irrigated wheat at $2,000 per year, equivalent to a government subsidy of about $1,400 for every metric ton of wheat produced.

Beset with rapidly increasing debts and stagnant export revenues, Nigeria resolved in 1985 to encourage the resubstitution of indigenous staples for wheat and to reduce wheat imports. It faces major hurdles in trying to do so: (1) several flour mills and thousands of bakeries have been established to produce bread for the Nigerian market; the milling companies and bakers form a potent lobby arguing for unrestricted imports; (2) consumers want to have access to cheap bread, particularly because of the high cost of locally grown staples; and (3) wheat imports have contributed to the decline in domestic agriculture. It will be difficult in the short run to fill the void created by a sudden reduction in food imports.

The Nigerian experience illustrates how apparently simple, short-run policy decisions about food supply and agricultural development may have far-reaching implications that are very hard to reverse.

Based on G. Andrae and B. Beckman. *The Wheat Trap*. London: Zed, 1987.

---

fluxes. However, there are heavy costs for becoming too dependent on food imports and aid (see, e.g., Vignette 12.1).

Famine

Famines, or "abnormal food shortages" as they are called euphamistically by the FAO, can no longer be considered truly "abnormal" in the contemporary African context. From the late 1960s to the early 1990s, hardly a year has passed without reports of famine in some part of Africa. Crop failure and famine were particularly widespread during 1983 to 1984 and 1991 to 1992. Both times, half of the countries of Africa south of the Sahara were designated by the FAO as having abnormal food shortages (Figure 12.4), and special appeals were launched to provide those coun-

Figure 12.3. Billboard promoting bread consumption, Nigeria. Advertising is one of the factors accounting for the rapid growth of bread consumption and the growth of Nigeria's "wheat trap." Photo: author.

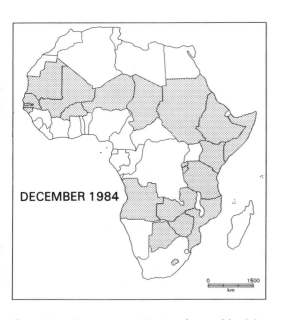

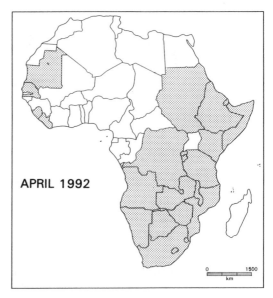

Figure 12.4. Countries experiencing abnormal food shortages, 1984 and 1992. Abnormal food shortages were reported in 24 countries during 1984 and 1992; they occurred in both years in 15 countries. Data sources: FAO. *World Food Report 1985.* Rome: FAO, 1985. FAO. *Food Outlook, 1992.* Rome: FAO, 1992.

tries with emergency food aid (see Vignette 12.2).

Famines are often associated with some ecological crisis serious enough to drastically reduce harvests. Drought is the most common of these ecological crises; but floods, volcanic eruptions, swarms of locusts or other insects, plant diseases, excessive rainfall may also cause crops to fail. Famines are also associated with political strife that disrupts normal economic activity. Beyond these immediate causes, a host of contributory factors may be identified. Each episode of famine increases susceptibility to subsequent crises, particularly among the poor. Food stores are exhausted,

debts are incurred, and land may have to be sold to acquire food. Smaller food reserves, coupled with debt and poverty, mean that crop failures that caused manageable hardship in the past result in famine today.

In drought-prone regions of Africa, where periodic famines have occurred since time immemorial, people rely on many strategies to cope with food shortages. Stored grain and famine foods (edibles that are consumed when other, preferred foods are not available) may provide immediate relief from hunger. Temporary interregional or rural–urban migration may provide a source of income to purchase food. In very serious crises, personal property

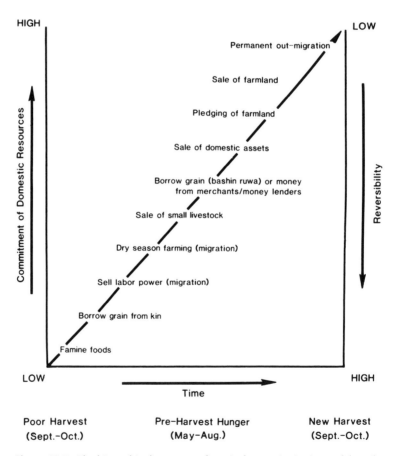

Figure 12.5. The hierarchical structure of survival strategies in times of drought: Northern Nigeria. As the effect of famine deepens, survival strategies shift, typically involving increased commitments of domestic resources and difficulty in reversing the strategy. Source: M. Watts. *Silent Violence: Food, Famine and Peasantry in Northern Nigeria.* Berkeley: University of California Press, 1983, p. 436. ©1983 by The Regents of the University of California. Reprinted by permission.

or land may be sold, or the family may even be forced to move away permanently. As Figure 12.5 shows, these strategies may be viewed as a hierarchy of responses, from those that are relatively easy to others with increasingly drastic and irreversible consequences.

The research of Michael Watts in northern Nigeria helps us to see how historical changes in political economy have changed the meaning of food shortages. He describes the workings of the 19th-century "moral economy," in which the ruling class received grain from the peasants as tax but were obligated in turn to provide relief during times of crisis. This moral economy provided a degree of security for the poor. During the colonial era the moral economy was irreparably damaged by heavy taxation, cash crop promotion, and the erosion of traditional values. Consequently, African rural communities today are less able to cope with crop failures and must rely increasingly on food brought from other countries as well as drastic such responses as outmigration to survive when severe food shortages occur.

It is hardly surprising that drought should recur in semiarid areas such as the Sahel, where rainfall tends to be highly variable from year to year. In such marginal environments the duration and regularity of precipitation is as important as the total amount. An unusually short rainy season or a long dry spell at any time before harvest can ruin crops.

Two things that have changed are (1) the number of people who depend on very marginal environments for their sustenance and (2) the "health" of semiarid ecosystems subjected to intensive utilization. The increased intensity of resource exploitation in the Sahel has coincided with the widespread displacement of farmers and pastoralists from their traditional milieus by cash cropping and by irrigation schemes developed in river valleys. The human dimensions of seemingly "natural" processes such as drought and desertification are discussed further in Chapter 21.

While food shortages in the Sahel have somewhat complex origins, it is impossible to miss the causes of the severe famines that devastated Mozambique for a decade, starting in the early 1980s. The country struggled with limited success to contain Renamo, an insurgent army sponsored at the time by South Africa as a means of destabilizing the Mozambique government. Renamo totally devastated the economy and social programs in rural areas, forcing many rural Mozambicans to abandon their homes and farms for the relative safety of protected encampments. Mozambique has a relatively favorable climate and plenty of arable land, but without peace and security, food production has fallen far short of need.

Chronic Undernutrition

Africa's most serious dilemma is not drought and mass starvation. Rather, it is the pervasive growth of undernutrition. Families, communities, regions, and nations in all parts of the continent are affected by chronically inadequate food supplies (Vignette 12.3). The patterns of undernutrition in society and space, and the factors that help to account for the growth of the crisis, are equally diverse. However, several generalizations may be made about chronic undernutrition in contemporary Africa:

1. Chronic undernutrition is extremely widespread.
2. It is both an urban and a rural problem.
3. Children and women are more likely to be undernourished than men.
4. It is often seasonal in nature.
5. It is not only, or even primarily, a production problem.
6. It is clearly linked to increasing levels of dependency.
7. The crisis has continued to deepen since the early 1970s when global attention was first drawn to the problem of food shortages in Africa.

No country and no ecological region is totally free from the problem of chronic undernutrition. Contrary to popular opinion, this is not merely a crisis of semiarid and arid en-

Vignette 12.2. Famine Relief for Ethiopia

With the airing of a dramatic television news report in October 1984, the global public learned that Ethiopia was being ravaged by famine. Governments and aid agencies had been aware of the crisis for some time, but the international response had been minimal until public concern began to mount.

The United Nations established an Office for Emergency Operations in Addis Ababa to coordinate the relief program. Food aid commitments totaling 1,273,000 t were made between December 1984 and December 1985. Over one-third of this food aid came from the United States. The European Community, Canada, Australia, and various United Nations agencies contributed most of the rest. Significant amounts of nonfood aid were pledged by several countries, most notably the USSR.

There have been few emergencies in which nongovernmental organizations (NGOs) played as large a role as in Ethiopia in 1984 to 1985. Eventually, some 63 NGOs from various parts of the world joined the effort. Some had been working in Ethiopia for many years, but most were new arrivals. The NGOs were responsible for the distribution of American, Canadian, and Australian food aid, some two-thirds of the total. The Ethiopian government's Relief and Rehabilitation Commission (RRC) distributed the rest.

The overwhelming response by governments and NGOs meant that the distribution of food, not its availability, was the primary challenge (Figure 12.7). It would be hard to imagine more difficult conditions for the administration of a relief program. The topography of Ethiopia is extremely difficult; it was often impossible to get across canyons and up cliffs to places only a few kilometers away. The network of roads, railways, and

Figure 12.6. Distribution famine emergency food, Ethiopia. The picture was taken during the massive international relief effort at the time of the 1985 to 1986 famine in Ethiopia. Photo: CIDA: D. Barbour.

cont.

Vignette 12.2. (cont.)

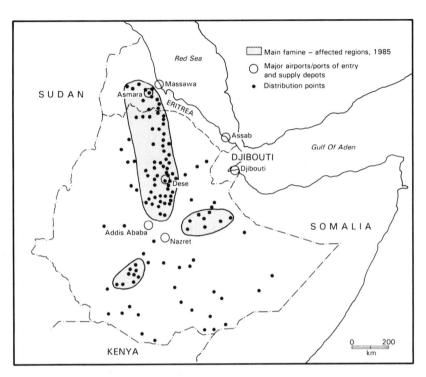

Figure 12.7. The distribution of food aid in Ethiopia, 1985 to 1986. The challenge of distributing a massive amount of food of food aid in extremely difficult circumstances necessitated diverse and innovative strategies.

airports was poorly developed and often unusable because of poor maintenance and war-related damage. Thus, much of the food had to be brought into makeshift airstrips or air-dropped into remote communities. Moreover, vehicles were in very short supply. Many donors sent food but made no provision for getting it to the people in need.

The greatest logistical problem was caused by the ongoing civil war in Eritrea, Tigray, and the northern Wollo Provinces, which included some of the worst famine areas. The RRC was unable to operate in many areas. With the Ethiopian government unwilling to agree formally to involving rebel groups in food distribution in rebel-held areas, much of that aid had to be brought along difficult routes via Sudan. Where road transport was possible in these insecure provinces, trucks had to move by convoy and remained at risk from hostile fire or land mines.

From a logistical standpoint, the relief effort of 1984 to 1985 was an outstanding success. By mid-1985, basic rations were being distributed to 7 million people. Intensive supplementary feeding programs focused on the special needs of infants, small children, and lactating mothers. The emergency effort could not, however, address the root causes of the famine. Further crises have occurred in Ethiopia since 1985 and are likely to persist. Can the world be counted upon to respond when the next emergency occurs?

Based on K. Jansson, M. Harris, and A. Penrose. *The Ethiopian Famine.* London: Zed, 1987.

Vignette 12.3. Four Families, Four Kinds of Hunger

Four brief sketches follow, each of which illustrates some of the diverse circumstances in which chronic undernutrition occurs in Africa south of the Sahara. The sketches refer to individual families, but their situations are virtually identical to those faced by millions of families in many parts of the continent.

A farm family in Gambia

Sorghum, millet, and groundnuts are cultivated on the family farm. Even with relatively intensive agricultural techniques, the farm seldom produces enough to feed the family for the year and provide income to cover essential costs. The father earns supplemental income working in Dakar as a porter during the dry season. Nevertheless, food is very scarce late in the dry season and early in the rainy season. This year's harvest was good, but one-quarter of it had to be sold to repay a loan obtained to purchase inputs to grow the crops.

A pastoralist family in Mali

Before the 1972 to 1974 drought, this Fulani household was considered to be prosperous, with a herd of 120 cattle and many sheep and goats. After four-fifths of the animals perished during the drought, the herd ceased to be economically viable. The family's dependence on cultivation increased subsequently, to the extent that over two-thirds of their dietary energy now comes from grain. When harvests were poor, young cattle had to be sold to finance food purchases. The family is caught in a vicious circle: Selling the young cattle prevents the revitalization of the herd and perpetuates the family's vulnerability.

A poor family in rural Lesotho

The meagre production of the family farm cannot support the family. Many families in Lesotho depend on remittances from members working in South Africa, but opportunities there for foreign migrant workers have become more restricted in recent years. Because no member of this family works in South Africa, food obtained by participating in food-for-work projects is crucial for making ends meet. The food distributed through food-for-work projects, food supplement programs for preschoolers, and school lunches is supplied from food aid.

A factory worker's family in Zaire

This family of seven lives in a squatter settlement on the outskirts of Kinshasa. The father supplements his wage as a factory worker with earnings from a part-time job as a waiter in a local bar. The mother is a petty trader; the older children often work with her. Family income has not kept pace with the cost of living. Austerity measures imposed by the International Monetary Fund as their prescription for Zaire's economic recovery have increased drastically the cost not only of imported food but also of locally produced staples. One meal per day has become the standard level of sustenance for Zaire's urban poor.

vironments. The United Nations has designated 24 low-income countries in Africa south of the Sahara as targets for food aid programs to alleviate their chronic food deficits. However, the problem extends even to South Africa, a major exporter of grains that nevertheless is beset with widespread and serious crises of undernutrition in many rural areas.

The extent and seriousness of undernutrition in urban areas is sometimes underestimated, perhaps because of the obvious visibility in the cities of food for sale. However, food tends to be extremely expensive in relation to the earning power of the urban poor; it is poverty rather than food production failures that prevents the urban poor from obtaining adequate sustenance. A variety of government policies, on issues as diverse as minimum wages, food imports, state monopoly pricing of commodities, and the maintenance of the transportation infrastructure, affect not only the volume of food in urban markets but also its affordability.

The adequacy of diet often varies within families. Young children, women, and the elderly are more likely than men to be undernourished. Custom often dictates that men should eat first, with women and children sharing what food remains. Men have access to more money than women and, thus, are in a better position to supplement their diet by purchasing prepared food. The effects of inequitable distribution on younger children and women are especially evident in times of increased food scarcity.

Undernutrition in Africa often occurs seasonally, especially in rural areas with a semiarid climate. Food production in such areas is virtually confined to a short rainy season. While food is relatively plentiful at harvesttime and people gain weight, the months before a new harvest are often characterized by food scarcity and hunger. Studies in several countries have shown that both body weights and general health status decline because of inadequate dietary energy. Because these food deficits are most acute during the farming season, when good health and plenty of energy are needed to undertake an onerous workload, the deficits may lead to reduced farm productivity.

It is hard to overestimate the importance of underdevelopment and poverty as explanations for chronic undernutrition in Africa.

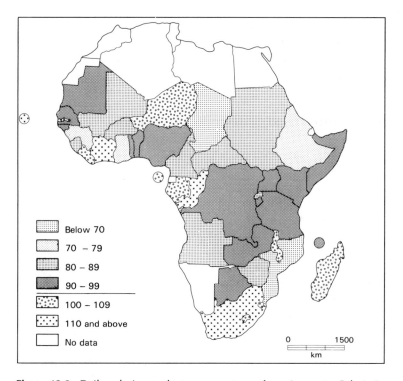

Figure 12.8. Daily calorie supply as a percentage of requirements. Calorie intakes reach FAO minimum standards in only a quarter of the countries of Africa south of the Sahara. Data source: World Bank. *World Development Report, 1990.* New York: Oxford University Press, 1990.

Hunger will be manifest in the midst of apparent food surpluses if part of the community lacks the means to purchase adequate sustenance or to grow its own food. Chronic indebtedness is often the key to hunger in rural Africa. Loans obtained to purchase food or to acquire seed and fertilizer usually are payable at harvest time when market prices are lowest. Thus, poor families sell their crops cheaply and then purchase food expensively at a later date. Deeply indebted households may be forced to sell the means of production, especially their land. A growing dependence on external resources has coincided with the deepening crisis of food shortages. Food imports and food aid have progressed from being short-term relief to being an integral part of national food budgets in most African countries. As Vignette 12.1 showed, food imports have stimulated changes in consumer tastes and have hurt local food producers. The imports have contributed to increasingly heavy government debt loads, which in turn have led to policies of restraint, for example, currency devaluation, wage controls, cuts in public services, and reduced food imports. For the poor, economic restraint often means eating less, and less nutritious, food.

Interpretations of Chronic Food Crises

It is generally agreed that the problem of chronic food shortages is highly complex, and that specific causes vary from country to country. However, there is considerable disagreement about the cause of Africa's apparent inability to feed itself adequately. Outlined below are five of the most widely circulated interpretations of the growth of chronic undernutrition in Africa south of the Sahara. Differences of interpretation are very important because each interpretation is associated with its own set of divergent policy prescriptions.

Effect of Climate Change on the African Environment

Since the late 1960s, drought has become almost commonplace in several parts of Africa south of the Sahara. The observed trends toward a hotter, drier climate in Africa's savanna and semidesert regions are consistent with the findings of recent research on climate change, that is, a global warming is underway.

The growing frequency of drought is clearly related to the deterioration of ecological resources, particularly vegetation and soil, in the more arid regions of Africa. Recent estimates suggest that moderate to severe desertification threatens a quarter of Africa's total land area and 85% of its drylands. As land degradation takes place, it becomes increasingly difficult for farmers and herders to produce enough to feed themselves.

Social scientists emphasize, however, that while desertification generally accompanies or follows the occurrence of drought, it is necessary to focus on the human response to drought to understand why this degradation of resources takes place. It is also important to consider why the human and animal populations of marginal environments have grown to such an extent that their use of the environment becomes unsustainable. This situation not only is a result of naive expansion during earlier times of above-average rainfall, but also is a result of the continuing displacement of pastoralists and farmers from highly productive areas, such as river valleys, because of agricultural development projects. Land degradation and related issues are discussed further in Chapter 21.

Rapidly Growing Population

While per capita food production has shown a steady decline in recent years, there has been an increase in the total amount of food produced (Figure 12.1). The implication of these data *seems* clear: If Africa's population was not growing so rapidly, there would be no food problem.

Few would dispute that a much slower rate of population growth is one of the keys if African countries are to have a reasonable chance of achieving real progress. However, if population growth was sufficient by itself to account for the shortage of food, rapidly growing countries in Latin America and Asia would also have growing food shortages; in reality their per capita food production has been increasing. Moreover, labor shortages in rural areas have at times been found to be a factor in declining production. Thus, the search for an explanation must go beyond population growth to consider a number of aspects of how food is produced in Africa.

Failure of the Peasants

According to this perspective, indigenous producers should be criticized for cultivation practices that allegedly cause harm to the environment and for their reluctance to adopt progressive farming methods. The solution is seen to lie in a restructuring of agriculture that uses some large-scale production system, such as plantations, state farms, or livestock ranches.

Although this perspective began to wane with the new emphasis in the 1970s on small producers, it continues to be enunciated, particularly by those who stand to profit from the promotion of large-scale, technological agriculture. The Reagan administration, for example, advocated large-scale international capitalist investment as a key component of its foreign-assistance programs.

Inappropriate Policies of African Governments

Many international agencies and development analysts have said that African governments should be blamed for the continent's food deficits. This perspective is most frequently identified with the World Bank, and especially its 1981 report entitled *Accelerated Development in Sub-Saharan Africa: An Agenda for Action*. Pricing policies have been identified as a pivotal issue. When governments import substantial quantities of food and fix its price below the market value for locally grown staples, they undermine domestic food production. Agriculture is also discouraged when state-run produce-marketing agencies pay farmers less than a fair market price for their crops; the price shortfall is in effect a hidden tax on rural-producers. Governments have been criticized

for inadequate maintenance of transportation networks, thus hampering both the distribution of production inputs to farmers and the flow of food to consumers. Finally, a whole range of "urban biases" in development policy are seen as inducements for young people to move to the city, where they become consumers rather than producers of food.

The World Bank advocates that governments phase out these counterproductive policies and focus their development efforts on small-scale farmers. The World Bank's IADP strategy, which was described in the previous chapter, emphasizes the provision of a wide range of production inputs to farmers and the improvement of rural infrastructures. This strategy includes short-run increases in foreign aid to finance the IADPs.

Relation of Commoditization of Agriculture to Declining Nutritional Status

Underdevelopment theorists have put special emphasis on the role of colonialism and of capitalist development in the postcolonial era as the causes of Africa's food crisis. *Commoditization* means increased dependency on purchased foods and reduced self-sufficiency. It may involve increased cash-crop production requiring a diversion of resources into nonsubsistence production, the incorporation of local farmers into large-scale production systems, or increasing dependence on wage labor after access to arable land is lost.

The key issue is the development of gross disparities in the distribution of land and other production inputs that occur with the commoditization of food systems. This process is fueled by the promotion of large-scale imported technologies and production systems, including those like the IADPs, which favor a few rural entrepreneurs while purporting to help small farmers. Thus, a large proportion of the population is left increasingly vulnerable to the effects of economic recession, wage controls, and crop failures.

The question of appropriate agrarian policies has proved to be more difficult for critics of commoditization. There is no clearly defined set of prescribed policy responses comparable to the IADP package of the World Bank. Liberals have tended to advocate small-scale, self-reliant rural development that uses local resources whenever possible to achieve greater equity. Marxists have tended to focus on the need for revolutionary change to reverse the processes giving rise to an inequitable distribution of wealth, and they typically advocate the reorganization of production according to socialist (collectivist) principles.

Many interpretations have been given for Africa's crises of food production and availability. That food crises have not only persisted but become steadily more pervasive, despite the attempt to implement myriad remedial strategies, points to the complexity of the problem. Simplistic explanations and the simplistic remedies that follow them should not be trusted.

The food crisis is multidimensional. The degradation of the African environment, which has contributed to declining food production in many parts of the continent, cannot be explained without reference to government policies that have increased the pace of commoditization of food. Likewise, the failure of the peasantry to produce enough food to meet demand may be attributed largely to policies that have given little support to farmers, have allowed rural–urban transportation linkages to deteriorate, and have responded to rising food prices by increasing imports of cheap grain from abroad. On the demand side, requirements for food have increased because of the rapid growth of population and policies that have encouraged or forced people to leave the land.

The policy response to food problems has often been too narrowly conceived and too often divorced from local realities. For example, the response to acute food shortages should address not only immediate needs (i.e., emergency food aid), as has so often been the case, but also longer-term needs (e.g., peace, reconstruction, and appropriate development policies for the agrarian sector). Moreover, responses not firmly committed to building on the strengths of indigenous systems of production, using local resources wherever possible, are unlikely to be sustainable.

Further Reading

The FAO publishes several sources that provide current data and descriptions of the world food situation:

Food Aid Bulletin (periodic).
Production Yearbook (annual).
Trade Yearbook (annual).
The State of Food and Agriculture (annual).

The following sources provide discussions of theoretical issues concerning the interpretation of Africa's food crises:

Berry, S. "The food crisis and agrarian change in Africa: A review essay." *African Studies Review,* vol. 27 (1984), pp. 58–112.
Bryceson, D. F. "Nutrition and the commoditization of food in sub-Saharan Africa." *Social Science and Medicine,* vol. 28 (1989), pp. 425–440.
Cathie, J. *The Political Economy of Food Aid.* Aldershot, England: Gower, 1982.
Eicher, C. "Facing up to Africa's food crisis." *Foreign Affairs,* vol. 61 (1982), pp. 151–174.
Knight, C. G., and R. P. Wilcox. *Triumph or Triage: The World Food Problem in Geographical Perspective.* Washington, DC: Association of American Geographers, 1976.

Seasonal aspects of hunger are discussed in the following source:

Chambers, R., R. Longhurst, and A. Pacey. *Seasonal Dimensions to Rural Poverty.* London: Frances Pinter, 1981.

The Sahelian drought has been studied in great detail. See the following source:

Franke, R., and B. Chasin. *Seeds of Famine: Ecological Destruction and the Development Dilemma in the West African Sahel.* Montclair, NJ: Allenheld and Osmun, 1980.

The following sources are individual or collected case studies of the many manifestations of the food crisis in Africa:

Lawrence, P., ed. *World Recession and the Food Crisis in Africa.* Boulder, CO: Westview, 1986.
Watts, M., and H. Bohle. "Hunger, famine and the space of vulnerability." *GeoJournal,* vol. 30 (1993), pp. 117–125. (See also M. Watts, *Silent Violence: Food, Famine and Peasantry in Northern Nigeria* [Berkeley: University of California Press, 1983].)
Wisner, B. "Nutritional consequences of the articulation of capitalist and non-capitalist modes of

production in Eastern Nigeria." *Rural Africana,* nos. 8–9 (1980–1981), pp. 99–132.

For discussions of policy issues concerning food, see the following sources:

Bryant, C., ed. *Poverty, Policy and Food Security in Southern Africa.* London: Lynne Rienner, 1988.

Harrison, P. *The Greening of Africa: Breaking Through in the Battle for Land and Food.* London: Paladin, 1987.

Raikes, P. *Modernizing Hunger: Famine, Food Surplus and Farm Policy in the EEC and Africa.* London: James Currey, 1988.

World Bank. *Accelerated Development in sub-Saharan Africa: An Agenda for Action.* Washington, DC: World Bank, 1981. (The book edited by Lawrence [see above] has a number of papers critical of the World Bank approach.)

URBAN ECONOMIES
AND SOCIETIES

While most Africans continue to live in rural areas, it is in urban Africa that the most rapid growth is taking place. The residents of Africa's cities now account for over one-quarter of the total African population. This rapid growth in the population of cities since independence has been accompanied by a comparable increase in the size and diversity of the cities' economic, cultural, and political roles. At the same time, the interpretation of this growth has continued to be the subject of debate. Some see the cities as dynamic centers of growth and innovation, taking the lead and showing the way for rural and small-town Africa. Others are critical of the "urban bias" that they see pervading most development theory and practice, and these critics see the cities as parasitic centers that drain the countryside of development capital.

Chapter 13 surveys the changing structure of African cities, from the precolonial cities that existed in several parts of the continent to the cities of colonial Africa to contemporary African cities. Looking at African urbanization in historical perspective highlights the dramatic changes in the size, functions, and social and spatial organization of the cities that have occurred and continue to occur.

The economic geography of African cities is discussed in Chapter 14. The chapter is structured around a comparison of the organization and significance of formal and informal economic activity in the cities. At the same time, it is important not to look at urban economic activity in isolation from that of rural areas. Not only are rural–urban economic linkages of increasing importance as urbanites continue their struggle to make ends meet during very difficult economic times, but also urban dwellers rely to a considerable extent on farming—the quintessential "rural" occupation—to survive.

Chapter 15 looks at housing in the urban environment and, in particular, the policy options used by governments to address the acute problems of housing that have inevitably occurred in conjunction with the rapid growth of Africa's cities. However, in the provision of housing, as with most other amenities, the efforts of government pale in comparison to the self-help efforts of countless millions of urban Africans who have constructed homes for themselves. Terms such as squatter settlements, which are often used to designate these self-housed communities, hardly do justice to the dynamism, ingenuity, and self-reliance that these places represent.

13

The Evolution of Urban Structure

This chapter provides a historical geography of urbanization in Africa, examining the changing size, spatial organization, and functions of cities in precolonial, colonial, and postcolonial times. Although urbanization has been a feature of the 20th century in most of Africa, the continent has had a long history of urban development. African cities are very diverse, resulting from the melding over many centuries of indigenous African, Arabic–Muslim, and European influences. Thus, standard North American theories of urban development and models of urban form must be used with caution in the African context. African urbanization can only be understood in the context of the diverse sources that have influenced its development on the one hand, and the political and economic histories of specific regions and societies, on the other.

The Precolonial City

Although most Africans in precolonial times lived in rural communities, there was a widespead and dynamic tradition of urban development (Figure 13.1). Urbanization first appeared in Africa south of the Sahara some 3,000 years ago in present-day Sudan. However, most precolonial urban development occurred between the 10th and 19th centuries

A.D. While Meroe, Great Zimbabwe, and many other early African cities exist today only as architectural ruins, some survived into the 20th century and remain important today. Ibadan, Kano, Kumasi, and Mombasa are all examples of modern cities that had been established and had flourished before the colonial era.

Most precolonial African cities were political capitals, the headquarters of powerful emperors or chiefs holding dominion over neighboring territories. The shrine and palace typically were situated close to each other, a symbol of the spiritual base of political power. As political centers, subject to attack from competing powers, early cities were often surrounded by a wall or located on an easily defended site. Residents of outlying villages could seek refuge in the walled city in times of danger.

Precolonial cities had important economic functions. Some were located near sources of vital raw materials; the first settlers in Kano, for example, exploited local deposits of iron ore. Manufacturing activities such as weaving, iron making, and metal casting were an important source of wealth. The products of these industries could be sold in local and regional markets, or internationally.

Precolonial African cities tended to be structured "organically" around the palace and re-

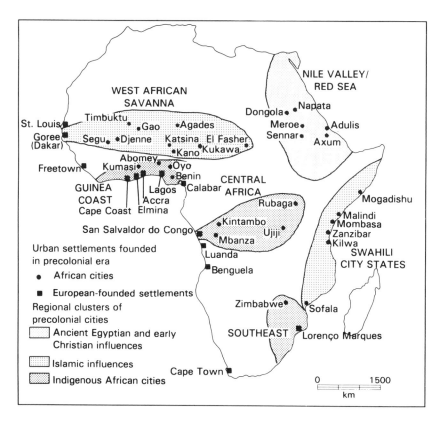

Figure 13.1. Precolonial urbanization in Africa. Precolonial urbanization was widespread. It reflected a variety of indigenous and external influences, specific to each of several regions of urban development.

ligious shrine as primary focal points (Figure 13.2). Particular occupational groups (e.g., blacksmiths, weavers, traders) were generally clustered in their own wards. Members of royal families and their associates tended to be concentrated near the locus of power—the palace. In some of these cities, the huge size and high walls of the royal compound created literally a city within a city.

The middle section of the Nile Valley has played a pivotal role in the history of urbanization. The development of cities in this region dates back 3,000 years to the founding of Napata and Meroe. The form and functions of these cities, most notably the construction of ceremonial temples and pyramids, reflected their close ties to Egypt. The Nile Valley later experienced distinct Christian (6th to 15th centuries) and Islamic (post–15th century) phases of urbanization.

The large, sprawling cities of Christian Nubia were replaced by compact cities of Islamic design, the most important of which were Sennar and Khartoum.

A separate tradition of urbanization evolved in what is now Eritrea and Ethiopia through cultural contact and synthesis between local African and migrant Arab populations. The port of Adulis, which became a very important trading center, was among the earliest of these cities. By the first century A.D., the city of Axum had been established as the political capital of the powerful state of Axum. The legacy of Axum's fourth-century conversion to Christianity includes the development of several cities as centers of trade, Christian worship, and rule. The founding of Addis Ababa in 1886 as a new capital marked the final phase of two millenia of premodern Ethiopian urban development.

Islamic cities were established in the West African savanna empires of Ghana, Mali, Songhai, and Borno, and in the Hausa states of Nigeria, starting in the ninth century. Most of these cities were located near the southern end of major trans-Saharan trading routes and developed in conjunction with the growth of economic and cultural linkages between West and North Africa. Their layout and architecture show a very strong North African Islamic influence. Many had separate districts inhabited by traders from North Africa. Manufacturing activities were concentrated in quarters occupied by specific types of artisans, while trade was centered within marketplaces. Mosques, the focal point of religious life, were located in the heart of the city. The most important of these cities were dynamic and sophisticated. For example, Timbuktu in the 15th and 16th centuries was a world-class city with impressive architecture, a bustling trading economy, and a renowned international university.

The writings of Heinrich Barth, a German explorer who visited Kano twice during the mid–19th century, provide a graphic description of the economic vitality of that city. Kano's economy was based on both manufacturing and commerce. The principal industry, the weaving and dyeing of cotton cloth, was undertaken during the dry season in the city and throughout the rich farming region nearby. Kano cloth was worn throughout savanna West Africa and across the Sahara in North Africa. According to Barth, the influx of foreign traders during the dry season caused a doubling of Kano's normal population of 30,000.

Kilwa, Mombasa, and some 40 other Islamic cities located in East Africa form an important part of the legacy of almost two millenia of commerce, intermarriage, and cultural synthesis between local African peoples and migrant traders from the Arabian Peninsula. These cities were established along the coast between Mogadishu and Sofala—near the southern limit of the seasonally reversing monsoon winds that allowed dhows (sailing vessels) from the Persian Gulf to travel to East Africa and back. The merchants, officials, and rulers, who were primarily of Arab origin, formed the elite in these Swahili cities. Using proceeds from a flourishing trade in slaves, gold, ivory, and other goods, they created planned urban landscapes, containing elaborate coral stone buildings, and lived in luxury. The bulk of the population was composed of Muslim artisans and traders of African origin and non-Muslim slaves. These city–states went into decline in the late 15th century, following the arrival of the Portuguese and the consequent disruption of trade.

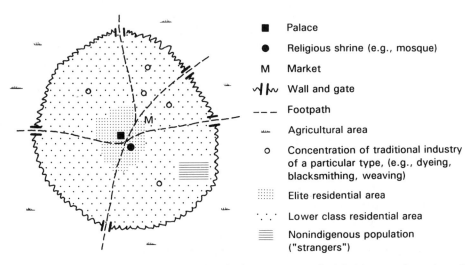

■ Palace

● Religious shrine (e.g., mosque)

M Market

Wall and gate

--- Footpath

Agricultural area

o Concentration of traditional industry of a particular type, (e.g., dyeing, blacksmithing, weaving)

Elite residential area

Lower class residential area

Nonindigenous population ("strangers")

Figure 13.2. Schematic map of the precolonial African city. Precolonial cities served a variety of economic, social, and political functions.

Indigenous (non-Islamic) African cities evolved in several regions, including Zimbabwe, the Kongo kingdom in present-day Zaire, and the forest zone of West Africa. These cities, having developed in diverse cultural and ecological settings, were more varied in form and function than the Islamic urban centers were.

The precolonial urbanization process was particularly well developed in the Yoruba kingdoms of southern Nigeria and in the neighboring kingdom of Benin. The earliest Yoruba city, Ife, dates back at least to the 10th century. Several Yoruba cities were founded as military camps, initially designed to ensure imperial domination over conquered peoples. Craft industries such as weaving, carving, and metalworking developed, with most towns having their own specializations. Nevertheless, the economies of Yoruba cities remained primarily agricultural. By the late 19th century, three Yoruba cities—Ibadan, Oyo, and Abeokuta—had populations of approximately 100,000; and 20 other urban settlements contained 10,000 to 60,000 people.

A number of European visitors to Benin, starting in the 15th century, described it as a very impressive city, with broad and straight avenues lined with neatly arranged and solidly constructed houses. The king's palace, which reportedly occupied as large an area as the Dutch town of Haarlem, contained numerous dwellings and huge galleries where bronze plaques portraying the history of Benin were on display. Merchants from Benin conducted large-scale trade in ironwork, weapons, ivory, and other goods throughout western Africa.

Europeans arriving for the first time found cities in many parts of Africa. In other regions, there was no urban development, even where conditions seemed to favor urbanization. For example, the Igbo of southeastern Nigeria did not build cities, despite their proximity to other urbanized societies, very high population densities, and relatively advanced social and economic institutions. It has been hypothesized that the absence of cities is related to the egalitarian structure of Igbo society: They had no chiefs and, therefore, had no

reason to build cities to house and glorify an aristocracy.

Starting in the late 15th century, Europeans established themselves at isolated points along the coast, the intention being to secure and protect regional trading rights and to provide refueling stations for ships en route to India. Fortifications were built at many these sites, and small settlements grew up around them. Modern cities such as Dakar, Accra, and Luanda grew rapidly during the colonial era at sites that Europeans had occupied for centuries. Other centers, such as Libreville and Calabar, emerged later in the precolonial era in conjunction with the growth in commodity trade and early efforts to liberate slaves.

The Colonial City

Although a large proportion of Africa's cities and towns originated in colonial times, only one-quarter of today's largest, most important cities had not been established prior to the colonial conquest. These previously existing settlements, of both African and European origin, grew as a result of expanded trade and new administrative functions. Elsewhere, particularly in the interior and in areas where there was little or no previous tradition of urbanization, Europeans established cities for the first time.

While most colonial cities in Africa performed a variety of economic and political functions, it is often possible to identify an initial one. Lusaka and Abidjan are among several cities established as colonial administrative centers. Other, generally smaller cities developed as provincial and district administrative centers in each country. The administrative capitals usually contained military garrisons, which represented the ultimate basis of colonial authority.

The exploitation of African resources was possible only because of the development of a transportation system. Port cities such as Douala, Matadi, and Beira were founded where good harbor sites were available. Railways were constructed to move minerals and

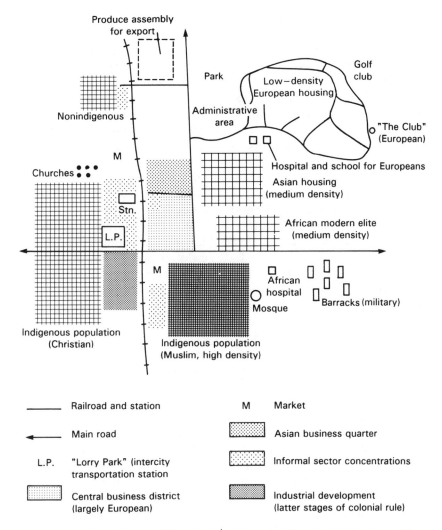

Produce assembly for export

Park

Golf club

Low–density European housing

Nonindigenous

Administrative area

"The Club" (European)

Churches

M

Hospital and school for Europeans

Stn.

Asian housing (medium density)

L.P.

African modern elite (medium density)

M

African hospital

Mosque

Barracks (military)

Indigenous population (Christian)

Indigenous population (Muslim, high density)

▬▬▬ Railroad and station	M Market
◀▬▬ Main road	▦ Asian business quarter
L.P. "Lorry Park" (intercity transportation station	▒ Informal sector concentrations
▦ Central business district (largely European)	▓ Industrial development (latter stages of colonial rule)

Figure 13.3. Schematic map of the colonial African city. The colonial city showed the influence of urban planning: a grid pattern of streets and a spatial separation of urban functions and population subgroups.

agricultural produce from the interior to the ports for shipment overseas. Cities located along the rail lines served as bulking points where produce from the hinterland could be gathered for export. In major mineral areas such as the Copper Belt of Zambia and Zaire, cities were developed to house and provide services for mine employees. Thus, many of Africa's colonial cities were created for economic reasons; administrative functions were clearly of secondary importance in these centers.

The face of cities established by Africans

in precolonial times was radically changed under colonial rule. Some cities, bypassed by the new transportation routes and rejected as administrative centers, declined into obscurity; examples are Kukawa and Abomey, the capitals of the kingdoms of Borno and Dahomey, respectively. Other precolonial cities gained new economic and governmental functions and prospered.

In the British colonies, the form of precolonial cities was left essentially intact; new colonial cities were grafted onto them. Kano is the classic example of a dual city, incorporating both a bustling modern sector and an ancient walled Islamic city (Vignette 13.1). In contrast, precolonial cities in French colonies were redesigned substantially in the European image. Most of the old cities were demolished and rebuilt with straight avenues, public squares, and other typically European features.

Urbanization during the colonial era reflected a concerted attempt to control the form, size, and function of cities and to achieve orderly development through the application of European town-planning principles. The grid pattern of streets, the central business district, and the architecture of public buildings were all reminiscent of Europe.

Other attributes of colonial cities reflected the particular concerns of Europeans living in Africa. Cities were deliberately and rigidly segregated on racial grounds. European, Asian, and African living and working spaces were placed in separate parts of the city. Segregation was justified on grounds of security and public health (see Vignette 13.2). Efforts were also made to segregate Africans of different religious and ethnic backgrounds, allegedly to reduce the likelihood of conflict. In reality, segregation permitted the colonialists to exert greater control by "dividing and ruling" groups that were potential sources of discontent and resistance. Economic functions were similarly divided among (1) a central business district catering to Europeans, (2) a so-called second-class business district occupied by Asian merchants who were "middle men" linking the African and European economic sectors, and (3) marketplaces for African traders.

Salisbury (now Harare), Lusaka, and Nairobi differed from most other colonial cities in that they were designed to cater to the needs of European settler populations. The urban structure and architecture of these cities were very similar to those in Europe. There were not many signs (especially in the central business district and in European residential districts) that these cities were located in Africa. Their European character was protected by means of legislation to strictly control rural–urban migration and, thus, to limit both the number of African residents and their location in the city.

Because of the heavy emphasis given to export-oriented agriculture in African economic development, it is hardly surprising that colonial authorities did not encourage migration to urban centers. Colonial urban economies were dominated by European commercial companies and Asian (primarily Lebanese and Indian) merchants, as a rule leaving rather limited opportunities for African traders. The public sector also provided few job opportunities for Africans.

While the history of South African urbanization reflects the unique character of its racially mixed population and its dynamic capitalist economy built upon mineral exploitation, there are strong parallels between South African and colonial African urban development. The implementation of apartheid as an official policy after 1950 was the culmination of decades of policies like those of colonial Africa that attempted to limit the migration of Africans to the city and intensified segregation within the city (see Vignette 13.2). In Cape Town (Figure 13.9) and other cities, the quest for a strictly segregated city involved uprooting vast numbers of people from their homes and sending them to locations designated by the state. While these measures have now been discontinued in conjunction with the dismantling of apartheid, the legacy of past policies will remain indefinitely. The end of apartheid has permitted some Africans, mostly wealthier and middle-class people, to move to areas formerly reserved for other groups, but the vast majority cannot afford housing outside of the townships or the massive squatter settlements that have mushroomed in recent years.

The Contemporary African City

As of the early 1960s, Africa south of the Sahara had few substantial cities. Of the 25 countries gaining independence between 1960 and 1964, only 3 had a city with at least 300,000 people: Nigeria (Lagos and Ibadan), Zaire (Kinshasa), and Senegal (Dakar). The popu-

Vignette 13.1. Kano: Quintessential African City

The urban landscapes of Kano reflect over 1,000 years of development and change. The early history of the city is quite well known, in part because of the detailed reports of several Arab and European visitors over the centuries and in part because of the Kano Chronicle, a unique written record of the political and economic history of the city under 42 kings between the 9th and 19th centuries.

Kano grew at the base of Dala Hill, where iron was being smelted as early as the 7th century. The old city is surrounded by a wall, first constructed between 1095 and 1134 and subsequently enlarged three times. Kano, and particularly Kurmi Market in the heart of the city, became the center of a booming trade in textiles, slaves, ivory, and other goods. Kano trade networks extended across the Sahara to North Africa, south into the forest zone, and across the savannas from present-day Sudan to the Atlantic. By the 19th century, Kano had become probably the most important manufacturing and trading center of black Africa, a cosmopolitan city of 30,000 permanent residents.

Under colonial rule, the traditional trade patterns of Kano were severely disrupted. However, the construction of the railway to Lagos created new opportunities; Kano became the center of a regional economy based on exporting groundnuts and importing manufactured goods. The structure of the old city was not significantly changed during the colonial era. However, a new city was established outside the walls, containing a modern central business district, administration and transportation facilities, and new residential areas for Europeans, migrants from southern Nigeria, and newcomers from other parts of the north.

The city continued to expand after independence, and particularly after the establishment of Kano State in 1967, surpassing 1 million inhabitants during the 1980s. The economy has diversified considerably beyond the traditional economic base in trade. Manufacturing has become increasingly important, as well as education and administration. The form of the city has continued to evolve. Newer residential areas increasingly reflect class divisions in the society, rather than ethnicity. The emergence of squatter settlements, occupied for the most part by the poor, is a new phenomenon. Elsewhere, middle- and upper–middle-class suburbs have been constructed to house civil servants, professionals, and businessmen. With the proliferation of cars, traffic has become a major

a    b

Figure 13.4. Photographs of Kano, Nigeria. (a) Kofar Kansakali, the best preserved of the gates of the 20-km-long old city wall, dates from the 14th century. (b) The Central Mosque, along with the Emir's Palace and Kurmi Market, are the most important focal points in the old city. *cont.*

c

d

(c) In the central business district the informal sector (in this case, bicycle repairs) and the formal sector (here the multinational Bata Shoe Company) exist side by side. (d) Kano State Ministry of Home Affairs, an example of government-related functions that have been among the most important "growth industries" since the 1967 founding of Kano State.

e

f

(e) Gwagwarwa, a working-class suburb established about 1920, is inhabited mainly by northern Nigerian Muslims. (f) Sabon Gari is a neighborhood established in colonial times to house southern, largely Christian, Nigerians. The building shown here combines commercial and residential space.

g

h

(g) Kurna, a lower-class squatter settlement that grew up during the 1970s and 1980s, is located directly under the main flight path to the airport. (h) An upper middle-class residence in the newer suburb of Gyadigyadi. Photos: author.

cont.

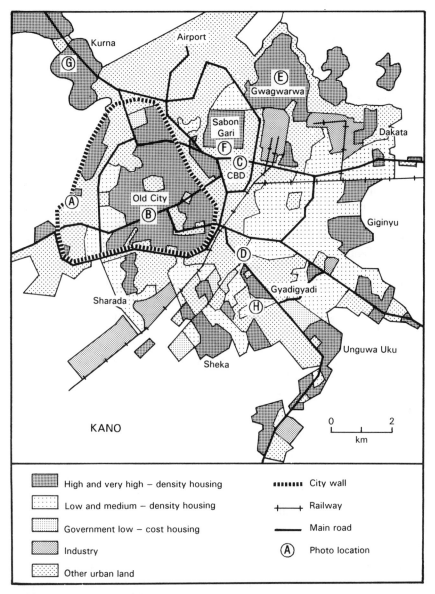

Figure 13.5. Kano, Nigeria. The urban landscapes of Kano reflect a thousand years of history and the effect of burgeoning growth in recent years. After H. A. C. Main, "Housing problems and squatting solutions in Metropolitan Kano." In R. B. Potter and A. T. Salan, eds., *Cities and Development in the Third World*. London: Mansell, 1990, pp. 12–31.

problem. Nevertheless, away from the few main thoroughfares, the old city remains a place apart, most of it accessible only along a circuitous maze of footpaths.

The accompanying photographs (Figure 13.4) show a variety of Kano landscapes. Their locations are indicated by letters on the map (Figure 13.5) corresponding to those for each photograph.

Vignette 13.2. Sanitation and Urban Planning

The spatial form of African cities still shows the influence of policies that sought to protect the health of whites from the allegedly unhealthy Africans. These measures, which grew out of the discovery of the relation between ill health and crowded, filthy environments, took a very different form in Europe and in the colonies. Massive investment in piped water and sewage systems did much to improve public health in European cities. In Africa, racial segregation brought health benefits to few.

In Cape Town, South Africa, epidemics of bubonic plague at the turn of the century provided a pretext for the government to forcibly relocate nonwhites from their inner-city homes to remote, barren sites outside the city. Thus, apartheid in this formerly integrated city began with the labeling of nonwhites as a threat to the health of whites.

In Freetown, Sierra Leone, the British decided to segregate African and European residents to protect the health of colonial officers, in the wake of the discovery in 1898 that malaria was spread by the bite of the *anopheles* mosquito. Ronald Ross, who had made this discovery, organized an expedition to Freetown, reputedly the most malarious place in the British Empire, to advise the government on malaria control. Ross made a number of policy recommendations, starting with the elimination of mosquito breeding sites. However, the Colonial Office chose a different approach, namely, the segregation of Europeans away from mosquito-breeding sites and from the African neighborhoods where most of these sites were to be found. A new European settlement, the Hill Station, was constructed overlooking the city.

The alternatives rejected by the Colonial Office, such as insect elimination and swamp drainage, would have contributed to better health for both Africans and Europeans. The choice of segregation as a strategy meant that only Europeans would benefit.

On closer examination, the racist underpinnings of the segregation policy become evident. Africans were blamed for being too lazy and primitive to maintain sanitary conditions in the town. Also cited as a justification for segregation was the alleged costs of providing "civilization" to Africans. But the implementation of segregation was not permitted to interfere with the basic comforts of European life; officers were permitted to have resident domestic servants for their Hill Station homes.

Sanitation regulations are no longer enforced with a view to the maintenance of racial segregation. Nevertheless, the distinctive appearance of the old European and African neighborhoods, sometimes still separated by open space – the former *cordon sanitaire*, or "sanitary barrier," where no development was permitted (see Figure 13.6) – are reminders of how and why early colonial cities were designed.

Based on Frenkel, S., and J. Western. "Pretext or prophylaxis? Racial segregation and malarial mosquitos in a British tropical colony: Sierra Leone." *Annals of the Association of American Geographers*, vol. 78 (1988), pp. 211–228; and Swanson, M. W., "The sanitation syndrome: Bubonic plague and urban native policy in the Cape Colony, 1900–1909," *Journal of African History*, vol. 18 (1977), pp. 387–410.

lation of the largest city was under 100,000 in 11 countries, and in 4 countries the largest city had fewer than 30,000 people. In all but 2 of these countries, Cameroon and Mauritania, the administrative capital was the largest city. Lessor urban centers were generally much smaller than the capital city, except where these urban centers were the site of a major economic activity like a mine or a port.

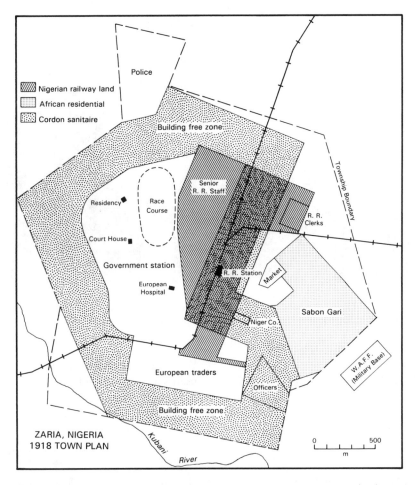

Figure 13.6. Proposed plan for Zaria, Nigeria. Note the open space completely surrounding and "protecting" the European residential area. After A. W. Urquhart. *Planned Urban Landscapes of Northern Nigeria.* Zaria, Nigeria: Ahmadu Bello University Press, 1977, p. 39.

The pace of rural–urban migration–and, consequently of urban population growth,–quickened following the attainment of independence. By the mid-1980s, approximately 115 million people, representing about one-quarter of the population, lived in African cities south of the Sahara. Twenty years earlier, only 15% of the population had been urban. These exceptional rates of urban growth reflect economic stagnation crises in the countryside and the widely held perception that fame and fortune are attainable in the city.

The rapidity of urbanization is reflected in patterns of growth of specific cities (Figure 13.10). Lagos, which had only 0.76 million people in 1960, had grown to 4.45 million by 1980 and has a projected population of 12.5 million in 2000. Kinshasa had grown from 0.45 million in 1960 to 2.24 million in 1980; its projected population in 2000 is 4.35 million.

One of the consequences of very rapid growth has been the acute shortage of affordable housing in many contemporary African cities. The scarcity and high cost of housing

Figure 13.7. Central business district, Lusaka, Zambia. A well-developed central business district and railway are both typical elements of colonial-era cities in Africa. Photo: author.

has forced many poor families to occupy only one rented room. Others have responded by building their own dwellings in squatter settlements where they have no formal tenure.

While data on the growth of squatter settlements are poor, largely because of the problem of defining precisely what they are, surveys suggest that between half and four-fifths of the

Figure 13.8. Keren, Eritrea. Two elements that show the colonial origins of this small town are its layout, radiating from a central plaza, and the Italian influences visible in the architecture of some of the buildings. Not surprisingly, the cities of different colonial powers varied somewhat in layout and appearance. Photo: M. Peters.

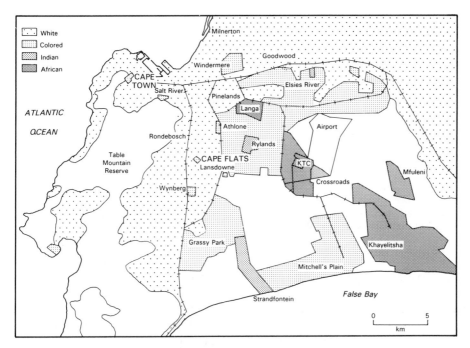

Figure 13.9. Cape Town: The racial division of space in an apartheid city. Sprawling black and colored squatter settlements such as Khayelitsha, Mitchells Plain, and Crossroads are located far from the urban core, until recently reserved for whites. After D. M. Smith. *The Apartheid City and Beyond.* London: Routledge, 1992, p. 126.

residents of large, national cities live in slums and squatter settlements. The rapid growth of cities has put immense pressure on urban infrastructures, including schools, water and sewage systems, and transportation. As a result, urban residents—and, in particular, people living in densely populated squatter settlements on the edge of the city—expend much time and money trying to get access to services that they need (see Vignette 13.3).

The modern African city looks quite different from its colonial predecessor. Apart from the very obvious difference of size, there are important structural and functional differences. Formal racial segregation, one of the fundamental principles of colonial urban design, has been superseded by informal divisions reflecting the class structure of society. African elites have moved into higher-class districts where only whites had formerly lived. Class-based segregation also extends to the middle and lower classes, who tend to occupy separate neighborhoods.

Modern African cities contain a substantial range of public services and administrative functions. There are not only far more primary and secondary schools but also universities and technical colleges that had previously existed in only a handful of colonies. In national and regional capitals, the construction of tall office buildings reflects the massive growth of state bureaucracies that direct and control so many aspects of political, economic, and social development in modern Africa.

The central business districts of the leading cities in the more prosperous countries have large stores, a few skyscrapers, and traffic jams reminiscent of cities in industrialized countries. The names of transnational corporations—Toshiba, Mitsubishi, Sheraton, and Hilton—are very evident, while the names of colonial trading companies such as UAC (United Africa Company) and CFAO (Compagnie Français d'Afrique Occidental) have become much less prominent. The central business districts are no longer the exclusive

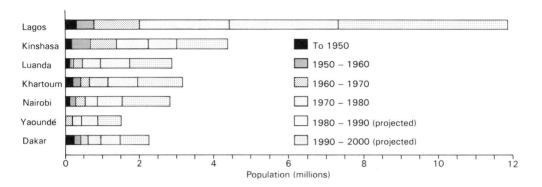

Figure 13.10. Past and projected growth of selected cities. Data source: *Prospects of World Urbanization 1988*. New York: United Nations, 1989.

preserve of expatriate companies. African entrepreneurs have developed sizable companies by taking advantage of expanding business opportunities and, in many cases, laws restricting expatriate involvement in certain types of activities. The streets of the central business district also contain many petty traders plying their wares. This type of informal street trade in the central business district had been strictly controlled, and usually prohibited, during the colonial era. Petty trading and other informal-sector enterprises are certainly not confined to the central business district. Small-scale businesses making available an infinite variety of goods and services are found along major thoroughfares, in markets, and almost everywhere in the poorer neighborhoods, where these informal sector jobs are so crucial for making ends meet.

Colonial industrialization was very rudimentary, mostly involving the primary processing of local products for export. Now, the outskirts of larger African cities have substantial industrial estates where a variety of goods are manufactured for domestic markets. These estates, along with national buildings, modern sports stadia, and universities, are not merely business ventures and places of employment but also symbols of national development and hope for the future.

The symbolic importance of modern urbanization is especially important in a handful of new, planned cities established since independence. The port city of Tema, developed as the focus for the anticipated industrial development of Ghana in the early 1960s, was the first of these postcolonial planned cities. New capital cities have been established in Malawi (Lilongwe), Côte d'Ivoire (Yamoussoukro), and Nigeria (Abuja). These cities have taken their inspiration from Brazil's futuristic capital on the frontier, Brasilia. In each case, their locations—away from the old centers of power—their planned designs, and their focal buildings were intended to evoke an image of hope for a brighter future (see Figure 13.11).

While it is important to look for generalizations that can be made about the cities of Africa and their postcolonial development, the limitations of generalized statements must be stressed. Many of the leading cities in African nations have developed into bustling metropolitan centers, but other cities bear the stamp of persistent economic and political crises that have stifled modern urban development, though not the growth of urban population. The contrast in appearance and economic vitality between economically stagnating cities like Maputo, Conakry, Freetown, and Kampala, and the entrepreneurial hives of activity like Nairobi, Abidjan, Lagos, and Douala, is far, far greater than at the time of independence. Between these two extremes are cities like Lusaka and Dar es Salaam where relative prosperity and rapid urban development in the early independent years has since given way to decline and stagnation.

Vignette 13.3. The Accessibility Problem:
Urban Transportation in Freetown, Sierra Leone

As the populations of African cities mushroom, the availability, convenience, and cost of public transport become increasingly important. This is particularly the case for the urban poor. Not only are they unlikely to have their own means of transportation, but the distances from their homes to places of work may be too great to use a bicycle even if each had one. Housing is more affordable in less desirable locations on the urban fringe or in ex-urban villages, but the rental savings may be largely offset by a dependence on high-cost public transport.

Freetown grew from 276,000 in 1974 to 690,000 in 1990, about 6% per year. The development of the city is spatially constrained by its location on a peninsula in the narrow space between the sea to the north and the mountain range to the south. The city has assumed an increasingly elongated form; new residential growth is concentrated on its eastern and western fringes and in numerous villages beyond the city. As a result, public transportation has become more and more important as a means of linking the city center and the growing suburbs.

Like most larger African cities, Freetown has a thriving public transportation industry. It consists of three main types of transit: a government-operated bus system, minibuses locally known as poda-podas, and taxis. Most poda-podas and taxis are owned by individuals and rented to drivers who purchase their own fuel and provide the owner with a guaranteed return. Unlike the buses, poda-podas and taxis do not necessarily travel along a fixed route. Poda-podas and taxis charge at least twice the official fare but carry the great majority of passengers. About two-thirds of the bus fleet is off the road because of a lack of spare parts, reflecting the scarcity of foreign currency.

Buses on the cross-city routes move at a snail's pace, about 8 to 12 km per hour. The slowness of traffic results from extreme congestion along the few available routes into the city. The deteriorating condition of the roads, street trading along the main routes, and failure to enforce regulations against on-street parking all contribute to the congestion.

Without the financial means to undertake road maintenance and construction, obtain spare parts and fuel for vehicles, and improve the quality of city administration, the transportation problem in cities like Freetown cannot be solved. Meanwhile, continuing high rates of rural to urban migration ensure future urban growth and, in turn, an escalating problem for the poor who must endure the inconvenience and high cost of moving about in the city.

Based on R. Barrett. *Urban Transport in West Africa*. Washington, DC: World Bank, 1991.

The discussion above has focused primarily on national cities, almost all of which are capitals. It has been in these cities that the postcolonial transformation has been most dramatic. The development of smaller urban centers has been much less spectacular, reflecting the tendency of governments and the business community to concentrate in national cities administrative functions, nation-al institutions like universities, and modern industrial facilities. Many secondary urban centers have also experienced considerable growth since the 1960s. Several states have made some effort to encourage the development of these smaller centers through administrative decentralization, transportation development, and the siting of public-sector facilities and enterprises away from the nation-

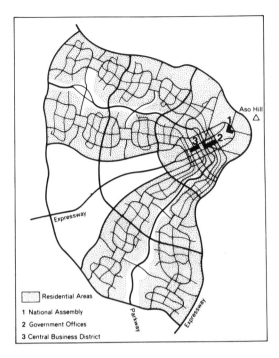

Figure 13.11. Abuja: Nigeria's new capital. Source: W. T. W. Morgan. *Nigeria.* Harlow, England: Longman, 1983, p. 155. ©1983 by W. T. W. Morgan. Reprinted by permission.

al capital. Still, with very few exceptions, the more cosmopolitan and better-serviced capital cities continue to attract much more investment and many more migrants than secondary urban centers.

Most African societies remain predominately rural. However, cities in all parts of Africa south of the Sahara have grown explosively, especially in the three decades since independence. Urban centers have increasingly become the primary hub not only of political affairs but also of change in national economies and societies. This concentration of wealth and power ensures that Africa's leading cities will continue to grow in size and importance within their respective countries.

It has been noted that many residents of contemporary African cities struggle to make ends meet and to secure basic amenities—in particular, adequate shelter. Governments must also grapple with these same challenges, that is, striving to achieve economic growth and stability and ensuring that housing and

other amenities are available. Planning for the future is the easiest part; the real challenge is to find ways of bringing about orderly and progressive development when resources are so scarce and when urban residents simply choose to get on with meeting their own needs, paying no heed to utopian official plans. The next two chapters examine in greater detail individual and official responses to problems of urban economic development and the provision of housing for urban residents.

Further Reading

Reference sources on African urbanization include the following sources:

O'Connor, A. *Urbanization in Africa: An Annotated Bibliography.* Boston: G. K. Hall, 1982.
Stren, R., and C. Letemendia. *Coping with Rapid Urban Growth in Africa: An Annotated Bibliography.* Montreal, Quebec: McGill University, 1986.

Two journals that focus specifically on African urban questions are *African Urban Notes* and *African Urban Quarterly.*

Various aspects of the development of African cities are discussed in the following sources:

Coquery-Vidrovitch, C. "The process of urbanization in Africa (from the origins to the beginning of independence)," *African Studies Review,* vol. 34 (1991), pp. 1–98.
Hanna, W. J., and J. L. Hanna. *Urban Dynamics in Black Africa: An Interdisciplinary Approach.* 2nd ed. New York: Aldine, 1981.
Mabogunje, A. L. "Urban planning and the postcolonial state in Africa." *African Studies Review,* vol. 33 (1990), pp. 121–203.
Miner, H. *The City in Modern Africa.* New York: Praeger, 1978.
O'Connor, A. *The African City.* London: Hutchinson, 1983.
Parkin, D. J. *Town and Country in Central and Eastern Africa.* Oxford: Oxford University Press, 1976.

Precolonial urbanization is discussed in the following sources:

Davidson, B. *The Lost Cities of Africa.* Boston: Little, Brown, 1959.
Hull, R. W. *African Cities and Towns before the European Conquest.* New York: Norton, 1976.

Winters, C. "Traditional urbanism in the north-central Sudan." *Annals of Association of American Geographers*, vol. 67 (1977), pp. 500–520.

The effect of colonialism on African urban development is discussed in the following sources:

King, A. *Colonial Urban Development*. London: Routledge and Kegan Paul, 1976.

Southall, A. "The impact upon urban development in Africa." In V. Turner, ed., *Colonialism in Africa, Profiles of Change: Society and Colonial Rule*, pp. 216–255. Cambridge: Cambridge University Press, 1971.

The following are case studies that examine a particular African city:

Lloyd, P. C., A. L. Mabogunje, and B. Awe. *The City of Ibadan*. Cambridge: Cambridge University Press, 1967.

Pons, V. *Stanleyville: An African Urban Community under Belgian Administration*. London: Oxford University Press, 1969.

Skinner, E. P. *African Urban Life: The Transformation of Ouagadougou*. Princeton: Princeton University Press, 1974.

Western, J. *Outcast Capetown*. London: Allen and Unwin, 1981.

Urban dynamics in South Africa are discussed in the following source:

Swilling, M., R. Humphries, and K. Shubane, eds. *Apartheid City in Transition*. Cape Town, South Africa: Oxford University Press, 1991.

14

✳

Urban Economies

The previous chapter discussed the explosive growth that has been characteristic of African urban centers, especially since 1960, and pointed out that rapid urbanization is likely to continue for the forseeable future. The focus now turns to how urban Africans make their living and to the broader characteristics of the urban economies within which Africans work. This chapter also discusses policy options that governments may use to stimulate or regulate urban economic activity. While most of these initiatives were once directed at the development of large-scale projects in the formal economic sector, the focus has increasingly shifted to the informal initiatives of small-scale traders, artisans, and the like, which account for the majority of economic activity.

The Structure of Urban Economies

Economists speak of four basic types of economic activity:

1. Primary production, which involves the harvesting of products of the environment by farmers, fishers, forestry workers, and miners
2. Secondary production or manufacturing, which transforms products into more valuable and useful forms

3. Tertiary activities, entailing the provision of services, such as health care, entertainment, and the sale of goods to consumers
4. Quaternary activities, including government and other administrative services

Although *primary production* is usually associated with rural economies, it also plays an important role in many African cities. Several large cities have developed as a result of mineral exploitation. Johannesburg and Kimberley in South Africa, Ndola and Kitwe in Zambia, and Lubumbashi in Zaire are examples of urban centers that started as mining towns and where mining remains important. Primary producers engaged in farming, fishing, and forestry are to be found in virtually all African cities. In certain regions, including traditional Yoruba cities like Ibadan and Oyo, farmers migrate between permanent residences in the city and seasonally occupied farmsteads. Elsewhere, small market gardens have been developed within and adjacent to cities to contribute to family food supplies and to take advantage of a growing demand for fresh produce. A recent study of urban agriculture in Nairobi (Vignette 14.1) demonstrates the prevalence of this long-ignored activity and its importance to the well-being of families and the economy.

Secondary production ranges in sophistication from simple handicrafts to modern manufactures. While small-scale handicraft production is prevalent in both urban and rural settings, large-scale manufacturing is essentially an urban-based activity in Africa south of the Sahara. In most countries, between 65 and 90% of industry is located in the primate city, with virtually all of the rest being in smaller, regional centers.

Certain *tertiary activities* are heavily concentrated in cities. For example, interregional transportation services and import–export and wholesale trade are clustered in large port cities where transportation routes converge. Financial services such as banking and insurance are also largely urban based.

Quaternary activities are perhaps the most urban focused of all. African governments tend to be highly centralized in the national capital, and to a lesser extent in state or regional capitals. Many African states operate a variety of parastatal corporations – companies established by governments to engage in particular business ventures – and oversee the establishment and management of schools, hospitals, and other social institutions. Government jobs are eagerly sought because they generally offer higher wages and greater job security than are found in other sectors and because the state and its agents wield immense power.

Formal and Informal Economies

Until the early 1970s, studies of urban economies in Africa and other parts of the Third World focused almost exclusively on modern, large-scale economic activity. Development specialists emphasized the role of transportation networks to facilitate the movement of people and goods, factories to manufacture valuable products, and commercial enterprises to distribute goods and services. Meanwhile, the "subsistence" economic activities of the poor were virtually ignored.

Later, it was recognized that many urban residents obtained few benefits from standard modernization strategies and had to look after their own basic needs with virtually no official assistance. The poor constructed their own houses, manufactured a wide variety of products, often from recycled materials, and earned a living as self-employed sellers of an infinite variety of goods and services. In some Third World cities, as many as 90% of urban workers are active in this "informal economy."

The urban informal economy consists of small-scale, labor-intensive enterprises, heavily reliant on family capital, skills, and labor. To derive precise definitions – exactly how small and how dependent on family resources, for example – would probably be a futile exercise. Rather, definitions of the informal economy have emphasized ways in which formal and informal economies differ (Table 14.2).

While the contrasts between formal and informal economies are evident, it is important to remember that they are part of a total urban economy and are neither as clearly differentiated nor as functionally-separate as Table 14.2 seems to imply. All cities contain enterprises such as medium-sized, locally owned retail outlets and industries that fall between the definitely formal and definitely informal sectors. There are also many forms of interaction between the formal and informal economies that are not reflected in this dualism. Labor moves back and forth between the two sectors, transferring skills as well as raw materials and finished products from one to the other.

The Formal Economy: Manufacturing

Africa south of the Sahara remains the least industrialized part of the world, accounting for only 1% of global manufacturing value added. Colonial policy retarded the development of an industrial sector; manufacturing was quite simply incompatable with Africa's assigned role of supplying raw materials. The only notable exceptions were a few raw-material processing enterprises, such as cotton ginneries, vegetable-oil mills, and mineral concentrators.

Newly independent governments invested heavily in industrial development in the 1960s. The case for rapid industrialization was stated by Kwame Nkrumah in *Africa Must Unite*

Vignette 14.1. Making Ends Meet: The Significance of Urban Agriculture

Most studies of the urbanization process have assumed that migrants from rural areas abandon agriculture when they move to the city. Recent studies, however, are finding that urban agriculture is both prevalent and economically significant. Table 14.1 (based on Freeman, p. 129) shows something of the importance of farming in three of Kenya's largest cities.

Table 14.1. Urban Agriculture in Three Kenyan Cities

	Kisumu	Mombasa	Nairobi
HH[a] with food-growing land in city	28%	15%	11%
HH growing food on urban or rural land	70%	55%	65%
HH selling urban crops	18%	21%	21%
Median quantity produced	90 kg	125 kg	29 kg
HH keeping livestock	55%	47%	51%

[a]HH, households

Evidence of the activities of urban farmers is to be seen in virtually all parts of Nairobi, even in the heart of the central business district. These vegetable gardens, or *shambas,* are on average about 2,300 sq m in size, ranging from 5 sq m to over 6 ha. Private residential land is used by about one-third of cultivators; most others farm roadsides, riversides, and other public spaces. Private land, when available, is more secure from theft, but the alluvial soil found in river floodplains is likely to be more fertile.

Two-thirds of urban cultivators in Nairobi are female, but otherwise they vary greatly in income, age, education, employment status, and duration of urban residence. Close to half had no job at the time of the survey.

A wide variety of crops are grown on urban *shambas*. The most important is maize, produced on over half of all farms. Beans, potatoes, cocoyams, various types of vegetables, and bananas are also grown by many. While most urban farmers (70%) consume all that they grow, there is also a significant market component to agriculture in Nairobi. It was found that 13% of those surveyed sold half or more of their crop.

The contributions of urban agriculture to the local and national economy and to the social well-being of the urban poor are only starting to be recognized. Freeman has observed that farming benefits the community economically in five ways by (1) contributing to urban productivity (with an estimated aggregate production for all Kenyan cities of 25 million kg); (2) generating employment, not only on the plots themselves but also through the sale of agricultural inputs and produce; (3) giving women entrepreneurs entry into the informal sector; (4) exploiting a vacant niche in the urban economy, focused on the food needs of the urban poor; and (5) valorizing vacant and often derelict urban land.

Urban farming is a practical, self-reliant, and sustainable response to people's pressing needs for an adequate diet, a job, and extra income. For Nairobi's poor, the *shambas* represent, according to Freeman, "gardens of hope, not wastelands of despair" (p. 121).

Based on D. B. Freeman. *A City of Farmers: Informal Agriculture in the Open Spaces of Nairobi, Kenya*. Montreal, Quebec: McGill-Queen's University Press, 1991.

Figure 14.1. Urban agriculture, Kampala, Uganda. Africanists have only recently begun to appreciate the extent and importance of agricultural production by urban dwellers. Photo: author.

(1963): "We have here, in Africa, everything necessary to become a powerful, modern, industrialized continent. . . . Every time we import goods that we could manufacture if all the conditions were available, we are continuing our economic dependence and delaying our industrial growth" (p. 112).

Rates of industrial growth have declined during the 1970s and 1980s, reflecting the very serious effect of rising petroleum prices, falling export revenues, and growing debts. Table 14.3 demonstrates that the downturn has been especially severe in low income countries, where there was no growth in output between 1975 and 1980 and, with the exception of semiarid countries, where there was significant decline between 1980 and 1987. The most significant decline since 1980 has been among oil exporters; the collapse of oil prices has been instrumental in bringing about a decline of 2.5% per annum in industrial output, compared to an annual growth of 11.5% during the boom years of the late 1970s. Industrial crisis is manifest in the abandonment

Table 14.2. Attributes of Formal and Informal Economies

Informal sector	Formal sector
Ease of entry	Difficult entry
Predominantly indigenous inputs	Overseas inputs
Predominantly family property	Corporate property
Small scale of activity	Large scale of activity
Labor-intensive activity	Capital-intensive activity
Adapted technology	Imported technology
Skills from outside school system	Formally acquired (often expatriate) skills
Unregulated/competitive market	Protected markets (e.g., tariffs, quotas, licenses)

Table 14.3. Growth of African Manufacturing Output, 1960 to 1987 (percentage per annum at constant 1970 prices)

	1960–1965	1965–1970	1970–1975	1975–1980	1980–1987
Low income countries					
semiarid	4.8	9.7	1.8	0.4	2.9
other	9.3	8.2	2.4	−0.2	−2.7
Middle income countries					
oil importers	7.5	7.6	7.7	4.2	NA
oil exporters	3.7	15.9	6.6	11.5	−2.5
Total of sub-Saharan Africa	7.3	9.3	5.3	4.4	−1.2

Sources: W. F. Steel and J. W. Evans. *Industrialization in Sub-Saharan Africa: Strategies and Performance.* Washington, DC: World Bank, 1984, p. 33. World Bank. *From Crisis to Sustainable Growth: A Long-Term Prospective Study.* Washington, DC: World Bank, 1989.

and underutilization of industrial capacity. "Deindustrialization" has been particularly severe in several countries, including Ghana, Zaire, Benin, and Tanzania, some of which are using as little as 30% of installed industrial capacity.

Industry in underdeveloped economies tends to be concentrated in the largest urban centers, where energy supplies, transportation, communications, and other infrastructural resources are most accessible. The largest cities also contain better educated and more experienced workers, as well as the most affluent consumers. The extreme concentration of Senegal's manufacturing in the capital city of Dakar (Vignette 14.2) is typical of industrial development in Africa. South Africa and Nigeria are the only countries in which industry is fairly well dispersed.

The composition of Senegal's manufacturing is typical of the African pattern. Manufacturing in most countries consists almost exclusively of export-processing and import-substitution enterprises. The first category includes ore concentrators, vegetable-oil mills, fruit canneries, sawmills, and other facilities preparing primary goods for export. Import-substitution industries make various consumer goods for local markets using either local or imported raw materials.

Capital-goods industries producing inputs utilized in other types of production are poorly developed except in South Africa. While Africa has significant deposits of coal and iron ore,

only South Africa has a functioning, integrated iron-and-steel complex. Nigeria's steel complex, begun in 1976 at Ajaokuta, has been plagued by technical difficulties and fiscal crisis. Ghana, Cameroon, and Guinea have major aluminum smelters, but their products are almost all exported as unfinished aluminum rolling stock. Although several countries have petroleum refineries producing fuels and basic petrochemicals, only South Africa has a well-developed chemical industry.

Africa south of the Sahara has not yet attracted much export-oriented manufacturing investment, unlike Thailand, Mexico, and several other Third World countries, which have usually specialized in textiles, clothing, electronics components, product assembly, and similar industries requiring considerable unskilled labor and relatively unsophisticated technology. A number of African countries, including Senegal, Togo, Liberia, Tanzania, and Sudan have established free ports where tariffs and other regulations are relaxed for companies producing for export. However, none has had more than limited success attracting exporting industries. Africa has no real advantages of location, labor costs, or skills compared to competing locations in Latin America and Asia. The continent's reputation for political instability and for inadequate infrastructures and unreliable support services are major disincentives to large-scale foreign investment.

The relative immaturity of African indus-

Vignette 14.2. Industrial Development: A Case Study of Senegal

By the standards of Africa south of the Sahara, Senegal is a moderately industrialized country. It lags well behind Nigeria, Côte d'Ivoire, Kenya, and Zimbabwe in volume and diversity of industrial production. However, it is more industrialized than most African countries, including some more populous ones like Tanzania and Ethiopia. Manufacturing accounted for 17% of Senegal's GDP (see glossary) in 1983 but provided jobs for only 35,000 employees, representing only 1% of the economically active population.

Approximately 85% of Senegal's manufacturing activity is located in Dakar (Figure 14.2). Most of the remainder is established within 150 km of Dakar in the provincial towns of Thies, Kaolack, and Diourbel. The remainder of the country has only two sizable factories.

Senegal's industries process local raw materials for export and produce import-substituting goods for the domestic market. Food processing, which accounts for almost half of industrial production, includes groundnut-oil mills, fish canneries, and a sugar refinery (export processing), as well as breweries, flour mills,and confectionaries (import substitution). Textiles, metal products, and chemicals and allied products each account for 12 to 14% of total industrial production. While some local raw materials are used in these industries—cotton for textiles and phosphates for fertilizers, for example—most industries depend on imported raw materials such as unrefined petroleum or imported parts for local assembly.

Although Senegal possesses a good variety of basic industries producing goods for local consumption, there are almost no capital-goods industries; the exceptions are plants that refine petroleum, make fertilizer, and assemble agricultural machinery. Senegal's domestic market is presently neither large enough nor wealthy enough to support a more sophisticated industrial base. Because of this, the government has emphasized the development of industries to process and add value to its own raw materials such as phosphates, fish, and groundnuts. A free-trade zone has been established in Dakar to attract foreign industry geared to export production, but so far it has had very little success.

Senegal's manufacturing sector is of considerable importance to the domestic economy—more in relation to the value of production than the amount of employment—but nevertheless remains very small, even within the regional context of West Africa. The size and composition of the industrial sector are unlikely to change significantly in the forseeable future.

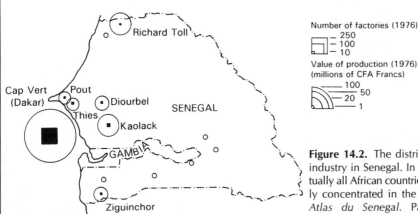

Number of factories (1976)
- 250
- 100
- 10

Value of production (1976)
(millions of CFA Francs)
- 100
- 50
- 20
- 1

Figure 14.2. The distribution of modern industry in Senegal. In Senegal, as in virtually all African countries, industry is highly concentrated in the largest city. After *Atlas du Senegal*. Paris: Atlas Jeune Afrique, 1980.

Figure 14.3. Inside a modern aluminum smelter, Douala, Cameroon. Regions with an abundance of hydroelectic power have some comparative advantage in producing aluminum for export. Photo: CIDA: R. Lemoyne.

trial development does not reflect official disinterest. In fact, African governments have often put undue emphasis on manufacturing as the foundation for modern development. Many governments have given generous incentives to industrialists, have entered into partnerships with transnational companies, and have established industrial parastatal corporations. The record of state involvement in manufacturing has been mixed. Incentives and partnership arrangements have helped at times to overcome the reluctance of transnational corporations to undertake risky investments. However, hundreds of industrial "white elephants" provide clear evidence that sound economic reasoning has often been bypassed.

The extent of direct involvement by governments in manufacturing varies considerably, from perhaps one-tenth of industrial capacity in countries such as Kenya and Côte d'Ivoire that are committed to development of a free market economy to almost 90% in socialist Mozambique and Tanzania. Much of the early industrialization was undertaken by large European trading companies. Since independence,

transnational corporations with no longstanding involvement in Africa have become much more prominent, especially in countries with mixed economies. Industrial ventures in Kenya, Nigeria, and, to a lesser extent, elsewhere are being undertaken by indigenous entrepreneurs with increasing frequency. Some of the impetus for this indigenous involvement is due to limitations imposed on foreign ownership by many states.

Industrialization is having a significant effect on the shape of modern African societies. Workers from diverse backgrounds are brought together and share common concerns about wages, working conditions, and job security. One result has been the growth of a working-class conciousness that transcends ethnic, regional, and religious cleavages. Working-class solidarity typically becomes stronger as a result of union membership and of collective actions like strikes and protests against government policies that are harmful to labor. Nevertheless, the participation of workers in national affairs is constrained by restrictions imposed on unions in the majority of African states.

The Informal Economy

While the emerging industrial sector has received careful attention and many favors from African governments, the informal sector has continued to function in relative obscurity. As previously mentioned, the informal sector consists of small-scale enterprises producing and selling a wide variety of goods and services, using comparatively simple technology and resources mobilized primarily from within family units.

The urban informal sector resembles, but is distinct from, the traditional craft industries and petty trading found throughout rural Africa. As a rule, craft production in rural areas is done seasonally by people who depend primarily on farming for their livelihood. Most of those employed in the urban informal economy are, by necessity or by choice, almost totally dependent on nonagricultural income. However, there are tangible connections. For example, migrants from the countryside often enter the urban informal economy by employing or adapting their rural skills.

Most descriptions of the urban informal economy have focused on its role in household subsistence. However, the urban informal economy also makes an enormous contribution to the larger economies of cities and nations. A very significant proportion of the manufactured goods utilized by Africans is produced by informal-sector workers. These items provide lower cost alternatives to the products of large-scale industries; and in the smaller, less industrialized countries, these items constitute the majority of manufactured goods produced domestically.

Four brief case studies of informal-sector activities are given below. These examples should illustrate both the diversity of the informal sector and the ingenuity and adaptibility of its entrepreneurs. They also touch upon several aspects of the interdependence of formal and informal economies.

Leather Workers in Dakar

Leather workers produce a variety of goods, including shoes, handbags, and amulets that are worn as protective "medicine." The majority of traditional leather workers are artisans who work individually and sell their products directly to consumers. Some work cooperatively in larger workshops and sell their goods through petty traders and small businesspeople.

Adaptability is crucial to the survival of the informal economy; entrepreneurs must be able to adjust, for example, to changes in raw-material supply and customer demand. In the past, Dakar shoemakers worked with leather purchased from Mauritanian women who tanned hides in the traditional manner. After the Senegalese government granted the transnational Bata Shoe Company a virtual monopoly to purchase leather, local shoemakers lost their source of raw materials. The local shoemakers solved this problem by using plastic from Europe. However, a tiny number of importing firms control the trade in plastic, leaving the local shoemakers more vulnerable to interruptions in supply and increases in price. Although these shoemakers have retained a large share of the local market, the plastic goods that they now make bring a lower price than those made of leather.

Souvenir Makers in Lusaka

Wherever there are tourists, Africans have found various opportunities to make a living. Utilitarian objects like blankets and carved utensils traditionally made for local use, carvings that replicate traditional ceremonial objects, and modern handicrafts are sold as souvenirs. In Zambia, decorative objects like jewelry and figurines are crafted from malachite, a bright green copper ore obtained in the Copper Belt. Other craftspeople create wonderfully realistic miniature bicycles from pieces of wire and rubber tubing. While some craftspeople sell directly to tourists, most rely on itinerant traders and small shopkeepers to sell their wares.

Street Traders in Kano

Petty traders occupy a variety of niches in the urban environment. They dash into the streets

a

b

Figure 14.4. The informal sector at work. (a) Cassette seller, Kano, Nigeria: Locally (illegally) duplicated tapes are sold by this mobile vendor. He advertises his wares by playing music on the tape recorder. (b) Children selling peanuts and cigarettes, Asmara, Eritrea: Children are heavily represented in the informal sector. Their earnings, even if they are small, are often crucial for the family budget. Photos: (a) author, (b) M. Peters.

at busy intersections to sell anything from newspapers to screwdrivers to motorists stopped for a traffic light. Other traders are itinerants, carrying their wares from place to place looking for customers. Table traders, kiosk owners, and small shopkeepers operate from fixed points along the street.

In the highly competitive trading environment, keys to success are accessibility and visibility to potential customers and selling wares that are in demand and competitively priced. The itinerant cassette vendor (Figure 14.4a) possesses many of these attributes. By playing music on the tape recorder, he attracts the attention of customers as he moves from one likely location to another. The cassettes he sells include "genuine" recordings, cheaper pirated versions in packages closely resembling the original version, and cheap homemade recordings in plain packages. Actual selling prices are established by bargaining. These mobile vendors may be independent entrepreneurs or agents selling on commission for a larger trader.

The Entertainment Industry in the Mathare Valley, Nairobi

Men and women frequently specialize in different informal-sector enterprises. Women are often attracted to businesses that operate out of the home and that therefore can be combined with domestic work.

Some 90% of the women in the Mathare Valley, a squatter community in Nairobi, work in informal-sector jobs. Many women brew local beer from maize in their rooms or houses. While home brewing is illegal, it is attractive as a fairly lucrative business requiring low capital inputs, readily available raw materials, and skills that are already known to many women. The beer is generally sold from tiny informal bars located on the same premises. Independent women may also supplement their incomes through sexual liasons with men whom they meet as customers.

It is sometimes forgotten that informal economic activity is not a new phenomenon, either in African or non-African cities. Figure

14.5 shows the periods of existence of several informal-sector enterprises in Johannesburg and illustrates how the structure of the informal economy continues to evolve in response to changes in the larger economy and society. As certain opportunities wane, others emerge and are exploited by innovative entrepreneurs.

When the importance of the informal sector was finally recognized, programs were initiated by international agencies, notably the International Labor Organization (ILO), and by governments to foster its development. These institutions have provided improved access to credit, relaxation of legal restrictions affecting the informal sector, and technical assistance. Still, the view persists in many countries that the spontaneous development of the urban informal economy is incompatable with sound planning. Attempts to regulate the informal sector have had little success, since the first "law" of the informal sector is that opportunities must be exploited where and when they occur, irrespective of whether officialdom approves.

Making Ends Meet in the City

Julius Nyerere, former President of Tanzania, commented on the difficulties of urban dwellers in a 1968 speech: "The vast majority even of our town dwellers live extremely poorly, and in most cases they are worse off . . . than the people in rural areas could be. An unskilled worker . . . earns wages which are hardly sufficient to enable a family to eat a proper diet and live in a decent house."

The prospects for most urban dwellers are much grimmer in the 1990s than they were when Nyerere made this statement 25 years ago. For most urban Africans, life is a constant struggle to make ends meet. Whereas rural Africans are able to produce most of their own food, urban Africans must rely primarily on earned income to survive. They are vulnerable to market fluctuations and have no real protection when crop failures, changes in government policy, or hoarding drive up prices. As shown in the case study described in Vignette 14.1, many urbanites produce some of their own food. However, for the majority, including most of those who are especially vulnerable, lack of access to land and other agricultural inputs means that farming is not a viable option.

In many African countries, the IMF has imposed severe economic-restraint programs, forcing governments to reduce public-sector employment, to remove subsidies that had ensured the availability of relatively cheap imported food, and to devalue the currency. A Ghanaian teacher's monthly salary of 2,000 cedis does not go far when a chicken costs

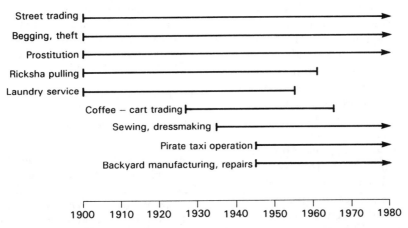

Figure 14.5. The evolution of the urban informal sector in Johannesburg, South Africa. After C. Rogerson. "Johannesburg's informal sector: Historical continuity and change." *African Urban Quarterly,* vol. 1 (1986), pp. 139–151.

over 1,000 cedis and a meal of yams about 300 cedis.

How do people make ends meet? They do so by severely curtailing consumption, by finding ways to supplement their incomes, and by making use of social networks. Few families can afford to rely on a single income. Workers in the formal sector commonly supplement their earnings with part-time informal sector jobs, such as taxi driving or petty trading. Housewives contribute to the family income by keeping a garden, trading, preparing food for sale, and minding other people's children. In poorer families, the children work, often as messengers or street hawkers (Figure 14.4b).

The cultivation of social networks is crucial for survival. Relatives, friends, neighbors, and colleagues at work may provide invaluable information about when and where housing, employment opportunities, and scarce commodities may be found. Close linkages are also maintained with relatives in rural areas. Urban residents may remit small sums of money when possible and provide temporary lodging for visitors and new migrants to the city, in return for occasional gifts of firewood and food and their assistance in times of crisis.

Life in the African city is not easy. In recent years, government cutbacks and the deteriorating economic situation have brought about the elimination of many formal-sector jobs in manufacturing and civil service. The cost of food, shelter, transport, and other necessities has kept increasing. It has become harder and harder to make ends meet.

Despite this gloomy picture, the city's "bright lights" still shine for many Africans. The city still exemplifies opportunity—the possibility of achieving something better than what can normally be expected in the countryside. For the great majority, opportunities in the city can only be realized by ingenuity and hard work. These qualities are clearly evident in the informal-sector artisans, traders, and service providers at work in every conceivable location. While this ever-changing, ever-adapting informal economy may be an urban planner's worst nightmare, it is also a hopeful symbol of African self-reliance and ingenuity.

Further Reading

For a general overview of urban economies, see the following source:

International Labor Organization (ILO). *Abidjan: Urban Development and Employment.* Geneva, Switzerland: ILO, 1976

The following sources are concerned with industrial development. (Dicken's book is an excellent study of industrial location at a global scale; the other sources are specific to Africa):

Dicken, P. *Global Shift: Industrial Change in a Turbulent World.* London: Harper and Row, 1986.
Mabogunje, A. L. "Manufacturing and the geography of development in tropical Africa." *Economic Geography,* vol. 49 (1973), pp. 1–20.
Mytelka, L. "The unfulfilled promise of African industrialization." *African Studies Review,* vol. 32 (1988), pp. 1–72.
Perkins, F. C. "Technology choice, industrialization and development experiences in Tanzania." *Journal of Development Studies,* vol. 19 (1983), pp. 213–243.
Selwyn, P. *Industries in the South African Periphery: A Study of Industrial Development in Botswana, Lesotho and Swaziland.* London: Croom Helm, 1977.
Steel, W. F., and J. W. Evans. *Industrialization in sub-Saharan Africa: Strategies and Performance.* Washington, DC: World Bank, 1984.
United Nations Industrial Development Organization. "The changing role of manufacturing in African economic development: Trends, prospects and issues." *African Development,* vol. 2 (1982), pp. 126–141.

The following sources focus on the emergence of an African working class and consider the significance of this development:

Lubeck, P. *Islam and Urban Labour in Northern Nigeria: The Making of a Muslim Working Class.* Cambridge: Cambridge University Press, 1986.
Peace, A. *Choice, Class and Conflict: A Study of Southern Nigerian Factory Workers.* Atlantic Highlands, NJ: Humanities Press, 1979.
Sandbrook, R., and R. Cohen, eds. *The Development of an African Working Class.* Toronto, Ontario: University of Toronto Press, 1975.

The following sources are recommended as introductions to the urban informal sector:

Bromley, R., ed. *Planning for Small Enterprises in Third World Cities*. Oxford: Permagon, 1985.

Bromley, R., and C. Gerry, eds. *Casual Work and Poverty in Third World Cities*. New York: Wiley, 1979.

Gerry, C. "Petty production and capitalist production in Dakar: The crisis of the self-employed." *World Development*, vol. 6 (1978), pp. 1147–1160.

Rogerson, C. "Johannesburg's informal sector: Historical continuity and change." *African Urban Quarterly*, vol.1 (1986), pp. 139–151.

Santos, M. *The Shared Space: The Two Circuits of the Urban Economy in Underdeveloped Countries*. London: Methuen, 1979.

Sethuraman, S. V., ed. *The Urban Informal Sector in Developing Countries: Employment, Poverty and Environment*. Oxford: Permagon, 1985.

15

Housing Africa's Urban Population

The urban population of Africa south of the Sahara has undergone an eightfold increase over the past 40 years, growing from 19.8 million in 1950, to 54.8 million in 1970, and to 164.8 million in 1990. It has been projected that the urban population will have grown to 441 million by 2010, an increase of 167% over 1990. Such explosive growth exerts tremendous pressure on urban infrastructures. More people means more demand for health care and education. It means more vehicles, both private and public, on the roads, as well as more passengers crowding onto public transportation. It means increased demand for water and, thus, the probability of shortages affecting both domestic consumers and industry. It means a scarcity of reasonably priced housing. Where are newcomers to the city, most of whom are poor, to find shelter?

The impress of rapid urban growth varies in different parts of the city. In the older central districts, land use tends to become more intensive. One- and two-story houses and shops are replaced with multistory commercial and residential buildings. On the periphery, services have to be expanded to cater to the needs of emerging suburbs. Government officials and urban residents face the same challenges, namely, coping with contemporary crises of strained infrastructure and trying to predict and plan for future needs.

This chapter surveys the housing challenge in Africa's cities and examines responses to it from the often opposed perspectives of consumers and officials.

Housing and Social Class

The geography of social class intersects closely with the geography of housing. The size and style of houses, along with their location within the city, are powerful indicators of wealth and status (Vignette 15.1). Even if the residential spaces occupied by the rich and the poor are not far removed from each other, rich and poor seldom trespass on the others' turf and rarely live side by side.

The impress of class in relation to housing is manifest in many obvious ways:

- location within the city (residential segregation)
- the appearance (design) of houses
- building materials used to construct houses
- space, both interior and exterior, and privacy
- amenities in the house—piped water, toilets, kitchens
- quality and quantity of nearby community services
- occupants' control of the property (owners and tenants)
- extent of government support and subsidization

The extent of these differences and some of their implications become evident when the housing situations of Africa's elite, the middle class, the working poor, and the unemployed populations are compared.

Elite Housing

During the colonial era, housing was built by the government for expatriate administrators and military officers on large lots in estates well separated from African townships. The houses were European in design and very spacious. However, elite neighborhoods have long since ceased to be the exclusive preserve of European government officials. African civil servants, professionals, and entrepreneurs predominate, although quite a few expatriate business people, diplomats, and contract employees are still present, especially in national capitals. Architectural styles have changed, and the lots tend to be smaller than during the colonial era. Still, the houses are fundamentally the same: They are very spacious (and sometimes huge), are essentially European in style, and are situated in pleasant, landscaped surroundings. High security walls and guarded entrances are common and speak of the contemporary elites' wariness of the possibly restive masses.

An increasing proportion of the housing in upper-income neighborhoods is privately owned. Nevertheless, most African governments have continued to allocate a disproportionate share of scarce resources to providing housing for higher officials. An exception is Tanzania, which has treated government housing for officials as a low priority.

Middle-Class Housing

The term *middle class* in Africa is used loosely to refer to middle-level civil servants such as teachers, clerks, soldiers, and policemen. Middle-income employees of companies and middle-level independent professionals and businesspeople may also be included.

Colonial governments provided basic housing for many of its African employees. In the newly established colonial cities, especially "European" cities like Salisbury and Lusaka, companies took an active role in providing housing for their African employees. Much less of this type of housing was erected in established precolonial cities like Kano.

In the postcolonial era, the proportion of middle-level civil servants and employees living in government and company housing estates has declined greatly. The main exceptions would be police and military personnel, who are still usually housed in barracks. The middle classes have also tended to be the primary beneficiaries of so-called low-cost public-housing projects that have been developed by many governments as a response to the urban housing crisis. Nevertheless, the majority of the middle classes look after their own housing needs.

Many middle-class families are able eventually to afford their own homes. They may benefit from low-interest loans from government or company sources and tend to receive favored treatment when governments make building lots available for sale to the public. Such assistance is seldom available to the poor. Middle-class homes range in size from modest two- to four-room single family homes to larger dwellings that often contain accommodation for members of the extended family, space for a small shop, and rooms for rent to supplement the household income. Population densities in middle-class neighborhoods may be quite high, especially where there are many partly rented, multistoried homes.

Housing for the Working Poor

Housing the poor was a very low priority during colonial times. Basic housing was provided for the servants of Europeans. Many of the large mining companies built barracks to house their employees, but often not the employees' families. These types of housing clearly were designed to benefit expatriate employers rather than African employees.

The housing available to the poor in most African cities still provides little more than the minimal requirements for shelter. Tenants pay a substantial portion of their incomes to rent this rudimentary housing. The accommoda-

Vignette 15.1. Residential Landscapes in Lusaka

Like all colonial and postcolonial cities, the residential areas of Lusaka are structured according to social class. The dominant elites have their own elite neighborhoods, separated spatially from those of the less well off. At the other end of the scale, the poor provide their own housing, often in squatter settlements with little in the way of modern amenities.

The photographs show typical housing in different parts of Lusaka. They are accompanied by small maps showing the layout of the same or similar neighborhoods, and giving some indication of the density of development. The letters on the map show the approximate locations of the detailed layout maps.

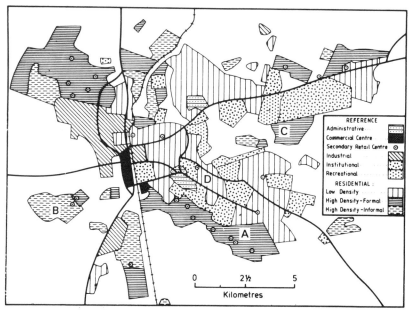

Figure 15.1. Social class and housing in Lusaka, Zambia. The inset maps below show the layout of various residential districts and highlight the magnitude of difference in house size and density in relation to social class. (Scale of inset maps: 1 cm = 100 m.)

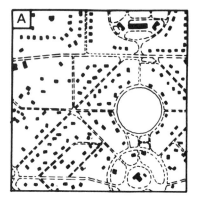

(a) Housing constructed during the colonial era for African workers.

Colonial housing in Old Chilenje.

cont.

Vignette 15.1. (cont.)

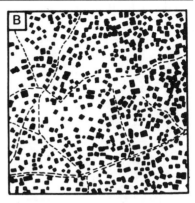

(b) Postindependence squatter settlement, occupied mostly by lower-class residents.

Squatter settlement at Kanyama.

(c) A newly developed site-and-service scheme provides opportunities for lower middle-class people to build houses which serve their own needs.

Site-and-service center at Mtendere.

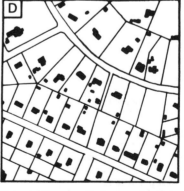

(d) Hidden by a wall and surrounded by gardens, the opulent home of either a wealthy Zambian or an expatriate.

Colonial low-density European housing at Ridgeway.

Source (city map and inset maps): G. Williams. *The Peugeot Guide to Lusaka*. Lusaka: Zambian Geographical Association, 1983. Photos: (a), (b) G. Williams; (c), (d) author.

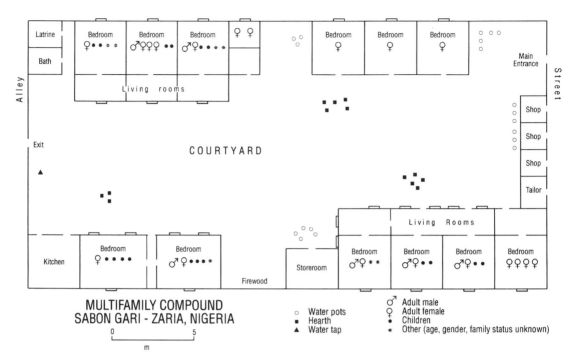

Figure 15.2. The layout of a typical multifamily compound in the Sabon Gari district of Zaria, Nigeria. Sabon Gari ("new town") was established during colonial times as a residential area for migrants from southern Nigeria. After A. W. Urquhart. *Planned Urban Landscapes of Northern Nigeria.* Zaria, Nigeria: Ahmadu Bello University Press, 1977, p. 49.

tions of the poor of Nairobi (Table 15.1) are fairly typical of the shelter available to Africa's urban poor—namely, a one-room house made of scrap materials or a single, rented room in a larger dwelling, with kitchen and bath shared by several families. Figure 15.2 shows the layout of a multifamily dwelling in a working-class migrant suburb of Zaria, Nigeria.

Table 15.1 shows the results of an exten-

sive housing survey conducted in low-income districts of Nairobi. The great majority of respondents were tenants rather than owner-occupiers. Their homes were very small and crowded; over 90% of dwellings had only one room. Individual kitchens and toilets were found in very few homes, especially in the intermediate and peripheral zones of the city. Few of the houses in the newer low-income suburbs were constructed of permanent build-

Table 15.1. Some Characteristics of Housing in Low-Income Districts of Nairobi

Location (sample size)	Central city (234)	Intermediate zone (663)	Peripheral zone (597)
Owner-occupied dwellings	4.0%	13.2%	27.5%
Houses with one room only	83.8%	90.4%	99.0%
Occupants per room	4.1	3.3	3.6
Houses of permanent materials	82.2%	3.9%	20.8%
Houses with individual kitchens	18.8%	2.1%	2.8%
Houses with individual toilets	16.6%	1.4%	1.1%

After J. W. Muwonge, "Intra-urban mobility and low income housing: The case of Nairobi, Kenya." In M. Morrison and P. Gutkind, eds., *Housing the Urban Poor in Africa.* Syracuse, NY: Maxwell School, Syracuse University, 1982, pp. 57–80.

ing materials. However, even rudimentary housing of this sort was very costly in relation to the earnings of the urban poor.

The poor must also make do with very inadequate public sevices. Local schools and health clinics, if available, are likely to be very overcrowded and understaffed. The inadequacy of water supply and disposal systems for sewage and refuse poses a threat to health. Widespread cholera epidemics in the early 1970s provided dramatic evidence of this health threat, but less dramatic illnesses such as gastroenteritis and dysentery regularly cause still greater levels of sickness and death. The extremely high population densities found in many poorer districts of contemporary African cities increase the concentration of pollution and facilitates the spread of epidemic disease.

Governments have done little to alleviate the housing difficulties faced by the urban poor. The occasional governmental low-cost housing project has virtually no effect on the availability of housing for the working poor. In most large cities, there is an acute shortage of affordable, legally registered building plots. The poor suffer not only from the scarci-

and high cost of legal plots but also from regulations governing plot development. Rules stating that homes must be constructed of permanent materials and finished within a specified period are an insurmountable barrier for citizens with modest incomes. The poor have often responded by building their own houses on land they do not legally own. These squatter settlements tend to be found on the outskirts of large cities, often on waste land.

Housing for the Unemployed

The cities of Africa south of the Sahara contain significant populations of desperately poor unemployed people. Many of them find shelter with relatives. Others may stay in house entranceways and courtyards, often doing casual work for the house owner. Still others are forced to sleep on the street, in markets, or in other public spaces.

The majority of the unemployed population consists of men. Some are unmarried while others have left their families at home in the countryside. There are also families who lack basic housing. Drought, armed conflict, and other crises that force people to leave their

Figure 15.3. Shelters occupied by refugees, Addia Ababa, Ethiopia. As "internal refugees," these Ethiopians displaced from Eritrea, when it was still part of Ethiopia, were not recognized as refugees by UNHCR and, thus, are not entitled to assistance. Photo: M. Peters.

rural homes are likely to increase the number of homeless families in the city (Figure 15.3).

The unemployed are very poorly served, not only because they have no housing of their own, but also because they have extremely poor access to amenities and social services. Many live in environments that are literally health threatening.

The Cultural Meanings of Housing

The quality of housing cannot be evaluated by using only utilitarian indices, such as number of rooms, amenities, and building materials. Appropriate housing not only provides shelter but also facilitates the expression of the community's cultural values and the maintenance of traditional lifestyles. The cultural dimension is clearly evident in the design of houses in rural communities and often in older, indigenous neighborhoods in cities.

For an example of how cultural values are reflected in house design, we may consider the houses of Islamic societies in countries such as Mali and Sudan. Islam permits polygynous marriages and calls for the seclusion of wives (purdah). Seclusion is accomplished with windowless walls surrounding the compound, as much to exclude men as to keep women within. Separate rooms are constructed for each wife around a central courtyard. The communal courtyard space and shared cooking facilities symbolize the common identity of household members and the importance of cooperation.

Housing in the modern African city, particularly housing normally available to the poor, is often ill designed in relation to cultural values. Single-room apartments and houses provide little privacy from other family members and neighbors. Outside space for food preparation and socializing is very cramped, if it is available at all. The high cost of adequate housing may force poor men to leave their children or wives in the countryside with relatives. Housing problems may also serve as a disincentive for people to have the culturally preferred number of children.

Public-housing projects have often been criticized for ignoring cultural values. The clearest examples are provided by the all-male company barracks for migrant workers in South Africa. Those accepting employment must leave their families behind; "normal" family life is only possible during brief visits every few months or after retirement from the mines. However, even the luxurious houses that governments provide for senior civil servants may be ill suited for traditional lifestyles. Modern kitchens may be poorly designed for food preparation that involves such tasks as grinding grain or pounding yams. Even the spatial arrangement and directional orientation of houses may convey unintended cultural meanings. Architects and planners need to become better educated about cultural values in order to design better houses and communities.

Despite the importance of cultural values, the poor are very pragmatic about their housing. For many of the poor, more spacious and culturally appropriate housing is a lower priority than other needs, including longer-term "investments" such as school fees for their children. Moreover, those able to set aside some money do not necessarily invest it in urban housing; many urban Africans with strong ties to their rural communities of origin prefer to construct a village home. In doing so, they reaffirm the importance of kinship and also provide themselves with some security for their retirement years.

Housing Policy Alternatives

The conventional wisdom about housing policy has changed radically since the mid-1970s. Previously, governments paid little heed to the housing needs of the majority of the urban population. As the limitations of the generally favored strategy of building public-housing projects became evident, more emphasis was placed on site-and-service schemes and squatter settlement improvements.

Many governments have endeavored to develop public-housing estates, in theory to help the poor. Unfortunately, these have not provided the answer to the urban housing crisis, in part because high costs have prevented the construction of enough units to make a difference. So-called low-income housing usually has been priced beyond the means of the majority who earn no more than a few hundred dollars annually. In some projects, undemocratic allocation procedures have favored the relatives of those in power and have excluded those without connections.

The housing crisis has been worsened by the shortage of affordable plots where private-sector housing could be built. The shortage of plots has been more acute in East, central, and southern African cities, where colonial policies had established strict planning guidelines to limit migration and urban growth, than in older West African cities, where legal access to plots could be obtained through traditional channels as well as from current urban administrations.

In South Africa, policies designed to restrict the growth of African urban populations and to effect strict residential segregation by race were intensified following the adoption in 1950 of apartheid as an official doctrine. Acute disparities in housing availability and quality (Table 15.2) are an important part of the continuing legacy of four decades of apartheid. As Vignette 15.2 shows, there are no easy, effective policy options that can alleviate this housing crisis, which is bound to intensify now that South Africa has entered the postapartheid era.

One response by Africans denied access to an affordable, registered building plot has been to erect a house on someone else's land in contravention of planning regulations. These illegal communities, often called squatter settlements, have mushroomed, particularly in marginal areas like floodplains, rocky hillsides, or forest reserves, within or just beyond urban boundaries. Sometimes, a landowner might illegally subdivide and sell his holding. These illegal and unplanned settlements usually have very inadequate provisions of water and other services.

Officials have tended to view squatter settlements as unhealthy eyesores that subvert the entire planning process. The common response has been to bulldoze them, often with no warning, as a means of reaffirming "the rule of law." Despite official disapproval and harsh penalties for building illegally, squatter settlements continue to proliferate. The bulldozers only provoke public outrage and deepen the housing crisis by destroying homes without providing alternate shelter.

The adaptive and dynamic nature of squatter settlements has gradually come to be recognized. The initial scrap-material shacks gradually disappear and are replaced by more elaborate dwellings made of permanent building materials. After a few years, there may be little apparent difference between planned suburbs and squatter communities. This upgrading process typically takes place in several stages as home owners put aside savings and become more confident about their tenure. Some governments and aid agencies have begun to assist in this process by providing low-interest loans to finance home improvements and by installing services for community use.

The primary result of this reevaluation of squatter housing has been the development of so-called site-and-service schemes, in which the government begins to develop a new suburb by surveying plots, constructing roads, and installing water, electricity, and other basic services. After obtaining a plot, prospective home owners are free to build their own houses, appropriate to their needs. Since the costs to the state are much lower than with public-housing projects, site-and-service schemes can be developed on a large scale. Nevertheless, demand for serviced lots has exceeded supply and the costs of buying a plot and building a house remain beyond the means of many of the working poor and certainly the unemployed. Thus, illegal squatter settlements continue to proliferate, and most of the poor continue to live in cramped quarters or even remain homeless.

Intervention by governments and development agencies has not been limited to the creation of new site-and-service suburbs. Programs to upgrade existing squatter settlements have also been implemented in several countries. Upgrading schemes typically involve the development of improved public infrastructures and incentives for individual

Vignette 15.2 Khayelitsha: Housing Policy and the Struggle for Shelter in an Apartheid City

Under apartheid, Cape Town, like other South African cities, was divided into zones for allocation to each racial group (Figure 13.10). Coloreds, who composed over half of Cape Town's population, were allocated only 27% of the land. The fate of residents of the long-established inner-city neighborhood called District Six was typical of that of tens of thousands of coloreds. They were uprooted from their homes and sent to an isolated, desolate plain 20 km from downtown. The new community had virtually no housing or services. Authorities attempted to exclude Africans from the city by forcing all migrant workers into barracks and severely restricting family housing. Not only squatters but also people with legal tenure were evicted from their homes.

As Table 15.2 shows, a massive housing crisis emerged as a result of forced removals, rapid population growth, and a grossly inadequate housing policy. The government eventually responded to this crisis with a number of remedial measures, one of which was the establishment in 1983 of the new town of Khayelitsha to house Africans legally residing in Cape Town. The town was to grow in a gradual and orderly fashion, with families moving in as new public housing was built. However, Africans protested being forced to move into 14.4 sq-m "houses" in a distant suburb with few services, virtually no possibilities for employment, and no rights to land ownership. By 1985, the government had relented, dropping the idea of moving all Africans to Khayelitsha and adding site-and-service plots where people could construct their own homes.

A survey in 1988 estimated that between 110,000 and 189,000 people were living in Khayelitsha. By late 1990, the number of persons in Khayelitsha had swollen to 450,000, only 14% of whom were in formal housing. A further 54% occupied serviced and partly serviced sites. The remainder consisted of squatters who illegally occupied whatever space they could find. The squatter areas receive no services of any kind. The rapid growth of Khayelitsha, despite its remoteness, unattractive appearance, lack of jobs, and very inadequate services, reflects the virtual absence of viable alternatives for the vast majority of Africans in Cape Town.

The African population of Cape Town is growing at 14% annually, fueling demand for an estimated 300,000 to 500,000 additional housing units during the 1990s in Cape Town alone. The state cannot hope to meet such a demand for new housing itself. Without effective, innovative new policies, the unplanned and unserviced squatter settlements will continue to mushroom. The best alternative may be a diverse set of policies to assist self-help in housing by stimulating the growth of employment, removing barriers to the construction of self-help housing, and providing training to upgrade construction skills.

Based on G. P. Cook. "Khayelitsha: New settlement forms in the Cape Peninsula." In D. M. Smith, ed., *The Apartheid City and Beyond*. London: Routledge, 1992, pp. 125–135.

Table 15.2. Housing Inequalities in Cape Town, South Africa

Group	% of total population	Units No.	Units %	Families on waiting lists	% of units under 3 rooms	Persons per room
White	23	197,671	48	–	<1	0.8
Colored	48	195,114[a]	47	65,048	87	2.3
African	27	20,108[b]	5	90,000	85	2.6

[a]Plus 2,916 informal units.   [b]Plus 43,785 informal units.
Source: G. P. Cook. "Cape Town." In A. Lemon, ed., *Homes Apart*. Bloomington: Indiana University Press, 1991, p. 31.

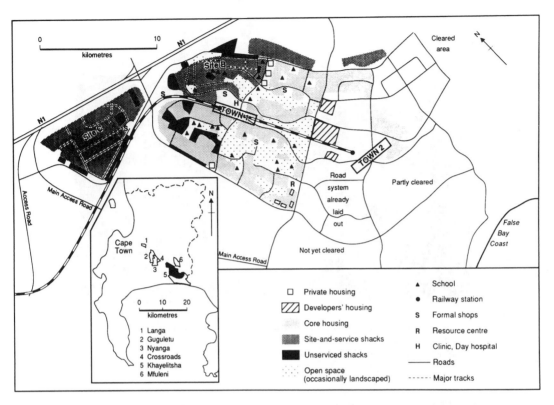

Figure 15.4. The development of Khayelitsha, a Cape Town suburb. This rapidly growing community is primarily a squatter settlement, but has some private and site-and-service scheme development. Source: G. P. Cook. "Cape Town." In A. Lemon, ed., *Homes Apart: South Africa's Segregated Cities.* London: Paul Chapman, 1991, p. 31. ©1991 by Paul Chapman Publishing Ltd. Reprinted by permission.

Figure 15.5. Crossroads, Cape Town, South Africa. The housing of Crossroads is typical of that of the mushrooming squatter settlements on the peripheries of large South African cities. Photo: D. Bowen.

Figure 15.6. Uncollected garbage in a residential area, Kano, Nigeria. Inadequate sanitation, often a characteristic of poorer districts in Africa's largest cities, is a health hazard and an aesthetic eyesore. Photo: author.

householders. These incentives may include granting legal title to squatter properties and providing low-interest loans for renovation work. Improvements to a community's infrastructure are often accomplished by mobilizing local voluntary labor to work on roads, drainage systems, schools, and community centers with materials supplied by the organizing development agency.

Upgrading programs have contributed substantially to better living conditions in many of the communities where the programs have been launched. Still, comprehensive upgrading schemes can be quite expensive and only infrequently have they been considered a high priority by governments. Not uncommonly, these schemes show up as demonstration projects in the capital city, to give the impression that something is being done.

The housing crisis in African cities mirrors a wider crisis of access to basic needs. The poor are severely disadvantaged in their quest for adequate water, education, transportation, health, and other services. Although "basic needs" strategies of urban development have helped to improve service accessibility, the scarcity of resources and the self-interest of ruling classes have limited their effect. Where governments have failed to meet poor people's basic needs, the poor have had to find ways of providing for themselves.

Further Reading

The following sources provide overviews of housing problems in contemporary African cities:

Amis, P., and P. Lloyd, eds. *Housing Africa's Urban Poor*. Manchester, England: Manchester University Press, 1990. (See in particular the Introduction and Part 1.)

Morrison, M., and P. Gutkind, eds. *Housing in Third World Cities*. Syracuse, NY: Maxwell School, 1982. (See Chapters 1, 2, 6, and 8.)

O'Connor, A. "Housing." Chapter 6 in *The African City*. London: Hutchinson, 1983.

Policies to address housing crises by developing site-and-service schemes and upgrading squatter settlements are discussed in the following sources:

Burgess, R. "Some common misconceptions about self-help housing policies in less developed countries." *African Urban Quarterly*, vol. 2 (1987), pp. 365–378.

Gilbert, A. "Self-help housing and state intervention: Illustrative reflections on the petty commodity production debate." In D. Drakanis-Smith, ed., *Urbanization in the Developing World*, pp. 175–194. London: Croom-Helm, 1986.

Laquian, A. A. *Basic Housing: Policies for Urban Sites, Services and Shelter in Developing Countries.* Ottawa, Ontario: International Development Research Centre, 1983.

Obudho, R. A., and C. C. Mhlanga, eds. *Slum and Squatter Settlements in Sub-Saharan Africa.* New York: Praeger, 1988.

Payne, G. K. *Low Income Housing in the Developing World: The Role of Sites and Services and Settlement Upgrading.* Chichester, England: Wiley, 1984.

Ward, P. M., ed. *Self-Help Housing: A Critique.* London: Mansell, 1982.

The larger concept of "basic needs," which includes self-help housing policies, is critically assessed in the following source:

Sandbrook, R. *The Politics of Basic Needs: Urban Aspects of Assaulting Poverty in Africa.* Toronto, Ontario: University of Toronto Press, 1982.

Much has been written about the experiences with housing policy in particular African countries. Examples include the following sources:

Adeniyi, E. *Housing the Urban Masses in Nigeria.* Ibadan, Nigeria: Nigerian Institute of Social and Economic Research, 1977.

Bamberger, M., B. Sanyal, and N. Valverde. *Evaluation of Sites and Services Projects: The Experience from Lusaka, Zambia.* Washington, DC: World Bank, 1982.

Faruquee, R. *Social Infrastructure and Services in Zimbabwe.* Washington, DC: World Bank, 1981.

Grootaert, C., and J. L. Dubois. *The Demand for Housing in the Ivory Coast.* Washington, DC: World Bank, 1986.

Lemon, A., ed. *Homes Apart: South Africa's Segregated Cities.* Bloomington: Indiana University Press, 1991.

Smith, D. M., ed. *The Apartheid City and Beyond: Urbanization and Change in South Africa.* London: Routledge, 1992. (Part 2 and Part 5 each have a number of chapters on housing.)

Stren, R. "Urban policy." In J. Barkan and J. Okuma, eds., *Politics and Public Policy in Kenya and Tanzania*, pp. 179–208. New York: Praeger, 1979.

SOCIAL GEOGRAPHY

The discussion in the following three chapters may be situated within the welfare school of social geography. This approach, originally conceptualized by David Smith as the "study of who gets what where," examines social and spatial variations in human welfare. However, the social-welfare approach goes beyond mere description to search for the underlying causes of social injustice, whether historical, economic, cultural, or political. It is a policy-oriented approach in which the ultimate objective is to show how more equitable future states might be attained.

Chapter 16 explores the social geography of African women. The substantial and diverse economic roles played by African women are finally being recognized. However, while development agencies have responded by supporting women's development projects, there continues to be disagreement about whether this aid is a harbinger of changing attitudes toward women or mere tokenism. The chapter also considers how the role of women is defined within the context of African culture and the implications for African women when increasing access to education and other changes in a modernizing society subject traditions like early marriage and circumcision to greater scrutiny.

Chapter 17 looks at the uneven development of education in Africa south of the Sahara. These inequities are traced from the colonial legacy of unequal development to the continuing rural–urban and class inbalancess in access to education. Various attempts have been made to develop more relevant and accessible education systems. However, while most countries have invested heavily in education as a foundation for development, the returns on this investment have often seemed disappointing.

In Chapter 18, the focus shifts to health, particularly to the policy debates that have surrounded the development of health services in Africa. In recent years, as the African economic crisis has deepened, it has become increasingly necessary for governments to reexamine how health care is provided and financed; several new approaches have been developed to address these problems. Finally, the chapter examines how the rapid spread of AIDS has created a number of new challenges to health care systems.

16

❋

African Women and Development

Until quite recently, very little attention had been paid by scholars and development planners to the social, economic, and political roles of women in Africa. Implicit in this silence were the assumptions that what women did was not of great importance and that their interests were adequately served by conventional "gender-neutral" development strategies. Since the early 1970s, the quantity, quality, and diversity of feminist scholarship on "gender and development" have continued to grow, leaving no room for doubt about the fundamental significance of gender relations for development.

At the same time, the voices of African women, speaking individually and as members of women's organizations, have begun to be heard. One of their greatest contributions has been to insist that the values, opinions, and objectives of African women be respected and used as the basis for development initiatives. Vigorous debate continues to take place among women in both Third World and industrialized countries about the nature of women's oppression and the preferred directions for change.

This chapter examines distinctive features of the geography of African women, looking at selected economic and social issues affecting women in Africa, particularly the effect on women of conventional approaches to de-velopment. This is not to imply that there is a single, unified geography of African women. On the contrary, the situations and strategies of African women are extremely diverse, reflecting differences in social class, ethnicity, religion, and place of residence.

It has been said that African women have suffered under two "colonialisms": that of Europe and that of men. European officials and missionaries brought with them their own notions of the proper social and economic roles for women. The Victorian ideal was that women should stay at home and concentrate on child rearing and domestic labor. If the African reality clashed with these values–as it usually did–then measures should be taken to change the Africans! Hence, for example, taxes were seen as an incentive for men to assume their "proper" role as farmers. European policies did not challenge the strong traditions of patriarchal control of women in African society; indeed, such policies often strengthened those traditions.

The end of colonial rule seldom brought substantive changes to either of the "colonialisms." Women have continued to suffer disadvantage and discrimination in many facets of their personal lives, in options accessible to them in the community, and in their treatment by the nation–state. At the same time, it must be emphasized that while African women are disadvantaged in many ways, they should not be seen as merely passive victims either of male domination or of larger economic forces. Women play vital roles in development and struggle in various ways to exercise greater control over their own destinies and to maximize opportunities for themselves and their families.

The economic contribution of African women has tended to be forgotten and ignored, in part because so much female economic activity is classed as housework or subsistence— and, hence, is not recorded in such macroscale measures of economic activity as the gross national product. This devaluation— indeed, denial—of the quantity and value of women's work has been characteristic of industrial societies as well. In most African societies, it is appropriate to portray women as family "breadwinners," not only because they grow most of the food but also because it is women, not men, who take ultimate responsibility for seeing that basic needs are met. In Africa, women work longer hours than men, rural women work longer than urban women, and women of the poorest countries work the longest hours simply to provide the basic needs of food, shelter, and clothing for their families.

The Double-Double Workload of African Women

Most studies of women's work have stressed the importance of women's double work load: in reproduction (the domestic sphere) and in production (paid labor in the public sphere). The term *double workload* refers not only to the dual focus of women's work but also to the amount of work performed by women. The double-workload construct, the validity of which is now increasingly questioned even by feminists interested in industrial societies, has always been of uncertain value for the analysis of women's work in the Third World. As a general rule, African women work longer and harder, do more types of work, and struggle against more formidable barriers than women in industrial societies—hence, the reference

above to their "double-double" workload. Much of the work of African women cannot easily be categorized as either reproductive or productive, in the usual sense of these terms. Moreover, the nature and productive significance of women's work varies greatly both between societies and within specific societies.

In the discussion that follows, four broad categories of women's work are considered:

1. Child rearing, the preparation of meals, and other types of domestic labor centered primarily in the home
2. Tasks such as farming, collecting fuelwood, and fetching water—household subsistence activities, usually done by women, that are undertaken outside the home
3. Money-earning activities centered in the informal economy, including the preparation of goods for sale, the provision of services, and retail trade
4. Employment in the formal economy—in factories, as civil servants, and so on

Only a small minority of women are involved actively in all four of these types of work. As a rule, there are significant rural–urban and class distinctions. Rural women have few, if any, opportunities to work in the formal economy, and the various subsistence tasks centered outside the home are much more likely to affect rural than urban women. As for social class, the poorer the household, the greater the likelihood that women will be forced to undertake many types of work.

The strength of women's economies is important not least because of the precarious situation of older women who have been widowed or divorced. With virtually no social security and relatively poor prospects for remarriage, unmarried older women must find ways of supporting themselves, perhaps with some support from family and friends.

Domestic Labor Centered Primarily in the Home

Women have responsibility for a wide variety of work that is particularly associated with

Figure 16.1. "A woman's work is never done": the daily tasks of women in Botswana. (a) Bringing water home from the village borehole. (b) Fetching firewood for use as fuel for cooking and warmth. (c) Working together on the farm. (d) Winnowing grain. (e) Preparing food using a mortar and pestel. (f) Caring for children. Photos: (a) R. Dixey; (b) to (f) CIDA: B. Paton.

the home. These tasks include, among other things, preparing and serving meals, keeping house, and caring for children and those who are sick.

The great majority of Africans would undoubtedly assert that bearing and rearing children is women's most important role. This role involves a tremendous commitment of time and energy. African women give birth, on average, six or seven times, and may breast-feed each of their babies for 18 to 30 months. Thus, many African women spend perhaps 15 to 20 years of their lives bearing or breast-feeding children. This is not to imply that caring for an infant brings much relief from other types of work—quite the opposite. Carrying their babies with them wherever they go, women continue to cook meals, fetch water, work in the fields, carry goods to market, and do whatever else needs to be done.

As a rule, men do not participate in domestic work, including child rearing—such tasks are considered to be the exclusive domain of women. While men in some societies are obliged by custom to provide their wives with sufficient money to cover the costs of food and other day-to-day household costs, in other societies, particularly in cases where women farm, men's obligations regarding household maintenance are more ambiguous. It is a common complaint that men do not take sufficient responsibility for providing for their families but rather treat the income that they earn as theirs to spend.

The burden of combining child care and other work tends to be more severe in poorer monogamous households than in polygynous households, especially where there are no older children and few relatives living nearby to lend assistance. In polygynous households, there are opportunities for co-wives to share the burden of domestic work, including child care.

Many African cultures traditionally practice polygyny and consider it to be the preferred form of marriage. Polygyny is sanctioned by Islam, but Christian denominations based in Europe and North America have always strongly condemned it. The preference for polygynous marriages, especially among men, relates primarily to its value as a symbol of status and wealth. With the costs of marrying and supporting more than one wife increasingly beyond the means of men with modest incomes, polygyny may well become less common, but its image as a status symbol is unlikely to diminish.

Household Subsistence Activities Outside the Home

In addition to their home-centered activities, African women do the majority of household subsistence work consisting of tasks outside the home. According to an International Labor Organization study by Ruth Dixon-Mueller, African women contribute 70% of the total hours spent in agricultural production, as well as doing 50% of the care of livestock, 80% of the collection of wood for fuel, and 90% of water collection for household use.

Women compose the majority of agricultural workers in Africa and do most of the farm work. Rural women in Gambia, for example, spend an average of 159 days working on the farm. In Uganda, the majority of women—approximately 70% in most districts—reported that their husbands seldom or never assisted them in their work on the farm.

In one common gender division of labor, which arose with the emergence of a cash economy during colonial rule, women assume sole responsibility for food-crop production, while men concentrate on cash crops. The sale of cash crops was essentially equivalent to the sale of labor; both were methods of earning money to pay taxes and obtain consumer goods. As men focused increasingly on work to generate income, they left to women a larger proportion of nonmonetarized work, such as growing food for household consumption. Not only did women have difficulty obtaining cash, but they often suffered losses because colonial strategies converted more productive lands to cash-crop production (Vignette 16.1). Most women were traveling farther and working harder to produce the same amount of food on soils that were becoming less fertile.

While the majority of food production is undertaken by rural women, this gender division of labor is not universal. In some Islamic cultures, where most women stay in purdah, the only women actively involved in agriculture are older widows or women from the poorest, most labor-deficient households where survival has to take precedence over preferred religious practice.

Vignette 16.1. Changes in the Gender Division of Labor under Colonialism

How colonialism changed the lives of rural women depended on a variety of factors, such as types of export crops introduced, extent of labor migration, the control of land, and cultural traditions about the division of labor. What follows is a brief comparison of changes in four groups: the Luo and Kikuyu of Kenya, the Mandinka of Gambia, and the Ewe of Ghana.

Among the Kikuyu and Luo, men cleared the land and women were responsible for planting, weeding, and harvesting of food crops. As male labor migration became more common and longer-term, men often failed to contribute their traditional share of labor, forcing women to work harder. Because men thought that providing food was women's responsibility, women had to find ways of earning their own cash income to buy supplemental food. Luo women became more involved in trading, while Kikuyu women began to modernize farming practices and relied on traditional forms of cooperative craft production. Women lost some of their best land when it was taken over for settler agriculture and came under further pressure with the 1955 land-tenure reform that created individual ownership and made it possible for absent husbands or sons to sell farms without women's consent.

During the colonial era, Ewe men increasingly shifted land and labor from yam cultivation to cocoa production and also engaged in labor migration. As men laid claim to the most fertile land for their cocoa farms, women found it harder to get access to land to grow food. Women lost traditional rights to use lineage common lands and had to get permission from individual men to use fallow areas. Because of the shortage of male labor for farm clearance, women had to use land that was less densely forested and thus, easier to clear; this land also tended to be the least fertile. They increasingly turned to growing cassava and to petty trading to compensate for the shortfall in yam production. While women's workload increased, family nutrition suffered because of cassava's low protein content.

Among the Mandinka of Gambia, women traditionally concentrated on swamp-rice cultivation, while men were responsible for upland crops like millet and sorghum. Mandinka men migrated infrequently during the colonial era; instead, they intensified their cultivation of groundnuts as a cash crop. Competition for land was less of a problem since men and women made use of different types of land to grow their crops. However, Gambian women had to grow more rice to compensate for the declining production of men's staples, which necessitated using more distant and less attractive swamplands.

Specific effects and adaptive strategies varied, but in each case, described above, women had to find ways of producing more food with less support from their husbands and often with decreased access to land. Moreover, women continued to have responsibility for other tasks like child rearing, food preparation, and fuelwood and water collection. The double workload of women was redoubled.

Based on E. Trenchard. "Rural women's work in sub-Saharan Africa." In J. Momsen and J. Townsend, eds., *Geography of Gender in the Third World*. Albany: SUNY Press, 1987.

Women in rural areas lacking easy access to water must spend hours each day carrying heavy water jugs from distant streams and shallow wells. The work is onerous, and time spent carrying water must be taken from other tasks. Compromises have to be made, an example of which is the substitution of relatively easily cultivated but less nutritious crops like cassava for other, more demanding, food crops.

Collecting fuelwood for cooking, heating, and income-producing activities like smoking fish is a time-consuming process, almost entirely performed by women and children. In the forest zone, women spend an average of 45 to 60 minutes per day collecting wood. In savanna and semidesert environments, especially where population densities are quite high, considerably more time may be needed to collect sufficient fuel. Population growth, the expansion of agriculture, the cutting of fuelwood for sale in urban markets, and in some cases government restrictions on tree felling are forcing women to spend longer hours and to walk farther to obtain enough wood for household needs.

Labor migration has generally increased the burden of work for rural women. With many, and sometimes most, of the able adult men absent, women have been forced to do additional, "male" tasks, like the clearance of farmland. The situation of rural women has been especially precarious in the former homelands of South Africa, since South Africa until recently prevented the wives and families of black migrant workers from accompanying their husbands to the city.

Money-Earning Activities Centered in the Informal Economy

In Ghana, as in several other parts of Africa, to enter a marketplace is to witness the economic power of women. Most of the traders are women. Moreover, many of the goods that women sell also have been produced, processed, and transported to market by women. For example, in Ghana, every stage in the processing and marketing of fish, except the actual fishing, is likely to have been done exclusively by women.

Although the majority of economically active women operate small, marginal enterprises from their homes, very few African women have become wealthy entrepreneurs controlling major trading, contracting, and manufacturing enterprises. The market women of Togo, Ghana, and southern Nigeria are legendary for their economic savvy and wealth (Vignette 16.2).

Even in Islamic societies practicing strict purdah, women prepare handicrafts and foods for sale, participate in trade, and act as ethnomedical practitioners. In the city of Kano, where very few married women of childbearing age ever venture outside the house except on ceremonial occasions or for medical care, nine-tenths of women are involved in income-producing activities. Women's economic activity may account for one-third of the total economy of Kano. This "hidden trade" by secluded women relies largely on using children as messengers and sellers. These often forgotten women's economic activities may be eroded by government licensing requirements and even by otherwise progressive social legislation; making school attendance compulsory in Nigeria, for example, deprived many secluded women of the labor they needed to carry on their economic activities.

Women use the income they earn for a variety of purposes, ranging from personal needs, to children's school fees, to gifts on ceremonial occasions, to collateral for future business ventures. Women may have to dip into their own savings to cover the cost of basic household necessities if their husbands fail to meet their obligations. With the continuing, severe decline in real incomes in recent years, the earnings of women and children have become essential for survival in more and more households.

The economic activities of women are characterized by the development of mutual-support mechanisms. One example is the revolving credit system, in which a group of women pool a specified amount of money; members in turn collect the total sum and use it for projects of their choice. Such institutions can easily be used as the basis for organizing cooperatives to undertake projects beyond the scope of individual members.

Employment in the Formal Economy

Women in urban areas, particularly those with education, are beginning to face new economic challenges. Many of these women work in the

---

Vignette 16.2. The 'Nanas-Benz' of Togo

Who are the 'Nanas-Benz'? These venerable ladies are Togolese cloth merchants. Relatively elderly—some as old as 75—and often illiterate, they are nevertheless canny businesswomen who certainly know their numbers. 'Nanas-Benz' is a combination of two words: nana, meaning 'established woman' or 'woman of means' and Benz from their passion for the Mercedes Benz.

The major feature distinguishing the Nanas from other female cloth merchants is the sheer volume of their businesses. The most successful have been known to turn over the equivalent of $600,000 per month. The location of a Nana's business—which may be an important stall in the Grand Marché of Lomé, Togo's capital, or a well-known boutique in the street of a neighboring quartier—contributes as much to her prestige as to her sales volume. Status also depends on buying power, ability to negotiate, and size of clientele. The Nanas-Benz act as agents between the importers and a wide-ranging clientele in West Africa. About 85 per cent of the cloth delivered to Lomé is sold to buyers from other West African countries. Togo's low rate of customs duties allows buyers from neighboring nations to purchase more cheaply in Lomé than in their own countries, even after transportation costs are taken into account.

The Nanas select their fabrics from samples created by European designers, who sometimes follow their suggestions. Batik cloth arrives on container-ships. The bolts are addressed to the particular Nana and distributed on the importer's premises. Boat arrivals are irregular: up to eight months may elapse between order and delivery, so the Nanas must rely on intuition and foresight in anticipating the tastes of their clients and trends of fashion.

At the top of Togo's cloth trade are the wholesale dealers and major retailers—that is, the Nanas and a few others. All of them take in retail clerks or assistants, who are not paid but are given room and board. Often they come from the same village as the owner, and become trusted associates—sometimes they even take over the business. At the bottom of the scale are pedlars who criss-cross the market, selling fabric by the piece. They pay their employers only after making a sale, so the relationship is based on mutual trust.

All successful 'Nanas-Benz' make sure their children attend university. Girls study economics, management, and administration; boys become architects, teachers, or bankers. These women consider it important to have female children, partly to inherit the business. If no daughter exists, they often leave the enterprise to a niece or cousin. In this way, a kind of family matriarchy is created within a social system which is both patriarchal and polygynous.

On Lomé's *Grand Marché*, that wonderful gathering-place for women, the only men seen behind the stalls are butchers. And any other men here are merely clients, strollers, or relatives of the lady merchants.

Exerpt from M. Crouillère. "The 'Nanas-Benz.'" *Development*, Spring, 1987, pp. 7–8.

---

formal sector as teachers, health-service personnel, factory workers, and the like. Their concerns include such workplace issues as promotion, job security, scheduling, and maternity leave, as well as such public concerns as the reliability of public transportation systems and the quality of education. Most of these formal-sector jobs are considered very desirable, although many do not command especially high rates of pay.

While the number of women employed in the formal sector is small in relation to the total population of women in Africa, these women are becoming more numerous and influential. Not all African women lead the lifestyle typical of rural women, nor are women's priority issues the same in all parts of the continent.

Social and Political Issues

In Africa, as elsewhere, each society has its unwritten rules—guidelines that are neither so rigid that change is impossible nor so flexible that "unacceptable" behavior will go unchallenged. The direction of change reflects struggles between conservative factions determined to protect cultural tradition and radicals striving for a new order. Tradition remains a very powerful force limiting the choices open to African women. Strict adherence to culturally defined rules of behavior is seen as the individual's and society's best defense against misfortune. The defense of tradition also provides the ultimate rationale for the exercise of power by chiefs, elders, priests, and other "traditional" leaders.

Those arguing for greater choice for women must also confront a generally ambivalent attitude from most men who consider themselves to be progressive. Many men are preoccupied with other issues and do not really wish to change fundamentally the subservient status of women, both within the family and in the broader society. Moreover, African women are divided about the extent to which tradition should give way to greater choice; many influential women argue that the best guarantees for women's fulfillment lie in careful adherence to culturally defined norms.

The debate about women's choice has been particularly heated on the issue of female circumcision. In many African cultures, some form of surgical alteration of females' genitalia is performed as a rite of passage. The surgical procedures used vary, and the practice is not universal (Figure 16.2). Many Western feminists have strongly condemned female circumcision, perjoratively (from the African perspective) calling it female genital mutilation. African women are divided about whether these practices should be retained, modified, or abolished, not least because the underlying cultural meanings of the surgery are complex. Most African women are united, however, in condemning outsiders' intervention in a matter that they wish to see settled in Africa, by Africans, and in accordance with African values.

Controversy also surrounds the issue of female choice in marriage. Customarily, most African cultures prefer to have their girls marry early—at or even before puberty. Because customary marriages are not easily compatible with female education at the postprimary level, conservative parents agonize about whether their daughters' marriage prospects will be hindered or improved by allowing them to attend

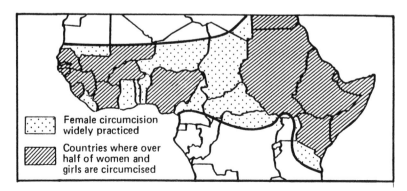

Figure 16.2. The practice of female circumcision. After J. Seager and A. Olson. *Women in the World: An International Atlas.* London: Pan Books, 1986.

school. Marriages are traditionally arranged by the family, with the bride having little or no say about her future husband. Young African women are increasingly assertive about their right to reject an arranged marriage that they dislike. Bride-wealth payments customarily are given to the parents of the bride. Parents are inclined to demand whatever the market will bear, thus forcing poorer families to go into debt and to delay marriage for years until bride wealth is accumulated. Where revolutionary governments have been established, laws to abolish forced marriages and the payment of bride wealth have received early assent but have also suffered from widespread public resistance.

Providing opportunities to all for education is very important for women's progress. Literacy gives access to an infinite range of written material, and vocational and postprimary education opens new employment opportunities to women. There has been real progress in Africa south of the Sahara in expanding educational opportunities, including those for women. Females accounted for 45% of students in African primary schools in 1989, compared to only 32% in 1960. At the secondary level, they composed 41% of students, up from 26% in 1960. Still, much remains to be accomplished. Within both the African family and the modern state, traditional thinking dies hard that attaches higher priority to the education and the posteducation employment of boys than girls.

The economic and social policies that benefit women will inevitably be shaped within the political arena. Thus, if women are to advance, they must succeed in having a meaningful influence in politics.

Political power and influence are not entirely new to African women. History records several examples of women, such as Queen Amina of Zaria (Nigeria), who were influential leaders. In certain matriarchal societies, such as the Ashanti of Ghana, women play an important role in political affairs. The Queen Mother holds a position of great honor in Ashanti society and heads an organization of women who participate in the selection of new kings. During the era of colonial rule, African women often took the lead in protesting taxes and other government measures that they considered to be unfair.

Achieving real political influence in present-day Africa will not be easy, given the male domination of the media, politics, the civil service, and the military. Women face the greatest barriers in military states, where political agitation is discouraged, if not prohibited, and in one-party states, where there is no alternate political vehicle if the party gives low priority to women's concerns. Women have made the greatest strides toward political equality in states such as Eritrea and Guinea-Bissau where independence was won through armed struggle. Progress in these states evolved from the recognition that anti-imperial struggles could not succeed without the full commitment of women and that full commitment was impossible as long as women suffered under "two colonialisms." However, most states provide few opportunities and little encouragement for female political activism. Although many countries have appointed female cabinet ministers, only a handful, such as Tanzania and Zimbabwe, have made serious attempts to involve women in the political process. In Ghana, President Rawlings's election victory in 1992 owed much to his prolonged efforts to mobilize women's support, particularly in rural areas, by emphasizing the benefits to women of water supply and other rural development projects.

The evolution of a more active political role for African women has been assisted indirectly by developments in the international women's movement. The United Nations. Decade for Women and associated conferences, particularly the concluding World Conference held in 1985 in Nairobi, served as a catalyst for the growth of national women's organizations in several countries, the discussion of women's concerns, and the exchange of ideas about programs to benefit women.

Women and Development

In 1970, Ester Boserup published her ground breaking book, *Women's Role in Economic De-*

velopment. Boserup's analysis began with a survey of the crucial economic role played by women in the Third World, a role, she noted, that was usually discounted and forgotten because of the exclusion of domestic and subsistence work from economic statistics. She showed how the crucial work of women had been ignored by governments and development agencies, both during and after the colonial era. Moreover, she argued, the "development" process had contributed to a decline in the situations of many women. Not only was the colonial promotion of cash cropping directed at men, excluding women from the income so derived, but women were often displaced from their best and most accessible farmland to make way for cash crops.

Following independence, women's agriculture was further marginalized when national economic policies and foreign aid programs put even more emphasis on cash crops to increase foreign exchange earnings. This reflected not only a bias toward export crop production but also a belief that food production would continue to "look after itself"–as well as the unquestioned assumption that males as heads of households controlled whatever happened on the farm. Thus, women continued to work almost invisibly, using traditional, labor-intensive technology to produce food, mainly for household consumption.

When growing food shortages and rising prices for food finally focused attention on food production in the 1970s and 1980s, the solutions proposed–irrigation schemes, large-scale farming, and land-tenure reform, for example–often favored men instead of women. Land, traditionally a communal resource in most parts of Africa, was converted to private title in a number of countries, in part to permit its use as collateral for loans. Men have often obtained title to land normally farmed by women, in the process eroding women's customary rights of use.

Boserup did not critically examine the dominant model of development; her point was that women needed to be included in the development process. The publication of her book stimulated interest for the first time in

projects specifically for women. Development agencies established "women-in-development" programs that typically attempted to improve domestic skills and methods of crafts production. These types of projects were attractive because they did not challenge the economic domain of men–and, thus, were politically and culturally "safe."

The limitations of disjointed, token, "women-in-development" projects soon became evident. Domestic work and crafts generate comparatively little money relative to the work effort and tend to reinforce the stereotypical view of "women's work." Moreover, rural women usually lack the time, energy, and financial means to take full advantage of development opportunities intended to be of benefit to them.

More ambitious projects for women's development also failed when not designed with enough attention to local sociocultural realities. A case in point is the Yagoua rice-culture modernization project (SEMRY) in Cameroon, which attempted to give women necessary assistance to produce rice. In Cameroon, women traditionally produce sorghum and men produce the more valuable crop, rice. The SEMRY project failed to meet its objectives because planners had failed to realize that, unlike sorghum, men controlled rice income even when it was produced by women.

More recent approaches have emphasized the inclusion of women in integrated community-development projects. While women may be less visibly "ghettoized" in these integrated projects, questions remain about whether women's voices are truly heard and whether women reap their fair share of benefits. In most cases, men continue to dominate and control what happens at the local level, and women continue to do more than their share of the work.

It would be wrong to conclude that development programs cannot be of substantial benefit to women. For example, the provision of safe, accessible water not only contributes to improved family health but may also reduce the time that women spend hauling water, thus freeing them up for other things. Maternal- and child-health programs that address women's

Figure 16.3. Woman in the Oodi Weaving Cooperative, Botswana. Oodi tapestries are internationally renowned for their beauty. The Oodi cooperative was a notable success among the early "women-and-development" aid projects. Photo: CIDA: B. Paton.

concerns about the birth and survival of children also contribute to the well-being of women.

Since the mid-1980s, there has been significant growth in the number of women's organizations, operating at all levels from the local community to the international. These organizations are helping to initiate a feminist transformation in the way in which women's development is done. At the international and national levels, the analysis is often explicitly feminist, focusing on gender relations as the key to understanding women's oppression and as the necessary starting point for progressive, liberating development. Where overt political activity is possible, feminist strategies increasingly center on ensuring that the political voice of women is strong and effective. Even in local communities, women are adopting strategies that are at least implicitly feminist. Women not only are forming their own local organizations to address needs that they themselves have identified as important, but also are insisting that women remain in control of these initiatives and that women reap whatever benefits can be derived.

As pressure on African societies increases because of population growth and environmental degradation and as governments become less and less able to respond to urgent development needs because of declining revenues and increasing debt, the hardships that confront the majority of African women continue to grow. Metaphorically, the geographic landscape for African women is a rocky terrain. Nevertheless, African women are not be pitied as passive victims. Rather, they are proud, innovative, and assertive within the contraints imposed by their societies, and they are increasingly determined to shape their own destinies.

Further Reading

For an insightful and provocative feminist overview of the "world of women," see the following source:

Seager, J., and A. Olson. *Women in the World: An International Atlas*, London: Par, 1986.

Economic issues associated with "women and development" are discussed in the following sources:

Boserup, E. *Women's Role in Economic Development*. London. Allen and Unwin, 1970.

Dixon-Mueller, R. *Women's Work in Third World Agriculture*. Geneva, Switzerland: ILO, 1985.

Gladwin, C. H., K. A. Staudt, and D. E. McMillar. "Providing Africa's Women Farmers Access: One Solution to the Food Crisis." *Journal of African Studies*, Winter 1986–1987, pp. 131–141.

Obbo, C. *African Women: Their Struggle for Economic Independence*. London: Zed, 1980.

Parpart, J. L., and K. A. Staudt. *Women and the State in Africa*. Boulder, CO: Lynne Rienner, 1989.

Plewes, B., and R. Stuart. "Women and development revisited: The case for a gender and development approach." In J. Swift and B. Tomlinson, eds., *Conflicts of Interest*, pp. 107–132. Toronto, Ontario: Between the Lines, 1991.

Stamp, P. *Technology, Gender and Power in Africa*. Ottawa, Ontario: International Development Research Centre, 1989.

Selected political and social issues concerning African women are discussed in the following sources:

Charleton, S. E. M., V. Everett, and K. Staudt, eds. *Women, the State and Development*. Albany: SUNY Press, 1989.

Coles, C., and B. Mack, eds. *Hausa Women in the Twentieth Century*. Madison: University of Wisconsin Press, 1991.

Cutrufelli, M. R. *Women of Africa: Roots of Oppression*. London: Zed, 1983.

Hosken, F. *The Hosken Report: Genital and Sexual Mutilation of Females*. Lexington, MA: Women's International News, 1982.

Oppong, C. *Female and Male in West Africa*. London: George Allen and Unwin, 1983.

Qunta, C., ed. *Women in Southern Africa*. London: Allison and Busby, 1987.

Robertson, C.; and I. Berger. *Women and Class in Africa*. New York: Holmes and Meier, 1986.

The lives of African women are explored in a diverse body of nonfictional and fictional literature. As a starting point, see the following sources:

Smith, M. F. *Baba of Karo: A Woman of the Muslim Hausa*. New Haven. Yale University Press, 1954.

Schipper, M. "Women and Literature in Africa." In M. Schipper, ed., *Unheard Words: Women and Literature in Africa, the Arab World, Asia, the Caribbean and Latin America*, pp. 22–58. London: Allison and Busby, 1984.

Emecheta, B. *Second Class Citizen*. London: Fontana, 1974. (Other novels by the same author include *Double Yoke*, *The Bride Price*, and *The Slave Girl*.)

17

✴

Education:
Who Gets What Where?

The view that education is *the* key to unlocking Africa's potential is widespread and deeply held. It prevails within development agencies such as the World Bank as well as among national political leaders. In many African families, scraping together money for childrens' school fees takes precedence over all but the most crucial of other needs.

It is imperative, however, to look critically at the role of education in national development. In part, this is because the focus on education as modern, formal schooling neglects the contribution of various kinds of indigenous education. It is also because there has been too little careful consideration of important education-related issues, such as basic objectives, curriculum structure, resource allocation to various parts of the educational system, and the fate of graduates. These factors ultimately determine the extent to which investment in education can have an effect on social and economic development in particular settings.

Indigenous Education

One of the greatest myths about African development is that education was a European gift. Although formal Western education was introduced in colonial times, it is also true that education, formal as well as informal, had existed long before the arrival of Europeans.

The most widespread form of education is the learning that occurs informally as children observe and explore the environment in which they live. They do so at play and while assisting their parents and elder siblings with work on the farm or in the household (see Vignette 10.1). Working alongside elders provides countless opportunities to learn by example and by word of mouth.

African societies traditionally relied on oral communication to convey traditions, beliefs, and values, as well as information, from one generation to the next. Stories, songs, and proverbs are used to convey fundamental moral messages. Riddles serve as a test of mental dexterity and imagination. Into the ceremonial process of initiation into adulthood, some African societies incorporate formal instruction in the rituals, beliefs, and traditions of the clan or community.

In areas where Islam was important, formal Koranic schools were established (Figure 17.2). Instruction in the Arabic language made it possible for children to study the Koran and to read other books on Islamic belief and practice. The more gifted students could continue

Figure 17.1. Rural school, Mwanza, German East Africa (Tanzania), circa 1910. Even schools as rudimentary as this one were few and far between in most parts of Africa during the early colonial period. Photo: O. Haeckel.

with higher Islamic studies, specializing in areas such as Islamic law or training to become religious leaders and teachers. These scholars occupied positions of great prestige in society.

It should be emphasized that forms of indigenous education are still widely practiced. While their importance has declined with the spread of Western education, especially in the cities, they are still the basic mechanisms by which African values and knowledge are passed on from generation to generation.

Education in Colonial Africa

Despite the lofty rhetoric of the "civilizing mission" of colonialism, education was not a high priority for the British, French, Belgian, and Portuguese colonial rulers of Africa. Colonial administrators did recognize the need to train a cadre of local people who would be literate in the European language, capable of doing numerical calculations, familiar with European "ways of doing things," and perhaps trained to be mechanics, nurses, or practitioners of some other trade. Graduates could assume lower-ranking positions within the colony, for

example, as secretaries and administrative assistants in government offices, as teachers and nurses, and as clerks in commercial enterprises. On the other hand, it was feared that educated Africans could become a focus of political dissent, questioning the authority of both colonial rulers and traditional leaders who collaborated with them. As a rule, colonial regimes planned to construct just enough schools to meet the demand for trained personnel.

The shortage of funds and the involvement of missionaries in the educational field provided justification for the official neglect of education. The widely held view that too much schooling would "spoil" the African further justified this policy. In the novel *Mister Johnson,* by Joyce Cary (formerly a District Officer in Nigeria), the educated African is portrayed as caught between two worlds – divorced from his traditional culture but not part of the modern culture. Johnson struggles in his job as a clerk in a local administrative office, then loses his job and the status that went with it, and finally suffers a tragic death.

As time went on, the approach taken in most British colonies increasingly differed from that used in the French and Portuguese colonies. The French and Portuguese facilitated the creation of a very small class of "assimilated" Africans who were given special privileges by virtue of an elite education that sometimes included a period of study in Europe. It was hoped that this assimilated class would identify with the colonial power and reject anticolonial movements. The educational system in British colonies was somewhat less elitist and did not aim explicitly to create a class of officially assimilated Africans.

Missionary societies did not have the same ambivalence as the colonial state about the expansion of education. Schooling was identified as a powerful tool for spreading the Christian gospel. Schools, especially boarding schools, provided an atmosphere in which Christian beliefs and attitudes on marriage (monogamy), lifestyle (a rejection of traditional beliefs and practices), and work ("discipline") could be inculcated. In short, establishing schools was seen by missionary societies as a means to an end, rather than an end in itself.

The missionary involvement in education began very early. In present-day Senegal, Sierra Leone, Ghana, and Nigeria, a number of mission schools were established in the early 1800s. The spatial pattern of educational development that evolved reflected the nature and extent of missionary involvement in particular regions. Where missions with an active interest in education were established at an early date, a relatively high proportion of children went to school. Where there were few missionaries, often because of official restrictions on their activities, schooling tended to lag behind. Each missionary society had its own preferred model of educational development; some, for example, did considerable vocational training while others focused on literacy, obedience, and religious instruction.

The colonial neglect of educational development was very evident at the university level. Outside of South Africa, there were only five independent universities in 1960, located in Liberia, Ethiopia, Sudan, Senegal, and Congo-Léopoldville (Zaire). There were also 10 more colleges, all of which still operated as affiliates of European universities. This

Figure 17.2. Koranic school, Niger. Traditional Islamic education, conducted in the Arabic language, focuses on the study of the Koran and other religious texts. Photo: CIDA: R. Lemoyne.

Figure 17.3. Scene in a modern primary school, Niger. There is a vast difference in the curricula, both formal and informal, of the modern school and the Koranic school shown in Figure 17.2. Photo: CIDA: R. Lemoyne.

group included such notable institutions as Fourah Bay College in Sierra Leone (founded 1827), Makerere University in Uganda, and University of Ibadan in Nigeria. The total number of university students from black Africa, as of 1961, was only 27,500, of whom 13,000 were studying abroad. A total of 438 students graduated from Nigerian institutions in 1961; this included only 25 in engineering, 35 in medicine, and 21 in agricultural science.

Education in Contemporary Africa

Since independence, the countries of Africa south of the Sahara have invested heavily in education. The results of this effort have been impressive, particularly when the achievements in education are compared to those in other sectors.

Between 1960 and 1989, the number of children in primary schools increased more than fivefold, from 12 million to almost 61 million in Africa south of the Sahara (excluding South Africa). The gains in secondary enrolment were even more impressive—from almost 800,000 to almost 12 million. The numbers enrolled in postsecondary courses rose from 21,000 to 600,000, almost a 30-fold increase. To make these gains possible, African countries have invested vast sums in physical infrastructures (e.g., buildings, books, and supplies) as well as human capital (e.g., teachers). While substantial amounts of foreign assistance were received for educational development, the bulk of resources has come from within.

The state of educational development varies considerably from country to country (Figure 17.4). For example, less than one-third of adults are illiterate in 11 countries, while more than two-thirds are illiterate in another 13 countries. For the region as a whole, the enrollment in primary schools represents 71% of the primary school–aged population. The range of values is from 15% in Somalia and 23% in Mali to more than 100% in a few countries (the enrollment of some children younger and older than the usual school ages accounts for the occurrence of percentages over 100). The disparities between countries are even greater at the secondary and college

Table 17.1. Access to Education in Selected African Countries

	Adult illiteracy 1990 (%)	Primary school enrollment (1,000)		Gross enrollment ratios 1989[a] (# in school/# in cohort) × 100		
		1960	1989[a]	Primary	Secondary	College
Angola	58.3	104	1,041	95	11	0.7
Burkina Faso	81.8	57	472	35	7	0.7
Congo	43.4	116	503	NA	87	5.6
Ethiopia	44.8	224	2,856	38	15	0.8
Kenya	31.0	781	5,124	93	23	1.6
Lesotho	26.3	136	348	110	26	4.8
Mali	68.0	65	324	23	6	0.8
Nigeria	49.3	2,913	13,777	70	19	3.3
Rwanda	49.8	264	1,059	70	7	0.6
Zaire	28.2	1,550	4,356	77	24	0.5
Totals for Africa S. of Sahara	41.8	11,853	60,689	71	20	2.4

[a]In certain cases, latest data are for years other than 1989.
Sources: World Bank. *Education in Sub-Saharan Africa.* Washington, DC: 1988. UNESCO. *World Education Report 1991.* Paris, 1991. UNESCO. *Statistical Yearbook 1992.* Paris, 1992.

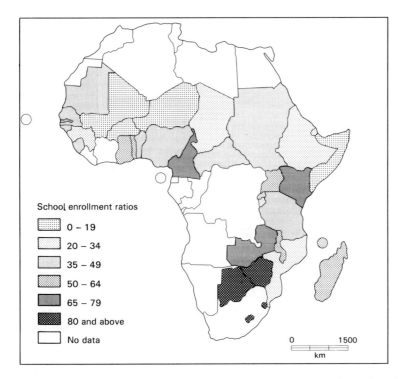

School enrollment ratios

- 0 – 19
- 20 – 34
- 35 – 49
- 50 – 64
- 65 – 79
- 80 and above
- No data

Figure 17.4. School enrollment ratios, 1986 to 1988. The ratios are for combined primary and secondary enrollments, and are based on the proportion of children of school age who are attending school. Data source: UNDP. *Human Development Report, 1991.* New York: Oxford University Press, 1991.

levels. For example, the enrollment ratios for secondary education are below 10% in 11 countries. In some cases, such as Tanzania, this reflects a policy decision to concentrate scarce resources in primary schools. In other cases, such as Mali and Somalia, educational development at all stages lags well behind the continental norm.

These national data do not tell the whole story, however. They do not identify the extent of disparities in access to schooling *within* particular countries in relation to gender, class, or region. Nowhere has this disparity been more evident than in South Africa where the education system not only reflected but worked to reproduce the apartheid ideology of separate and unequal development of officially designated racial groups (Vignette 17.1). National data do not address the important subject of the quality and relevance of the education being provided. Moreover, they do not show that in recent years school enrollments have been falling. These issues and some of their implications are discussed below.

Who Gets What Where?

Who?

Once Western education became established in an area, it was usually seen as the surest pathway to improving one's economic status. This was certainly the case for some, who gained access to positions of influence by virtue of an education. Often, the greatest opportunities for mobility of this sort came in the early years after independence, when there were many jobs available to Africans for the first time and few well educated people to fill them.

Education as a strategy for social mobility has now become much less attractive, especially for the poor. There are fewer public-sector jobs than in the past, and there are many more educated applicants for these positions. Many African countries have a considerable number of unemployed teachers, engineers, and other educated professionals, in large part because governments have been forced by means of IMF and World Bank lend-

ing conditions to cut back drastically on public-sector employment, regardless of need.

These adjustment programs have reduced available funds for education and have resulted in the imposition of much higher tuition fees that have excluded those unable to pay. Meanwhile, access to the best schools, admission to a university, and the probability of being appointed to a public-sector job are increasingly dependent on wealth and social contacts in circles that count. In short, education today is more an instrument for the perpetuation of class cleavages – a means for the ruling classes to consolidate their position – than an opportunity for social mobility.

Opportunities for education do not only vary in relation to social class. Gender is an important determinant of life chances in education; the data in Table 17.3 show that African women are at a consistent disadvantage compared to men in the same society. Female illiteracy rates are significantly higher than those for males in every country of Africa south of the Sahara. In 15 of the 34 countries for which 1990 UNESCO data are available, more than three-quarters of adult females are illiterate. While the proportion of female students in primary-, secondary-, and college-level courses has increased in the region and in most individual countries, large disparities remain. The gaps are greatest at the college level, where only one-quarter of students are women, and at the secondary level, where women compose one-third of students.

Restricted educational opportunities for women reflect patriarchal attitudes entrenched in both African and European (colonial) society. Because women have generally been thought destined to bear children and keep house, female education has been accorded low priority. Moreover, African families have tended to look upon modern education as an investment, wherein the graduate could secure a well-paying job and contribute to the support of the extended family. Because young women take their training and earning power with them when they marry, education for girls has often been seen as a poor investment. Most ordinary African families cannot afford the considerable cost of educating every child

Vignette 17.1. Education in South Africa: Separate and Unequal

Strict separation of school systems on the basis of race (as defined under apartheid) served for decades as a bulwark of the apartheid system. Ex-Prime Minister H. F. Verwoerd, speaking in 1954, emphasized that the role of "Bantu" education was to ensure that Africans would know their place and not aspire to any role beyond needed kinds of labor within the white community.

The government of F. W. de Klerk (1989 to 1994) distanced itself from the extremes of rhetoric that were formerly used to characterize the system. However, the reforms that it made did not fundamentally change the system.

The separate education systems were characterized by large disparities in levels of funding and in the provision of human and material resources. The gap in funding between white schools and others has been narrowing in recent years but still remains large. The unequal provision of resources, as Table 17.2 shows, is reflected in levels of matriculation and literacy that vary significantly, particularly between whites and blacks.

The phasing out of the clear and rigidly enforced separation of educational systems has taken place as a part of the broader process of dismantling apartheid. Universities are now free to admit any student who meets entry requirements, irrespective of race. About one-quarter of students in the major English-language "white" universities are nonwhite. Private primary and secondary schools may admit students without regard to race. However, there was widespread disagreement within de Klerk's government on how to proceed with the reform of the system as a whole, so as to remove visible racial barriers and improve nonwhite educational opportunities, while at the same time not disrupting the "nature and character" of existing schools. In short, de Klerk's language of reform was meant to reassure whites that their schools would remain, for all intents and purposes, white.

While the legal basis for the spatial segregation of races has been abolished, the racial composition of most neighborhoods is unlikely to change in the forseeable future. School fees will keep all but the wealthiest African families out of private schools. What seems most probable is a system in which segregation will be on the basis of class and wealth, rather than strictly race. The inequities in the system may diminish, but they are unlikely to disappear for a long time.

Table 17.2. Education Resources and Attainment, 1988 to 1989

Group	Per capita expenditure	Pupil–teacher ratio	Rate of matriculation (%)	Adult literacy (%)
African[a]	R[b] 666	38:1	57	45
Colored	R 1221	18:1	66	68
Indian	R 2067	19:1	95	80
White	R 2882	14:1	96	97

[a]African population living in white-designated areas only.
[b]R is Rand, the South African currency.
Source: South African Institute of Race Relations. *Race Relations Survey, 1989–90.* Johannesburg, South Africa: 1990.

Table 17.3. Women's Education in Selected African Countries

| | Females as % of total enrollment | | | | | | Female illiteracy | |
| | Primary | | Secondary | | College | | As % of adult females | As % of male illiteracy |
	1960	1989[a]	1960	1989[a]	1960	1989[a]		
Angola	33	48	40	33	NA	17	72	161
Burkina Faso	29	38	27	38	NA	23	91	126
Congo	34	48	28	44	7	17	56	187
Ethiopia	24	39	14	40	5	18	NA	NA
Kenya	32	49	32	41	16	28	42	205
Lesotho	62	55	53	60	22	72	NA	NA
Mali	28	37	17	29	NA	13	76	129
Nigeria	37	45	21	43	7	27	61	160
Rwanda	31	50	35	42	NA	19	63	174
Zaire	27	42	24	32	NA	9	39	240
Totals for Africa S. of Sahara	32	45	26	41	12	25	NA	NA

[a]In certain cases, the latest data are for years other than 1989.
Sources: See Table 17.1.

beyond the primary level. As Table 17.3 shows, women's opportunities have suffered in the process.

Gets What?

In Africa south of the Sahara, as elsewhere, education means much more than learning the three Rs. In addition to the formal curriculum, there is an "informal curriculum" of ideas and values that are conveyed even if they are not taught explicitly. One of the most important elements of the hidden curriculum is the message that indigenous African culture and knowledge is not important—that everything worth knowing comes from Europe

The powerful words of Franz Fanon, in his book *Black Skin White Masks* (New York: Grove Press, 1967), focus on why the language of instruction is a potent symbol of what education represents:

Every colonized people—in other words, every people in whose soul an inferiority complex has been created by the death and burial of its local cultural originality—finds itself face to face with the language of the civilizing nation; that is with the culture of the mother country. The colonized is elevated above his jungle status in proportion to his adoption of the mother country's cultural standards. He becomes whiter as he renounces his blackness. (p.18)

Three decades after the demise of colonialism, European languages remain preeminent, even in the first year of primary school. Indigenous languages are used in early primary classes in 13 of 15 countries formerly ruled by Great Britain but are used in only 4 of 15 former French colonies and in none of the former Portuguese territories. Somalia and Tanzania are the only countries where an indigenous language is used for at least part of the instruction at the postprimary level. While the great number of indigenous languages spoken and the lack of published materials in most local dialects are barriers to the use of many African languages in schools, the most important barrier has been a reluctance to fundamentally rethink priorities in education.

Julius Nyerere's essay on education and self-reliance (see Vignette 17.2) provides an insightful critique of the objectives and methods of conventional education, as well as a clear vision of an alternate approach that gives priority to local needs and pays homage to indigenous wisdom. Nevertheless, schooling still tends to be mostly a process of sorting academic abilities, that is, identifying those capable of proceeding to the next level, rather than teaching what is most relevant to local needs. For this reason, education has sometimes been called the "enemy of the farm," since so many graduates of rural school seem determined to

Vignette 17.2. Education for Self-Reliance

In 1967, Julius Nyerere who was then prime minister of Tanzania, set forth a new vision of education as a basis for development in his essay "Education for Self-Reliance," published in his book *Ujamaa: Essays on Socialism* (Oxford: 1968). The proposal was widely debated, both within Tanzania and beyond. Attempts were made to implement the proposals in Tanzania, but the longer-term effect has been much less than the revolutionary restructuring of education that Nyerere had in mind. Nevertheless, more than two decades after it was published, "Education for Self-Reliance" is still an important and thought-provoking essay.

Nyerere begins with a critique of the existing colonial system of education, saying that it was deficient in four ways:

1. The colonial model is elitist—designed to meet the needs of a very small proportion of those in the school system.
2. The school has developed separately from society, rather than as an integral part of it.
3. Students come to believe that all useful knowledge comes from books or from "educated" people.
4. Youth do not learn as they work; they simply learn. They are consumers of scarce resources and do not contribute as they should to national output.

The following exerpts from "Education for Self-Reliance" convey both Nyerere's basic philosophical orientation as well as a few of the practical measures that he proposed as part of a revised educational system that would be more responsive to the needs of a poor country committed to rapid but socially just development.

The education given in our schools must be a complete education in itself. It must not continue to be simply a preparation for secondary school. Instead of the primary school activities being geared to the competitive examination, which will select the few who go on to secondary school, they must be a preparation for the life which the majority of the children will lead. Similarly, secondary schools must not be simply a selection process for the university, teacher's colleges, and so on. They must prepare people for life and service in the villages and rural areas of this country. (pp. 61–62)

Schools must, in fact, become communities—and communities which practice the precept of self-reliance. This means that all schools, but especially secondary schools and other forms of higher education, must contribute to their own upkeep; they must be economic communities as well as social and educational communities. (p. 64)

The education provided by Tanzania for the students of Tanzania must serve the purposes of Tanzania. It must encourage the growth of the socialist values we aspire to. It must encourage the development of a proud, independent and free citizenry which relies upon itself for its own development, and which knows the advantages and problems of cooperation. It must ensure that the educated know themselves to be an integral part of the nation and recognize the responsibility to give greater service the greater the opportunities they have had. (p. 74)

Excerpts ©1968 by Mwalimu Julius K. Nyerere. Reprinted by permission.

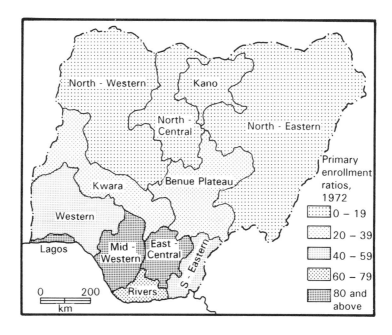

Figure 17.5. Disparities in primary-school enrollment in Nigeria, 1974. Vast north–south differences in education characterized Nigeria prior to the implementation of Universal Primary Education. Data source: Nigeria. *Annual Abstract of Statistics.* Lagos: Federal Office of Statistics, 1975.

Vignette 17.3. Redressing the Imbalance: Universal Primary Education in Kano State, Nigeria.

Hadejia Emirate is typical of many parts of northern Nigeria as well as of other parts of Africa where there was little investment in education. Treated as an unimportant backwater by the colonial government and passed over by missionaries because of the strength of Islam and government restrictions, Hadejia had only 9 primary schools and no post-primary institution at the time of independence. Four-fifths of the population of about 500,000 resided more than 5 km from the nearest school.

During the period 1960 to 1975, the number of primary schools increased 11-fold, from 9 to 99. However, only 11% of primary-school–aged children were in attendance and almost half of the population still lived more than 5 km from a school in 1975. Most schools were located in the larger villages, which meant that rural residents had very limited access to education.

Table 17.4. Access to Education in Hadejia Emirate

	1960	1976	1980
No. of schools	9	99	392
% of population within 5 km of school	20	55	95+
Total enrollment	2,200	15,100	66,000
% of school-aged children in school	2	11	48

cont.

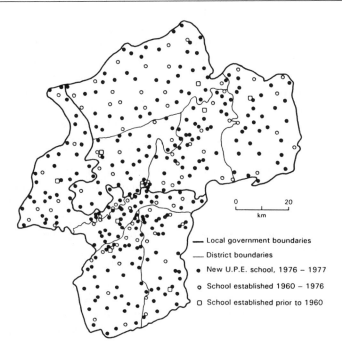

Vignette 17.3. (cont.)

Figure 17.6. UPE in Hadejia Emirate, northern Nigeria. UPE brought a fourfold increase in the number of schools in only 2 years.

When Nigeria's head of state announced in 1975 that primary education would become free and universal, Hadejia was confronted with massive logistical problems. During 1976 to 1977, 293 new primary schools were built, and other schools were expanded to accommodate the anticipated influx of students. School furniture, equipment,and books had to be obtained. Teachers had to be found to fill the new classrooms.

The Universal Primary Education program (UPE) succeeded in greatly increasing access to Western education. Virtually all people now lived within 5 km of a school, and schools were now to be found in many of the smaller villages, rather than in the more populous places. The initial enrollments were higher than expected, reflecting the new-found sense of "ownership" that many people had in their local schools. There was much less resistance to sending girls to school than had been anticipated. Between 1976 and 1980, total enrollment increased by 437%.

Unfortunately, initial successes have not been maintained. The discovery that UPE was more costly than had been expected coincided with economic crisis as oil prices collapsed. Many school buildings became damaged, often because of poor construction, and were left unrepaired. There were growing shortages, not only of books and other supplies but also of trained teachers. Moreover, the introduction of school fees further discouraged parents. The loss of momentum in the UPE program is revealed in the enrollment data for 1984, which shows that 38% of classes in Grade 1 and a quarter of those in Grades 2, 3, and 4 were untaught.

Source: R. Stock. "The rise and fall of UPE in Northern Nigeria." *Tijd. Econ. Soc. Geog.*, vol. 76 (1985), pp. 277–87.

pursue their dreams in the city, irrespective of how scarce jobs may be there.

Not only the content–implicit and explicit–of African education but also its quality have been called into question. Not surprisingly, the quality of education has been jeopardized by the economic crises affecting virtually every country. There is a crucial shortage of books and supplies; expenditure on educational materials at the primary level averages only 60 cents per pupil per year. Many school buildings are closed because there is no money for essential repairs. Because of very poor salaries, teachers have to juggle their teaching duties with other income-producing activities in order to make ends meet.

The effect of educational cutbacks has been very uneven. The wealthy purchase books for their children, patronize private schools, and hire personal tutors. They are also well placed to secure the limited education resources available to the state. The poor, particularly the rural poor, get whatever remains.

Where?

Significant spatial variations in access to education first emerged during colonial times and still persist. As a rule, urban areas have received proportionally more investment in education than rural areas have; this has been particularly true at the secondary and tertiary levels. For rural students, not having a nearby school may mean having to bear additional costs for room and board in town or being unable to attend.

Many African countries have large regional disparities in school attendance, literacy, and other measures of educational status. Nigeria provides an excellent illustration of how such regional inequities in educational development came into existence. In southern Nigeria, the missions were very active at an early date. In 1912, there were 32,000 students in voluntary agency primary schools in southern Nigeria compared to about 4,000 in government and Native Authority schools. By 1957, there were 2,343,000 students enrolled in 13,473 primary schools in southern Nigeria. Demand

for schooling was so great that the regional governments of Eastern Nigeria and Western Nigeria had attempted to implement universal primary education in 1955, a move which proved too costly. In northern Nigeria, a region containing more than half of Nigeria's population, there were fewer than 1,000 students in primary schools in 1912 and only 185,000 in 1957. Missionaries had been virtually excluded by the colonial authorities from the Islamic northern part of the region; it was argued that local rulers would object to a Christian presence. What schools were established in the Muslim areas were run by the government. Missionaries in northern Nigeria were concentrated in the non-Muslim areas, mostly in the southern part of the region.

The extent of the consequent inequities is revealed in enrollment data from 1972 when Nigeria launched its Universal Primary Education program. Three states in northern Nigeria had less than 10% of primary school-aged children in school, while three southern states had well over 80% enrolled (Figure 17.5). The northern states have moved decisively to close this educational gap (see Vignette 17.3), but it will take generations to do so. In the meantime, these disparities have contributed substantially to the ongoing social, political, and economic tensions within Nigeria.

The rapid expansion of education in Africa south of the Sahara has been one of its greatest achievements of the past three decades. Enrollments in primary schools grew more than fivefold between 1960 and 1989, and secondary and college education expanded even more rapidly. African governments, supported by aid agencies, have viewed expenditure on education as the best possible investment for the future. Unfortunately, the expansion of education has often failed to bring expected benefits.

Government cutbacks in education expenditure have occurred because of recent economic difficulties, and access to education has suffered as a result. The challenge for African governments is to educate a school-aged population growing at approximately 3% annually using fewer resources. To do so successfully will require a rethinking of educational objectives and methods. Progress in education involves much more than constructing new schools; African states need to look closely at "Who gets what where?" as a starting point for assessing how education can be made more relevant and effective.

Further Reading

For statistics on African education, see *Statistical Yearbook* and *World Education Report* published annually by UNESCO.

The following source contains a fascinating study of indigenous education:

Katz, C. "Sow what you know: The struggle for social reproduction in rural Sudan." *Annals of Association of American Geographers*, vol. 81 (1991), pp. 488–514.

Colonial educational policies are discussed in the following sources:

Clignet, R. "Education and elite formation." In J. Paden and E. Soja, eds., *The African Experience*, vol. 1, pp. 304–330. Evanston, IL: Northwestern University Press, 1970.

Mugomba, A. T., and M. Nyaggah. *Independence without Freedom: The Political Economy of Education in Southern Africa*. Santa Barbara, CA: ABC-Clio, 1980.

Tibenderana, P. Z. "The emirs and the spread of Western education in northern Nigeria, 1910–1946." *Journal of African History*, vol. 24 (1983), pp. 517–534.

The following case studies examine the problems and achievements of the Universal Primary Education program in Nigeria:

Bray, M. *Universal Primary Education in Nigeria*. London: Routledge Kegan Paul, 1981.

Stock, R. "The rise and fall of Universal Primary Education in peripheral Northern Nigeria." *Tijd. voor Econ. en Soc. Geografie*, vol. 76 (1985), pp. 277–287.

Various aspects of the relation between education and development are discussed in the following sources:

Freire, P. *Pedagogy of the Oppressed*. New York: Seabury, 1970.

Nyerere, J. "Education for self-reliance." In J. Nyerere, *Ujamaa: Essays on Socialism*, pp. 267–290. London: Oxford University Press, 1968.

Simmons, J. "Education for development, reconsidered." *World Development*, vol 7 (1979), pp. 1005–1016.

Thompson, A. R. *Education and Development in Africa*. London: Macmillan, 1980.

World Bank. *Education in Sub-Saharan Africa: Policies for Adjustment, Revitalization and Expansion*. Washington, DC: World Bank, 1988.

For a case study applying geographical methods to educational planning, see the following source:

Gould, W. T. S. *Planning the Location of Schools: Ankole District, Uganda*. Paris: UNESCO, 1973.

On the dismantling of apartheid education in South Africa, see the following sources:

Morris, A., and J. Hyslop. "Education in South Africa: The present crisis and the problems of reconstruction." *Social Justice*, vol. 18 (1991), pp. 259–270.

South Africa Institute of Race Relations (SAIRR), *Race Relations Survey*. Johannesburg, South Africa: SAIRR, published annually.

18

✳

Social Policy: The Health Sector

In Africa, as in all other parts of the world, there is gross inequality of risk and of opportunity. This chapter looks at the provision of health care, particularly the kinds of health-policy responses that have come from governments. The choice of strategy–or rather, in many countries, the lack of a coherent policy–has serious implications for public health, especially the health of comparatively vulnerable groups such as women, children, and the poor.

The chapter examines policies concerned with the delivery of health care, whether curative or preventative, and how such policies affect people's health. It starts by identifying several long-standing controversies about how African health care systems should be developed. Debates about these issues continued throughout the colonial era, during the first two decades of independence when health systems were being expanded and more recently when cost control has become a top priority. To be effective, health policies have to look beyond the provision of services to address a full range of factors–environmental, economic, social, and political–that profoundly influence levels of risk. The importance of a broader definition of health policy is addressed in the latter part of the chapter.

Health Policy Issues

There has been a sense of continuity in policy debates about health, dating back to the early colonial period. The specific issues of greatest concern to the state and the public have varied at different times, as have the approaches favored by medical and social scientists and policy makers. Nevertheless, the key debates for the most part have been about the same issues. Five of these controversies are outlined below.

Health and Other Priorities

While few indeed have ever disputed the importance of having a healthy population, the question of the appropriate commitment of resources by the state to health promotion has long been a matter of controversy. Health may be important, but so too are the construction of roads, education, and many other things. Those who argue that health be given priority point out that health-status improvements bring other benefits, such as greater productivity and lower levels of fertility. However, investment in education, for example, is also an investment in future development. In making their budget allocations, governments signal where their priorities lie. The unevenness of governments' commitment to health is reflected in significant variations in health expenditure, especially in comparison to other sectors, such as military spending. The role of the state has remained especially important in Africa because of the uneven and usually weak development of the private sector as a source of health-related initiatives.

General versus Targeted Programs

The allocation of health expenditures and how to achieve desired benefits at an acceptable cost have long been subjects of controversy. According to one school of thought, maximum benefits may be obtained with disease-specific programs to control or even eliminate certain diseases with carefully structured mass campaigns. The successful eradication of smallpox 25 years ago was the best known and most successful of these campaigns. Critics of the targeted-disease strategy argue that far broader and longer-lasting benefits can be obtained from general programs that address the full range of health problems. Closely related to this debate about whether programs should be general or more narrowly focused is the question of whether health care resources should be distributed as uniformly as possible, or if selected areas, usually cities, should be given priority. Unlike in colonial times when the state provided health care for a few select groups and areas, all governments now pay lip service to universal access to health care as a goal. However, the actual distribution of resources often tells a different story.

Preventative versus Curative Medicine

The gap between theory and practice is frequently evident in the commitment to preventative health interventions, such as the provision of safe water, mass vaccination of children, and health education. Often, governments that talk about the importance of prevention allocate the great majority of resources to health care facilities that focus on curative medicine. On the other hand, because the demand for curative services seems limitless, it is always difficult to find ways of freeing more resources for prevention without appearing to jeopardize curative care.

The Necessity of Modern Technologies and Advanced Training

Controversy also surrounds the subjects of modern technology and advanced medical training. African countries, at least in theory, have access to a full array of modern medical technology, ranging from CT-scanners to the latest pharmaceuticals. It is often argued, especially by the medical establishment, that these technologies are needed if teaching and specialist hospitals are to function effectively. The counterargument is that expensive advanced modern technologies not only fail to address the major health problems of African nations but also drain scarce resources from other, more pressing needs. The debate about technology extends to the training of health care personnel. Should physicians and other medical professionals continue to be trained to Western standards in conventional medical schools, or should resources be reallocated into programs to train large numbers of paraprofessional health workers?

The Role of Traditional Healers

Another debate revolves around the role of traditional healers. Few would dispute that African healers play a very active role in the treatment of illness. Rather, there has been disagreement about whether such treatments have therapeutic value or are a threat to the patients' health; whether the practice of traditional medicine should be severely restricted, tolerated, or encouraged, and whether institutions should be fostered to enable traditional and modern practitioners to work together.

Health Care: The Colonial Legacy

The primary objective of colonial health policy was quite clear: It was designed to protect the

Figure 18.1. Traditional healer and patient, Botswana. Ethnomedicine accounts for a substantial majority of the health care obtained by Africans. Photo: R. Dixey.

health of Europeans in the "white man's grave." Hospitals were constructed in the major cities to care exclusively for white patients. Public health measures, ranging from the strict segregation of African and European residential areas (see Vignette 13.2) to drainage and vegetation clearance as a means of reducing insect populations, were designed to protect Europeans from the threat supposedly posed by "unhealthy" Africans.

Basic health care was often made available to Africans employed by colonial governments or European companies. These services were concentrated in such areas of economic growth as mining enclaves or export cropping zones where health care expenditure could increase worker' productivity. In poorer rural areas, colonial regimes gave scant regard to health care.

In much of the continent, the only health care was provided by Christian missionaries who linked proselytizing to medical care. Missionary medicine was very unevenly distributed; few missionaries went to Muslim areas, for example. In areas of indirect rule, such as northern Nigeria, a few simple dispensaries were constructed by African local governments and financed by tax levies. At the end of the colonial era, most of rural Africa had effectively no access to Western health care. Moreover, the few existing facilities were very rudimentary, in most cases small clinics staffed by a dispenser trained to give basic first aid and vaccinations.

Since time immemorial African societies have had their own healers charged with responsibility for the health of the community. Far from being nurtured by colonial governments, indigenous medicine was seen as either irrelevant or primitive and dangerous. In many colonies, certain kinds of healing rituals were banned because such ceremonies were thought to be potential foci of anticolonial resistance.

Colonial governments launched campaigns against specific diseases, in particular yellow fever, sleeping sickness, leprosy, malaria, and yaws. While a few of these campaigns achieved some success, most were paralyzed by their uneven implementation, the crudeness of available technologies, and Africans' widespread skepticism about colonial public health interventions. It was often assumed that the government had ulterior motives in mind —increased taxation, for example—when it implemented public health measures. Moreover, some of the problems that these campaigns were designed to alleviate were themselves the product of ill-conceived colonial development policies. For example, the rising incidence of sleeping sickness resulted in no small part from the establishment of resettlement schemes in high-risk environments, the creation of forest reserves that became potential disease "hot spots," and the increased mobility of infected people and disease vectors along newly built transportation routes.

The health care systems that the colonialists bequeathed to newly independent governments were fragmented in structure, very biased in favor of urban areas, oriented to curative instead of preventative medicine, and organized to serve colonial interests. The colonial neglect of health care for Africans was exemplified by the case of the Congo (Zaire), which at the time of its independence in 1960 did not have a single indigenous graduate in medicine in the country.

The 1960s and 1970s: Growth (and Development?)

Following independence, African governments moved to upgrade health services but had to contend with the scarcity of resources to build new facilities, train health workers, and initiate new policies. Compared to the increasingly difficult years that followed, the 1960s and 1970s were times when African governments were able to strive for growth and development in the health sector. The approach adopted by most countries reflected the still predominant faith in modernization theory and the lack of critical evaluation of conventional models of health care delivery. Highest priority was given to the establishment of medical schools to train doctors and other medical professionals. Foreign aid donors gave financial support for the construction of modern "disease palace" teaching hospitals that reproduced the technological medicine of industrial countries and paid scant attention to ordinary but absolutely crucial health problems, such as intestinal parasites, malaria, and malnutrition. These hospitals proved to be so

Figure 18.2. Village dispensary, Jigawa State, Nigeria. For most rural Africans, access to modern health care means a walk of several kilometers to a small clinic staffed by two or three primary health care workers. Photo: author.

expensive to staff and operate that little was left for the health needs of the population. For example, half of Liberia's entire health budget goes to one such facility, J. F. Kennedy Hospital in Monrovia. Such inequities in the distribution of resources conform to the prediction of the "inverse care law" (Figure 18.3), which states that there tends to be an inverse relation between the availability of medical care and the needs of those served.

Most African countries attempted to enhance health services in the previously neglected rural areas. Kenya developed a "Basic Health Services" (BHS) model to improve rural health services by developing a network of spatially accessible health centers and clinics catering to the needs of local and regional populations. The BHS approach envisaged the creation of a hierarchy of services centered on a rural health center where primary (basic, first-stage) health care would be provided, to more seriously ill patients referred from nearby clinics. However, BHS brought no substantive changes in the old biases favoring urban centers. The 1973 to 1974 expenditure per capita on curative medicine was 77.4 pounds in Nairobi, but only 3.6 to 14.1 pounds in the other provinces.

The Kenyan BHS model was emulated in several other countries. In practice, it was far too expensive to be widely implemented, even in relatively wealthy Nigeria. Nigeria's ambitious BHS plan proposed to cover the country with local networks of 20 clinics, four primary health centers, and one comprehensive health center for every 150,000 people.

However, the actual cost of 8 million naira per unit was 16 times the budgeted estimate. In Kano State, only one-tenth of the planned facilities were constructed. Seven years after Nigeria launched its BHS plan, there were only 30 doctors to serve 8.7 million people in the rural districts of Kano State (Figure 18.4).

In 1978, the Alma-Ata Conference of the World Health Organization (WHO) ended with a declaration that "health for all" should be a reality by the year 2000. Primary health care (PHC) was identified as the approach most likely to make this goal attainable. Many of the ideas associated with the PHC model came from the experiences of China. A notable example was their program of training "barefoot doctors"—ordinary citizens who receive basic medical training and are given responsibility for community public health and the treatment of common illnesses. Priority is given to the development of local solutions using local resources. The PHC strategy emphasizes preventative health care and health education, and it stresses the importance of addressing diverse factors affecting well-being—clean water, universal education, and agricultural development, among others.

The PHC approach has the potential to quite radically change the state of health and health care. When local health workers are selected by the community and supported, materially and morally, by it, the health worker becomes accountable to the community. However, while lip service is often paid to this ideal, governments and aid agencies seldom

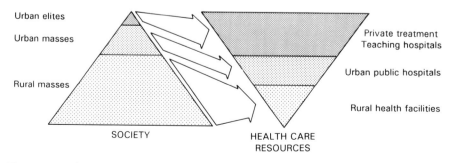

Figure 18.3. The "inverse care law" of health care provision. Resources tend to be distributed in inverse proportion to need.

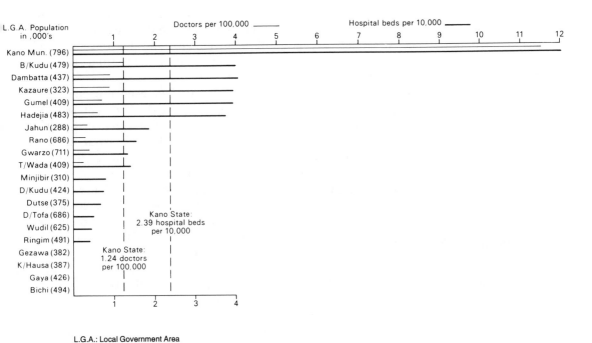

Figure 18.4. Urban–rural disparities in access to physicians and hospital beds, Kano State, Nigeria, 1980. Urban–rural disparities, albeit often less dramatic than in the case of Kano State, are characteristic of African health care systems. Data source: Kano State Ministry of Health, unpublished data.

have any real commitment to empowerment at the grassroots; among other things, it is widely feared that empowerment is an invitation to dissent. In countries such as Kenya and Côte d'Ivoire with a strongly entrenched capitalist ruling class, PHC has had a disappointing effect. The urban elites continue to obtain good-quality care from private physicians, teaching hospitals, and even from overseas clinics, while many rural areas still have no modern health care at all.

The health care systems of Guinea-Bissau and Mozambique were developed differently. During the prolonged struggle against the Portuguese, the liberation movements organized social services in the areas they controlled. The PAIGC (African Party for the Independence of Guinea and Cape Verde), for example, operated a PHC system with nine hospitals and over 500 health workers. The PHC model continued to be applied after victory, with emphasis given to preventative programs such as immunization and sanitation and to the training of village health workers. During the early 1980s the commitment of Guinea-Bissau and Mozambique to health as a basic right and first-order priority was reflected in their ranking as the two African countries allocating the highest proportion of government expenditure to health. Unfortunately, these countries have more recently had to reduce expenditure on health to address other pressing economic and political concerns such as the loss of aid from the Soviet Union and its allies and, in the case of Mozambique, the devastating effects of the Renamo guerrilla campaign.

Post-1980: The Challenge of Doing More with Less

As the 1980s progressed, African governments faced growing economic pressures resulting from rising debt loads and declining terms of trade that forced them to reexamine their development priorities and strategies. Meanwhile, the ongoing growth and redistribution of population and the emergence of new sources of demand, most notably from the spread of AIDS, has brought increased pressure on health care systems. In short, governments are having to find ways of doing more with fewer resources. The discussion that follows looks at some of the approaches that have been used to address these challenges.

New Strategies for Organizing and Financing Health Care

The deteriorating economic situation has left governments with very little money for the maintenance of existing health infrastructures, or for the purchase of drugs and other supplies. Cutbacks in public-sector spending, often done at the behest of the IMF, has resulted in large staff layoffs and significant salary reductions. The result has often been hospitals that have become, in the words of Nigeria's President Babangida, "mere consulting clinics" without drugs and sometimes without medical staff. Many facilities were closed because of staff shortages or the lack of funds for needed repairs. Cutbacks that forced health workers to take second jobs to make ends meet resulted in increased absenteeism and poorer care. Many doctors left the public service, and some took advantage of their international-standard training to emigrate. There are reputedly more Malian physicians practicing in Paris than in Mali itself.

Primary health care, like the BHS approach that preceded it, was criticized as being too expensive for the majority of African countries. An alternate approach, selective primary health care (SPHC), was promoted by the major international agencies as being more cost-effective. The SPHC approach involves the priorization of programs to address a small number of targeted diseases that are the most important causes of mortality in each country. There is heavy reliance on low-cost interventions such as child immunization, oral rehydration therapy (the use of a simple so-lution of salt and water to counteract dehydration in infants with diarrhea), the promotion of breast-feeding, and the provision of clean water to reduce mortality from the targeted diseases.

The selective approach has been very popular among the major development agencies because it focuses attention on manageable parts of the larger health issue, is target oriented (i.e., programs can be evaluated in relation to a numerical goal such as an $x\%$ increase in immunization), and puts its faith in a set of technological "magic bullets." However, SPHC has been widely criticized, among other things, for its failure to address the root causes of of ill health in Africa and for its top–down, technological approach that does not empower communities to tackle their own health problems.

Selective is the operative word in evaluating SPHC, which has involved the selective application of selected technologies to selected health problems and has brought about *selective* progress–reductions in infant mortality, for example. However, its piecemeal approach provides no basis whatsoever for a long-term, comprehensive strategy to improve the health of Africans. As well, where inadequate provision has been made for maintaining SPHC gains, the benefits have been quite temporary. For example, Tanzania's program of developing rural water supplies has been jeopardized by the lack of funds for maintenance, with the result that an estimated half of all wells are now inoperative.

Another approach to maintaining services has been to focus on strategies for governments to recover some or all of the cost of providing health care. Consultation fees have been introduced in virtually all countries where treatment was formerly free. Patients are expected to purchase their own drugs and supplies, and the families of in-patients are often expected to provide meals and routine care. While lip service is paid to alleviating the effects of user fees on the poor, the reality is that fees are, for many, a formidable obstacle to obtaining care (see Vignette 18.1). Cost recovery has also been pursued by establishing community revolving drug schemes, in

---

Vignette 18.1. Health Care User Fees: What Benefits? What Costs?

The effect of prolonged economic crisis and rising debt in Africa south of the Sahara has been an acute shortage of money for health care programs. Governments have often been unable to maintain existing services, much less to initiate new programs. For many Africans, health care means going to a hospital where there are no drugs and quite possibly no doctor. Moreover, the true extent of such cutbacks, hidden by inflation and currency devaluation, is often greater than it seems.

The World Bank and other development agencies have promoted user fees ("cost recovery") as a strategy for generating revenues for the health sector. Users of the health care system are charged a small fee that can be used to purchase drugs and finance new health services. It is argued that patients will readily accept such fees, especially if the quality of care is improved as a result. Fees are also justified as a means of discouraging unnecessary visits, thus bringing more efficiency.

The World Bank acknowledges that fees may have a negative effect on the ability of the poor to obtain care. It proposes that very poor families or poor communities be exempted from the fees and suggest that fees not be charged for certain services.

The imposition of user fees has major implications for the affordability of health care—and consequently, on utilization. When Swaziland imposed modest user fees, attendance at government health facilities declined by 32% and the use of mission-run clinics fell by 10%. Visits for childhood vaccination and for the treatment of sexually transmitted diseases fell by 17% and 21%, respectively. Studies in Mali, Côte d'Ivoire, and elsewhere have also shown that user fees cause people to delay treatment or to do without it and that higher disease and death rates occur as a result.

The health benefits from user fees have been very small indeed. The monies collected generally contribute no more than 5 to 15% of national health budgets, an amount that can hardly justify either (1) the allocation of scarce resources to collect the fees, or (2) the health, social, and economic costs of excluding so many of the poor from access to basic services.

The solution to the funding crisis in health lies, not in collecting small user fees from patients, but in focusing on the root causes of crisis, particularly the effect of debt repayment on the ability of African governments to deliver even rudimentary health services. Debt forgiveness is not the entire answer, but it is an obvious starting point.

---

which drugs are provided for sale at near cost and funds received are used to purchase replacement supplies.

Mozambique was one of the first countries to initiate a basic-drugs purchasing program as a means of reducing the high cost of imported pharmaceuticals. Companies are invited to submit tendered bids for supplying large quantities of generic (not brand-name) drugs that are deemed most crucial to treating the country's major diseases. Basic drugs schemes have saved money and facilitated more cost-effective treatment.

The "Discovery" of Ethnomedicine

Ethnomedical practitioners exist in every African society and continue to provide the bulk of health care for most Africans. Several distinct healing traditions, including herbalism, midwifery, bone setting, and spiritual healing, are practiced in each African culture. In stable rural communities, where medical knowledge is passed from one generation of healers to the next, the reputations of healing families are established through their accomplishments over many decades. Traditional healers are popular, not only because they are so much more numerous and accessible than modern health care facilities, but also because people trust and value the cures that these healers provide. Healers and patients come from the same cultural milieu and share the same basic ideas about appropriate cures and the nature and causes of ill health.

Until recently, African ethnomedicine was dismissed, particularly in the scientific community, as mere superstition. Scientific research has now begun to prove the efficacy of many herbal medicines and to better understand the importance of the healer–patient relationship for social–psychological healing. The WHO and several African governments, responding to the problem of shortages in the formal health care system as well as to the new scientific interest in ethnomedicine, have shown increasing interest in programs that involve healers in national health care systems. There are various potential avenues for involving healers, ranging from programs to upgrade the skills of village midwives to initiatives in which spiritual healers assist graduate psychiatrists in the treatment of mentally ill patients. Such programs are still relatively rare and small-scale, but they have opened the door for further integration in the future. They represent an important attempt to look beyond Western technology to indigenous knowledge and resources in the search for more cost-effective and culturally relevant solutions to Africa's development needs.

New Pressures on the Health System: The Challenge of AIDS

The rapid growth of HIV infectivity rates and mortality from AIDS was discussed in Chapter 8. As of 1992, an estimated 7.5 million Africans were HIV positive, over 60% of the estimated 12 million infected worldwide. Four-fifths of the world population of HIV-infected women is African. Rates of infection vary greatly from country to country, and between high risk populations in both rural and urban areas. In Uganda, one of the most seriously affected countries, surveys showed that three-quarters of high risk urban women (e.g.,

prostitutes) and one-quarter of urban women considered to be at low risk were HIV positive in 1992.

Governments have responded to AIDS quite differently. While Kenya has sought to minimize publicity about its large AIDS epidemic to protect its lucrative tourist industry, Uganda has been quite open in acknowledging its AIDS problem and welcoming external assistance in research and program development. This openness has not been without a cost, however, since Uganda has been subjected to prolonged international scrutiny as a "global AIDS capital" and as a laboratory for new interventions. Such publicity has often seemed to imply incorrectly that the fight against AIDS is in the hands of outsiders, with Africans as mere passive recipients. In reality, African health care workers, non-governmental organizations, and communities have remained in the forefront in the struggle against AIDS.

AIDS presents several major challenges to the orderly development of the health care system. Because of its rapid growth, very scarce resources in the health care system may be diverted from other needs to the fight against AIDS. In countries such as Uganda, AIDS patients are occupying a growing proportion of hospital beds and consuming more and more of the time and energy of health workers. Because of the high profile of AIDS, development aid in the health sector is often channeled into AIDS programs. Experienced researchers and specialists focus on AIDS to the detriment of other health needs. Finally, AIDS threatens to rob Africa of scarce medical expertise because doctors and other health workers are susceptible to infection themselves, not least because of the nature of their work.

This is not to imply that AIDS is not an extremely important health problem or that the needs of HIV-positive people and AIDS patients should be ignored. Rather, it reflects the danger that the high profile of AIDS will result in the even greater neglect of less publicized health problems such as malaria, tuberculosis, and measles that still cause far more deaths than AIDS.

There is also a danger that AIDS will continue to be viewed too narrowly by health professionals and planners as a *biomedical* rather than a *social* disease that poses a greater threat to family, community, and national well-being than as a direct cause of death (Vignette 18.2). Viewing AIDS from a holistic perspective is essential to the development of appropriate health care policies for the future.

Toward an Integrated Approach to Planning for Health

The WHO has defined health as "a state of complete physical, mental and social well-being and not merely the absence of disease or infirmity." This is a very utopian definition, not just for Africa; but it helps to direct our attention beyond curative medicine to a much wider view of health and health promotion. Ideas about how to improve health conditions in Africa and other parts of the Third World have changed radically, especially since the late 1970s. The following exerpt from a speech by Margaret Catley-Carlson, president of the Canadian International Development Agency to the Canadian Public Health Association (1984) clearly identifies the nature of the task at hand:

To understand world health, we have to turn our normal ideas upside-down. When we help developing countries, with pathetic health budgets, to follow expensive Western medical models, we can—without wanting to, or meaning to—deprive babies and children and mothers and peasants. When we bring their brightest medical students here, to learn the most specialized skills and use the most advanced facilities, the ultimate effect can be to take better health care away from their future, and profiteer on their sick. The big opportunities for health progress in our world lie not in exotic procedures and high-tech breakthroughs, but in very simple, basic measures—clean water and sanitation, improved diet, immunization, campaigns against vector-borne mass diseases such as malaria and half a dozen others. The Third World can save more lives with the 200 drugs on WHO's basic list than it can with the wild assortment of 25,000 now being pushed there. There will

never be enough resources to provide the current Western model for all the world's people—a medical approach focused intensely on the individual patient. We need to absorb the profound paradox that, to save more individuals, we must put priority on the social, environmental and preventative aspects of human health.

Despite the ringing call of the WHO for "health for all the world's people by the year 2000," the reality has been very different: health for some and good health for the privileged few. Scarcity of resources is a real problem, but one that may be overcome with adequate commitment to social justice and sustained external support at a modest level. Unfortunately, the intregal connections between health and productivity usually receive too little attention. People who are ill cannot work effectively. Women who spend their days fetching unsafe water from distant sources have less time for farming and other activities. Expenditure on health, therefore, should be seen as a cost-effective investment, not as a burden. In fact, it should be unnecessary to resort to economic arguments; effective access to basic health care is a fundamental human right that every state has a duty to make possible.

There continue to be large disparities between countries in the provision of health services. The population with access to health services (Figure 18.5) varies from under 30% in Mali, Somalia, and Zaire to over 75% in 10 countries, including Tanzania, Lesotho, and Gabon. While these data must be interpreted cautiously because the definition of *accessibility* may vary from country to country, the same cannot be said for the percentage of children that are immunized. As Figure 18.6 shows, the gap between the highest and lowest rates of vaccination coverage is as high as that for access to health care.

The priority given to safe water provision says much about the commitment of governments to the health of their people. The absence of safe water means that people are exposed to the risk of a host of infectious and parasitic diseases. When water is not readily available, sanitation inevitably declines. Yet, the construction of a borehole to provide ac-

---

Vignette 18.2. AIDS and the Social Side of Health

AIDS has usually been viewed as a medical and public-health problem. However, AIDS also has important social dimensions. This social side of AIDS refers to the "ripple effect" that it may have on the health of individuals, families, and communities living in the shadow of the disease. These effects tend to remain unrecognized until they manifest themselves as costly health problems.

Caring for an AIDS patient can deal a crippling financial blow to an African family. Medicine, when it is available, is prohibitively expensive in most countries. Even the cost of repeatedly washing and replacing soiled clothing and bedding may represent a major cost when family budgets are stretched to the limit. Moreover, income may be adversely affected, particularly if the victim is a wage earner or if a household member has to give up a job to stay home and provide care. One study in Kinshasa showed that a child's hospitalization costs on average three times the average monthly income, while funeral expenses for a child consumed the equivalent of 11-months' earnings.

When AIDS causes family expenses to increase dramatically or income to be reduced, the health of other family members is adversely affected. Because less money is available for food, nutritional status declines and opportunistic infections like tuberculosis and pneumonia become more prevalent.

The most dramatic health effects occur among children who have been orphaned as a result of AIDS. Rakai District in southern Uganda had an estimated 24,000 AIDS orphans as of 1989. When extended families and whole communities have been ravaged, traditional mechanisms for the care of orphans–elder siblings or aunts and uncles assuming a parental role–may break down. Elderly grandparents, who are no longer able to do strenuous work, may be the only available guardians.

It is important that health policy and program measures begin to recognize the broader effects of AIDS on health. AIDS is not simply a biomedical problem, amenable to scientific solutions. Rather, a balanced social and medical effort is needed in which interventions are designed to assist whole communities in coping with the diverse effects of the disease rather than focus only on AIDS patients and their immediate families.

Based on E. M. Ankrah. "AIDS and the social side of health." *Social Science and Medicine*, vol. 32 (1991), pp. 967–980.

---

cessible and unpolluted water for a community costs only a few thousand dollars.

Table 18.1 suggests that national wealth is a very poor predictor of investment in safe water projects. Despite their poverty, Tanzania, Gambia, and Burkina Faso have done as much or more to provide good water for their citizens than have Kenya, Cameroon, and Botswana, which are among Africa's more prosperous nations. The poorer nations have done particularly well in providing water for their rural citizens.

Medical professionals, interacting with elite interests, have often been a barrier to real progress toward health for all. They have argued for the preservation of expensive, curative medicine based in hospitals and against a redistribution of resources into programs that are designed to give the most benefit to the most people. The few governments–Mozambique and Zimbabwe, for example–that have attempted to redistribute resources out of hospitals and into the community have been resolutely opposed by medical interests. In most countries, the approach has been to add new preventative programs without challeng-

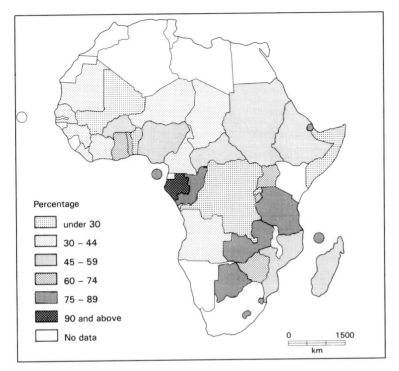

Figure 18.5. Population with access to health care services. "Access" to health care is an important determinant of quality of life but is very hard to quantify meaningfully. The actual percentages on the map need to be treated cautiously. However, they show clearly that access to health care is uneven and often very inadequate. Data source: UNDP. *Human Development Report, 1991.* New York: Oxford University Press, 1991.

ing the hegemony of doctors. The results have been predictable: underfunded and ineffective token programs and policies that do not address the root causes of ill-health.

Selective primary health care has become popular because interventions can be arranged on a massive, resource-efficient scale. However, SPHC is a top–down strategy that confers no power on communities over their own health, except for the dubious "opportunity" to pay for their own health care through user fees. In the final analysis, any initiatives

Table 18.1. Access to Clean Water in Selected African Nations

Country	GNP per capita 1989 (U.S. $)	% of population with access to safe water	
		Urban	Rural
Tanzania	130	75	46
Gambia	240	92	73
Burkina Faso	320	44	72
Kenya	360	61	21
Central African Republic	380	13	11
Cameroon	1,000	43	24
Botswana	1,600	70	46

Source: UNDP. *Human Development Report, 1992.*

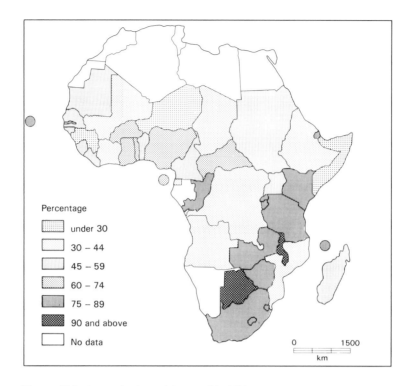

Figure 18.6. Immunization of 1-year-old children, 1988–1989. Data source: UNDP. *Human Development Report, 1991*. New York: Oxford University Press, 1991.

Figure 18.7. Village well, Mozambique. An accessible, safe, and dependable supply of water, one of the cheapest and most effective defenses against a host of diseases, is still only a dream for the majority of rural Africans. Photo: CIDA: B. Paton.

Figure 18.8. Health promotion posters, Nigeria. These posters in the Hausa language promote breast-feeding and vaccination. Photos: author.

that are not structured around the reality of peoples' daily lives cannot be a solid base for real development.

Life expectancy and the quality of life are only partly a matter of chance. They are not primarily a reflection of the hostility of the natural environment, as many once believed. Life expectancy and the quality of life are significantly affected by the choices made by governments—their priorities for development in general and for health policy in particular. The question, "Who gets what where—and why?" goes to the heart of how to assess states' policies toward and on behalf of their people.

Health involves much more than the provision of curative medical care. Good health policy cannot be formulated apart from policies to improve nutrition, sanitation, housing, education, and general well-being. Good health policy is politically grounded in a firm commitment to socially just development and the empowerment of communities to work for the improvement of their own situation. Such a commitment is an essential ingredient, but good intentions are hard to put into practice when sufficient resources are unavailable.

Thus, the future development of health depends as much on the general improvement of Africa's economic health as on specific policies in the health sector.

Further Reading

On the relation between underdevelopment and health, see the following sources:

Stock, R. "Health care for some: A Nigerian study of who gets what where and why." *International Journal of Health Services,* vol. 15 (1985), pp. 469–484.

Turshen, M. *The Political Economy of Health in Tanzania.* New Brunswick, NJ: Rutgers University Press, 1985.

World Bank. *World Development Report, 1993.* Washington, DC: World Bank, 1993.

Approaches to the provision of health care in the Third World are discussed in the following sources:

Gesler, W. *Health Care Delivery in Developing Countries.* Washington, DC: Association of American Geographers, 1985.

Stock, R., and C. Anyinam. "National governments and health policy in Africa." In T. Falola and D. Ityavyar, eds., *The Political Economy of*

Health in Africa. Athens, OH: Ohio University Center for International Studies, 1992.

There is a large literature on primary health care in theory and in practice. See, for example the following sources:

Bloom, G. "Two models for change in the health services in Zimbabwe." *International Journal of Health Services*, vol. 15 (1985), pp. 451–468.

Freund, P. "Health care in a declining economy: The case of Zambia." *Social Science and Medicine*, vol. 23 (1986), pp. 875–888.

Gish, O. "The political economy of primary health care and 'health by the people': An historical exploration." *Social Science and Medicine*, vol. 13C (1979), pp. 203–211.

Green, R. H. "Politics, power and poverty: Health for all in 2000 in the Third World?" *Social Science and Medicine*, vol. 32 (1991), pp. 745–755.

Jelley, D., and R. J. Madeley. "Primary health care in practise: A case study of Mozambique." *Social Science and Medicine*, vol. 19 (1984), pp. 773–780.

The effect of user fees and more generally, of structural adjustment on access to health care, are discussed in the following sources:

Anyinam, C. "The social cost of the IMF's adjustment programs for poverty: The case of health care in Ghana." *International Journal of Health Services*, vol. 19 (1989), pp. 531–547.

UNICEF. *The State of the World's Children*. Oxford: Oxford University Press, published annually.

Yoder, R. A. "Are people willing and able to pay for health services?" *Social Science and Medicine*, vol. 29 (1989), pp. 35–42.

There are numerous studies of African traditional medicine. The following sources are particularly recommended:

Good, C. M. *Ethnomedical Systems in Africa*. New York: Guilford, 1987.

Anyinam, C. "Availability, accessibility, acceptability and adaptability: Four attributes of African ethnomedicine." *Social Science and Medicine*, vol. 25 (1987), pp. 803–812.

RESOURCES

African economies remain firmly based on primary production. Most African workers are engaged in farming, mining, forestry, and fishing. The primary sector is the direct source of sustenance for the majority of African families and generates the great majority of export earnings. Moreover, other elements of the economy, purchasers of primary products, suppliers of goods, and services to primary producers, are intimately linked to the primary sector. Thus, the spatial distribution of natural resources, the quantity and quality of these resources, and who controls their development are all important determinants of economic strengths and of political and social stability.

Chapter 19 focuses on the development of Africa's rich but unequally distributed mineral and commercial energy resources. While Africa is an important world producer of several minerals. African governments remain hostage to the realities of foreign ownership and the uncertainities of the international market for minerals. Mineral exploitation has brought relative prosperity to several countries, but it has been a dependent prosperity with an uncertain future.

Chapter 20 explores the role of Africa's fauna in the development of local, regional, and national economies. The role of Africa's wildlife in providing a basis for tourism is well known, but fauna are also an important source of food and other economically useful products. Much of this fauna is increasingly threatened, directly as a result of increased human utilization of these resources and indirectly as a result of the destruction of natural habitats.

Chapter 21 examines the diverse uses of vegetation, as a source not only of export earnings—the logging and wood processing industries—but also of food, traditional medicines, building materials, and fuel. The growing threat—indeed, reality—of environmental degradation implies the loss of a crucial resource base upon which many Africans depend. The development of appropriated policies to address the deterioration of the resource base depends initially on a better understanding of why degradation is occurring.

19

✳

Mineral and Energy Resources

Gold and diamonds, more than any other substances, symbolize opulence and solid, inflation-proof wealth. Yet, while about half of the world's gold and almost three-quarters of the world's diamonds are mined in Africa south of the Sahara, the continent is known for its poverty, not its prosperity. Gold and diamonds glitter for few Africans.

This chapter examines why Africa's mineral and energy resources have not stimulated real economic development in the continent outside of South Africa. It points to stark contrasts in the organization and significance of mining in precolonial times and after the colonial conquest. The mining industry in Africa, as elsewhere in the world, is controlled by large, global companies whose decisions reflect corporate self-interest rather than Africa's welfare.

Mining in Precolonial Africa

Inherent in the myth of "darkest Africa" was the denial of indigenous development; European capital and expertise were said to have been essential for the development of African resources. Yet, Africans have exploited the minerals of the earth's crust for thousands of years. Iron, gold, copper, and tin were mined in significant quantities in the precolonial era

and were used for making a variety of utilitarian and ceremonial objects.

Minerals were a very important component of interregional and even intercontinental trade during precolonial times. Gold from the headwaters of the Niger River and from present-day Ghana was reaching North Africa and Europe as early as the eighth century A.D. and brought extraordinary wealth and fame to the empires of Ghana and Mali. Similarly, gold from Zimbabwe was traded as far afield as the Persian Gulf, India, and China.

Iron making and the crafting from iron of agricultural tools, weapons, and utensils took place in many parts of precolonial Africa. The technology of iron making reached Nok in central Nigeria between the seventh and fourth century B.C., apparently having spread from Carthage via Saharan Berber nomads. In Nubia (in present-day Sudan), iron making had begun by the fifth century B.C. and was crucial to the prosperity of the kingdom. Recent archeological evidence points to the independent invention of ironmaking in the Lake District of East Africa prior to the third century B.C. and perhaps as early as the seventh century B.C. Knowledge of iron making spread gradually from these initial sites to other parts of West, East, central, and southern Africa in conjunction with the Bantu migrations.

Copper, primarily from the Copper Belt of

Figure 19.1. Traditional mining of alluvial tin deposits, Jos Plateau, Nigeria. Photo: author.

Zaire and Zambia, and tin, primarily from central Nigeria and eastern Zaire, were mined and used in bronze casting to make ceremonial and utilitarian objects. The intricate bronze art of Ife and Benin demonstrate the vitality of these precolonial African metalworking industries.

Salt was one of the most important commodities of precolonial African trade; thousands of caravans moved annually from Saharan producing centers such as Bilma into the savanna and forest regions where salt sources were unknown. Salt was so valuable that it was used as a medium of exchange. The Saharan mines produced many types of mineral salts used as medicine, food additives, and raw materials for tanning and dyeing. Although it has declined steadily in importance during the 20th century, the salt industry still continues to function much as it did in precolonial times. In many coastal areas, salt has long been extracted by evaporation from sea water for local use and as a valued trading commodity. This ancient industry remains alive in some places, for example, along the coastal lagoons of Ghana.

Development of the Modern Mining Industry

Although Europeans had long been aware that Africa contained rich stores of minerals, these resources remained firmly in African control prior to the colonial conquest. The rulers and merchants of the ancient empire of Ghana had managed to prevent Arab traders and visitors from learning the source of their vast supplies of gold. Likewise, early European explorers found Africans extremely reluctant to show them locations from which strategic and valuable materials were obtained.

Interest in the mineral potential of Africa rose to a fever pitch following the discovery of diamonds and gold in South Africa. Thousands of fortune seekers lured by stories of huge diamonds rushed to the Kimberley area in 1870 and 1871. Small mining operators soon gave way to capitalist mining companies, which in turn fought each other for an increased share of mineral property and market share. The ultimate victor was Cecil Rhodes's company, De Beers Consolidated Mines. By 1890, De Beers had sufficient control of the world diamond market to be able to control prices by restricting supply.

Gold was found in the Witwatersrand in Transvaal in the mid-1880s. The deposits were huge, but special technology was needed to exploit them because of their depth and the difficulty of extracting gold from the local bedrock. The investments needed to develop these gold deposits came from large companies, including the diamond mining conglomerates. Cecil Rhodes was again the most prominent capitalist in this new mining venture. The hope of finding even greater mineral wealth spurred Rhodes to expand northward. Using deception and military force, territory in present-day Zimbabwe and Zambia was seized for the British South African Company and was named Rhodesia. In the long run, the copper mines of Northern Rhodesia proved to be much more lucrative than the gold deposits of Southern Rhodesia. Large-scale mining did not occur until the late 1920s, stimulated by increased global demand and inflated prices for copper.

A similar pattern of occupation and mineral exploitation took place in Katanga, the region of the Belgian Congo adjacent to the Rhodesian Copper Belt. During the 1920s copper boom, the Belgian consortium Union Minière emerged as the third largest copper producer in the world. Other companies were established to exploit Congolese diamond and tin deposits. Where mineral deposits were found elsewhere in Africa, the pattern of exploitation was similar, although usually on a smaller scale. Concession mining companies invested in diamond mines in Angola, South-West Africa, the Congo, and Sierra Leone; tin mines in Nigeria; and gold and manganese mines in the Gold Coast. Investment and production fluctuated in response to world demand, collapsing during the depression of the 1930s, but growing rapidly during and after World War II.

In territories where mining development occurred, there were diverse economic, social, and political effects. Railroads were constructed from mineral deposits to ports or previously existing lines, and new towns were established

to house the mine work force. The new urban, wage-based economy of the mining communities was suddenly inserted into the midst of agricultural subsistence economies. While coercion was often needed in the initial stages to recruit migrant labor for the mines, the attraction of wage employment and the stagnation of traditional economies made labor recruitment increasingly simple. Except in South Africa, permanent mine workers gradually replaced seasonal workers who returned home to farm for several months each year.

During the 1950s, an expansion of the mining industry was made possible by a new wave of investment from the United States as well as the colonial powers. Greatly increased prospecting resulted in the discovery of new ore bodies, both in the established mining regions and in other parts of the continent. Many new mines were opened in South Africa, Southern and Northern Rhodesia, and the Belgian Congo. Major iron-ore mines were established in Liberia, Mauritania, and Angola; the world's largest deposits of bauxite were tapped in Guinea; and Gabon became an important producer of uranium and manganese. Perhaps the most important development was the discovery of petroleum in the Niger Delta of Nigeria and along the western coast in Angola, Congo, Gabon, and Cameroon. The subsequent improvement of technology for offshore drilling has facilitated exploitation of large offshore petroleum and natural gas reserves in the region.

There have been relatively few significant new mining developments since independence. The most notable exceptions have been new copper–nickel and diamond mines established in Botswana, new uranium mines in Niger, and large new iron mines recently developed in Guinea near the Liberian border. However, while the contribution of mining to the African economy doubled from 5 to 10% during the 1960s, the 1970s brought mixed fortunes. Petroleum producers profited greatly from the successful manipulation of marketed supply and prices by the Organization of Petroleum Exporting Countries (OPEC), but producers of most other miner-

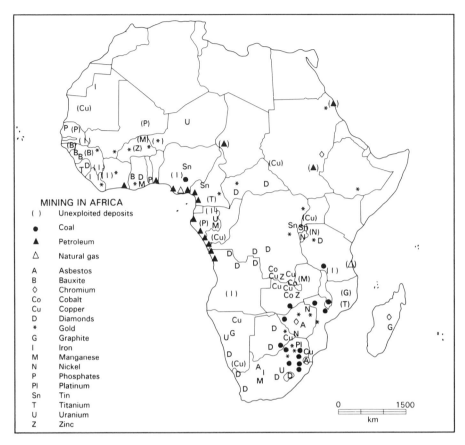

Figure 19.2. Mineral exploitation. Many of the mining operations shown on the map operated on a small scale, often intermittently. Data source: *Minerals in Africa: 1990 International Review.* Washington, DC: Bureau of Mines, 1992.

als were badly hurt by global recession and reduced demand for industrial raw materials. Production declined, and marginal mines were closed. During the 1980s with the weakening of OPEC, petroleum producers suffered a similar slackening of demand and collapse of market price.

Africa's Minerals and the World Economy

Africa contributes substantially to the global supply of minerals, with a total production valued at over $35 billion. Except for South Africa, which has a large and diverse industrial sector, most African production is exported. Nigeria and South Africa together account for well over half of the total value of mineral production. Angola, Zaire, Botswana, Gabon, and Zambia occupy a second tier in the production hierarchy, each having mineral exports valued at between $1.3 billion and $2 billion in 1989 (Table 19.1). A further 11 countries have between $100 million and $950 million of mineral sales annually.

Africa is an important source of several minerals and is the dominant source of supply for a few mineral commodities (Table 19.2). It produces half or more of the world's diamonds, platinum, and cobalt and 30% or more of the world's chromium, manganese, and uranium. It supplies at least one-tenth of the world's copper, bauxite, and rutile. Phosphates (8% of the world's supply), iron ore (7%), and petroleum (6%) are also produced in large quantities.

Table 19.1. Major Exporters of Minerals in Africa, 1989

	Value of exports (million U.S. $)	Share of exports (%)	Leading product
1. South Africa	11,500	65	Gold
2. Nigeria	7,508	90	Petroleum
3. Angola	2,154	95	Petroleum
4. Zaire	1,930	86	Copper
5. Botswana	1,510	>90	Diamonds
6. Gabon	1,500	79	Petroleum
7. Zambia	1,320	92	Copper
8. Cameroon	950	48	Petroleum
9. Zimbabwe	752	45	Gold
10. Namibia	750	75	Diamonds
11. Congo	701	76	Petroleum
12. Guinea	428	>90	Bauxite
13. Niger	235	68	Uranium
14. Liberia	215	49	Iron ore
15. Ghana	195	29	Gold
16. Mauritania	193	45	Iron ore
17. Togo	141	43	Phosphates
18. Sierra Leone	100	80	Rutile

Primary source: U.S. Bureau of Mines. *Mineral Industries of Africa*. Washington, D.C. 1989.

A portion of Africa's mineral production has been considered to be strategically important for Western military and industrial production because the major alternate source for chromium, gold, manganese, platinum, and cobalt is the former Soviet Union. The perceived importance of South Africa's strategic minerals contributed to the reluctance of the Western alliance to implement strong sanctions against South Africa for its racial policies. However, the demise of the Soviet Union has weakened Africa's position as a necessary source of strategic minerals.

Several episodes of neocolonial intervention in African political affairs have been related to the perceived importance of African mineral resources. In the 1960s, Western mining companies supported the attempted secession of the mineral-rich Katanga Province from Congo-Kinshasa, which had a leftist government at the time. More recently, troops from Belgium and France have intervened to support General Mobutu's repressive dictatorship when dissident Zairean troops threatened to disrupt mineral production and dislodge Mobutu from power. Direct and indirect foreign intervention in civil wars in Chad, Nigeria, and Angola has been related to the strategic

importance of mineral resources–petroleum in Nigeria and Angola and uranium in Chad.

Mining and Underdevelopment

Minerals provide substantial export revenues in about half of the countries of Africa south of the Sahara. In 17 countries, more than half of export earnings are from the sale of minerals. Angola, Botswana, Gabon, Guinea, Zambia, and Nigeria are countries where at least 90% of exports consists of minerals. However, despite the importance of African minerals in the world economy, African nations have not become wealthy as a result of mining development. They remain heavily dependent on exporting primary commodities and are therefore vulnerable to changes in world mineral markets.

South Africa is an exception in that mineral resources have clearly been instrumental in its growth as an industrial power. Several factors distinguish South Africa from other countries on the continent. Its mineral resources are diverse and vast, and this has bestowed considerable leverage in world markets, especially for diamonds, gold, and chromium. In-

Table 19.2. Africa's World-Ranked Mineral Producers

| | % from Africa | | World rank of leading African producers | | | | |
| | 1981 | 1989 | | 1981 | | 1989 | |
				Rank	(%)	Rank	(%)
Diamonds	72	50	Zaire	1	(29)	2	(20)
			Botswana	2	(21)	3	(16)
			South Africa	4	(16)	5	(10)
Cobalt	66	76	Zaire	1	(51)	1	(58)
			Zambia	3	(10)	2	(16)
Gold	54	35	South Africa	1	(50)	1	(33)
Platinum	>40	49	South Africa	1	NA	1	(48)
Chromium	38	38	South Africa	1	(32)	1	(32)
			Zimbabwe	5	(5)	5	(5)
Uranium	33	31	South Africa	3	(12)	3	(10)
			Niger	4	(10)	5	(9)
			Namibia	6	(8)	6	(9)
Manganese	23	33	South Africa	2	(13)	2	(18)
			Gabon	4	(9)	3	(14)
Copper	17	12	Zambia	5	(7)	6	(5)
			Zaire	6	(7)	5	(5)
Bauxite	16	20	Guinea	2	(15)	2	(16)
Rutile	14	20	Sierra Leone	3	(14)	2	(20)

Primary source: (UNCTAD). *Commodity Yearbook, 1990.*

digenous capital, rather than colonial or trans-national corporations, took the lead in the development of the South African mining industry. These mining companies later used their profits to diversify into other industrial enterprises. The profitability of the South African mining industry is also attributable to government regulations that strictly controlled wages and working conditions for African miners.

Even during the years when economic sanctions were in place, South African mining capital managed to exert strong, if not growing, regional and international influence in sectors of the world mineral economy. The best example is the virtual monopoly of De Beers in the production and trade in diamonds. Even Angola and Tanzania, two of the most fiercely antiapartheid countries, had to market their diamond production through De Beers, on terms set by the company. South African mining companies are directly involved in other mining ventures outside of South Africa, an example being the involvement of the Anglo-American Corporation in the development

of Botswana's Selebi-Pikwe copper–nickel mine.

Except in South Africa, most mining regions have remained essentially enclave economies without strong linkages to other sectors. Their products are destined for overseas markets, and machinery and other inputs necessary for mining are virtually all imported. Relatively little value is added between the mine and the port; ore concentrates and in some cases refined metals, not manufactured products, are exported. The most important linkage has been the employment of unskilled and semi-skilled labor. However, increasing mechanization is now reducing the job-creation potential of mining development.

The share of mineral wealth accruing to governments through taxes, royalties, and profit sharing has remained small in relation to the value of production. For example, during the late 1970s, iron-ore mining constituted 40% of Liberia's gross domestic product and 60% of its exports, but contributed only 13% of government revenues, a mere $14 million, in 1977. The contribution of funds from

Vignette 19.1. Botswana's Mineral-Based Economy: Success or Illusion of Success?

When Botswana became independent in 1966, it was considered to be one of the poorest countries in Africa. Its population of 500,000 was scattered over an area of 660 million sq km. Exports in 1968 amounted to only $10 million. The domestic economy was based on cattle herding and remittances from migrant workers in the mines of South Africa.

Shortly after independence, a series of important mineral discoveries were made (Figure 19.3). Large, productive diamond deposits were found at Jwaneng and Orapa. Botswana now ranks third in the world in the volume of diamonds produced, and it leads in the value of output. A major copper–nickel deposit was discovered in 1966 at Selebi-Pikwe near the Zimbabwean border (Figure 19.4). The mining of this deposit commenced in 1973. Coal production in 1989 amounted to 633,000 t. Smaller mining operations have been inaugurated more recently (1989 to 1991) to exploit gold deposits near Francistown and soda ash at Sua Pan. Potash and salt have also been discovered, and exploration for petroleum has been started.

The development of the mining industry has brought such startling growth to Botswana that it has been characterized as one of Africa's greatest economic success stories. The 1989 GNP per capita was $1,600, among the highest in Africa south of the Sahara. The value of exports grew from $22 million in 1970 to $503 million in 1980 and $1.4 million in 1988. Diamonds account for over 80% of export earnings and 63% of government revenues. Although imports have grown rapidly, the balance of payments situation is still very positive.

The rapidity of growth has not brought prosperity to all Botswana, however. A small elite of perhaps 10,000 officials, managers, and businesspeople have become extremely wealthy. Another 190,000 are supported by reasonably well-paying jobs in the mines, the military, and public service. The remaining 600,000, including many young, unemployed males, live in dire poverty.

The gap between rich and poor has increased markedly as the economy has grown, in large part because of the way mineral-derived wealth has been spent. Botswana's elites have invested heavily in cattle ranching and the infrastructure to support it, particularly private boreholes. The number of cattle increased by 76% during the 1970s, reaching 2.9 million in 1980. Numbers have since declined by about 10%, as a result of drought and damage to rangelands. As the rich were accumulating an increasing proportion of land and cattle, 80%

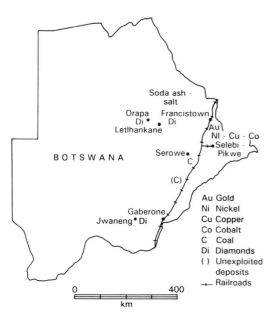

Figure 19.3. Mining in Botswana. After *Minerals in Africa: 1989 International Review*. Washington, DC: Bureau of Mines, 1989, p. 26.

cont.

Vignette 19.1. (*cont.*)

Figure 19.4. Open-pit copper mine, Selebi-Pikwe, Botswana. The production of this mine has contributed substantially to the growth of Botswana's GNP since the mid-1970s. Photo: CIDA: C. McNeill.

of the rural population was being relegated to less productive lands. Many poor rural families have been forced to seek urban employment to make ends meet.

The rapid growth in water demand for cattle ranching, mining, and urban development has coincided with several years of drought. Shortages, especially in the more developed southeastern part of the country, have become increasingly serious. The supply of water may become a major limiting factor with respect to further, if not existing, development.

Despite the growth of cattle ranching, Botswana's food production has declined. Cereal production has fluctuated between 14,000 t in 1983 and 109,000 t in 1988, but average production has fallen much below the levels recorded in the early 1970s. Even when harvests are excellent, Botswana falls far short of the 250,000 t of cereal production needed for self-sufficiency. While the decline in food production is in large part the result of drought, the effect of increasing societal inequalities of access to scarce economic resources in rural areas has been even more significant. Food imports have increased markedly, reaching 150,000 t in 1988. Over one-third of imported food has been in the form of food aid. In 1984, an estimated 60% of the population was receiving supplementary food aid.

Another dimension of Botswana's vulnerability is its growing dependence on South Africa. Despite Botswana's initial resistance to South African involvement in mining development, the role of South African capital has continued to grow. The diamond mines are controlled by a subsidiary of De Beers, and the copper–nickel deposits were only brought into production after the Anglo-American Corporation was allowed to make a major investment. South African companies are also heavily involved in Botswana's other

cont.

Vignette 19.1. (*cont.*)

---

mining ventures. Moreover, Botswana has become increasingly dependent on energy imports from South Africa to fuel its commercial economy. In all, 86% of the country's imports originate in South Africa.

Botswana tried to be pragmatic in its relation with apartheid South Africa. Measures such as the improvement of transportation linkages with Zambia and the establishment of a national currency independent of the South African rand have been designed to lessen its vulnerability. At the same time, the government avoided harsh criticism of apartheid. During the 1980s, a series of incidents occurred in which South Africa attempted to coerce Botswana into signing a nonaggression pact. In the most serious incident, South African security forces raided Gaberone, the capital, and killed 15 people, on the pretext that African National Congress guerrillas were infiltrating into South Africa from Botswana.

The dismantling of apartheid in South Africa may give Botswana greater security from South African interference. On the other hand, every sign points to Botswana remaining a very underdeveloped country, though it is very wealthy by African standards.

Primary source: R. L. Curry. "Poverty and mass unemployment in mineral-rich Botswana." *American Journal of Economics and Sociology*, vol. 46 (1987), pp. 71–88.

---

the mining sector to national development—to improve education, transportation, and health care, for example—has been small, indeed, given that Liberia was one of the world's 10 largest iron-ore producers for 25 years. Now, Liberia's importance as an iron-ore producer has declined, because of the depletion of higher grade ores and the effects of political instability.

In countries highly dependent on mineral exports, the mining industry has tended to distort national economic priorities; the needs of the mining sector that "pays the bills" take precedence over other needs. Government neglect of agriculture and the lure of mine wages stimulate outmigration and economic decline in rural areas. It is a vicious circle; agricultural decline ensures even greater dependence on mineral export revenue to finance development projects and pay for imported food.

The world market for minerals is extremely unstable and characterized by major fluctuations in demand and price. These fluctuations are illustrated in Table 19.3 with data on copper exports from Zambia in the years 1968 to 1988. Zambia's copper production declined from 20% to 4.8% of the world's total between 1968 and 1991. The value of copper exports has fluctuated from year to year and has shown no general upward trend. Meanwhile, the price index for the cost of imports increased sixfold between 1968 and 1991. Therefore, apparent increases in the value of imports actually translate into far fewer goods. The growing imbalance in trade has been offset, in the short run, by increasing levels of debt. However, falling government revenues and growing costs of debt servicing have, in turn, forced drastic cutbacks in basic services such as health care.

The declining size of high-grade reserves, coupled with the high cost of production in Zambian mines (in 1989, $1.22 per pound of refined copper in Zambia versus an average of $0.63 in all major producing countries) indicates that further declines in Zambia's copper industry are to be expected.

Contemporary changes in the structure of the mining industry have steadily undermined the bargaining power of national governments. The relatively small, venture-capital mining companies that established the first modern mines in Africa have virtually all been absorbed

Figure 19.5. Loading bauxite for export, Guinea. Most African minerals received only primary processing before being exported. Photo: CIDA: P. Chiasson.

and eliminated by transnational corporations. As mining operations have become larger and more mechanized, smaller companies have been unable to compete. Because the transnationals control mineral deposits in various parts of the world, they are able to concentrate production where profits are greatest. They have no particular commitment to any of the countries where they operate.

New technologies have made it feasible to exploit formerly uneconomic ore deposits, often located much closer to European, American, and East Asian markets. Increased exploitation of these low-grade deposits has depressed market prices and reduced demand for minerals from Africa. With very few exceptions, African countries have spent very little on exploration to find new mineral deposits. The neglect of exploration investment is not surprising in light of the precarious financial position of governments that must address many urgent needs with stable or declining resources. However, it means that as old mineral deposits are depleted, new operations seldom take their place.

Meanwhile, the poor state of the political "enabling environment" has discouraged new international investment in African mining ventures, with the notable exception of petroleum. Mining companies have become

Table 19.3. Trends in Value and Cost Structure of Zambian Trade

	1968	1973	1978	1983	1988	1991
Share of world copper exports (%)	20	16	11	7	5	<5
Exports (U.S. $ million, in constant 1980 prices)	1,363	1,406	1,382	1,346	966	1,165
Price index for mineral exports (1980 = 100)	56	82	63	74	118	105
Imports (U.S. $ million, in constant 1980 prices)	456	532	628	690	848	1,612
Price index for all imports (1980 = 100)	19	34	69	95	110	115
External debt (U.S. $ million)	NA	823	2,585	3,770	6,498	7,279
Real govt. health expenditure per capita (in Zambian Kwacha)	NA	19.0	14.9	11.9	NA	NA

Sources: World Bank. *World Tables 1989–90.* Washington, DC: World Bank, 1990. World Bank. *World Tables 1993.* Washington, DC: World Bank, 1993. P. Freund. "Health care in a declining economy." *Social Science and Medicine,* vol. 23 (1986), pp. 875–888.

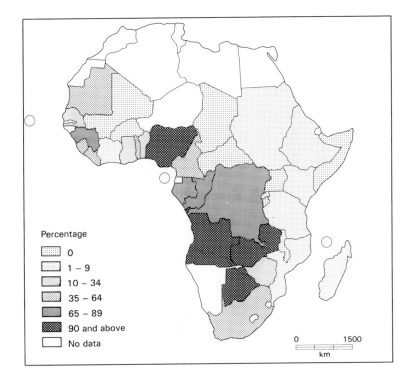

Figure 19.6. Fuels, minerals, and metals as a percentage of all exports. The economies of a dozen countries are highly dependent on exports from the mining sector. Data source: World Bank. *World Development Report, 1991.* New York: Oxford University Press, 1991.

wary about longer-term political stability in most African countries. Companies have also chosen to invest elsewhere because of ownership, taxation, and profit-repatriation legislation that they consider too restrictive and because of the failure of governments to appear willing and able to create a profitable business environment. The result is that Africa south of the Sahara, excluding South Africa, now supplies only 10% of the Third World contribution to the global trade in nonenergy minerals, compared to 23% in 1960.

Commercial Energy

A significant proportion of Africa's mining industry is devoted to the extraction of mineral fuels, namely, petroleum, natural gas, coal, and uranium. In addition, Africa has a huge, barely tapped potential for the development of hydroelectric energy. Paradoxically, while Africa south of the Sahara has vast resources of commercial energy, it remains energy poor.

The commercial energy resources of African countries have several distinguishing characteristics:

- Commercial energy resources are very unevenly distributed, with some countries having large surpluses and many having no commercially viable energy resources.
- Most of Africa's commercial energy resources are *potential* resources that have not been developed; this is particularly true of hydroelectricity.
- Most benefits of already developed commercial energy have gone to foreign interests and a small minority of Africans.

Ordinary Africans in both urban and rural areas get their fuel from biomass (firewood, crop refuse, and charcoal). While biomass and commercial energies are interchangeable for many purposes, the economic organization of

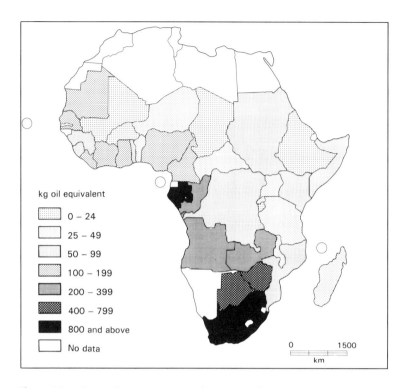

Figure 19.7. Per capita consumption of commercial energy. In all but four African countries, per capita consumption of commercial energy is less than 5% of that in the USA. Data source: World Bank. *World Development Report, 1991.* New York: Oxford University Press, 1991.

their production differs. Most fuelwood and charcoal are produced, distributed, and utilized within the informal economy. Commercial-energy projects are large scale, capital intensive, and technologically complex, and they serve primarily the formal (modern) economy. Consumption per capita of commercial energy can be used as a measure of economic activity, particularly in the formal sector. The data offer dramatic evidence of the depth of African underdevelopment; whereas consumption averages 7,794 kg per capita of oil equivalent in the United States, it is only 17 kg per capita in Chad and Burkina Faso, 20 kg in Ethiopia, and under 100 kg in all but 15 countries (Figure 19.7). Consumption per capita of commercial energy exceeds 1,000 kg oil equivalent only in Gabon and South Africa.

The majority of African countries are dependent on imported energy for all, or virtually all, of their commercial energy needs. Conversely, five countries—the major petroleum producers—export most of the energy that

they produce. In six countries, including South Africa, production and consumption of commercial energy are approximately equal. Even though levels of consumption are very low in the importing countries, their total dependence on imported energy has retarded development. After petroleum prices increased sharply in the 1970s, these countries simultaneously faced increased debt, slackened demand for their exports, and reduced ability to purchase oil and other imports.

Commercially viable deposits of hydrocarbons—petroleum, natural gas, and coal—are found in only a quarter of the countries of Africa south of the Sahara. Except for a small field at Enugu, Nigeria, Africa's exploited coal deposits are all in the south central and southeastern parts of the continent. South Africa, Zimbabwe, and Mozambique exploit large reserves of good quality coal; whereas Zambia, Zaire, and Tanzania have minor coal mining industries based on small, low quality deposits.

Africa's only major coal producer is South Africa. Large deposits occur in thick seams near the surface in Transvaal and Natal. The low cost of exploitation is crucial for South Africa, which uses coal in the iron and steel, transportation, and mining industries, to generate thermal electricity and manufacture synthetic petroleum. Because South Africa has no petroleum fields, the apartheid state was highly committed to its petroleum-from-coal industry that made South Africa less susceptible to possible international economic sanctions.

Petroleum production is concentrated in Nigeria (which has about two-thirds of production) and in four other countries in west-central Africa. Petroleum benefits the producing countries primarily as a source of export income, rather than as a major energy resource for indigenous development. Natural gas occurs along with the petroleum, but most of it is flared, because of high development costs and competition from cheap Russian, North African, and North Sea gas in the European mar-

ket. Relatively small deposits of petroleum and natural gas have been found along the West African coast between Benin and Côte d'Ivoire, near Lake Chad, and in Sudan.

Africa has vast potential for hydroelectric development; an estimated 40% of the world's potential hydroelectric resources are located in Africa. The continent, particularly in "High Africa" (Figure 2.1), is bordered by major escarpments, over which or through which rivers must pass to reach the ocean. Where large rivers cut through axes of uplift or where they cross erosion-resistant rock formations, there are deep gorges and waterfalls or rapids that provide ideal sites for dam construction.

The greatest potential is in the Congo basin. In the lower reaches between Kinshasa and Matadi, the Congo River's average flow of 40,000 cubic meters per second is exceeded only by that of the Amazon. In this 350-km stretch, the river drops 270 m through a series of 30 rapids and waterfalls. Only 1.3% of the total capacity of 103 million kW (kilowatts) has been harnessed. In all, Zaire has about

Figure 19.8. Major hydroelectric projects. Africa has several very large hydroelectric dams. Nevertheless, only a fraction of Africa's potential has been harnessed.

Figure 19.9. Akosombo Dam, Ghana. This dam, constructed in the 1960s, was expected to become the cornerstone of Ghana's drive for modernization. The development that occurred fell far short of expectations. Photo: CIDA: B. Paton.

16% of the world's total potential hydroelectric resources.

Africa south of the Sahara has 15 substantial hydroelectric installations with capacities of 100 to 2,000 MW (megawatts) and numerous small installations. The largest, in order of size, are Cabora Bassa in Mozambique, Kariba on the Zambia–Zimbabwe border, Inga 2 in Zaire, Kainji in Nigeria, and Akosombo in Ghana.

Each of these dam megaprojects was undertaken in a unique political context. Akosombo, constructed in the early 1960s on the Volta River, was to be the cornerstone of Ghana's drive for modernization and industrialization. A large aluminum smelter was established, but otherwise there were few tangible industrial spin-offs. Cabora Bassa on the Zambezi was constructed during the last years of Portuguese colonial rule. The mutual self-interest of South Africa and Portugal lay behind the project – electricity for South Africa and assured South African support for Portuguese colonialism. Independent Mozambique has continued to sell Cabora Bassa power to South Africa, despite the protracted, bitter conflicts between the two countries that repeatedly disrupted power transmission.

Despite their very high construction costs, large dams have been coveted as keystone development projects. Dam projects *seem* to promise multiple benefits, including flood control, irrigation, navigation, and hydroelectricity. Hydroelectric power provides a base for industrialization and a means of reducing dependence on imported hydrocarbon energy. However, as the many anticipated benefits from these massive investments have generally failed to materialize, it should be asked whether scarce resources could not be put to better use. The development of smaller-scale projects generating energy from the sun, from wind, and from local, small-scale, hydrogenerating facilities eventually may provide Africa with a more cost-efficient and less environmentally damaging alternative to large dam projects.

Future Prospects

The exploitation of African commercial energy and mineral resources is big business, with big benefits for industrial countries and, except for South Africa, uncertain benefits for Africa and its people. Mineral resources are nonrenewable, and when the higher-grade ores become depleted—as has happened in Zambia—income from mineral sales declines. On the other hand, it would be hard to argue that Botswana, for example, would have been better off without its booming mining industry and the dilemmas of dependent development that have accompanied its rapid growth.

In the long run, international capital may be attracted to the continent to harness its hydroelectric resources for smelting and other industries with high-energy requirements. For now, the excessive cost of dam projects rules them out for the debt-ridden majority of African countries.

African governments lack the resources to undertake effective mineral exploration and the development of resources on their own. As for the mining industry, there is certain to be extreme caution about large-scale investment because of concerns about the political and economic environment in Africa for business and because of the weak global market for most minerals. Thus, the prospects are that the African mineral industry will continue, with very few exceptions, to stagnate.

Further Reading

For recent data on the production, trade, and use of minerals and energy, see the following sources:

"Major commodities of Africa: Minerals." *Africa South of the Sahara*. London: Europa Publications, published annually.

United Nations. *Energy Statistics Yearbook*. New York: United Nations Department of International Economic and Social Affairs, published annually.

U.S. Bureau of Mines. *Minerals Yearbook*. Washington, DC: Department of the Interior, published annually.

The following sources provide useful overviews of the mining industry in Africa:

Fozzard, P. M. "Mining development in sub-Saharan Africa: Investment and its relationship to the enabling environment." *Natural Resources Forum*, vol. 14 (1990), pp. 97–105.

Labys, W. C. *The Mineral Trade Potential of the Least Developed African Countries*. New York: United Nations Industrial Development Organization (UNIDO), 1985.

Lanning, G. *Africa Undermined: Mining Companies and the Underdevelopment of Africa*. Harmondsworth, England: Penguin, 1979.

Ochola, S. A. *Minerals in African Underdevelopment*. London: L'Ouverture, 1975.

Ogunbadejo, O. *The International Politics of Africa's Strategic Minerals*. London: Frances Pinter, 1985.

UNIDO. *The Mineral Industry of Developing Africa: A Brief Review of Some Current Issues*. Vienna: UNIDO, 1983.

There are innumerable case studies of mining in particular settings in Africa. The following sources are examples:

Cunningham, S. *The Copper Industry in Zambia: Foreign Mining Companies in a Developing Country*. London: Praeger, 1981.

Freund, B. *Capital and Labour in the Nigerian Tin Mines*. Atlantic Highlands, NJ: Humanities, 1981.

Greenhalgh, P. *West African Diamonds: An Economic History*. Manchester, England: Manchester University Press, 1985.

Innes, D. *Anglo-American and the Rise of Modern South Africa*. London: Heinemann, 1984.

For two contrasting views on South Africa and the world mineral economy, see the following sources:

Bolton, B. "Illusions of dependence: South Africa's minerals in the global economy." *Raw Materials Report*, vols. 2–3 (1983), pp. 10–23.

Malan, W. W. "South Africa: A reliable source of strategic minerals." *Mining Survey*, vols. 3–4 (1983), pp. 28–33.

Energy planning in the Third World is discussed in the following sources:

Bradley, P. N., N. Charangi, and A. Van Gelder. "Development research and energy planning in Kenya." *Ambio*, vol. 14 (1985), pp. 228–236.

Hosier, R., P. O'Keefe, B. Wisner, D. Weiner, and D. Shakow. "Energy planning in developing countries: Blunt axe in a forest of problems?" *Ambio*, vol. 11 (1982), pp.180–187.

Studies of hydroelectric developments in Africa include the following sources:

Lazenby, J. B., and P. Jones. "Hydro-electricity in West Africa: Its future role." *Energy Policy*, vol. 15 (1987), pp. 441–455.

Middlemas, K. *Cabora Bassa*. London: Weidenfeld and Nicholson, 1987.

20

*

Fauna and Economic Development

When non-Africans think of Africa, chances are that their first and clearest images will be of vast herds of animals grazing on the savannas. Perhaps thoughts will turn to individual species, such as the lions popularized in the book and film *Born Free*, or the mountain gorillas described in Dian Fossey's articles in *National Geographic* magazine and portrayed in the film *Gorillas in the Mist*. With the exception of the Galapagos Islands, it is hard to think of another region where wildlife plays such an important part in popular perceptions of place.

The popular image is hardly representative. Large herds are typical only of certain game reserves and national parks, mostly in East Africa. Moreover, the large animals that command so much attention—the elephants, zebras, giraffes, lions, and gorillas, for example—represent only a minute portion of Africa's fauna. Each ecosystem contains countless species of mammals, birds, insects, fish, reptiles, and other fauna, as well as many kinds of plants, which together constitute an interdependent web of life.

Wildlife Habitats

At a very general level, five wildlife habitats—three terrestrial (forest, savanna, and desert) and two aquatic (the oceans and freshwater environments)—may be identified. At a more local scale, there are countless ecosystems with distinctive and interdependent communities of fauna. Energy transfer occurs through the operation of food chains, which begin with the growth of plants through the process of photosynthesis that uses solar energy to convert water and carbon dioxide into biomass. Plant life provides sustenance for herbivores, which in turn are consumed by carnivores. Omnivores consume both animals and plants. In addition to the primary food chain, each ecosystem has a decomposer food chain, consisting of microorganisms such as fungi and bacteria that consume dead organic material.

In reality, the structure of food chains is very complex, with each species having a limited range of potential and preferred foods. The food preferences of each species in a given ecosystem are distinct and complementary, that is, foods preferred by one species are often ignored by others. Many species of wildlife also undertake seasonal migrations, enabling them to use different spaces and sometimes different foods at different times of the year.

The fauna of forest and savanna ecosystems each have their own distinct characteristics. The vertical stratification and botanic diversity of the forest create not only many niches that fauna can exploit but also a tremendous variety of available foods. In contrast, savanna and desert ecosystems have much less diversity. Vegetational diversity is correlated with faunal diversity; forest ecosystems have significantly more species of fauna than savannas. However, despite the luxuriant growth of vegetation in forest environments, its total animal biomass tends to be significantly less than that supported by savanna ecosystems. Forest species also tend to be less able than savanna life to adapt to habitat disturbance.

The fauna of the island of Madagascar deserve special mention. Despite its relative proximity to continental Africa, Madagascar's animal life has developed in isolation over millions of years and is mostly unique to the island; it has been estimated that 90% of the species in Madagascar's tropical forests are found only there. The lemurs are among the most fascinating of Madagascar's wildlife. These primates have evolved into some 25 different species occurring in a variety of ecological niches that, on the African continent, are normally occupied by monkeys and apes. The continuing destruction of the island's natural environments, in conjunction with the expansion of agriculture and pastoralism, has seriously jeopardized the survival Madagascar's of unique fauna.

Fauna–Human Interactions in the Environment

Human societies have always coexisted with, and often competed with, fauna. In precolonial East Africa and elsewhere, animal populations were significantly reduced whenever humans and animals competed for territory. Wildlife habitat was affected by the growth of agriculture and the widespread use of fire by farmers, herders, and hunters. Animals were hunted, for food, skins, ivory, and to secure grazing resources for livestock. Reducing wild animal populations also made possible the control of tsetse and other disease-carrying insects. East African pastoralists were well aware of the dangers of tsetse for their livestock; their survival depended on the maintenance of some degree of ecological control.

East Africa's wildlife multiplied during the colonial era, but the cost for Africans was frequently high. Substantial areas were set aside as wildlife sanctuaries and forest reserves, often after people and their livestock had been forced to move out. The control of fires and livestock in the reserves allowed vegetation to flourish and animals to proliferate, creating ideal conditions for the spread of tsetse. Virulent epidemics of sleeping sickness subsequently appeared in human populations in East Africa and in many other parts of the continent. Livestock populations were decimated by trypanosomiasis in tsetse-infested areas. Colonial officials generally saw these epidemics as further evidence of the pervasive unhealthiness of Africa. Seldom was there any recognition of the ways in which colonial policies had contributed to the disaster.

The balance between humans and wildlife has continued to shift since the end of the colonial era, the result of continuing alterations to the environment. Large areas of previously undeveloped land have been appropriated for agriculture to feed rapidly growing populations and to supply export markets. For example, irrigation schemes have been established in river valleys and have eliminated wetlands crucial to the survival of waterfowl and some animal populations. The increasing utilization of pesticides and herbicides, including chemicals such as DDT that have been banned in most industrialized countries, threatens the survival of some fauna.

The multifaceted human modifications of the environment—for example, the clearance of tropical forests; the deliberate use of fires in savannas by farmers, herders, and hunters; intensive grazing by livestock; and the construction of dams and reservoirs—has significant effects on fauna. Some species, most notably the larger wildlife for which Africa is so famous, have been forced to retreat and some species may ultimately disappear. Other fauna thrive in human-created environments. For example, monoculture encourages the proliferation of pests. The agricultural chemicals commonly used to control these pests in turn endanger a broad spectrum of species.

So far, the discussion has focused on ways

Vignette 20.1. Termites and Tillage

Termitaria, structures that contain nests of termites, are a common feature of African ecosystems, particularly in moister savanna areas. Africa has many species of termites, each of which has a distinctive type of nest. Certain species construct mounds of varying shapes and sizes to contain their nests. Some of these termitaria are pillarlike and up to several meters high, whereas others are large, relatively flat mounds up to 30 m across. The density of termitaria varies in relation to local environmental conditions; a Zambian study found an average of two to three mounds per hectare.

The activities of termite colonies enhance soil fertility in and around their nests. Termitaria often contain concentrations of fertile clays, brought up from many meters below the surface to construct the mound. They are rich in organic matter and nutrients derived primarily from plant materials collected as food and from the cycle of life within the colony. In the process of digging through heavy laterite soils, termites significantly improve the soil's drainage and aeration.

African farmers recognize that termitaria, whether occupied or disused, have exceptionally fertile soils. In large fields, areas around termitaria stand out as having visibly healthier and higher yielding crops. In some farming systems, special crops or farming techniques are used to take advantage of termitaria soils.

Figure 20.1 shows land use in a small study area with a large concentration of termitaria near Lusaka, Zambia. The preferred use for these soils is maize, a crop requiring fertile soils to yield well. It is apparent that maize is being cultivated on many of the termitaria and that numerous other termitaria had been used to grow corn in the past. Very little of the land between termitaria, and virtually none in the poorly drained lowland areas, are under cultivation.

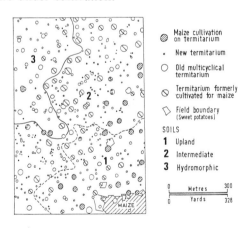

Maize cultivation on termitarium
New termitarium
Old multicyclical termitarium
Termitarium formerly cultivated for maize
Field boundary (Sweet potatoes)

SOILS
1 Upland
2 Intermediate
3 Hydromorphic

In the simple process of constructing its nests and sustaining colony life, the lowly termite modifies the African landscape, enhances the fertility of soil, and contributes immeasurably to the well-being of millions of Africans.

Figure 20.1. Termites and tillage in Zambia. Many termitaria are, or were formerly, under cultivation. Source R. A. Pullan, "Biogeographical studies and agricultural development in Zambia," *Geography*, vol. 59 (1974), pp. 309–231. ©1974 by The Geographical Association. Reprinted by permission.

Based on R. A. Pullan. "Termite hills in Africa: Their characteristics and evolution." *Catena*, vol. 6 (1979), pp. 267–292.

in which human alterations of the environment affect fauna. Fauna can also affect the environment in significant ways, some of which are beneficial for humans, while others are harmful. For example, scavengers such as vultures and hyenas quickly consume the flesh of dead animals, thus reducing the risk of disease. Predators help to control pests that might otherwise threaten crops or human health. In constructing their nests, termites improve soil

Figure 20.2. Termite mound, Nigeria. Cassava has been planted around the base of the mound to take advantage of the more fertile soil created by the termites. Photo: CIDA: B. Paton.

quality and enable farmers to get better yields (Vignette 20.1).

On the negative side, fauna as varied as elephants, quela birds, and locusts can utterly destroy crops. Fauna are also intregally linked to the transmission of many diseases that afflict humans. Mosquitoes, tsetse, and fleas, among others, spread infectious diseases. Wildlife also act as a reservoir of infection for certain diseases that can be passed directly (e.g., rabies) or indirectly (e.g., sleeping sickness) to humans.

Fauna as an Economic Resource

Africa's wildlife is an important natural resource that contributes significantly to national, regional, and local economies. It is a vital source of food, a source of other valuable products, and is a key resource for the tourist industry.

Fauna as Food: Meat from Wild Animals

Wild-animal meat is the most important source of dietary animal protein in many parts of Afri-

ca, particularly where heavy infestations of tsetse preclude livestock production. Consumers of "bush meat" have very eclectic tastes; thus, a wide range of animals, birds, and other kinds of fauna may suffer from hunting stress. Compared to East and central Africa, such stress is much more evident in West Africa, where human populations have been larger for a longer time and where wildlife habitats are shrinking. In regions where considerable wild-animal meat is consumed, it forms an important component of rural–urban, interregional, and even international trade. Thus, pressures on wildlife may not necessarily be a reflection of hunting for local food needs.

Game cropping and game ranching have been explored as alternatives to traditional hunting. Game cropping involves a regulated harvest of selected species of wildlife in designated areas, whereas game ranching involves the semidomestication of wildlife. Game cropping and ranching schemes have focused on several species of ungulates like the eland, wildebeest, and zebra. Although experimental game ranches established in Zimbabwe,

Kenya, and Tanzania have had promising results, this strategy has not become widespread. Game cropping has been quite widely practiced in East and south central Africa but is much less important than unregulated hunting as a source of food.

There has been considerable interest in improving wildlife management to achieve higher productivity, especially since wild animals have several advantages over domestic livestock. Wildlife populations adapt more readily to varying environmental conditions, especially in marginal areas. They are more tolerant of heat stress, utilize a wider range of fodder resources, and are better able to survive when fodder and water are scarce. Consequently, the ungulate carrying capacity, as measured by the total weight of animal populations that can be sustained in a given savanna environment, is several times greater than the domestic livestock carrying capacity in the same environment. Finally, resistance to certain diseases affecting domestic animals, especially trypanosomiasis, enables wild animals to thrive in areas where domestic livestock could not survive.

Fauna as Food: Fish

Fish are consumed in large quantities in much of Africa, especially along the coast and near lakes and large rivers where substantial inland fisheries exist. The nutritional significance of these fisheries is very great because many of these areas have a scarcity of domestic livestock. The importance of the inland fisheries is often underestimated. However, the landlocked countries of Chad and Uganda, with annual catches of well over 100,000 t each, have substantially larger catches than the majority of coastal states.

The traditional fishing industry is large and very labor intensive. A variety of fishing techniques are used, including fish traps, gill nets, and hooks and lines. Fishing is often done cooperatively, with several members of a family or community working together to drive fish into traps or to handle larger nets. Societies where fishing is important often practice resource conservation by observing traditions that regulate fishing seasons and that control access to key fishing locations. These measures are particularly important in inland fish-

Figure 20.3. Commercial fishing, Côte d'Ivoire. Commercial fishing has only begun to achieve its potential in most coastal African states. Photo: CIDA: M. Faugere.

eries where fishing is commonly a seasonal activity.

Development agencies have attempted to improve the efficiency of these traditional fisheries. For example, larger and stronger nets enable fishermen to increase their catches, while improved preservation techniques can greatly reduce spoilage and enhance the quality of marketed fish. Introducing better fishing boats has aided the coastal and lacustrian fishing industries. Development agencies have also promoted fish farming by using fast-growing species like talapia as a strategy for increasing protein supplies. Fish-farming has often been undertaken as a secondary enterprise in conjunction with irrigation projects.

Off the northwest and southwest coasts of Africa, the cool Canary and Benguela currents have created some of the world's richest fishing grounds. The mixing of cool and warmer waters over the continental shelf provides ideal conditions for plankton, the tiny marine plants that are the first link in the oceanic food chain. These areas teem with massive schools of small fish like mackerel, sardines, and pilchards. Elsewhere along the African coast, the catches tend to be smaller but often include higher value species like tuna and shrimp.

It is ironic, given the low levels of protein in most African diets, that most of the fish caught off African coasts is bound for Europe, Japan, and North America, rather than for Africa itself. Moreover, the majority of the fish caught in the rich zones of the Canary and Benguela currents is used as fish by-products, like fish oil and fish meal for fertilizer and animal feed for the industrialized world, rather than as human food.

Japanese, Korean, Russian, Portuguese, and Spanish fishing fleets are very active in African waters. These countries send large factory ships capable of processing and storing the catches of several accompanying fishing vessels. Their fleets are virtually self-sufficient, so there are few economic benefits for countries adjacent to the main fishing areas. Several African coastal nations, including Mauritania, Senegal, Nigeria, and Angola, have laid claim to 320-km-wide territorial waters and have attempted to regulate fishing within these zones.

However, regulations are only as good as their enforcement; African nations are not in a strong position to control the world's fishing superpowers. Without adequate control, overfishing may result in long-term damage to the resource base. While this has not yet become apparent off the African coast, it has occurred in other major fishing regions. For example, overfishing contributed to a dramatic fall in fish harvests off the west coast of South America in the late 1970s and more recently has been linked to the demise of the cod fishery on Canada's Grand Banks.

South Africa has a large and long-established modern fishing industry concentrated off the Namibian coast. During colonial times, Angola had a well-developed fishing industry linked to a huge Portuguese fishery. The tonnage landed by Angola-based fishers has declined since independence but is still substantial. Several West African nations have been attempting to increase their harvest of ocean fish, both for export and domestic consumption. Senegal and Mauritania have developed large fishing industries generating export earnings for each of about $150 million annually. Nigeria has also invested in a fishing fleet, almost entirely to supply the domestic market. Nigeria's annual catch of over 500,000 t is second only to that of South Africa. Côte d'Ivoire and Ghana have also developed fairly large fishing industries that produce for both export and local consumption.

Fauna as a Source of Valuable Products

Africans have obtained hides and skins, ivory, and other items from fauna since time immemorial. Hides and skins were made into clothing, utensils, weapons, and musical instruments, and various animal parts were used in medical preparations. Ivory was carved to make ceremonial objects and was also, for many centuries, one of Africa's most valued exports. It was an important component of the trans-Saharan trade and the Atlantic-coast trade with Europe. From East and south central Africa, ivory was exported to the Middle East, India, and China.

Vignette 20.2. How to Protect Africa's Elephants: The Debate

In October 1989, the Convention on Trade in Endangered Species (CITES) voted to enforce a complete ban on international trade in ivory, in an attempt to reduce the poaching that had brought about such a drastic reduction in the population of African elephants. Subsequently, all of the major importers of ivory agreed to abide by the ruling and have suspended ivory imports.

The decision to ban the ivory trade came as a result of the failure of attempts to use a quota system to limit the slaughter of elephants. The quota system was not applied in a consistent and ecologically rational way. Each country was able to set its own quota without due consideration to its elephant population; the CITES-approved quotas of 1986 totaled 108,000 tusks, up to ten times the sustainable level of harvest. Moreover, the quotas did not apply to worked ivory. The extremely high market prices for ivory ensured that poachers were willing to take ever greater risks in order to cash in.

Kenya was among the strongest supporters of the CITES ban on ivory exports. Its government argued that only a total ban would allow effective policing of the ivory trade and would bring about a drop in prices sufficient to dissuade poachers. As a symbol of its determination, the Kenyan government staged a public burning of its entire, huge stock of ivory seized from poachers.

The ban on the ivory trade has been strongly opposed by several countries in southern Africa, including Zimbabwe, South Africa, and Botswana. These countries all have stable, if not growing, herds of elephants, which the governments of these countries attribute to careful management of the resource. They argue that selective killing is necessary to maintain the health of the herds and of the ecosystems supporting them. Moreover, the sale of ivory can be used as a means of financing rigorous wildlife conservation and antipoaching programs; the wildlife services of most African countries are notoriously underfunded and underequipped.

The debate on how to save the elephant resumed at the March 1992 meeting of CITES in Kyoto, Japan. The supporters of the ban pointed to the collapse of the price of ivory on the world market since 1990 and argued that a continuation of the ban was needed

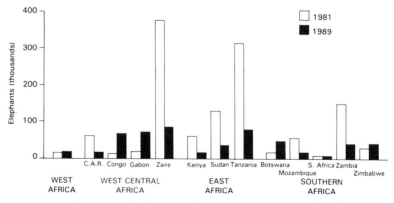

Figure 20.4. Changes in elephant populations, 1981 to 1989. Although elephant populations have virtually collapsed in several of the countries that once had the largest herds, some populations show signs of growth in certain other countries. After *World Resources, 1990–91.* New York: Basic Books, 1991.

cont.

Vignette 20.2. (*cont.*)

Figure 20.5. Elephant herd, northern Cameroon. The debate continues about what strategies will provide the most effective protection for Africa's wildlife and, thus, for Africa's important wildlife-based tourist industry. Photo: CIDA: R. Lemoyne.

to allow for the elephant herds in East Africa to recover. The southern African countries with more stable elephant populations claimed that they were being penalized for their good management and again argued that a controlled harvest of elephants and limited legal sale of ivory made sense, both ecologically and economically. CITES voted to extend the 1989 total ban on ivory sales, a decision that the southern African states called "political," that is, more influenced by a conservationist climate in Europe and North America than by good scientific data.

It is too early to ascertain whether the ban will allow the elephant populations to increase. This debate shows that the conservation of African wildlife is a complex issue that needs to be addressed at the local, national, and international levels. Policies that seem to work in one jurisdiction and for one particular species may not be appropriate for others. Our understanding of the science, economics, and politics of conserving Africa's wildlife is still very rudimentary.

During the colonial era, there was a flourishing trade in animal products, especially ivory and the hides and skins of animals like the leopard, crocodile, and zebra. Wealthy hunters from Europe and North America came in search of exotic trophies. Africa's fauna was also trapped for live export to zoos and circuses. This extensive trade in African animals and animal parts posed a threat to the survival of some species and certainly resulted in reduced ranges for animals in areas where wildlife numbers were low and hunting very intense. For example, the greatly reduced ranges of the leopard and cheetah reflect the intensity of hunting pressures on these valued species.

The trade in Africa's endangered wildlife and wildlife products continues on a massive scale, despite the prohibition of such trade in CITES. Many countries, both in Africa and other parts of the world, have not ratified the treaty. Even where CITES is in effect, a flourishing underground trade persists, catering to the insatiable appetites of those willing to pay the price.

During the 1980s, the African elephant population fell from 1.3 million to about 600,000. In Angola alone, 100,000 were killed by the Unita guerrillas to fund their insurrection against the central government. Between half and two-thirds of the very large elephant populations of Kenya, Tanzania, Zambia, and Zaire have been eliminated. The implications of this slaughter extend far beyond the diminishing opportunities to see elephants in the wild. When elephant herds uproot trees and otherwise "damage" natural vegetation, they are helping to diversify the environment and, thus, are enhancing its capacity to support many species. Fewer elephants may lead to a decrease in wildlife numbers and species diversity.

The devastation of Uganda's wildlife provides a case study of the implications of poaching. The two largest national parks in Uganda lost over 95% of their elephants between the early 1970s and mid-1980s. Despite a total ban on elephant hunting since 1980, 280 t of ivory were exported from Uganda in 1987. The quest for rhinoceros horn, used to make dagger sheaths in Yemen, has resulted in the total elimination of the rhinoceros from Uganda. Endangered species like the Nile crocodile and leopard continue to be hunted illegally for their skins. The country's exceptionally rich bird life has also come under increasing pressure from poachers.

In Uganda, as elsewhere, the devastation of wildlife needs to be interpreted in relation to the broader political and economic situation and not seen as merely the work of unscrupulous individual poachers. During two decades of civil unrest, the massive disruption of the "normal" economy and the need for

funds to finance guerrilla campaigns provided an incentive for wildlife poaching, while the disorganization of the Ugandan state left it unable to manage its national parks effectively.

African wildlife is in crisis, even in countries fully committed to conservation. Conservation officers must patrol vast territories and guard highly mobile wildlife. The poachers are very determined and often armed with high-powered automatic weapons. Although poachers receive only a tiny portion of the final market value of the wildlife products, the profits are very attractive in desperately poor countries with few lucrative job opportunities. Zimbabwe has tried to protect its once large rhinoceros population in the Zambezi Valley from poachers, many of whom are based in Zambia. Despite extensive and sophisticated surveillance and a policy of shooting to kill when poachers are encountered, the slaughter continues. Zimbabwe's wild rhinoceros population has declined by more than 90% since 1970.

Fauna and Tourism

Shortly after the colonial annexation of Africa at the turn of the century, the first tourists began to arrive. The massive game populations of East and southern Africa proved irresistible to the aristocrats and capitalist tycoons from America and Europe. While some came only to view and photograph the fauna, many came to collect trophies. These early safaris were lavish affairs, befitting the expensive tastes of the clientele.

Advances in air transportation have been crucial to the development of tourism in Africa. As airplanes have become larger and faster, and air travel relatively less costly, more and more people have been able to fulfill their childhood dreams of seeing Africa's fauna in the wild.

In recent years, African countries have done more to promote historical sites like Great Zimbabwe and the temples of Axum, as well as the rich cultural heritage of the continent. New oceanside resorts have been developed in several countries, including Senegal, Gambia, Sierra Leone, Côte d'Ivoire, and Kenya.

Vignette 20.3. Point(P)/Counterpoint(C): Should African States Promote Tourism?

Much controversy surrounds the issue of treating tourism as an industry for priority development. The proponents of tourism emphasize its potential for employment creation and profit, as well as other anticipated benefits. Its critics see it differently. Some of the specific areas of debate about the advantages and disadvantages of tourism are explored below.

P1: Tourism is a major source of foreign exchange that provides earnings of over $25 per inhabitant in Gambia and Botswana. It is the most important earner of foreign exchange in Kenya ($410 million in 1988). Other countries, many of which have economies too dependent on agriculture or mining, would do well to take advantage of tourism's potential as a source of funds for development.

C1: A tourist industry can only be established after considerable investment in hotels, transportation systems, and other infrastructures. Because visitors insist on "all the comforts of home," inputs ranging from food and drink to hotel furnishings must be imported. Much of the apparent earnings accrues to airlines, travel companies, and hotel chains, many of which are foreign owned. In short, the profits from tourism are often illusory.

P2: The infrastructure developed in conjunction with tourism is of benefit to other sectors of the economy. Improved air services and hotel accommodations, for example, assist not only the tourism industry but also other sectors of the economy. Tourism is an effective means of publicizing opportunities for investment; every planeload of visitors represents a new chance to acquaint potential investors with what Africa has to offer.

C2: Investment in tourism diverts funds from education, health, agriculture, and other sectors where greater benefits could be realized. Tourist development tends to be highly concentrated in a few places—resorts, national parks, and the capital city—and, thus, increases regional disparities in development.

P3: Tourism is an employment-intensive industry and is thus very beneficial for countries where unemployment is high and where there are few modern-sector job opportunities.

C3: Tourism creates menial and poorly paying jobs—as cooks, waiters, cleaners, and drivers, for example—that perpetuate the stereotype of Africans as willing servants. Illegal professions like prostitution and drug-dealing thrive in tourist areas.

P4: Tourism is a way of making visitors from the industrialized world more aware of the accomplishments and problems of Africa. For example, people who have visited Africa are a potential source of support in wealthier countries for the continuation of foreign aid.

C4: Most tourists get a very partial and distorted picture of the African continent. They visit only a few places, most of which have been chosen for their wildlife or beaches. Relatively few visitors are interested in seeing the disturbing realities of African underdevelopment. Tourist facilities are so segregated, in both social and spatial terms, that visitors have few opportunities to meet ordinary Africans.

P5: The development of tourism may help in the preservation of indigenous culture. For example, dances and other cultural ceremonies can be adapted to entertain visitors. Threatened craft industries may survive and even flourish.

cont.

Vignette 20.3. (*cont.*)

C5: What is promoted is often a caricature of African culture. The ceremonies, taken out of their cultural context and choreographed for tourist interest, lose their significance. Indigenous culture is frequently described by travel agencies in degrading terms. Consider these exerpts from a tourist brochure: "This tour is designed for viewing the African people . . . visits are made to primitive areas where one must expect inconvenience. . . . The most fascinating of the West African countries is the Cameroons where native behavior has existed without interruption since the beginning of time . . . two-thirds of the population still practices the ancient pagan religion of ritual figures, magic men and evil witches."

However, for most Europeans and North Americans, tourism in Africa is synonymous with the wildlife safari.

There are three zones where tourism is well established:

1. Along the West African coast from Senegal to Benin, where the emphasis has been on sun, sand, and sea (Senegal and Côte d'Ivoire attract some 200,000 tourists annually, mostly from France.)
2. In East Africa, especially Kenya and Tanzania (Kenya had 677,000 visitors in 1988, 60% of whom came from Europe to see wildlife and visit other tourist attractions.)

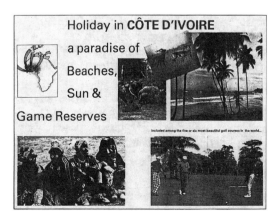

Figure 20.6. Tourism advertisement from Côte d'Ivoire. The traditional attractions of the African tourist industry—wildlife, sand and surf, and indigenous culture—are featured.

3. In South Africa and its English-speaking neighbors (Zambia, Zimbabwe, and Botswana each have over 100,000 visitors per year, most from South Africa. Wildlife viewing and the magnificent Victoria Falls are the primary attractions in Zimbabwe and Zambia. Lesotho and Swaziland and, until their demise in 1994, some homelands within South Africa, allowed the development of "sin tourism" catering to South Africans. Sun City in the now defunct Bophuthatswana Bantustan, sometimes referred to as "South Africa's Las Vegas," is the best known resort.)

International tourism remains quite insignificant in most of the rest of Africa south of the Sahara, even in Nigeria, Sudan, Zaire, and Ethiopia. There are diverse reasons for the dearth of tourists, including in certain cases economic decline and civil war. Large-scale tourism depends on the availability of infrastructural resources such as hotels and transportation systems acceptable to international tourists; such facilities are poorly developed in most of Africa.

The establishment of national parks and wildlife reserves has provided an environment in which wildlife populations have some protection from poachers and expanding human occupance. Nevertheless, the effect of poaching has increased as wildlife numbers beyond park boundaries have declined. Many of the sites chosen for parks are also places of unique

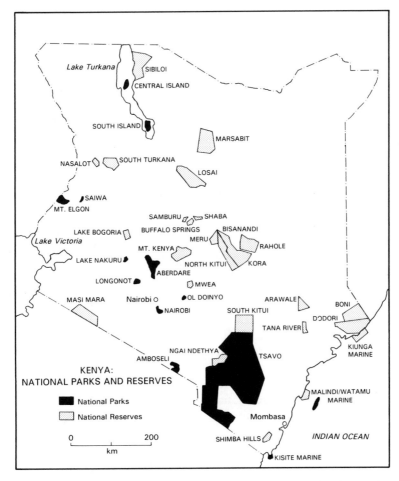

Figure 20.7. National parks and game reserves in Kenya. Several of these parks are the focal points of the country's thriving tourist industry. After *Msindi,* vol. 4, no. 1 (1993), p. 1.

scenic beauty. In Kenya, for example, national parks and reserves (Figure 20.7) are located beside scenic lakes, on the slopes of huge volcanic peaks, and within rift valleys, providing spectacular settings for wildlife observation.

In Africa, as in other parts of the Third World, tourism is widely seen as a potentially lucrative source of foreign exchange. However, there has been considerable debate about the amount of money that should go into tourism and about the nature of tourism's socioeconomic effects. Contrasting perspectives on five key points of debate are summarized in Vignette 20.3.

People versus Wildlife?

From afar, the question of protecting African wildlife and the environments that sustain it may seem like a simple matter of recognizing the importance of wildlife and having a strong commitment to protecting the resource. It is seldom so simple. Wildlife and humans are often in competition for the same scarce environmental and financial resources.

The utilization of wetland habitats provides an excellent example of the people-versus-wildlife dilemma. Africa's wetlands are crucial ecological resources. For example, a few relatively small wetlands located south of the Sahara are absolutely essential staging points for many species of migratory birds from Europe. However, these areas are also extremely important for primary producers, since they have fertile soils and water for irrigation. Farmers and herders seldom have viable alternatives to using these areas, even though the wildlife habitat is likely to be damaged in the process. "Debt-for-conservation" swaps, in theory, provide a means of protecting vulnerable wetlands. The problem, however, is that rural populations whose livelihoods are affected by such conservation efforts seldom receive just and adequate compensation.

In a similar way, the crisis of declining wildlife numbers from illegal and inadequately regulated hunting reflects a wider social and economic malaise. The traditional control over hunting formerly exercised by African societies as a means of resource management has been effectively eroded. Moreover, the declining economic situation provides a strong incentive for wildlife to be slaughtered for sale or for food. In short, the fate of Africa's wildlife and wildlife habitats cannot be separated from the political and economic condition of Africans.

Further Reading

The following sources are excellent introductions to zoogeography:

Attenborough, D., et al. *The Atlas of the Living World*. Boston: Houghton-Mifflin, 1989.
Durcell, L. *The State of the Ark*. Garden City, NY: Doubleday, 1986.
Kingdon, J. *East African Mammals: An Atlas of Evolution in Africa*. London: Academic, 1982.

The impact of colonial policy on wildlife is considered in the following sources:

Kjekshus, H. *Ecology, Control and Economic Development in East African History*. London: Heinemann, 1977.
Matzke, G. *Wildlife in Tanzanian Settlement Policy*. Syracuse, NY: Maxwell School, 1977.

The significance of wild game as food and experiences with game ranching are discussed in the following sources:

Jewell, P. A. "Ecology and management of game animals and domestic livestock in African savannas." In D. R. Harris, ed., *Human Economies in Savanna Environments*, pp. 353–381. London: Academic, 1982.
Pullan, R. A. "The utilization of wildlife for food in Africa: The Zambian experience." *Singapore Journal of Tropical Geography*, vol. 2 (1981), pp. 101–113.
Walker, B. H. "Game ranching in Africa." In B. H. Walker, ed., *Management of Semi-Arid Ecosystems*. Amsterdam, Netherlands: Elsevier, 1979, pp. 55–81.

The conservation of Africa's endangered species is discussed in the following sources:

Musambachime, M. "The fate of the Nile crocodile in African waters." *African Affairs*, vol. 86 (1987), pp. 197–207.
Penny, M. *Rhinos: Endangered Species*. New York: Facts on File, 1988.
Swanson, T. M., and E. Barbarier, eds. *Economics for the Wilds: Wildlife, Wildlands, Diversity and Development*. London: Earthscan, 1992.
Thornton, A. *To Save an Elephant: The Undercover Investigation into the Illegal Ivory Trade*. London: Doubleday, 1991.

Issues concerning the implications of conservation for rural communities are discussed in the following sources:

Child, G. F. T., and R. A. Heath. "Unravelling national parks in Zimbabwe: The implications for rural sustainability." *Society and Natural Resources*, vol. 3 (1990), pp. 215–222.
Dries, I. "Conservation of wetlands in Sierra Leone: Farmer's rationality opposed to government policy." *Landscape and Urban Planning*, vol. 20 (1991), pp. 223–229.
Enghoff, M. "Wildlife conservation, ecological strategies and pastoral communities: A contribution to the understanding of parks and people in East Africa." *Nomadic Peoples*, nos. 25–27 (1990), pp. 93–107.
Hackel, J. H. "Conservation attitudes in southern Africa: A comparison of KwaZulu and Swaziland." *Human Ecology*, vol. 18 (1990), pp. 203–209.
Kiss, A., ed. *Living with Wildlife: Wildlife Resource Management with Local Participation in Africa*. Washington, DC: World Bank, 1990.

21

✳

Vegetation as a Resource

Vegetation is an important source of products for both local and national economies. This chapter examines the use of botanic resources by the timber industry and in local economies as a source of energy, food, and raw materials. Finally, some of the economic and ecological implications of inappropriate development in vulnerable environments are considered.

The Economic Importance of Vegetation

Statistics on production in the forestry industry do not distinguish clearly between products produced and sold in the formal economy and those produced and sold within the informal sector. However, only 10% of the total production of industrial roundwood is exported; nine-tenths of what is harvested is destined for local use as building materials, furniture, and other products made of wood.

What is clear from Table 21.1 is that forestry is extremely important in both forested and savanna areas. Only 4 of the 10 largest producers of industrial roundwood have substantial areas of tropical forests. Countries like Kenya and Ethiopia are major wood producers, although they are, for the most part, arid. Thus, the future availability of adequate for-

estry resources will depend on the careful management of all ecosystems, not just the tropical forests.

Processed wood products–sawn wood and panels (plywood and similar products) and pulp and paper–account for only a small proportion of the industrial roundwood production in most African countries. It is only in South Africa, Nigeria, Côte d'Ivoire, and Cameroon that a substantial proportion of harvested wood is processed. In South Africa and Swaziland, the production of pulp and paper using softwood species is the most important sector in the forestry industry.

The Timber Industry

Some of the strongest, hardest, and most beautiful woods available to humankind are harvested from tropical forests. Mahogany, widely used to construct fine furniture and paneling, is the best known of the tropical woods. Tropical forests also contain dozens of other species that are exploited commercially for a variety of specialized uses.

The leading exporters of tropical hardwood, which together account for 80% of supplies, are Indonesia, Malaysia, the Philippines, Côte d'Ivoire, and Gabon. Although two African nations are among the top five exporters, Africa produces only 12% of tropical hardwoods

Table 21.1. Major Producers of Roundwood and Wood Products in Africa South of the Sahara, 1987 to 1989

| | Industrial Roundwood | | Processed wood products | | | |
| | | | Sawn wood | | Panels | |
	(1,000 m³)	Rank	(1,000 m³)	Rank	(1,000 m³)	Rank
South Africa	12,168	1	1,827	2	398	1
Nigeria	7,868	2	2,714	1	233	3
Côte d'Ivoire	3,362	3	775	3	260	2
Cameroon	2,730	4	652	4	80	5
Zaire	2,715	5	121	12	53	8
Sudan	2,030	6	13	–	2	–
Tanzania	1,947	7	156	10	13	12
Uganda	1,800	8	26	–	3	–
Ethiopia	1,759	9	39	–	15	11
Kenya	1,711	10	189	7	45	9

Source: World Resources Institute. *World Resources, 1992–93.* Oxford: Oxford University Press, 1992.

entering international trade. Most hardwood is exported from Africa as unprocessed logs, rather than as sawn lumber, plywood, or veneer. Among the leading exporters, only Côte d'Ivoire and Ghana sell less than half of their product as unprocessed logs (Table 21.2).

The responsibility of the timber industry for the destruction of forest ecosystems is a matter of some debate. The timber companies stress, correctly, that far more damage is done by agricultural clearance than by logging. Ecologists, however, point to the disproportionate damage caused by a timber industry that is only interested in a few select species scattered at extremely low density throughout a forest. While extracting these desired species, other vegetation is severely damaged; one study found that 55% of large trees were irreparably damaged by logging activities in which only 10% of large trees were harvested.

Not only are the ecological costs of logging very high, but the economic returns are surprisingly low. The price paid to producers of tropical hardwoods is negligible. The relatively small economic contribution of the timber industry is evident in Table 21.2; only five African countries derive more than 10% of their total export earnings from the sale of timber.

Longer-term prospects for tropical timber exports are poor. The desired species are increasingly scarce in accessible areas. They also take many decades to grow and are difficult to propagate artificially. Once the commercially valuable timber is gone, the timber trade will end, and some exporters may have to import hardwood. Zaire is the only African country with very large resources of yet unexploited timber. Although Zaire has the third largest

Table 21.2. Major African Exporters of Tropical Timber, 1989

	1989 Exports (U.S. $ million)	% Change 1979–1989	Logs as % of exports	Timber exports as % of all exports
Côte d'Ivoire	236	− 39.2	30.5	7.9
Gabon	131	+ 5.8	87.8	11.3
Congo	123	+202.0	82.9	14.5
Cameroon	100	− 31.0	72.0	11.1
Liberia	78	+ 2.6	89.7	21.1
Ghana	76	+ 80.9	31.6	7.5
Central African Republic	16	− 51.5	50.3	17.4

Source: FAO. *Forest Products Yearbook, 1990.*

Figure 21.1. Tropical hardwood for export, southern Côte d'Ivoire. While timber is Côte d'Ivoire's third largest export, longer-term prospects for the industry are poor because of the rapid depletion of Ivoirian forests. Photo: author.

area of tropical forest in the world, it produces only about 0.3% of Third World timber exports. The relative inaccessibility of the regions where these forests are found has thus far protected them from exploitation. However, as Amazonian and Southeast Asian forests are depleted, the forests of Zaire inevitably will be opened for business.

Vegetation as a Resource in Domestic Economies

Timber for export represents only a small proportion of the economic contribution of the forests. Natural vegetation is a source of countless useful products ranging from fever remedies and fishing nets to farming tools and fencing. Forest resources are particularly important in indigenous subsistence economies where the forest is literally equivalent to the building supply store, the specialty food shop, and the pharmacy.

The forest provides timbers and sawn wood for the construction of houses and other buildings. The thatch roofs of traditionally constructed houses are made from tall grass or, in the forest, from very large tree leaves. Most furniture is constructed out of wood by local carpenters. Various kitchen utensils, gardentools, and decorative objects are made from wood, gourds, seeds, and other products obtained from natural vegetation. Ceremonial objects such as masks, statues, and walking sticks are most frequently fashioned out of wood.

Fruits, nuts, tubers, and leaves from uncultivated plants are an important source of vitamins, minerals, fiber, and carbohydrates in African diets. Where natural foodstuffs are extensively used, diets are quite varied and are likely to be more nutritionally balanced than where such foods are seldom consumed. The natural environment is the source of many famine emergency foods–edibles that are seldom consumed except when preferred foodstuffs are unavailable–that have always been crucial for survival in drought-prone regions.

The Hausa people of Nigeria and Niger refer to the forest as "God's medicine cabinet," reasoning that cures for any human ailment are to be found there. In all African cultures

Figure 21.2. Local sawmill, eastern Zaire. Enterprises processing timber for local use make an important contribution to local and regional economies. Photo: A. Harder.

extensive use is made of herbal remedies. These traditional medicines continue to be extremely important, not only because of the inadequate development of modern health care but also because of patients' confidence in them. Modern science, knowing that many herbal medicines have verifiable medical effects, is increasing its research on tropical plants as a source for new drugs. While traditional healers are the true guardians of herbal knowledge, most rural Africans have some basic knowledge of how to prepare common herbal remedies.

A substantial proportion of these forest products is gathered, processed, and used within the household. While not bought or sold, these products are important to household self-sufficiency and sometimes even household survival. These same products are also gathered, processed, and sold as a source of income. While much of this trade occurs within local and regional markets, long-distance trade in forestry products is becoming increasingly important. This long-distance trade includes not only construction timbers, charcoal, and other products one would expect to be traded, but also forest foods and

traditional medicines; Nigeria, for example, has a bustling interregional and even international trade in wholesale quantities of herbal medicines to supply healers with ingredients that are not available locally.

Unlike the export timber trade, the domestic forest-based production is fully integrated into local economies and is labor intensive. Thus, the loss of areas of natural vegetation owing to human encroachment may pose a serious threat to household self-sufficiency as well as to the viability of forest-based production and trade.

Fuelwood

Africa is heavily dependent on wood as a source of energy. Wood accounts for only 10% of Asia's and 20% of Latin America's total energy consumption, but constitutes some three-quarters of the energy used in Africa. Biomass (wood, charcoal, and crop refuse) accounts for over half of the total energy consumed in every country except South Africa, Zimbabwe, and Botswana. In Tanzania, Ethiopia, Burundi, and Central African Republic, more than 90% of total national energy supply is from biomass.

The size of a country's population is closely related to the amount of fuelwood and charcoal that it produces and consumes. Nigeria, with a population of 90 million, accounts for almost one-quarter of the fuelwood and charcoal production of Africa south of the Sahara. Ethiopia, Sudan, Tanzania, and Kenya produce much more fuelwood and charcoal than countries such as Cameroon and Côte d'Ivoire, which, although better known for their forest resources, are also considerably less populous.

A major reason for the dominance of biomass energy is that wood was available until quite recently as virtually a free commodity. Even in urban areas, wood and charcoal have remained the cheapest sources of domestic energy. Moreover, the increased cost of petroleum during the 1970s severely limited the growth of fossil-fuel consumption. Thus, urban households and small industries that might have been expected to convert to more modern fuels have continued to rely on biomass energy.

While most biomass energy is used as a fuel for cooking, it is also an important source of energy for light industrial production. Smaller commercial enterprises—bakeries, brickworks, potteries, and metal forges—commonly use wood or charcoal as their primary source of energy. In Tanzania, where industry accounts for 17% of national energy consumption, biomass accounts for over four-fifths of the energy used by manufacturers (Table 21.4).

Table 21.3. Leading Producers of Fuelwood and Charcoal, 1987 to 1989

	Production (million m³)
1. Nigeria	97.1
2. Ethiopia	37.1
3. Kenya	32.5
4. Zaire	31.5
5. Tanzania	30.0
6. Sudan	19.6
7. Ghana	15.9
8. Mozambique	15.0
9. Uganda	12.1
10. Zambia	11.4
11. Cameroon	9.9
12. Côte d'Ivoire	9.4

Source: World Resources Institute. *World Resources, 1992–93.* Oxford: Oxford University Press, 1992.

With the rapid growth of cities, the business of selling wood and charcoal has become increasingly lucrative. As the hinterlands of major cities have been progressively deforested, particularly in drier savanna regions, wood has to be brought to the cities from farther and farther away. The consequent increases in transportation costs have raised the cost of fuelwood to urban consumers and encouraged the substitution of charcoal for unprocessed wood. Charcoal is much less bulky and thus, is less costly to transport. Unfortunately, using traditional African techniques, perhaps 60% of the energy contained in wood is lost when it is converted to charcoal.

As wood has become increasingly expensive and scarce and the ecological effects of

Table 21.4. Tanzania's Energy Usage (as Percentage of Total Consumption)

	Rural households	Agriculture	Urban households	Industry	Transport	Services	Total
Petroleum	1	1	1	2	5	*	10
Electricity	0	0	*	*	0	*	–
Coal, natural gas	0	0	0	*	0	0	–
Fuelwood	53	3	9	13	0	7	85
Charcoal	*	0	3	1	0	*	4
Other (e.g., crop refuse)	2	0	0	*	0	0	2
Total	55	4	13	17	5	7	

*Insignificant amount.
After B. Munslow, P. O'Keefe, A. Pankhurst, and P. Phillips. "Energy and development on the East African coast." *Ambio,* vol. 12 (1983), pp. 333–337.

Vignette 21.1. Farmland Trees

African farmed landscapes, whether in the tropical forest or the savanna, very commonly include a variety of randomly spaced trees that have been planted or have been permitted to grow naturally. These trees and shrubs provide a tremendous variety of foodstuffs, medicines, and other useful products. Products obtained from farmland trees may also provide substantial income; the locust-bean trees commonly found on savanna farmlands yield fruits that are used as a condiment and can provide several hundred dollars of income per year. A number of species are maintained because they contribute to soil fertility and improved crop yields. Research has shown that yields of sorghum and millet are doubled in the presence of the white acacia, which fixes nitrogen in the soil, provides humus through leaf fall, and attracts grazing cattle that fertilize the land with manure.

It is only recently that agricultural economists have begun to fully appreciate the importance of farmland trees for rural societies and economies. From their research has come a series of policies designed to encourage the development of agroforestry in Africa. Agroforestry is, in essence, a strategy for sustainable development encouraging the systematic integration of trees into farming systems. It is an attempt to understand, promote, and extend the use that African farmers and pastoralists have made of trees for thousands of years. As such, agroforestry builds upon the strengths of indigenous knowledge and methods of utilizing the environment and provides additional scientific justification for the protection of vegetation.

Table 21.5. Common Uses of Selected Farmland Trees of the West African Savanna

Silk cotton	• Kapok (silky fibres from seed pod) is used to make mattresses. • Wood is preferred for carving into utensils and tools. • Branches are "harvested" as firewood.
Baobab	• Young leaves are used as a green vegetable. • Fruits are eaten. • Inner bark is used to make rope.
Tamarind	• Fruits are used to flavor food. • Bark and leaves are used to treat stomach ailments. • It is preferred as a shade tree.
White acacia	• It is valued highly because it increases crop yields by fixing nitrogen in the soil. • Bark and roots are medicinal. • Leaves are dry-season fodder for livestock.
Shea butter	• Fruits provide an oil used for cooking, soap-making and as a medicine. • Dead wood is harvested as fuel.
Locust bean	• Fruits are used as a condiment. • It is leguminous and, thus, improves soil.

excessive fuelwood harvesting have become apparent, the fuelwood crisis has attracted more attention from development planners. Several approaches are being used to alleviate the crisis. In the short run, the development of more energy-efficient stoves helps to conserve energy. These stoves are up to five times as efficient as open fires for cooking. Nevertheless, the popularity of stoves has been limited because they are much less effective than open fires in providing warmth and light. Programs of tree planting for fuelwood use have been widely implemented to increase wood supplies (Vignette 21.2). Tree

Figure 21.3. Farmland trees, Jigawa State, Nigeria. Trees such as the white acacia and baobab, shown in the above photo, provide a variety of economic benefits for rural Africans. Photo: author.

planting is a useful medium-term solution, especially when it is integrated into peasant production systems. Large-scale tree planting in government or commercial plantations may help to improve fuelwood supply in urban areas. In the longer term, other types of energy such as hydroelectric, coal, solar, and wind, should increase in importance, especially for commercial enterprises and higher income households in urban areas.

Figure 21.4. Vegetation clearance, Côte d'Ivoire. The use of fire to clear brush has some immediate benefits for farmers and herders but has major environmental costs, such as the elimination of some species and increased soil erosion. Photo: CIDA: M. Faugere.

Vignette 21.2. Women's Tree-Planting Groups in Uganda

For rural women in Uganda, as elsewhere in Africa south of the Sahara, the environment is a vital source of resources to sustain themselves and their families. Because women are responsible for obtaining fuelwood, deforestation and the resulting scarcity of wood is of particular concern. In some parts of Uganda, rural women and children spend up to three hours per day gathering fuelwood.

The government of Uganda has become increasingly concerned about environmental protection and has stepped up efforts to increase public awareness of these issues. The formation of the Uganda Women's Tree Planting Movement(UWTPM) occurred in response to the government's public-education campaign. The objectives of UWTPM include encouraging women to plant trees as a source of energy and other useful products and increasing public awareness of the importance of environmental protection.

In Mpigi District near Kampala, women have responded to the messages of UWTPM and the government by coming together to form 34 tree-planting groups. These groups are small in size (from 10 to 35 members each) and have only women as members. The women have done so to ensure that their projects, and the expected benefits from tree planting, remain under their own control. One women explained it this way: "When you work with men, they make you do all the work and they have all the benefits."

The tree-planting groups in Mpigi District have experienced a number of difficulties. Some of these difficulties have been technical in nature, reflecting a lack of previous experience growing and transplanting seedlings. A number of the groups were able to address these problems by getting help from the District Forestry Officer. Another problem for many groups has been the severe shortage of land suitable for tree planting in this densely-populated region. Finally, since tree planting is a very long-term investment, the members have had to find ways to sustain their projects for several years until they have an opportunity for returns from the sale of fuelwood or other products. Some members have done so by selling seedlings, but this option has only been viable in communities located near the main roads where potential customers can be found.

Despite these problems, the organization of women's tree-planting groups has been a very positive development. The international media has helped to create the perception that Africans are the passive victims of environmental crises beyond their control and that the only potential solutions to these problems are coming from international aid agencies. This case study shows that Africans are very much involved in addressing issues of environmental degradation, mobilizing their own local resources to address local needs.

Based on D. H. Kasente. "Performance of Uganda Women Tree Planting Movement." Unpublished research report, Makerere University, Kampala, Uganda, 1991.

Ecological Concerns

Environmental research, the agitation of environmental pressure groups like Greenpeace and Friends of the Earth, and international symposia like the 1992 Earth Summit in Rio de Janeiro have heightened global concern about environmental degradation. The destruction of tropical rain forests and desertification have been identified as particularly important threats to the future of the planet. Yet, as Table 21.6 shows, all African ecosystems have suffered severe degradation. According to the study on which this table is based, over the course of human history human intervention is responsible for the loss of about six-

Table 21.6. Impact of Humans on African Ecosystems

	Original area (km²)	Area remaining (km²)	Percentage remaining	Percentage protected
Dry forests	8,216,808	3,415,988	41.6	15.0
Moist forests	4,699,704	1,867,629	39.7	7.1
Savanna	6,954,875	2,835,196	40.8	10.5
Scrub/Desert	176,600	172,630	97.8	10.1
Wetland/Marsh	61,700	43,770	70.9	5.4
Mangroves	87,870	39,182	44.6	2.9

Based on World Resources Institute. *World Resources, 1990–91.* Oxford: Oxford University Press, 1991, p. 124.

tenths of the potential area of each of the three major nondesert ecosystems of Africa south of the Sahara.

Deforestation

It has been estimated that the global area of tropical forest decreases by an average of 157,000 sq km annually, an area equal to that of England and Wales. If the present rate of deforestation is maintained, it is projected that all tropical forests may disappear by the middle of the 21st century. In Brazil, Indonesia, and elsewhere, vast areas of tropical forest are threatened by schemes, sanctioned by national governments and supported by some international development agencies, to clear land for peasant resettlement, plantations, and cattle ranches.

The clearance of tropical forests has global as well as local implications. Tropical-forest ecosystems have incredible biological diversity; when plant species become extinct, humanity is deprived forever of their potential benefits—for example, the discovery of significant new medicines. Moreover, the removal of forest cover facilitates increased soil erosion and soil compaction, thus reducing agricultural productivity. Regional climatic change, including higher temperatures and lower rainfall has been observed in deforested environments.

As noted in Chapter 2 (Vignette 2.2), deforestation has also been linked to predicted changes in the climate of the earth—the greenhouse effect. With forest clearance, carbon stored in vegetation is released into the atmosphere, while the forest's capacity to create oxygen is reduced. Higher concentrations of greenhouse gases are expected to produce hotter and drier climates in the savanna and semidesert ecosystems of Africa and other parts of the world. Vegetation will come under increasing stress, not only because of the harsher environmental conditions but also because of the effects of increasing human populations and decreasing agricultural productivity.

Although there have been no development projects in Africa comparable in size to those in Brazil and Indonesia, Africa's tropical forests are nevertheless under threat. Between 1980 and 1990, Africa lost an estimated 5 million ha of tropical forest per annum, a loss of 0.8% of the total area each year. In West Africa, the forest has been in retreat for centuries. However, the rate of deforestation has accelerated—to 2.1% annually—because of an ever-growing demand for farmland to support relatively high population densities. Forests in West Africa are also in danger because they occupy fairly small blocks of territory. In contrast, Zaire's forests are less immediately threatened; they occupy a huge area, have very low population densities, and are difficult to penetrate because of poor transport development.

Desertification

The Sahelian drought of the 1970s caused greatly increased concern about environmental degradation in general and desertification in particular. Was the Sahelian drought evidence of larger changes in world climate? Was the Sahara literally advancing southward, envelop-

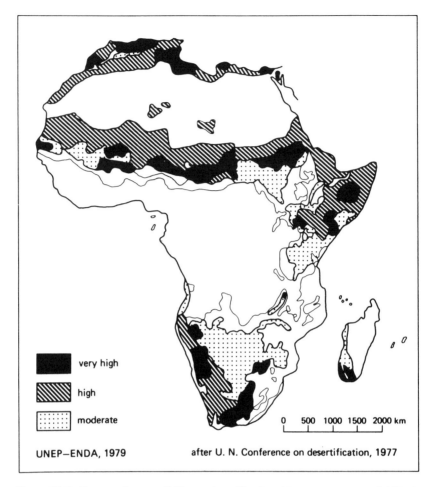

Figure 21.5. Degree of susceptibility to desertification. Up to one-quarter of Africa's land area, including large areas not located along the desert fringe, is susceptible to degradation. Source: Environmental Development Action (ENDA). *Environment and Development in Africa.* Oxford: Oxford University Press, 1981, p. 9. ©1981 by United Nations Environment Programme (UNEP) and ENDA. Reprinted by permission.

ing communities along the way? To what extent were human activities responsible for the apparent growth of desert-like conditions? Could the process of desertification be reversed, or at least controlled?

Desertification is characterized by a range of changes to ecosystems, including soil erosion by wind, the formation of sand dunes, the disappearance or degradation of vegetation, and the loss of soil moisture. The cumulative effect of these changes is "the diminution or destruction of the biological potential of the land," ultimately producing desertlike conditions of soil and vegetation in

areas beyond the climatic desert. This definition, which came from the United Nations Conference on Desertification held in Nairobi in 1977, did not end the debate about the meaning of desertification. Some studies have used the term to mean the *process* of land degradation, whereas others view it as the *end result* of a process of change. All agree that desertification has both climatic and human dimensions; social scientists and climatologists often disagree, though, about the relative importance of the two dimensions. Climatologists are also divided as to whether desertification is linked to climate variability (recur-

Vignette 21.3. The Causes of Desertification: A Kenyan Case Study

Who is to blame for land degradation in marginal environments? Is it the people who inhabit these regions or does the blame lie elsewhere? The case of the Rendille pastoralists who live east of Lake Turkana in northern Kenya is relevant to the questions posed above.

The Rendille occupy a marginal semidesert environment with average annual rainfall ranging from 200 to 300 mm per annum. Much of the area that they occupy shows signs of severe stress. During the droughts of the early 1970s they lost large numbers of camels, goats, sheep, and cattle upon which they are dependent.

Taken at face value, resource management decisions made by the Rendille seem to account for the widespread ecological damage. Grazing lands are used unevenly; perhaps one-fifth of the Rendille's territory is overgrazed, but considerable grazing land remains virtually unused. This uneven pattern of grazing is related to the following factors:

- The Rendille opt for grazing areas relatively close to springs or easily accessible waterholes and only as a last resort move to pastures where much effort is needed to get water.
- They avoid areas where cattle raiding occurs most frequently.
- The development of permanent settlements has contributed to uneven use and ecological damage around settlement sites.

Analyzing the behavior of the Rendille from their own perspective suggests other conclusions, however. They seem less the careless destroyers of their own sustenance base than the victims of policies and systems over which they have no control. Far from urban centers and dependent on small, uncertain local markets to sell their animals, the Rendille are forced to maintain large herds and maximize their gains in good years to survive through periodic droughts. They receive poor prices for their livestock—one-third to one-half of the Nairobi price—but must pay very high prices for the products that they purchase. These very unfavorable terms of trade are a strong disincentive for the Rendille to invest extra labor and capital to open up new pastures and watering holes in underutilized areas.

For the Rendille, government policies have been part of the problem, not the solution. When the first development projects were initiated in the late 1960s, the focus was on cattle ranching. Not only were cattle a dubious choice for these vulnerable lands, but government planners virtually ignored the existing Rendille economy with its focus on raising camels, goats, and sheep. Moreover, restrictions on livestock exports and policies designed to ensure low food prices for urban consumers have condemned the Rendille to continuing poverty.

In Rendille country, as in other parts of Africa threatened with ecological disaster, policy makers must recognize the need for solutions that address both facets of the ecological crisis: Not only do fragile lands need to be protected, but the fragile societies and economies dependent on these resources need careful assistance if they are to survive.

Based on M. O'Leary. "Ecological villains or economic victims: The case of the Rendille of northern Kenya," *Desertification Control*, no. 11 (1984), pp. 17–21.

rent droughts) or to a longer term process of climate change (global warming).

The following definition attempts to bridge the gap between the scientific and development communities: "Desertification, the process of land degradation characteristic of arid, semi-arid and sub-humid areas of the world, is largely human-induced and is normally exacerbated by adverse climatic conditions such as prolonged drought or dessication, which enable it to strike at the land resource base by weakening the physical, biological and economic potential of the land, thereby severely reducing or curtailing overall productivity" (R. S. Odingo. "The definition of desertification and programmatic consequences for UNEP and the international community." *Desertification Control Bulletin*, no.18 (1990), p. 47).

The human processes that may give rise to desertification are very diverse. Most explan-

ations of ecosystem degradation have focused on the pressures exerted by the rapid growth of human and animal populations and the resultant need to extend and intensify resource utilization. Serious, if not irreversible, ecological damage results when more land is cleared for agriculture, more firewood is harvested, and more livestock is kept.

Michael Mortimore has put forward a model that indicates how the recurrent cycles of land degradation and deepening economic crisis may be initiated in marginal environments with substantial numbers of farmers and herders (Figure 21.6). Under natural conditions, the environment is able to recover without lasting harm after a year of drought. With human occupancy, however, things are different. To survive in the wake of crop failures and animal deaths, farmers and herders are forced to sell whatever property they have and to cut firewood for sale, thus putting the surviving

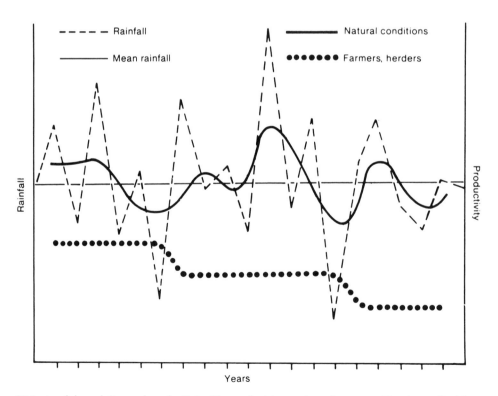

Figure 21.6. Land degradation and productivity. Times of crisis may force farmers and herders to liquidate natural capital in order to survive; the end result is a reduction in the environment's carrying capacity. Source: M. Mortimore. "Shifting sands and human sorrow: Social response to drought and desertification." *Desertification Control Bulletin,* no. 14 (1987), pp. 1–14. ©1987 by UNEP. Reprinted by permission.

Figure 21.7. Cultivating tree seedlings, Ethiopia. Massive tree-planting campaigns have been pursued aggressively in several countries as a strategy for protecting endangered environments. Photo: M. Peters.

woodland under increasing pressure. In subsequent seasons, crop yields decline because manure is inadequate. More land has to be cultivated to compensate for lower yields, fallow periods decline, and the area of unfarmed woodland decreases. Meanwhile, pastoralists increase their herds rapidly to replace animals lost during the drought. Subsequent droughts bring about further decreases in productivity and increasing social and economic crisis for the communities affected. Rapid population growth brings further destabilization to this unstable system.

The population of the Sahel and of other dry savanna regions began to increase markedly during the latter part of the colonial era. Farmers and herders were encouraged to occupy more and more of these marginal environments by three decades of above-average rainfall in the Sahel, by relatively good prices for groundnuts and other crops, and by the construction of roads and wells in sparsely populated areas. Moreover, migration out of more densely settled areas was stimulated by increasing pressure on the resource base.

It is not enough, however, to attribute the degradation of arid ecosystems only to overpopulation and naive development. Despite recurrent droughts, large-scale investments in cattle ranches and irrigation schemes to produce for export markets have occurred in certain marginal, semidesert regions (e.g., in Senegal and Botswana). Such investments have been possible only because of the compliance of some African governments and the support of international development agencies. Feasibility studies for such projects have often discounted both the wider ecological implications of intensive, large-scale development, and the effect of these projects on peasant farmers and pastoralists. Local farmers and pastoralists have been displaced from the most productive lands and forced to occupy marginal areas susceptible to ecological damage, where the risks of crop failure and hunger are especially high.

Sustainable Alternatives

African ecosystems, particularly in tropical rain forests and drier savannas, are in imminent

Figure 21.8. Tending a new windbreak, Burkina Faso. Windbreaks improve crop yields by reducing both soil erosion and evapotranspiration; they also provide a source of fuelwood. Photo: CIDA: D. Barbour.

danger of irreversible damage. Vast areas have already suffered irreparable damage because of inappropriate use of vulnerable environments.

Africa's natural resources are vital to the health – indeed the survival – of rural societies and economies and, in a more general sense, the well-being of every African nation. What distinguishes Africa from most other global regions threatened by environmental degradation is the large number of people living in African regions where the productivity of the land has already declined markedly and where very few resources are available to cope with crisis situations or to implement appropriate changes.

One encouraging development in recent years has been the growing understanding among development planners of the importance of vegetation in African rural economies. Research on agroforestry has begun to develop promising new techniques to permit development that is environmentally and economically sustainable. The development of alley cropping as a stable alternative to shifting cultivation has been an especially important innovation. Establishing shelter belts and helping communities to undertake tree-planting projects help to address the related problems of desertification and fuelwood shortage.

What is much more important than new technology, however, is a commitment to sustainable approaches to development – approaches that are holistic in orientation, that are compatable with the needs, financial resources, and cultural perspectives of ordinary Africans, and that are highly sensitive to possible immediate and longer term effects on the environment.

Further Reading

For data on forest industries and studies on the economic development of forest resources, see the following sources:

FAO. *Yearbook of Forest Production*. Rome: FAO, published annually.

Christianson, C., and J. Ashuvud. "Heavy industry in a rural tropical ecosystem." *Ambio*, vol. 14 (1985), pp. 122–133.

The nature and importance of agroforestry is discussed in following sources:

Agroforestry Systems (journal).

Chambers, R., and M. Leach. "Trees as savings and security for the rural poor." *Unasylva,* no. 161 (1990), pp. 39–52.

Cook, C. C., and M. Grut. *Agroforestry in sub-Saharan Africa: A Farmer's Perspective.* Washington, DC: World Bank, 1989.

Raintree, J. B. *Land, Trees and Tenure.* Madison, WI: Land Tenure Center, 1987.

The following sources focus on Africa's fuelwood crisis:

Baidya, K. N. "Firewood shortage: Ecoclimatic disasters in the Third World." *Journal of Environmental Studies,* vol. 22 (1984), pp. 255–272.

Cline-Cole, R., H. A. C. Main, and J. Nichol. "On fuelwood consumption, population dynamics and deforestation in Africa." *World Development,* vol. 18 (1990), pp. 513–518.

Foley, G, "Wood fuel and conventional fuel demands in the Developing World." *Ambio,* vol. 14 (1985), pp. 253–258.

Leach, G., and R. Mears. *Beyond the Woodfuel Crisis: People, Land and Trees in Africa.* London: Earthscan, 1988.

Patterns and processes of deforestation are discussed in the following sources:

Guppy, N. "Tropical deforestation: A global view." *Foreign Affairs,* vol. 62 (1984), pp. 928–965.

Plumwood, V., and R. Routley. "World rainforest destruction: The social factors." *The Ecologist,* vol. 12 (1982), pp. 4–22.

Tropical Forests: A Call for Action. New York: World Resources Institute, 1985.

Whitlow, R. "Man's impact on vegetation: The African experience." In K. J. Gregory, and D. E. Walling, eds., *Human Activity and Environmental Processes.* Chichester, England: Wiley, 1987.

For more information about desertification, see the following sources:

Bullwinkle, D. A. "Drought and desertification of the African continent: A bibliography." *Current Bibliography on African Affairs,* vol. 16 (1983–1984), pp. 279–297.

Glantz, M. H., ed. *Desertification: Environmental Degradation in and Around Foreign Lands.* Boulder, CO: Westview, 1977.

Grainger, A. *Desertification.* London: Earthscan, 1982.

Hare, F. K. "Recent climatic experiences in the arid and semi-arid lands." *Desertification Control,* no. 10 (1984), pp.15–22.

Mortimore, M. "Shifting sands and human sorrow: Social response to drought and desertification." *Desertification Control Bulletin,* no. 14 (1987), pp. 1–14.

Odingo, R. S. "The definition of desertification and programmatic consequences for UNEP and the international community." *Desertification Control Bulletin,* no. 18 (1990), pp. 31–50.

AFRICAN ECONOMIES

The chapters in this section survey several aspects of African economic development at three levels: Africa within the world economy, national economic development, and community/local development.

Chapter 21 examines why Africa occupies such a marginal and vulnerable position in the global economy. The dependence on a small number of primary-product exports, which are subject to uncertain demand and prices in the global marketplace, has remained a source of economic weakness since the colonial era. More recently, Africa's position has become even more tenuous owing to cutbacks in aid and investment and a growing debt burden. The economic weakness of African countries helps to account for their difficulty in achieving the sustained progress for which all have struggled.

In Chapter 22, the relation between ideology and development is explored. During the first three decades of the postcolonial era, African countries experimented with three broad approaches to development, each characterized by its own set of priorities, strategies, and outcomes. Socialist states such as Tanzania and capitalist countries such as Kenya purposefully followed very different development paths, which are clearly reflected in the economic, social, and political institutions. In recent years, structural adjustment has emerged as a new "unifying" ideology, supplanting the old ideologies of development in most countries. However, structural adjustment may be seen as not just a set of strategies or even an ideology, but rather as a negation of African sovereignty.

In Chapter 24, the focus shifts to development at a local level. The recent growth of enthusiasm among development specialists in grassroots development initiatives needs to be examined critically. On the one hand, "development from within" correctly recognizes that communities can achieve much when they mobilize their own resources to address their own self-identified needs. On the other hand, the emphasis on self-reliance threatens to become an excuse for African governments and international development agencies to absolve themselves of responsibility for local development. While the recognition of what local groups can accomplish is important, it is neither a panacea nor a substitute for appropriate macroscale initiatives.

22

Africa in the World Economy

In a 1976 article entitled "The Three Stages of African Involvement in the World-Economy," Immanuel Wallerstein forecasted an African future shaped by a global economic crisis of excess industrial capacity, economic contraction, and depression. He predicted that the African states with the greatest industrial and strategic raw-material capacity–notably South Africa, Nigeria, and Zaire–would prosper and experience industrial growth. For the truly peripheral areas, he forecast declining demand for nonessential exports, increasingly serious food crises, acute suffering, and social and economic disintegration. This would set the stage for the future development of mechanized primary production, controlled by multinational and state corporations, ready to supply raw materials whenever the next stage of world economic growth began.

Almost two decades later, much of what Wallerstein predicted seems to be taking place. The global organization of industry has changed, with production increasingly shifting from the old cores to newly industrializing countries. The African periphery has had a dramatic decline in economic fortunes, as well as increasingly serious crises of survival. What has not transpired is the predicted growth and relative prosperity of Africa's stronger economies. In Nigeria, for example, lower demand and lower world prices for petroleum have brought increased indebtedness, reduced industrial production, and a growing range of social problems.

This chapter examines a number of aspects of Africa's involvement in the world economy, focusing especially on trade, aid, debt, and the role of multinational corporations. It shows not only that Africa is peripheral to the world economy, but also that its position has become progressively weaker. As countries have become less and less able to exert meaningful control over their own destinies, new forms of neocolonial control of African development have emerged.

The Role of Africa South of the Sahara in World Trade

As noted above, Africa's role in world trade as a supplier of raw materials and a consumer of imported industrial goods was established in the precolonial era and solidified after the colonial conquest. Much of colonial policy was preoccupied with bringing about an increase in raw-material production and exports by whatever means necessary. The development of industry, except for the primary processing of raw materials for export, was actively discouraged; African-based industry would provide unwelcome competition for the

Vignette 22.1. If Countries Were Companies: The Wealth of African Nations

The New State of the World Atlas, by Michael Kidron and Ronald Segal, contains many thought-provoking maps. Figure 30 in the book compares the sales incomes of the world's largest companies to the gross domestic products of countries for the year 1981. The map underscored the relative poverty, and hence, economic and political weakness of many states, particularly in the Third World.

Figure 22.1 provides a similar comparison of countries and companies, in this case relating the GDPs of African nations to the sales incomes of the 500 largest American companies in 1989. According to *Fortune,* General Motors, with sales of about $127 billion, was the largest American company in 1989. Affiliated Publications ranked 500th, with annual sales of $543 million.

Equating GDPs and sales incomes, only 2 countries in Africa south of the Sahara would rank among the top 25 American corporations. South Africa had a GDP of about $80 billion in 1989, equivalent to 4th place among American corporations (between Exxon and IBM). Nigeria's GDP of about $29 billion is equivalent to the sales of the 12th-ranked corporation. Only two more countries, Cameroon and Zaire, have GDPs as large as the

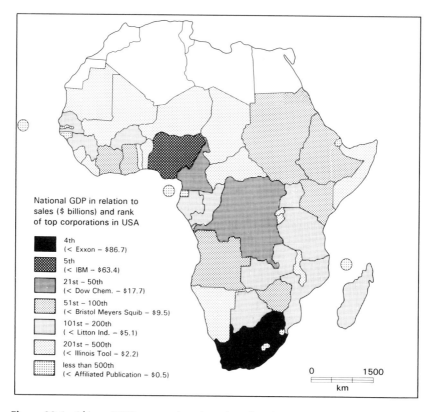

National GDP in relation to sales ($ billions) and rank of top corporations in USA

- 4th (< Exxon – $86.7)
- 5th (< IBM – $63.4)
- 21st – 50th (< Dow Chem. – $17.7)
- 51st – 100th (< Bristol Meyers Squib – $9.5)
- 101st – 200th (< Litton Ind. – $5.1)
- 201st – 500th (< Illinois Tool – $2.2)
- less than 500th (< Affiliated Publication – $0.5)

Figure 22.1. African GDPs equated to the sales of major corporations in USA, 1989. Even the largest African economies pale in comparison to the sales of major corporations in USA. Data sources: "The Fortune 500." *Fortune.* April 23, 1990. World Bank. *World Development Report, 1991.*

cont.

Vignette 22.1. (cont.)

---

almost $9.5 billion sales of Bristol-Myers Squibb that was ranked 50th among American corporations. A total of 22 African countries have GDPs greater than the approximate $2 billion in sales of Illinois Tool Works, *Fortune's* 200th-ranked American company. Eight countries, including Lesotho, Swaziland, and Gambia, would not make the top 500 if they were corporations.

Data such as these highlight several important facts. First, they show the immense economic power wielded by large corporations and demonstrate why these corporations have been able to exercise such great political influence. Second, they provide dramatic evidence of the economic and, hence, political weakness of African states. It is little wonder, given the paucity of resources at their command, that African states have been unable to address more than a portion of the myriad demands of their citizens for social and economic development. Third, the data show a large gap between the resources available to the largest and best-developed economies—in particular South Africa and Nigeria—and those of the smallest and least developed countries. These disparities help to account for the different levels of influence of various African countries, both on the continent and in the world.

---

colonialists' own industrial enterprises. In short, each colony was established as a fully dependent satellite of its colonial metropole in matters of trade and economic development.

Despite more than three decades of efforts by African countries to escape the straight jacket of dependent trade relation, there has been little fundamental change. African countries continue to be dependent on trade relation over which they have no real control. Overall, their position in the world economy has declined, rather than grown stronger. In fact, during the 1980 to 1989 period, the value of exports from Africa south of the Sahara (excluding South Africa) declined by an average of 4.5% per year. Its share of total world primary commodity exports fell between 1980 and 1990 from 10.4 to 4.1%.

As of 1990, 10 countries obtained at least 95% of their export earnings from the three leading export commodities. The largest single commodity accounted for 95% or more of exports in 4 countries: Nigeria (petroleum), Uganda (coffee), Zambia (copper), and Guinea (bauxite). There were only 15 countries in which the three leading exports accounted for less than two-thirds of the total; in 7 of

these countries less than half of total earnings came from the top three exports (see Figure 22.2).

Countries that are highly dependent on one or a small number of export commodities are vulnerable to demand and price fluctuations on the world market. An increase in the price may bring temporary prosperity but also may bring higher inflation and debt that accentuate the effect of subsequent price declines. In the case of agricultural economies, countries depending on one or two export commodities may be severely affected by droughts, crop diseases, or other natural disasters that reduce the quantity or quality of the harvest.

Several countries, most notably Côte d'Ivoire and Kenya, have been very successful in diversifying their farm exports. However, their recent economic difficulties show that diversification provides very imperfect protection from swings in the world market, in large part because demand and prices for broad categories of commodities tend to rise and fall in unison. Meanwhile, a number of other countries have become progressively less, rather than more, diversified over time. Nigeria is a good example: Although its export economy was quite small but diversified prior to

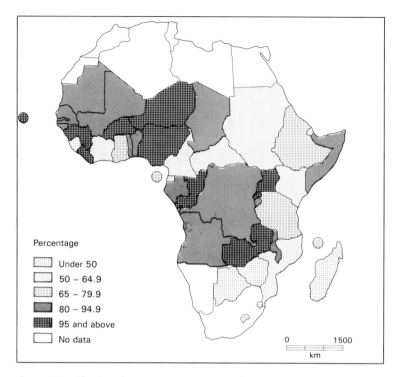

Figure 22.2. The three largest exports as a percentage of total exports. Most countries are highly dependent on earnings from three or fewer export products. Data source: United Nations Conference on Trade and Development (UNCTAD). *Commodity Yearbook 1990.* New York: United Nations, 1991.

the mid-1960s, its exports now consist almost entirely of one commodity, petroleum.

One of the problems with diversification has been that it has tended to involve the production of a wider range of "traditional" agricultural and mineral commodities. As such, diversification may succeed primarily in increasing market supply and lowering the world price for a particular commodity. The more marginal producers of the commodity become the main losers, no longer able to compete effectively. Market shifts that result in minor gains for commodity *consumers* may spell disaster for *producers* who have "all of their eggs in one basket."

Most African commodities tend to be price inelastic; declines in price do not usually bring large increases in demand. This inelasticity applies both to foodstuffs such as coffee and cocoa and to industrial raw materials such as copper and iron ore, demand for which depends much more on the overall health of the

world industrial economy than on the cost of raw materials. The development of lower cost or more adaptable substitute materials has been a further source of trouble for some commodities.

Producers of several commodities, including coffee, cocoa, copper, and petroleum, have attempted to establish cartels to regulate market supply and price. In the 1970s, OPEC had some notable success, but, in general, the establishment of cartels has not brought the stability and prosperity that commodity producers had envisaged.

The overall effect of dependence on selling in a world market is evident in Table 22.1, which shows trends in selected countries' terms of trade (value of exports relative to the value of imports) and purchasing power of their exports (i.e., combining world price and total production). While terms of trade improved markedly for some, especially the petroleum producers until the early 1980s, the

Table 22.1. Terms of Trade and Purchasing Power of Exports for Selected Countries, 1970 to 1989 (Index: 1980 = 100)

	Terms of trade					Purchasing power of exports				
	1970	1975	1980	1985	1990	1970	1975	1980	1985	1990
Oil producers										
Angola	45	63	100	102	68	75	88	100	135	170
Nigeria	19	56	100	93	64	16	53	100	60	43
Mineral producers										
Liberia	161	126	100	101	104	137	118	100	85	52
Zaire	179	98	100	90	86	173	90	100	67	52
Agricultural producers										
Côte d'Ivoire	83	76	100	85	62	56	66	100	106	81
Kenya	79	85	100	91	66	100	88	100	76	68
Mozambique	95	113	100	94	99	218	132	100	31	39
Tanzania	94	100	100	89	65	187	126	100	78	71

Source: UNCTAD. *Handbook of International Trade and Development Statistics 1992.* New York: United Nations, 1993.

terms have since declined for virtually all countries. In the mineral-dependent economies of Liberia and Zaire, the terms of trade declined quite dramatically from 1970 to 1990. The primary problem for Africa is simple: The prices of both exports from Africa and imports to Africa are effectively established in London, New York, and other major centers of the world economy. African countries cannot predict, much less control, the value of their commodities on the world market, and so cannot undertake medium- to long-range development planning with any certainty.

Table 22.1 shows the dramatic decline of

Figure 22.3. The port of Dar es Salaam, Tanzania. The major seaports are critical points of linkage between the externally oriented modern economies of Africa and the outside world. Photo: CIDA.

purchasing power in African economies owing to lower export returns, especially during
the latter part of the 1980s. In Nigeria and
Mozambique, the purchasing power of 1990
exports was well under half of what it had been
in 1980. Although the decline in export purchasing power was less severe in the other
countries considered, it has been sufficient in
all to retard economic development and to create severe balance of payments problems.

Trade between the countries of Africa and
the members of the European Community has
been governed since the mid-1970s by a series of agreements known as the Lomé Conventions. These agreements have been
notable for their recognition of some of the
problems identified above. Under the Lomé
Conventions, tariffs and other trade barriers
restricting African access to European markets, particularly for certain semiprocessed
goods, have been progressively removed. As
well, a stabilization fund has been established
to compensate countries whose major exports
are adversely affected by declining market
prices. While the Lomé Conventions have at
least tried to address a number of important
issues, they have not been sufficient to alleviate Africa's steadily deteriorating trading position in the world marketplace.

African countries have attempted since independence to reduce their dependence on
imported goods through a strategy of import
substitute industrialization. Industrial production has certainly increased, and many consumer goods and some products for the
industrial sector are now made in Africa.
However, this industrialization has brought a
new form of dependency—namely, a dependency on imported technology, expertise, and,
in many cases, production inputs. For example, spare parts to keep machinery in working condition are available from very few
sources. With the economic downturn in recent years, funds for the purchase of spare
parts and other essential inputs for industrial
production have been in short supply. As a
result, the majority of the industrial capacity
of numerous African countries is now idle.

Africa accounts for only 0.4% of total world
exports of manufactured goods. The continent
has remained virtually untouched by the global
reorganization of production that has brought
about the rapid industrialization of East Asia,
Mexico, and certain other countries.

Compared to the colonial era, African countries are much less closely tied to a single trading partner. A significant portion of African
trade now is with the newer industrializing
countries of Brazil, India, Korea, and China,
but over three-quarters of African exports still
go to the older industrialized countries. The
long-held aspiration of African countries to
reduce their dependency on outsiders by increasing intra-African trade has not made great
progress. Less than 7% of trade is between
countries within Africa south of the Sahara.

Aid, Debt, and Adjustment: In One Hand and Out the Other

Since the late 1970s it has become increasingly difficult to discuss meaningfully the role
of foreign aid in African development without
reference to the subjects of debt and structural adjustment. Most official development

Table 22.2. Official Development Assistance to Selected Countries, 1990

	U.S.$ million	U.S.$ per capita	As % of GNP
Nigeria	234	2.0	0.7
Ethiopia	888	17.4	14.6
Ghana	456	31.2	7.4
Zambia	438	54.0	14.0
Mozambique	946	60.2	65.7
Lesotho	138	78.0	24.5
Botswana	148	118.2	5.5
All of Africa S. of Sahara	16,538	33.1	10.0

Source: World Bank. *World Development Report, 1992* (Table 20).

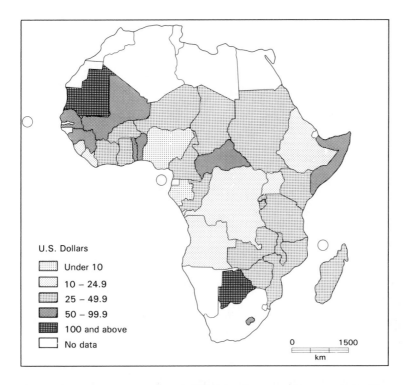

Figure 22.4. Receipts per capita of official development assistance, 1989. Data source: World Bank. *World Development Report, 1991.* New York: Oxford University Press, 1991.

assistance to Africa has, in recent years, been targeted toward the alleviation of debt-related crises, rather than such "development" objectives as improving social welfare and increasing the productive capacity of regional, national, and local economies. Of course, this critique would be disputed by many development planners, especially those working for the IMF and World Bank. They argue that current aid and structural-adjustment policies are creating the preconditions for economic growth and progress and that without appropriate adjustment Africa's economic crises will only deepen.

In 1989, Africa south of the Sahara received a total of $16.5 million in official development assistance (ODA). This amounted to $33.10 per capita, or 10.1% of the GNP of the continent (Table 22.2). This assistance was very unevenly distributed, ranging from only $2 per capita in Nigeria to over $100 per capita in Botswana. While ODA is equivalent to less than 15% of the GNPs of most countries, it

equals almost two-thirds of the GNP in war-ravaged Mozambique.

Despite the often repeated commitment of aid donors to give priority to the least developed countries in the allocation of assistance, the correlation between need and the distribution of ODA funds is very weak. Botswana, with a thriving mining sector and GNP per capita of $2,500, received about seven times as much ODA per capita as Ethiopia, a country coping with extreme economic, social, and environmental crises and having a per capita income of only $100.

The provision of aid changed dramatically in the mid-1980s, following the emergence of the Third World debt crisis. Mexico announced that it would be forced to default on its loan-repayment commitments. It became obvious that the international banking system was seriously threatened by the possibility of a mass default by several major borrowers. This crisis had developed in the 1970s and early 1980s when international banks had lent

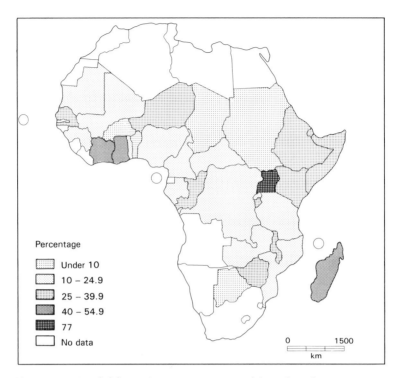

Figure 22.5. Total debt service as a percentage of the value of exports, 1989. Data source: World Bank. *World Development Report, 1991.* New York: Oxford University Press, 1991.

huge amounts to the Third World, often for very risky ventures. The Mexican crisis of 1985 was patched over by means of the Baker Plan, whereby an additional $40 billion was to be lent to the most heavily indebted nations—thus, in effect, buying time for the banks. American financial support for this scheme was made contingent upon the World Bank's and IMF's forcing recipient countries to implement harsh structural adjustment policies. Failure to adhere to the prescribed policy regimen would result in a total withdrawal of financial support from all donors. Thus, heavily indebted nations had little option but to accept the neocolonial intrusion of the IMF and World Bank into their affairs. An increasing proportion of ODA was, in effect, new loans to meet repayment and interest obligations on old loans.

The data in Table 22.3 point to the changing role of the IMF and World Bank. Since the mid-1980s both have been net *recipients* of funds from Africa south of the Sahara. In 1989 they collected $1.1 billion more in debt repayment and interest than they provided in new loans. The decline in net transfers from the IMF and World Bank has been offset by increased lending from the International Development Association (IDA). Support from the IDA is mostly targeted at the poorest countries and is on somewhat more favorable terms, but it is still in the form of *loans* that will have to be repaid. Meanwhile, loans from bilateral (country to country) and multilateral (e.g., United Nations agencies and the European Community) sources have not increased. Although grants appear to have grown during the 1980s, much of this assistance was in forms that did not contribute directly to African development—emergency food aid and military assistance, for example.

Much has been written about the dilemmas of aid: for example, about the costs to recipients of tied aid programs designed as much to provide a market for donor nations' products as to bring development to the Third World.

Table 22.3. Net External Transfers to Africa South of the Sahara from the IMF, World Bank, and Other Sources (U.S.$ million)[a]

	1980	1983	1985	1987	1989
IMF/IDA/World Bank					
International Monetary Fund	730	879	−434	−863	−728
International Development Association	403	593	802	1,570	1,574
World Bank	72	270	31	− 75	−391
Other net transfers (long-term debt)					
Multilateral	707	664	487	709	607
Bilateral	1,657	2,295	472	1,194	945
Private	2,818	270	−2,648	−213	−428
Grants	3,057	2,844	4,514	5,030	6,570
Direct foreign investment	20	882	1,059	1,167	2,301

[a]Net transfers = gross disbursements − repayments and interest.
Based on G. K. Helleiner. "The IMF, the World Bank and Africa's Adjustment and External Debt Problems: An Unofficial View." *World Development*, vol. 20 (1992), pp. 779–792.

The dilemmas also extend to the question of who benefits and who should benefit from aid; large-scale projects such as irrigation development and mechanized farming have been criticized because they tend to confer major benefits to indigenous elites and multinational companies and, at the same time, to displace or disrupt the lives of ordinary people and threaten the environment, often in the name of anticipated benefits that do not bear close scrutiny. Vignette 22.2 describes the Tanzania–Canada wheat program, a project that serves to illustrate several of these dilemmas of aid.

Transnational Corporations and African Underdevelopment

The growth in size, economic and political influence, and spatial reach of transnational corporations has been one of the most important developments of the late 20th century. The major transnational corporations have more economic power than all but the largest countries. Decision making by these companies is based entirely on opportunities for profit; as such, transnationals have no inherent commitment to any particular country or enterprise. Transnational corporations have taken the lead in the global restructuring of production, one

result of which has been the transfer of increasing amounts of industrial production to parts of the Third World to take advantage of cheap labor, low levels of taxation, and weak environmental legislation.

Transnational corporations have been widely criticized for distorting the economic development of poorer nations. They represent a heavy drain on resources because most transnational corporations rely heavily on imported technology, production inputs, and expertise. Instead of encouraging indigenous development through strong local economic linkages, transnational corporations often compete with and squeeze domestic companies out of the market. These corporations tend to make very large profits, which are either repatriated or reinvested in order to acquire an ever-increasing share of the country's productive capacity. For example, data from the United Nations Centre on Transnational Corporations indicates that between 1970 and 1980 Nigeria received $3.8 billion in foreign investment, but experienced a net loss of $2.7 billion because of the repatriation of $6.5 billion in fees, royalties, and profits.

Compared to most other parts of the world, the presence of transnational corporations in Africa south of the Sahara is extremely small. Net direct foreign investment in Africa south of the Sahara amounted to $882 million in

Vignette 22.2. Wheat at What Cost?
An Assessment of the Tanzania–Canada Wheat Program

Since the early 1970s, $200 million of Canadian aid money has been invested in the development of seven large, mechanized wheat farms in Tanzania, operated by Tanzania's National Agriculture and Food Corporation (NAFCO). These farms produce some 40% of Tanzania's wheat requirements and have been judged a major success by Canadian and Tanzanian government officials. It is said to have reduced Tanzania's dependence on imported wheat. From Canada's perspective, it has been an opportunity to put Canadian expertise and technology to good use.

A closer analysis of the Tanzania–Canada Wheat Program raises important questions about the true benefits and costs of this project and about large-scale development schemes in general. Who benefits from projects of this sort, and who does not? What are the opportunity costs associated with investing huge sums in these projects? To what extent should foreign aid donors accept responsibility for the negative social, economic, and environmental effects of projects they fund?

Critics of the Tanzanian wheat program point to its excessive costs. Four-fifths of Canadian aid to Tanzania is tied to the purchase of Canadian goods and services. The use of imported technology on the large wheat farms has provided many benefits for Canadian manufacturers but has created an expensive, long-term dependency for Tanzania. When the true costs of energy and other inputs are considered, the project has been demonstrated to be uneconomic. Moreover, it encourages Tanzanians to consume more wheat, ultimately increasing Tanzanians' dependency on imported food (see Vignette 12.2).

The Tanzania-Canada Wheat Program has also been expensive as far as foregone economic opportunities are concerned. Wheat still accounts for only 1% of Tanzania's food consumption, but the wheat program has brought over 20% of Canadian aid to Tanzania. The focus on large-scale wheat production has drawn scarce resources away from other crucial needs and from more appropriate and economic approaches to growing wheat. Although the large, mechanized farms have been shown to be uneconomic, there are long-established smallholder wheat farms elsewhere in Tanzania that are economically viable producers of wheat.

The Tanzania–Canada Wheat Program has negative effects on the lives of ordinary Tanzanians living in the project area. The concerns of one such group were outlined in a 1989 "open letter" to the Canadian people, exerpts from which appear below:

> We, the Barabaig of Tanzania, are a poor and troubled people. We are a pastoral minority dependent on our livestock for survival. Every day we strive to sustain our herds and secure a better future for ourselves and our children. We are few in number and live in scattered communities.
>
> Traditionally, we live on the plains that surround Mount Hanang in Hanang district of Arusha region. We have done so for well over a hundred years. Here we build our homes, herd our livestock, cultivate our plots, and live our lives. In colonial times we cleared the land to control the tsetse fly. Today we burn the pasture to control ticks and improve the grazing. Some of the land is sacred. Our esteemed elders are buried here in graves that are tended and visited for generations. We value and respect the land. We want to preserve it for all time.
>
> People are continuously moving in to grow crops on our pastures. They take the best land which we rely on to sustain our herds. The loss of this land has resulted in a drastic reduction of our livestock and a decline in production that causes us great suffering. If the land continues to be taken we shall have to move away or perish.

cont.

Vignette 22.2. (*cont.*)

The government has taken more than 100,000 acres for a wheat scheme. Official approval for this was given without our consent. We were just told that the project needed land and we would have to move. We have not been compensated for the loss of this land. The growing of wheat on what was once our pasture is destroying the environment. By stripping away the vegetation cover with mechanized cultivation, the soil is laid bare to be carried away by flash floods, creating deep gullies and silting up water sources in our sacred Lake Basotu. The area of land we are left with is generally less fertile and too small for our needs. It is becoming denuded by overgrazing. The vegetation has changed, making pastures less productive than they were before.

Canadian aid is as much valued by us as by other Tanzanians. We are not opposed to your involvement in the development of this country. In fact we would welcome your continued support for development in Hanang district. Our problem is with the project and its impact on our lives and land. Through this letter we want to inform you what is currently being done with your aid. You can see how you have been party to the wrongs inflicted on us. With what you now know we hope you will be moved to use whatever means are available to resolve the conflict.

We would also like to consider how the wrongs inflicted on us might be redressed. We want our land back. We want our customary rights observed. We want no further destruction of the land. Our hope is that you will be motivated to provide better human and livestock health facilities, and basic infrastructure and services would do much to overcome the underdevelopment we have endured. We want the opportunity to participate in our own development.

Based on C. Lane. "Wheat at what cost? CIDA and the Tanzania-Canada Wheat Program." In J. Swift and B. Tomlinson, eds., *Conflicts of Interest: Canada and the Third World.* Toronto: Between the Lines, 1991, pp. 133–160. Excerpt © 1991 by Between the Lines. Reprinted by permission.

1990, only 0.5% of total world investment. While the amount of net direct foreign investment in Africa was only slightly less in 1990 than the average for 1980 to 1985, its share of the world and Third World totals diminished greatly during the same period (Table 22.4). The role of transnational corporations is especially evident in the mining and energy sectors. However, the influence of these corporations extends to all facets of the modern economy, including manufacturing, banking, trade, and transportation.

Total investment by transnational corporations is concentrated in a few countries, especially such oil producers as Nigeria, Gabon, and Cameroon, and in other centers of comparatively rapid growth, including Côte d'Ivoire, Botswana, and Kenya. Liberia has an exceptionally large foreign investment for its size, chiefly because it has one of the world's largest "flag-of-convenience" merchant fleets. However, foreign investment in South Africa is still the largest in the continent, despite massive divestment by many companies during the 1980s in response to economic sanctions and the growth of worldwide antiapartheid sentiment.

Africa south of the Sahara, excluding South Africa, has attracted less than 3% of American and 1% of Japanese foreign investment. It accounts for about one-tenth of British and one-quarter of French foreign investment, reflecting those countries' colonial histories. This is evident in the distribution of investment; that of France is concentrated in Côte d'Ivoire, Gabon, and Senegal, while British investment is heaviest in Nigeria, Kenya, and Zambia. In certain southern African countries, including

Table 22.4. Trends in Net Direct Foreign Investment, 1980 to 1985 and 1990

	Net direct investment (U.S.$ million)		% of world total investment		% of Third World total investment	
	1980–1985	1990	1980–1985	1990	1980–1985	1990
Developed countries	37,179	151,970				
Developing countries	12,634	31,776				
Africa S. of Sahara	1,004	882	2.8	0.5	7.9	2.0
Oil producers	524	457				
South Africa	83	−5				
Other African	297	430				

Source: *World Investment Report 1992: Transnational Corporations as Engines of Growth.* New York: United Nations, 1992.

Namibia, Botswana, and Lesotho, South Africa is the main source of foreign capital.

As of 1982, the capital stock of foreign firms operating in Botswana was equivalent in value to 42% of the GNP, or $342 per person. In Nigeria, the proportional influence of foreign companies is less, but still large. The holdings of foreign companies were equivalent in 1982 to only 6% of the GNP, or $51 per Nigerian. However, these 1,200 foreign-owned companies employed 166,000 Nigerians.

Patterns of foreign investment shift constantly, reflecting such factors as changes in world supply, demand, and price of minerals and other commodities and reflecting the business community's comparative assessment of risks and opportunities. The great majority of new investment in 1990 was in only two countries, Nigeria ($558 million) and Botswana ($148 million). Gabon, Côte d'Ivoire, and Angola, countries that had attracted considerable investment prior to the mid-1980s, suffered a combined net loss of $236 million in investment during 1990.

The activities of the Lonrho Corporation indicate the pervasive role of transnational corporations in the modern economies of Africa. The Lonrho Group consists of more than 800 companies operating in over 80 countries. Its sales have grown from $180 million in 1967 to $7.8 billion in 1988. Lonrho is involved in a wide range of businesses – commercial agriculture, mining, tourism, motor vehicle distribution, general trade, publishing, and financial services. It is the largest distributor of motor vehicles in Africa, with agencies for ten major automakers. It farms and ranches 810,000 ha of land in Africa and the USA and is Africa's largest commercial food producer. It has major mining investments in South Africa, Zimbabwe, and Ghana.

Lonrho is unusual among transnational corporations in that its primary locus is in Africa. Although Africa south of the Sahara accounted for only 18% of Lonrho's gross sales during 1985 to 1988, it provided half of its pretax profits. Almost 70% of Lonrho's 98,000 employees are in Africa. One of the keys to Lonrho's success has been the strong connections that its executive director maintains with ruling African elites. The company continued to wield considerable political and economic influence, even when antiapartheid concern was at its height, despite its maintenance of large and profitable investments in South Africa.

Irrespective of the distorting effects on development that transnational corporations may have, they are an integral and growing part of the African economic landscape. They exert great influence not only in strongly capitalist countries like Botswana and Côte d'Ivoire but also in countries like Angola that have tried to develop according to socialist principles.

The Changing World Economy: Effects on Development

The deterioration in recent years of African economic and social conditions cannot be understood without reference to the marginalization of the continent in the global economy.

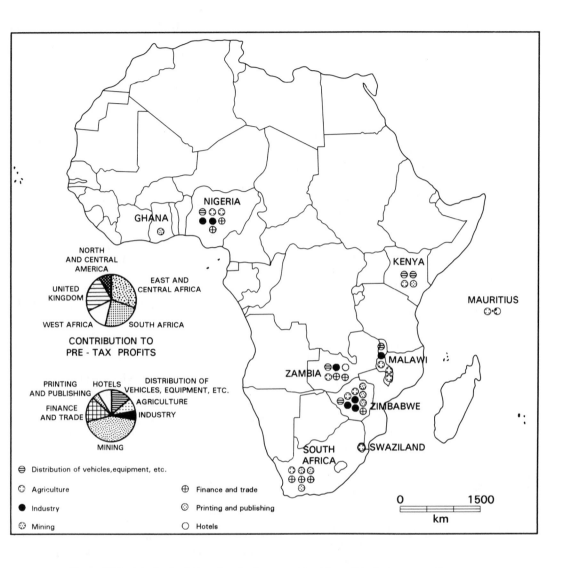

Figure 22.6. Lonrho in Africa. Lonrho has considerable political clout as well as economic power in several African countries. Source: J. P. Dickenson, C. G. Clarke, W. T. S. Gould, R. M. Prothero, D. J. Siddle, C. T. Smith, E. M. Hope-Thomas, and A. G. Hodgkiss. *A Geography of the Third World.* London: Methuen, 1983, p. 154. ©1983 by Methuen and Co. Reprinted by permission.

The sharp decline in world prices for Africa's primary products is tied to the growth of the debt crisis, which has in turn brought about a progressive loss of sovereignty to the IMF and World Bank. Transnational corporations continue to make substantial profits in countries where there is no money for school books and where hospitals function without medicines.

African countries have been given no choice but to focus on short-term objectives related to balance of payments and debt servicing. The social and economic costs of these policies have been very high for the African people. Moreover, Africa's longer term recovery has been seriously jeopardized by the damage done to economic and social infrastructures through the diversion of scarce resources overseas. Under present circumstances, achieving broadly based, socially just development is indeed very difficult.

Further Reading

For overviews of Africa's role in the world economy, see the following sources:

Ake, C. *A Political Economy of Africa*. New York: Longman, 1982.

Cooper, F. "Africa and the world economy." *African Studies Review*, vol. 24 (1981), pp. 1–86.

Hopkins, A. *An Economic History of West Africa*. London: Longman, 1973.

Seidman, A. W., and N. Magetla. *Outposts of Monopoly Capitalism: Southern Africa in the Changing Global Economy*. Westport, CT: Lawrence Hill, 1980.

Wallerstein, I. "The three stages of African involvement in the world-economy." In P. C. Gutkind and I. Wallerstein, eds., *The Political Economy of Contemporary Africa*, pp. 30–57. Beverley Hills, CA: Sage, 1976.

On patterns of trade involving African countries, see the following sources:

Frey-Wouters, E. *The European Community and the Third World: The Lomé Convention and Its Impact*. New York: Praeger, 1980.

"Major commodities of Africa." *Africa South of the Sahara*. London: Europa publications, published annually.

Issues related to debt, aid, and the role of international lending agencies are discussed in the following sources:

Freeman, L. "CIDA and agriculture in East and Central Africa." In J. Barker, ed., *The Politics of Agriculture in Tropical Africa*, pp. 99–123. Beverley Hills, CA: Sage, 1984.

George, S. *A Fate Worse than Debt*. London: Penguin, 1988.

Helleiner, G. K. "The IMF, the World Bank and Africa's adjustment and debt problems: An unofficial view." *World Development*, vol. 20 (1992), pp. 779–792.

Humphreys, C., and J. Underwood. "The external debt difficulties of low-income Africa." In I. Husain and I. Diwan, eds., *Dealing with the Debt Crisis*, pp. 45–68. Washington, DC: World Bank, 1989.

Mistry, P. *African Debt: The Case for Relief for Sub-Saharan Africa*. Oxford: Oxford International Associates, 1989.

World Bank. *Sub-Saharan Africa: From Crisis to Sustainable Growth*. Washington, DC: World Bank, 1989.

The role of multinational corporations is considered in the following sources:

Cronje, S., M. Ling, and G. Cronje. *Lonrho: Portrait of a Multinational*. Harmondsworth, England: Penguin, 1976.

Dicken, P. *Global Shift: Industrial Change in a Turbulent World*. London: Harper and Row, 1986. (See, in particular, Chapters 3 and 4.)

Langdon, S. *Multinational Corporations in the Political Economy of Kenya*. London: Macmillan, 1981.

Onimode, B. *A Political Economy of the African Crisis*. London: Zed, 1988. (See Chapters 3 and 4.)

Wells, L. T., Jr. *Third World Multinationals: The Rise of Foreign Investment from Developing Countries*. Cambridge, MA: MIT Press, 1983.

23

✳

Ideology and
Economic Development

The first years of independence were characterized by great optimism about Africa's future. Africans would at last be able to reap the just rewards of their labor and use their resources to achieve national development. The United Nations declared the 1960s to be the Development Decade and set lofty objectives such as a minimum of 5% annual growth for national incomes. Three decades later, the expectations of imminent development have proved to be sadly inappropriate. Fortunes have varied, from strongly qualified success in some countries to decay and disintegration in many others.

The question of how Africa could achieve the greatest progress was the focus of a famous wager in 1957 between Presidents Nkrumah of Ghana and Houphuët-Boigney of Côte d'Ivoire. Nkrumah called for aggressive, nationalistic policies to foster independence, whereas Houphuët-Boigney favored pragmatic policies emphasizing investment and growth. While the more impressive growth of the Ivoirian economy suggests that Houphuët-Boigney may have won the original bet, the controversy continues unabated about the best strategies to foster development in African countries.

This chapter provides a brief review of the approaches used by African nations since independence to order and shape national development. The following issues are particularly important:

- The political ideologies that have informed African development since 1960
- The influence of ideology on development priorities and strategies
- Some of the achievements and failures of each approach
- The effect of IMF and World Bank structural adjustment packages on development planning

Ideology

There is no universally accepted classification of African political ideologies, but that of Crawford Young has been used widely. He identified three dominant approaches: capitalism, populist socialism, and Afro-Marxism. African capitalist countries have maintained relatively open economies in which the private sector has played a leading role. Afro-Marxist countries have used state interventions to reshape the economy according to Marxist–Leninist principles. Populist socialist states have tended to emphasize nationalist and socialist development goals, while distancing themselves from Marxist ideology.

The question of ideology, and the extent to which it will continue to influence the shape of development, seems much less certain now than during the 1980s. The demise of the Soviet Union and of communist regimes in Eastern Europe has effectively removed the main source of both ideological inspiration and development aid for Afro-Marxist states and has narrowed the options of every country. The increasing involvement of the World Bank and IMF in African economic affairs has also contributed greatly to a narrowing of policy options. The implementation of these agencies' structural adjustment programs has increasingly become a condition for international assistance. The major thrust of these packages has been to remove internal restrictions on the operation of a free-market economy, promote export production, encourage foreign investment, and reduce the public-sector role in economic and social matters. These intrusions on national sovereignty have been bitter pills that virtually every African country has had to swallow.

African Capitalism

Among the most prominent of African capitalist states have been Côte d'Ivoire, Kenya, Nigeria, Gabon, and Zaire. In these countries, the private sector has been encouraged to take a leading role in economic development. Foreign investment has usually been welcomed, particularly in areas of the economy in which indigenous companies have little expertise. At the same time, African capitalism differs considerably from that of the United States and most other advanced

Figure 23.1. Two faces of life in Côte d'Ivoire. (a) Modern office towers in Abidjan. (b) Rural women preparing food. Photos: CIDA: R. Lemoyne.

Vignette 23.1. Côte d'Ivoire: A Case Study in African Capitalism

Côte d'Ivoire has remained Africa's leading beacon of free enterprise. In the words of President Houphuët-Boigney, who maintained total domination of the political system from the 1950s until his death in 1993, "We are not socialists in that we do not believe in giving priority to the distribution of wealth but wish to encourage the creation and multiplication of wealth first of all. We are following a policy of state capitalism."

During the first two decades of independence, Côte d'Ivoire maintained an astonishing rate of economic growth. The GNP grew by an average of 11% per year during the 1960s and by 7% in the 1970s. During the 1980s, the economy grew by only 1.2% annually, well below the 3.9% annual rate of population growth. Nevertheless, the country has gone from one of the poorest countries prior to the 1950s to one with the eighth-highest GNP per capita in Africa south of the Sahara in 1990.

Ivoirian growth has been strongly based in the agricultural sector, especially in coffee and cocoa production. The country is the world's leading producer of cocoa and the fifth-ranked producer of coffee. These crops are grown primarily on some 600,000 family-owned plantations averaging 3 to 4 ha in size, most of which were established in the 1940s, 1950s, and 1960s. The wealthiest planters are very prosperous and have played a dominant role in Ivoirian political and economic life. Houphuët-Boigney himself rose to prominence as a wealthy plantation owner.

The government has had considerable success in promoting the diversification of the agricultural economy. Côte d'Ivoire is one of the world's top producers of palm oil, Africa's largest rubber producer, third-largest cotton producer, and a major producer of bananas and pineapples. While much of the production of these crops has come from smaller farms, there has been an increasing emphasis on large-scale plantations operated by parastatals (government-owned companies) or foreign investors.

Timber represents the third-largest source of export earnings, but the continuing decimation of the resource base threatens its long-term viability. Petroleum production began in the late 1970s, but has now virtually stopped owing to the high cost of production and the small size of deposits.

Côte d'Ivoire has a relatively diversified industrial base, accounting for about one-eighth of the GDP. Most industries process primary products for export and produce import-substitution goods. While most manufacturing was in the hands of foreign investors at independence, the Ivoirian state now controls about half of all equity in manufacturing. The eagerness of the state to join in collaborative ventures has proved to be a strong incentive for foreign investors.

The economy is characterized by gross urban–rural and regional disparities in wealth and development. With the exception of cotton, all of the major cash crops are produced in the forest regions of southern Côte d'Ivoire. The forestry and petroleum industries are also southern based. Modern sector development in the form of industry, commerce, transportation, and government are highly concentrated in the south, particularly in the major city of Abidjan. Little has happened to change the original role assigned to the north, namely, as a source of cheap migrant labor for the southern region.

Côte d'Ivoire has benefited from its position of dominance relative to neighboring states. A quarter of the population consists of migrants, mainly from Mali and Burkina Faso, who do most of the menial work. They represent the backbone of the rural economy, doing the majority of work on the cash-crop plantations. Yet they form a permanent underclass in Ivoirian society; legislated wage levels for agricultural workers are very low

cont.

Vignette 23.1. (*cont.*)

---

relative to urban workers. Migrant workers have little security and are ready scapegoats for Ivoirian problems.

In quality-of-life measures such as infant mortality and rates of access to social services, Côte d'Ivoire lags behind many poorer African countries. According to the *Human Development Report*, 8.3 million of the total Ivoirian population of 17.6 million lacked access to health care, 9.8 million lacked access to safe water, and 7.2 million lacked access to sanitation in the late 1980s. The services that are provided are distributed very unequally. For example, health services were available to 11% of rural and 61% of urban populations.

Because of the rapid growth and diversification of the Ivoirian economy, especially before 1980, it has often been cited as one of Africa's great success stories. This view has many critics, however, who point to the gross disparities in wealth and quality of life and who criticize the country's heavy dependence on foreign capital and expertise. For Africa's economic nationalists, Côte d'Ivoire is one of the ultimate examples of neocolonial underdevelopment, where growth has greatly benefited foreign capital and indigenous elites at the expense of the poor, especially migrant workers.

The Ivoirian economic miracle became increasingly tarnished in the 1980s. The prices paid on the world market for most of its farm products stagnated or fell, causing a reduction of export earnings. Meanwhile, the cost of servicing the debt incurred to finance economic growth continued to rise. By 1991, the total national debt stood at almost $19 billion; this debt was equivalent to 223% of the GNP, compared to 59% in 1980. Debt-servicing costs represent 43.4% of the value of exports.

Because of the worsening economic situation, Côte d'Ivoire has implemented a structural adjustment package. Tax increases, public-sector cutbacks, and fee increases for social services have increased public discontent, especially among civil servants and others who had been the major beneficiaries of the country's growth. Public protests have forced the government to permit opposition parties to be formed for the first time.

The death of the omnipotent Houphuët-Boigney in 1993 has left Côte d'Ivoire's political future in doubt, even though the immediate transition of power to his hand-picked successor went smoothly. The new leader is likely to face persistent challenges from opposition forces and those adversely affected by the weak state of the economy. To survive, the new leader will need all the political skill that Houphuët-Boigney displayed in his four decades of power.

---

capitalist countries in that the African state has tended to take a very active role in the development process. Governments not only have attempted to create a climate favorable to investment by offering incentives to foreign investors but also have become directly involved as partners or as major shareholders in new ventures. Many states have also taken steps to increase the role of indigenous firms in the economy by passing laws reserving some types of economic activity for local com-

panies, requiring other companies to train and employ Africans in supervisory and management positions, and creating incentives for the development of local supply linkages.

Capitalist countries, inspired by classical economic theory, have tended to emphasize economic growth in the economy as their primary objective; as such, there has been less concern with issues of urban–rural, regional, and class-based equity in the distribution of benefits. Thus, while development by the pri-

Figure 23.2. Communal farm work, Tanzania. The encouragement of communal production was one of the primary goals of Tanzania's populist socialist government. Photo: CIDA: D. Barbour.

vate sector has tended to be highly concentrated in both spatial and social terms, it is assumed that the benefits of growth, in the form of increased trade and employment opportunities and more money for social expenditure, will eventually "trickle down" to benefit initially disadvantaged regions and social groups.

The distribution not only of wealth but also of social welfare—in particular, safe water, health care, adequate nutrition, and education—has tended to be very uneven in African capitalist states. While the small elite population of top political figures, civil servants, and entrepreneurs control a disproportionate share of wealth and have access to the very best in education, health care, and other social amenities, almost everyone else struggles to make ends meet and often has no access at all to even the most basic social services. These disparities are evident not only in the most overtly corrupt and repressive states like Zaire but also in countries like Côte d'Ivoire and Nigeria that have been comparatively more open.

Populist Socialism

During the 1960s and 1970s, many regimes claimed to be following a socialist path of development. Espousing socialism helped to create distance from the capitalism of former colonial masters. However, there was a gap between socialist rhetoric and capitalist reality in several countries, a prime example being Kenya.

One of the earliest and most influential attempts to implement populist socialism was in Ghana under Kwame Nkrumah. Nkrumah aimed to create "a welfare state based on African socialist principles, adapted to suit Ghanaian conditions, in which all citizens, regardless of class, tribe, color or creed, shall have equal opportunity." Thus, Nkrumah argued that it was perfectly acceptable to borrow ideas from all parts of the world although these ideas would have to be reshaped to reflect local conditions and local priorities. He saw African traditional society as inherently socialist: Land and other resources were owned communally, work was often organized

Vignette 23.2. Tanzania: A Case Study in African Socialism

Tanzania, under the leadership of President Julius Nyerere, became somewhat of test case for the populist-socialist model. Nyerere's clearly articulated vision of self-reliant, egalitarian development caught the imagination of people worldwide. While the Tanzanian approach has been criticized widely in recent years, by radicals and conservatives alike, few dispute the importance of Nyerere's ideas.

The turning point for Tanzania occurred in January, 1967 with the adoption of the Arusha Declaration by TANU, the ruling party. The declaration set forth a commitment to socialist development and established a series of principles and policies for the implementation of the objective. The declaration reserved a prominent role for the state and at the same time limited the role to be played by the private sector.

The cornerstone of Tanzania's rural-development strategy was the *ujamaa* village. The scattered rural population was encouraged to move into nucleated settlements, where services could be provided more efficiently, communal production organized, and involvement in political affairs encouraged. The program began as a voluntary process and was quite successful at first; by 1974, 2.5 million people were occupying 5,000 *ujamaa* villages. However, the pace was deemed inadequate and remaining peasants were coerced into forming *ujamaa* villages. Problems began to multiply because of the inadequacy of support services to identify the best locations for new settlements and to make available all of the needed resources. The communal farms failed in many villages, partly because of peasant disinterest in communal work and partly because marketing and technical support were often inadequate. Tacitly recognizing the limitations of the program, the state reduced pressures for communal production and began to use price incentives to encourage more production from farmers' private plots. Since the early 1980s, what remained of the communal aspects of the *ujamaa* approach has been undercut by IMF-designed structural adjustment.

Tanzania established numerous parastatal companies to undertake and manage a wide range of enterprises in produce marketing, transportation, and manufacturing, among other things. By the latter part of the 1970s, four-fifths of all investment was by the state, and four-fifths of large and medium-sized enterprises were under state control. While the overall performance of the parastatal sector was solid, most of these companies have now been privatized.

The Arusha Declaration emphasized the importance of creating an egalitarian society. Disparities in wages between top officials and ordinary workers were reduced, and restrictions were placed on the involvement of public officials in private business activities. Another initiative that was justified on egalitarian grounds was the transfer of the capital from Dar es Salaam to the small, regional center of Dodoma where, it was argued, civil servants would be less able to isolate themselves from the everyday realities of the lives of ordinary Tanzanians.

Investment in health care, education, and other social services received high priority. Tanzania played a pioneering role in developing primary health care, a strategy that was adopted because it was a very cost-effective and appropriate method of addressing the basic health needs of the majority of Tanzanians living in rural areas where health care had previously been unavailable. This concern for social equity is evident in Tanzania's Human Development Index score. While the country only ranks 122nd in the world, this ranking is 29 positions higher than its ranking for GNP per capita. By comparison, Côte d'Ivoire ranks 21 places *lower* for human development than for per capita income.

cont.

Vignette 23.2. (cont.)

The Tanzanian approach has received criticism from both conservative and radical sources. Conservatives point to the failure of communal farming projects and criticize the high costs of bureaucratic inefficiency in parastatal enterprises. They have advocated opening the economy to give more freedom and incentives for peasants and urban entrepreneurs. Radicals have criticized Tanzania's overdependence on foreign aid and the government's failure to pay enough attention to class divisions in society; it has been argued that the problems of Tanzanian socialism were attributable to the uncooperative attitudes of many entrepreneurs, wealthier peasants, and professionals.

The debate about the Tanzanian model has virtually stopped following the progressive dismantling of socialist policies under the watchful eye of the IMF. The involvement of the IMF began as a result of a balance of payments crisis in the late 1970s and early 1980s, caused by a large decline in the price of coffee and other agricultural commodities and by the high cost of Tanzania's war with Uganda. Responding to a Ugandan attempt to annex some Tanzanian territory, Tanzania had invaded Uganda and brought about the collapse of the despotic regime of Idi Amin. However, the war proved to be very costly, not only because of the $300 million direct cost to Tanzania but also because IMF intervention had to be accepted in the war's aftermath.

The achievements of Tanzania since Arusha deserve to be recognized. These achievements have been made in a country that has a poor natural-resource base and that had few development initiatives before independence. Undoubtedly, the greatest accomplishments have been in the social sector and in the narrowing of disparities between urban and rural, rich and poor, Tanzanians. Unfortunately, these gains are threatened by structural adjustment. For example, although 93% of the primary school-aged population was in school in 1980, the percentage was only 64% in 1988.

Economically, the 3.7% annual growth in GDP between 1960 and 1985 was slightly above average for Africa south of the Sahara. During the 1980 to 1989 period, under the direction of the IMF and World Bank, Tanzania's economy grew at 2.6% per year, below the 3.4% annual growth of population.

---

collectively, and citizens felt a sense of obligation to contribute to the welfare of extended family members, neighbors, and even strangers.

Ghana's experiment with populist socialism ended in failure with the overthrow of Nkrumah. However, there have been other countries where the commitment to socialist development has been more enduring. Tanzania and Zambia have been particularly influential as models of populist socialist development. Each had a charismatic president who led the fight for independence and who clearly articulated a vision of egalitarian, self-reliant development. While the policies that the leaders of these two countries advocated often failed to achieve the intended results, they did provide a vision of a better African future that inspired many.

Populist socialism has remained strongly rooted in ideas about the importance of communities in traditional African society. The individualism and competitiveness of capitalism were criticized as being alien to African traditions of communal ownership of land, cooperative production, and shared responsibility for welfare. Instead, community mobilization for self-help projects and communal production were encouraged. These socialist regimes tended to be partial to rural development, perhaps because the values that they espoused were thought to be best preserved in rural communities. Because self-reliance was considered to be a precondition for real independence, there was heavy reliance on state-owned industrial and trading companies, as well as strict controls on foreign investment.

While populist socialist regimes have recognized the importance of economic growth, they have differed from capitalist nations in not treating economic growth as their pre-eminent objective and in not accepting the assurances of "trickle down" economics that growth will ultimately benefit all, irrespective of where it takes place or who controls it. They have given priority to the provision of social services, particularly for rural areas.

In many cases, state-initiated projects in agriculture, industry, and trade have been costly failures, for reasons that range from poor planning and management to peasant resistance. These projects have also shared in the adverse effects of the external threats to Africa's economic well-being, principally declining terms of trade for their goods on the world market, which have forced them to adopt major revisions in their development strategies as the price for IMF support. While a few states, such as Uganda under President Museveni, continue to use much of the rhetoric of African socialism, their policies clearly reflect the guiding hand of the IMF and World Bank.

Afro-Marxism

Until the late 1980s, there were several African regimes that maintained an explicit commitment to Marxism–Leninism. Certain of them, including Mozambique and Angola, were forged through a process of armed struggle leading to independence. The evolution of other once Afro-Marxist regimes, including those of the Congo Republic, Benin, Burkina Faso, and Ethiopia, was more complex. Although these regimes declared an explicit commitment to Marxist–Leninist ideology, they emerged, not as a result of prolonged revolutionary struggle, but as a result of military coups staged by lower-ranking soldiers, disaffected with the corruption and elitism of entrenched interests.

Afro-Marxist regimes remained committed

to gaining control of the "commanding heights" of the economy–commercial agriculture, industry, banking, trade, and commerce–through state direction. The Soviet Union, China, Cuba, and other communist states provided not only the model but also the financial, technical, and, in several cases, military aid to make it possible. The heavy reliance on assistance from communist states was necessary because these regimes could not attract substantial aid and investment from the West. Moreover, the dependence of several of these regimes was significantly increased because of the debilitating effect of insurrections supported by hostile outside interests, most notably South Africa and the United States.

Most Afro-Marxist regimes made significant efforts to achieve social, as well as economic, transformation. Primary health care programs were implemented, mass literacy campaigns organized, and initiatives taken to improve the status of women in society. While the social and economic transformation has occurred in a "top–down" fashion, most regimes were strongly committed to the mobilization of "grassroots" participation in the process of change.

As a general rule, Afro-Marxist regimes failed to achieve their objectives of rapid economic growth and comprehensive social and economic transformation. Nevertheless, their failures need to be put into perspective. While in many cases failure may be attributed to the naive application of inappropriate models and bad management, the importance of Western hostility to these experiments should not be underestimated. Very limited access to Western aid and investment, trade embargoes and ongoing attempts at political destabilization created a severe disadvantage for these regimes and their development agendas. Prolonged droughts also did much to weaken Afro-Marxist regimes in several countries, most notably those in Ethiopia and Mozambique.

The collapse of Afro-Marxist regimes in Somalia and Ethiopia in 1991 virtually ended, at least for the time being, three decades of experimentation with Marxism–Leninism

Vignette 23.3. Mozambique: A Case Study of Afro-Marxism

The roots of Afro-Marxism in Mozambique lie in five centuries of Portuguese exploitation and the prolonged struggle of the Mozambican people for independence. Prior to the late 19th century, when large tracts of land were given to settlers to start plantations, Portugal's primary interest was the acquisition of slaves. The colonial state supported the settlers by implementing brutal policies of land expropriation, heavy taxation, forced labor, and violence against the indigenous population. The Portuguese also signed an agreement with South Africa under which Mozambicans were sent to work in the mines and most of their earnings remitted to the colonial government. In short, it is hard to think of a colonial regime that exploited its people more and did less for them in return.

The liberation movement called Frelimo, which came into existence in 1962 through an amalgamation of three smaller movements, drew inspiration from a long history of resistance to Portuguese colonialism. Frelimo gradually expanded the spatial and political extent of its activities from its initial base in the northern part of the country. Frelimo's strategy was to advance slowly, preparing the way for guerrilla activity with the mobilization of political support among the rural population. After expelling the Portuguese in a district, Frelimo moved to establish its own state apparatus, including provision for schooling and health care. The struggle was long and bloody, but Frelimo eventually triumphed, gaining independence for Mozambique in 1975.

The departing Portuguese left the country in shambles. By 1976, four-fifths of the 200,000 Portuguese settlers had gone. The number of doctors, for example, fell from 550 in the early 1970s to only 80 in 1976. Not only did the settlers leave, but in many cases they also destroyed their property. Crops were burnt, domestic animals killed, and farm machinery and buildings wrecked. The new state inherited very little in the way of infrastructure and even less in the way of formal training and preparation for the task at hand.

Frelimo's attachment to Marxist–Leninist ideology had developed gradually over the course of the liberation struggle. However, by 1975 there was a strong commitment to implementing a total economic, social, and political transformation to erase the profound underdevelopment caused by colonial exploitation. This commitment was particularly strong in agriculture, where priority was given to the establishment of large, mechanized state farms, initially on the settler estates and later in other parts of the country. Some 3,000 tractors and 300 combine harvestors were imported for these farms at a cost of $100 million. The program was a costly failure; the state lacked adequate management expertise to run the farms, the equipment was underutilized and ill-suited to the country's needs, and many peasants were not very interested in collectivized farming. The state also provided some assistance for agricultural cooperatives but initially chose to neglect the independent, small-scale farmers who constituted the base of the country's rural economy. These policies helped to deepen the crisis in agriculture brought about by the departure of the Portuguese and later by drought.

The development of social services, virtually ignored by the Portuguese, was a high priority of the Frelimo regime. The training of some 4,500 health care workers between 1975 and 1982 permitted the state to extend basic health care to most parts of the country, often providing services where none had existed before. By 1980, health was receiving one-tenth of state expenditure. While significant strides were made in the areas of maternal and child health care, there was often a gap between a well-developed socialist rhetoric and a less well-developed practice. Doctors and others working in the formal

cont.

Vignette 23.3. (*cont.*)

---

health sector resisted a restructuring of the health care system that shifted the main locus of intervention away from them. Moreover, as security in the countryside worsened, many rural health workers abandoned their posts.

The gravest threat to Mozambique's development efforts has come from the Mozambican National Resistance called Renamo. Renamo was organized in the late 1970s, with direction, funding, and material support from the governments of Rhodesia and South Africa and from former Portuguese settlers. South Africa's objective in supporting Renamo was to destabilize and ultimately destroy Frelimo. South Africa was very successful. An estimated 1 million Mozambicans lost their lives as a result of Renamo's insurrection, 1.5 million others were to flee to other countries as refugees, and 2 million more were dislocated within the country. Agricultural production declined by at least one-third, and interregional trade has been severely resticted. The state was forced to allocate up to 40% of its budget to defense in an unsuccessful effort to achieve a military victory. In 1984, the government was forced to sign a humiliating accord with South Africa under which support for Renamo was to cease in return for various Mozambican concessions. However, Renamo continued to receive external support. After years of negotiations between Renamo and the government, a peace accord was signed in 1992. Since then, there has been slow but encouraging progress toward peace and the staging of multiparty elections. Still, there are reasons enough to fear that there are many setbacks yet to come along the road to peace.

The growing political and economic cost of the war, the effect of severe droughts, the failure of its economic policies, and the virtual absence of Western aid forced Frelimo to modify and then effectively to abandon its commitment to Afro-Marxism. The implementation of structural adjustment forced the dismantling of the state farm program, the introduction of free-market pricing, currency devaluation, and drastic cutbacks in public-sector employment and social-service expenditure. The social costs of adjustment are proving to be high. The government has had to slash per capita expenditure on health from $4.70 in 1982 to $.90 in 1989 and to increase user fees at hospitals more than 10-fold. Economic reforms have brought some increases in available food supply to a few areas, but very few people can afford the costs. The IMF's program, never before attempted under such adverse conditions, has proved to be a dismal failure; it has done much more to weaken Frelimo and the country as a whole than it has done to bring about economic recovery.

---

in Africa south of the Sahara. In several countries, the cumulative effects of many years of externally funded insurrection forced governments to compromise their espoused principles and to sue for peace. The worsening economic circumstances forced several states to accept IMF and World Bank recommendations and move toward an open-market economy with a much reduced role for the state. The withdrawal of support from the Soviet Union and its Eastern European allies left the remaining Afro-Marxist states with no option but to attempt to reach out to Western aid agencies and investors. These trends are still quite recent; it remains to be seen whether this represents the

Figure 23.3. Billboard advertising Frelimo's fifth party congress. Photo: CIDA: B. Paton.

end of Afro-Marxism or only a temporary demise.

SAP and AAF-SAP:
The New Orthodoxy and
an African Alternative

During the 1980s there was an increasing convergence in the economic policies of African states. This convergence came about through the growing debt crisis and the insistence of creditors that strict conditionalities established by the IMF be applied before countries could be considered for debt rescheduling or further loans. Virtually every country of Africa south of the Sahara has had to accept the intervention of the IMF and the World Bank and to implement the structural adjustment programs prescribed for them. The preceding discussion has pointed to the policy implications of this process in capitalist, socialist, and Afro-Marxist states. What follows is a summary of how the strategy of structural adjustment is supposed to work, according to the IMF and World Bank, together with a critique of this

strategy and an alternative approach to restructuring proposed by United Nations Economic Commission for Africa.

Structural adjustment programs reflect to some extent the political, economic, and social realities of the individual countries in which they are implemented. However, what is much more striking is the uniformity of policy direction that has been established through these structural adjustment packages. In general, adjustment programs attempt to increase the solvency of debtor states through policies designed to stimulate economic growth and investment and to reduce the cost of government by cutting back on the public sector. The ultimate objective of these policies is to ensure that African debtor states will be able to meet their debt-repayment commitments.

The specific policy directions established through structural adjustment programs generally include the following:

- Massive currency devaluation
- Reduction of internal and external government deficits by limiting the growth of credit and money supply

Figure 23.4. Convoy of trucks, Mozambique. The activities of Renamo virtually paralyzed the transportation system and, in turn, the entire economy of Mozambique. Photo: CIDA: B. Paton.

- Liberalization of the economy, guided by "market forces" domestically and "comparative advantage" internationally
- Encouragement of foreign investment
- Removal of high tariffs and quotas to encourage a more efficient allocation of resources in the economy
- Elimination of price controls and subsidies to encourage increased productivity, especially in agriculture
- Increasing export producer's share of world market prices
- Cutbacks in the state sector, including privatization of state enterprises and reductions in public-sector employment
- Introduction of cost recovery (user fees) in health care, education, and for other social amenities

Structural adjustment has imposed onerous social, political, environmental, and economic costs on Africa south of the Sahara. Among others, UNICEF has shown how the higher cost of food and reduced access to health care have increased malnutrition and infant mortality. The poor, women, and children have suffered the most as a result of reduced social expenditure. The political costs have often been considerable for governments forced to implement such policies as increased food prices that affect peoples' very means of survival. Structural adjustment has helped to accelerate the environmental crisis by forcing both families and governments to liquidate ecological capital–cutting trees, for example–to make ends meet. As for the economy, adjustment programs have significantly distorted economic planning by focusing only on short-term, balance-of-payments objectives at the expense of longer-term planning for balanced and equitable development. The few countries identified by the IMF and World Bank as adjustment success stories, of which Ghana is a notable example, have experienced some increases in the volume (not value) of exports and have met debt-repayment commitments with the help of further loans and debt rescheduling.

Structural adjustment as development orthodoxy has come under increasing criticism by academics, international social agencies, and African governments. How can programs that exact such a heavy price for such questionable gains be considered a success? The United Nations Economic Commission for Africa in 1989 set forth an alternative approach, the African Alternative Framework to Structural Adjustment Programs for Socio-Economic Recovery and Transformation (AAF-SAP). The philosophy of the AAF-SAP is that IMF and World Bank policies divert attention from, rather than address, the causes of African underdevelopment. These policies have eroded African sovereignty and undermined the ability of African states to plan and implement rational development policies. The very survival of the African social fabric is threatened by adjustment. The key to a resolution of this deepening crisis, according to AAP-SAP, is for African governments in partnership with the people to regain control of economic and social policy. Adjustment needs to be accompanied by measures to facilitate longer-term socioeconomic transformation. These measures include increasing the development of intra-African trade as an alternative to the outward orientation of present trading patterns; strengthening productive capacity especially to grow more food; and giving priority to equity considerations in growth and in the provision of basic needs.

We have seen that the social and economic landscapes of African countries show the evidence of a diversity of approaches to development. Experiments in Marxist, socialist, and capitalist development have been implemented with enthusiasm, but in all cases with mixed results. More recently, the implementation of structural adjustment policies has resulted in a convergence of development policies. However, structural adjustment has been externally dictated and designed to address the concerns of Africa's creditors rather than the development needs of the African people. The costs of adjustment have been high and the benefits have been dubious.

Future directions in development policy remain uncertain. Nevertheless, as external attempts to achieve a one-formula restructuring of African economies become thoroughly discredited, there will be few alternatives but to leave it to Africans to decide for themselves what their countries' priorities and policies should be. National development policies may well become as diverse in the future as they were in the past.

Further Reading

Excellent introductions to the role of ideology in African development are given in the following sources:

Saul, J. "Ideology in Africa: Decomposition and recomposition." In G. M. Carter and P. O'Meara, eds., *African Independence: The First Twenty-Five Years*, pp. 300–329. Bloomington: Indiana University Press, 1985.

Young, C. *Ideology and Development in Africa*. New Haven: Yale University Press, 1982.

Studies of capitalist development in Côte d'Ivoire include the following sources:

Den Tuinder, B. *Ivory Coast: The Challenge of Success*. Baltimore, MD: The Johns Hopkins University Press, 1978.

Lubeck, P. M., ed. *The African Bourgeoisie: Capitalist Development in Nigeria, Kenya and the Ivory Coast*. Boulder, CO: Lynne Rienner, 1987.

Marcussen, H. S., and J. E. Torp. *Internationalization of Capital: Prospects for the Third World*. London: Zed, 1982.

On the Tanzanian approach of populist socialism, see the following sources:

Hyden, G. *Beyond Ujamaa in Tanzania: Underdevelopment and an Uncaptured Peasantry*. London: Heinemann, 1980.

Msambichaka, L. A. "State policies and food production in Tanzania." In T. Mkandawire and N. Bourenane, eds., *The State and Agriculture in Africa*. Dakar, Senegal: Codesria, 1987.

Nyerere, J. *Ujamaa: Essays on Socialism*. London: Oxford University Press, 1968.

Raikes, P. "Rural differentiation and class formation in Tanzania." *Journal of Peasant Studies*, vol. 5 (1978), pp. 285–325.

Mozambique's attempt to implement Afro-Marxism is discussed in the following sources:

Hanlon, J. *Mozambique: The Revolution Under Fire*. London: Zed, 1984.

Hanlon, J. *Mozambique: Who Calls the Shots?*. London: James Currey, 1991.

Huffman, R. "Colonialism, socialism and destabilization in Mozambique." *Africa Today*, vol. 39 (1992), pp. 9–27.

Isaacman, A., and B. Isaacman. *Mozambique: From Colonialism to Revolution, 1900–1982.* Boulder, CO: Westview, 1983.

Kyle, S. "Economic reform and armed conflict in Mozambique." *World Development,* vol. 19 (1991), pp. 637–649.

There is a vast literature on the nature and effect of structural adjustment packages of the IMF and World Bank. For example, see the following sources:

Cornia, G., R. Jolly, and F. Stewart, eds. *Adjust-*

ment with a Human Face. 2 vols. London: Clarendon, 1987.

Havenevik, K., ed. *The IMF and the World Bank in Africa: Conditionality, Impact and Alternatives.* Uppsala, Sweden: Scandinavian Institute of African Studies, 1987.

Onimode, B. *The IMF, the World Bank and African Debt.* vol. 1: *The Economic Impact.* vol 2: The Social and Political Impact. London: Zed, 1989.

World Bank. *Africa's Adjustment and Growth in the 1980s.* Washington, DC: World Bank, 1989.

24

✳

Development from Within:
Local Self-Reliance in Development

For too long, development theory and practice have failed to pay sufficient attention to the strong tradition of self-help within local African communities. One of the basic premises of modernization theory, for example, was that the traditional economies had no real future and that their present role was confined for the most part to contributing labor and savings in support of the emerging modern economy. In the early 1970s, the World Bank and other development agencies proclaimed their discovery of the importance of small farmers, but the "bottom–up" development model that they advocated remained "top–down" in practice. Attempts to transform rural economies were usually based on introducing imported technologies that were too expensive for most people, often inappropriate for local conditions, and based on outsiders' assumptions about the needs and objectives of local residents.

The failure of conventional, top–down models of development brought calls for a different approach in which development is defined, implemented, and controlled by the residents of local communities. Universal solutions were rejected in favor of approaches that are of necessity diverse because they are grounded in the particular ecological and socioeconomic conditions of particular localities.

In *Development from Within*, Fraser Taylor and Fiona Mackenzie explore issues related to development at the local level. They identify participation and territoriality as fundamental characteristics of genuine, progressive local development. Territoriality, which refers to the physical–environmental, social, and political boundaries delimiting a community, arises out of Africans' strong attachment to place. In short, development is undertaken within distinct, locally recognized communities, not in spatial and social aggregates defined by outsiders. Participation involves community mobilization in an organized struggle to gain more control over resources. It may develop as a defense mechanism whereby marginalized groups come together to fight against threatening initiatives promoted by outsiders or local elites.

Local Initiative and the Development Process

The support for local initiatives in development belatedly recognizes the importance of what African communities have done since time immemorial, namely, to attempt to improve the quality of their own lives by making use of locally available resources. Unlike the predominant Western model emphazing individual initiative, ownership, and economic gain, African societial traditions tend to emphasize collective ownership of resources, common security, and cooperative forms of production. Land and other key resources are communally owned; making one's livelihood from it brings an inherent obligation to protect resources for the use of future generations.

Collective security in precolonial African societies was achieved through working and celebrating together. Among the Langi of Uganda, for example, collective security was formalized through *wang-tic*, an institution in which members of the community came together at a member's request to undertake larger agricultural tasks such as bush clearing, weeding, or granary construction. Participants were rewarded with food and millet beer and the right to assume that the beneficiary would honor their own future requests for assistance. Cooperative farming of this sort, involving an extended family or members of the community, not only spreads the workload in times of heavy labor demand but also reaffirms the interdependence of the group. In times of crisis, those who are better off have a moral obligation to share their resources with relatives and neighbors who are in need.

The African tradition of sharing also extends to the products of specialized knowledge. Persons who know how to prepare medicines for particular illnesses, for example, carefully guard the secret but willingly share their concoctions with others in need. Thus, the community benefits from the collective expertise of all its members.

Colonial and postcolonial policies, sometimes deliberately and at other times unwittingly, undermined traditional values and institutions and encouraged Western-style individualism. Among the Langi, the cooperative traditions of *wang-tic* were weakened by the increasing importance of cotton, a labor-intensive commercial crop. With the large-scale cultivation of cotton by merchants, many of whom were also moneylenders, *wang-tic*

evolved into what was often essentially a forced labor team in which poorer farmers were obliged to provide labor on demand, but did not benefit from reciprocal assistance of equal value.

Several countries sought to take advantage of the tradition of community self-reliance as a means of addressing the high expectations of the early postindependence period. The Kenyan government encouraged and often gave material support to communities, mostly rural, to undertake self-help projects to speed development. These local *harambee* projects account for over two-thirds of Kenya's secondary schools, as well as a large proportion of its rural health facilities and water-supply systems. Although individual *harambee* projects varied in terms of their viability and longer-term success, collectively they contributed greatly to Kenyan rural development, at relatively low cost to the state. However, the dynamic self-reliance of the early phases of *harambee* was increasingly undermined by the Kenyan government's determination to control and direct local development initiatives to suit its own political purposes.

Like Kenya, Ethiopia sought to mobilize rural resources for its development projects. After the 1973 drought, it launched a massive program to rehabilitate highland areas decimated by soil erosion and forest clearance. Erosion removes an average of 100 t of topsoil per ha per year, causing a steady decline in crop yields in an area inhabited by almost three-quarters of Ethiopia's population. With the backing of the World Food Program, the government organized a conservation program that involved some 35 million person-days per year of community labor. In a decade, over 200,000 km of stone terraces were constructed and 20,000 ha of land were reforested. Entire watersheds were rehabilitated by building stone terraces from top to bottom on hillsides (see Figure 24.1), erecting small dams, and planting elephant grass to control gully formation.

While the massive scale and accomplishments of Ethiopia's conservation program deserve to be recognized, much more could have been done if there had been sufficient

Figure 24.1. Terraced and partially reforested hillside, Tigray Province, Ethiopia. Ethiopia has undertaken a massive program of land conservation through terracing and the mobilization of communal labor. Photo: M. Peters.

commitment by the government to fostering a strong sense of community project ownership. Control of soil-conservation projects was nominally in the hands of local peasant associations that mobilized the labor, but its direction remained very much in government hands. The official allocation of grain provided by the World Food Program to pay local conservation workers on a "food-for-work" basis effectively determined where projects would be undertaken. Instead of initiating their own community conservation projects, peasants preferred to wait in anticipation of future food-for-work support from the government. Lacking a strong sense of "ownership," villagers often failed to maintain previously completed terraces and reforestation plots.

Kenya's *harambee* projects and Ethiopia's soil-conservation programs indicate the potential benefits of development initiatives that mobilize, rather than ignore, local resources. However, because these programs were ultimately controlled and even initiated from above, their full potential as an empowering, self-sustaining strategy for development was not realized. In contrast, the success of the

Naam Movement in Burkina Faso shows how community development may take place in a way that not only mobilizes local resources but also educates and empowers those who become involved.

The Naam movement, first established in 1967 by a local teacher, had been established in 1,350 Burkinabe villages by the mid-1980s. Naam was modeled on the traditional cooperatives that were organized around annual planting and harvesting activities. The philosophy of the movement is to make each participating village responsible for its own development, to base development on what the peasant knows and wants, and to rely as much as possible on locally available, low-cost materials and tools. An integral part of the development process is village-level "animation," through which communities may analyze their own situations and develop collective responses. The locally selected animators also help to educate villagers by setting up demonstration projects and informal schools. Although technical and material support from external sources is now available for Naam chapters, the key to the movement's success has been that projects continue to be locally conceived and locally controlled.

Naam communities have undertaken a wide variety of projects, including planting trees, controlling erosion, digging wells, establishing primary-health programs, and organizing cereal banks that purchase and store grain as a protection against seasonal price increases and shortages. One of the most successful initiatives has involved building low stone barriers along slope contours to reduce soil erosion and trap runoff to grow crops and trees. Simple "water-harvesting" methods are of vital importance in areas that receive marginal amounts of precipitation and that experience frequent drought. Constructing stone barriers is a traditional technique for collecting water among the Mossi of Burkina Faso. Naam-sponsored animation informed villagers about how these structures could be more effectively built; individual Naam groups made the decision about whether this would be their immediate priority for development and organized the work themselves using their own resources.

The Naam movement, while firmly based at the grassroots level, still operates at a much larger scale than the great majority of local development groups. Collectively far more important are the countless thousands of small-scale initiatives relating to particular local concerns in communities across Africa. Very few of these are ever publicized beyond the local level, much less being externally supported. They include the work of village improvement associations that undertake the construction of places of worship, schools, feeder roads, and other amenities using their own pooled resources. They include the work of cooperatives, ranging from small-scale revolving credit schemes popular among women (see Chapter 16) to larger ventures in which community resources are pooled to provide a means of exploiting, processing, or marketing local products. They include the efforts of groups such as the Ada Salt Miner's Cooperative (see Vignette 24.1) that come together as grassroots political movements to protect local interests that are seen as threatened from the outside.

Figure 24.2. Communal work on the construction of a channel to bring rainwater to farmland, Niger. Photo: CIDA: R. Lemoyne.

Vignette 24.1. Community Mobilization and the Struggle for Resources: The Salt Miners' Cooperatives of Ada, Ghana

For centuries, the people of Ada on the coast of Ghana have exploited salt deposits produced by the evaporation of seawater. A French visitor in the late 18th century noted that attached to each household was a storage hut capable of holding at least 50 tons of salt. Salt was traded widely and at times was as valuable as gold. Chiefs and priests regulated the collection of salt, in the process ensuring that the entire community had fair access to the resource. In return, chiefs and priests received a substantial share of the salt that was collected.

In the early 1960s, ecological changes in the lagoons caused by the construction of the Akosombo Dam reduced natural salt production and severely damaged the traditional industry. A decade later, local chiefs granted exclusive mining rights to two commercial companies in return for promises of royalty payments. The people of Ada effectively lost access to their resource base.

Conflicts erupted in the early 1980s between the mining companies, which had fared poorly in their attempts to exploit the salt deposits on a commercial scale, and the local population. In order to fight for their rights to gather salt, 3,000 residents of Ada came together to form a Salt Miner's Cooperative Society. Their fight pitted the cooperative against local chiefs and elements in the government that favored commercial development of the resource.

The ensuing struggle was long and bitter. Many members of the cooperative were jailed and one person was shot and killed. The government finally agreed in 1985 to grant open access to the salt lagoons. The cooperative's struggle continues to ensure that the hard-won right to mine salt is not lost. The cooperative's adversaries in this struggle have included not only the commercial companies but also local and national governments. Following the early financial success of the salt cooperative, the District Council and local Council of Chiefs both attempted to impose new taxes on salt mining. Factions within the Ghanaian government clearly continue to support the claims of a remaining commercial company to exclusive rights over the deposits.

The evolution of the salt cooperative illustrates that development from within involves much more than local communities undertaking their own small projects. Genuine development from within is a political exercise that may well pit communities against outside interests, including those of the state. It may also divide communities, in this case on class lines. Still, the political dimension of the struggle at Ada may be seen as one of its greatest strengths. The people of Ada fought and won this battle for themselves and in the process learned much about the power of working together to achieve a common goal.

Based on T. Manuh. "Survival in rural Africa: The salt cooperatives in Ada District, Ghana." In D. R. F. Taylor and F. Mackenzie, eds., *Development from Within: Survival in Rural Africa*. London: Routledge, 1992, pp. 102–124.

The 1990s: The New Case for Local Development Initiatives

The importance of encouraging communities to undertake their own self-help initiatives has emerged, particularly since the mid-1980s, as one of the most popular themes of the "development industry." At the most basic level, local development initiatives are seen as a necessary survival strategy, given the current state of crisis in Africa. The effect of declining terms of trade, together with the imposition of structural-adjustment programs, have reduced significantly the ability of governments to maintain existing programs, much less address unmet needs. Because governments have been unable and often unwilling to provide adequate development support to enable local people to improve the quality of their lives, communities are having to become as self-reliant as possible.

The proponents of development from within often refer to the failure of conventional, top–down approaches and argue that universal solutions should be rejected in favor of strategies that are grounded in the ecological and socioeconomic realities of specific places. Because people at the local level are acutely aware of the importance of the health of the environment, it is argued that environmental degradation is much less likely to occur out of ignorance or greed, which might be the case with large-scale, externally initiated projects. Local communities have a vital interest in sustainability, since they have to live with the consequences of whatever development takes place.

Local control may help to ensure that development initiatives reflect local realities; but knowledge, needs, and priorities also vary *within* communities. The result is an increase in opportunities and resources, like the varied kinds of indigenous knowledge found at the local scale. Moreover, it may be possible to increase the involvement of women, who are often excluded from power and influence within government circles. Women have their own formal and informal organizations that may serve as vehicles for discussing and acting upon their own aspirations. Likewise, disad-

vantaged minorities may be able to achieve some of their objectives by organizing locally.

This diversity of local communities results in a dynamic that is likely to be very complex and politically sensitive. Different classes, ethnic groups, genders, and age cohorts have distinct, often divergent, aspirations. As for working together, actual communities are seldom perfect models of caring and sharing. It is dangerous to assume, for example, that they are homogeneous units of people sharing one history and one set of objectives. It cannot be taken for granted that the entire community will benefit, and certainly that its members will benefit *equally*, from community-development initiatives. Local elites usually have command of much more than their fair share of resources, and benefit most from the majority of development initiatives. Women continue to be dominated by men, and subordinate socioeconomic groups remain disadvantaged. It is common, for example, for women to do most of the work on projects that are ultimately of greater benefit to men (see Vignette 21.2 on women's tree-planting groups in rural Uganda).

The World Bank, now tentatively acknowledging some of the limitations of its past macroeconomic policies, has shown increasing interest in community-based initiatives. The World Bank's argument for this shift includes concern about the limited resources and limited administrative capacity of African governments. The hope is that decentralization and devolution of control to the local level may alleviate some of the inefficiencies and other limitations of central planning. The World Bank also rests its case for local development initiatives on the importance of ensuring that development builds upon peoples' historical traditions. The World Bank stresses that a more "participatory" approach to development builds upon robust African traditions of grassroots initiatives for community and group welfare.

The vision of locally based development promoted by the World Bank and other large agencies is quite different from that envisioned by radical and populist supporters of local development, including such early proponents as E. F. Schumacher (*Small is Beautiful*) and Paulo Freire (*Pedagogy of the Oppressed*). Freire's popular-education techniques, for example, were designed to help people to analyze their own situations as a basis for mobilization and change. As such, it is an intensely political exercise, likely to result in the kinds of challenges to authority that occurred in conjunction with the organization of the Ada Salt Miner's Cooperative. Conversely, the World Bank's vision of local development is apolitical; communities mobilize their own resources, work together to solve local problems, and do not really question or challenge the status quo. Thus, the political component that is inherent in genuine community empowerment is left unmentioned.

Primary health care is an example of a program that seems well suited as a vehicle for community mobilization and development. The rhetoric of primary health care emphasizes the importance of community empowerment – that communities should take responsibility for identifying and rectifying situations that threaten their collective health and should select a primary health care worker locally and contribute funds to pay his or her salary. For the development agencies, emphasis has been placed on the contribution of funds by communities, as opposed to community empowerment. The result has been a series of schemes to recover the costs of providing services, coupled with the promotion of the generally *disempowering* selective primary health care model (Chapter 18). In the end, rural areas usually get inferior care that they pay for themselves, while most government resources continue to go into highly subsidized conventional hospitals in urban areas.

Development from within emphasizes what communities can do for themselves, but there are limits to what they can accomplish without active government support. For a number of years, youth groups in several wards of Kano organized community clean up campaigns to remove accumulated garbage and to clear drainage channels. Frustrated by the municipal government's lack of support and failure to remove the collected refuse, community groups began to pile it in the middle of major roads,

forcing the government to respond with better arrangements for refuse collection. Communities continue to resort to blocking roads with garbage whenever regular garbage collection is interrupted.

One of the assumptions implicit in much of the writing about local development initiatives is that African communities have substantial resources, whether of land, labor, or money, that can be tapped for local development. In reality, many African communities exist near the limits of survival and have few resources to spare. Thus, for example, the imposition of apparently modest user fees for health care and education have brought about notable reductions in utilization. Even the availability of free labor cannot be taken for granted; people may be able to participate in communal work only at certain times during the year between farming seasons.

Local Development Initiatives: What Role for the Future?

The recent wave of enthusiasm about community self-help as a strategy for development needs to be examined critically. After all, it is but the latest of several approaches to development that have promised to succeed where earlier models had failed. In each case, early enthusiasm gave way to more sober assessments and ultimately to widespread disillusionment. There is no reason to believe that the newly popular approach provides the last, best answer to the development question. What follows is a summary of some key strengths and limitations of development from within as a model for African development in the 1990s.

1. *Development from within addresses some of the most glaring weaknesses of earlier approaches to development.* Arguably the most pervasive feature of past development models has been a shared arrogance about the assumed benefits and universal relevance of imported, packaged, designed-by-experts solutions to African development problems. Despite differ-

ences in the scale and objectives of various approaches—top-down progress through industrialization versus bottom-up development through IADPs, for example—all were conceived, driven, and controlled from above and outside. Local communities were virtual bystanders; local needs and realities were seldom given due consideration.

Development from within talks of redirecting control back to local communities, so that initiatives can be shaped in relation to local priorities, resources, and customs. The many potential benefits of this approach, ranging from the development of a sense of community "ownership" of the project to the application of indigenous knowledge, were reviewed earlier in this chapter. Unlike top-down strategies that rely heavily on external inputs, these local initiatives that are tailored to the availability of local resources have a better chance of long-term sustainability. Of the various benefits, the political mobilization of marginalized communities through genuine grassroots development provides the greatest potential for fundamental social and economic change.

2. *Development from within is extremely complex and unpredictable.* Genuine community development happens at its own pace and develops its own unique, local dynamic. It cannot be "willed" to happen. The complexity of the process is largely due to the great diversity of local communities. Different groups in the community, defined in relation to gender, age, class, and ethnicity, have their own histories and agendas, as well as differing abilities to participate in and benefit from particular initiatives. In the end, these divisions may frustrate efforts toward broadly based community development.

Difficulties arise not only because of divisions within local communities but also because of the determination of many governments and external agencies to control and direct community-development efforts. There is a pervasive suspicion of genuine grassroots mobilization that could question or challenge the political status quo. The continuing arrogance of educated outsiders, who assume that the ignorant peasants need guidance, is

often a problem. As the example of the Ethiopian conservation program suggests, it may be possible to achieve temporary successes through externally manipulated mobilization of local resources, but not a deeper, longer-term transformation.

3. *Local communities are not isolated, autonomous entities.* Individual African communities are not autonomous islands, divorced from wider political and economic dynamics. The linkages of local economies to the broader regional, national, and global economic spheres provide opportunities to strengthen local initiatives but at the same time are key to understanding the marginalization of people and places in the African periphery.

One of the most important institutions linking local economies to the world beyond is the periodic market (Figure 24.3). At the level of the local economy, markets provide a venue for the exchange of a wide range of goods and services, as well as opportunities for people to exchange information and to socialize. However, as the degree of incorporation of rural Africa into regional, national, and international economies has increased, the role of rural markets has progressively shifted away from local exchange toward urban–rural and interregional exchange. Locally produced primary goods are purchased by urban-based traders for resale in the city, in other regions, or abroad. Manufactured goods of many kinds move in the opposite direction, destined for sale to rural consumers.

While the terms of trade in the local marketplace represents only one factor determining the economic health of families and communities, it is an important one. Terms of trade strongly influence decisions about what to grow—cash crops or food crops, for instance. When world market prices for African primary products decline, the negative effects are felt at the local as well as the national level. When cheap imported manufactured goods flood the marketplace, the viability—and, ultimately, the survival—of local craft industries is at stake.

Economic linkages to the wider economy extend far beyond those centered in the marketplace. Local economies obtain some bene-

Figure 24.3. Periodic market. Niger State, Nigeria. Photo: author.

fits from the urban–rural and interregional exchange of people, goods, monetary resources, and knowledge. Remittances by family members working away from home represent an important source of funds for local development, especially in poorer areas that have long served as labor reserves for Africa's islands of modern economic development (Figure 24.4).

These wider economic linkages—in particular the health of regional, national, and global economies—significantly affect the ability of African communities to mobilize resources for local development. "Development from within" depends partially or primarily on "resources from without."

4. *Development from within must not be allowed to become merely development on the cheap.* The new enthusiasm for locally initiated, locally funded development comes at a time when governments have few resources to undertake new development initiatives. Local self-reliance is being endorsed at a time when foreign aid to Africa continues to be reduced and when there is an increased emphasis on debt repayment and balancing national budgets.

Critics of development from within have suggested that the enthusiasm for this approach has more to do with the desire of governments and development agencies to absolve themselves of their responsibility to facilitate development than with any commitment to progress at the grassroots level. In essence, development from within threatens to become "development on the cheap."

The possibilities for greater self-help at the community level in no way absolves governments of their responsibility to facilitate development at all levels, from the local to the national. The initiatives of individual communities are undertaken within the context of social, economic, and political policies established by the state. Does the state take seriously its responsibility to bring development to all regions and all peoples, or does it serve only a portion of its citizens? Does the state strive to create an atmosphere of peace and harmony, or does it resort to terror and "divide-and-rule" tactics? Does the state encourage independent action by community groups or is it threatened by it? These are but a few examples of the crucial role the state plays in creating, or suppressing, an en-

Figure 24.4. Modern house under construction, Jigawa State, Nigeria. This house, being built for an urban-based banker in his home village, symbolizes the importance in many rural communities of migrant remittances as a source of funds for local development. Photo: author.

abling environment for community-based development.

5. *The role of the international community remains important, but needs to change.* Just as the growth of community initiatives does not absolve African governments of responsibility for development, neither does it absolve the global community of its moral responsibility to support the quest for social justice and development in Africa. Moreover, despite the end of the Cold War, the self-interest of the West will not be well served by policies that abandon Africa and ensure deepening crises of underdevelopment.

The shift toward local development initiatives creates new opportunities for aid givers to direct assistance to regions and groups that have the greatest need. The shift toward local development initiatives also presents opportunities to ensure that the involvement of aid givers supports local institutions and is designed to endure.

As interest in local development initiatives grows, there may be increasing opportunities for local nongovernmental groups to establish

linkages with international development agencies and gain access to valuable financial, technical, and material assistance. There are dangers, however, when outside agencies attempt to direct support to areas of greatest need. This support may have a distorting effect, deliberately or unwittingly "directing" development toward objectives determined outside the community or providing the means for one faction in the community to prevail at the expense of others.

One of the most valuable roles for external agencies may be to support research and development into appropriate, low-cost technologies that have the potential to help local communities to become wealthier and more self-reliant. New, appropriate technologies such as alley cropping, energy-efficient stoves, and simple but reliable hand pumps have not always achieved their anticipated potential, but they do help to overcome specific impediments to development, at a cost that most, if not all, families can afford.

As a rule, the most important weaknesses of past research and development have not been technological but cultural. The key to success lies in finding ways of building upon indigenous technologies and within indigenous institutions, rather than imposing packaged solutions developed elsewhere, as if in a cultural vacuum. Such research must start with studies of traditional knowledge and methods in particular settings that seek to better understand how such knowledge and methods function, as a prelude to considering how they might be improved. Unfortunately, the importance of starting with and building upon local knowledge and resources is still too often ignored by outsiders.

In conclusion, development from within—initiatives within particular communities that have arisen through genuine participation—help to address the urgent needs of communities at a time when governments are able to do less and less. Successful local movements help to build a sense of empowerment among ordinary people, and with it the hope of further progress.

Governments and external agencies remain ambivalent, generally welcoming, on the one hand, initiatives in which communities donate resources to do things for themselves while asking for little or no external assistance, but responding, on the other, with suspicion and often hostility to popular initiatives that present a real challenge to the status quo.

Development from within is not new; African communities have since time immemorial worked cooperatively to achieve collective development goals. Nor is it a panacea. It cannot take the place of a well-conceived, carefully-implemented national strategy for development. It cannot by itself overcome the negative effects in peripheral regions of deteriorating terms of trade in the global economy. It is not an alternative to addressing the root causes of African underdevelopment. Without fundamental changes in the political–economic relation that underlie the current crisis in Africa, development from within is unlikely to achieve more than small, sporadic victories for the disadvantaged majority.

Further Reading

As an introduction to the literature on local development, consult the following source:

Dow, H., and J. Barker. *Popular Participation and Development: A Bibliography on Africa and Latin America.* Toronto, Ontario: University of Toronto Centre for Urban and Community Studies, 1992.

Some of the precursors of the contemporary interest in local development initiatives include the following sources:

Freire, P. *Pedagogy of the Oppressed.* New York: Seabury, 1970.
Lipton, M. *Why Poor People Stay Poor: Urban Bias in World Development.* London: Temple Smith, 1977.
Schumacher, E. F. *Small is Beautiful.* London: Abacus, 1978.

The case for community-based rural development is made in the following sources:

Ake, C. "Sustaining development on the indigenous." *Background Papers: From Crisis to Sustainable Development.* Washington, DC: World Bank, 1989.
Brokensha, D. W., D. M. Warren ,and O. Werner, eds. *Indigenous Systems of Knowledge and Development.* Lanham, MD: University Press of America, 1980.
Chambers, R. *Rural Development: Putting the Last First.* Harlow, England: Longman, 1983.
Chambers, R. "The state and rural development: Ideologies and an agenda for the 1990s." *IDS Discussion Paper 269,* University of Sussex, 1989.
Goulet, D. "Participation in development: New avenues." *World Development,* vol. 17 (1989), pp. 165–178.
Harrison, P. *The Greening of Africa.* London: Paladin, 1987.
Taylor, D. R. F., and F. Mackenzie, eds. *Development from Within: Survival in Rural Africa.* London: Routledge, 1992. (Chapters 1 and 10 are overviews, Chapters 2 to 9 case studies.)

On the World Bank's approach to community-based development, see the following sources:

World Bank. *Sub-Saharan Africa: From Crisis to Sustainable Growth.* Washington, DC: World Bank, 1989.
World Bank. *World Development Report, 1990: Poverty.* Washington, DC: World Bank, 1990.

Case studies that examine the problems and prospects of local development initiatives include the following sources:

Chambers, R., A. Pacey, and L. A. Thrupp. *Farmer First: Farmer Innovation and Agricultural Research*. London: Intermediate Technology, 1989.

Mackenzie, F. "Local initiatives and national policy: Gender and agricultural change in Murang'a District, Kenya." *Canadian Journal of African Studies*, vol. 20 (1986), pp. 377–401.

Swanson, R. "Development interventions and self-realization among the Gourma (Upper Volta)." In D. W. Brokensha, D. M. Warren, and O. Werner, eds., *Indigenous Systems of Knowledge and Development*, pp. 67–91. Lanham, MD: University Press of America, 1980.

For a thought-provoking overview of the importance of appropriate technology for Third World development, see the following source:

Smillie, I. *Mastering the Machine: Poverty, Aid and Technology*. London: Intermediate Technology Publications, 1991.

POLITICAL GEOGRAPHY: REGIONAL CASE STUDIES

In contrast to the thematic approach used in previous sections, the last three chapters are structured regionally. They explore aspects of the contemporary political geography of Africa south of the Sahara that have unfolded, and continue to unfold, in specific countries and regions. These processes have profound implications for the future shape and "health" of African societies and economies.

Chapter 25 surveys the political geography of Nigeria since independence. The stability of Nigeria, with Africa's largest population and second largest economy, is important not only for Nigeria itself but also for Africa as a whole. Nigeria has survived a civil war, several coups d'état, and various other crises. It is argued in the chapter that a series of policies designed to accommodate diversity has contributed significantly to its ability to survive. Most other African countries face similar challenges of accommodating diversity and have used some of the same strategies that Nigeria has used.

Chapter 26 focuses on South Africa in the early 1990s as it grapples with the immensely complex problem of dismantling apartheid. The chapter provides an historical overview of the evolution of apartheid, leading up to its demise. Nevertheless, while the changes are certain to be dramatic, one can still only speculate about the future social and economic geographies of South Africa. The end of apartheid will affect not only South Africa's future prospects but also those of surrounding countries—and, ultimately, of the continent as a whole.

The regional effect that South Africa has had—and may be expected to have in the future—is considered in Chapter 27. Economically, South Africa has long dominated its smaller and weaker neighbors through diverse mechanisms ranging from the structure of trade and transportation systems to the survival of a century-old system of labor migration to South African mines and farms. During the 1970s and 1980s, South Africa resorted to terror and intimidation in a futile attempt to preserve apartheid by weakening its neighbors. Coincidentally, the countries of Southern Africa came together to form the Southern African Development Coordination Conference (SADCC) in an attempt to counteract South African influence through regional cooperation. The SADCC experiment is of wider interest, since the development of greater regional cooperation has often been proposed as a means of improving Africa's economic prospects.

25

✳

Nigeria: The Politics of Accommodating Diversity

The nations of Africa south of the Sahara have all faced the challenge of nation building – the challenge of creating a sense of national identity and common resolve among their disparate peoples. African countries are characterized not only by ethnic, linguistic, religious, and cultural diversity, but also by colonial histories in which "divide-and-rule" tactics often heightened the tensions caused by this diversity. Moreover, the economies of these arbitarily defined national entities developed very unevenly during the colonial era; economic disparities were increased by the concentration of modern development in a few enclaves.

There are few nations in which the complexities of nation building are more obvious than in Nigeria. The political history of Nigeria has repeatedly revolved around such problems as the regional and ethnic divisions of power and wealth and the search for balance between the demands of special interests and of national unity. The bloody civil war of 1967 to 1970 provides ample proof that the process has sometimes been very traumatic. Nevertheless, as this chapter shows, Nigeria has managed to survive, in large part because of a series of measures like the creation of new states that have been designed to reduce tensions by accommodating diversity.

Diversity

Nigeria was, and still remains, a creation of British imperialism. The country did not come into existence until 1914, when the protectorates of Northern and Southern Nigeria were amalgamated. Previously, Southern Nigeria had been formed by joining together the Colony of Lagos, Niger Coast Protectorate, and territory administered by the Royal Niger Company. Nigeria's international borders were not "natural," in that they followed neither major physical features nor preexisting political borders. Moreover, the negotiations in Europe that drew Nigeria's borders brought about the separation of several groups between neighboring countries, for example, the Hausa–Fulani between Nigeria and Niger, the Kanuri between Nigeria, Niger, and Chad, and the Yoruba and Bussawa between Nigeria and Benin.

The rather artificial creation known as Nigeria brought together a great diversity of peoples. *Nigeria in Maps,* by Barbour et al.

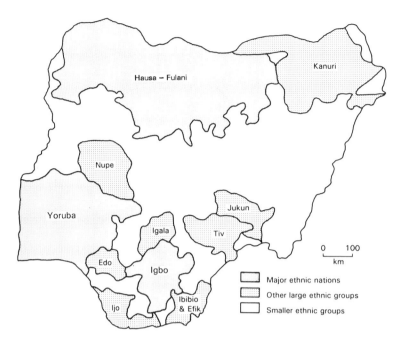

Figure 25.1. Major ethnic groups in Nigeria. There is a strong regional dimension to ethnic power in Nigeria, particularly in relation to the three largest groups.

(New York: Africana, 1982) indicates that the country has 395 indigenous languages belonging to 10 different major language groupings. The diversity of peoples also extends to religion, including both indigenous religions still widely practiced in some parts of the country and the introduced religions of Christianity and Islam.

Nigeria is often characterized as an amalgum of three ethnic nations: the Hausa–Fulani in the North, the Yoruba in the southwest, and the Igbo in the southeast. According to the 1963 census, these three ethnic nations accounted for two-thirds of the Nigerian population; the Hausa–Fulani made up 29.5%, the Yoruba 20.3%, and the Igbo 16.6% of the population. Yet Nigeria also has several other large ethnic groups, including the Kanuri in northern Nigeria; the Tiv and Nupe in central Nigeria; and the Ibibio, Edo, and Ijo in southern Nigeria (Figure 25.1). Each of these groups makes at least 1% of Nigeria's population, variously estimated at 88.5 million to 115 million (Vignette 25.1). The remaining ethnic groups together represent less than 20% of the total population.

Each of these major ethnic nations evolved with its own cultural, religious, and political traditions. The Hausa culture developed in a series of autonomous city–states that were incorporated into the Fulani-ruled Sokoto Empire in the early 19th century. Although Islam had been practiced among the Hausa for hundreds of years, it was only after the ascendancy of the Sokoto Empire that strict adherence to Islamic teachings became the foundation upon which all aspects of Hausa-Fulani life were structured. The Kanuri of northeastern Nigeria also have a long Islamic history and political development, as illustrated by the empire of Kanem-Borno which lasted from from the ninth century A.D. until the colonial conquest.

In southern Nigeria, the Yoruba and Edo were organized into a network of large and sophisticated semi-independent city–states. Conversely, the Igbo in precolonial times lived in spatially dispersed communities that functioned democratically without chiefs and other strong traditions of centralized government. Christianity made strong inroads during the colonial era in southern Nigeria, especially

Vignette 25.1. How Many Nigerians?

Few issues have evoked greater and more lasting controversy than that of the census; the question is not only how many Nigerians there are but also where they live. Population figures are important because they are the primary determinant of revenue allocations and parliamentary representation during civilian times. The distribution of population also has a strong psychological effect, related to the concern of most southerners about "northern" control, and vice versa.

Conducting a census in Nigeria has always been a difficult task. It is a very populous and diverse country. Prior to the 1970s and particularly during colonial times, there was a strong incentive to avoid being counted because of the perceived relation between the census and taxation. Moreover, it has always been hard to get an accurate count in Islamic areas where the strict seclusion of women in purdah is widely practiced. Since independence, concern about the regional distribution of political and economic benefits has provided a powerful incentive for localities and states to inflate their populations, not least because of the belief that there will be cheating in other parts of the country—cheat to avoid being cheated.

The 1952–1953 colonial census recorded 30.4 million Nigerians, which is usually considered to have been an undercount. The Northern Region accounted for 55% of the total. The first postindependence census in 1962 proved to be a political bombshell; the population of the Eastern Region and Western Region was recorded as having increased by 70% in one decade, compared to only 30% growth in the north. With northern hegemony clearly at stake, the government rejected the 1962 figures and ordered a recount. The new 1963 census showed a population of 55.6 million, including nearly 30 million in the north. This time, even more people were found; the Northern Region's population was 67% higher than in 1952–1953, the Eastern Region was 65% higher, and the Western Region was almost 100% above the 1952–1953 figures.

While the 1963 census results were widely rejected by demographers, the Nigerian government had little choice but to use them. Unfortunately, the next census to be accepted by the government did not take place until 1991. For three decades, Nigeria's national and regional populations were estimated using the 1963 figures as a baseline for projections. Nigeria has been forced, in effect, to "plan without figures."

Nigeria's next census, undertaken in November 1973, provided still more in the way of surprises. The preliminary figures gave a national population of 79.8 million, more than 40% above the inflated 1963 total. Moreover, major regional differences in growth were recorded; while two of the northern states allegedly had almost doubled in population between 1963 and 1973, two of the southern states had lower populations. These trends could not possibly have been attributable to interregional migration or differences in natural increase. The release of the preliminary 1973 census results sparked a predictable response of outrage, especially in the southern states. The government had no option but to rule the 1973 census null and void.

A number of nationwide programs during the 1970s and early 1980s provided partial population data suggesting that the 1963 totals might not be as inaccurate as once believed. Universal Primary Education was implemented in 1976, comprehensive vaccination programs were undertaken for smallpox and later for childhood diseases, a national fertility survey was completed, and voters were enumerated in 1978–1979 and 1982–1983. A total of 47.5 million electors were enumerated in 1979, suggesting a national population of perhaps 90 to 100 million.

cont.

Vignette 25.1. (cont.)

Until 1992, there was general agreement that Nigeria's population was well over 100 million, and perhaps as high as 125 million. The World Bank's estimate for 1990 was 117.4 million. The release of preliminary figures from the 1991 census provided yet another shock. Only 88.45 million Nigerians were enumerated, at least 20 to 30 million less than anticipated. Large regional disparities in growth between 1963 and 1991 were found. In general, the rate of growth was higher in the northern states than in several of the southern states, thus confirming the numerical superiority of the north.

With an election campaign in progress at the time, it is hardly surprising that some claimed that the population had been undercounted in their parts of the country. However, the public response to the release of these figures was, in general, quite positive. The government was seen to have made every effort to depoliticize the process and to ensure as accurate a count as possible. United Nations representatives who obser016erd the census exercise have expressed confidence in the results.

Nigerians responded with ambivalence to the news that their national population was much lower than previously thought. On the one hand, Nigeria's national ego has been linked in no small part to its enormous size. On the other hand, the smaller population figure implies that the problems of rapid population growth may be less acute than previously believed.

For Nigerian officials, having widely accepted population data will facilitate more effective development planning. It means that one of the country's most divisive political issues can be set aside for at least a decade. However, no one familiar with the chaotic history of previous Nigerian censuses is likely to predict what surprises and controversies might emerge when the results of future censuses, in 2001 and beyond, are released.

Based on R. M. Prothero. "Nigeria loses count." *The Geographical Magazine*, vol. 47 (October 1974), pp. 24–28. P. Idowu, N. Adio-Saka, and B. Olowo. "A game of numbers," *West Africa*, (March 30–April 5, 1992), pp. 539–541.

---

in Igboland. Among the Yoruba, there are more or less equal numbers of Muslims and Christians, as well as many adherents of indigenous religions.

The territories separating the major groups are occupied by a profusion of smaller groups with varied cultural and religious backgrounds. These groups represent a particularly important element in the Middle Belt, the zone located between the Hausa–Fulani heartland in the north and the Igbo and Yoruba homelands in the south.

The administrative structure, under which the colony was divided into three regions (Northern, Eastern, and Western Nigeria), helped to intensify regional differences. This framework tacitly, if not explicitly, legitimated the domination of the various minority groups by the Hausa–Fulani, Igbo, and Yoruba. As a result, there was considerable discontent among the ethnic minorities in each region. This was particularly the case in Northern Nigeria where the implementation of indirect rule meant that Muslim Fulani emirs continued to exercise considerable authority over many non-Muslim minority peoples.

The colonial administration of the three regions differed in a number of respects, the most important being the decision to give low priority to Western education and to limit the work of Christian missionaries in Islamic parts of northern Nigeria. These policies created a

Figure 25.2. Groundnut pyramids, Jigawa State, Nigeria. Nigeria's colonial-era export economy, based on the export of agricultural products, has faded into insignificance since the rise of the petroleum economy in the 1970s. Photo: author.

large north–south gap in levels of education and development. At independence, southern Nigeria had 12 times as many primary-school students and 10 times as many secondary students as equally populous northern Nigeria. Interregional distrust intensified, and southerners, even in northern Nigeria, continued to hold most jobs in the public sector.

Nigeria since Independence

Nigeria became independent in October 1960, after several years of strenuous debate about the future shape of political institutions. Under the new constitution, considerable power was reserved for the regional governments of the federation. The British parliamentary system provided the organizational model for federal and regional governments. Much to the consternation of the southern politicians who had fought long and hard for independence, the first government was dominated by conservative elements from northern Nigeria who had been relatively inactive in the independence movement. Interregional–and, to a lesser extent, intraregional–tensions arose concerning, among other things, the allocation of funds for development, access to

government jobs, the alleged rigging of census figures, and electoral abuse.

With Nigeria's fragile political institutions near collapse, a number of junior officers staged a bloody coup d'état in January 1966 and established an Igbo-dominated military regime. A northern countercoup occurred in July 1966, leading to the installation of Lieutenant Colonel Gowon as leader. Disillusioned by this turn of events and the occurrence of widespread, bloody riots directed against Igbos living in northern Nigeria, the Eastern Region declared itself the independent Republic of Biafra in May 1967.

For the next two and a half years, a bitter civil war was fought over the future shape of Nigeria. At stake was not only its territorial integrity but also the question of who would benefit from the recently discovered large petroleum deposits in the Niger Delta. While there was widespread public sympathy for the Biafran cause, most governments supported the Nigerian campaign to reunite the country. To do otherwise, it was argued, would call into question the legitimacy of almost every African border and nation state. However, the international support that Biafra received from France, South Africa, and Portugal prolonged the war and increased the level of suffering.

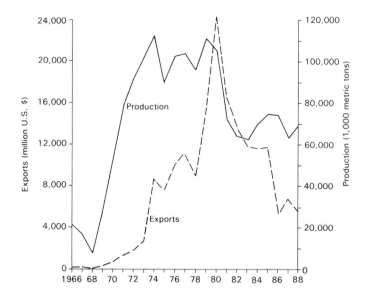

Figure 25.3. Petroleum in Nigeria's export economy, 1966 to 1988. Data source: UNCTAD. *Commodity Yearbook.* New York: United Nations (various years).

The Biafran resistance ended in January 1970, and the breakaway region was reincorporated into Nigeria with surprisingly few recriminations.

Military rule continued until 1979, when a new, elected civilian regime took power. Between 1970 and 1979, there were actually three military regimes. General Gowon retained power until July 1976, when he was overthrown. General Murtala Mohammed ruled for only seven months before he was assassinated in an attempted coup staged mostly by military personel from Gowon's home base in the Middle Belt. Murtala's former deputy, General Obasanjo, then assumed power and presided over the return to civilian rule.

The 1970s brought hitherto unimagined growth to the Nigerian economy. Petroleum exports increased from 150 million barrels per year in 1966 before the war to 1.1 billion in 1980, and the value of oil in the world marketplace grew rapidly with the formation of the Organization of Petroleum Exporting Countries (OPEC). The expanded income was used by both federal and state governments to undertake many social and economic projects throughout the country. Although most of the growth took place in the various capital cities, a few initiatives such as Universal Primary Education were implemented in every corner of the nation, often in areas that had been bypassed in the expenditures of previous governments. Industry and commerce experienced rapid growth and diversification. The 1970s also saw the growth of conspicuous consumption among those able to gain access to oil wealth. The rapid growth of revenue, and the military government's policy of equitably distributing these funds to all states, led to a period of comparative political peace.

Civilian rule was reestablished in 1979 with a constitution modeled on that of the United States. The election was contested by five parties, each of which had a strong regional base. The relatively conservative and northern-based National Party (NPN) won, gaining strong support from most of the minority regions. The NPN was reelected in very controversial elections in 1983. It was felt by many that Nigeria's second experiment with democracy had been grossly abused, especially by a clique of NPN insiders, popularly known as the Kaduna Mafia, who distributed wealth and privileges to themselves and their friends at an unprecedented rate. Falling government revenues because of the collapse of the international petroleum market, the proliferation of wasteful public spending, and large increases in the volume of nonessential imports brought about a deepening economic crisis that the government refused to acknowledge.

The NPN government was overthrown in a northern-dominated coup on December 31, 1983. This military intervention was widely seen as a necessary response to the worsening economic and political situation. However, the new regime headed by Major General Buhari lost much of its public support as it revealed itself to be inflexible and autocratic. His regime was deposed in August, 1985 in a coup led by Major General Babangida. Babangida's regime had its share of controversies and opposition, including two serious abortive coups d'état, but it brought back a degree of stability to the country. Having inherited a massive foreign debt (most of which was incurred during the 1979 to 1983 period), much reduced export earnings, and a stagnating domestic economy, Babangida was forced to undertake a massive devaluation of the currency and to greatly reduce public-sector spending. In essence, Nigeria avoided having to accept unpalatable IMF conditions by implementing its own package of IMF-type reforms. Babangida displayed considerable political skill in managing to "sell" these highly unpopular measures to Nigerians.

Babangida took several initiatives to bring about a return to civilian rule in 1992 to 1993. Perhaps most controversial was the creation of a two-party system in which party ideologies were imposed by the military government. Babangida argued that specifying the shape of political institutions would break the cycle of ethnic, religious, and regional rivalries in the political arena that had caused Nigeria so much past grief. The mid-1993 presidential election was relatively orderly, the old regional voting patterns were much less intense, and one of the candidates, Chief Abiola, won decisively. Nigerian democracy seemed on the verge of a major triumph, but Babangida had another surprise in store. He

Figure 25.4. Oil rig, Niger Delta, Nigeria. Photo: CIDA: B. Paton.

annulled the election and declared that he would retain power, while vaguely promising another election.

The last few months of 1993 were very chaotic. Faced with strong opposition, both within Nigeria and internationally, Babangida resigned, and put a hand-picked civilian president into office. Given the new president's absolute lack of legitimacy, it was hardly a surprise when Major General Sani Abacha, who had been the head of the armed forces throughout Babangida's years in power, staged a bloodless coup in December 1993. Back to square one.

In mid-1994, the political climate of Nigeria became increasingly tense. Chief Abiola, winner of the annulled 1993 election, was imprisoned after declaring himself president. Prodemocracy forces launched a campaign of civil disobedience, including a general strike that crippled the vital petroleum industry and other sectors of the economy. The military

government responded to the challenges of
the prodemocracy movement by steadily increasing the level of intimidation and repression. Because the campaign against the
northern-dominated military government was
centered in the southern states, it has served
to revive long-standing regional, ethnic, and
religious antagonisms. Nigeria's political future
has seldom been in greater doubt.

Accommodating Diversity

Nigerian governments since independence, in
their quest for political stability, have used
several specific strategies and a stated commitment to equitable sharing of government
resources, development, and power. A number of the strategies used by the Nigerian state
have clearly defined spatial dimensions to
them. Three of these, the creation of new
states, the commitment to an equitable formula for sharing revenues and other benefits
dispensed by the federal government, and the
decision to relocate the capital city, are discussed below. In every case, political imper-
atives have sometimes conflicted with
economic rationality. It may be argued,
however, that it has been a necessary price
to pay for a united Nigeria.

The Formation of New States

Nigeria inherited a very unwieldy political
structure at independence. The Northern,
Eastern, and Western Regions were large and
powerful enough to be semiautonomous. Development tended to be highly concentrated
and large areas were virtually ignored. Minority
groups felt excluded from decisions and believed that any sign of political insubordina-
tion would result in even greater marginalization for their homelands.

The creation in 1963 of the Mid-Western
Region in part of the Western Region was the
first step in the dismantling of the old political structure, but long-standing appeals for the
creation of regions in minority-dominated
areas were not addressed. In 1967, the Nigerian government announced the formation of

a new 12-state structure. This decision was
taken hastily in response to the imminent
threat of Biafran secession. The move was
justified as a response to the aspirations of
minorities, but in reality it was designed to
deprive the rebellious Eastern Region of much
of its territory, economic base, and population. For convenience, the boundaries of the
new states followed existing provincial boundaries within the regions.

The 12 newly created states varied greatly
in area (1,381 to 105,300 sq mi), population
(1.5 to 9.5 million), and resource endowment.
For example, while some states had a surplus
of qualified personnel, the development of
other states was slowed because of an acute
shortage of well-educated workers. Most of
the states' revenue was derived from federal-
government transfer payments. Each new
state faced a unique set of challenges in these
early days – challenges that were more daunting because the federal government was preoccupied with problems related to the civil war.

The 1967 reform of the political map did
not end the clamor for additional states. Indeed, the end of the civil war and Gowon's
promise of a return to civilian rule intensified
demands for statehood in many aggrieved
regions. The basis of these demands varied;
among the most common complaints were alleged discrimination or neglect by the existing state governments, long-standing emnities
between ethnic groups, the righting of colonial
wrongs, the need for balanced development,
and the large size of certain states compared
to others. Predictably, the creation of more
states was one of the first promises made in
1975 following the Murtala coup d'état. The
number of states was increased subsequently
to 19, 10 of which were located in the north.

With the return to civilian rule in 1979, and
particularly at the time of the 1983 election,
the clamor for still more new states reached
a fever pitch. A senate committee recommended a total of 45. However, the growing
economic crisis forced the government to
postpone any decision. Following the 1983
coup, the new military government banned all
efforts aimed at creating new states. Nevertheless, under Babangida's administration, 2 new

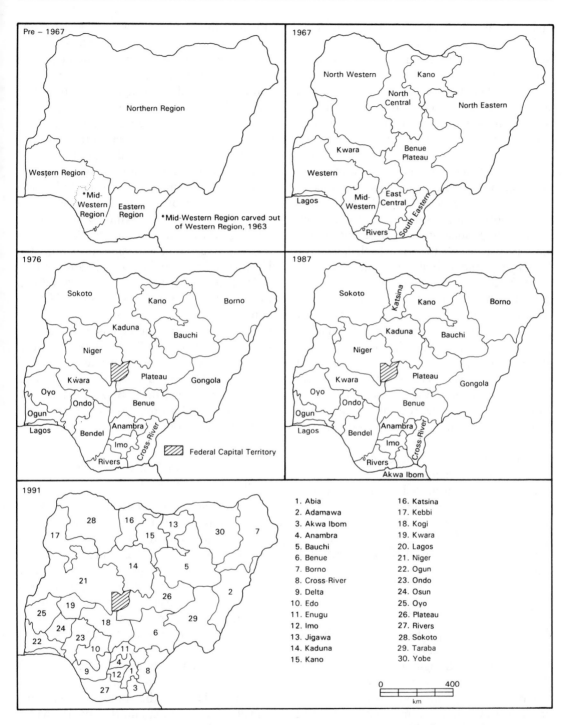

Figure 25.4. The evolution of Nigeria's political map, 1960 to 1992. Nigeria's political map has been in a state of constant flux since independence. Nevertheless, many regional and ethnic interest groups aspire to have even more states created.

states were added in 1987 and 9 more in 1991. Nigeria now has 30 states, varying considerably in size, wealth, and prospects for future development.

The proliferation of states may be seen as a valid response to political reality or as a massive waste of scarce resources. On the one hand, it addresses the aspirations of many minority groups and peripheral regions. It has brought about a much more even distribution of development than would have been likely with the old regional structure. Moreover, the subdivision of large, wealthy states has contributed to political stability by ensuring that no state will be able to seriously challenge the authority of the federal government. On the other hand, the growing number of states is a heavy financial burden that Nigeria can ill afford. The use of scarce resources to pay more civil servants' salaries and to build more government office towers should not be a high development priority. Among the strongest proponents of state creation have been entrepreneurs, civil servants, and politicians—groups whose self-interest in gaining more direct access to government-related opportunities and funds is obvious.

The proliferation of states has helped to diffuse regional, religious, and ethnic hostilities and has contributed to the dispersion of oil wealth and economic growth in previously neglected areas. On balance, this expensive and often wasteful exercise has done much to make possible the survival of Nigeria.

Creating a New Capital

Lagos, Nigeria's capital city, was for long the subject of controversy. Some argued that Lagos was too strongly associated with the Yoruba and that the capital city should be a symbol of all Nigerians. Even in colonial times, it was a crowded, rather unattractive city. The oil boom of the 1970s brought rapid population growth and much new development—commercial, industrial, and institutional. Day-to-day activities and longer term planning became increasingly difficult in this already congested city. Nigerian government offices were situated in crowded downtown locations where orderly expansion was difficult.

In 1976, the government established a commission to consider the capital-city question. It recommended establishment of a new capital at Abuja, at the time a small village located north of the confluence of the Niger and Benue rivers. The area around the new city was designated the Federal Capital Territory in order to differentiate it from any one state. The choice of Abuja, centrally located within the country and away from the Hausa, Yoruba, and Igbo heartlands, symbolized a new beginning for the nation. The plan (see Figure 13.9) envisaged an imposing inselberg, Aso Hill, as the focal point for the new capital.

Abuja has been an expensive undertaking; by 1986, the costs had reached some $4.5 billion. Moreover, many civil servants have been reluctant to move from the cosmopolitan city of Lagos to the still developing Abuja. Nevertheless, the project has been welcomed as an important symbol of progress, much in the same way that most Brazilians had welcomed the establishment of their new capital two decades earlier.

Governing According to the "Federal Character" of Nigeria

For each Nigerian government, one of the most daunting challenges has been to allocate resources and rewards to the various parts of the country in a way that minimizes the inevitable charges of regional and ethnic bias. In a country where the federal government controls the vast majority of public wealth, the question of revenue allocation is bound to be crucial and controversial. The Nigerian government provides about 90% of the revenue needed by state governments, including a 70% share from a common pool of oil revenues. Half of this money is allocated equally to each state, and the rest is divided in proportion to each state's population.

What has remained much more open to debate has been the allocation of other rewards—ranging from positions in the federal cabinet, civil service, and military; to the allocation of scholarships and admissions to universities; to the location of such federally funded projects as new industries, colleges, and roads. It is seldom possible to treat all states equally in such undertakings; and even if equal distribution were possible, it would often be counterproductive, with efficiency and other reasonable criteria being sacrificed in the quest for equality.

The constitution of the Second Republic (1979 to 1983) was explicit about how the "federal character" of Nigeria was to be protected by providing for the appointment of at least one cabinet member from each state and specifying that ambassadors and the armed forces should also reflect the nation. The principle of equity was even extended to scholarships and admission to federal training programs. However, even the inclusion of these provisions in the constitution did not stop the bickering and charges of favoritism, especially from states governed by parties not included in the federal coalition.

Planning on the basis of political/equity principles has produced some dubious results. A glaring example concerns the location of rolling mills to process output from the new steel complex at Ajaokuta near the junction of the Niger and Benue rivers. Mills have been established at Oshogbo, Katsina, and Jos; all three are badly underutilized. These cities have very little other industry and are not well located to supply what the existing steel-utilizing industries need.

As states continue to proliferate, the problems of adhering to established equity principles increase. In the late 1970s, there was a major expansion of the national university system to ensure that institutions of higher learning would be located in every state. It is doubtful that a further expansion of this system to open more universities in the most recently established states can be justified, given the outstanding needs of existing universities and the scarcity of resources.

Unresolved Controversies

Nigeria has survived through three tumultuous decades of independence. The future promises to be no less challenging. The discussion turns briefly to three key questions that will remain unresolved for a long time to come.

The Future Role of the Military

Nigeria's third experiment with democracy and civilian rule was terminated by the military, even before a civilian authority had come to power. In general, military governments have been more successful than their civilian counterparts in quelling regional bickering. Nigerian civilian regimes have found equity concepts especially troublesome owing to inevitable charges of "political favoritism." It remains to be seen what the current military leaders will have to offer. The 1992 constitution seemed to have paved the way for a breaking of traditional alliances and the regional bickering that went with them. However, that opportunity for political reform has been lost. It would be very hard to replicate these reforms, not least because the Nigerian people will be very skeptical indeed about the motives of the military in light of what happened in 1993.

Given the military's past history of repeatedly intervening in politics, Nigeria is unlikely to have seen its last coup. The nature of future military regimes cannot be taken for granted. Nigeria has been fortunate to have had military rulers who were relatively competent and committed to national unity. The Abacha regime's increasingly divisive and repressive response to the prodemocracy campaigns of 1994 represents a new and disturbing trend in Nigerian military rule. All military rule is ultimately based on the power of the sword; there is always a tangible risk that this power may be used as an instrument of terror and oppression.

Religious Fundamentalism and Intolerance

Religious tensions, which played a prominent role in events leading up to the civil war, have shown signs of recurring. The most serious cause of these tensions has been the growth of fundamentalism among both Muslims and

Vignette 25.1. 'Yan Tatsine: Anatomy of an Islamic Protest Movement

With so much attention given to interregional, interethnic, and interreligious tensions in Nigeria, there has been a tendency to see these broad categories as homogeneous and fixed regarding attitude and behavior and as much more important than various dimensions of class conflict. The 'Yan Tatsine protests that rocked Kano and several other northern cities in the early 1980s point to the naïveté of such a view.

The 'Yan Tatsine were followers of an unorthodox and outspoken religious leader, Alhaji Mohammed Marwa Maitatsine. The meaning of the name Maitatsine in Hausa is "the one who damns," which alludes to his frequent, bitter public condemnation of the Nigerian state and the effects of growing modernization and corruption on northern Nigerian society. His greatest wrath was directed at the conspicuous consumption of the wealthy elites and the police, whom he accused of being the elites' agents.

Maitatsine became increasingly influential during the 1970s, especially among unemployed migrants and among the gardawa – young adult males who study the Koran and also work part-time to support themselves. The group divorced itself from the mainstream and congregated around the home of their leader. Confrontations with police and "nonbelievers" became more frequent and violent.

On December 18, 1980, Maitatsine and his followers staged an uprising, taking over a part of the old city of Kano and for 10 days fighting off the police. The uprising was finally quelled by the armed forces following several hours of artillery fire. The official death toll was 4,177 'Yan Tatsine, several police and military personnel, and numerous civilians. Maitatsine himself was killed as he and his followers attempted to escape.

The 'Yan Tatsine did not disappear with the death of their leader. Similar uprisings occurred in a number of other cities in northern Nigeria between 1981 and 1985.

To the religious, political, and economic elites of Kano, Maitatsine was a fanatic and infidel who had espoused false Islamic beliefs and had falsely proclaimed himself a prophet. The Nigerian government argued that these uprisings were mounted by non-Nigerians and sponsored by foreign Islamic fundamentalists intent on destabilizing Nigeria. However, the official inquiry noted that the vulnerability of unemployed and alienated migrant youth had contributed to the uprising.

In his article, Paul Lubeck discusses changes in Kano's society and economy as they pertain to the alienation of the gardawa and their desperate protest in 1980. The traditional hospitality and material support accorded to itinerant Islamic scholars and their students began to disappear in the 1970s; they were increasingly labeled as vagrants and vagabonds. With conditions in the rural economy deteriorating, more gardawa came to Kano and stayed for a longer time. However, many of their jobs in the informal economy were disappearing. Their hitherto free housing in the entryways of homes became increasingly scarce. Meanwhile, the elites were busily engaged in an orgy of accumulation, seemingly unconcerned about either the misery of the poor or the state of Islam.

Based on P. Lubeck. "Islamic protest under semi-industrial capitalism: 'Yan Tatsine explained." Africa, vol. 55 (1985), pp. 369–89.

Christians. Fundamentalism has encouraged a much less tolerant attitude toward "unbelievers" and a more aggressive approach to proselytizing. Tensions have been especially great in communities where both faiths have been competing for converts, as in the Middle Belt. In short, the geography of power has not changed; the middle is still caught in the multifaceted struggle between northern and southern interests. Religious riots have erupted several times and in several places, especially in northern Nigeria, during the past decade. A considerable number of lives have been lost, but in the longer run the most important casualty may have been Nigerians' trust in their ability to live together in harmony.

Another long-standing religious controversy concerns the future role of the Islamic legal code, *shari'a*, in the country. In past constitutional discussions, Muslims, especially in northern states, have demanded that the Islamic legal code to be used in cases involving Muslims. Needless to say, non-Muslims have strenuously rejected the notion of adopting *shari'a*, even in limited circumstances. There are widespread fears, however exaggerated, that a northern-dominated government could attempt to widen the application of the code to Christians. The example of the Sudan, where attempts by an Islamic government to impose Islamic institutions in the south have led to civil war, is a potent symbol for many Nigerians of why *shari'a* must be opposed as a threat to the religious freedom of Nigerians.

The Sustainability of Nigerian Development

Modern Nigeria has been built with petroleum revenues. Petroleum accounts for over 90% of exports by value; the old economy based on agricultural exports has all but disappeared. Petroleum has made a few Nigerians very wealthy, but it has not made Nigeria a wealthy nation. Nigeria's 1989 per capita income of $250 was the 13th lowest in the world.

The prospect of a future Nigeria with rapidly declining petroleum reserves, few other sources of wealth, and an economy addicted to large petroleum subsidies is very real. It will be a Nigeria with a much larger population than today and inevitably still coping with the same problems of accommodating diversity. It will be a Nigeria with disparities of wealth and power even greater than today, in which the poor will be even more left to their own

devices. The shape of a future Nigeria without substantial oil wealth is very much uncertain.

Further Reading

Good introductions to the geography of Nigeria are found in the following sources:

Barbour, K. M., J. S. Oguntoyinbo, J. O. C. Onyemelukwe, and J. C. Nwafor. *Nigeria in Maps*. New York: Africana, 1982.

Buchanan, K. M., and J. C. Pugh. *Land and People in Nigeria*. London: University of London Press, 1955.

Morgan, W. T. M. *Nigeria*. London: Longman, 1983.

Oguntoyinbo, J. S., O. O. Areola, and M. Filani, eds. *A Geography of Nigerian Development*. Ibadan, Nigeria: Heinemann, 1978.

Udo, R. *Geographical Regions of Nigeria*. London: Heinemann, 1970.

On the colonial history of Nigeria, see the following sources:

Crowder, M. *West Africa under Colonial Rule*. Evanston, IL: Northwestern University Press, 1968.

Lugard, F. D. *The Dual Mandate in British Tropical Africa*. London: George Allen and Unwin, 1922.

On the development of the modern Nigeria state, see the following sources:

Ajayi, J. F. A., and B. Ikara. *Evolution of Political Culture in Nigeria*. Ibadan, Nigeria: Ibadan University Press, 1985.

Graf, W. D. *The Nigerian State*. Portsmouth, NH: Heinemann, 1988.

Kirk-Greene, A. M. H., and D. Rimmer. *Nigeria Since 1970: A Political and Economic Outline*. London: Hodder and Stoughton, 1981.

Peil, M. *Nigerian Politics*. London: Cassell, 1976.

Sklar, R. *Nigerian Political Parties*. New York: Nok, 1983.

Aspects of the political economy of contemporary Nigeria are explored in the following sources:

Bienen, H., and V. P. Diejomaoh, eds. *The Political Economy of Income Distribution in Nigeria*. New York: Holmes and Meier, 1981.

Ihonvbere, J. O., and T. M. Shaw. *Towards a Political Economy of Nigeria*. Brookfield, WI: Avebury, 1988.

"Oil, debts and democracy in Nigeria." *Review of African Political Economy*, no. 37 (1986), pp. 1–105.

Williams, G., ed. *Nigeria: Economy and Society.* London: Rex Collings, 1976.

Zartman, L. W., ed. *The Political Economy of Nigeria.* New York: Praeger, 1983.

Several Nigerian leaders have published their memoirs; while they vary in quality and insight, they are interesting reading:

Awolowo, O. *The Strategy and Tactics of the People's Republic of Nigeria.* London: Macmillan, 1970.

Obasanjo, O. *My Command: An Account of the Nigerian Civil War.* London: Heinemann, 1981.

Odemugwu-Ojukwu, E. *Because I Am Involved.* Ibadan, Nigeria: Spectrum, 1989.

Shagari, S. *My Vision of Nigeria.* London: Frank Cass, 1982.

On problems related to boundaries and state formation, see the following:

Adejuyigbe, O. *Boundary Problems in Western Nigeria: A Geographical Analysis.* Ife, Nigeria: University of Ife Press, 1976.

Sada, P. O. "The Nigerian twelve state structure." *Nigerian Geographical Journal,* vol 14 (1971), pp. 17–30.

26

✳

South Africa:
Apartheid and Beyond

The year 1994 will be remembered as a turning point of epic importance in the history of South Africa. The prolonged struggle of the majority of South Africans for freedom and an end to apartheid culminated in April 1994 in the country's first truly democratic election. Despite its undeniable symbolic importance, this election represents but one step in what will inevitably be a long and extraordinarily difficult process to unravel 300 years of white domination and close to half a century of the relentless pursuit of an apartheid society by the South African state.

Apartheid is the system of institutionalized racism under which South Africa's black majority was denied a wide range of fundamental political, social, and economic rights under the guise of promoting separate development. Apartheid was a complex system that grew out of a long history of racial oppression and that operated on many levels to shape South African society into its present form. Irrespective of the legal status of apartheid, the geography of South Africa will continue to reflect apartheid's legacy in countless ways.

Apartheid in Historical Perspective

While the implementation of apartheid as official ideology began in 1948 following the electoral victory of the Afrikaner-based National Party, discrimination and separation by race had been integral to South African society for a very long time, legitimized through a series of increasingly discriminatory laws. To understand the nature of apartheid, it is important to examine the deep historical roots of racism in South African society.

The development of South Africa may be divided into five historical periods: the precolonial era, the era of conquest, the era of segregation, the era of apartheid, and the transition to a postapartheid society. There has been long-standing, fundamental disagreement between the defenders of apartheid and its liberal and radical critics about the nature of South African society and the significance of events that took place. With the transition to a postapartheid society, the focus of debate, and particularly the role of the South African government in it, is shifting. This is not to say that present debates about South Africa's history and future development are any less intense.

The Precolonial Era

Conventional histories of South Africa have perpetuated the convenient fiction that the history of South Africa began in 1652 with the establishment of the first European settlement at what is now Cape Town. For apartheid-era governments, this version of history provided a key justification for the European occupation of South Africa and the pursuit of "separate development." If, as they argued, blacks and whites had arrived in South Africa at the same time, no group had a prior claim to the country.

Archeologists have shown this claim to be completely false. At the time when Europeans first arrived, there were four main groups of indigenous South Africans:

- Khoikhoi pastoralists living near the Cape
- San hunter–gatherers of the semiarid interior
- Nguni peoples, including the Zulu, Swazi, and Xhosa, living in the Natal coastal plain and the interior
- Sotho and related groups occupying the central interior

The Khoikhoi and San are closely related peoples descended from the earliest Stone Age

inhabitants of southern Africa. South African sites have yielded early australopithecine remains and diverse Stone Age artifacts (Figure 26.1a). The Nguni and Sotho are peoples of Bantu origin. Iron Age sites dating from as early as A.D. 270 have been found in South Africa, providing clear evidence of the antiquity of Bantu settlement. Centuries before the arrival of Europeans, most of the fertile valleys in the eastern part of the country had been occupied by farmers and herders. Iron, copper, and tin were being mined, smelted, and traded in large quantities. Oral histories and linguistic evidence both point to the antiquity of trading contacts between the Nguni and Khoikhoi.

The Era of Conquest

In the two centuries following the arrival of Europeans, there was a gradual diffusion of white settlement into the interior, accompanied by the alienation of land for white farms and the imposition of colonial rule. Poorer whites of Dutch origin (the Boers) began the

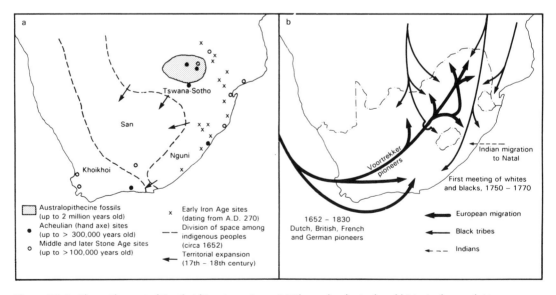

Figure 26.1. The settlement of South Africa: two views. (a) The archeological and historical record. Human occupation of South Africa began hundreds of thousands of years ago. All parts of modern South Africa were settled prior to 1652. (b) The official view under apartheid. The configuration of arrows suggests falsely that whites found an unpopulated land when they arrived at the Cape and only made contact with Africans much later and far from Cape Town. After *Multi-National Development in South Africa: The Reality.* Pretoria, South Africa: State Department of Information, 1974, p. 21.

Figure 26.2. Johannesburg. The goldmine pithead in the foreground and the impressive skyline in the background, remind us of the importance of the mining industry for the development of modern South Africa. Photo: Chamber of Mines Library. Johannesburg (courtesy of J. Crush).

push inland to establish large farms; by the late 1700s, the line of white settlement had reached the Great Fish River in the east and the Great Escarpment in the north. In 1795 the Cape was annexed by the British. The Boer migration out of the Cape quickened after the arrival of a large number of British settlers in 1820 and the abolition of slavery in 1833. The Boer quest for their own territory, free of British control, culminated in the Great Trek of the late 1830s and 1840s when about one-quarter of the Cape's white population moved north into lands beyond the Orange River. The independent Boer republics of Transvaal and Orange Free State were founded there in 1854.

The Boer expansion into the interior was fiercely contested. Between 1779 and 1846, there were six major battles between the Xhosa and white settlers. The armed conquest of African kingdoms continued until the end of the nineteenth century.

Among the Africans, this was a time of great change, known as the *mfecane* ("the crushing") or, among Sotho speakers, as the *difaqane* ("the

scattering"), characterized by a series of bitter wars, the emergence of formitable military states, economic crises, and large-scale migrations. Previously, these events were explained in relation to the assumed emnity of rival ethnic groups and the predatory militarism of the Zulu kingdom led by Shaka, whose campaigns against neighboring chiefdoms were said to have created a chain reaction of conquest and state formation among other groups. Recent scholarship explains the *mfecane* as the result of severe ecological crises and profound economic and social changes affecting southern African societies early in the 19th century. Prolonged droughts gave rise to famine and, ultimately, struggles over scarce food and still productive land. These ecological crises were manifested unevenly in space and within societies; the most vulnerable often had to seek help and protection from the powerful to survive. European demand for ivory, and, later slaves provided a direct stimulus for warfare and enslavement—and, increasingly, so did the white quest for land.

The northward expansion of the British also

resulted in conflict with African kingdoms. The resistance of the powerful Zulu army was especially strong, but the British eventually prevailed in the battle of Ulundi in 1879, following a devastating loss to the Zulu at Isandhlwana.

The Era of Segregation

The political and economic transformation of South Africa began with the discovery of diamonds at Kimberley in 1874 and of gold at the site of Johannesburg in 1886. These discoveries brought a massive influx of capital and technology as well as many white immigrants. The economic base of the region, hitherto exclusively in agriculture and trade, shifted increasingly to mining, with its promise of vast fortunes for those who were the luckiest, most astute, and ruthless.

The conquest of African territory continued, until the entire region had been carved up. Conquered peoples lost their land and livelihoods and were increasingly confined to scattered pieces of marginal land known as reserves. Laws were passed that increasingly restricted blacks' freedom of movement and rights to employment. Many blacks sought work at the mines and in the mining towns. While some were attracted by opportunities to accumulate wealth, increasingly they came because the alienation of their land left them with no viable alternative to labor migrancy (see Vignette 9.2).

The British seized control of South Africa following the Boer War of 1899 to 1902. In 1910 the Union of South Africa was formed through the amalgamation of the formerly separate colonies of Cape of Good Hope and Natal and the republics of Transvaal and Orange Free State. Under the new government, discrimination against blacks continued to intensify. Legislation was passed that reserved skilled mining jobs for whites, declared illegal the occupation of land by blacks outside their reserves, and decreed the segregation of white and black residential areas in cities.

Blacks actively resisted the imposition of segregation, and through the African National Congress (ANC) pressed for the establishment of a democratic, nonracist South Africa, although racist laws excluded blacks from parliament. Blacks also pressed their claims for justice by engaging in strikes, protests, and innumerable forms of passive resistance. As a rule, however, their successes were partial and temporary. The South African state continued to intervene in support of agricultural and mining capital in its insatiable quest for land and labor.

The Era of Apartheid

While the government of South Africa continued to strengthen the legislative basis for racial segregation, these measures were deemed insufficient by extreme nationalist elements among the Boers. Inspired largely by the nationalist ideology of Nazism, these Boers formed the "Purified" Nationalist Party in 1934 to fight for a South Africa fully organized according to apartheid principles. After winning the 1948 election, they moved to implement their more extreme vision of South Africa.

The National Party government based its case for implementing apartheid on the premise that different groups need to live and develop separately, each at its own pace, and in accordance with its own cultural heritage, resources, and abilities. To do otherwise would defy the natural laws of peaceful coexistence between peoples. Through a policy of "creative self-withdrawal" (i.e., the creation of tribal homelands), the national aspirations of the various African groups would be resolved peacefully, in a way that protected the identity of white South Africans. The government, it was claimed, was sincerely committed to protecting the best interests of all residents of the country. In short, apartheid was said to exemplify ideals of fairness, justice, and freedom, and had nothing to do with exploitation.

The reality of apartheid for the majority of South Africans was far removed from this picture of benevolence, harmony, and universal progress. President Verwoerd's dream became a nightmare for black South Africans.

The popular perception of the nature of

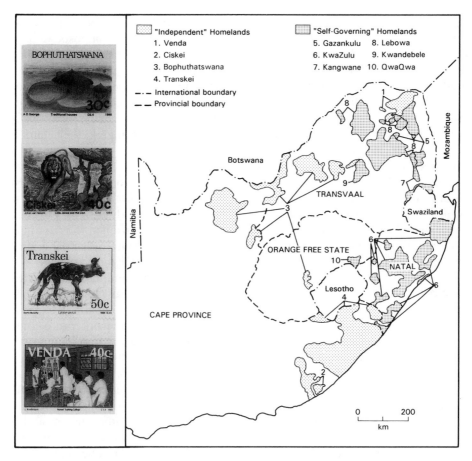

Figure 26.3. South Africa's homelands. Of the many effects of apartheid on South Africa's space economy, none rivals the creation of ethnic homelands as incipient "nations." The fact that only South Africa recognized their independence did not deter the "independent" homelands from acquiring some of the symbolic trappings of nationhood, such as the issuing of their own stamps.

apartheid has tended to focus on the strict racial segregation of beaches, buses, sports teams, and the like. Most such measures, often categorized as petty apartheid, disappeared during the 1980s, as pressure for the abolition of apartheid mounted. Much more fundamental, and much more resistant to change, has been the ruthlessly enforced macroscale division of space and resources between the country's officially designated racial groups. In his book *Endgame in South Africa*, Robin Cohen identified four major pillars upon which apartheid was constructed: the white monopoly of political power, the manipulation of space to achieve racial segregation, the control of black labor, and urban

social control. These measures are outlined below.

Apartheid South Africa repeatedly contrasted its own democratic institutions with the undemocratic regimes governing many African countries. However, it was hardly a model democracy. Whites monopolized political power, effectively excluding the other 85% of the population. Asians and Coloreds were granted limited political rights in 1983, but the exclusion of blacks from the political system continued for a decade more. Blacks supposedly had political rights in the homelands, but most of these territories were ruled with an iron fist by puppets of the government.

When apartheid was proclaimed in 1948,

the government set out to reorganize the so-cial–political map of the country. It commenced a program of forcibly removing blacks from their long-established homes in areas now designated for white use and dumping blacks in remote, unhospitable relocation areas, with little or no provision for their welfare. As many as 3.5 million people had been moved and a further 2 million remained under threat of displacement when removals ceased in the late 1980s. Most removals were from "white" farming areas and areas of black-owned farmland in the "white" countryside that dated from before the passage of the Native Lands Act of 1913. The spatial reconstruction of South Africa according to apartheid principles also occurred in urban areas, resulting in the removal of over 200,000, often from older communities within the city to remote periurban ghettos.

Forced resettlement in remote and marginal locations created a vast pool of unemployed workers with few viable options. This dependent, tightly controlled pool of migrant labor has been fundamental to ensuring that South African mines and farms would remain profitable. The state implemented a series of policies known as influx controls to severely limit the mobility of black South Africans.

Blacks were forced to carry passbooks indicating where they were supposed to be. Anyone found without a passbook or found to be illegally present in an urban area was subject to prosecution. A series of labor acts put severe limits on the terms of employment of African workers, for example, prohibiting migrant workers from bringing their families with them.

Apartheid defined several categories of black workers. Urban workers were those who had been residents of one particular city since before 1945. From their homes in segregated, high density townships, they commute daily to jobs in the white industrial and commercial economy. Migrant workers, who leave their families behind in the rural areas while employed in 1-year contracts, are found in many sectors of the economy. Especially large numbers of migrant workers are employed in the mining industry; the gold mines alone employ some 500,000 black miners. There are also hundreds of thousands of frontier commuters—residents of the (former) homelands who commute to jobs in white areas of South Africa, spending up to six hours per day on the bus between home and workplace (see Vignette 26.1). The apartheid state encouraged frontier commuting with subsidized

Figure 26.4. Housing in Botshabelo, South Africa. Botshabelo, a new rural city of 600,000 located east of Bloemfontein, has developed as a "dumping ground" for workers made redundant by farm mechanization. There are virtually no local employment opportunities. Photo: C. Badenhorst.

Vignette 26.1. Frontier Commuting from KwaNdebele:
An Example of Apartheid in Practice

Joseph Lelyveld's book *Move Your Shadow* relates the details of how the daily lives of ordinary South Africans have been shaped by the perverse and pervasive force of apartheid. The following exerpts, in which he gives us a glimpse of the "life" of John Masango, a resident of the KwaNdebele homeland and a long-distance commuter to work in South Africa, provides a revealing glimpse of the absurdities of apartheid in practice.

KwaNdebele had been Putco's most important growth area for five years. In that time the population of this obscure tribal enclave had nearly doubled to 465,000. Or so the chief minister had boasted. Others say it is 300,000. Possibly no one knows. The last accurate count had been taken at the time of the 1970 census, before there was a KwaNdebele, and then only 32,000 people had lived in the area.

But the population explosion in KwaNdebele, unlike the wider world, has little to do with breeding and practically everthing to do with apartheid. In a period in which South Africa is alleged to be changing and phasing out apartheid, the expansion of Putco into the *bundu,* or bush, of the homeland provides as accurate a measure as can be found of the real thrust of change. The bus company had to draw its own maps, for its new routes were on roads that had just been cut; its buses came in right behind the bulldozers. In 1979 Putco started to run two buses a day from Pretoria to the resettlement camps of KwaNdebele. By 1980 there were 66 a day, which jumped to 105 in 1981; to 148 a day in 1982; then 220 a day in 1983 and 263 a day in 1984, when the government was expected to pay Putco a subsidy of $26.5 million to keep its buses rolling to the homeland. That worked out to about $25 a head a week, more than $1,000 for each "commuter" a year: a negative social investment that went up in gas fumes when it might just as easily have gone into new housing for the same black workers nearer the industrial centers if that had not violated the apartheid design. It was the price the white government was willing to pay—and go on paying, year after year—to halt the normal process of urbanization. The KwaNdebele bus subsidy—the government's largest single expense in the development of this homeland—was higher than the KwaNdebele gross domestic product. This is basic apartheid economics. It had to be so high because KwaNdebele, a state supposedly on the way to independence, was utterly devoid of a productive economy or resources. The racial doctrine sets the priorities: First you invent the country; then, if you can, an economy. In the meantime, there are buses to carry the homeland's citizens to jobs in the nearest industrial center. In KwaNdebele's case that meant Pretoria, which is fifty-five miles distant at the homeland's nearest point.

At two-forty in the morning, number 4174 left the depot and headed north and east, *away* from Pretoria, to pick up its first passengers at a place called Kameelrivier. In the Ndebele homeland, it seemed, all place-names were still in Afrikaans—the names, mostly, of the white farms the state had bought up in order to ghettoize the bush. The headlights showed six men and four women waiting patiently beside the dirt road, in what appeared to be the middle of nowhere, when the bus made its first stop, ten minutes late, at two-fifty.

John Masango, the first man on board, said he worked six days a week at a construction site near Benoni, an industrial town forty miles on the far side of Pretoria, taking three buses each way. Even at the concessional rates arranged by the authorities for KwaNdebele, the total bus fares he paid out in a week gobbled up one-quarter of his wages. He was fifty-three years old, and on days when he was not required to work overtime, he could get back to Kameelrivier by eight-thirty at night. Only on Sundays did he ever see his home or his family in the light of day. Most nights, after washing, eating, and, as he put it, "taking care of family matters," he was able to get to sleep by ten or

cont.

Vignette 26.1. (cont.)

---

ten-fifteen. With four hours' sleep at home and a couple of hours' sleep on the bus, he managed to stay awake at work. It was important not to be caught napping; you could lose your job. While I was thanking him for his patience, John Masango reached into a bag he was carrying and extracted a little rectangle of foam rubber about the size of a paperback book. He then pulled his blue knitted cap over his eyes and, leaning forward, pressed the foam rubber to the back of the seat in front of him; in the final step of this procedure, he rested his head against the foam rubber and dropped his hands to his lap. As far as I could tell, he was out like a light.

Exerpt: J. Lelyveld. *Move Your Shadow*. New York: Penguin, 1985, pp. 122–129. ©1985 by Random House, Inc. Reprinted by permission.

---

bus systems and incentives for industry to locate close to this pool of labor.

In recent years, especially after the elimination of pass laws, huge periurban squatter settlements have sprung up (see Figures 26.4 and 26.7). The emergence of these settlements has given rise to a new category of commuters, distinguished from frontier commuters by living in homes located in (formerly) "white" South Africa and by the absence of state approval or subsidization.

The employment of large numbers of migrant workers from countries other than South Africa predates the rise of apartheid but served apartheid well. The presence of foreign miners enabled the state and employers to use divide and rule tactics to keep all workers, foreign and South African alike, vulnerable and compliant. The migrant labor system, extremely profitable for employers, has had a devastating effect on family life in rural communities wherever this system has operated.

Social control, the fourth pillar of apartheid, was perpetuated through three types of institutions:

- The state's control of the army, police, and secret service as instruments of coercion and oppression
- The more subtle ideological role of institutions such as schools and churches in justifying the state's control
- Control of the bureaucratic state apparatus

that administered the complex maze of apartheid laws and regulations.

The police, secret police, and armed forces, whose role was allegedly to maintain law and order, repeatedly and blatantly used their power to terrorize black citizens, murder key leaders of the resistance movement, and foment violence between various groups, especially in the urban townships. Much more subtle than the "stick" of police and military terror was the "carrot" of ideological manipulation of ideas, exercised through the schools, churches, and state-allied media. These channels were used to perpetuate and legitimate the official line that apartheid was rational and necessary for orderly development and peace.

The Struggle to End Apartheid

The fight to end racial discrimination in South Africa began long before the formal initiation of apartheid. The ANC, founded in 1912, was active in protests against the Native Land Act of 1913. At the same time, campaigns against racial discrimination were being organized by Mahatma Gandhi, later the leader of India's long but successful fight for independence.

The campaign of racial discrimination intensified with the inception of apartheid in 1948. The popular history of that struggle has focused for the most part on certain places where horrific events dispelled any illusions that the world might have had about the nature of apartheid–places such as Sharpeville and Soweto and, more recently, Bisho and Boipatong. The popular history of the struggle has also focused on the role of a few of its key leaders, among them Steve Biko, Desmond Tutu, and, above all, Nelson Mandela. Yet the heart of the struggle remained the daily resistance of millions of ordinary South Africans to the oppression of the system. For example, the abolition of the pass laws resulted from the mass disobedience of these laws that ultimately made them impossible to enforce. Likewise, when the government attempted to coopt Asian and colored people by giving them limited political rights, they responded with a mass boycott of elections.

The armed struggle against apartheid led by the ANC's military wing *Umkhonto we Sizwe* proceeded sporadically. Nevertheless, there were some notable successes, such as the successful bombing of the strategic Sasol oil-from-coal plant, which served as a reminder that guerrilla warfare in the white South African heartland was a real possibility.

The workplace was one of the most important points of struggle against apartheid. In 1973 a series of strikes by black workers paralyzed mines and industries. These strikes paved the way for significant concessions, including higher wages, improved trade-union rights, and the removal of some regulations that had strictly limited access to skilled jobs. Following these changes, there was a massive expansion in black trade unions and increasingly frequent industrial action. The success of the ANC-sponsored general strike of 1992 again showed the importance of the workplace as a focus of antiapartheid struggle.

Worldwide campaigns against apartheid contributed greatly to apartheid's demise. International organizations such as the United Nations and its member agencies, the Commonwealth of Nations, and the OAU repeatedly passed resolutions condemning apartheid. However, as the nature of apartheid became more widely known, the most important source of international pressure proved to be the growing force of public opinion. Public opinion forced Western governments to speak out more clearly against apartheid and to move

Figure 26.5. National Union of Mineworkers meeting. Strikes and protests by black workers, especially by members of the National Union of Mineworkers, played a crucial role in the struggle against apartheid. Photo: *The Star.* Johannesburg (courtesy of J. Crush).

toward implementing increasingly comprehensive political and economic sanctions against South Africa. Public opinion sparked organized campaigns for shareholders to divest in companies profiting from apartheid and caused many international companies to reconsider their otherwise profitable South African investments.

As opposition to apartheid grew in the late 1970s, the South African state fought a losing rearguard battle to preserve apartheid. Attempts were made to suppress black political development by force under the terms of the 1985 State of Emergency legislation that gave sweeping powers to the police and army. Divide-and-rule tactics were employed among the black population by promoting anti-ANC groups such as Inkatha and buttressing the fragile powers of the homeland governments. In response to internal and international opinion, a series of limited reforms were announced that ended specific types of discrimination. There were attempts to deflect international attention to other issues, through tactics such as the prolonged defiance of United Nations resolutions calling for Namibian independence. Meanwhile, South Africa was promoting itself as a strategic bastion for the West in a supposedly Marxist-dominated southern Africa.

Despite these measures, internal and international pressures on the South African state continued to intensify. Increasing pressures for a political settlement that would end the country's growing isolation and prevent a bloodbath, while protecting white privilege as much as possible, came from white liberals and from the boardrooms of South Africa's largest companies, whose futures were increasingly threatened by sanctions and divestment.

The pace of change quickened with the accession to power of F. W. de Klerk in 1989. Unlike his rigid predecessors, de Klerk recognized that fundamental reform was necessary and showed a willingness to take bold initiatives. Several ANC leaders, most notably Mandela, were released from detention, the draconian state-of-emergency law was repealed, and informal negotiations with the ANC were begun. Formal negotiations concerning majority rule commenced in 1992 after de Klerk won a substantial victory in a referendum asking white voters to endorse this process.

At first, the prospects for reform seemed very much in doubt. The initial positions of the ANC and the government were far apart on virtually every substantive issue. Both Mandela and de Klerk enjoyed majority support from their constituencies but seemed to have limited room for compromise. The ANC leadership was under pressure from growing militancy within the movement, especially among its younger members. The government was under pressure not only from right wing opposition groups but also from many moderate whites who remained ambivalent about reform.

In spite of these obstacles, the negotiating parties made major concessions, setting the stage for the historic World Trade Center Agreement of November 18, 1993, regarding a new constitution for South Africa. Under the agreement, the newly established National Assembly was to be chosen by proportional party representation, thus eliminating such contentious issues as constituency boundaries. The Senate was to be appointed by the legislatures of the nine newly created regions (Figure 26.6) that incorporated both the former provices and all of the homelands. A stipulation that all parties gaining at least 5% of the vote would be represented in the Cabinet ensured that smaller political—and racial—groups would not be totally marginalized as a result of the reforms. Among the many other provisions in the Constitution were a comprehensive Bill of Rights, the naming of 11 official languages, and arrangements for restructuring the armed forces.

Although the new constitution was supported by most political groups and the majority of the population, there continued to be significant opposition. Right-wing Afrikaner groups remained resolutely opposed to the transition to majority rule and continued to insist that their rights be protected through the establishment of an Afrikaner "homeland" (Vignette 26.2). Opposition also came from elements within the black population. The

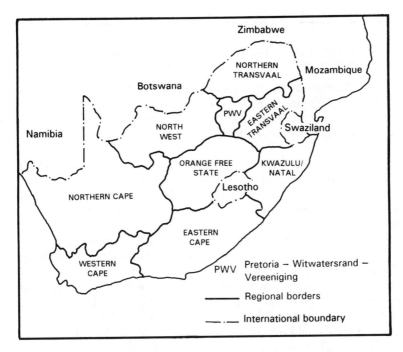

Figure 26.6. Political divisions in postapartheid South Africa. The map shows the nine provinces created as part of the constitutional agreement of November 1993, replacing the old provinces and homelands.

radical Pan-African Congress rejected the principles of negotiation and compromise with the white minority and accused the ANC of selling out black interests. The other major source of opposition was the Zulu-based Inkatha Freedom Party and its leader, Chief Buthelezi, who argued for much stronger guarantees of regional autonomy, if not full independence, for KwaZulu.

Speculations on the Geography of Postapartheid South Africa

The transition to a postapartheid era is certain to bring profound changes. A fundamental restructuring of the country's space economy is well underway. Change has often occurred prior to, or in anticipation of, the formal abolition of apartheid regulations. For example, some black families had begun to occupy dwellings in white-designated urban neighborhoods well before this practice became legal. While the changes now occurring will be massive, it is only with time that

their true nature, extent, and implications will unfold. This uncertainty reflects, among other factors, the limited capacity of the state to control the nature and direction of change. Change, especially in the less regulated environment of the new South Africa, will reflect, not simply government policy, but future decisions made by millions of individuals.

Political Transitions

The 1993 constitutional agreement has transformed the political map of South Africa. Gone are the old provinces, each with its own history predating the formation of the country. Gone as well are the homelands, including the four that had been designated independent. This is not to say that the regional question is dead. Indeed, both the conservative Afrikaner parties and Inkatha continue to aspire for territorial autonomy for their own constituencies.

The reconstruction of the political map is an attempt to dismantle the tribal identities

Vignette 26.2. The Dream of a White Homeland

Many white South Africans, primarily Afrikaners, remain deeply committed to the apartheid system. They felt abandoned by the rest of the world and betrayed by the National Party as it dismantled apartheid and negotiated with the hated ANC. They mobilized to fight for their land, their culture, their world—a world that seemed under attack from all sides.

The struggle to preserve apartheid was reflected in the steady growth of support for right-wing, ultranationalist movements, most notably the Conservative Party led by Andries Treurnicht and the extremist Afrikaner Resistance Movement of Eugene Terre Blanche. Support for these organizations threatened to weaken the position of the less conservative National Party.

The fears of white nationalists gave new life to the idea of restructuring the South African map to enable whites to exercise power within a "white" territory. One proposal called for the creation of a small Afrikaner homeland where blacks could neither live nor work. A more radical proposal envisaged the creation of a white state that would have in effect resurrected the former Boer republics of Transvaal and Orange Free State. This proposal would have ensured that the heartlands of both Afrikaner culture and the South African economy would remain under white control but disregarded the fact that whites would be a small minority in the population of such a state.

The vision of an independent Afrikaner state, where racial separation and the preservation of traditional Afrikaner values would remain unchallenged, grew out of the history and collective identity of the Afrikaner people. Many saw the Great Trek of the 19th century, in which the Boers sought to preserve their way of life by migrating to the isolation of the frontier, as a symbol of what was needed again. Moreover, despite their origins in Europe, many Afrikaners see themselves as *Africans* with "nowhere else to go" and with nonnegotiable rights to freedom and territory in Africa. Finally, some argue that the Afrikaner presence in Africa is sanctioned by divine covenant. According to Terre Blanche, "We do not have an agreement with the United Nations over land. We have an agreement with God himself. We are white because God made us that way. From far away, you can recognize us as the bearers of God's light in Africa."

Conservative Afrikaner groups refused to participate in the 1993 constitutional talks. As it became increasingly clear that progress was being achieved, the Afrikaner coalition stepped up its demand for a white homeland. However, the ANC continued to reject outright the principle of allowing citizenship in any area to be based on race or ethnicity.

It is unlikely that the dream of a separate white state will ever become a reality. There is no clear, undisputed territorial basis for the creation of such a state, and most whites now accept the evolution of South Africa into a majority-ruled unitary state. However, this may not stop those committed to apartheid and the preservation of Afrikaner values from waging a fierce, quite possibly armed, fight to secure their own safe haven.

of the former territories, especially the homelands, so carefully nurtured under apartheid. The long-term success of this endeavor will depend to a great extent on the government's ability to achieve rapid and very broadly based development. It is a profound challenge.

The maintenance of peace and security in a postapartheid South Africa is certain to be an important issue. Much has been made in the international press of "black-on-black" violence. The problem is very real; thousands of innocent people have lost their lives in recent years. Nevertheless, the issue is much more complex than press reports have suggested. The violence has grown out of a long history of divide-and-rule tactics employed by the South African state. There is also strong evidence that some elements in the security forces and others intent on preventing the demise of apartheid orchestrated incidents of black-on-black violence for their own political ends. The violence has also grown out of fundamentally different visions of South Africa's future; the ANC is the largest and most broadly based political movement, but it does not speak for all South African blacks, much less for all South Africans. Future political debates, and the future political tactics of various groups, inevitably will reflect what the postapartheid government achieves, as well as how it responds to the inevitable challenges to its authority.

Social Transitions

Apartheid guaranteed that even the poorest of whites had privileges that set them apart from and above blacks. Opportunities for advancement according to ability were severely limited by employment barriers, legislated wage differentials, and restricted spatial mobility.

South African society is being transformed into one structured according to social class as well as race. The old racial divisions remain, but a new set of class divisions, both overall and within each of the racial groups, has been superimposed on them. The removal of employment barriers and restrictions on movement have helped to stimulate the growth of a black middle class with a lifestyle bearing closer resemblance to that of middle-class whites than that of most blacks. At the same time, there is evidence of increasing poverty and unemployment among some segments of white society caused by decreased subsidies for small farmers, the general economic decline, and increased opportunities for blacks.

Middle-class blacks and poor whites still represent relatively small proportions of the total population. However, the direction of present and likely future change is increasingly apparent. Whatever happens, white South Africans can be expected to continue to control a vastly disproportionate share of wealth, while the majority of blacks can be expected to constitute a very large, poverty-stricken underclass with few prospects.

South African cities are beginning to reflect the removal of restrictions on mobility and place of residence, together with the growing wealth of part of the black population. A small number of affluent black families have begun to purchase homes in white suburbs. Less affluent families have begun to move in increasing numbers into working-class neighborhoods formerly reserved for whites, as well as into the inner cities. The reasons for this migration include the acute shortage of housing in the black townships and the desire for upward social mobility.

Few blacks have nearly the level of wealth needed to live in areas formerly reserved for whites. Yet they have been pouring out of the overcrowded homelands and out of white farming areas where many jobs have been lost and have been heading for the cities where most work opportunities exist. This migration started to occur during the mid-1980s, accelerated rapidly after the abolition of influx-control laws, and is likely to continue at a rapid pace indefinitely. The acute shortage of suitable, affordable housing has forced many new migrants to build their own shelters in vast squatter settlements on the peripheries of major cities.

Durban provides a striking example of the scope of this unregulated surge to the cities during the 1980s. The high-density squatter settlements that mushroomed on the periphery of Durban (Figure 26.7) are estimated to house 1.7 million people, a number that is expected to double in the near future. These settlements first sprang up in KwaZulu but had spread onto white-designated territory long before the demise of apartheid.

Separate and grossly uneven social services, particularly education and health care systems, were inherent in the apartheid system. Progress toward the eradication of these inequalities will be a leading priority – but also

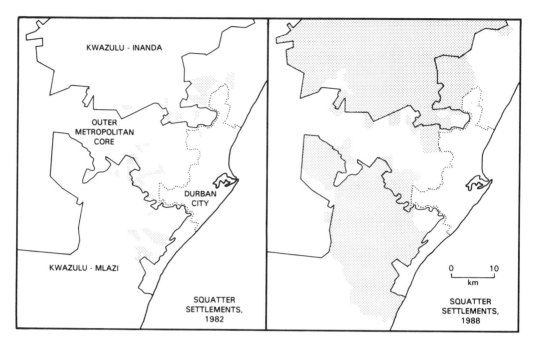

Figure 26.7. The growth of squatter settlements around Durban, 1982 to 1988. The rate of illegal urbanization mushroomed during the 1980s owing to the deterioration of economic conditions in the countryside and the relaxation of influx-control measures. After D. V. Soni and B. Maharaj. "Emerging urban forms in rural South Africa." *Antipode,* vol. 23 (1991), pp. 47–67.

an extremely taxing one–for the postapartheid state. A massive commitment of resources will be needed to train new teachers and health workers and to establish adequate facilities to make services accessible to all. Huge gaps in access to services and quality of life are likely to persist for generations to come. Moreover, the real struggle in the quest to improve social well-being extends far beyond the realm of service provision to include adequate income, housing, sanitation, and nutrition. Thus, the objective of postapartheid governments must be an overall improvement in the conditions of life of all South Africans, but particularly those most victimized by apartheid.

The very dimensions of the challenge provide interesting possibilities for the development of innovative strategies such as primary health care, an approach that not only can be cost effective but also can facilitate community mobilization and control. The question of redistributing social-service resources is likely to be very contentious. White South Afri-

cans, and particularly medical and educational professional groups, are certain to resist any attempt to implement a significant redistribution of resources to achieve a more equitable system.

The dismantling of apartheid has been accompanied by the emergence of a new class-based segmentation of social services. There is very heavy demand, for example, from wealthy whites and blacks for places in private schools for their children. Private institutions are very expensive, but they provide a means by which the wealthy can insulate themselves from a possible deterioration in the quality of public-sector services.

Economic Transitions

Under apartheid, South Africa's prosperity depended heavily on foreign investment and the ability of businesses to make huge profits, in large part because of state-enforced control over labor. Both long-term labor migrancy and frontier communting have exacted a heavy toll on African community and family life. Despite the repeal of influx-control laws in 1986, these forms of labor mobility have continued on a large scale. In addition, companies locating within or adjacent to the homelands received large subsidies. It remains to be seen whether postapartheid regimes will continue to encourage rural industrialization in order to alleviate unemployment where it is greatest, or to renounce it as a legacy of apartheid.

The ANC has made a concerted effort to reassure the business community. The ANC's socialist roots, as set out in its Freedom Charter (1955) and Constitutional Guidelines for a Democratic South Africa (1988), have been downplayed. What is now emphasized is the party's commitment to stability and repect for the rights of private businesses. The party also seems to have distanced itself from its long-standing commitment to end the migrant labor system, perhaps to ensure economic stability while moving toward a gradual, orderly phasing out of the system.

The business community, both within South Africa and internationally, has responded positively to these reassurances. It has excellent reasons for remaining and expanding: rich natural resources, Africa's wealthiest market, the prospect of increased economic activity following the end of sanctions, reopened markets in neighboring countries, and the increased purchasing power of 30 million black South Africans.

The ANC has long been committed to an affirmative policy of land reform that not only would abolish racial restrictions on land ownership but also would provide redress for the victims of forced removals under apartheid. A land reform that carved out small farms from European farms would also provide an attractive option to address the needs of residents of the homelands. The land reforms undertaken previously in the White Highlands of Kenya and in Zimbabwe provide precedents for such an initiative.

The extent and shape of land reform remain very much in doubt. Firstly, there is the difficult question of resolving conflicting claims to specific parcels of land—for example, where

blacks were removed from their farms in "black spot" areas, often many decades ago. Secondly, there is the question of compensation for white farmers displaced under land reform. Thirdly, the model for rural development under land reform remains unresolved. How large would the farms be? Would the state provide substantial assistance for the establishment of commercial farms, or would it prefer a system of large-scale cooperatives?

The geography of South Africa has developed over centuries, but especially since 1948, as the applied geography of racism. The extent to which racism was institutionalized as the guiding principle of an entire society has set South Africa apart from other nations. Now, all facets of South African life are in a state of transition as the country moves into its post apartheid era. One can only speculate about the future shape of South Africa's political, social, and economic institutions and about how they will evolve on the ground. The emerging South Africa will be a very different country, albeit one that will continue for many generations to reflect its troubled past.

Further Reading

The following reading list is but a tiny sample of the vast literature on South Africa, on the impress of apartheid and, more recently, on prospects for a postapartheid era.

On the history of South Africa, see the following sources:

Davenport, T. R. H. *South Africa: A Modern History*. London: Macmillan, 1982.

Frederickson, G. M. *White Supremacy: A Comparative Study in American and South African History*. Oxford: Oxford University Press, 1981.

Maylam, P. *A History of the African People of South Africa: From the Early Iron Age until the 1970s*. London: Croom Helm, 1986.

Van Onselen, C. *Studies in the Social and Economic History of the Witwatersrand 1886–1914*. London: Longman, 1982.

Wright, H. M. *The Burden of the Present: Liberal-Radical Controversy over South African History*. London: Rex Collings, 1977.

General discussions of apartheid include the following sources:

Cohen, A. *Endgame in South Africa?* London: J. Currey, 1986.

Lemon, A. *Apartheid in Transition*. London: Gower, 1987.

Lipton, M. *Capitalism and Apartheid*. Aldershot, England: Gower, 1985.

Murray, M. *South Africa: Time of Agony, Time of Destiny*. London: Verso, 1987.

Smith, D. *Living under Apartheid: Aspects of Urbanization and Social Change in South Africa*. London: Allen and Unwin, 1986.

Aspects of the enforcement of apartheid are examined in the following sources:

Lelyveld, J. *Move Your Shadow: South Africa, Black and White*. New York: Penguin, 1985.

Freund, B. "Forced resettlement and the political economy of South Africa." *Review of African Political Economy*, no. 29 (1984), pp. 49–63.

Jeeves, A., J. Crush, and D. Yudelman. *South Africa's Labor Empire*. Boulder, CO: Westview, 1991.

Unterhalter, E. *Forced Removal: The Division, Segregation and Control of the People of South Africa*. London: International Defence and Aid Fund for Southern Africa, 1987.

The following sources speculate about South Africa's future:

Collins, P., ed. *Thinking about South Africa: Reason, Morality and Politics*. New York: Harvester Wheatsheaf, 1990.

Pickles, J., and D. Weiner, eds. *Rural and Regional Restructuring in South Africa* (theme issue). *Antipode*, vol. 23, no. 1 (1991).

Smith, D. M., ed. *The Apartheid City and Beyond: Urbanization and Social Change in South Africa*. London: Routledge, 1992.

Wilson, F., and M. Ramphele. *Uprooting Poverty: The South African Challenge*. Cape Town, South Africa: David Phillip, 1989.

A useful handbook that provides comprehensive annual updates of the South African situation is *Race Relations Survey*, published annually by the South African Institute of Race Relations.

27

*

The Politics and Economics
of Surviving
in South Africa's Shadow

For countries in southern Africa, surviving in South Africa's shadow has been a continuing dilemma. This chapter examines the nature of this dilemma and attempts by South Africa's neighbors to overcome it through political and economic cooperation.

The relation between South Africa and neighboring states has continued to evolve since the establishment of colonial rule. Despite the attainment of independence and strategies to reduce economic vulnerability, there has not been any fundamental change in the dependency of neighboring states on South Africa. Even with the attainment of majority rule in South Africa, the implications for states at South Africa's periphery remain uncertain. Paradoxically, the end of apartheid could make the states of southern Africa even more dependent on their large and powerful neighbor.

Political and Economic Linkages

The creation of the British colonies of southern Africa – Bechuanaland (now Botswana), Basutoland (Lesotho), Swaziland, and

Rhodesia (Zimbabwe, Zambia, and Malawi) – took place within a broader context of political and economic events in South Africa. The British colonization of the BLS countries (Botswana, Lesotho, and Swaziland), completed under the guise of protecting them from Boer expansion, was part of a larger British strategy to encircle and ultimately defeat the Boer republics and, thus, secure control of the republics' vast gold and diamond deposits. The BLS colonies were neglected by the British; linkages to South Africa were consolidated through the development of labor migrancy centered on the Witwatersrand mines and the incorporation of BLS into a monetary and customs union controlled by South Africa.

The colonization of Rhodesia was undertaken by Cecil Rhodes, a mining baron based in South Africa, through his British South Africa Company. By the time the company relinquished control to Great Britain in 1923, strong linkages had been established with South Africa by means of white settlement, investment by South African–controlled mining companies, and migrant-labor ties to South Africa. The alienation of African land, especially in Southern Rhodesia, ensured a ready supply of labor for both local and South African employers.

South Africa forged even stronger ties with South West Africa (Namibia). After World War I, South Africa was granted a League of Nations mandate over the former German colony, which became a de facto colony of South Africa. Mutually advantageous ties, based initially on the supply of migrant workers to South Africa, were established between South Africa and the Portuguese colonists in Mozambique and Angola.

Many of the ties established during the colonial era have remained intact; often they have intensified. The BLS countries are still part of the South African Customs Union (SACU). Labor migrancy continues on a large scale and, for a number of countries, is a crucial source of foreign-exchange earnings, and tourism from South Africa is growing in importance. South African investment in the region, especially in mining and industry, has continued to grow. South Africa remains by far the most important trading partner of countries located on its periphery.

As in the rest of the continent, the colonial transportation system in southern Africa was designed to facilitate the export of commodities rather than to serve as the basis for balanced internal development. Thus, rail lines linked major cash-crop and mining areas to the nearest suitable port (Figure 27.1). The purpose of railways that crossed international borders was to provide access to landlocked states rather than to stimulate intercolonial trade. Except for the Tazara railway from Zambia to Tanzania, new routes have not been added since independence.

The colonial transportation system in much of southern Africa developed as an extension of the South African system. The BLS countries are almost completely dependent on South African routes and ports. Further north, the main colonial transportation linkages were with ports in Mozambique and Angola. As a result of South African–sponsored insurrec-

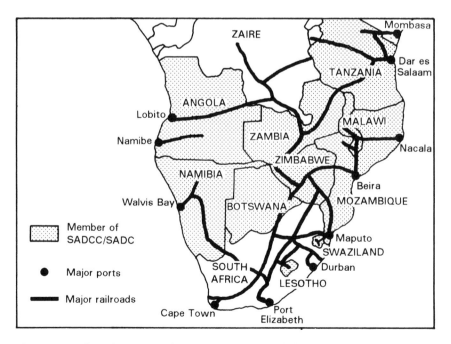

Figure 27.1. The railway network in southern Africa. While there are several routes to the sea that bypass South Africa, insurgencies have made most of them impassable since the mid-1970s.

Table 27.1. Some Linkages between South Africa and Its Neighbors

	Migrant workers in S. Africa		% of trade with S. Africa, 1984		Visitors from S. Africa, 1983	
	1965	1986	Imports	Exports	No.	% of total
Botswana	59,000	28,244	78	9	363,840	43
Lesotho	117,000	138,193	97	40	232,488	96
Swaziland	39,000	21,914	90	37	189,209	70
Namibia	ND	ND	ND	ND	ND	ND
Zimbabwe	27,000	7,304	23	18	238,909	38
Zambia	16,000	2,421	15	<1	4,460	3
Malawi	80,000	31,411	24	4	ND	ND
Mozambique	161,000	73,186	12	<1	ND	ND
Angola	11,000	22	–	–	ND	ND
Tanzania	–	–	–	–	ND	ND

ND, no data available; –, value close to 0.
Note: More recent data are unavailable owing to economic sanctions.
Sources: South African Institute of Race Relations. *Race Relation Survey, 1987–88.* Johannesburg, South Africa: 1988. R. Gibb. "The effect on the countries of SADCC of economic sanctions against Republic of South Africa." *Transactions of Institute of British Geographers,* vol. 12 (1987), pp. 398–412. *Yearbook of Tourism Statistics, 1992.* Madrid: World Tourism Organization, 1992.

tions in these countries, these routes were blocked. By the mid-1980s, approximately 70% of the region's trade was passing through South Africa, compared to only 20% a decade earlier. South African ports handled 85% of Zimbabwe's trade and 93% of Malawi's. The costs involved were economic as well as political. For example, it is three times as far from Harare to Durban as from Harare to Beira. Transit charges earn South Africa some $350 million annually.

South Africa continued to hold a dominant position in the external trade of several southern African countries (Table 27.1). In the mid-1980s, trade with South Africa accounted for over 90% of the imports of Swaziland and Lesotho and more than 35% of their exports. South Africa was also the largest trading partner of Namibia, Zimbabwe, and Botswana. The imposition of economic sanctions against South Africa had no effect on trade within SACU and reduced, but did not stop, trade with its other neighbors. In addition to the overt trade between South Africa and its neighbors, hidden but significant trade dependencies remained in existence. Angola and Mozambique, both staunchly anti-apartheid states that suspended direct trade with South Africa, continued to market their

diamond production through the South African de Beers Corporation, thus acceeding to that company's global diamond monopoly.

With the lifting of sanctions in the early 1990s, South Africa quickly reestablished its dominance of trade in southern Africa. The reappearance of South African wines in shops in many parts of Zambia and Tanzania symbolizes the return of business as usual, with South African products, especially consumer goods, openly dominating the market throughout the region.

The century-long flow of migrant workers from southern African countries to South Africa has remained a very important linkage. The number of migrant workers going to South Africa still exceeds 250,000. Colonial and some postcolonial governments made arrangements with the contracting agencies that allowed them to appropriate directly a significant part of migrants' earnings. Lesotho provides an extreme example of dependence on income from migrants, whose earnings still contribute almost half of Lesotho's GDP.

A different form of population mobility, namely, that of tourists, is creating new linkages of dependency. During the 1970s and 1980s, there was heavy investment in the BLS countries to develop a tourist industry cater-

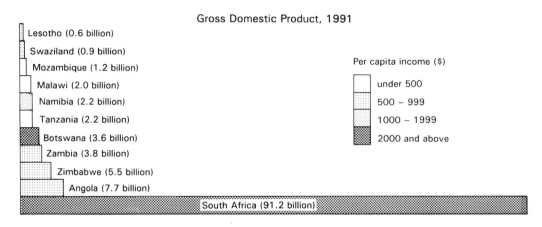

Figure 27.2. South Africa in southern Africa: national GDPs in U.S. dollars. Even when combined, the economies of SADC member states are no match for that of South Africa. Data source: World Bank. *World Development Report, 1993.* New York: Oxford University Press, 1993.

ing to South African visitors. Zimbabwe also receives many South African visitors – 239,000 in 1983. Mozambique, with support from the World Bank, has begun to refurbish its colonial-era hotels in an attempt to attract South African tourists. That Mozambique launched this initiative at a time when South African–sponsored destabilization was still taking place is a clear indication of the lack of attractive income-earning options available to the countries in the region.

Foreign investment has been a crucial mechanism of South African control over its neighbors. South African capital has been heavily involved in mining, and there are substantial South African investments in manufacturing, retail and wholesale trade, large-scale agriculture, and tourism. Five of Zimbabwe's 10 largest industries are controlled by or associated with South African companies. South Africa's stake in the regional economy continues to grow. Botswana, for example, has continued to get three-quarters of new investment capital from South Africa.

Based on patterns of economic linkage, it is possible to distinguish three groups of countries in the southern African periphery. The linkages of the BLS countries to South Africa are so comprehensive that they have no option but to develop as, in effect, South African economic dependencies. Mozambique, Zimbabwe, Malawi, Zambia, and Namibia form

a second group of states. All have substantial linkages to South Africa that continued after the imposition of sanctions, despite strong antiapartheid sentiments in all except Malawi. All suffered economic hardship as a result of sanctions against South Africa and from South African destabilization policies. Nevertheless, their economies are sufficiently independent that they have development possibilities that do not entail further dependency on South Africa. Angola and Tanzania form a third group. While these countries do not have major investment, transportation, trade, and labor ties to South Africa, their development has been influenced by South Africa. Angola's prospects for development have been especially retarded by South African destabilization.

Regional Destabilization

Guerrilla forces fighting for the independence of Mozambique and Angola made significant territorial gains during the 1960s and early 1970s. The escalating human and financial cost of the war and growing international isolation led to the collapse of the Portuguese dictatorship and its withdrawal from Africa in 1975. With the withdrawal of Portugal, the white minority regime of Ian Smith in Rhodesia was South Africa's only remaining ideological ally in the region. Linkages to South Africa ensured that comprehensive international sanctions to dislodge Smith's government would fail. Trade and investment with South Africa increased and important military assistance was provided. Nevertheless, the growing success of the liberation movements and international pressure for an "internal settlement" led to the demise of Rhodesia and the emergence of an independent Zimbabwe.

During the 1970s and 1980s, South African interference in the affairs of its neighbors escalated into a full-scale policy of regional destabilization. This change coincided with the growing international isolation of South Africa. A series of United Nations resolutions condemned apartheid, declared South Africa's occupation of Namibia illegal, and called for sanctions. Between 1975 and 1979, the end of white minority rule in Angola, Mozambique, and Zimbabwe deprived South Africa of its protective "shield" of allies and diversionary targets for international attention. The governments of these newly independent countries embraced a Marxist development model and made a strong commitment to the liberation of South Africa. The inauguration of the

Southern African Development Coordination Conference (SADCC) in 1980 was seen as a further threat since it brought together moderate and radical states in the region with the objective of lessening dependence on South Africa.

South Africa's regional strategy shifted significantly in 1978 with its decision to forge a regional "constellation" of moderate states. The policy was based on the premise that black rule in the region would not threaten the South African status quo as long as neighboring countries could be kept weak, dependent, and compliant. A primary objective was to isolate and ultimately to defeat Marxist governments and liberation groups in the region. South Africa also hoped to coerce its neighbors into expelling the ANC and softening their antiapartheid stances. It was hoped that a gradual acceptance of the "independence" of the homelands would develop within the regional alliance. The new strategy also sought to consolidate the region's economic dependence on South Africa by increasing trade and investment.

The newly installed moderate transitional government of Zimbabwe, led by Bishop

Figure 27.3. Government troops on patrol, Mozambique. Destabilization wreaked havoc on the economy of Mozambique for almost two decades. Photo: CIDA: B. Paton.

Muzorewa, was seen as the key to convincing other non-Marxist states to join South Africa in a regional alliance. Muzorewa, considered by most Zimbabweans as a mere figurehead serving white interests, was swept aside in the election of April 1980. During the same month, nine countries signed the Lusaka Declaration that created SADCC. From this point, South Africa turned increasingly to violence to destabilize its neighbors and to advance its own regional interests.

The policy of destabilization by violence was unleashed in full force against the Afro-Marxist governments of Mozambique and Angola. South Africa increased its military and material support for Unita, a guerrilla organization based in southern and eastern Angola, and South African troops made increasingly frequent military incursions into Angolan territory (Vignette 27.1). South African troops remained in continuous occupation of parts of southern Angola until 1989, repeatedly penetrating up to several hundred kilometers inside the country.

In Mozambique, South African strategy revolved around support for Renamo, an antigovernment group originally nurtured by the white government of Rhodesia in the late 1970s. Material and logistical support was provided to increase the capacity of Renamo to destroy the Mozambican economy by attacking villages, farms, and the transportation system. The devastating effect of these attacks, coupled with a serious drought and other economic problems, forced Mozambique to negotiate with South Africa. Under the terms of the Nkomati Accord of March 1984, Mozambique agreed to prevent the ANC from operating in the country, while South Africa pledged to withdraw support for Renamo. Ignoring the nonaggression treaty it had signed, South Africa continued to support Renamo and to otherwise ensure the total destabilization of Mozambique.

A variety of strategies were applied elsewhere in southern Africa. Swaziland was induced to sign a secret nonaggression pact in return for the transfer of a small amount of South African territory. Lesotho, totally surrounded by South Africa, was subjected to increasing pressure, including threats of prohibiting Lesotho citizens from working in South Africa, restrictions on the movement of its goods and people through South Africa, and attacks by commandos on targets in Lesotho. Following the imposition of a virtually total blockade in 1986, the Lesotho government was deposed in a military coup and replaced by a more compliant regime that soon agreed to sign a nonaggression treaty. Botswana was also subjected to increasing pressure to sign a nonaggression pact. The tactics against Botswana included repeated border incursions and threatened economic penalties. Commando raids were also launched against targets in Zambia and Zimbabwe and attempts were made to disrupt their economies by restricting the flow of their goods through South Africa.

Throughout the 1980s South Africa continued to resist international pressures to implement United Nations resolutions calling for Namibian independence. More frequent and more comprehensive military actions were undertaken with the objective of destroying SWAPO. Meanwhile, attempts were made to create a compliant pseudoindependent state that would exclude SWAPO and pose no threat to South Africa.

South Africa's "total strategy" of control in southern Africa was a product of desperation and was almost certain to fail. However, it was a coordinated attempt not just to destabilize the region but ultimately to create a South African–controlled alliance of dependent regimes. For example, attacks on transportation routes in Mozambique and Angola also weakened other countries, notably Zambia and Zimbabwe, and increased dependence on South Africa. Threats and actions against individual countries not only affected the target but also served as a warning to others in the region.

In the late 1980s, and particularly after the accession to power of de Klerk, South Africa's regional strategy was pursued much less aggressively. South Africa's desperate attempts to elect a more moderate regime were thwarted when SWAPO won the elections leading up to Namibian independence. Military incur-

Vignette 27.1. Regional Destabilization: The Case of Angola

Few countries have experienced as sustained an assault on their territory and sovereignty as Angola. The Angolan case helps to illustrate the scope and persistence of destabilization by South Africa under apartheid, and its disasterous effect on the countries affected. However, the Angolan story is ultimately about the failure of destabilization to save apartheid.

Following the collapse of the Portuguese dictatorship in 1974, South Africa became concerned about Angola, especially when it became clear that the Marxist Popular Movement for the Liberation of Angola (MPLA) was prevailing over its rival guerrilla groups, the National Front for the Liberation of Angola (FNLA) and National Union for the Total Independence of Angola (Unita). In a desperate attempt to prevent an MPLA victory, the South African Defence Force (SADF) invaded Angola. Its arrival coincided with that of Cuban troops and of aid from the USSR to bolster the MPLA. Up to 6,000 SADF troops launched a drive north from Namibia, penetrating to the outskirts of Luanda (Figure 27.4). Despite its initial success, the SADF beat a hasty retreat when confronted with the prospect of fighting a rapidly growing and better-armed Cuban contingent deep inside Angola.

From 1975 to 1978, South Africa continued to send aid to the beleagured remnants of Unita and made repeated raids allegedly in pursuit of Namibian (SWAPO) guerrillas. The SADF involvement escalated with the launching of several incursions into Angola in 1978 and 1980. Technically, SADF conducted two wars in Angola, one against SWAPO bases and the other in support of Unita. In reality, they were parts of a single strategy of resisting all pressures for Namibian independence. Military operations by Unita and SADF continued to become more frequent and were launched over a much wider area. The MPLA reported 53 SADF troop operations and 100 bombing raids in the first 11 months of 1981. More than 10,000 SADF troops continuously occupied a 70-km-wide strip of Cunene province, as a result creating 80,000 refugees.

The South Africans received an important boost in morale, as well as help for their Unita allies, after Reagan's election in 1980. The expulsion of Cuban troops from Angola, by whatever means necessary, became a primary goal of USA foreign policy. USA support for the enemies of the Angolan government continued to grow, especially after Reagan's reelection in 1984. In fact, it was only in 1993 that the USA granted diplomatic recognition to the MPLA government, 18 years after it had come to power.

South Africa experienced two key setbacks in 1983. First, its Unita allies

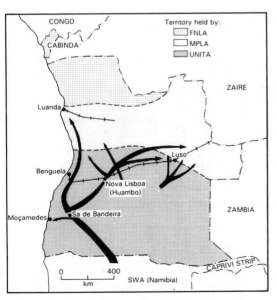

Figure 27.4. The South African invasion of Angola, 1975. After P. Moorcroft. *African Nemesis: War and Revolution in Southern Africa, 1945–2010.* London: Brassey's, 1990, p. 87.
cont.

Vignette 27.1. (cont.)

suffered a major defeat at Cangamba, despite strong support from SADF air and ground forces. Later, an SADF invasion force of 10,000 was repelled by Angolan and Cuban troops at Cuvelei, throwing SADF's supposed air superiority into doubt. Abruptly, South Africa changed course and proposed to withdraw its troops if Angola would end its support for SWAPO. However, despite agreeing to these terms under the Lusaka Accord, SADF continued to launch commando raids and to support Unita.

By 1987, the scale of SADF operations inside Angola had again escalated. As in previous campaigns, the government went to great lengths to maintain secrecy, largely because of growing concern at home about white casualties and general war weariness. A protracted battle at Cuito Cuanavale proved decisive. While SADF losses were small compared to those of the Angolan and Cuban forces, the battle again emphasized South Africa's dilemma. The cost of the war, in lives and in lost equipment, was escalating. The Angolan army showed every sign of becoming stronger rather than weaker. With few prospects of an early or easy military resolution to the conflict, both the USSR and the USA became increasingly insistent that a regional peace accord be reached.

The New York Accord of December 1988 established terms for a regional disengagement, including the withdrawal of both Cuban and South African troops from Angola. South Africa agreed to independence for Namibia and this time honored its promise. With Namibia's independence and the departure of Cuban troops, South Africa's main reasons for attempting to destabilize Angola were removed. Nevertheless, some covert assistance continued to be sent to Unita, the result of which has been to needlessly delay the achievement of a final end to the Angolan civil war.

Angola's first multiparty election, held in September 1992, pitted Unita against the governing MPLA. Not surprisingly, the support for these two parties was strongly based in their respective home regions. The MPLA won an overall victory; in the presidential election, President dos Santos gained 49.4% of the first round vote, just short of the absolute majority needed to win. Despite the assurances of international observers that the election had been conducted fairly, Unita refused to accept the results and resumed the armed struggle. United Nations mediators failed to bring about a negotiated end to hostilities, and fighting between the rival factions resumed.

Even though South Africa's direct intervention in Angolan affairs has ceased, the legacy of destabilization has continued. The Angolan people on both sides of the conflict can only hope that their long-cherished hope for peace will soon be achieved. However, two years after the elections that were to bring the war to an end, most of the Angolan people are suffering more than ever. Unita controls most of the countryside and many of the cities, even in the northern part of the country. The war has ravaged what was left of local and regional economies, and has made the delivery of now vital international relief extremely difficult. Militarily, there is a stalemate, with no end in sight.

Based on P. Moorcroft. *African Nemesis*. London: Brassey's, 1990.

---

sions came to an end and other forms of intimidation against neighboring states were greatly reduced. The focus shifted to South Africa itself and the quest there for majority rule.

The reduction of direct South African interference has not brought immediate peace and security to southern Africa. On the contrary, prospects for a lasting peace in Angola and Mozambique remain fragile and uncertain.

In Mozambique, Renamo continued for some time to receive "unofficial" support from the South African army and other South African sources that enabled it to pursue its brutal campaign of destruction. Meanwhile, other countries have paid a heavy price for the continuation of these wars, ranging from the on-going disruption of trade and transportation to the cost of caring for 1.5 million refugees from Mozambique and Angola alone.

SADCC: Effects on Dependence and Development

The SADCC was inaugurated as a formal organization in April 1980 with the signing of the Lusaka Declaration, entitled "Southern Africa: Towards Economic Liberation." The agreement was signed by delegates from Botswana, Lesotho, Swaziland, Zimbabwe, Zambia, Malawi, Tanzania, Angola, and Mozambique.

The Lusaka Declaration began by describing southern Africa as "fragmented, grossly exploited and subject to economic manipulation by outsiders". The declaration proposed that a coordinated strategy be developed to achieve economic liberation. Four development objectives were established by the signatories:

1. Reduction of economic dependence, particularly, but not only, on the Republic of South Africa
2. Forging of links to create a genuine and equitable regional integration
3. Mobilization of resources to promote the implementation of national, interstate, and regional policies
4. Concerted action to secure international cooperation within the framework of a strategy for economic liberation

The declaration identified transportation and communication, including both improved coordination of existing systems and the development of new regional facilities, as the key to economic liberation. The need for improved transportation linkages is clearly evident in the trading patterns of the member countries. At its inception, trade among the members of SADCC was relatively small; intra–SADCC trade amounted to well under 10% of the external trade of every member country (Table 27.2). While intra–SADCC trade increased from 2.7 to 4.4% of member countries' total trade between 1979 and 1984, its value remained small in comparison to South Africa's 18.5% share.

The poor state of most national economies and of transport linkages between SADCC members has significantly curtailed the growth of trade among member states. As Table 27.3 shows, Zimbabwe was SADCC's major beneficiary, in most cases exporting several times the value of the products it imports from its neighbors. Zimbabwe–Botswana trade seems to have been an exception, although these apparently high trade values may reflect efforts to circumvent sanctions restricting direct trade with South Africa. Zimbabwe's trading success within SADCC reflects the greater diversity and health of its economy, especially of its industrial sector.

Although increased trade was an important objective of SADCC, it was not a common-market or free-trade organization. This made it different from ECOWAS, which is the other major regional organization of Africa south of the Sahara. More recently, with the transformation in 1992 of SADCC into SADC (Southern African Development Community), member states have agreed to work toward the eventual establishment of a regional common market.

The formation of SADCC received widespread support from the West and from international development agencies. This interest was based on several considerations in addition to the concern about the region's dependence on South Africa and the possible effect that sanctions against South Africa would have on economies in the region. Southern Africa was recognized as having a strong resource base that could be further developed with appropriate investment, especially in transportation. SADCC could help to rationalize the allocation of aid and investment on a regional basis and provide economies of scale. Finally, SADCC was seen as a means

Table 27.2. Relative Importance of Intra-SADCC Trade, 1981

	Intra-SADCC exports			Intra-SADCC imports		
	Value (U.S.$ million)	% of all exports	Primary destination	Value (U.S.$ million)	% of all imports	Primary source
Angola	NA	NA	NA	NA	0.7	Zimbabwe
Botswana	35.8	9.0	Angola	43.0	6.0	Zimbabwe
Lesotho	NA	0.4	NA	NA	0	NA
Malawi	24.0	10.0	Zimbabwe	24.5	8.0	Zimbabwe
Mozambique	31.0	9.0	Zimbabwe	33.9	3.0	Zimbabwe
Swaziland	9.6	2.6	Mozambique	3.3	0.6	Zimbabwe
Tanzania	4.9	0.9	Mozambique	8.9	0.8	Mozambique
Zambia	39.8	4.0	Zimbabwe	54.4	5.0	Zimbabwe
Zimbabwe	138.2	10.0	Zambia	106.5	6.0	Zambia

Based on J. H. Wagao. "Trade relations among SADCC countries." In S. Amin, D. Chitala, and I. Mandaza, eds., *SADCC: Prospects for Disengagement and Development in Southern Africa*. London: Zed, 1987, pp. 147–180.

of limiting the growing influence of Afro-Marxist regimes and liberation groups, and their Soviet allies, in the region.

SADCC evolved into an important forum for consultation and consensus building. Annual conferences provided opportunities for leaders of the member countries to discuss issues of regional development and cooperation. Consultations were instituted with donor agencies to establish priorities for aid programs.

A host of cultural, professional, and service organizations emerged as forums for representatives from the SADCC countries to discuss issues of common interest.

One of the most important functions of SADCC was to serve as a "clearing house" for foreign aid to the region. Members of the SADCC would propose a range of priority development projects and enter into negotiations with development agencies to have the pro-

Figure 27.5. Benguela Railway, Angola. Transport system improvements have been identified as one of the keys to success for the SADCC. However, key existing routes such as the Benguela Railway had to be shut down for long periods because of the activities of South African–backed guerrillas. Photo: CIDA: B. Paton.

Table 27.3. Trade between Selected SADCC Members, 1988 (U.S.$1,000)

Source	Country of Destination					
	Botswana	Malawi	Mozambique	Tanzania	Zambia	Zimbabwe
Botswana	–	107	1,054	81	4,081	61,257
Malawi	41	–	3,856	833	1,429	3,194
Mozambique	NA	590	–	1,060	NA	590
Tanzania	NA	300	3,200	–	1,300	600
Zambia	3,000	5,000	100	7,300	–	17,100
Zimbabwe	74,500	22,800	51,200	5,000	40,300	–

Based on Economic Commission for Africa. *Foreign Trade Statistics for Africa.* New York: United Nations, 1991.

jects funded. In its first decade, 490 SADCC aid projects were funded with a about $2.5 billion. The major areas of project funding included transportation and communications, energy, food security, agriculture and animal husbandry, natural resources, and training and research. Assistance was obtained for the rehabilitation of railways throughout the region and ports in Angola and Mozambique, the linking of national power grids, programs to achieve regional self-sufficiency in basic foodstuffs and technical training programs.

Coordination offices for each of the major economic sectors were established in a different member country. For example, mining initiatives were coordinated from Zambia, tourism from Lesotho, energy from Angola, transportation from Mozambique, and food security from Zimbabwe. This structure seems to encourage the development of a strong cooperative spirit among members.

There is little evidence that SADCC has had much effect on the problem of dependency and underdevelopment that led to the organization's formation. Trade patterns remain as strongly oriented to South Africa as ever, particularly following the end of sanctions. Little has been done to develop regional economic growth based on the exchange of the diverse resources found in the SADCC/SADC countries. Member countries have acknowledged the limitations of a piecemeal "project" approach and in 1992 agreed to work toward the harmonization of economic policies, but have not succeeded in developing a more comprehensive integrated regional development strategy.

Radical writers have argued that the countries of SADCC merely substituted one dependence for another, by becoming increasingly dependent on Western aid. Meanwhile, many of the development projects, such as the rehabilitation of ports and railways, have done more to strengthen external rather than internal linkages. Critics of SADCC have pointed to the growing burden of debt associated with the development projects and suggest that in contracting this debt member countries have heavily mortgaged their future.

Many liberal writers acknowledge SADCC's lack of striking economic successes but regard as a major accomplishment the steady growth of cooperation and trust within a group of extremely diverse countries. The development of a strong sense of regional identity, as well as a solid institutional framework, provides a basis for further development in southern Africa. It has also been argued that SADCC has helped the region to attract more aid than would have been given to individual countries and that the aid has accomplished more because of SADCC coordination.

Prospects for Southern Africa in a Postapartheid Era

The people of southern Africa have long looked forward to the end of apartheid and, with it, attaining opportunities for a more stable and prosperous future. Without doubt, the end of apartheid can be expected to bring substantial benefits to the region as a whole, particularly to Angola and Mozambique that have suffered so greatly from South African aggression. Nevertheless, the effects of an end to

Figure 27.6. Cattle receiving water at a borehole, Botswana. Many rural development projects have been undertaken under the auspices of the SADCC. Photo: CIDA: B. Paton.

apartheid may not always benefit other countries in the region.

The black majority government in South Africa is under extreme pressure to address the urgent needs of its own citizens. In particular, there are pressures to ensure that South Africans are employed before consideration is given to foreigners. However, any move by South Africa to expel hundreds of thousands of migrant workers from neighboring countries would have a devastating effect on the economies of Mozambique and Lesotho and, to a lesser extent, on other countries in the region.

It remains to be seen what effect South African majority rule will have on the flow of aid to the region. With the demise of apartheid, South Africa's neighbors will no longer be seen

as threatened. Aid projects, long justified as a means of reducing South African domination, may well diminish. At the same time, aid is being diverted to South Africa to assist in its postapartheid development efforts and to enable donor countries to reestablish their presence in the rich South African market. Moreover, the objectives of aid donors may change from promoting intra-SADCC cooperation to encouraging the development of a regional economic constellation anchored by South Africa.

With the prospect of majority rule in South Africa becoming increasingly likely, SADCC members confronted the controversial question of whether, and under what circumstances, South Africa might become part of the organization. Because of its very size, South Africa could be expected to dominate the organziation, leaving other members with a diminished role. Moreover, the ANC had said little about its anticipated future role in the southern African region, much less its expectations with respect to SADCC.

In August 1992, members of SADCC signed the Treaty of Windhoek, transforming SADCC into SADC. Their primary objective was to address the changing situation in South Africa. South Africa was invited to join SADC once an elected majority government was in place. The treaty envisaged that SADC would build upon SADCC's successes, with the intention of achieving increased economic and political cooperation among member states.

The ANC-led majority government of South Africa has not hastened to redefine formally the country's relations with its neighbors. Several months after its election, it had not yet taken up the standing invitation of SADC members to join the organization. Nevertheless, the regional impact of the changed political terrain in South Africa are already becoming evident. The implications for SADC members vary greatly. Whereas the effects on Tanzania and Malawi may be quite minor, those of some other countries, notably the BLS countries, are likely to be profound. In the case of Lesotho and possibly Swaziland, their very survival as independent nations may be at stake (Vignette 27.2).

Vignette 27.2. Lesotho: What Options in a Postapartheid Southern Africa?

All the countries of southern Africa have many ties to South Africa, but nowhere is this dependence more comprehensive than in Lesotho. Geographically, Lesotho is an enclave completely surrounded by South Africa. Moreover, with its monetary union with South Africa, its membership in the Southern Africa Customs Union and its extreme reliance on the earnings of migrant workers, Lesotho has what is in effect an enclave economy.

Lesotho has experienced numerous affronts to its sovereignty since it became independent. The most dramatic interference was the military blockade in 1986 that precipitated the replacement of the Lesotho government with one more to South Africa's liking. It has often been said that Lesotho's prospects will not change until the situation in South Africa changes dramatically. These dramatic changes have now occurred, but it is still unclear what effects the accession to power of a majority government will have on Lesotho. Three possible scenarios are outlined below.

Scenario 1: No Change
Under this scenario, Lesotho would seek to maintain its existing formal relation with South Africa, albeit in a friendlier way. However, it is far from clear that South Africa will wish to maintain the status quo. It is widely assumed that a black majority government in South Africa will seek to restrict the employment of foreign migrants, so as to give first opportunity to its own unemployed people. Such a move would have a devastating effect on Lesotho's economy. Moreover, it is not certain that the new South African government will wish to continue to maintain its monetary and customs agreements on the same basis, since their net costs to South Africa could increase.

Scenario 2: Incorporation
The idea of making Lesotho part of South Africa is not new; there was provision for it in the act that created the Union of South Africa in 1910. Incorporation would bring certain benefits for the majority of Lesotho's people. As South Africans, they would be free to move anywhere in South Africa and would have secure access to job opportunities there. Lesotho would probably experience a significant outmigration of people to South Africa's cities. The greatest costs, however, would be for the ruling elites and civil servants, many of whom would lose status and power and some of whom would lose their jobs.

Scenario 3: Economic Union
In an economic union, the existing customs and monetary arrangements would be extended to include the free movement of people and labor. This would secure the benefits of incorporation but also would allow Lesotho to remain a sovereign nation. Such an arrangement, which would be attractive to the Lesotho elites, is apparently of interest to South Africa as a model for its future relation with its neighbors. South African political influence in the region and access for South African capital would be secured, without the complications of formal incorporation. However, negotiating such a union would not be easy, given the deep-seated fears of South African domination.

Based on J. Cobbe. "Lesotho: What happens after apartheid goes?" *Africa Today*, vol. 38 (1991), pp. 19–32.

To summarize, SADCC/SADC represent a novel response to the unique set of circumstances that have prevailed in southern Africa. While the organization did not succeed in significantly lessening its members' dependence on South Africa, it has achieved modest success as a forum for regional consultation and cooperation. The long-awaited end of apartheid is now bringing substantial changes to the political and economic map of southern Africa, but it would be wrong to assume that these changes will necessarily bring greater independence and growth for all countries in the region.

Further Reading

South African destabilzation policies are discussed in the following sources:

Chan, S. *Exporting Apartheid: Foreign Policies in Southern Africa 1978–1988.* London: Macmillan, 1990.

Hanlon, J. *Beggar Your Neighbours.* London: Catholic Institute for International Relations, 1986.

Johnson, P., and D. Martin. *Apartheid Terrorism: The Destabilization Report.* London: James Currey, 1989.

Moorcroft, P. L. *African Nemisis: War and Revolution in Southern Africa (1945–2010).* London: Brassey's, 1990.

Picard, L. *South Africa in Southern Africa: Domestic Change and International Conflict.* Boulder, CO: Lynne Rienner, 1989.

On South African interventions in specific countries, see the following sources:

Bardhill, J. E., and J. H. Cobbe. *Lesotho: Dilemmas of Dependence in Southern Africa.* Boulder, CO: Westview, 1985.

Hanlon, J. *Mozambique: The Revolution Under Fire.* London: Zed, 1984.

Somerville, K. *Angola.* London: Pinter, 1986.

On the history of SADCC's development, see the following sources:

Abegunrin, L. "The Southern African Development Co-ordination Conference: Politics of dependence." In R. Onwuka and A. Sesay, eds., *The Future of Regionalism in Africa,* pp. 190–205. London: St. Martin's, 1985.

Commonwealth Institute. *SADCC: Development in the Region, Progress and Problems.* London: Commonwealth Institute, 1984.

Nsekela, A. J. *Southern Africa: Towards Economic Liberation.* London: Rex Collings, 1981.

The following sources describe and evaluate aspects of SADCC's programs for regional development:

Amin, S., D. Chitala, and I. Mandaza, eds. *SADCC: Prospects for Disengagement and Development in Southern Africa.* London: Zed, 1987.

Gibb, R. A. "The effect on the countries of SADCC of economic sanctions against the Republic of South Africa." *Transactions of Institute of British Geographers,* vol. 12 (1987), pp. 398–412.

Hay, R. W., and M. Rukuni. "SADCC food security strategies: Evolution and role." *World Development,* vol. 16 (1988), pp. 1013–1024.

Lee, M. *SADCC: The Political Economy of Development in Southern Africa.* Nashville, TN: Winston-Derek Publishers, 1989.

Martin, R. *Southern Africa: The Price of Apartheid.* London: The Economist Intelligence Unit, 1988.

Peet, R. *Manufacturing Industry and Economic Development in the SADCC Countries.* Stockholm, Sweden: Beijer Institute, 1984.

Weisfelder, R. "Collective foreign policy decision-making: Do regional objectives alter national policies?" *Africa Today,* vol. 38 1991, pp. 5–17.

CONCLUSION

Which Future?

As the 21st century approaches, Africa and its people struggle against imposing odds in their quest for survival and development. Three decades of disappointment have shown conclusively that African development is a much more complex undertaking than was once believed. The optimism of the 1960s has long since faded. Africa has continued to slide further into debt, and the prices obtained for its commodities on the world market have continued to decline. Previous social and economic achievements have been put in jeopardy, and African sovereignty has been compromised by the imposition of structural adjustment programs. For most African governments and for many communities and families as well, development has increasingly taken a back seat to survival.

Looking into the future, the foremost question is whether the current crisis can be reversed, so that development – a more balanced and sustainable development – can be anticipated. While prospects for such a change remain very much in doubt, the proven resilience of African societies and systems of production provide seeds of hope.

Will Things Fall Further Apart?

During 1992, international attention turned to the tragic state of affairs in Somalia. The previous government of Siad el Barre had been deposed in 1991, following a prolonged civil war. However, far from bringing peace and stability, the result was a descent into lawless chaos, in which the heavily armed supporters of rival factions continued to fight each other for control. With the Somali state effectively ceasing to exist, ordinary Somalis were left without protection. More than 1 million fled as refugees to neighboring countries. Famine threatened the very survival of the majority of Somalis who chose to remain or were unable to leave.

The international response to the Somalian crisis was, to say the least, disturbing. Despite reports from international relief agencies that a crisis of unprecedented proportions was unfolding, it was many months before Western governments, finally responding to growing expressions of concern from their own citizens, made any serious effort to help. The Western media briefly descended on the country, searching voyeuristically for stark images of suffering. However, their reports seldom made reference to the broader political context of present suffering, especially Somalia's now obsolete role as a Cold War ally of the West owing to its opposition to the Marxist government of Ethiopia, and the attendant large-scale shipment of arms into the country.

The large-scale deployment of troops from the United States and several other countries,

413

under the auspices of the United Nations, failed in its objective of imposing a quick and easy peace. Facing determined resistance and undeniable evidence that the conflict was much more complex than it had seemed, foreign troops were withdrawn and Western sympathy for Somalia and its people waned. Somali resistance may have prevented a de facto "recolonization" of the country, but at the probable price of Somalia's being left largely to its own fate for years to come.

The apocalyptic course of events in Somalia represents a worst-case scenario for Africa's future. Sadly, Somalia is not an isolated case. While the specific circumstances have varied, Liberia, Mozambique, Angola, southern Sudan, and Rwanda have all experienced similarly traumatic crises entailing widespread suffering and death, the destruction of most social and economic infrastructure and the virtual collapse of the state.

For many in the global community, these events will seem to justify abandoning Africa as a hopeless cause and a waste of time and effort. More than ever, Africans are seen as the authors of their own misfortune. After all, it is said, the rapid economic growth of countries in eastern and southeast Asia demonstrates that Africa's current state of crisis was not inevitable.

Another Future?

Sustainable development is a concept that has become increasingly fashionable in recent years. The Brundtland Report, *Our Common Future*, defined sustainable development as development that "meets the needs of the present without compromising the ability of future generations to meet their own needs" (p. 8). However, the sustainable development that international agencies have endorsed enthusiastically for Africa has had a rather different focus. Advocates of sustainable development in Africa have given priority to "the bottom line"; to be sustainable, it is argued, development must be affordable within the constraints imposed by the meagre resources available to African governments and communities. Calls for making development sustainable have coincided with policies designed to increase government revenues through export growth and user fees for basic social services.

The African environment, as the sustenance base for society, must be protected if sustainable development is to be achieved. However, the degradation of African environments is certain to continue as long as families and countries are forced to liquidate environmental capital in order to address immediate crises of survival. African environmental crises manifest themselves at the local and regional levels; but as previously noted, their primary causes are to be found elsewhere.

The Hausa of Nigeria have a proverb that says, "If the world was a just place, then the spindle would be clothed in a gown and trousers" (i.e., the spindle never tastes the fruits of its labor). For hundreds of years, Africa has been that spindle, the source of vast wealth that has benefited others but has brought Africa few and often fleeting rewards.

For Africa to achieve a lasting recovery from its present crisis requires fundamental changes in the relation of Africa to the global economy. The deepening marginalization of Africa within the global economy—declining terms of trade, the crushing burden of debt, and reduced flows of foreign aid—ensures that African governments can do even less than in the past to address the urgent needs of the people. Far from embracing the Brundtland Report's vision of the planet as a single, interdependent entity and development as a global responsibility, the fate of Africa is treated as something of little or no consequence to the West. The net flow of wealth in recent years has been *out* of Africa, not into it.

The proverb quoted above reminds us that in the future, as in the past, Africa cannot afford to pin its hopes for development primarily on expectations of fair play, much less of charitable acts, by outsiders. Inevitably, the focus of African development, if it is to be sustainable, must shift to local communities, enabling local people to decide for themselves local development needs and priorities and to encourage the utilization of local knowledge and resources. The shift to the local provides a ray of hope that initiatives will more often be appropriate and effective. In the past, indigenous perspectives on development have seldom been taken seriously. Instead, the expertise of the "development expert" has been taken for granted; model development projects have been replicated in diverse settings with little attention to local realities. In most cases, the results have been predictably disappointing.

Recent trends toward the democratization of African national political processes are cause for hope, since they may signal new possibilities for the empowerment of ordinary people to speak their minds and to work to improve their prospects. African traditions of community and of sharing provide a foundation for a renewed empowerment at the local level. However, empowerment implies changes well beyond a return to patriarchal tradition. Women and other traditionally marginalized groups in society are determined to have their voices heard and to reap their fair share of the benefits of their labor. Their struggle is no less important for Africa's future than the struggle for political liberation was in decades past.

Glossary

AAF-SAP (African Alternative Framework to Structural Adjustment): A set of strategies to address the current economic crises of Africa, proposed by UNECA in 1989 as an alternative to the structural adjustment programs of the IMF and World Bank.

African diaspora: The scattered peoples of African origin in other parts of the world, their dispersal primarily the result of the trade in African slaves in centuries past.

Africanity: A term coined by Jacques Maquet that refers to the cultural unity of the peoples of black Africa.

Afrikaners: White South Africans primarily of Dutch origin. The Afrikaner identity is rooted in the use of Afrikaans as a language, in affiliation with the Dutch Reformed church, and in a shared history of isolation from and often mistrust of Europe.

Alfisols: Moderately weathered, moderately fertile brown to reddish soils associated with humid and semihumid climates – in Africa, found primarily in savanna areas.

Alley cropping: An agricultural system that involves planting crops between rows of leguminous shrubs. It was developed through agricultural research as a stable alternative to shifting cultivation, primarily for tropical forest environments.

ANC (African National Congress): The multiracial, but primarily black-supported, party founded in 1912. The ANC led the struggle against apartheid in South Africa and won the 1994 election.

Apartheid: The official doctrine that formally institutionalized the separate development of racial groups in South Africa.

Aridisols: Soils found in dry environments, characterized by low organic matter and accumulations of soluble minerals (salts and carbonates).

Bantu: A term applied to a large family of African languages of the Niger–Congo group, as well as to the peoples who speak them. Over three millennia, Bantu peoples spread out from a point of origin in central Nigeria, eventually dominating most of Africa east and south of the Cameroon Highlands.

Bantustans (homelands): The 10 ethnic territories set aside under apartheid for the exclusive use of black Africans. Four of them became "independent" between 1976 and 1981. All were reabsorbed into South Africa in 1994 as part of the 1993 constitutional agreement.

Basic needs: The economist Dudley Seers argued that providing basic needs – notably food, shelter, employment and health – was the first priority for development. These ideas formed an integral part of "bottom–up" approaches to development that grew out of the rejection of modernization theory.

Berlin Conference: A gathering of European nations in 1884 that established the ground rules for the colonial carving up of Africa, following moves by King Leopold of Belgium to annex the Congo.

Bilateral aid: Aid agreements made between two countries, a recipient and a donor country. See also **multilateral aid.**

Biomass: The mass of living matter in an ecosystem. Biomass as a source of energy refers to fuelwood, charcoal, crop refuse, and dung–energy obtained from living (nonfossil) sources.

Biome: A large terrestrial ecosystem with a common type of vegetation, as well as broadly similar soils, climatic conditions, and animal life.

BLS countries: Botswana, Lesotho, and Swaziland

Cabora Bassa: A large dam on the Zambezi River in Mozambique, with Africa's largest installed hydroelectric capacity (18 billion kWh per year). Most of the power is sold to South Africa.

Cape to Cairo: The imperialist dream of Cecil Rhodes who promoted a vision of continuous British-governed territory from the northern and southern extremities of the continent.

Cassava: A high-yielding but nutritionally poor starchy root crop that is a widely grown and consumed staple in tropical Africa.

Chemical weathering: Decomposition and decay of constituent minerals in rock as a result of the minerals' chemical alteration.

Close-settled zones: Areas of high-density rural settlement, especially in the Hausa heartland of northern Nigeria (e.g., the Kano close-settled zone).

CIDA: Canadian International Development Agency.

CITES (Convention on International Trade in Endangered Species of Wild Fauna and Flora): An international agreement to strictly regulate or prohibit international trade in endangered species.

Copper Belt: A mineral-rich zone in southeastern Zaire (Shaba Province) and north-central Zambia, which produces some 10% of the world's copper as well as several other minerals.

Crude birth (death) rate: The annual number of births (deaths) per thousand persons in a population.

De Beers: A South African–based multinational corporation that exerts monopoly control over the global trade in diamonds.

Development from within: An approach to development, increasingly popular in the late 1980s and 1990s, that emphasizes the importance and untapped further potential of local self-reliance in development.

DES (Dietary energy supply): DES is usually expressed as the daily average number of calories consumed in a population.

Double workload: A term used primarily in feminist literatures to refer to the dual responsibilities of women for reproduction and production (of goods and services traded in an economy).

ECOWAS (Economic Community of West African States): An organization, founded in 1975, that links 16 countries of West Africa. The founding Treaty of Lagos made provision for the elimination of barriers to trade and mobility and aimed at promoting economic, social, and cultural cooperation.

EPI (Expanded Program of Immunization): A joint WHO–UNICEF program to achieve full vaccination coverage of Third World children against common diseases of childhood.

FAO (Food and Agriculture Organization of the United Nations)

Frelimo (Front for the National Liberation of Mozambique): The political–military front that organized armed resistance in Mozambique against Portuguese colonialism, from 1962 to 1975, and that has remained the governing party since independence.

Frontier commuters: Black South African residents of the Bantustans who, under apartheid, commuted daily, often over long distances, to jobs in South Africa. The South African government subsidized frontier commuting as part of its strategy to extend apartheid.

Game cropping: The practice of systematically harvesting wild animal populations (especially ungulates) as a source of food.

Gondwanaland: The ancient megacontinent that comprised Africa, South America, India, Australia, Antarctica, Madagascar, and Arabia and that began to break up some 250 million years ago, with the constituent parts slowly moving apart via continental drift.

GDP (Gross Domestic Product): Annual value of all goods and services produced in an economy, plus income earned by residents outside the country, minus incomes accruing to foreign residents of the country.

GNP (Gross National Product): Annual value of all goods and services produced in an economy.

Groundnuts: Peanuts–an important crop produced in savanna regions both for export and domestic consumption.

Harambee: A community self-help movement that flourished in Kenya in the early years of independence,the objective being to increase the pace of development by mobilizing local resources.

Hidden curriculum: Values and attitudes transmitted informally through the educational system that may have the effect of undermining indigenous cultures and economies.

Homeland: (see **Bantustan**)

HDI (Human Development Index): A multidimensional scale developed by the United Nations Development Program to distinguish between levels of development, defined as the range and quality of options available to people for shaping their own destinies.

IADP (Integrated Agricultural Development Projects): A development strategy, mostly associated with the World Bank, that uses intensive investment to improve rural infrastructures (roads, schools, etc.) and to promote new agricultural technology to spur development.

IITA (International Institute of Tropical Agriculture): One of a series of institutions doing research in tropical agriculture. It is located in Ibadan, Nigeria, and specializes in crops and farming systems of tropical-forest environments.

IMF (International Monetary Fund): An international agency, originally founded in 1944, that oversees the "credit worthiness" of nations and establishes terms for loans. In this role, it has forced most African countries to adopt structural adjustment programs.

Indirect rule: A strategy of colonial rule at the local level that involved retention of indigenous governments, closely supervised by colonial officials. It enabled the colonialists to rule with relatively few European personnel and to coopt African rulers as collaborators.

Infant mortality rate: The annual number of infant deaths per thousand live births in a population.

Inkatha: The predominantly Zulu political movement in South Africa, led by Chief Buthelezi. A vociferous opponent of the ANC and of African majority rule, Inkhatha was linked to much of the political violence before the 1994 election.

Inselberg: An "island mountain," a solitary dome of rock, resistant to chemical weathering and erosion, that rises above the surrounding plains. It is most common in savanna regions.

Intercropping: The practice of growing two or more crops side by side in the same field. It is commonly used in indigenous farming systems to capitalize on symbiotic relationships between certain species, to reduce erosion, and to maximize yields.

ITCZ (Intertropical convergence zone): The zone of low pressure located between the tropics, where air converges and ascends. The seasonal movement of the ITCZ governs the change of seasons in the tropics.

Labor reserves: Areas that were deemed by colonial administrators to have little potential for development and, hence, were exploited as source areas for migrant workers for mines, plantations, and so forth, elsewhere.

Laterite: Highly-leached, infertile soils of the wet tropics, often with a bricklike hardpan crust.

Legitimate commerce: The 19th- century term for trade in commodities such as palm oil, that superseded the slave trade in West Africa.

Lingua franca: A language used as a medium of communication by people whose native tongues differ. Swahili and Hausa are important regional lingua francas in Africa.

Lomé Convention: A series of agreements between the European Community and most African, Caribbean, and Pacific states to facilitate trade and development assistance.

Lusaka Declaration: The 1980 statement of strategy of nine southern African countries to lessen their dependence on South Africa–the founding document of SADCC.

Migrancy: A form of labor mobility in which workers and their families are dependent on both wage earnings and subsistence production to make ends meet. The term is particularly common in studies of South African migrant labor in which legal restrictions on where people could live ensured the continuation of migrancy.

Multilateral aid: Aid channeled through international agencies (e.g., UNICEF, United Nations Development Program) rather that from a specific donor country.

Neocolonialism: A term, devised by Kwame Nkrumah of Ghana, to describe the continuing economic control of Europe over its politically independent former colonies.

NGO (Nongovernmental organization): International or indigenous organizations, operating at arm's length from government. Their scope may be very broad (e.g., Oxfam) or specific, either to a particular type of activity or a single community.

Nitrogen fixing: The process in which certain species of plants (legumes) convert atmospheric nitrogen into organic nitrogen compounds that are accessible to all plants.

Onchocerciasis (river blindness): A chronic disease in which the proliferation of microfilariae (tiny worms). transmitted by the black fly called *Simulium damnosum*, cause the formation of skin nodules – and in extreme cases, reduced life expectancy, and blindness.

OAU (Organization of African Unity): An organization of 52 independent African states, founded in 1963, with the objective of promoting African solidarity.

Oxisols: Soils, found in very moist tropical environments, that are old, highly weathered, and of low fertility.

Pan-African Movement: An international political and intellectual movement of people of African descent, founded in 1900, that fought for black cultural and political liberation. Its slogan, "Africa for the Africans," is symbolic of the key role the movement played in setting the stage for African independence.

Parastatals: Companies or agencies established by governments and left to operate semiautonomously in a designated commercial or service field. Examples might include a state airline, a well-drilling company, or a state-established industry.

PAIGC (African Party for the Independence of Guinea and Cape Verde): The liberation movement that led the struggle against Portuguese colonial rule in Guinea-Bissau and Cape Verde, commencing in 1963 and concluding with independence in 1974.

Polygyny: The cultural practice of permitting a man to have more than one wife.

Populist socialism: A development ideology that emphasized African communal and/or cooperative traditions as the source of principles for modern development. Nyerere's Tanzania is the best-known example.

Primary health care: An approach inspired by the example of China and set out in the Alma-Ata conference of WHO in 1978, calling for health strategies at the community level that addressed local needs in accordance with local values and resources.

Primate city: A city that is much larger than other cities in the same country and that typically has a very high proportion of the nation's modern economic development and political power.

Pronatalist: Policies adopted by certain governments with the objective of maintaining high fertility rates, or of increasing fertility.

Purdah: The practice in orthodox Islamic societies of confining women to their homes, with opportunities to go out strictly regulated by husbands. The strictness of purdah varies in relation to religious orthodoxy, wealth, and class.

Remittances: Sums of money and other material aid that migrants send to their home communities, often to support their families or as investments in anticipation of their own return.

Removals: The South African policy under apartheid whereby people (mostly black) were forced to move off land designated officially for other groups. In the case of blacks, people were removed to their assigned Bantustan.

Renamo (Mozambique National Resistance): A guerrilla organization, supported throughout the 1980s by South Africa, that fought the Frelimo government of Mozambique, with devastating effects on the country's economy and society.

River blindness (see **Onchocerciasis**)

SACU (Southern African Customs Union): An agreement among South Africa, Lesotho, Swaziland, and Botswana that provides for free trade among member states and for a common set of customs duties with respect to foreign trade.

SADC (Southern African Development Community): The successor organization to

SADCC (see below), established in 1992 with the signing of the Treaty of Windhoek. It envisaged the development of SADC into a common market with growing political and economic integration, and the eventful inclusion of South Africa as a member.

SADCC (Southern African Development Coordination Conference): An organization founded in 1980 to reduce the dependence of countries in Southern Africa on South Africa through coordinated development planning. (See **SADC** and **Lusaka Declaration**)

Sahel: The semidesert region at the southern fringe of the Sahara, as well as the countries that fall within this region (usually defined as Senegal to Chad). Droughts in the 1970s and early 1980s focused international attention on the Sahel.

Schistosomiasis (bilharzia): A disease caused by blood flukes (*Schistosoma*) that mature in the liver, causing anemia and urinary problems. Bilharzia is often related to water-development projects, since its spread depends on the presence of certain freshwater snails.

Selective primary health care: A health care strategy, much promoted by development agencies in the late 1980s and 1990s, that focuses entirely on delivering a few, most cost-effective interventions (e.g., safe water, immunization) to as many people as possible.

Shifting cultivation: Also called swidden or slash and burn, it is an agricultural system in which farms are abandoned for extended periods after a short cycle of cultivation. It is suited to tropical-forest environments with poor soils and low population densities.

Site and service schemes: An approach to urban development that seeks to achieve cost-effective, orderly, and community-responsive growth. The government constructs the basic infrastructure (e.g., roads, and water) for a new suburb and sells low-cost lots to people who then build homes suited to their individual needs and resources.

Sleeping sickness (see **tsetse**)

Squatter settlement: A settlement located on land neither owned nor rented by the residents—and, hence, illegal.

State bourgeoisie: The comparatively well-off social class that has benefited from its close ties to (or control of) the postcolonial state. Members would include bureaucrats, soldiers, and entrepreneurs with government contracts.

Structural adjustment programs: A package of reforms, designed by the IMF and World Bank to restore nations' economic health through reforms to devalue currency, reduce public sector expenditure, and strengthen market forces. Structural adjustment programs have been implemented in virtually all African countries.

Swahili: The synthetic (African–Arab) culture of coastal East Africa, and especially the language that developed within this milieu. Although Swahili is the native tongue of relatively few, it is used as a lingua franca by the majority of East Africans.

SWAPO (South West African People's Organization): The leading nationalist organization in Namibia, SWAPO launched its armed struggle against South African occupation in 1966, ending in independence under a SWAPO-led government in 1989.

Tied aid: Aid programs that specify that certain or all inputs (e.g., machinery) be purchased from the donor country. Tied aid limits the ability of recipient countries to choose the cheapest and best technology, and fosters long term dependence (e.g., for spare parts).

Total fertility rate: The average number of births that a woman would experience in her lifetime if current age-specifc fertility rates persist.

Transnational corporations: Firms, usually based in the major industrial nations, that control operations in more than one country.

Triangular trade: Trade linkages, controlled by European powers, between Europe, Africa, and the Americas during the slave-trading era; slaves from Africa were the key commodity.

Trickle down: The assumed gradual spread of modernization and its benefits from large, national urban centers to the periphery. Trickle down was a key assumption underlying most development during the 1960s and contributed to an urban bias in development.

Tsetse: A fly that is the vector for a parasite (trypanosome) that causes typanosomiasis, or sleeping sickness, a serious disease affecting humans, cattle, and some wildlife species.

Ultisols: A suborder of Alfisols, associated in Africa with moist savanna environments; soils are weathered, reddish-yellow in color, and low in fertility.

UNDP (United Nations Development Program)

UNECA (United Nations Economic Commission for Africa)

UNEP (United Nations Environmental Program)

UNHCR (United Nations High Commissioner for Refugees)

UNICEF (United Nations Children's Fund)

Ujamaa: Literally "familyhood" in Swahili, an approach to development stressing cooperative effort and an ethic of sharing. *Ujamaa* was the philosophical basis for African socialism in Nyerere's Tanzania.

Unita (National Union for the Total Independence of Angola): Unita began as a guerrilla group fighting for independence. After independence (1975), Unita continued to fight the MPLA government, with South African backing. Attempts to end the conflict, including United Nations–backed elections in 1992, have failed.

UPE (Universal Primary Education): An ambitious scheme, launched by the Nigerian government in 1976, that attempted to make primary education universally available and compulsory. Universal Primary Education greatly increased enrollments, especially in the north, but fell short of its objectives.

White Highlands: The region of Kenya, located near Nairobi, that developed in colonial times as a center of European commercial farming and that was the focus of the Mau Mau struggle over land in the 1950s.

Witwatersrand: South Africa's economic heartland, centered on the city of Johannesburg. The initial development of the region was based on gold mining; mining remains the keystone industry.

World Bank: Established in 1944 at the same time as the IMF, the World Bank (originally the International Bank for Reconstruction and Development) aims at assisting member states in their development efforts with the provision of loans and technical assistance.

WHO (World Health Organization)

Xeralfs: A suborder of Alfisols, associated with Mediterranean climates.

INDEX

Abidian, Côte d'Ivoire, 139, 196, 206, 341
Abiola, Chief, 373
Acacia trees, 38, 312, 313
Achebe, Chinua, 54
Ada Salt Miners' Cooperative, 356–357, 359
Addis Ababa, Ethiopia, 37, 194, 227
Africa south of the Sahara
  aid to; *see* Foreign aid
  class structure in, 44, 47, 52–54
  climate of, 29, 30–34
  countries of, 14, 15
  and cultural identity, 42, 72, 88
  development of; *see* Development
  economy of, 4, 6, 97-98, 327–330, 414
  empires of, 62–65
  ethnic groups of, 6, 42, 44
  European exploration of, 73–74
  regional groupings in, 19, 21–22
  religions of, 43, 50–52
  size of, 13–14
African Alternative Framework to Structural
    Adjustment Programs for Socio-Economic
    Recovery and Transformation (AAF-SAP),
    351
African National Congress, 16, 287, 384, 389,
    393, 395, 408
African Party for the Independence of Guinea
    and Cape Verde (PAIGC), 267
Afrikaners, 390, 392
Afro-Asiatic language group, 46, 48
Afro-Marxism, 98, 339, 346–349, 401, 406
  models for, 346
Agriculture and colonialism, 145, 147, 161
  cooperative, 354
  development strategies for, 145, 168

and environmental conditions, 8–9, 29, 32,
    34–38
and indigenous knowledge, 5, 8, 147–159,
    162, 172, 188
  mixed, 148, 159, 162
  plantation, 147, 161, 187
  smallholdings, 81, 82, 84, 166
  systems, 149–154
  urban, 210, 212, 219
and wildlife habitats, 195, 305–306
women's role in; *see* Gender, and division of
    labor
AIDS, 4, 121, 122–123, 235, 268, 270–271, 272
  centers of infectivity, 122, 270
  and population growth, 123
"AIDS Belt," 122
Air circulation patterns, 30–31
Air pollution, 33–34
Akosombo Dam, 292, 357
Alley cropping, 171, 172, 320
Alluvial fans, 29
Amharic language, 48
Amin, Idi, 7, 46, 94, 345
Angola, 4, 15, 92, 106, 283, 329, 407, 414
  and Afro-Marxism, 98, 165, 346, 401
  Benguela Railway, 406
  civil war in, 3, 5, 6, 16, 96, 129, 302,
      403–404
  cold war adversaries' engagement in, 403
  elephant slaughter in, 302
  fishing industry in, 299
  independence of, 89, 346, 400
  and slave trade, 68
  and South Africa, 98–99, 399, 400–401,
      402–404